MACROECONOMICS

MACROECONOMICS

A Survey of Research Strategies

Edited by

ALESSANDRO VERCELLI
AND
NICOLA DIMITRI

OXFORD UNIVERSITY PRESS
1992

Oxford University Press, Walton Street, Oxford OX2 6DP
Oxford New York Toronto
Delhi Bombay Calcutta Madras Karachi
Petaling Jaya Singapore Hong Kong Tokyo
Nairobi Dar es Salaam Cape Town
Melbourne Auckland
and associated companies in
Berlin Ibadan

Oxford is a trade mark of Oxford University Press

Published in the United States
by Oxford University Press, New York

British Library Cataloguing in Publication Data
Data available

Library of Congress Cataloging in Publication Data
Macroeconomics: a survey of research strategies/edited by Alessandro Vercelli and Nicola
Dimitri
Includes bibliographical references and indexes.
1. Macroeconomics. I. Vercelli, Alessandro. II. Dimitri Nicola.
HB172.5.M33535 1992 339–dc20 92-20945
ISBN 0-19-877314 5
ISBN 0-19-877315-3 (Pbk.)

Typeset by Keytec Typesetting Ltd., Bridport, Dorset
Printed and bound in
Great Britain by Bookcraft (Bath) Ltd.,
Midsomer Norton, Avon

Preface

This book is an outgrowth of the first workshop organized by ISER (International School of Economic Research, sponsored jointly by the Consiglio Nazionale delle Ricerche and the University of Siena) on recent advances in macroeconomics. This workshop was held in November 1987 at the Certosa di Pontignano, a beautiful sixteenth-century Carthusian monastery currently owned by the University of Siena. This harmonious building, secluded from everyday routine and competition, provided an ideal ambience for calm meditation and serene discussion.

The philosophy of the workshops organized by this School has been much appreciated. The main purpose is to put very promising young researchers and University teachers in touch with the lively frontier of economic research. Therefore the Organizing Board each year chooses a topic which is considered particularly 'hot', and asks a few of the main recent contributors to the literature on the subject to prepare a critical assessment of the recent results and prospects for future research.

The hallmark of the School is the unusually wide range of perspectives gathered on the same topic. The only criterion followed is that of finding the best possible representatives on the frontier for each of the chosen lines of research, orthodox or heterodox as they might be perceived in different quarters. By so doing, of course, the School takes a risk. It is often believed that a serious debate on scientific issues can be constructive only if the participants share the same theoretical and methodological presuppositions. However we believe that this could dismember the scientific debate into a number of research lines which may never intersect. This would greatly impoverish the critical awareness of researchers and might also depress their creativity, particularly in the sense of their ability to introduce major innovations. This would be particularly misleading for young researchers and teachers who especially need to be 'exposed' to alternative methodological and theoretical perspectives, before their choices harden into irreversible and possibly divergent directions. Until now, this choice of pluralism has worked surprisingly well so that even the participants who were sceptical before have had to admit that the debate among teachers and pupils has been very stimulating and often quite exciting. One proof of this is that most of the students have applied more than once and most of our distinguished lecturers have declared themselves glad to come back.

The first workshop on *Alternative Approaches to Macroeconomics* was considered a very successful example of postgraduate intensive teaching by all the participants, and this reception suggested the idea of extending the audience through publication of the contributions presented at the workshop. However this book is meant to be something more than a volume of proceedings. All the authors have extensively revised and updated their papers, taking into account the lively debate which developed throughout the workshop. Furthermore, in writing the final draft of their papers, the contributors have considered the interaction with other chapters while trying to avoid possible overlaps. This explains why it took such a long time to complete the project. We believe that this delay is amply justified by the quality of the product. Let us thank very warmly all the contributors for their active and committed collaboration in the success of the workshop and the quality of the book.

The increasing need for high-level reference books on the recent advances in economic research is witnessed by an exponentially growing number of encyclopedias, handbooks, collections of surveys, etc. This volume may be less complete and systematic than some of them, but it is particularly lively being the result of the idiosyncratic choice of, and passionate interaction among, some of the macroeconomists who are presently pushing out the frontier of economic research. Unity of time and space turns out to be a golden rule not only in play-writing but also in scientific training and research. We hope that this volume will succeed in conveying some of the flavour of the intense but open-minded debate which went on at the workshop.

All the chapters of this book with only two exceptions, are revisions, sometimes very radical as in the case of Sargent and Goodwin, of the papers presented and discussed at the workshop. The chapter by Silvestre takes the place of the paper presented by Benassy, which was already committed to another publisher. It covers almost the same ground in a very lucid and stimulating manner. The first chapter, by Hicks, is a reprint of his last paper already published in the *Economic Journal* (100 (1990), 528–38; notice however that the two texts are not identical because of different editing of the same manuscript). There are many reasons for this due homage to Sir John. He participated very actively in the first two workshops and had to read this paper at the third one. He was always very keen on participating in the Siena workshops, where he could find a very high concentration of admirers and former students, and where he could enjoy the particular Sienese harmony between culture and nature of which he was so fond. In addition the general perspective of the School, open-minded and pluralistic, was certainly very much influenced by his attitude towards the economic disciplines. Hence we thank the *Economic Journal* and Basil Blackwell for permission to republish Hicks's paper.

We cannot end this preface without thanking very warmly Axel Leijonhufvud and Ned Phelps who, as foreign members of the Organizing Board, made a fundamental contribution to the successful starting-up of this School and to the organization of the first four workshops. We also thank the other members of the Organizing Board for their constant help. In addition we would like to express our gratitude to Max Alter, who organized the workshop, as well as to Barbara Engelmann and Joanna Warren for their help in preparing this book.

We wish to thank the Dipartimento di Economia Politica, which hosts the ISER and is the main scientific and operational partner; the Rector of the University of Siena Luigi Berlinguer, and the Authorities of the Consiglio Nazionale delle Ricerche—in particular the President, Luigi Rossi Bernardi, and the Chairman of the sub-committee for economic, social, and statistic disciplines, Luigi De Rosa—who signed the agreement which instituted the ISER, and spent a lot of energy towards its successful implementation.

We acknowledge the invaluable contribution to the success of the workshop given by the Ufficio Congressi of Siena University, and in particular by its director Mrs Palma Trefoloni, and her collaborators, especially Monica Masti and Maria Teresa Soldatini. We would also like to thank the personnel of the Certosa di Pontignano who greatly contributed to the well-being of all participants, and last, but not least, we wish to express our gratitude for their excellent work to Andrew Schuller, Enid Barker, Sue Hughes, and all the staff of OUP involved in this long and burdensome project.

AV and ND

Siena
December 1991

Contents

List of Contributors

RICHARD DAY, Professor of Economics, University of Southern California

NICOLA DIMITRI, Assistant Professor, of Economics, University of Siena

RICHARD GOODWIN, Emeritus Professor of Economics, University of Siena

DAVID HENDRY, Professor of Economics, University of Oxford

DANIEL HEYMANN, Professor of Economics, University of Buenos Aires

JOHN HICKS, formerly Drummond Professor of Political Economy, University of Oxford

DAVID LAIDLER, Professor of Economics, University of Western Ontario

AXEL LEIJONHUFVUD, Professor of Economics, University of California, Los Angeles

TZONG-YAU LIN, Associate Professor of Economics, Soochow University, Taipei

SIRO LOMBARDINI, Professor of Economics, University of Turin

ALBERT MARCET, Assistant Professor of Economics, Carnegie Mellon University

BENNETT MCCALLUM, H. J. HEINZ, Professor of Economics, Carnegie Mellon University

PIER MARIO PACINI, Assistant Professor of Economics, University of Pisa

EDMUND PHELPS, MCVICKAR, Professor of Political Economy, Columbia University

THOMAS SARGENT, Professor of Economics, University of Chicago

JOAQUIM SILVESTRE, Professor of Economics, University of California, Davis

JOSEPH STIGLITZ, Professor of Economics, Stanford University

JOHN TAYLOR, Professor of Economics, Stanford University

ALESSANDRO VERCELLI, Professor of Economics, University of Siena

MICHAEL WOODFORD, Associate Professor of Economics, University of Chicago

Introduction

In this introduction we do not aim to give a comprehensive résumé of the chapters of the book (which would be pedantic and of little use) or an appraisal of the value they have added to the existing economic literature (some hints to this end will be provided in Laidler's epilogue). What we want to do essentially is to clarify the editorial structure of the volume. This will provide a justification of the ordering of the chapters, but it will not exhaust by any means the great richness of interrelationships between the papers, of which the reader will see more in the epilogue.

Macroeconomics is as old as economics. Whenever economic theory considered themes referring to a community as a whole—the accumulation of national wealth, the fluctuations of economic activity, inflation, etc.—the ensuing analysis could be considered, using our modern language anachronistically, macroeconomic analysis. It is well known, however, that the word itself, as well as a clear distinction between macroeconomics and microeconomics, was introduced by J. M. Keynes, who was the first to conceive of macroeconomics as an autonomous discipline.

A methodological fracture between micro and macro had grown progressively since the neoclassical revolution when what we now call microeconomics began to be rigorously founded on general equilibrium models, while what we call macroeconomics was still related to simple theoretical constructs like the Quantity Theory of Money, or empirical regularities like the Gresham Law. Keynes did not solve this contradiction between the 'two faces of the moon', but tried hard to explore its hidden side, developing a new autonomous discipline which he christened macroeconomics. This was not only meant, as Lucas has recently maintained, to liberate aggregate economics from the discipline of general equilibrium under the pressure of the Great Crisis (Lucas, 1981: 220), but also to provide remedies for the shortcomings of the existing micro theory, in so far as aggregate phenomena were concerned. After all, in order to see the other face of the moon a point of view different from the earthly one is needed.

Part I

The first part of the book discusses the genesis and development of Keynesian macroeconomics. We cannot avoid that. Though Keynesian macroeconomics has been radically questioned in recent decades, the

different macroeconomic schools still define their own features and aims
in relation to Keynes's ideas, either as a development of some interpretation of his thought or as a restoration of some version of pre-
Keynesian 'classical thought'. This implies perhaps that macroeconomics
is not yet a mature discipline, since it has not managed to emancipate
itself completely from the influence of its founding father. Nevertheless,
many of his insights and methodological hints are still extremely
stimulating heuristic ideas which have not ceased to exert a powerful
influence on macroeconomic research (see e.g. Vercelli, 1991).

  1. It is very appropriate to begin the book with a contribution written
by Sir John Hicks who, for more than half a century, played a
prominent role in the interpretation, critical stimulation, and constructive development of Keynesian thought. This chapter is a sort of
illuminating 'prologue' to the 'plot' developed by the other papers. It
goes to the roots of macroeconomics, when the word itself had not yet
been forged and research on aggregate phenomena was not yet conceived as part of an autonomous discipline. However the problems were
already there and were somehow seriously analysed. In particular,
according to Sir John, the early development of 'social accounting' was
an important contribution to the genesis of macroeconomics. From this
point of view Hicks even sees a broad continuity between the 'Great
Classics' and Keynes, particularly that of *How to Pay for the War*
(1940), whose importance in the early development of macroeconomics
is here emphasized. The neoclassicists, on the contrary, never showed a
genuine interest in 'social accounting', probably because of their greater
faith in the virtues of the market. According to Sir John, this contributed to the modern fracture between the analysis of 'micro' problems
and the analysis of 'macro' problems which Keynes tried to remedy.
  Hicks's point of view is clearly at variance with that expressed
recently by the new classical economists who ascribe to Keynes the
responsibility for the chasm between microeconomics and macroeconomics and strive for a pre-Keynesian unitary 'economic theory' (see
Lucas, 1987: 107–8). This is the result not only of a different perspective
on the history of economic thought but—more profoundly—of a different way of conceiving the aims and scope of macroeconomics. Hicks's
Social Accounting view of macroeconomics connects it strictly to anti-
cyclical state intervention, while the classical and new classical views rely
as far as possible on the autoregulative virtues of the market. Of course
the particular perspective into which Keynes's contribution is put here
by Hicks is interesting but partial. Hicks himself has chosen a different
perspective on other occasions (see e.g. Hicks, 1974). Surveys of further interesting views on Keynes will be found in the other chapters of
Part I.

2. All critical surveys organize the subject-matter according either to a generic order or to a taxonomy. Hicks's chapter is essentially organized according to a generic order which leads to Keynesian macroeconomics. The second chapter, written by Axel Leijonhufvud, is organized by his well-known 'Swedish-flag' table which classifies business-cycle theories according to the hypotheses concerning the impulses that initiate fluctuations, and the propagation mechanisms that turn the impulses into persistent movements in aggregate variables. The Swedish flag provides a taxonomic principle for defining different macroeconomic approaches. But it is also used as a device for describing and clarifying the evolution of the macroeconomic debate after Keynes. In other words the 'Swedish-flag' table is conceived as a two-dimensional projection of that 'spiral staircase of increasing formal sophistication' along which we are 'coming back again and again to the same basic issues' (p. 28).

The fundamental issue, according to Leijonhufvud, is the co-ordination of individual economic choices and activities. The last well-established stage of the evolutionary process, new classical macroeconomics, permits a solution to the contradiction between micro and macro, but only by reducing macroeconomics to general equilibrium microeconomics. This is possible, in his opinion, only through the crucial assumption of a representative agent which defines away the problem of co-ordination that, according to Leijonhufvud, is the *raison d'être* of macroeconomics. Therefore, in his view, the spiral staircase should be continued resuming in a more rigorous way a few basic ideas put forward by Keynes, among which that of 'bounded rationality' will have to play a crucial role. In addition, more attention should be given to issues so far neglected by macroeconomists (including Keynes and his followers): in particular the implications of increasing returns.

3. Joseph Stiglitz examines in some detail the features and prospects of a recent approach (of Keynesian inspiration), generally called 'new Keynesian macroeconomics'. As the name itself suggests, the solution to the tension between micro and macro proposed by this school of thought is, in a sense, the opposite of that suggested by the new classical economists. According to this view, rather than reducing macroeconomics to Walrasian general equilibrium, microeconomics should be accommodated to macroeconomics by introducing a variety of real-life complications like limited information, bounded rationality, imperfect competition, and adjustment costs. This should eventually lead to a macro theory fully consistent both with a rigorous microeconomics and with the empirical aggregate evidence.

Now Keynesian economics, as conceived by Stiglitz, takes an agnostic view on the source of disturbances which may cause market failures but it emphasizes the intrinsic instability of actual market economies, since small disturbances may lead to large changes in output and employment (in particular because of the risk-averse behaviour of firms). This instability depends on a set of information problems that have a pervasive effect on labour, capital, and product market.

While defending the main tenets of the school, Stiglitz examines and criticizes a few crucial aspects of the main alternative approaches to macroeconomics. In particular, new classical economics is refuted on methodological and empirical grounds. As a matter of fact, he stresses that 'if one believes that some kinds of "market failures" are at the root of macroeconomic phenomena, one can hardly study these issues by using representative agent models; for when all individuals are identical there is no need for trades, and hence there are no consequences of the absence of markets' (p. 44). More specifically, the hypothesis of rational expectations is considered a useful bench-mark, as it clarifies to what extent market failures depend on 'irrational' expectations. However, rational expectations are not a guarantee of efficiency, as many important co-ordination problems pertain to the functioning of decentralized markets and are not excluded by the hypothesis itself.

4. Joaquim Silvestre defends the validity of a different Keynesian research programme often called non-Walrasian or disequilibrium macroeconomics. According to this author each market is an efficient allocative device within its own boundaries, but this does not rule out the possibility of co-ordination failures across markets because of the monetary nature of trade and the existing price rigidities. (On the contrary, Leijonhufvud and Stiglitz maintain that there may be co-ordination failures even inside a single market.) Under this approach the theoretical formulation of the co-ordination problem highlights the importance of quantities and 'excess effective demands' as signals driving exchanges out of equilibrium.

Silvestre underlines in particular the conceptual links between the non-Walrasian approach and the implications of market power. Price rigidities and quantity rationing can be seen as the implementation of an imperfectly competitive equilibrium. In general, the agent who is 'rationed' in the fix-price model is the one with market power in the imperfectly competitive model. Different regimes of disequilibrium can then be interpreted as different combinations of market power.

In the remaining part of the chapter Silvestre shows, through an example, how non-Walrasian analysis may be used in order to explore the properties of different institutional hypotheses. To this end he discusses the properties of a 'share' economy in which workers are paid a fixed share in the revenue instead of a fixed wage per hour. According to Weitzman, the share economy would have the same long-run features as the present 'wage' economy, but would maintain full employment during the short-run adjustment to external shocks. Silvestre shows that the superiority of the share economy depends on the instantaneous adjustment of prices. If we assume in the short run the rigidity of both the compensation scheme and prices, a share economy would still maintain full employment after a technology shock, but it would fail to do so after a shock in demand. Silvestre concludes, in partial agreement with Weitzman, that an economy-wide reform in the way workers are paid would never be disadvantageous to anyone.

As we have seen, the first part of the book examines a few Keynesian research programmes, while other Keynesian perspectives, as well as the anti-Keynesian or a-Keynesian research programmes, though often mentioned and discussed in the preceding chapters, are not presented in a comprehensive and self-contained way. This may sound unfair to many important schools of thought which made lasting contributions to macroeconomics, but space limitations prevented a broader coverage. A case in point is new classical economics, a school of thought which has played a crucial role in macroeconomic analysis since the early 1970s. As a matter of fact, Tom Sargent, who at the Siena Workshop illustrated and defended this research programme with great lucidity and breadth, preferred to contribute a more technical paper, written jointly with Albert Marcet, which addresses issues of great interest for assessing the robustness of the research programme of new classical economics, but which does not attempt to discuss explicitly and in general terms its strengths and purposes. (This paper is included in the second part of the book and will be discussed in the next section of this introduction.)

Whatever may have been Sargent's motivations, his choice is consistent with the scepticism recently shown by the main representatives of the new classical school towards comparative assessments of general research programmes. Lucas, for example, maintained: 'there is no doubt something to be learned by tracing the main ideological currents in macroeconomic research, but I myself find most of this discussion of crises, revolutions and so on, unintelligible, and almost wholly unconnected with the most interesting current research' (1987: 1). This attitude is somewhat puzzling in the light of Lucas's (and Sargent's) contributions of the late 1970s in which they did not hesitate to put the history of macroeconomic analysis and the role of their own contributions in the frame of a secular conflict between the classical research programme and the Keynesian one (see e.g. Lucas and Sargent, 1979; and Lucas, 1980).

The reader may however easily find elsewhere a few lucid accounts of the outlines and promises of this research programme (in particular in Lucas, 1981, and 1987, as well as in Lucas and Sargent, 1981). Moreover, many of the ideas brought forward by the new classical economists will be discussed separately in the following parts of the book, namely: the hypothesis of rational expectations, equilibrium business cycle, the degree of flexibility of prices and wages, and the Granger causality.

Part II

In the second part of the volume the importance of the hypothesis of rational expectations, already discussed in the first part of the book by Leijonhufvud and Stiglitz, is analysed in more detail by Phelps and Sargent. The idea, proposed by Lucas (1972), of introducing the hypothesis of rational expectations in macroeconomics, proved to be extremely far-reaching and contributed in a crucial way to the anti-Keynesian revolution of the new classical economists. It is true that 'John Muth's hypothesis of rational expectations is a technical model-building principle, not a distinct, comprehensive macroeconomic theory' (Lucas, 1981: 1), but this hypothesis offered a methodological paradigm which was gradually expanded and articulated in what is now known as 'new classical economics'. In particular it suggests how to maintain a crucial role for equilibrium under uncertainty without denying a complex stochastic dynamics around it. This offers the key for reconciling general equilibrium (in a stochastic version) with the business cycle and infla-tion. Of course the hypothesis is based on a few assumptions which appear rather remote from reality and thus very hard to swallow: perfect flexibility of prices and money wages, substantive rationality of decision makers, homogeneity of beliefs, etc. The debate on these issues has been, and still is, very lively.

5. Ned Phelps provides a broad sketch of the debate on the rational expectations hypothesis. He points out a few basic problems but recognizes that this hypothesis of expectations formation is in many respects better than the preceding ones and that it will be replaced only when a more convincing proposal is discovered and developed. However, in the mean time, we should be fully aware of its shortcom-ings. In particular, Phelps underlines that 'there is an element of farce when collectively we work with all these different theories and yet posit rational expectations as if there were only one model' (p. 137). In fact we should not forget that, as this book clearly—though partially—docu-ments, 'macroeconomics these days is virtually Balkanized', i.e. divided into different schools (in a recent book he defines at least seven of them: see Phelps, 1990).

According to Phelps, a hypothesis of expectations formation more general than that of rational expectations would be that each agent bases his forecasts not only on his own fundamentals and perceived exogenous factors, but also on his estimates of others' expectations on different fundamentals. But, in Phelps's view, the infinite regress which would ensue is not yet perfectly understood and mastered in analytical terms. This problem is also connected with that of sunspot equilibria, where other people's beliefs are important for the final allocation of resources in the economy (see Woodford's chapter below). Therefore the issue at stake is not only that of convergence through learning to the rational expectations equilibrium but also that of understanding to which equilibrium heterogeneous expectations would eventually converge.

6. Albert Marcet and Thomas Sargent provide a partial answer to the first question raised by Phelps. The hypothesis of rational expectations restricts the intrinsic indeterminacy of economic systems which are self-referential in the sense that 'outcomes depend partly on what people expect those outcomes to be' (p. 139). However Sargent recognizes that often there are pairs of expectations and outcomes that are consistent with the same specification of a model. A rational expectations equilibrium may be a plausible escape from indeterminacy only if undemanding learning schemes rapidly converge towards it. Moreover, the study of learning processes may further restrict the residual indeterminacy still looming under the rational expectations hypothesis by selecting only the most stable rational equilibria.

This chapter summarizes some of the main results on least-squares learning mechanisms in linear expectations models. In this particular class of models convergence often but not always obtains: there are cases in which there is no convergence towards a rational expectations equilibrium (as in Bray's model of 1982 for some parameter specification) or in which there is divergence from a rational expectations equilibrium (the bubbles equilibrium of Cagan's hyperinflation model).

These results are not yet very general as they strongly depend upon the assumptions adopted by this class of models (linearity of the model and the least-squares learning scheme). Moreover the behaviour of economic agents is assumed to be, in a sense, not fully rational (the sequential application of linear least squares to vector autoregressions is not rational for the above environments, as argued by Bray and Kreps (1987), and recalled by the authors of the chapter). In another sense it is too rational, as the agents are supposed to be using state-of-the-art 'adaptive control' techniques. Marcet and Sargent seem to admit, in their balanced conclusions, that the results of this literature do not yet have a great bearing on the plausibility and robustness of the hypothesis of rational expectations. However this line of research is necessary to understand its scope of application and the requisites of better hypotheses for expectations formation.

Part III

The third part of the book focuses the attention on one of the main areas of the macroeconomic debate in the 1960s and 1970s: the explanation and control of business cycles. After a period of decline of this subject during the long phase of steady growth of the 1950s and 1960s, since the late 1960s the business cycle has again attracted the attention of economists and policy-makers. The revival of interest manifested itself as soon as the inflationary tensions reappeared at the world level, followed by the oil shocks and the stagflation period. The traditional Keynesian approach appeared to be inconsistent with fluctuations dominated by supply-side switches and forward-looking swift learning processes. So, alternative theories were put forward in order to explain the empirical evidence and to identify the best policy rules to cope with the emerging turbulences.

The most influential new approach was without doubt that suggested by the equilibrium business-cycle models worked out by Lucas (the first articulated prototype may be found in Lucas, 1975). This approach promised to reconcile macroeconomic fluctuations with general equilibrium theory, by explaining the cyclical co-movements among economic time series as the outcome of exogenous shocks and transmission mechanisms such as the gradual adjustment to unexpected changes of capital stock and of agents' perceptions. However, many scholars committed to this methodology soon felt uneasy with the extreme monetarism of the first generation of equilibrium business-cycle models. In 1982 the first prototype of real business-cycle models was published (Kydland and Prescott, 1982), and rapidly became the most influential explanation of business cycles. It applies the basic equilibrium methodology codified by Lucas in his monetary model of the business cycle, but replaces Lucas's monetary impulses with technological shocks. Also the propagation mechanisms are conceived in a different way, as they are essentially related to the technological features of the system ('time to build') rather than to accelerator or learning mechanisms.

However, even this approach has been recently challenged, and so has the general methodology of equilibrium business cycles. These issues are discussed in some detail in Part 3 of the volume.

7. The first essay by Bennett McCallum offers a critical assessment of the real business-cycle approach to macroeconomic analysis. In these models economic fluctuations are often conceived as optimal responses to technological shocks which would render useless any sort of anti-cyclical policies. However, as McCallum emphasizes, Pareto optimality is not granted (p. 169). In addition, this sort of model rightly reminds us that the business cycle cannot be conceived of as a purely monetary

phenomenon, but it may be argued that it has gone too far in the opposite direction. Moreover, McCallum maintains that there is no reason to believe that monetary and fiscal-policy interventions should not be considered of significant importance in affecting the business cycle.

In the remainder of the paper McCallum suggests the need for a different approach to the business cycle, which is able to take into account, at the same time, the price sluggishness and the 'Lucas critique'. In the mean time, it should be possible to agree on a mix of monetary and fiscal policies that, for a wide range of models, would be able to virtually eliminate inflation, avoid possibly destabilizing policy surprises, and perhaps contribute to the dampening of real cyclical fluctuations.

8. Equilibrium business cycle models, either of the monetary or of the real variety, see economic fluctuations as purely exogenous or in the sense that without exogenous shocks there would be no economic fluctuations. This is not the only possible approach to the business cycle. Recently there has been a revival of interest in the endogenous models of economic fluctuations, i.e. fluctuations that would continue to occur even in the absence of exogenous shocks. Michael Woodford offers a thorough, critical assessment of the models of endogenous fluctuations and discusses their pros and cons *vis-à-vis* the models of exogenous fluctuations. He restricts his attention to the endogenous fluctuations produced by equilibrium models, i.e. assuming optimizing behaviour on the part of economic agents and perfect competition.

Woodford distinguishes two kinds of models of equilibrium endogenous fluctuations: those in which equilibrium is determinate but unstable and 'sunspot' models. Their main distinguishing feature is that of denying one or other of the two determinacy theses which, according to the author, underlie equilibrium exogenous fluctuations models: global weak determinacy and asymptotic strong determinacy. According to the 'global weak determinacy' thesis, the equilibrium values at any point in time do not depend upon 'irrelevant' (sunspot) components either of endogenous-state variables or of predetermined endogenous-state variables. According to the 'asymptotic strong determinacy' thesis, the equilibrium values depend only upon the realizations of the exogenous fundamentals, while asymptotically the initial conditions of the predetermined endogenous variables will have no effect upon the equilibrium values. The two determinacy theses together imply that persistent fluctuations in the endogenous variables must be explained by fluctuations in the exogenous fundamentals. But it is sufficient to deny one of the above theses to allow the possibility of endogenous fluctuations. Determinate but unstable dynamic models do not necessarily converge asymptotically towards a steady state, and thus contradict the 'asymptotic strong determinacy' thesis, but are consistent with the thesis of 'global weak determinacy'. On the other hand, sunspot equilibrium models deny the global weak determinacy thesis as they show that sunspot states may affect equilibrium values. The point with these models, according to Woodford, is that they show exactly that a 'well-posed' model, i.e. one that assumes maximizing behaviour and competitive equilibrium, is not necessarily in agreement with one or both determinacy theses.

Woodford explains why the traditional arguments against endogenous explanations of the business cycle are now considerably weakened by the recent advances of non-linear dynamics and econometrics. He also shows why the issue has a considerable importance for economic theory and policy. First it can be argued that an endogenous explanation of aggregate fluctuations generally implies that they are inefficient and that they should be repressed through apt policy interventions. He also argues that these results do not depend on this alleged inconsistency with rationality, equilibrium, and optimizing behaviour. However he maintains that the most plausible conditions under which either sunspot equilibria or determinate but unstable dynamics can occur would seem to be conditions under which such equilibria are possible only because of market imperfections.

9. An important class of endogenous fluctuations models, which would violate the global weak determinacy thesis proposed by Woodford, is founded on the so-called (deterministic) chaos theory. This is a branch of nonlinear dynamics which has received a lot of attention in the last two decades in many disciplines, including macroeconomics.

Though a rigorous theory of chaos began to be developed only in the 1970s (Li and Yorke, 1975), Richard Goodwin, a pioneer of nonlinear dynamics in economics, had already had a few insights into chaotic dynamics as early as the 1950s. Not surprisingly, Goodwin was one of the first to understand the relevance of this theory for economics. Here, together with Pier Mario Pacini, he gives a balanced survey of the literature, the problems it opens, and the implications for macroeconomic analysis and policy. The authors agree with Woodford that the endogenous explanation of economic fluctuations offered by deterministic chaos has great implications for both theory and policy. Their occurrence is a possibility which has seriously to be taken into account since its plausibility cannot be excluded either on theoretical grounds or by empirical tests. The robustness of the hypothesis strictly depends on the alternative definitions and mathematical language which have been used in this field. The authors clarify these options and show their implications and promise for future research.

In all cases chaos implies the inability to forecast perfectly, the practical impossibility of fine tuning, and the persistence of the effects of temporary disturbances. Moreover, interventions to eliminate or reduce chaotic fluctuations are bound to be structural: stabilization is impossible without changing the values of the structural parameters which govern the behaviour of the system.

According to the authors, the weak point of this literature is that in most cases observable chaos is not a generic property of the economic system, i.e. it applies only to particular values of the parameters. This requires a careful justification—both theoretical and empirical—of the plausibility of these special values and a particular caution in drawing conclusions. In any case, though very arduous, this research programme not only promises to clarify the conditions of applicability of existing models and theories (which require inexistence of chaos) but could also help us to give a consistent endogenous explanation for that part of behaviour that used to be banished as an unexplainable error of an unpredictable shock (p. 285).

10. Richard Day and Tzong-Yau Lin work out an example of a model economy exhibiting chaotic dynamics and explore in some detail its properties and implications. The model is an adaptive version of the standard neoclassical perfect-competition optimal-growth model. The traditional theory of optimal growth is considered by the authors to be a useful benchmark, but a bad approximation to empirical economic performance. Real economic agents never calculate over an infinite horizon and cannot easily find the optimal forecasts and the optimal strategies for this complex world. On the contrary, the basic insights of adaptive expectations have recently been rehabilitated by experimental and empirical work. According to the adaptive theory of competitive growth, 'perfect foresight eliminates intrinsic fluctuations but does not guarantee optimality' (p. 315). Without it, fluctuations may occur and persist even in the absence of exogenous shocks. These fluctuations may be periodic, irregular, or even chaotic. The 'adaptive theory' is thus considered more general than the standard theory of fluctuations and growth because it retains the optimal competitive equilibrium path as a special case, but offers a wider range of possible behaviours under different circumstances. Exogenous shocks of course may be somehow added to the adaptive prototype model presented by the authors, further enlarging the set of virtual behavioural patterns.

Part IV

The chapters in the first three parts of the book, though mainly theoretical or methodological in their inspiration, recognize that scientific judgement must be solidly anchored in a thorough empirical analysis. Unfortunately, owing to space limitations, only two examples of empirical analysis can be included in this book. They are strictly related to the themes treated in the other parts of the book.

11. The chapter written by John Taylor faces one of the crucial problems that loom large in the whole book and, indeed, in the macroeconomic debate: the degree of flexibility of money wages and prices. The classical point of view, old and new, has always assumed flexible wages and prices and has always interpreted the assumption of rigid, or sticky, wages and prices as the hallmark of the Keynesian point of view. However, in the Keynesian camp opinions on this point are divided, as we have seen in the first part of the book, but in any case perfect and instantaneous flexibility is always denied, at least as a general feature of modern economies.

The problem of nominal price flexibility, as in any serious empirical work, is carefully circumscribed in this chapter. The question analysed is specifically the empirical significance of synchronized wage determination as a source of the different degree of wage flexibility observed in different countries: Japan, USA, Canada, France, Germany, Italy, and the UK. The equations are fitted to quarterly data for the period 1972–86. The results indicate that synchronization significantly affects the behaviour of aggregate wages in Japan by eliminating much of the slow adjustment of average money wages resulting from overlapping contracts. However, much of the difference between aggregate nominal wage flexibility in Japan and other countries remains unexplained. Taylor, on the basis of previous work, excludes the idea that the residual can be ascribed to the bonus system and advances the hypothesis that the annual discussions surrounding the Shunto process itself may enhance aggregate wage flexibility in Japan.

12. The importance of institutional factors clearly emerges from the paper by Taylor, and plays a crucial role in the paper by Daniel Heymann. High inflation episodes have always been considered a sort of laboratory case for macroeconomics as their extreme conditions may help to clarify the relationships among a few aggregate variables: money, income, prices, wages, and expectations. Their study, besides the obvious practical importance it has for the countries affected, is also important for the general insights they provide not only on the causal relations among macro variables, but also about the role of monetary institutions, the resilience of markets, and economic behaviour under uncertainty.

The analysis of these episodes suggests that inflation is not simply a monetary phenomenon, and disinflation policies not only a matter of monetary rigour. There is a long tradition extending from the early discussion on German hyperinflation (Bresciani Turroni, 1937) to the structuralist and neo-structuralist approaches to Latin-American inflation, which stresses the role of relative price changes coupled with structural change and sectoral rigidities at the domestic and international levels. A fiscal crisis is very often found at the roots of high inflation and this frequently depends on political factors: 'it may be significant, in this respect, that high inflations often take place during the decline of authoritarian regimes, or in new democracies that have not yet developed well functioning fiscal institutions' (p. 342).

We do not intend to summarize and discuss here the complications of the real world which clearly emerge from the study of a set of concrete phenomena like high inflation. What we would like to stress, in agreement with the author, is a warning against over-simplifications regarding the nature of causal links in macroeconomics.

Part V

There is a well known trade-off between different degrees of abstraction. Theories must be simple enough to act as magnifying glasses which select a few crucial aspects of reality. But they are at the same time blinkers which may screen off important aspects of reality. On the other hand, accurate empirical analysis cannot be as simple as a good theory: the most important factors risk getting lost in a jungle of less crucial details. These problems are typical of all empirical sciences, but are particularly delicate in macroeconomics, where a satisfactory matching between theory and facts always results in something particularly puzzling. As Kalecky remarked long ago, we might say that economics is characterized by theoretical propositions that no one is able to verify and empirical regularities that no one is able to explain.

The increasing sophistication of econometric techniques has not improved the situation very much. It is still true, as Hendry has remarked, that 'the credibility of a great proportion of empirical econometric evidence depends on the prior credibility of the theoretical model from which it was derived, so when the theory fails so does most of the evidential basis' and 'that is not common to other disciplines' (p. 364). This methodological issue is a great obstacle to a balanced assessment of competing research programmes. The last part of the book specifically addresses this theme from different—but somewhat complementary—points of view.

13. Among the specific aspects analysed by David Hendry in his chapter, the discussion of the criterion of 'encompassing' for assessing the validity of rival models is particularly relevant for the general themes of the book. The intuitive idea has been used many times in the macroeconomic debates. Keynes maintained that his theory was more general than the classical theory since it led to the same results in full

employment equilibrium but was able to supplement a satisfactory
analysis in all the other cases too. The classical theorists reacted by
saying that the Keynesian model was just a special case of the classical
theory under the assumption of rigid wages. The neoclassical synthesis
strove for a macroeconomic theory able to 'encompass' both the
Keynesian and the classical theory. Hendry's 'encompassing' is a translation in technical and rigorous econometric terms of the traditional idea
of superior generality. It is thus a useful criterion provided we remember that the results of its application are relative to a specific theoretical
and methodological background.

14. Another important criterion of choice between rival models and
research programmes is that of causality. In particular the discussion
between Keynesians and monetarists in the 1960s, between Keynesians
and new classical economists in the 1970s, the shift from monetary
equilibrium business-cycle models to real business-cycle models in the
1980s have all been strongly influenced by different opinions on the
validity of causal arguments and tests. Alessandro Vercelli, from this
point of view, surveys the evolution of the main causality concepts
utilized by the economists. He shows that the different conceptions of
causality are deeply influenced by the epistemological presuppositions of
the researcher.

For instance, the debate about the superiority of recursive (causal)
systems versus interdependent systems which took place in the 1950s
and 1960s was affected by a conflict between two basic principles of
intelligibility: methodological individualism which inspired a stimulus-
response reductionism, and substantive rationality which inspired an
equilibrium reductionism. A preference for recursive systems was typical
of scholars who stressed the first principle and emphasized the role of
disequilibrium processes (as in the Wicksellian and Keynesian schools),
or the role of bounded rationality (as in the case of Simon), while a
preference for interdependent systems was typical of scholars giving a
central role to the second principle and emphasized equilibrium and
optimization (as for example, many general equilibrium theorists).

In particular, the different opinions on causality matters depend very
much on different views about the relationship between theory and
facts. The choice itself of the 'right' concept of causality and the
interpretation of the results of causality tests depend on this delicate
epistemological question. New classical economists prefer Granger causality tests to alternative causality concepts and tests because they are
inclined to believe that they are unconditional to theoretical hypotheses.
The author recalls why this claim is questionable. Facts are theory-laden
and there is no way to establish their existence and their properties
without a priori theoretical assumptions. In particular it is impossible to
exclude that a certain correlation is spurious only through empirical

tests, without assuming specific theoretical hypotheses. What Hendry had already maintained in his chapter is thus confirmed: 'neither theory nor evidence can claim precedence in scientific progress' (p. 364).

Therefore causality tests are not sufficient to enable a choice to be made between rival models and theories. However they are by no means useless. They help us to explore and compare the characteristics of the epistemological structures of different models and theories and the relationships entertained by empirical structures. Causal arguments enter legitimately into our appraisal of rival research programmes. But they only increase the weight of our arguments rather than 'proving' them.

15. Siro Lombardini also insists on the fact that theory and facts are mutually related in a very complex way. He goes deeper into a few aspects of this interaction (uncertainty, aggregation, rationality) to lament the unilaterality of existing economic research either because economic theorizing too often ignores a careful analysis of existing evidence or because it engages in econometric work oriented towards forecasting without caring enough about the plausibility and the biases of the assumed theoretical presuppositions.

A possible way out—according to Lombardini—can be envisaged in what he calls 'computational economics', i.e. a systematic use of simulation techniques made possible by the development of computer sciences. This would permit the use of models much more complex than the existing ones which are constrained by the requirement of analytic solutions. In particular this would offer new opportunities for the better integration of theories and facts. The new possibilities opened by the rapid development of computer sciences have been recently underlined by many other economists: for example Hendry in his chapter, or Hahn in a recent paper on the future prospects of economics (1991). The latter agrees that what Lombardini calls 'computational economics' will become very important and sees in that an opportunity but also a risk. In particular he fears that these developments may discourage further serious work on the theoretical foundations. Though this risk might be a real one and ought to be avoided, we must agree with Lombardini that simulation models will play an important role in the future, at least in the heuristic phase of economic research.

Part VI

The book ends with an epilogue written by David Laidler. The first draft of this chapter was presented as a summing-up at the Siena Workshop from which this book originated. The author takes this occasion for expressing his personal views on the state of the art in macroeconomics. He does so in a very stimulating manner picking up different threads which join or contrast the chapters of the book. This clearly shows that the conceptual structure of the book is not just a 'tree diagram' as might appear from our introduction, but something much more complex—a network, if not a web. Of course, Laidler's is just one of the possible conceptual webs which can be visualized in this book. Moreover his open-minded and balanced assessment of the contributions published in this book is inspired by his own research programme. This is not only unavoidable, but also an asset. Through the epilogue also the point of view of modern monetarism creeps into the book.

We conclude this introduction with a few observations on the meaning and role of pluralism in macroeconomics and the degree of consistency of this book with this guiding principle. We are fully aware that many important research programmes are not adequately mentioned, or not mentioned at all, in this volume. However, pluralism does not mean a complete coverage of the existing theoretical and methodological points of view on a certain subject (see Caldwell, 1982). In our view pluralism basically means a fundamental respect for different opinions, theories, approaches, and a sincere readiness to be convinced by interlocutors entertaining a different point of view.

The above attitude has been shared by the participants in the workshop, and the authors of the chapters. This, more than anything else, makes us optimistic about the future evolution of macroeconomics.

References

BRAY, M. M. (1982). 'Learning, estimation, and the stability of rational expectations'. *Journal of Economic Theory*, 26: 318–39.
—— and KREPS, D. (1986). 'Rational learning and rational expectations', in W. Heller, D. Starret, and R. Starr (eds.), *Essays in Honour of K. J. Arrow*. Cambridge, Cambridge University Press.
BRESCIANI-TURRONI, C. (1937). *The Economics of Inflation*. New York, Barnes and Nobles.
CALDWELL, B. J. (1982). *Beyond Positivism: Economic Methodology in the Twentieth Century*. London, Allen and Unwin.
HAHN, F. H. (1991). 'The next hundred years'. *Economic Journal*, 101 1: 47–50.
HICKS, J. (1974). *The Crisis in Keynesian Economics*. Oxford, Blackwell.
KEYNES, J. M. (1936). *The General Theory of Employment, Interest and Money*. London, Macmillan.
—— (1940). *How to Pay for the War*. London, Macmillan.
KYDLAND, F. E., and PRESCOTT, E. C. (1982). 'Time to build and aggregate fluctuations'. *Econometrica*, 50: 1345–70.

LI, T. J., and YORKE, J. A. (1975). 'Period Three Implies Chaos'. *American Mathematical Monthly*, 82: 985–92.

LUCAS, R. E., JR. (1972). 'Expectations and the Neutrality of Money'. *Journal of Economic Theory*, 42: 102–24.

—— (1975). 'An equilibrium model of the business cycle'. *Journal of Political Economy*, 83: 113–44.

—— (1980). 'Methods and Problems in Business Cycle Theory'. *Journal of Money, Credit, and Banking*, 12 4: 696–715.

—— (1981). *Studies in Business-Cycle Theory*. Cambridge, Mass., MIT Press.

—— (1987). *Models of Business Cycles*. Yrjo Jahnsson Lectures, Oxford, Basil Blackwell.

LUCAS, R. E., JR., and SARGENT, T. J. (1979). 'After Keynesian Macroeconomics'. *Federal Bank of Minneapolis Quarterly Review*, 3 2. Reprinted in Lucas, R. E. Jr., and Sargent, T. J. (1981). *Rational Expectations and Econometric Practice*, 295–329.

—— —— (eds.) (1981). *Rational Expectations and Econometric Practice*. London, Allen and Unwin.

PHELPS, E. S. (1990). *Seven Schools of Macroeconomic Thought*. Oxford, Clarendon Press.

VERCELLI, A. (1991). *Methodological Foundations of Macroeconomics. Keynes and Lucas*. Cambridge, Cambridge University Press.

PART I

Keynesian Macroeconomics: Foundations and Prospects

1

The Unification of
Macroeconomics

JOHN HICKS

1. Introduction

If we define *modern* macroeconomics as beginning with Keynes, it is to
more than his *General Theory* of 1936 that we should be referring. It is
nowadays accepted that there is something in his *Treatise on Money*
(1930) which belongs, but not so widely felt that there is a third which
completes the trilogy. This is his booklet *How to Pay for the War*
(1940). It was published at the beginning of the fateful year; he wrote it
to give advice on what he had then thought to be a quite transitory
problem, for he had no idea when writing how long the war was going
to last. Thus it is not surprising that in later years little attention has
been paid to it. I nevertheless maintain that it is the true turning-point;
for the Keynesian *method* is much more explicit in it than in his earlier
works. I propose in this *paper* to set that method in historical perspective. I shall show that he had mighty predecessors, the most important
being none other than Adam Smith himself.

The method in its Keynesian form depends on the table of 'social
accounts', or of 'National Income and Expenditure', as the first British
official estimate was called, to be produced that same year by Meade
and Stone under Keynes's influence.[1] The method is to take the table of
social accounts as it is in a particular period (a year), enquire into the
propensities and policies of the period which have made it what it is,
and ask how it would have been changed if these had been different.
This I believe is the general characteristic of Keynesian method; the
employment theory of 1936 is a particular application.

Now if we look back to the days of the dominance of those
economists, whom Keynes called the Classics but we call the Neoclassics, we find that they did not use this method, and there was a reason

---

[1] I was engaged in that work myself, though I was already working on closely related
subjects, as will be seen in the first *Wealth and Welfare* volume of my *Collected Essays*
(1981). My 'Valuation of the Social Income', included in that volume, appeared almost
contemporaneously, and my *Social Framework* textbook had its first edition in 1942. (I
wanted to call it 'Social Accounts', but this was too forward-looking for my publisher.)

why they did not do so. They did not have even rudimentary accounts of national income from which to start. The first estimates of British national income which have any authority were those made by Bowley and Stamp for the particular years 1911 and 1924. None of this was available to Marshall when he was doing his best work.

And one can explain why this should have happened. A *laissez-faire* economy, such as the British may be taken to have been for most of the nineteenth century, does not collect—it is in principle unwilling to collect—much information about macro magnitudes. So if Jevons, or the early Marshall, had tried to construct a social accounting table, they would have had little from which to start. By the close of the century, things were beginning to be different. It was in 1893 that a Liberal politician proclaimed, 'We are all socialists now'. Just enough information was beginning to be collected, through trade unions and an inquisitive income tax, for the statisticians to have something to bite on. And after what happened in the First World War, there was plenty.

Something like that must have happened in several other countries, in the twentieth but not in the nineteenth century.

2. Petty and Cantillon

If however we go further back, to what was already past history in the days of Adam Smith, we do find some particular occasions when material became available from which a statistician could have made a start. One of these was after the Norman conquest of England—the Domesday Book. Not surprisingly, nothing came of that. The one which is relevant is the English conquest of Ireland, for such it effectively was, in the 1650s under Cromwell. The conquerors were then a more sophisticated people than the conquered, but they had none of the moral scruples of some more recent colonizers. They just regarded Ireland as an estate which had come into their possession, so the ownership of it had to be divided up among them. They needed to find out just what it was to be divided. They needed to make a survey of the land of Ireland.

This is the (in our eyes disreputable) event from which macroeconomics is ultimately descended. For the official to whom the task of making the survey was entrusted was William Petty, who had already had a remarkable career, which had brought him into contact with the beginnings of modern science.[2] So when his survey was completed, he

---

[2] Particularly medical science. It was as medical officer to Cromwell's army that Petty originally went to Ireland; so he will have known about Harvey and the Circulation of Blood. (It is not unlikely that he was personally acquainted with Harvey.) His principal economic work is entitled *Political Anatomy of Ireland* (Petty 1671).

looked up from it and set himself the wider question: How could one measure the whole wealth of Ireland, its labour wealth as well as its land wealth? He had no income tax data at his disposal, and very little in the way of wage statistics; but even if he had had them, it is doubtful if he would have wanted to use them. For it was the normal value (rental value) of the land which he had been measuring, like any value nowadays, so it would have been the normal wage which he needed to set against it. How could one establish a relation between those normal values? How, as he put it, could one establish a par between land and labour?

This in Petty was little more than a question; the first attempt to answer it was made, more than a half century later, by Cantillon.[3] He also, in the first part of his book—the only part which concerns us—was proceeding as a social accountant. He clearly knew that in a closed economy (that qualification is quite explicit) the social product is equal to the sum of incomes, and that the equality is maintained by valuing each particular product at its inclusive cost in terms of productive factors. (The other equality—between income and expenditure—is less explicit, but in the course of his work it is evidently implied.)

Like modern social accountants, Cantillon divides his economy into sectors: town and country, it will be convenient to call them. Town labour, being thought of as handicraft labour, can produce without any co-operating factor; country labour, agricultural labour, cannot produce without having land on which to grow its 'corn'. Both sorts of labour have to be paid a subsistence wage, which may indeed be different in the two sectors. The supply of labour to each sector is taken to be perfectly elastic. 'Men multiply like mice in a barn if they have unlimited means of subsistence', as he puts it himself. So the wages of both sorts of labour are taken to be fixed in terms of corn.

The corn values of town products are therefore fixed, for they are equal to the corn-wage of the labour required to produce them. But, the product of country labour being corn itself, the value of a unit of corn in terms of corn must be unity, having no necessary relation to the corn-wage of country labour, except that it cannot be more than would swallow up the whole product. There is however no reason why it should not be less, as Cantillon, looking about him, sees that it generally is. So country labour, unlike town labour, produces a surplus, collectable as rent by the landowner.

[3] Richard Cantillon (1685–1734) has always been a man of mystery, not yet entirely dispelled by the facts collected by his industrious biographer, Antoin Murphy (1986). It used to be said that he is not the most famous economist who is known to have been murdered; but it now appears that the evidence for that is not conclusive. It may have been a disappearance, such as has been attempted by other financiers, not usually so successfully. His book, *Essai sur la nature du commerce en général*, stated to be translated from the English, did not appear until 1755.

So much for the earning (and distribution) of the social income: but what of the spending side? The division into sectors has thrown up that problem. The people who draw their incomes from a sector do not necessarily spend within that same sector: some is spent 'domestically' and some on 'imports' from the other. Taken together, the sectors constitute a closed system, in which income and expenditure must balance; if that also holds for the sectors separately (if each is 'balancing its budget'), the imports and exports of each sector must balance. By the imposition of this balance-of-payments condition, the system can be made to 'work'.

It is reasonable to suppose that most (if not all) of country demand for town products comes from landowners. Country labour spends nearly all its income on country products, so the labour sub-sector of the country sector is approximately a closed economy in itself. Thus it is mostly the spending of rents on town products which provides the export market for the town and thereby enables it to buy the food which it requires. One can certainly recognize that much in Cantillon.

Later economists have thought this to be an odd doctrine; but there are conditions, not only those of Cantillon's own environment, which it fits. It is still true, in some non-industrialized countries, that government is supported out of an agricultural surplus. Part of this is devoted to feeding, and clothing, the government's own servants; while part, in the modern case of a non-closed national economy, is sold abroad. Again, these exports pay for imports; so the goods needed by government (and indeed by other people in the national town sector) which cannot be produced at home are obtained by way of international exchange. It is still true, in such conditions, that the population, which can be employed at reasonable wages, will be larger the larger is the agricultural surplus. That is what Cantillon says.

3. The Physiocrats

Cantillon's book does not seem to have attracted many readers; but it had an important influence on that group who first took to themselves the name of 'economists', those who flourished in France between 1750 and the Revolution, and later became known as Physiocrats. I do not need to discuss their work in detail, but there is one deduction they made from the Cantillon model which deserves attention. It carries on from what has just been said.

Suppose that the demand on the landowners for town products increases, so that additional exports from the town are required. These could be provided by the town devoting more of its production to export, retaining less for its own consumption; but it does not seem very likely that this is the way it would react. (Remember that the supply of labour in the town is perfectly elastic, so that there is nothing to stop it increasing the output of its own products, if it is able to dispose of them. And here is an increased demand.)

Suppose that the fraction of their incomes which townspeople desire to spend on imports is k. (k must be less than 1.) Then, to maintain equilibrium in the balance of payments of the town sector,

Increase in exports = increase in imports = k × increase in income,

so that

$$\text{Increase in town income} = (1/k) \times \text{increase in exports},$$

and $(1/k)$ is necessarily greater than 1.

That an increase in exports should lead to an increase in incomes was not surprising; but the balance of payments shows that there is an extra increase arising from the spending of a part of the extra income upon home production. Just the same story as with the Keynesian multiplier! Why was there nothing of this in Adam Smith? Let us see.

4. Smith's Dynamic Method

It is commonly thought that the main way in which Smith's model differs from that of his predecessors is that he sectorializes differently. He also has two sectors, one producing a surplus, the other not. But his unproductive sector is much more restricted than the town sector of the Physiocrats, which it succeeds. Most of what in common parlance would be called town labour we would reckon as productive.

It is tempting to take this as a reflection of the more industrialized economy in which he was living; but when one remembers that the *Wealth of Nations* was published in 1776, while the date favoured by economic historians for the beginning of the Industrial Revolution in Britain is a bit later, that is not very convincing. I believe that a more important reason for the change goes deeper. He wanted to have the model he is using more firmly placed in time.

While a model such as that of the Physiocrats might do if one were making a comparison between the wealth of different nations, it would not do if one were interested in what we should now call 'growth'. And one can see that Smith, in his opening chapters on the division of labour, has committed himself to making that a large part of his subject. For surely the specialization to which he is attaching so much import-ance is something which comes into existence in the course of growth. So his model has to allow for that. The social accounts he has in mind must be accounts *of a period*, a period which has a past and a future which are not to be assumed to be just like the period itself, carrying on in a static manner.

So, on this matter Smith is on the side of Keynes; like Keynes, he is working with analysis of the behaviour of an economy during a period. But he does not have Keynes's advantage of an actual account of an economy he can look at; he has to construct it in his mind for himself. He does this quite well; nevertheless, it is an important consequence of his proceeding that he does not feel called upon to define characteristics of his account which do not seem to need to be specified for a particular purpose: he can afford (or thinks he can afford) to be quite reticent about them. An important case of this is the question of the length of the period.

Keynes certainly took his period to be of finite length, at least long enough for different decisions to have time to show some of their consequences. It would have been better if Smith had done the same. He is however influenced by the practice of Newtonian mechanics, in his day already well established: i.e. the study of motion by dividing time into periods of infinitesimal duration. One can see that, sometimes at least, he shows that he is thinking in that manner.

If he had worked with a period of finite length, his period would have started with a stock of goods (of all sorts) inherited from the past, and would have finished with a similar stock handed on to the future. The labour employed during the period would be reckoned to be 'product-ive', in his sense, if its product contributed to the final stock (or capital); labour which did not so contribute would be reckoned as 'unproductive'. But this is not what Smith says. He defines unproductive labour as that which 'perishes in the very instant of its performance' (1970 edn.: 330). This shows that he is thinking of a period of infinitesimal length. If it had been of finite length, then labour em-ployed during the period, the product of which was consumed later on within the period, should also be reckoned as unproductive.

5. Unproductive Consumption and Capital Accumulation in Smith

There is a more important matter which can also be cleared up by the method of Smith, once we allow him to have a period of finite length. It may be conveniently approached by asking, What exactly would Smith have said, or ought he to have said, was wrong with the physiocratic model we were previously discussing? Surely it would simply have been the static condition, of one period being just like another, which had been imposed upon it. The other assumptions were empirical and might or might not have been valid. As we saw, conditions are possible in which they would be fairly valid.

The only sector of the Physiocrats' model which would have been productive, in the sense of Smith, would have been its country sector, producing corn. The town sector would have been the unproductive sector. If one were allowed to have a period of finite length, the natural period to take would be the agricultural year, from harvest to harvest. It begins with a stock of corn, carried over from the preceding year. It is that which would be the initial capital.

Suppose (as we did with the physiocratic model) that country labour consumes nothing but corn. Then there are three things which can be done with the initial capital:

1. it may be 'fed' to the country (productive) labour;
2. it may be consumed directly by landowners;
3. it may be consumed by the unproductive labour in the town.

Both of these latter may be regarded as unproductive consumption, since neither makes any contribution to the growth of the capital stock.

Let K_0 be the initial capital (of corn). Let C be the unproductive consumption (of corn). Then $K_0 - C$ is the wages (in terms of corn) which can be paid to the productive labour. This produces a surplus, on physiocratic lines, so the output of corn in the current period is $(K_0 - C)(1 + s)$. It is this which forms the final capital stock (K_1). So the increment of capital, over the period, is

$$K_1 - K_0 = sK_0 - C(1 + s).$$

If there were no unproductive consumption, capital would increase, over the period, by the full value of the surplus product; if there is a 'leak' into unproductive consumption, that reduces the growth of the capital by more than itself, because it diminishes the *input* into 'production'.

I think it is clear that this was the model which Smith was generalizing. His initial capital was of course far more complex, comprising fixed capital goods, which might need replacement, as well as goods in process. All that is fairly well understood, and I need not go into it, since it does not affect the main points I want to make. The 'unproductivity consumption' and the 'production' of Smith will obviously transform into the 'consumption' and 'investment' of Keynes.

Nevertheless, it is a pity that Smith did not carry through the physiocratic exercise we have been doing for him. For he must then have noticed that there is another thing which might be done with the initial capital (of corn). It might just have been hoarded—in granaries—to go, perhaps after some deterioration, into the final stock, but not contributing to the increment of capital. It would be unproductive, but it would not be consumption. The growth rate to be attributed to it would have been zero, or perhaps less than zero. Still, it is a possibility which Smith clearly left out. If he had noticed it, he could not have been so dogmatic about his doctrine: 'Parsimony and not industry is the immediate cause of increase of capital' (1970 edn.: 337), for which he has so often been reproved. It seems useful to show that the exception could have been allowed for within the structure of Smithian economics.

Smith missed it; Ricardo, I think, also missed it; but we do find it appearing explicitly in the work of the third Great Classic, who in several ways completed their work, J. S. Mill. Mill actually talks of 'full employment'; but it is full employment of capital, not of labour, which he has in mind. He expressly states that the capital stock, carried over from the past, may not be fully used. It can be held up, as unsold stocks, in the process of exchange.

This perpetual non-employment of a large proportion of capital is the price we pay for the division of labour. The purchase is worth what it costs, but the price is considerable. (Mill 1884: 56)

And, again more decisively, at the end of the essay in which that passage occurs,

There can be no permanent excess of production, or of accumulation; though it must at the same time be admitted that, as there may be a temporary excess of any one article considered separately, so there may be of commodities generally, not in consequence of overproduction, but of a want of commercial confidence. (Mill 1884: 74)[4]

'Animal spirits' was an eighteenth-century expression which had gone out of fashion by the time of Mill, who could have found it helpful. Its reintroduction had to wait for Keynes. I mention it here, as I am showing that a place could be found for it in Great Classical economics.

6. Keynes: Money, Wages, and Savings

As I have shown, the later nineteenth century was a Dark Age, from the point of view of the tradition which I am discussing; so I may pass it over and go straight on to Keynes. What was the essential difference between his theory and Great Classical theory? Surely it is that Keynes's was a theory of employment and money, while theirs kept money

---

[4] These essays, although not published until 1844, are stated to have been written in 1829–30, not long after Ricardo died. I think one may assume, from a passage in Mill's *Autobiography*, that they were written for a seminar, held over breakfast by a group of Mill's youthful friends, before they dispersed to the offices in which they were employed. The same doctrine can be found in Mill's *Principles* (1848) but it is sharper and clearer in the *Essays*.

separate. Looking at Keynes's theory from their standpoint, how did he bring money in?

Surely it was by his treatment of wages. Keynes's wages are money wages. By saying that he is working in wage-units, he endeavours to protect himself from the accusation that he is assuming the money wage to be constant; but he nevertheless assumes that, in conditions of less than full employment of labour, it is determined exogenously—that it is not affected by changes in the variables he is discussing. It will be just the same whether unemployment is high or low. So the simplified form of his theory which was inevitably adopted by expositors did assume constant money wages. At the time when he was writing, this was fairly acceptable; for it had been a notable experience of the Great Depression of the elderly 1930s, both in Britain and in America, that in spite of the massive unemployment the fall in money wage rates was remarkably small. The experience of those particular years set its mark on Keynes's theory.

Later experience has been different. It has long been taken for granted now that a rise in the consumer price index makes an acceptable case for a corresponding rise in money wages; so a better simplification of modern wage behaviour would be to assume the real wage to be constant, or only to vary *above* a minimum. But that is just what the Great Classics assumed. The reason they gave for the assumption was different, more appropriate to the conditions of their time; but whether the minimum is a subsistence wage or a conventionally acceptable wage, it has the same effect. So the major difference between Keynes's theory and that of the Great Classics disappears.

So it is that we have discovered by experience the importance of the point that was made by Smith—the crucial point in his theory, as I have shown it to be. If employment is to be increased, with real wages held constant, it is not sufficient that labour should be available: the goods on which the wages of that labour will be spent must also be available, and these cannot be provided out of the product of the labour which is newly employed, for that is not yet ready. (That was where the physiocratic doctrine went wrong.) When Keynes's doctrine is applied to the case of an (open) national economy, it takes the form of saying that the first effect of an expansionary policy is a strain on the balance of payments; if the policy is to be successful, the country must have reserves, of one kind or another, to cover the deficit. In the case of a closed economy, of which both Smith and Keynes were of course thinking in the first place, the reserves will have to be *real* reserves, which indeed in a cyclical depression may have piled up (as Mill perceived). They will have piled up in the form of goods that are ready, or nearly ready, for sale but have not yet been sold. So this is the case in which the simple Keynes prescription is right. Otherwise the goods must be released from the existing productive process by an increase in saving. That may be done by 'fiscal policy', increased taxation, and a budget surplus, if institutions are such that its effect on consumption can be rapid.

So Smith was not so wrong in his statement about parsimony, so long as it is qualified by the possibility of drawing on reserves. It is then true, and it is important. Note that he is valuing capital at cost, as accountants—and social accountants—do to this day. If new projects are started without savings (or the release of reserves) to match them, capital is just transmuted from one form to another—into the capital that is embodied in the early stages of the new processes from that which was embodied in the late stages of the old. It is possible, though not inevitable, that in the new form it will in the end be more *useful*; but this does not show up during the period of construction. At this stage there is bound to be a strain.

I return to the case of the national economy, which is open to external trade and external finance. Consider as an example the 'underdeveloped' country, which is to be developed by a development scheme. Suppose that the scheme has been well devised, so that it should in the end be very productive. There will still be an intermediate stage, in practice often a long one, to which the doctrine of Smith will apply. The dam (or whatever it is) is not ready; to finish it more money will have to be borrowed; the borrowing power which at that stage will be available is quite a question. If like Smith we value the uncompleted dam *at cost*, this more or less exactly offsets the debt which has been incurred; both being allowed for, the capital of the country is neither increased nor diminished. But as the time of (planned) completion approaches, with the project not yet completed, the creditor will begin to ask himself, Will it be worth what it was planned to be worth when it is done? If the answer to that is satisfactory, all is well; but if it is not, the choice lies between lending more in order to complete the project, and closing it down. If the latter alternative is adopted, the project will have been proved to be worthless, but the debt which has been incurred to finance it continues. Taking both into account, there is a loss of capital, which must somehow be shared between lender and borrower. It is conceivable that it might all be taken by the lender, in which case on the account of the borrowing country there is neither gain nor loss, though it may well be that it must expect a loss of credit, or of ability to borrow in the future for similar purposes. If some is taken by the borrower, there may be less loss of credit, but the loss of capital in which it has involved itself is explicit.

It is true that, if the project is nearly completed, the further borrowing that is needed for completion may be rather easy. For the alternatives that are open at that point are just between completion and abandonment. Although the project might never have been started if the information now available had then been available, the gain from completion against abandonment may be large, and amply sufficient to cover the cost of the extra funds. Even so, the project will have been only partially successful; so some loss of credit is likely to result.

In practice, of course, such economic considerations are liable to be obscured by political cross-currents; much international lending is motivated by the search for political advantage. Even so, there are choices between political advantages. It is only too likely that what is an economic failure will be a political failure also.

7. Conclusion

I have a few more general points to make in conclusion. First, though I have tried to show that the teaching of Keynes and that of the Great Classics can be made compatible, so that it can be available to us as a coherent system of thought, I am not maintaining that it would have been enough to say on all those problems we might call macroeconomic. There would be other directions which would remain to be explored.

Some of these were explored by the Neoclassics, of whom I have had some hard things to say. What, for instance, about the 'price mechanism'? The doctrine that all economic problems can be solved by movement of prices has now, one hopes, been exploded. I don't think it would have been maintained by Smith, and by Keynes it was certainly rejected. It has now been put to sleep, on the purest theoretical level, by the work of Debreu. But it certainly does not follow that there are not some problems where movement of prices can be a help. My suspicion is that they are mostly 'micro' rather than 'macro', as I have shown in the chapters on the working of markets in my latest book (Hicks 1989).

Another quite different direction in which neoclassical economics went 'macro' in an interesting manner was in its concept of the utility optimum, with the valuation of the social product at market price, rather than cost, which goes along with it. This received its most important expression in the *Economics of Welfare* of Pigou.[5] The estimates of national income which were made by Colin Clark (1932 1937) were income in the sense of Pigou and thus carried on from it.

I may claim that I myself perceived (in 1940) that there were two senses of income that were coming up; and that they were not identical.

[5] Originally published as *Wealth and Welfare* (in 1912), given the title by which it is generally known in 1920, after which it went through several editions with not inconsiderable alterations.

In later work I kept both in play. But I gradually became convinced[6] that all that was of practical use on the welfare side was 'micro' rather than 'macro'. So there I am happy to leave it.

Returning to the period which has a past and a future, there is a related point concerning the past. We meet it in a chapter in the *General Theory*, which notoriously has not passed into Keynesian tradition, the chapter on user cost (Keynes 1936: ch. 6, app.). If a machine that is in constant use had a market price both at the beginning and at the end of the period, over-use during the period would show up as a fall in that market price. But the bulk of such machines do not change hands, so as to have at each such point in time a market price. There is nothing then to be done, as businessmen in practice have discovered, but to allocate to the period a share in original cost. But that allocation, being based on original cost, is not a price of the period; so it must be the same whatever is done, or might be done, during the period. Thus, for the application of the Keynesian method, comparing what is done and might have been done during the period, it can do no harm to leave it out; whence the gross investment and gross product with which we have become familiar. But except for this application, it can hardly be claimed that gross product is a concept which makes much sense.

Rather similarly for the future. The form in which the terminal stock is left will make no difference to the accounts of the current period. But in practice it may make a considerable difference. Keynesians have not (to my knowledge) done much on this 'continuation' theory; perhaps that is why their doctrine has got the reputation of being short-sighted. Ricardo, however, did attend to it, in the difficult chapter on machinery which he added to the last edition of his book which he himself prepared. Though some of his immediate followers did consider it, in the days of the Neoclassics (and Keynesians) it got lost. I myself, particularly in my later work,[7] have gone on worrying about it. I have approached it from several angles, none perhaps very successfully. I can nevertheless claim that I have made some explorations.

But there is much more to be done. So I would like to end this paper, which has been so much concerned with the past, with a call to others (it will have to be others) to continue with continuation—into the future.

---

[6] In the course of writing several essays that are reprinted in my *Wealth and Welfare* volume (Hicks 1981).

[7] It begins with some unsatisfactory chapters (16 and 22) in my *Capital and Growth* (1965); appears again in the final chapter and Appendix of *Theory of Economic History* (1969); has in effect a volume devoted to it in *Capital and Time* (1973), of which Ch. XII, which uses a different method, should be separately noticed; the whole of these writings being reviewed in my *Economic Perspectives* (1979: 184–95).

References

CANTILLON, RICHARD (1955). *Essai sur la nature du commerce en général.* New York: Augustus M. Kelly.

CLARK, COLIN (1932). *National Income.* London: Macmillan.

—— (1937). *National Income and Outlay.* London: Macmillan.

HICKS, JOHN (1942). *Social Framework.* Oxford: Clarendon Press.

—— (1965). *Capital and Growth.* Oxford University Press.

—— (1969). *A Theory of Economic History.* Oxford University Press.

—— (1973). *Capital and Time: A Neo-Austrian Theory.* Oxford: Basil Blackwell.

—— (1979). *Economic Perspectives.* Oxford University Press.

—— (1981). *Collected Essays on Economic Theory,* i: *Wealth and Welfare.* Oxford: Basil Blackwell.

—— (1989). *A Market Theory of Money.* Oxford University Press.

KEYNES, J. M. (1930). *A Treatise on Money.* London: Macmillan.

—— (1936). *General Theory of Employment, Interest and Money.* London: Macmillan.

—— (1940). *How to Pay for the War.* London: Macmillan.

MILL, J. S. (1844). *Essays on Some Unsettled Questions of Political Economy.* London: Parker.

—— (1848). *Principles of Political Economy.* London: Routledge & Kegan Paul, 1965 edn.

MURPHY, ANTOIN (1986). *Richard Cantillon, Entrepreneur and Economist.* Oxford: Clarendon Press.

PETTY, WILLIAM (1671). *Political Anatomy of Ireland,* in *Economic Writings,* ed. C. Hull. New York: McKelley.

PIGOU, A. C. (1912). *Wealth and Welfare.* London: Macmillan.

RICARDO, DAVID (1817). *The Principles of Political Economy and Taxation.* Cambridge University Press, 1951 edn.

SMITH, ADAM (1776). *The Wealth of Nations.* Oxford: Clarendon Press, 1970 edn.

2

Keynesian Economics: Past Confusions, Future Prospects

AXEL LEIJONHUFVUD

1. Introduction

The complaint has become widespread in recent years that macroeconomics is in a confused state. Theory and practice have lost virtually all connection. The approaches generating all the theoretical excitement offer almost no guidance on stabilization policy. Policy practice proceeds on the basis of theories in which we no longer have much confidence. Keynesian and Monetarist beliefs continue to contend with New Classical ideas with no clear-cut resolution in sight.

One way to find an intelligible pattern in this confusing contention among alternative approaches is to take them in historical sequence and consider, again, the grounds on which some substantial segment of the profession decided to transfer its allegiance from one camp to another. This is the tack taken here. The sketch that follows cannot be comprehensive: it is selective, which means, of course, that it is in some degree subjective.

2. The Swedish Flag

Consider first the following 'Swedish Flag' taxonomy. This classifies business cycle theories according to the hypotheses they make about the *impulses* that initiate fluctuations and about the *propagation* mechanisms that turn the impulses into persistent movements in output and employment.

A nominal impulse (N) is a disturbance to the system such that the re-equilibration of the economy requires (only) a change in nominal scale, i.e. an adjustment of the money price level, leaving real magnitudes unaffected. Purely nominal impulses are neutral, in other words. A helicopter drop of fiat money in a Patinkin model free of distribution effects is an example. A real impulse (R), on the other hand, requires some reallocation of resources between industries or occupations, and therefore also some corresponding change in relative prices. If it is a 'pure' case of a real disturbance, it will not require a general deflation or inflation in order to restore equilibrium (see Fig. 2.1). For the immediate purposes of the Flag, we deal throughout with a particular sub-category of real impulses, namely the intertemporal ones.

Close real-world approximations to the pure cases may be relatively rare, so the Flag is drawn to recognize 'mixed' categories on both the impulse and the propagation side. Our historical review of macroeconomic debates will not compel us to discuss them, however.

3. R/R (Keynes) and N/N (Friedman)

How propagation comes in is best explained by going directly to the relevant cases. Start at R/R in the lower right-hand corner of Fig. 2.1 with 'the economics of Keynes'. Various events may cause firms to change their views about the profitability of investment, i.e. of employing present productive resources for the purpose of augmenting future output. If this shift of the 'marginal efficiency of capital', as Keynes called it, is in a pessimistic direction, for example, they will plan to reduce investment, thereby creating an excess supply of present resources and, implicitly, an excess demand for future goods. This disequilibrium Keynes liked to describe in terms of quantities ('saving exceeds investment'), while Wicksell preferred to describe it in terms of prices ('the market rate exceeds the natural rate'). The appropriate system response should be that real rates of interest fall (so as to raise the price of future goods in terms of present goods). The Keynesian propagation hypothesis is that speculation prevents the real rates of interest from falling sufficiently to equate saving and investment at full employment. With the failure of the relevant relative price to co-ordinate intertem-

		Propagation		
		Nominal	Mixed	Real (intertemporal)
Impulse	Nominal	N/N		N/R
	Mixed			
	Real (intertemporal)	R/N		R/R

Fig. 2.1

poral activities, the excess supply of present resources is removed by a decline in output and employment.

In the upper left-hand corner, at N/N, we find the monetarism of Milton Friedman or of Brunner and Meltzer, i.e. the monetarism before New Classical economics. The typical disturbance is an exogenous change in the fiat money supply; the failure of the money wage to adjust immediately propagates the shock to real magnitudes so that real income and employment (and not only nominal prices) co-vary with the money stock. Note carefully that the stickiness of money wages is *essential* to this theory: without it, the history of the US money stock is not to be transformed into a history of US business fluctuations.

4. The Monetarist Debate that Never Happened

A monetarist controversy between the N/N and R/R positions would have been relatively straightforward. The theoretical cores of the two are easily grasped. The N/N theory asserts that the typical disturbance is nominal and that the problem with the system is that nominal prices do not adjust promptly. The R/R hypothesis asserts that real disturbances require changes in intertemporal prices but that the capitalist system has peculiar difficulty in producing this particular adjustment when it is needed. In each case, there is a straightforward correspondence between what the impulse requires and what the system won't do.

Note that the two theories are not mutually exclusive. It is perfectly reasonable (at least a priori) to take the eclectic view that certain episodes in our macro history were of the N/N type, others were of the R/R type, and yet others, indeed, were 'mixed'. But one can easily imagine a debate between two camps, one insisting on a 'real', the other on a 'monetary', interpretation of the historical record. That debate never took place.

5. The 'Keynes and the Classics' Debate

Before the Monetarists came on the scene, internal developments within the Keynesian camp had already shifted the Keynesian position into the bottom left (R/N) corner of the Flag. The Keynesian economics that filled the textbooks for three decades retained the hypothesis that shifts in the marginal efficiency of capital were the typical cause of changes in income but stressed money-wage 'rigidity' as the cause of unemployment. It is curious that 'Keynesian' economics should have ended up in this position, since the wage rigidity explanation of unemployment was one that Keynes had done his best to dispute. Moreover, it is not at all obvious that the mix of a real disturbance hypothesis with a nominal inflexibility hypothesis results in a coherent theory.

This, however, was the outcome of the so-called 'Keynes and the Classics' debate, which sought to isolate and define the fundamental difference between Keynes's 'revolutionary' new theory and previously accepted 'classical' theory. At one stage (Modigliani 1944) two 'causes' of unemployment were distinguished in the discussion: (1) the traditional one of a money-wage level too high in relation to the nominal scale of the economy (as determined by an exogenously set money supply), and (2) Keynes's novel one of an interest rate too high for savings not to exceed investment at full employment. But the Pigou-effect argument, it was eventually agreed, demonstrated that this second explanation also depended on nominal-wage inflexibility and therefore should not be accepted as a distinct and independent case. In thus reasserting the generality of the classical unemployment explanation, this brand of Keynesianism lost sight of the difference between an unemployment state that could be cured by a money-wage correction of a few percentage points (so as to bring wages into the equilibrium relationship with the nominal scale of the system) and one of similar extent that would require a horrifying never-yet-experienced deflation (in order to produce a sizeable wealth effect on saving out of the increased real value of the outside money stock).

This shift of the Keynesian position switched the theoretical focus from the role of intertemporal relative prices in the co-ordination of saving and investment over time to the relationship between current aggregate money expenditure and money wages.

6. The Monetarist Controversy

The Keynesian–Monetarist controversy started, therefore, with the Keynesians in this muddled R/N position being attacked by Monetarists from an N/N position. The Keynesians found the defence difficult. To cover all the issues and all the various stages of this thirty-year debate is not feasible here. Consider first two examples from the later stages which, although hardly central to the controversy as a whole, serve to show how the discussion was affected by the Keynesian shift from R/R to R/N.

First, consider the Keynesian response to Friedman's so-called 'natural rate of unemployment' hypothesis. This hypothesis was not one of the original issues in the debate but was added rather late in the game. For present purposes, it may be stated as follows:

> Employment has a strong tendency to converge rapidly on equilibrium employment. What ensures this result is simply the ordinary

supply-and-demand mechanism operating on the price in the relevant market. Unemployment will be found to diverge from its
'natural rate' only when, and in so far as, the money-wage rate
temporarily lags behind its equilibrium value.

From the standpoint of Keynes's R/R theory, this is true if and only if
intertemporal equilibrium is already assured—but false whenever saving
does not equal investment at full-employment income. Any Keynesian
would have said so in the 1940s. But when, in the 1960s, Friedman
added the 'natural rate of unemployment' hypothesis to the structure of
monetarist beliefs about the world, the intertemporal co-ordination
problem was out of sight and out of mind among his Keynesian
opponents. No one brought it up! It was not even mentioned.

So what retort was left to them? The answer given was, in effect, that
Friedman was right: only lagging wage adjustment stands in the way of
full employment—but money wages are *more inflexible* than he or any
other Monetarists would like to believe! In this way, Keynesian economics became so strongly wedded to the notion of wage inflexibility that,
by now, most of the profession thinks of it as *the* characteristic that
distinguishes it from other brands of macroeconomics—and also as the
basis for its advocacy of active stabilization policies. The irony of all this
is of course palpable: money-wage inflexibility is down-played by the
side that necessarily needs the hypothesis in the context of its own
(N/N) theory; it is insistently played up by the side that has stumbled
into the hypothesis only by mistake!

Second, consider the Keynesian response to Robert Barro's (1974)
so-called Ricardian equivalence theorem. This theorem asserts that the
present value of future taxes has the same effect on aggregate behaviour
as an equivalent amount of current taxes; consequently, there is no
reason to delay taxation, and the Keynesian proclivity for bond-financed
deficit spending, rather than simply balanced budget spending, has no
rational basis.

The natural Keynesian (R/R) retort to this should have been to insist
that the discussion keep to the original context for these characteristic
Keynesian fiscal policy recommendations. That context was, of course,
one of unemployment arising from intertemporal disequilibrium. With
real interest rates at a level that will not allow saving–investment
co-ordination at full employment, the result will be an excess supply of
present factor services and an implicit excess demand for future goods.
Spending now will reduce this excess supply; taxing later will reduce the
excess demand. The temporal structure of the Keynesian policy fits the
temporal maldistribution of excess demands left uncorrected by intertemporal price adjustments.

Barro's Ricardian theorem presupposes intertemporal general equilibrium. This is not a state of affairs that needs to be 'stabilized'. Nor has anyone ever suggested that activist fiscal policies should be used in such circumstances. Moreover, the only thing of much interest that can be said about the calculation of wealth at a market rate different from Wicksell's natural rate is that *everyone* will get the wrong result.

But, again, no one brought it up. Having lost track of Keynes's saving–investment problem, the critical replies to Barro accepted his intertemporal equilibrium assumption but argued that his aggregative conclusions might still be invalidated by distribution effects. Admittedly, intergenerational distribution effects are somewhat more interesting and slightly more amenable to empirical study than the run-of-the-mill distribution effects that always surround any macro-theoretical proposition with a penumbra of doubts. But Keynesian fiscal policy doctrine cannot be restored on this ramshackle foundation.

7. Successive Monetary Regimes and the Monetarist Controversy

Although conflicting beliefs about the economy's capacity for 'automatic' self-equilibrating adjustment bedevilled the debate from beginning to end and made progress even towards some 'agreement to disagree' difficult, the explicit issues at the core of the controversy concerned the role of money in the determination of income (both nominal and real) and the effectiveness of monetary policy. The debate on these issues did not take place in the safe isolation of some ivory tower. Instead, the course it took was strongly influenced from the start by external events and, in particular, by the monetary regime changes of the last fifty years.

The experience of the 1930s formed the economic world view of early American Keynesianism in more ways than one. With regard to money, the formative memories were of a banking system that, in the wake of the Great Crash and deflation, found few of its potential borrowers credit-worthy and seemed to have an almost insatiable new taste for excess reserves. Monetarism, as it first emerged, was primarily a challenge to the doctrine of monetary policy ineffectiveness that Keynesians had distilled from this experience and had carried over into a postwar world that was very different.

The younger men who were about to assume leading roles in Keynesian economics after the war—Tobin, Modigliani *et al.*—were not wedded to this ineffectiveness notion, however. Their differences with Friedman ran deeper. Basically, these Keynesians thought of changes in the money stock as changes in bank credit that had their effects on investment, output, and employment via changes in real interest rates.

In contrast, the Monetarists thought of changes in the money stock as changes in the 'nominal scalar' of the real economy. The actual rescaling dictated by a particular nominal impulse would, however, come about with 'long and variable lags'; in the mean time, nominal impulses had real effects. These two competing perceptions of 'what money does' fit—to the extent that they do fit—quite different monetary regimes.

Consider two basic, inherited ideas of how a society may achieve predictability and stability of the nominal price level. We may refer to them as 'convertibility control' and 'quantity control', respectively. The macroeconomic theory appropriate to a regime relying for its nominal stability on convertibility differs in important respects from the one appropriate to a regime relying on government control of the stock of money.

The main points are as follows. Under commodity convertibility, the government fixes the nominal price of gold (for example) and leaves it to the banks and their customers to determine the corresponding equilibrium stocks of money and other liquid assets. Under quantity control, the monetary authorities fix the quantity of money and allow the markets to determine the corresponding equilibrium level of nominal prices. From the standpoint of the government, the first is a 'price-fixing, quantity-taking' and the second a 'quantity-fixing, price-taking' strategy.

The constraints that convertibility imposes on the behaviour of the monetary authorities prevent them from bringing about sizeable changes in the equilibrium price level. In general, therefore, monetary policy cannot be very 'effective' if by that we mean causing large changes in nominal income. The commitment to redeem money in gold (or foreign currency) on demand means forgoing the option of controlling the money stock. Roughly speaking, the money stock is determined by demand rather than supply. In a system where the money stock adjusts to the price level rather than the other way round, however, the central bank can worry about the price and availability of credit and their effects on real activity in the economy. If convertibility were generally to be seen to guarantee the price level, the public will have 'inelastic expectations'; that is, whenever the price level departs a bit from the longer-term trend set by the supply and demand for gold, people expect it to return to trend. The inelasticity of price expectations reduces the amplitude of fluctuations in money prices and money wages (even when these are perfectly 'flexible'). With such expectations, changes in the central bank discount rate change the real price and changes in bank reserves change the real volume of credit supplied. The monetary authorities therefore have some limited leverage over output and employment in such a system.

Clearly, much of this has a distinctly Keynesian ring to it. But the match between the two theories is not perfect. The standard Keynesian model did not have an endogenously varying but an exogenously fixed money stock, just as did the monetarist one (see, however, Tobin 1963). And Keynesians in general have not regarded the validity of their theory as in any way restricted to convertible regimes.

Monetarist theory is best suited to the pure-quantity control case. When the economy is on a pure fiat standard, control over some nominal stock is necessary in order to provide the system with a nominal anchor. If the authorities try to govern real credit, and do not keep track of the money stock, they are likely to fail at their primary task of providing nominal stability. Interest rate targeting of monetary policy, which is a natural tactic when convertibility takes care of the price level, threatens total loss of control over the price level under these conditions. Monetary policy is obviously 'effective' under quantity control in the sense that it can bring about large changes in money income (by changing the money stock and letting the price level adjust). What is not so clear is whether it can have a reliable, predictable effect on real activity.

Now, Keynesian economics evolved in the heyday of the Bretton Woods system (of which Keynes, not so coincidentally, had been one of the principal architects). This meant that, until the late 1960s, Keynesian economics dealt with a world in which the monetary regime was such as to avoid exposing the economy to sizeable nominal shocks—one that behaved in most respects as the convertibility model. Keynesian theory came to embody, therefore, the ingrained analytical habits of interpreting money stock changes in effect as changes in the real volume of credit, and of treating monetary policy as operating chiefly through its effect on real rates of interest. As the Bretton Woods system crumbled and was swept away, however, these were no longer the most appropriate mental habits. On the whole, Keynesians adapted only slowly and reluctantly to the inflationary environment of the 1970s. The monetarist analytical habit of interpreting money stock changes not as endogenous responses to real income movements, but as nominal shocks requiring, albeit with long and variable lags, a corresponding adjustment in the nominal scale of the economy, now came into its own. Monetarists were more ready than Keynesians for a world in which nominal scale varied almost altogether independently of real variables. Keynesians tended to dwell on stagflation as a puzzling phenomenon and to hang on too long to the belief in predictable and exploitable Phillips trade-offs. This Keynesian unpreparedness to deal with an inflationary world thus handed the Monetarists a series of easy victories at this stage of the debate.

8. New Classical Economics

The New Classical movement began with Lucas's attempt to construct a micro-theoretically founded model of Friedman's theory. In that theory, movements in employment could be generated by assuming either that the labour market did not clear, or else that it cleared but on the basis of asymmetric expectations between the two sides of the market. For methodological reasons, Lucas did not want to make either assumption. Instead, he first produced a monetarist version of Phelps's 'islands' model. This model still belongs at N/N in the Flag taxonomy, but Lucas soon shifted to a N/R model in which nominal impulses led to changes in the intertemporal prices perceived by transactors, who would respond by reallocating their supply of labour and their consumption of leisure between the present and the future.

For several years following its appearance, Lucas's intertemporal equilibrium business cycle model was the 'leading edge' in macroeconomic debates. Thus the late 1970s offered the odd spectacle of a sort of Keynesian–monetarist controversy on the 'wrong' diagonal. By now, a few years later, it seems unclear whether much of substance was learned from this clash of the two combinations of mismatched hypotheses—the supposedly 'Keynesian' R/N theory and the Lucasian N/R theory.

This N/R theory did not become a lasting position for the New Classicals, however. Their Minnesota wing led a withdrawal from the nominal inpulse hypothesis. Sims (1983) showed that the empirical support for it was much weaker than previously thought, while work by Wallace (1981), Sargent (e.g. 1987), and others subverted its quantity theory foundations. These attacks from a new quarter on monetarism in all its versions opened the way for Kydland and Prescott's 'real business cycle theory', in which exogenous changes in anticipated productivity govern the variations in employment. This is an equilibrium model in the New Classical sense, so the fluctuations in activity that it exhibits are optimal. Propagation here becomes a matter of explaining not departures from equilibrium, but the persistence of (relatively) high or low activity states. The hypotheses favoured among the real business cycle theorists use the durability of capital or its gestation period ('time-to-build') to spread out the effects of productivity shocks through time.

The Kydland–Prescott theory is also intertemporal. In equilibrium models where information is not dispersed, we deal in effect with a representative agent (or social planner), so the basic story can be put in time-honoured Robinson Crusoe form. We may imagine that Crusoe's island has seasonal weather and that there are certain planting seasons when the future return to present effort is particularly high. Robinson's dynamic programme will then tell him to behave like farmers through the ages, that is, to work long hours in the planting season and to take his leisure at times when his productivity is lower. (For Lucas's N/R theory, in contrast, we would have to imagine that the powers that be rain fiat money on him from time to time and that, whenever this happens, Robinson will draw the unwarranted conclusion that the planting season has arrived.)

In Kydland and Prescott's model employment is high, in effect, when the 'marginal efficiency of capital' is high. So we are back at R/R. But something has gone askew in this slow (fifty-year) dance around the Flag. Consider the positions now. To many erstwhile Keynesians, resistance to the New Classical economics has centred on their market-clearing assumption: resistance, in other words, is based on wage stickiness once more. At the same time, the inflationary world of the 1970s has taught them to regard changes in the money supply as the principal cause of changes in nominal income. These New Keynesians, therefore, have arrived more or less at Friedman's old position at N/N (almost as soon as it had been vacated by the New Classicals). But they use it as a base for asserting the need for active stabilization policy. Meanwhile, the New Classicals have arrived at R/R, once a Keynesian position, from which they argue that no stabilization policy is needed because observed fluctuations in activity are to be interpreted as optimal.

9. Keynesian Theory and the New Equilibrium Approach

The real business cycle (RBC) version of the New Classical economics would seem to be the leading research programme in macroeconomics today (cf. also Hansen 1985). At present, therefore, an appraisal of the prospects of Keynesian economics requires a redefining of that tradition in relation to this contemporary vanguard in economic theory. I choose not to consider the 'Keynesian economics' (at R/N), but to restrict myself to 'the economics of Keynes'. The two theories to be juxtaposed, therefore, are both at R/R.

For nearly three decades, Keynesians (of whatever description) have had to struggle with the task of defining their differences *vis-à-vis* evolving monetarist doctrines. This time monetarism—all of a sudden—is out of it. Or so it seems. Not, certainly, because it was vanquished by decades of Keynesian opposition but, instead, because it was abandoned by the younger generation that at one point was taken to be the heirs of Friedman and Brunner. The startling, dramatic thing about the New Classical school, in fact, is the speed with which, in a few years, it has moved from a monetarist N/N position to one that is, if not diametrically, then at least 'diagonally', opposed at R/R. In terms of the history of business cycle theory, these are two very different views of the world between which we have seen unending controversy. Continuity, in this school, is not a matter of tenaciously held beliefs about the real world: it is provided, instead, by shared (and tenacious) beliefs about what is 'good economics' or good ways of doing economics.

It is not obvious that either Keynesian economics or New Classical RBC economics has absorbed the lessons that should be learned from monetarism. But this time we may leave the monetarist issues aside. What seems intriguing, at present, is that the vanguard has come around to R/R—which is where we started with Keynes fifty years ago. No public rehabilitation for Keynesian economics results from this late-coming coincidence; for, in New Classical (NC) eyes, it wasn't 'good economics'. It was never done properly, as equilibrium theory.

What was done improperly in Keynesian theory can all be encapsulated in the complaint that the Keynesians created a macroeconomics distinct from, and certainly not rigorously derived from, microeconomics. The New Classicals do insist on building macroeconomics from first principles—meaning essentially from postulates of 'rational' behaviour. The distance from individual rationality to aggregative systemic rationality is often taken in quick stride (in part because the rational capabilities postulated for the typical agent are anything but modest). Thus the NC–RBC models describe cycles as efficient, perfectly co-ordinated dynamic responses to exogenous perturbations in productivity. (Since these responses are 'rational' from a systemic point of view, they do not require any policy intervention.) The New Classicals obeyed this same imperative in deserting the nominal shock hypothesis, finding it difficult, in the end, to believe that rational agents would not keep fully informed about changes in the money stock.

Making a methodological principle of the rational behaviour postulate may seem harmless or in any case unobjectionable to economists. But instructions on how to do things also tell you what things to do. So the methods deemed successful for obtaining answers in microeconomics are now determining what questions get asked in macroeconomics. And, for the first decade or so of New Classical economics, the old question— 'How good is the market system at co-ordinating activities?'—has not been one of them.

How does this come about? At the risk of over-simplifying and thus failing to do justice to the New Classical programme, let me try loosely to sketch the modelling strategy that has driven the programme.

The starting point is 'rational behaviour', conceived of as individual choice between perceived alternatives and represented, of course, in terms of optimization subject to constraints. It is unnecessary at this point to rehearse familiar reservations about the underlying cognitive assumptions. New Classical economics, however, adds a couple of lemmas to the rational behaviour postulate, namely:

1. The rational agent will have learned not to make systematic mistakes but will know the structure of the economy (at least one step ahead of economists).
2. Rational agents will not leave any gains from trade unexploited.

Broadly interpreted, the second lemma says that economists have no social function while the first says that they are the last to learn, anyway. Oh, well, a little humility will do us no harm!

Now, it was supposed that the first of these lemmas more or less does away with discrepancies between the subjectively perceived and the objectively existing reality and also, therefore, between the expectations of different agents. (Note, however, the effective challenge to this supposition by E. S. Phelps 1983.) When the pre-reconciliation of expectations can in this way be taken for granted, the second lemma will, under competitive conditions and with complete markets, transfer the rationality of the representative agent to the economic system as a whole. When gains from trade are exhausted, markets clear and are efficient. Most importantly, the law of one price will hold everywhere and will ensure that anyone using a resource takes into account its value to all other agents in the system and, therefore, that resources move without fail into their highest valued uses. The Modigliani–Miller theorem is in this broad sense an instance of the law of one price.

On the finance side of the New Classical economics, the hunt is on for other applications of Modigliani–Miller reasoning that may also have surprising or perhaps counter-intuitive implications (cf. Sargent 1987). The Ricardian equivalence theorem (Barro 1974) may be regarded as belonging in this class; so does the irrelevance theorem for open-market operations (Wallace 1981). Both theorems state, in effect, that the government accomplishes nothing by swapping what in the end will amount to perfect substitutes with the private sector. The irrelevance of the open-market operations proposition is one prong of a more comprehensive New Classical attack on the quantity theory. Wallace's 'legal restrictions' theory of money is another (Wallace 1983). The related Black–Fama–Hall theory is a third. It envisages a financial system in which, once legal restrictions impeding competition were removed, money would not be distinguishable from other securities, its quantity would therefore not be definable, and debts would be settled basically in barter deals for securities (Black 1970; Fama 1980; and for dissenting views O'Driscoll 1986; White 1984).

Thus, individual optimization with the two lemmas of rational expectations and exhaustion of the gains from trade produces a perfectly co-ordinated system—one that for most modelling purposes may be represented by one rational representative; and it is a system with no function for 'money' to perform. This should sound at least vaguely familiar. We have been here before.

From all this recent work, we have learned quite a lot about how to model dynamic systems based on intertemporal optimization and so on. Perhaps we have also learned to see more clearly some of the properties of perfectly co-ordinated systems. But on some spiral staircase of increasing formal sophistication, we are obviously coming back again and again to the same basic issues.

The dissatisfaction over the incongruous relationship of Keynesian macro to neo-Walrasian micro was not first felt or voiced by the New Classicals. The conceptual tension between value and allocation theory and monetary and cycle theory preoccupied Frank Knight, Friedrich Hayek, Erik Lindahl, John Hicks, and many others in the decade or so before the *General Theory*. From the standpoint of analytical method, the *General Theory* is itself an attempt to find an acceptable resolution. *Values and Capital* is another such attempt.

Note also that these authors did not see the problem of the relationship between equilibrium value theory and business cycle theory simplistically in terms of the contrast between stationary and fluctuating processes. To them, seasonal fluctuations were not part of business cycle theory precisely because they understood them to be equilibrium motions governed by (what we today call) rational expectations—and therefore not worth worrying about.

More to the point, perhaps, neither did they see this problematic relationship in terms of market-clearing *v.* non-market-clearing models. Lindahl and Hicks, in particular, constructed models in which all markets 'cleared' in each period. They, and Hayek also, regarded the fulfilment of expectations (between points of time) as the troublesome aspect of the equilibrium assumption.

Those of us who came out of graduate programmes in the early 1960s had been taught a micro and a macro theory that could not have applied to the same world at the same time. So this problem was of intense concern to many of us. Our label for it was the 'microfoundations of macroeconomics'. Quite a lot was written about it at one time (cf. Weintraub 1979).

Robert Lucas resolved this tension between micro and macro by declaring that the problem did not really exist. The appearance of a problem was due simply to the fact that macroeconomics had not been done right. The microfoundations problem would evaporate once we decided to do macro theory in strict obedience to micro-theoretical modelling principles.

That cut the Gordian knot, all right. But why was this path not taken before? Let me give a personal answer: because macroeconomics (I thought) is about system co-ordination, and one should not adopt a method that threatens to define away the main problem. The New Classical economics has the priorities the other way around—and carrying through from individual optimizing behaviour, it all but eliminates the co-ordination problem.

10. The Co-ordination Question

The co-ordination question, simply stated, is this: Will the market system 'automatically' co-ordinate economic activities? Always? Never? Sometimes very well, but sometimes pretty badly? If the latter, under what conditions, and with what institutional structures, will it do well or do badly? I regard these questions as the central and basic ones in macroeconomics.

The market system does very well with seasonal fluctuations, obviously. But that is surely in large measure because of their recurrent, predictable nature, which allows people to plan ahead in a co-ordinated fashion. Kydland and Prescott have the right modelling strategy for seasonal fluctuations. Maybe most business cycles are 'very much like' seasonal fluctuations—one should not pretend that the answer to that one is obvious. But the end of the First World War, or the Great Depression, or the first oil shock, or the international debt crisis— those, surely(?), were not 'like' seasonal fluctuations.

The point of the co-ordination question is this: Will the market mechanism work 'automatically' even if people are not so smart? Will it work even in cases of unprecedented, non-recurrent 'historical' developments whose consequences are difficult (even for smart people) to foresee? Indeed, if people were no more farsighted and calculating than Pavlovian dogs—or Battaglio's pigeons—would a system of 'free markets' co-ordinate their actions?

That is what we want to know about the market system. One is not much enlightened on this question by learning that an economy would work just fine if people were so smart and knowledgeable that they did not need market feedback to adjust their behaviour. In rational expectation models, people do not learn about changing relative scarcities from price movements: price movements merely reflect what they have all already learned more directly.

Perhaps not much is gained by ranting on about co-ordination in general terms. Consider, then, a specific example of a Keynesian question that is not being worked on at present. My choice is 'Effective Demand Failures'. The effective demand failure (EDF) question concerns the 'market forces' that act on prices (and on output and consumption rates) when people have not succeeded from the outset in setting those general equilibrium prices that would have co-ordinated all activities.

Suppose that, in a situation of this sort, we construct the vector of 'notional' market excess demands. This is done by asking what quantities people would have liked to buy and sell at those prices and then aggregating these magnitudes. Let us suppose that we could be assured of arriving at a perfectly co-ordinated general equilibrium state if price adjustments were governed by these 'notional' excess demands. Then the EDF question (or one variant of it) is: Do the 'effective' excess demands — that is, the actual market forces acting to force revisions of those 'incorrect' prices — always have the same sign as the notional excess demands?

The Keynesian answer is that the effective excess demands can differ in sign from the corresponding notional excess demands in cases where financial constraints are binding (Leijonhufvud 1973). This result throws doubt on traditional general equilibrium (GE) stability propositions — and therefore on simplistic beliefs about the 'automaticity' of the market system. It seems that we cannot be certain that people will always come to learn that which they did not know to begin with.

Note that there are two types of theoretical structures that will not allow you to analyse the EDF question:

1. the fix-price GE models, commonly called 'Keynesian disequilibrium' models;
2. the New Classical models.

The question, 'What EDs govern price adjustments?' does not make sense, either in models where prices do not adjust or in models where there are no meaningful excess demands. So the EDF question is an example of a question, central to Keynesian theory, that is excluded from analysis by current methodologies.

11. Beyond New Classical Theory

For those who would like to revive the co-ordination questions, the choice would seem to be between three strategies *vis-à-vis* the currently dominating New Classical economics.

11.1 *'Try to beat them at their own game'*

This would mean finding some hole in the New Classical deductive structure that lets genuine co-ordination difficulties seep back in, despite rational agents, rational expectations, and market-clearing. The interest of the New Classicals themselves in system-states that depart from perfect co-ordination has centred on the possibility of the rational private sector facing a government of more doubtful calibre that is either trying to take 'unanticipated' (usually inflationary) actions or else simply exhibiting time-inconsistent behaviour. Other possibilities for generating non-Pareto-optimal solutions include various asymmetric information and/or externality assumptions. Here the logical possibilities are almost endless—the problem is to come up with information asymmetries that are obviously important in explaining not steady-state aspects of system structure, but variations over time in how well the system is co-ordinated, or with externalities that 'truly rational' agents cannot in the end get around.

There seem to be two fronts where an opening may be sought. One is the 'Phelps problem' (Frydman and Phelps 1983), i.e. that agents must form expectations not just about parametric disturbances to the system but about each other's expectations as well. Keynes's beauty contest parable was an instance of this general problem. (Cf. also the reference to Haltiwanger and Waldman below.) The other is the recent literature on incomplete markets and multiple equilibria in general equilibrium models. Recent contributions have made these general equilibrium indeterminacies look much less like the improbable curiosities that they did at first. With incomplete markets, the model economy is likely to have equilibria in which financial constraints are binding on subsets of agents; it may then be possible to Pareto-rank the different equilibria, showing some of them to be inefficient (e.g. Levine 1989/1991). These multiple-equilibrium systems also open the theoretical door to exogenous shifts in the expectations of rational agents—such as that old Keynesian sunspot, the 'change in the marginal efficiency of expectations' (Farmer and Woodford 1984; Woodford 1988).

11.2 *'Refuse to play by their rules'*

In the present context, this means backing away from the 'unbounded rationality' postulate in some way. Only the experimentalists and those with a firm interest in other behavioural sciences seem willing to contemplate this at present. But note that Hart (1987), for example, is quite emphatic that the observed incompleteness of contracts cannot be rationalized in a context of unbounded rationality; progress in this area is held back by the lack of a satisfactory formalization of bounded rationality. Lucas (1986) sees no pressing need for a departure in this direction but takes a tolerant wait-and-see attitude—if someone gets a

firm handle on how to model 'bounded rationality', he will take an
interest in it. If we exclude Herbert Simon, the positive theoretical
record of prominent critics of *Homo economicus* has not been encouraging. But, in my opinion, there is now reason to be encouraged by the
recent work of Heiner (1983, 1986) and Leland (1988). It is worth
noting also that interesting results can be obtained by assuming that only
a subset of transactors falls short of unbounded rationality (Haltiwanger
and Waldman 1985, 1989).

11.3 *'Raise a different topic altogether'*

If the equilibria of the New Classical models (that we have been
exposed to so far) look 'too nice', perhaps it is due in part to
conventional general equilibrium assumptions that have nothing to do
with the knowledge and information assumptions on which most of the
discussion has centred. Surely, for instance the assumption of universally
diminishing returns has been suspect all along? A number of people are
already busy in this area (cf. especially Romer 1987).

12. Increasing Returns

So, I turn finally to a topic that has been neglected by Keynes and by
Keynesians but which I think has the potential for illuminating some
traditional Keynesian concerns: namely, increasing returns to scale.

The production theory that totally dominates in macroeconomics still
has the Ricardian farm as the representative production unit: constant
returns when both land and labour can be varied, smoothly diminishing
returns when labour is varied with land constant. If effective demand
failures can be disregarded, the unemployed Ricardian farmworker need
only adjust his asking price to his marginal product in order to induce
some farmer to take him on. Finding the farm where his marginal
product is the highest may take a bit of trudging around the countryside,
but such search-unemployment would not constitute a social problem of
great consequence. Similarly, a farmer who finds himself making losses
need only cut back output to raise the productivity of his variable inputs
until they earn their keep.

The macroeconomy consisting of Ricardian farms has a smoothly
convex transformation surface. When events in the surrounding world
economy require it to change its output mix, it suffices that some

farmers move a bit of land out of corn and into wine or vice versa in the direction of the higher land-rent; the adjustment can be gradual—no one needs to make a large, discontinuous move.

Suppose, instead, an economy made up of Smithian factories (Leijonhufvud 1986). Here, 'the division of labour depends upon the extent of the market'. Increased division of labour is productive so that the average product of inputs increases with the rate of output. A highly articulated division of labour, moreover, tends to be associated with a high degree of complementarity between inputs. Picture an economy consisting of assembly lines where a whole line comes to a halt if one machine breaks down or one worker leaves his work-station.

Market-clearing becomes an unclear notion in this setting. Decreasing-cost producers will be price-setters, not price-takers, and will normally always want to sell more than their current sales at the prices they have posted. It does not make sense to treat these markets 'as if' they were auction markets.

The Smithian factories form a nonlinear input–output system where each firm produces under increasing returns to scale and also uses one or more intermediate products produced by other increasing-returns firms. Structures of this kind can be enormously productive at high levels of activity but are, by the same token, incapable of a proportional scaling down of activities. For concreteness, suppose that the typical firm has the simple production structure of two parallel assembly lines with some work-stations in common, so that some machines and some operatives serve both lines. In recession, this firm shuts down one of the lines, cutting output in half; but it cannot lay off half the work-force because the common work-stations must still be manned. Thus, Okun's law is a result not of labour-hoarding, but of the increasing-returns technology in this system. At the reduced activity level the firm's real unit costs are higher, but it cannot compensate itself by charging a higher (relative) price since its customer firms are all in the same position. Everyone is making losses in the recession, and while the losses may be limited, profitability cannot be restored by reducing output further.

Note that the direction of causation here goes from changes in the activity level to changes in productivity and not, as in New Classical real business cycle theory, from productivity to activity.

The Smithian factory worker who has been laid off cannot induce the firm to start up the idle assembly line by lowering the real wage at which he offers to work. An individual worker is not able to expand the number of production jobs by this tactic. All he might achieve is to bid the job away from someone who is still working. Implicit contracts dictating lay-offs by inverse seniority, and strong social sanctions against scabbing, are likely to evolve in this setting.

The representative firm is itself in a situation precisely analogous to that of its representative worker. It cannot induce an expansion of the entire input–output structure by cutting the supply price of its product. And a small country that is highly integrated into the international division of labour may similarly find that it is easy to inflate but, acting alone, difficult to expand real activity. These Smithian input–output systems depend on 'the extent of the market'—that is, on demand in the final goods sector—to maintain the high levels of activity required for them to show high productivity and correspondingly high real incomes. But in a highly integrated world economy, a country's final goods sector is not always under domestic control. International policy co-ordination looks far more important in a system of this sort than it does through Heckscher–Ohlin (Samuelson–Stolper) glasses.

In part, these economies of scale will be internal to the firm, but to a large extent they are external. The internal scale economies dictate that firms will accumulate capital not continuously, but in discrete, sizeable 'lumps'. Investment decisions are correspondingly riskier and the timing of investments trickier. The external economies mean that the profitability of one firm's investments depends upon the scale at which its suppliers and customers will be operating. Economic development in such a system does not repeat past patterns, but evolves through progressive differentiation of functions and through the gradual achievement of economies of scale in more and more of these functions (Young 1928).

In a system of this sort, major changes in the allocation of resources cannot be made by continuous adjustment following some gradient procedure in the direction of the optimum. We have this problem at present. The current (1987) pattern of the international division of labour has evolved in a setting of exchange rates that could not be sustained indefinitely because they required one-way capital flows of large magnitude that could not cumulate indefinitely. Thus, the world economy cannot continue to grow in the pattern set over the last fifteen years or so. The result is tremendous investment uncertainty. We do not know whether the future will be one of free or of protected markets, of monetary stability or of inflations and financial crises. How much capacity to add—and where in the world to put it—are questions that may have to be answered more by 'animal spirits' than by rational calculation in this difficult transitional period.

Again, the assumptions of the analysis just sketched certainly are not Keynesian (by any definition of the term). But perhaps that means no more than that Keynesian economics has missed an avenue that it could profitably have taken. The implications that the analysis suggests do not clash with a Keynesian view of the world—the situation of the laid-off worker, the counter-cyclical behaviour of productivity and profits, the significance of investment uncertainty, the importance of final goods sector demand all seem to fit.

13. The Prospects

Does Keynesian economics have a future? My answer is 'Yes', for two reasons. First, because the co-ordination question is a real question that cannot be kept off the agenda indefinitely. Presumably, the current generation of theorists will pursue it with methods that are as New Classical as is at all possible; but, as they come to grips with it, the substance of the work will become Keynesian, not classical (see especially Roberts 1987). Second, because, sooner or later, we really must open up our theoretical structures so that results from the other behavioural sciences can be utilized in economics. Then the 'unbounded rationality' postulate will have to go. This, too, will have the effect of moving us away from the systemic rationality of classical economic models and readmitting the 'irrational' system-states of Keynesian economics.

References

BARRO, ROBERT J. (1974). 'Are Government Bonds Net Wealth?' *Journal of Political Economy*, 82: 1095–117.

BLACK, FISHER (1970). 'Banking and Interest Rates in a World without Money: The Effects of Uncontrolled Banking'. *Journal of Bank Research*, 1/2: 8–20.

FAMA, EUGENE G. (1980). 'Banking in the Theory of Finance'. *Journal of Monetary Economics*, 6: 39–57.

FARMER, ROGER E. A. and WOODFORD, MICHAEL (1984). 'Self-fulfilling Prophecies and the Business Cycle'. CARESS Working Paper no. 84–12, April.

FRYDMAN, ROMAN and PHELPS, EDMUND S. (eds.) (1983). *Individual Forecasting and Aggregate Outcomes: 'Rational Expectations' Examined*. New York: Cambridge University Press.

HALTIWANGER, JOHN and WALDMAN, MICHAEL (1985). 'Rational Expectations and the Limits of Rationality: An Analysis of Heterogeneity'. *American Economic Review*, 75: 326–40.

———— (1989). 'Limited Rationality Synergism: The Implications for Macroeconomics'. *Quarterly Journal of Economics*, 104: 463–83.

HANSEN, GARY D. (1985). 'Indivisible Labor and the Business Cycle'. *Journal of Monetary Economics*, 16: 309–28.

HART, OLIVER (1987). 'Incomplete Contracts'. In *The New Palgrave: A Dictionary of Economics* London: Macmillan.

HEINER, RONALD A. (1983). 'The Origin of Predictable Behavior'. *American Economic Review*, 73: 560–95.

—— (1986). 'Uncertainty, Signal-detection Experiments, and Modelling Behavior'. In Richard Langlois (ed.), *Economics as a Process: Essays in the New Institutional Economics*. New York: Cambridge University Press.

KYDLAND, FINN and PRESCOTT, EDWARD C. (1982). 'Time to Build and Aggregate Fluctuations'. *Econometrica*, 50: 1345–70.

LEIJONHUFVUD, AXEL (1968). *On Keynesian Economics and the Economics of Keynes: A Study in Monetary Theory*. New York: Oxford University Press.

—— (1973). 'Effective Demand Failures'. *Swedish Economic Journal*. Reprinted in Leijonhufvud (1981*a*).

—— (1981*a*). *Information and Coordination: Essays in Macroeconomic Theory*. New York: Oxford University Press.

—— (1981*b*). 'The Wicksell Connection: Variations on a Theme'. In Leijonhufvud (1981*a*).

—— (1986). 'Capitalism and the Factory System'. In Richard Langlois (ed.), *Economics as a Process: Essays in the New Institutional Economics*. New York: Cambridge University Press.

—— (1987). 'Whatever Happened to Keynesian Economics?' In David A. Reese (ed.), *The Legacy of Keynes*. New York: Harper & Row.

LELAND, JONATHAN W. (1988). 'A Theory of "Approximate" Expected Utility Maximization'. Carnegie Mellon University Working Paper.

LEVINE, DAVID K. (1989). 'Efficiency and the Value of Money'. *Review of Economic Studies*, 56: 77–88.

—— (1991). 'Asset Trading Mechanisms and Expansionary Policy'. Journal of Economic Theory, 54: 148–64.

LUCAS, ROBERT E. JUN. (1972). 'Expectations and the Neutrality of Money'. *Journal of Economic Theory*, 4: 103–24.

—— (1975). 'An Equilibrium Model of the Business Cycle'. *Journal of Political Economy*, 83: 1113–44.

—— (1986). 'Adaptive Behaviour and Economic Theory'. *Journal of Business*, 59: 5401–26.

MODIGLIANI, FRANCO (1944). 'Liquidity Preference and the Theory of Interest and Money'. *Econometrica*. Reprinted in *The Collected Papers of Franco Modigliani*, i, ed. Andrew Abel. Cambridge, Mass.: MIT Press.

O'DRISCOLL, GERALD P. (1986). 'Deregulation and Monetary Reform'. *Federal Reserve Bank of Dallas Economic Review*, July: 19–31.

PHELPS, EDMUND S. (1983). 'The Trouble with "Rational Expectations" and the Problem of Inflation Stabilization'. In Frydman and Phelps (1983).

ROBERTS, JOHN (1987). 'An Equilibrium Model with Involuntary Unemployment at Flexible, Competitive Prices and Wages'. *American Economic Review*, 77: 856–74.

ROMER, PAUL M. (1987). 'Growth Based on Increasing Returns Due to Specialization'. *American Economic Review*, 27: 56–62.

SARGENT, THOMAS J. (1987). *Dynamic Macroeconomic Theory*. Cambridge, Mass.: Harvard University Press.

SIMS, CHRISTOPHER A. (1983). 'Is There a Monetary Business Cycle?' *American Economic Review*, 73: 228–33.

TOBIN, JAMES (1963). 'Commercial Banks as Creators of Money'. In Deane Carson, *Banking and Monetary Studies*. Homewood, Ill.: Richard D. Irwin.

WALLACE, NEIL (1981). 'A Modigliani–Miller Theorem for Open Market Operations'. *American Economic Review*, 71: 267–74.

——(1983). 'A Legal Restrictions Theory of the Demand for "Money" and the Role of Monetary Policy'. *Federal Reserve Bank of Minneapolis Quarterly Review*, Winter: 1–7.

WEINTRAUB, E. ROY (1979). *Microfoundations: The Compatibility of Microeconomics and Macroeconomics*. New York: Cambridge University Press.

WHITE, LAWRENCE H. (1984). 'Competitive Payments Systems and the Unit of Account'. *American Economic Review*, 74: 699–712.

WOODFORD, MICHAEL (1988). 'Expectations, Finance and Aggregate Instability'. In Meir Kohn and S. C. Tsiang (eds.), *Finance Constraints, Expectations, and Macroeconomics*. Oxford: Clarendon Press.

YOUNG, ALLYN (1928). 'Increasing Returns and Economic Progress'. *Economic Journal*. Reprinted in K. Aaron and T. Scitovsky (eds.), *Readings in Welfare Economics*. Homewood, Ill.: Irwin, 1969.

3

Methodological Issues and the New Keynesian Economics

JOSEPH E. STIGLITZ

1. Introduction: Two Views of Capitalism

For two centuries, economics has presented two divergent views of the capitalist system. One, focusing on its less benign aspects, earned our profession the reputation as the dismal science: it saw the capitalist economy as characterized by (among other evils) periodic recessions and grave inequality. The other, following along the tradition of Adam Smith, emphasized its efficiency. Smith's vision was, of course, far broader than the view reflected in the fundamental theorem of welfare economics; for Smith stressed—as have most non-economist advocates of market economies since—the market's striving for innovation.

1.1 *Three alternative resolutions*

There is an obvious intellectual tension between these alternative views. The Smith view dominated in microeconomics, where one of the central theorems was the fundamental theorem of welfare economics, a formulation of Adam Smith's 'invisible hand' conjecture concerning the efficiency of competitive markets; while the problems of unemployment were the focus of a quite separate sub-discipline, macroeconomics. The tension between the two approaches has been addressed in three different ways.

(a) *The neoclassical synthesis*

The most popular view during the quarter-century following the Second World War was Samuelson's neoclassical synthesis, which held that,

Section 5 of this paper is based partly on joint work undertaken with Bruce Greenwald and Andrew Weiss, to whom I am greatly indebted. Parts of the joint work have previously been reported in the papers by Greenwald and Stiglitz cited in the references, i.e. Greenwald *et al.* (1984); and Stiglitz and Weiss (papers cited in the references). Financial support from the National Science Foundation and the Hoover Institute is gratefully acknowledged.

once the government stabilizes the economy, the old 'classical' laws prevail—the basic insights of Smith still hold. The neoclassical synthesis was put forward as an assertion. It was believed because economists wanted to believe it; they did not want to discard what they had previously learned (in spite of the fact that one of the first lessons they teach their students was that bygones were bygones). But is there any scientific basis for the neoclassical synthesis, which claims that, once the government corrects the problems posed by unemployment, the economy behaves efficiently? Is there any reason to believe that market failures come only in big doses, rather than (the alternative hypothesis) that depressions and recessions are but the most obvious symptoms of more pervasive market failures, and that correcting the most obvious symptom is by no means equivalent to correcting the underlying problem? The great advantage of the neoclassical synthesis was that it allowed these two disparate views to be bound within the same text. The conventional practice, followed in most colleges and universities, of having different instructors teach the macroeconomic and microeconomic sections absolved each instructor of having to reconcile the seeming inconsistencies in the two approaches; and the natural tendency of students to compartmentalize what is taught in different courses meant that, even if they should have noticed the disparity in the approaches, most students felt little if any intellectual tension.

The lack of intellectual foundations for the neoclassical synthesis has led, during the past fifteen years, to two new attempts to reconcile macroeconomics and microeconomics.

(b) New Classical models

One set of approaches drops the 'synthesis' from neoclassical synthesis. It does not try to combine Keynesian insights with neoclassical analysis, as Samuelson tried to do. It argues that all that one needs to understand macroeconomic activity is the neoclassical model. In effect, it attempts to make macroeconomics more like microeconomics. Currently, this view is most ardently represented by the 'real business cycle' theories, which claim that the economy's fluctuations can be explained by exogenous 'shocks' to its productivity. In the late 1970s and early 1980s, New Classical economics, emphasizing the importance of rational expectations, dominated.[1]

(c) New Keynesian models

The other approach attempts to change microeconomics, to make it possible to derive from 'correct' microeconomic principles commonly

[1] Later I shall comment more extensively on these two approaches.

observed macroeconomic phenomena. To accommodate microeconomics to macroeconomics, it introduces doses of imperfect information, imperfect competition, and adjustment costs. It looks for a variety of explanations of wage and price rigidities; it seeks to explain both the causes and consequences of these rigidities—consequences that extend beyond the macroeconomic fluctuations to which they may give rise.

1.2 *The New Keynesian approach and objections to the neoclassical approach*

Though different economists disagree about the relative weight that they assign to the variety of forms of imperfections (imperfect risk and capital markets, imperfect information, imperfect competition, adjustment costs), New Keynesian economists all agree that these 'imperfections' exist, are important, and, together, can account for macroeconomic phenomena—and the effect of government policy—better than the alternative 'perfect market' models.

The objection to the 'perfect market' models, however, is broader than just its inability to explain macroeconomic phenomena. As is by now well known, the concept of the market economy embodied in the Arrow–Debreu paradigm is basically inconsistent with that associated with modern industrial economies, in which innovation plays a central role, and in which entrepreneurs and business managers are constantly engaged in a process of obtaining information, to enable them to make decisions to adapt to the constantly changing economic environment. (See e.g. Stiglitz 1987*a*, *b*, 1990, 1991.)

Economics is, or is supposed to be, an empirical science: how could economists' views be so divergent? Were these so-called scientists studying the same economy? Were they—or should I say, are we— simply ideologues looking for justifications for our political biases, or (no less worse) technicians, taking the assumptions provided to us by our ideologue brethren and exploring their consequences, trusting that the models we are analysing bear some semblance to the world, because we have been told so by others? (Indeed, it is curious that macroeconomists took hold of the 'perfect markets' microeconomic model just as microeconomists began abandoning that model, recognizing the pervasiveness of, for instance, informational imperfections and the absence of perfect risk markets.)

These are among the thoughts that have occurred repeatedly to me as I have been engaged on a research programme over the past two decades, attempting to explore systematically the problems posed for capitalist economies by imperfect information, and the costly quest for information and knowledge (innovation and invention).

Out of that work has developed a picture of the capitalist economy in which market failures are endemic: Arrow and Debreu seem to have found the singular case (perfect information, complete markets) in which the economy is Pareto-efficient. There exist, in general, interventions in the market (taking into account the costliness of information and of markets) that could make everyone better off (see Greenwald and Stiglitz 1986, 1988e). But while this work may have decreased our confidence in the efficiency of the market economy, other studies focusing on the workings of government have simultaneously decreased our confidence in the ability of the government to remedy these deficiencies. Unfortunately, theory can take us this far, but not much further: theorems which say that the economy cannot be improved upon absolve us from the necessity of much enquiry into the nature of government or the magnitudes of the alleged market inefficiencies; but theorems which say that the economy *can* be improved upon are subject to the natural question, But how important are these inefficiencies? The true colours of the ideologues are quickly revealed; for they are willing to assert the unimportance of these inefficiencies without doing the necessary empirical investigations, though I have great confidence in their ability to 'show' the unimportance, given enough time to do the appropriate data-mining. Still, it is curious that the same 'scientific' scepticism is not raised at those papers that purport to show the efficiency of the market, inevitably assuming *no* technical change and, at most, limited forms of imperfect information: should they not have similarly asked, How do we know that these results are robust to such considerations?

But there is one arena in which I would have thought the 'facts' would speak for themselves: surely the Great Depression, as well as the periodic episodes of unemployment experienced by the United States and Western Europe over the past two centuries, are evidence of some kind of market failure? How could a theory that predicts that there should be full employment (except when wages are zero) be taken seriously?[2]

2. Methodological Remarks on Macroeconomics

Over the past few years, I, along with several of my co-authors, have been attempting to construct macroeconomic models with consistent

---

[2] The standard answer—that the 'perfect market' models are only intended to explain the 'normal' economic fluctuations, not the Great Depression—is unconvincing. As I comment later, the big experiments like the Great Depression provide the best tests of alternative theories: under normal circumstances, it is difficult to distinguish among competing hypotheses.

microeconomic foundations. Of course, this is not the only such attempt
that has been made in recent years, or even the only one in which
informational imperfections have played a critical role. Indeed, it seems
by now almost obvious that, in the absence of transaction/information
costs,[3] market economies must be Pareto-efficient, and that, in particular, the kinds of massive under-utilization of resources associated with
recessions and depressions simply could not occur.

One approach has emphasized the signal extraction problem, the
difficulties that, say, General Motors had in 1980 in ascertaining
whether the decline in the demand for its cars was due to a monetary or
a real shock. (Evidently GM executives of the company were unable to
read the newspaper, to find out what was happening either to monetary
policy or, for that matter, to Japanese imports; and their economists and
marketing people were evidencing the same kind of incompetence that
we have come to expect of government officials. Of course, part of the
problem may lie in the fact that the monetary statistics are of limited
relevance for making inferences—which, if true, should have direct
implications for the econometric work using such data.) The work in this
tradition has, however, assumed that, while the signal extraction problem greatly complicates the analytics of the problems facing firms and
individuals, the institutional structure of the economy is essentially
unaffected.

By contrast, I have been focusing on a set of information problems
that have pervasive effects on how labour, capital, and product markets
function. They affect the mechanisms by which risks get shared, by
which information gets conveyed, and by which individuals and firms are
provided with incentives.

Before setting out the details of these theories as they relate to the
output and employment market, however, I want to spend some time
discussing a range of methodological issues that arise in macroeconomics.

2.1 *Relationship between micro and macro theory*

There is now a general consensus that good macroeconomics must be
built upon solid microfoundations. But this perspective is often confused
with an argument that there is a particular set of microfoundations upon
which it should be built: namely, competitive markets with rational
agents operating with rational expectations in environments in which
adverse selection and incentive (moral hazard) problems are largely

---

[3] With some further assumptions, such as the absence of any monopoly power on the
part of any agent.

absent. That is one set of hypotheses that may deserve exploration, though I am not very sanguine that such an approach will yield important insights into the questions at issue. But economics is, or at least should be, a behavioural social science. We know, for instance, from the work of Tversky and others, that there are systematic errors in individuals' perceptions. The work of Akerlof and Yellen has shown that these misperceptions can systematically get reflected in economic behaviour. Exploring the causes and consequences of these seems to me an item which should have a high order on the research agenda.

Some qualifications on the role of microfoundations

Trade-offs in modelling Like all doctrinal positions, the contention that macroeconomic work should begin with a specification of the microeconomic foundations can be carried too far. No one should be more aware of the existence of trade-offs than economists; solving signal extraction problems is no mean task; it is perhaps regrettable that explicit solutions can be obtained only with parameterizations whose empirical implications can be quickly rejected. But my concern here is that focusing on *that* problem diverts attention from other problems. We can, perhaps, all agree on our eventual goal: the construction of models that incorporate all of our concerns. But I hardly need to remind readers that the purpose of model construction is not the replication of reality: rather, it is the development of a set of lenses through which we can see the essential aspects of any phenomena. And here, as I have already indicated, is where New Keynesian and neoclassical economists differ: I see the centrepiece of such a construction lying in a more thorough understanding of how informational considerations affect the functioning of labour, capital, and product markets. And one cannot develop an understanding of how those markets function from models based on representative individuals, no matter how complicated are the dynamic programmes they might be solving.

First principles? Moreover, it is to be hoped that our discipline is a *cumulative* science. Not every piece of research has to begin at the beginning. We know that there are good reasons, based on problems of adverse selection and moral hazard, why equity markets may not function well.[4] We also have ample empirical evidence that firms make limited use of equity markets; and event studies confirm that, when they do raise additional capital through the issue of equities, stock prices are

---

[4] See e.g. Myers and Majluf (1984), Greenwald *et al.* (1984), Stiglitz (1982*a*); Gale and Stiglitz (1989).

lowered significantly. It thus seems perfectly appropriate for macroeconomic studies to begin with the hypothesis that equity markets do not function efficiently. For some purposes it may not matter what the precise source of this market failure is; in other cases it will, and a good macroeconomic theory will try to distinguish between these cases.

Is microeconomic analysis helpful at all? There is a view that is even more sceptical of the role of 'simple' representative agent microeconomics in macroeconomic analysis. It is based on the results of Debreu (1974), Mantel (1974), and Sonnenschein (1972, 1973), which show that any set of market excess demand functions satisfying Walras's law can be derived from utility-maximizing individuals. Essentially, the rationality hypothesis puts no restrictions on observed behaviour.

Of course, when economists say that a particular parameterization of behaviour should be 'derived' from microeconomic principles, what they mean is something different: they mean that a particular parameterization can be derived as the behaviour of a *single* individual. But why should the economy behave as if there were a single individual? The Debreu–Mantel–Sonnenschein theorem simply reminds us that there is no reason why this should be so. Casual empiricism suggests many reasons why this should not be so, some of which I shall come to shortly.

Limited usefulness of the representative agent model for macroeconomic analysis More generally, the representative agent models, useful as they may be for teaching, have serious drawbacks when applied to macroeconomic analysis (or to more serious microeconomic analysis, for that matter).

First, they are of limited use in investigating problems arising from information asymmetries and co-ordination failures. Presumably, asymmetric information could be reconciled with a representative agent model only by assuming a particular kind of schizophrenia on the part of the representative agent.

Second, if one believes that some kinds of 'market failures' are at the root of macroeconomic phenomena, one can hardly study these issues by using representative agent models; for when all individuals are identical, there is no need for trades, and hence there are no consequences of the absence of markets. For instance, risk markets entail the transfer of risk from one individual to another; but if all individuals are identical, the absence of risk markets has no consequences: there would be no trade on those markets, even if they existed.

Indeed, even the standard method of 'solving' for market equilibrium within representative agent models cannot easily be extended: conventionally, the equilibrium is solved by finding the allocation that maximizes the welfare of the representative agent, and using the fundamental theorem of welfare economics to interpret the resulting optimum as a market solution. But the Greenwald–Stiglitz theorem (1986) shows that, in the presence of imperfect information and incomplete markets, market equilibrium is not even a constrained optimum.[5]

What is at issue is more than theoretical niceties. Credit constraints arise if one individual would like to borrow from another but cannot. But if all individuals are identical, there is no scope for intertemporal trades. Even if prices are wrong, so that all individuals believe that they would like to borrow, the real resource allocations may be unaffected: there is no one from whom they could borrow, even if prices were right.

2.2 *Generality and specificity in macroeconomic models*

Macroeconomics faces a problem that much of microeconomics does not: while much of microeconomics is concerned with abstract questions such as the existence and efficiency of equilibrium, macroeconomics seeks to 'explain' certain phenomena.

One of the major lessons to emerge during the past quarter-century— both from the capital-theoretic controversies of the 1960s and from the Debreu–Sonnenschein–Mantel theorem to which I referred earlier—is that restrictions on 'rationality', even if combined with restrictions on technology (such as convexity), do not suffice to establish many qualitative results of interest. Some further restrictions are required. The question is, Which ones? And this is a matter of judgement. As I have suggested, assuming that all individuals or firms are identical is to impose too much structure on the economy, at least when it comes to asking questions about the short-run movements in the economy. For other questions, it may not be inappropriate; for some purposes, assuming an aggregate production function may yield insights of value.

'Solubility'

Tractability has been a long honoured criterion for the selection of assumptions. Another criterion for choosing assumptions in much recent work has been 'solubility'—whether, with the given parameterizations,

---

[5] One may be able, of course, to create an 'artificial' maximization problem, such that the market equilibrium corresponds to the solution to this maximization problem. Grossman's 'social Nash optimality' concept was intended to define the sense in which economies with an incomplete set of risk markets are optimal. The analysis of Newbery and Stiglitz (1981), Stiglitz (1982b) and Greenwald and Stiglitz (1986) makes clear exactly how artificial that maximization problem was. None the less, the techniques of analysis can be used to 'solve' for the market equilibrium.

solutions can actually be calculated. This represents a change in perspective. Economists' lack of confidence in precise parameterizations (and in the values of the parameters in those parameterizations) had previously led most economists to attempt to derive qualitative properties, based on qualitative restrictions (e.g., they asked, What can we say simply assuming convexity or concavity?). Obviously, by imposing additional restrictions, one can make stronger statements; one can derive a more complete characterization of the economy. The problem is again one of trade-offs: the parameterizations that are soluble have properties that—on theoretical grounds alone, without engaging in much fancy econometric work—can be rejected. For instance, much work has employed the constant absolute risk aversion utility function ($U = -\exp(-\alpha Y)$). Such a utility function is simply unacceptable as a description of individual behaviour: it implies, for instance, that the wealth elasticity of demand for risky assets is zero, and that all individuals hold exactly the same portfolio of risky assets. Of what interest is it that a few of the properties generated by that model (say, the time series of output) are consistent with the data, when there are other predictions of the model that can be easily rejected?

2.3 Plausible magnitudes and judging the 'reasonableness' of an explanation

I have argued that, to derive results in macroeconomics, one has to impose assumptions beyond the minimal assumptions associated with rationality and convexity of technology. The problem remains, What are 'reasonable' assumptions? What makes this problem so difficult is that to answer the question we must make quantitative judgements about qualitative effects: in general, there are many 'effects'—economic behaviour might plausibly be affected by a myriad of variables. But some of these effects are likely to be small, too small to account for the magnitude of changes in output or employment that we observe.

Three examples will illustrate what I have in mind.

(a) Real balance effects

In much of the macroeconomic literature following the Second World War, real balance effects played a central role. They figured prominently in Patinkin's classic book (Patinkin 1965). Even today, in a sometimes hidden form, they play a prominent role in the fixed-price models. (In those models, a fall in wages and prices will normally lead to an increase in output and employment, precisely because of the real balance effect.) Recent years have seen the real balance effect questioned on many grounds. It is only outside 'money' and government debt that matters for the real balance effect; since it is money that we 'owe' ourselves—government debt, if internally held, is just money that we owe to ourselves—what we gain on one side (as holders of the debt) we lose on the other (as taxpayers, liable for repaying the debt).[6,7] But whether one takes these 'sophisticated' views or not, it is hard to see, even under the most optimistic view, the quantitative significance of the real balance effect for short-run macroeconomic analysis. Assume that prices were to fall by as much as 10 per cent in a year (this has happened only a few times in the last century): if the (outside) money supply were to remain unchanged (and if we believe that an increase in real balances is treated by households as an increase in their real wealth), and if real balances represented roughly 25 per cent of total physical assets, and total physical assets represented 25 per cent of total assets (including human capital), and if the elasticity of consumption with respect to real wealth were 10 per cent (it is probably more like 6 per cent), then the percentage change in consumption from the real balance effect would be

$$10 \times 0.25 \times 0.25 \times 0.1 = 0.06\%.$$

Hence to increase consumption by 25 per cent would take roughly 400 years. The point is that the time scale for the real balance effect to be significant is not commensurate with the appropriate period of analysis for macroeconomic models. As a first, or even second approximation, it is far better to ignore it.

(b) Cost of adjusting prices

In recent years, there has developed a huge literature attempting to explain price rigidities on the basis of adjustment costs. The title of this literature, 'menu costs', appropriately signals the unimportance of these adjustment costs (at least as conventionally modelled). (It seems as if the advocates of this approach thought that, by being their own first critics, they would disarm the sceptical, and establish the validity of their approach.) The recent spread of computers to the restaurant

---

[6] There are further issues concerning the dynamics of price declines. Falling prices gives rise to intertemporal substitution effects. If price declines are expected to continue, or to increase, these intertemporal substitution effects may lead to less consumption and investment. See below, and also Grandmont (1983) and Neary and Stiglitz (1982).

[7] To the extent that parents do not take fully into account their children's welfare in determining the magnitude of bequests, there may be intergenerational effects, leading to increased consumption by the current generation and reduced consumption in future generations—but this may lead to increases in consumption at the current time.

industry, allowing hourly printing of relatively fancy menus at almost zero cost, should—if the theory is correct—have eliminated price rigidities in the restaurant industry. In industries in which there are no published price lists, presumably there would be no price rigidities. On the face of it, it would seem that the costs of adjusting prices are simply too small to account for significant price stickiness—of a magnitude that could cause large unemployment.[8]

Worse still for the theory is the fact that what we should be concerned with is explaining the relative rigidity of prices and the relative variability of output and employment: but surely, costs of adjusting output and employment are greater than the menu costs of adjusting prices?[9]

(c) The mechanisms by which monetary and debt policy exerts its influence

Recent years have seen several general results asserting that government financial policy has no real effects on the economy (see Barro 1974, or Stiglitz 1988). In establishing those results, several assumptions are made; dropping any of the assumptions will result in government financial policies having real effects. But many of these effects would seem to be too inconsequential to account for the magnitude of the effects of public financial policy. For instance, government financial policy could operate through redistribution effects across generations or within a generation—but is this a plausible mechanism? Similarly, changes in government tax rates will have deadweight loss effects. If a tax is increased in one year and decreased in another, and if the tax rates in different years differ, then the increase in deadweight loss in one year will not just offset the decrease in another: there will be real consequences of the change in total deadweight loss. But is this significant? Is this the mechanism by which government financial policy affects the economy? I think not.

---

[8] To be sure, the literature has attempted to show how small costs of adjustment could lead to large macroeconomic effects. Much of this literature is based on a more basic result: whenever the economy is not at a (constrained) optimum, a deviation of an individual or firm from its optimum (which has a second-order effect on the individual) has a first-order effect on the economy (since the economy is not at its global maximum). Thus, small adjustment costs on output and employment could have large effects on aggregate welfare.

[9] There are other objections to the theory—e.g. the fact that there appears to be more inertia in the rate of inflation than in the level of prices. A rather different explanation of price rigidities is provided in Greenwald and Stiglitz (1989a), who emphasize the difference in the costs and risks of decisions concerning changes in the level of prices *v.* changes in quantities. (In some sense, of course, these decision costs can be simply viewed as a particular form of menu costs.)

2.4 *Ad hocery in macroeconomic analysis*

It is currently fashionable to 'derive' all the functions entering into a macroeconomic analysis from first principles, within the model. I have already given two objections to that approach: there are general theorems saying that any market excess demand function could be derived from rational individuals, and it seems hardly necessary to begin every paper from first principles. Macroeconomists should be able to borrow qualitative insights obtained in earlier papers.

Still, there is something very healthy about economists striving to understand better each of the assumptions that underlies their analyses. For instance, many older models simply assumed wage and price rigidities. Now we seek to explain them.

But several further caveats are in order, lest we become too unbounded in our enthusiasm for this more 'rational' approach.

(a) How primitive are the assumptions?

First, frequently, we push back the frontier only slightly—though that by itself is valuable. For instance, sometimes price and wage rigidities are related to the market failure of the absence of certain insurance markets; but the absence of the insurance markets needs itself to be explained.

(b) Pseudo explanations

The fact that we can find *some* model in which the particular assumption can be 'explained' should give us little solace, if our objective is explaining *our* economy. For instance, some economists have put a considerable amount of effort into explaining the cash-in-advance constraint—a constraint that is obviously not binding for most transactions (which can be conducted with credit rather than cash). In understanding that constraint, one presumably would want to understand better why certain activities normally require cash in advance, while most activities do not. (Of course, since most activities do not require cash in advance, understanding why those that do may make only a limited contribution to understanding macroeconomic fluctuations.)

It is easy to construct a model that explains the cash-in-advance constraint. Assume, as some recent models have done, that all individuals meet each other only once. If you borrow from someone, you will never see him again to repay him. Credit is infeasible: cash is required. But so what? In our economy, we have a myriad of financial institutions which enable parties who never meet to borrow and lend to each other. What faith do we have that any propositions derived in the artificial economy in which individuals meet at most only once and there are no intervening financial institutions have any validity for our economy? These are, of course, matters of judgement: I suspect you can tell what my beliefs are.

(c) Inexplicable phenomena?

There are some phenomena that are difficult to explain, at least within a model presuming rational individuals. Let me give two examples. My local bank once offered a new current account, which was identical to the old except that it offered a higher interest rate. You had to sign a form to switch your accounts. Many individuals did not switch their accounts. It seemed as if they kept their wealth in an asset that was dominated by another asset. Of course, one could tautologically say that the transaction cost (psychic or shoe-leather or postage) exceeded the gains.

This is only a less subtle form of a more widespread phenomenon of individuals holding dominated assets. Cash management accounts (CMAs) provide, at almost zero cost, a way of holding government bonds that are perfectly liquid; the bonds can, in effect, instantaneously and costlessly be converted into 'money' (current accounts), and yield a higher return than current accounts at banks. It is hard for any economic theory to explain why such accounts did not exist twenty-five years ago, and it is hard for any economic theory to explain why they are not even more widespread today. Nor can any economic theory explain well why home equity loans (allowing individuals to write cheques against the equity of their house) developed only recently, or even why the typical forms that mortgages take today in the USA did not exist a quarter-century ago, or why they differ from those found in many European countries.

There are other phenomena that are difficult to explain: we do not have good reasons why contracts are not made contingent on many of the seemingly relevant and easily observable variables.

Some economists have responded to such inexplicable phenomena by suggesting that, because we cannot explain them, they do not exist. It is as if a biologist, finding it difficult to explain how blood can be pumped to the head of a giraffe, were to assume that it therefore must have a short neck. The fact of the matter is that contracts are *not* indexed; individuals hold assets that *are* dominated, etc.

In the absence of an explanation, it is better to use descriptively accurate assumptions (contracts are not fully indexed, equity markets are limited) than to ignore the phenomena.

(d) Two cautionary notes

Two caveats to this approach, however, need to be made. First, we must be cognizant of the possibility that a change in the economic environment may lead to unpredicted changes. Take, for instance, the assumption of rigid wages, which has played such a central role in macroeconomics, and recall the days before we had good explanations of that rigidity. For most purposes, it would have been better, I argue, to assume that wages are rigid, even though we could not explain that rigidity, than to assume that they were perfectly flexible. But in some circumstances the assumption of perfect wage rigidity can lead to misleading results—a cautionary note on the use of fixed-price models. For example, an increase in unemployment compensation will, in many of the efficiency wage models, lead to a rise in the real wage and an increase in the unemployment rate, a result that would not have been anticipated by the fixed-wage models.

Second, sometimes things are not as they seem. Economists are used to looking behind the scenes to see what is 'really' going on. For example, the absence of explicit provisions for indexing contracts does not mean that there is no indexing: there could be *implicit* indexing. Whether there is or not is often difficult to ascertain. (Often, I think, economists play this game too ardently.)

2.5 *Validation of a theory*

This brings me to the final methodological remark. There is a popular view that the empirical verification of a theory requires a statistical test of the goodness of fit of the model, to see whether the predictions of the theory conform with the facts. Broadly stated, this position seems unobjectionable. But, operationally, such a view is often translated in macroeconomics into testing the conformity of some time-series predictions of the theory. Unfortunately, there appears to be a plethora of theories that do reasonably well on these criteria: careful selection of statistical techniques, data sources, and years has enabled a succession of economists to show not only that their theory does well, but that it is superior to at least certain specifications of competing hypotheses.

But the validity of a theory rests on the conformity not of one or two of its predictions to reality, but on all of its predictions. Our micro-based theories have micro predictions as well as macro predictions. We all recognize that a theory can be a useful theory even if some of its underlying assumptions are not verified. We do not need to see atoms to believe in the atomic theory. But if there were some predictions of the theory that are 'falsified' (to use Popper's term)—including its predictions about the behaviour of micro units—the theory must be rejected, or at least patched up. (The patching-up process provides a forum for the demonstration of cleverness; in the end, a judgement must be made about whether these have produced a more refined theory, or merely a Ptolemaic exercise.)

Thus, the implicit contract theories that were so popular in earlier days, while predicting wage rigidities, yielded predictions of full employment. Attempts to extend these theories by including considerations of asymmetric information yielded, alternatively, over-employment or, under specifications where the worker provided insurance to the firm, under-employment in all states of nature except one. The theory predicted that laid-off workers were better off than retained workers; that contracts carefully specified how the firm could dispose of its capital; and that they were indexed to a host of variables—industry and aggregate measures—providing information about market conditions. The inconsistency of these predictions[10] with the facts provides the basis for a rejection of this theory, no less than would an econometric test. Of course, the fact that these theories (at least in these forms) provided an inadequate basis for understanding unemployment does not mean that some of the insights provided by these theories have not proven, or will not prove, useful in other contexts.

Later I shall describe some of the 'facts' that a good theory needs to explain. For now, let me summarize the basic argument of this section as follows.

1. There should no more be a separate macroeconometrics from a microeconometrics than there should be a separate macro theory from a micro theory.

2. A model is persuasive only to the extent that all of its predictions are consistent with observations. At the very least, one needs to ask, of a model that has implications that are inconsistent with the facts, Are there models that are consistent with *more* of the facts than the given model?

3. Goodness of fit may not be the most persuasive test of a model. Whether a model can explain certain 'critical facts' may be far more important. Thus, in the test of relativity theory versus Newtonian mechanisms, on an R^2 test, based on ordinary experience, it would have been difficult to distinguish the two. The convincing evidence for relativity lay in the crucial tests where the theories had markedly different implications.

---

[10] To the extent that the contracts were implicit, it is hard to verify whether or not these conditions were satisfied. A theory, most of whose predictions concern unobservables, has in this sense a certain advantage over theories that generate predictions about observables! For further discussion of these issues, see Newbery and Stiglitz (1987).

3. Some More Detailed Issues in the Construction of Macroeconomic Models

In the preceding section I outlined a set of methodological issues which, while relevant to economic theory in general, are I think particularly important within macroeconomics. In this section I want to raise six more detailed issues that arise in the construction of macroeconomic models. They are modelling problems. We noted earlier the difficult trade-offs that macroeconomists face: they want a model that is specific enough to derive results, but general enough to capture what is going on. These are subtle matters. Reasonable people may disagree about the best research strategies.

3.1 *Aggregation of individuals and firms*

I have already inveighed strongly against the excessive aggregation of individuals, the use of representative agents. It is well known that the conditions under which one can legitimately form aggregates, e.g. an aggregate consumption function, ignoring distribution, are very restrictive. Essentially, what is required is that all consumption functions be linear in income (with the same slopes). Clearly, this is an assumption that is not likely to be satisfied in the economy. For macroeconomic analysis, of course, the relevant issue is not whether this is a 'correct' or 'incorrect' assumption. It is obviously incorrect. Doing rigorous, sophisticated analysis with an obviously incorrect assumption does not make it any more correct. But that is not my objection. The question is, Does it lead to misleading results, or at least, does it preclude considering some important aspects of the economy? I think it does. Liquidity constraints introduce an important source of nonlinearity, which needs to be taken into account. To put it another way, if the mechanism by which monetary policy operates is to reduce consumption of those who are facing liquidity constraints, the distribution of assets in the economy is crucial in determining the effect of a change in present income on present consumption, and a representative agent model—by assumption—precludes considering this possible channel for monetary policy.

Aggregation of firms

Assuming that all firms are identical may similarly lead to difficulties. If all firms are assumed to be identical, there is, for any job, either an excess number of applicants or an insufficient number of applicants.

Thus, there is no ambiguity about what is meant by involuntary unemployment: if some (all) firms have vacancies, anyone who does not work is voluntarily unemployed: he has chosen not to work. But, conversely, if some (all) firms have excessive applicants, anyone who applies for a job and does not get it is involuntarily unemployed. In real economies, however, there exist simultaneously vacancies and excessive applicants for some jobs. To analyse this, we cannot assume that all firms are identical. In such a world an individual could, at the same time, be both voluntarily and involuntarily unemployed. That is, he could have applied for a number of jobs for which he was perfectly well qualified (i.e. as qualified as the individuals who obtain the jobs) and not obtained them, and in this sense his unemployment would be due not to his choice but to the random selection of the market; but at the same time, he could have chosen not to apply for a job that he might have obtained, and in this sense he would be voluntarily unemployed. In the end, I suspect that appending the term 'voluntary' or 'involuntary' to unemployment in such situations is not very helpful (although we are more likely to be sympathetic to 'involuntary' unemployment than to 'voluntary' unemployment). The important point is that the structure of the economy is such that individuals who in other situations would have been gainfully employed are not working. The equilibrium of the economy is inefficient, and there are government policies that can make improvements. (We shall return to these questions later.)

Much of the New Keynesian economics is concerned with problems of imperfect information, of situations where there are important differences among individuals and firms, but which cannot be easily observed (directly). Again, assuming that all individuals or all firms are identical makes it impossible to analyse the central issues.

But if the use of the representative individual or firm seems too limiting, the alternative, employed in conventional general equilibrium analysis, of simply denoting different firms and individuals by different superscripts and subscripts, and forming aggregate demands and supplies by summing up, seems too general.

Good macroeconomic theory requires the judicious choice of the appropriate level of aggregation, of introducing just enough complexity to be able to explain the phenomena at hand.

3.2 *Aggregation of commodities and assets*

Keynes, and most subsequent writers, focused on two financial assets, usually 'money' and 'bonds' (usually long-term bonds or perpetuities). Equities were aggregated, presumably, with long-term bonds, and short-term bonds with money. Clearly, one wants to aggregate assets that are close substitutes to each other; but long-term bonds tend to increase in value in recessions, while equities tend to decrease in value — they are negatively correlated. Hence these two assets are complements rather than substitutes. (One serves as an insurance policy for the other.) This aggregation error has important implications for the mechanisms by which monetary policy affects investment.

Indeed, another central theme of New Keynesian economics is that (a) bank loans may differ from government bonds — firms may be credit-rationed, so that the market interest rate on bonds may not be relevant for determining the level of investment; and (b) equity and debt (as well as the form that debt takes) have fundamentally different implications for firm behaviour — equity entails risk-sharing, while debt imposes a risk of bankruptcy on the firm.

3.3 *Adjustment speeds*

The central role of dynamics in macroeconomic analysis is now generally recognized. Good macroeconomic theory must not only specify clearly what assumptions it is making about relative speeds of adjustment, but it must also provide an explanation of why certain variables seem to adjust so slowly. In the Great Depression, wages fell. Why did they not fall faster?

(a) *Explaining dynamics*

Traditional economic theory assumed rational maximizing equilibrium behaviour, but imposed *ad hoc* adjustments. (This is clearly apparent in Samuelson's classic, *Foundations of Economic Analysis,* 1963.) If there are adjustment costs, they should be part of the maximization problem.

Recent theories of investment (adjustment of capital) and pricing have done precisely that (see e.g. Abel 1982, and the menu cost literature to which I referred earlier). But the heart of the matter is not the existence of adjustment costs, but the relative speeds of adjustment. Formal models, analysing one decision at a time, cannot address that issue. That is why, in recent work, Greenwald and I (1989a) have attempted to develop a portfolio theory of firm behaviour, in which all of the actions of the firm are considered simultaneously.

Intuitively, as was suggested earlier, it would seem that costs of adjustment for employment and output are much greater than for wages and prices, and hence simple 'menu' adjustment cost theories cannot provide a convincing explanation of the relative speeds of adjustment.

(b) Exploring the consequences of relative speeds of adjustments

As was noted earlier, macroeconomics often proceeds simultaneously on several different planes. Even if we do not have a completely convincing explanation for why wages and prices adjust more slowly in the short run than output and employment, the fact is that they do, and a central objective of macroeconomics is to explore the consequences of this.

The traditional Keynesian model generated what is usually referred to as a short-run equilibrium; that is, given the values of the exogenous variables, there was a (usually unique) solution for the current endogenous (usually flow) variables. It was assumed that these were attained in a relatively short time: a change in some exogenous variable would imply that there would be a new set of equilibrium values for the endogenous variables, and it was believed that the economy quickly adjusted to this change. At the same time, it was recognized that there were economic forces leading the exogenous variables to change.

The most obvious example, perhaps, was the capital stock: in the Keynesian model there was investment, but the capital stock remained unchanged. Whether that was a good assumption or not depended on (*a*) how fast the capital stock changed, and (*b*) how important (in its effect on the equilibrium values of the endogenous variable) a change in the capital stock was. If the average life of capital was fifty years, then the change in capital stock occurring over one, or even five, years might be quite small; but if the average life is ten years, then the change occurring in five years would be quite large. A change in the capital stock shifts the employment–output relationship; and the nature of the complementarity between labour and capital, as well as the extent of embodiment of technical change,[11] are both important in determining the effect of a change in the capital stock on the employment–output relationship.

Thus, any short-run macroeconomic model can be viewed as 'cutting into a dynamic process', of saying that some variables adjust more rapidly than others. More particularly, it is assumed that the present values of certain variables adjust fully to their 'equilibrium' values— equilibrium, *given* the values of certain other variables. Other variables are assumed to adjust, but too slowly to worry about for short-run analysis.

Any meaningful macroeconomic analysis will likely entail some division of economic variables according to the speed of adjustment, but considerable care needs to be exercised in the decision of which variables are to be treated as 'fast'-adjusting and which as 'slow'.

---

[11] Technical change is 'embodied' in capital if the introduction of new techniques requires a change in capital (machines); see Solow (1957).

Formally, we have suggested that any macroeconomic system can be described by a set of dynamic relations:

$$\dot{\mathbf{x}} = f(\mathbf{x}, \mathbf{y}) \tag{1}$$

$$\mathbf{y} = g(\mathbf{x}) \tag{2}$$

where $\mathbf{x}$ is the vector of variables that adjust slowly, $\mathbf{y}$ is the vector of variables that adjust instantaneously to the values of the remaining variables. The short-run macroeconomic equilibrium is concerned with equation (2).

Of course, it is not obvious that having two categories is an adequate simplification: one might want to consider at least three categories, in which case one would discuss 'short-short-run equilibrium', 'short-run equilibrium', and 'long-run equilibrium'.

For instance, consider the case where (1) takes on the form

$$\dot{x}_1 = a(x_1 - x_1^*) + b(x_2 - x_2^*), \qquad a < 0, b > 0 \tag{1a'}$$

$$\dot{x}_2 = e(x_2 - \alpha - \beta x_1), \qquad e > 0 \tag{1b'}$$

If e is very large and a and b are small, we can 'approximate' the dynamics by letting

$$\dot{x}_1 \approx a(x_1 - x_1^*) + b(\alpha + \beta x_1 - x_2^*) = (a + b\beta)(x_1 - x_1^*).$$

Figure 3.1 presents the phase diagram depicting the dynamics of equations (1a') and (1b') for different values of e. As e increases, the paths approach the $\dot{x}_2 = 0$ line more and more quickly. In the limit, the

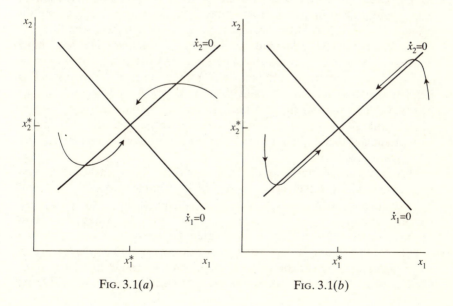

FIG. 3.1(a)   FIG. 3.1(b)

dynamics can be described as first going, for the given value of x_1, to the equilibrium value of x_2, and then moving along the $\dot{x}_2 = 0$ curve until the stationary point is attained.

The relative speeds of adjustment of different variables is important, not only for understanding the dynamics of the economy, but also for understanding the short-run consequences of any policy change. In many instances, one can show that the short-run and long-run effects on some important economic variable of certain policy measures are just the opposite. Differences in policy prescriptions may, in some cases, be attributed to differences in judgements concerning the dynamics of adjustment.

What is clear, however, is that much of the macroeconomic theory of the past fifty years has made a set of particularly unpersuasive implicit assumptions concerning dynamics. In much of the earlier literature, real balance effects played a crucial role. As I argued earlier, in the time scale that would be required for real balance effects to play any significant role, it is inappropriate to assume that capital stock, expectations, money supply, etc., are constant.

Let me further illustrate the importance of assumptions concerning relative speeds of adjustment with three additional examples. One important class of macroeconomic models takes wages and prices as the 'state variables', the exogenous variables to which everything else adjusts. Assume that all markets except the labour market are in equilibrium; i.e., the goods market is in equilibrium in the sense that supply equals effective demand. (It is not, however, in the Walrasian equilibrium.) Consider, then, the effect of a 10 per cent reduction in wages and prices in an economy that is at an unemployment equilibrium. This will leave real wages unchanged and, hence, employment unchanged. Effective demand at any given interest rate will have increased because of the real balance effect, so that, for equilibrium in the goods market to be attained, the rate of interest must rise. The implicit dynamic sequence is that the fall in prices and wages leads to increased consumption (in real terms), leading to reduced real savings, since at the given real wage output remains unchanged. The lower real savings means that investment demand exceeds savings, and hence the interest rate rises.

This is obviously markedly different from the effects in the short run in a model where prices are assumed to be flexible and there is a real balance effect. Then, a fall in wages and prices would initially increase consumption, leading to a rise in prices relative to wages, i.e. to a decline in real wages and an increase in employment.

The second example is concerned with expectations. Keynes (and most post-Keynesians) could never make up his mind to what extent expectations ought to be treated as a state variable. For the most part they were treated as exogenous. Expected quasi-rents did not depend (evidently) on current wages or prices or output. If they did, the *IS* curve would have had a quite different shape than that usually depicted (see Akerlof and Stiglitz 1966).

Similarly, interest rates were expected to return to their normal level, suggesting that long-run interest rate expectations were exogenous. On the other hand, the argument about why the price of a long-term bond was inversely proportional to the (short-term) interest rate usually makes use of the hypothesis that the short-term interest rate is expected to prevail in the future. Clearly, subsequent developments, particularly the accelerator model, have made extensive use of an endogenous expectations theory, i.e. that current output is crucial in determining expected output in the future and, hence, desired investment.

The third example is one that was at the centre of discussion of 'money and growth' dynamics some years ago (but which, for no good reason, seems to have been of little interest recently). Some money and growth models have taken the price level as an exogenous variable, and some have taken it to be an endogenous variable. In the former it is prices next period (or, implicitly, prices in the future markets) that adjust to clear the market today; in the latter, these expectations are usually taken as given and current prices adjust. The differences in stability properties of the various models are due at least partially to these differences in specification.

The point of these examples is to emphasize that the choice of which variables are to be taken as state variables (treated as exogenous at any moment) is crucial in determining the behaviour of the system and in predicting responses to various kinds of changes.

A good macroeconomic theory must not only specify clearly what assumptions it is making about relative speeds of adjustments, but must also provide an explanation of why certain variables seem to adjust so slowly. Keynes attempted to provide an institutional explanation for the rigidity of money wages, but this explanation, although clearly part of the story, is of only limited use: it does not explain why, in the Great Depression, wages fell by as much as they did. Nor does it explain the difference in wage rigidities between different periods. Clearly, whatever the institutions are that make wages rigid, they do not make them perfectly rigid. But what puts a limit on the degree of flexibility? Recent 'implicit' contract theories have attempted to provide an explanation that is better grounded in economic theory, but, as I shall comment below, this theory too is not very persuasive. Elsewhere we provide an explanation based on information-theoretic concepts (Greenwald and Stiglitz 1989*a*).

It is important to understand the determinants of the speeds of adjustment, not only to confirm that one has made a plausible story about relative speeds of adjustment, but also because it is conceivable, or even likely, that many economic policies affect speeds of adjustment; i.e., some variable that normally adjusts slowly without government intervention could respond very rapidly to certain types of perturbations, or conversely.

In the view that is taken here, the central issue of macroeconomics is not whether there exists an unemployment equilibrium, i.e. a configuration of wages, prices, etc., such that there is no mechanism by which the economy returns eventually to full employment, although elsewhere we have, in fact, shown that to be the case: rather, the central issue is, Are there reasons to believe that adjustment speeds in the response to, say, unemployment are sufficiently slow that the restoration of full employment is a slow and lengthy process? In this sense, the reconciliation of traditional microeconomic general equilibrium analysis and macroeconomic analysis becomes an easier task; for the traditional general equilibrium analysis either does not concern itself with the question of how equilibrium is to be attained, or, if it does, postulates an adjustment process that is no less *ad hoc* and no more convincing than those underlying traditional Keynesian analysis.

3.4 *Equilibrium and market-clearing*

Keynes argued that the economy could be in equilibrium and one of the markets—that for labour—might not clear (if there was an excess supply of labour). Those who believed in the classical model argued that, although this might be a characteristic of a short-run equilibrium, it could not be part of a long-run equilibrium.

Analytically, the distinction is seen clearly in our simple model of equations (1) and (2). A short-run equilibrium is characterized by a solution y for a given set of state variables x. If one of the current variables is the unemployment rate, then the question of existence of a short-run unemployment equilibrium is simply whether, for some values of the state variables, the solution to (2) entails a positive unemployment rate.

The long-run equilibrium of the economy is the situation where nothing changes; i.e.,

$$\dot{x} = f(x^*, g(x^*)) = 0 \quad \text{and} \quad y^* = g(x^*).$$

The existence of unemployment in the long run, then, is concerned with whether (again interpreting one of the variables, y, as unemployment) it is possible that, when the state variables are at their long-run equilibrium value, there can be positive unemployment.

If one takes this view, and then postulates that whenever there is excess supply of labour wages fall, then in the long-run equilibrium *by definition* unemployment cannot exist. Similarly, if one postulates that wages do not fall even when there is excess supply of labour, it is not hard to see that, even in the long run, there may be unemployment. This analysis seems to suggest that the question of whether there can be unemployment in the long run is almost a definitional matter: it seems to follow almost immediately from the dynamic assumptions one makes. Matters are, fortunately, somewhat more interesting than this would suggest.

First, I would argue that the existence of a long-run equilibrium with unemployment is not necessary for there to be an 'interesting' Keynesian problem: does it make much difference whether the response to unemployment is a fall in the wage at an infinitesimally slow rate or if it does not occur at all? Does one get much insight from remarking that, in the former case, the unemployment is present only in the short-run equilibrium, not in the long run?

Second, we can construct models in which the economy converges to a 'quasi-steady' state—in which real variables may be constant but monetary variables are always changing. In such an economy, wages and prices could be falling or rising but real wages, employment, etc., could be constant. In such a model, the question of whether there exists unemployment in the long run is an analytical one, and does not follow (at least quite) immediately from the assumptions. Elsewhere Robert Solow and I have constructed such a model (Solow and Stiglitz 1968). In these models unemployment may be a function of real wages, and real wages, if they adjust, adjust slowly.

Third, and most importantly, there is a sense in which *the economy is always in the short run*. The economy never settles down to the mythical steady state. Analytically, to capture this we need to formulate a stochastic model;

$$\dot{x} = f(x, y) + z_1, \tag{3}$$

$$y = g(x) + z_2, \tag{4}$$

where z represents a set of stochastic terms (the distributions of which may in fact be a function of the state variables). In this model the economy is never at rest: it is always subjected to changes. There is a steady state (if the disturbances are stationary over time). In the long run we can characterize the distribution of x and y; we can ask how these distributions will change with changes in the distribution of the stochastic terms or of the 'structure' of the economy (as represented by the functions f and g).

In this model unemployment can occur periodically even in the long run. The question of whether it can persist becomes simply a question—Is unemployment an 'absorbing state', i.e. a state which, once one enters it, one cannot leave? Most reasonable hypotheses would clearly make it not so. The question of whether in the long run unemployment is possible is simply the converse: i.e., If one is in a full-employment state, can one ever leave it? And again, most reasonable hypotheses would make full employment not an absorbing state. The question then becomes, What can one say about the kinds of disturbances that lead the economy from full employment to unemployment, and what kinds of processes (and disturbances) then lead to a return of full employment? How frequently can we expect unemployment, and with what duration?

Equilibrium and disequilibrium

Much of the confusion over the question of whether there can exist a short- or long-run equilibrium with unemployment arises from confusions about the meaning of equilibrium.

Quite often, the term 'disequilibrium' is used to suggest that if some feature of the world were changed, but others were not, the given values of certain economic variables would not occur; for instance, the sentence, 'The capital stock is not in equilibrium' quite often means, 'If there were no costs associated with adjusting the capital stock, then the capital stock we would have is not the capital stock we presently have', or 'If two years ago we had had perfect information concerning the level of demand today, we would have installed more capital'. I am not sure that identifying such situations and labelling them as 'disequilibrium' adds much insight.

(In a rather different context, Grossman and Stiglitz (1976, 1980) have considered the behaviour of a stock market with costly information. They show that prices in the market will reflect the information of the informed but will not be perfectly arbitraged; for if they were, speculators (arbitrageurs) would be unable to procure a return on their expenditures to obtain information—there must be 'an equilibrium degree of disequilibrium'. That is, prices differ systematically from what they would have been had information been free. But information is not free, and the economy is in equilibrium in the sense that no one has an incentive to change his behaviour.)

Since by their very nature the stochastic elements represent contingencies that could not be foreseen (i.e. that were not perfectly dependent on the state variables), individuals will persistently find themselves in situations to which they have to make adjustments: they are never in 'equilibrium'. But at the same time, if at each moment they take the best actions they can, subject to the information they have available, is it not equally meaningful to describe their behaviour as always in 'equilibrium'?

I have written equations (1)–(4) without having time appear explicitly in the right-hand side. In particular, I have characterized the disturbances to the economy by stationary distributions. This allows me to solve for steady-state distributions, distributions that describe the long-run equilibrium of the economy. This is the sense in which I have engaged in 'equilibrium analysis'. I have not, in other words, analysed the effects of particular disturbances, e.g. the Watergate affair, except as they can be subsumed as particular outcomes of the random processes. This, it seems to me, is more properly the affair of economic history than of economic theory.

Of course, once one admits the possibility that one market is not in equilibrium (in the sense that supply does not equal demand in that market)[12] — in the short run or the long run — one must contemplate the possibility that more than one market is not in equilibrium.[13] Indeed, we argued earlier that there were convincing reasons to believe that the goods market was not in equilibrium.[14] Not only would assuming that the goods market was in equilibrium imply that real wages should have risen far more in the Great Depression than, in fact, they did (if they rose at all), but also, it would imply that, were one to have asked a businessman in the middle of the Great Depression if he would be willing to sell more of whatever he was producing at current wages and prices, he would have said 'No'.[15] Casual evidence suggests the contrary. The analysis of economies in which markets other than labour are not in equilibrium is one of the main subjects of my paper with Solow (Solow and Stiglitz 1968) and the subsequent fixed-price literature (Barro and Grossman 1971; Benassy 1975, 1982; Grandmont 1983, 1985; and Malinvaud 1977).

[12] I hesitate even to use the vocabulary of 'market equilibrium' with 'demand equalling supply'. In any full account, demand and supply are both dynamic concepts. The observed level of, say, employment may differ from what a simple static demand and supply analysis might suggest; yet each individual or firm, at that moment, is doing what it wishes to do, given the economic environment. It is in a 'momentary' equilibrium. This state of affairs is, of course, perfectly consistent with changing behaviour over time (both in response to changes in the external environment, and as a consequence of previous actions taken by the individual or firm). (Whether it is appropriate to describe any shortfall in employment as 'involuntary unemployment' is a question I take up below.)

[13] Standard Walrasian analysis provides another example of the ambiguities in the concept of equilibrium. In standard expositions, we often say that Walras's law implies that, if one market is out of equilibrium, at least one other market must also be. If the labour market is out of equilibrium, either the goods market or the bond market is out of equilibrium. But, of course, standard Keynesian effective demand analysis says that the goods market may be in equilibrium, *given* the quantities of goods individuals and firms actually demand. It seems quite reasonable that participants in the goods market might respond more effectively to demands they actually see than to the kinds of 'conjectural' demands associated with Walrasian analysis — that is, the demands they would perceive if, say, the labour market cleared.

[14] In the 'effective demand' sense.

[15] An alternative explanation to assuming that the goods market was not in equilibrium is to assume that all firms possess some monopoly power. But there is little basis to suggest that market power changes significantly in recessions.

Just as alternative assumptions concerning relative speeds of adjustment have important implications for the effects of different policies, so
do different assumptions concerning which markets are and are not
'clearing'. For instance, let us return to the first example discussed
above, where wages and prices were assumed rigid and the goods
market was assumed to clear.

As a contrast, consider a model where employment, wages and prices
are taken as state variables in the short-short run and the goods market
is assumed to be out of equilibrium in the sense that the level of
effective demand is less than the amount that firms are willing to supply
at the given real wage. Then the immediate effect of a lowering of
wages and prices is an increase in output, since effective demand is
increased (as a result of the real balance effect).

And, as in the earlier discussion of the relative speeds of adjustment,
it is important to know why markets are not clearing, if it is assumed
that they are not. Is it, for instance, simply because wages and prices
are rigid? The failure of markets to clear follows, then, as a corollary of
the analysis of adjustment speeds.

In Greenwald and Stiglitz (1989a) we argue that, at least from the
perspective of firms (who, after all, are the primary agents responsible
for adjusting prices and quantities), the decision of how much to adjust
each of the variables can be viewed as part of a general dynamic
'portfolio' problem. There are risks and returns associated with each
adjustment. There are short- and long-run consequences. And the firm
must take into account all of these, as well as the interrelations among
them (as reflected, for instance, by the variance–covariance matrix).

3.5 Information and controllability

The next question, about which I shall have only a limited amount to
say, concerns the controllability of the economy. To understand the
issues, we need to expand our basic model (as represented by (1) and
(2) in the non-stochastic case and (3) and (4) in the stochastic case) by
introducing a set of control variables, say c. For the non-stochastic case,
we write

$$\dot{\mathbf{x}} = f(\mathbf{x}, \mathbf{y}, \mathbf{c}) \tag{5}$$

$$\mathbf{y} = g(\mathbf{x}, \mathbf{c}), \tag{6}$$

c being the vector of variables under the control of the government.
(We shall ignore the questions of the free will–predestination variety,
and assume that the government can, in fact, choose c at will.) In the

non-stochastic environment described by (3) and (4), the question of controllability is a simple one. In general, a change in c will affect various private decisions (various y and $\dot{x}$). The question is, Can the private sector completely offset the actions of the government so that all the variables of fundamental interest, e.g. output and unemployment, remain unchanged? For instance, if commercial paper was a perfect substitute for bank loans for some large corporations, then a policy that restricted the availability of credit through the banking system might well shift large corporations into the commercial paper market, but leave all real aggregates unaffected. In this example, the government lacks controllability. If, however, the government has control of some commodity ('bank loans') for which there exist no close substitutes, then controlling the supply of that commodity can affect the equilibrium in the same way that the behaviour of any large producer who restricted the supply of the commodity that he produced could and indeed would affect the equilibrium by the actions he took.

What I want to argue now is that, in a stochastic environment, the argument that the government cannot significantly affect the equilibrium of the economy is even weaker. We then formulate the government's behaviour as a policy, a rule, which describes the action to be taken in response to the observation of certain variables. The argument has been put that eventually the individuals will discover the fundamental relations describing the economy (including the policy of the government), and, having discovered these relations, will take offsetting actions to negate any governmental policy. That is, in a 'rational expectations equilibrium', government policy is ineffective. Several questions may be raised concerning this view.

First, I would argue that the assumption that the economy is in a rational expectations equilibrium, though analytically useful, is not always empirically convincing. There are numerous instances of individuals basing behaviour on beliefs that are either not supported by the facts or, indeed, incongruent with them. There are numerous instances (e.g. the corn–hog cycle) in which individuals' expectations appear to be far from 'rational'. Second, it takes time to discover certain relationships, so that the attainment of a 'rational expectations equilibrium' following a change in certain structural variables may take a long time. Indeed, one might argue that one of the objectives of economics research is to discover relationships that have not been previously discovered.

If we are concerned with describing the behaviour of the economy, then it may be best to model the economy as if it were not in rational expectations equilibrium. Moreover, once one recognizes that obtaining, storing, and analysing information is costly, it is not clear that the distinction between rational and non-rational expectations is either meaningful or insightful. For instance, a 'myopic' equilibrium in which individuals look only at current values of a variable is 'rational' if observing other potentially relevant variables is very costly and if storing past data is also very costly.

More generally, for the private sector to be able to offset completely the actions of the government, the lags between the observation of a variable and the implementation of a policy-dependent variable must be no greater (for any variable or policy) for the private sector than for the public sector; the lag between the event and the observation of the event must not be greater in the private sector than in the public; and the cost of observation and implementation of the offsetting actions must be precisely zero.

Schematically, we can represent the process of the government action and the private sector's offsetting action in Fig 3.2. Clearly, if the private sector's lags exceed those of the government sector, then the government policy can have an effect. Note that what is crucial is the observation-plus-action lag. Thus, it is conceivable that the private sector does not observe the event at all, but only observes the government action; but if it could instantaneously respond with counter-vailing action '$-c$' the government's effects would be only fleeting.

We need to emphasize also the importance of the assumption of costless information and costless implementation of the offsetting action. The argument is the familiar one: if it is costly to monitor the government's action, then those who monitor it must receive compensation for doing so. But if the effects of the government action were perfectly arbitraged out, those who monitor government action would receive no compensation; hence they cannot be completely arbitraged out.

These arguments are all strengthened if the government pursues a stochastic policy. Assume that what the government in effect announces

Event is
observed by   **Action: c**
public sector

Event   Net outcome: 0

Event is
observed by   **Action: $-c$**
private sector

Fig. 3.2

is a stochastic policy that, for a particular fraction of the time, when the state variables are 'such and such', reserve requirements will be changed. If it requires time to develop the alternative financial instruments, then the change in the reserve requirement may have a substantial impact on the short-run equilibrium. This may be true even if policy of using reserve requirements is known in advance (but obviously, the stochastic disturbance leading to the state in which it is employed is not); for the states in which the alternative financial instruments would be used occur sufficiently infrequently that it may not pay to develop them (or develop them completely) in anticipation of this stochastic event.

At a conceptual level, then, there seems to be no argument but that the government can, in principle, have an effect on the macroeconomic equilibrium of the economy. This, of course, does not answer either the question of whether, in fact, policies in the past have had a significant effect (although the evidence seems fairly clear that they have had a significant effect, although not always in the right direction), or, even if government policies *have* had limited efficacy in the past, whether there exist policies that are more effective.

3.6 *Rational expectations*

During the 1970s and early 1980s, there was much discussion of a rational expectations revolution in macroeconomics. Like any important set of ideas, it had many variants, but among the widely cited tenets were that:

1. government intervention was not necessary, because markets were efficient and cleared; and
2. in any case, government intervention was ineffective, because private actors perfectly offset the actions of the government; the inefficacy is unimportant, because without government intervention markets are already efficient.[16]

---

[16] While the 'rational expectations' approach is closely associated with the 'Chicago School', not all 'Chicago' economists agree with the second tenet. Friedman (1968), for instance, has argued that monetary policy is responsible for much of the economy's fluctuations. In this sense, he is in many ways closer to the Keynesians than to the real business cycle theorists. He believes, for instance, that there are short-run rigidities (e.g. wage and price rigidities) such that any action by the monetary authority cannot immediately and costlessly be offset by changes in the price level. He differs from most Keynesians in his judgement about the ability of the government to improve the economy, and, in certain circumstances, on the relative magnitudes of certain key parameters.

At one level, the rational expectations model represented the natural extension to a stochastic environment of the 'perfect foresight' models that had been extensively employed (and criticized) in the preceding decade in which growth was a central object of study by economists. The 'perfect foresight'–rational expectations assumptions can be viewed as a convenient benchmark. They enable us to engage in a thought experiment: To what extent do any results derived depend on 'irrational' expectations, e.g. myopia, and to what extent do they depend on other assumptions, e.g. concerning how markets function?

The use of the rational expectations model as a description of the economy is quite another matter. One might view it as an empirical hypothesis to be tested—and there has been considerable work over the past decade and a half doing precisely that. In some cases the data seem consistent with rational expectations; in many others they do not. Most observers think that the fall in the stock market price by 20 per cent in October 1987 could not possibly be interpreted as a 'rational' response to a change in fundamentals occurring within the span of a day or two. But, even more fundamentally, the special nature of the economic circumstances that the economy finds itself in, year after year, casts doubt on the usefulness of the rational expectations hypothesis as a description of important aspect of many important decisions, including the investment decisions of firms. Consider the stock market crash of October 1987. There had been only one similar stock market crash in this century. A sample of one is clearly too small to have much confidence for purposes of statistical inference. And the economic environment of 1987 was much different from 1929—the legal and regulatory environment, for example, had changed markedly. Accordingly, there was no relevant historical sample.

Similar issues arise in other contexts. How will rivals respond to a change in my prices? The international environment today is different from what it was a decade ago. Do Japanese firms respond the same way as American firms?

What are the consequences of the Tax Reform Act of 1986? We had never had a tax change of that magnitude. Not even the experts could agree on the consequences of some parts, e.g. the incidence of the corporate income tax. How, then, are we to believe that the behaviour of the economy should be described as if the responses of the economy were common knowledge—that is, as if all individuals knew the responses, and all knew that everyone else knew those responses, etc.?

The issue is not whether there is *some* experience that might be relevant. After all, firms must make predictions, and those predictions must be based on some inferences from previous behaviour. But there is no simple formula for distilling out of the past the relevant experiences. Deciding on what are the salient characteristics of the environment cannot be—or, at least so far, has not been—reduced to a straight-forward statistical procedure. It requires business judgement. From this perspective, the issue may not be so much whether the expectations of businessmen are 'rational', but whether they—or their aggregate consequences—can be described by a simple statistical model of expectations formation.

Unfortunately, we almost never test a model of expectations formation in isolation (we could, by looking at survey results on expectations, but such surveys tend not to lend much support to the rational expectations hypothesis, and accordingly get dismissed), but rather test it in conjunction with some model of a particular market. When the resulting test of the rational expectations model fails, we thus can only reject the joint hypothesis.

But my concern here is not so much with the hypothesis of rational expectations, and in particular with the testing of that hypothesis, but rather with the 'joint' hypotheses characterizing much of the rational expectations literature.

That literature has raised some fundamental questions, which we need to address, at least briefly:

1. To what extent do traditional Keynesian models depend on 'irrational' expectations?
2. To what extent do the conclusions of the rational expectations literature concerning the efficiency of markets and the impotency of government depend on the 'expectations' assumptions, rather than on other structural assumptions that they have employed?
3. To what extent can those particular joint hypotheses be supported?

Clearly, as we have already commented, Keynes employed a peculiar set of expectational hypotheses. Sometimes he assumed static expectations, sometimes a regression towards 'normality'. But the New Keynesian economics (see e.g. papers by Greenwald and Stiglitz 1986, and Neary and Stiglitz 1982) has shown clearly that:

1. even with rational expectations, market equilibrium may not be efficient (it is not even constrained Pareto-efficient): there are welfare-enhancing government interventions, which take into account both the costs associated with establishing and running markets and the imperfections and costs of information;
2. with rational expectations, there may be unemployment;
3. with rational expectations, small disturbances may give rise to large consequences; and
4. in particular, there may be significant multipliers associated with government actions, both monetary and fiscal policy: not only may government actions have real effects, but those effects may be larger than they would have been in the absence of rational expectations.

The intuition behind the latter result is simple: a major limit on the magnitude of the effect of an increase in expenditure today are leakages associated with savings. But, to the extent that increased saving leads to increased consumption in some future, demand-constrained period, it leads to increased output in that period; and that increased output and employment has, if rationally anticipated, effects in earlier periods. It has a spill-over back to the current period.

Thus, the results on the efficiency of the market depend on the special representative agent with a perfect—information assumption, an economic environment in which the absence of markets has few if any consequences. New Classical economics obtains results similar to old classical economics, not because it has added a new set of insights, derived from rational expectations, but because it has retained an old set of assumptions, concerning perfect markets and market-clearing.

When the joint hypotheses underlying much of the analysis are subjected to rigorous testing, they do not fare well. Recent econometric work has, for instance, cast doubt on the validity of the permanent-income hypothesis: there appears to be excessive sensitivity to current income, of a kind that is consistent with credit rationing on the part of some individuals. Micro data are consistent with this perspective. Similarly, investment studies show the importance of financial constraints; for firms accounting for much of the variability of investment, the neoclassical investment model appears to be rejected.

4. The Questions of Macroeconomics

Macroeconomics, as I have said, is concerned with interpreting, and predicting, the movements in the aggregates that describe the economy—output, employment, price levels, etc. In this paper I am concerned particularly with the short-run movements in the *real* variables which describe the economy. (As I suggested earlier, it may not be possible to separate completely these short-run movements for longer-run changes; still, it is necessary to cut somehow into any complicated interrelated system.)

There are a number of ways of dividing the issues which any good (complete) macroeconomic theory must address.

4.1 *The short-run dynamics of the economy*

One formulation stresses a study of the changes in the economy. The three questions which it stresses are:

1. What are the sources of the shocks to the economic system?[17]
2. What is the mechanism by which shocks get transmitted from one firm to another, from one sector to another, and perpetuated?
3. Why is it that shocks get amplified, rather than dampened (as they normally would through the price mechanism)? That is, as Fig. 3.3 illustrates, in the conventional demand and supply diagram, a disturb-ance—say, an exogenous increase in demand—leads to an increase in the price, so that the equilibrium increase in output is smaller than the initial disturbance.

Keynes did not have a clearly articulated theory of the sources of disturbance, and much of the later business cycle literature suggested that in fact there were no external sources of disturbance. The internal structure of the economy itself led to fluctuations. The more recent 'real business cycle' literature has emphasized the role of technology shocks; but, as standard criticisms of that literature point out, it is hard to see (given the postulated structure of the economy) how the kinds of observed technology shocks translate into the magnitudes of observed cyclical movements; and in particular, it is hard to find (except in a tautological sense) the negative technology shocks associated with the Great Depression and the other major downturns of the economy.

There is an interesting conflict between the two major neoclassical schools in this respect: while the New Classical economists and monetar-

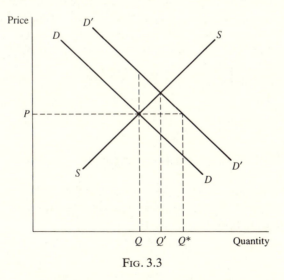

FIG. 3.3

[17] It should be clear, however, that I am not precluding here the possibility that downturns arise not from exogenous shocks, but from the internal dynamics of the economy, as emphasized in traditional business cycle theory.

ists see monetary policy as the major exogenous disturbance—it is hard to see any other disturbance large enough to account for the economy's fluctuations—'real business cycle' theorists believe monetary policy is irrelevant (only real variables matter).

The Greenwald–Stiglitz version of New Keynesian economics, on the other hand, takes a more agnostic view of the source of disturbances: i.e., there may be real or monetary disturbances. But what it emphasizes—and where it differs from the traditional neoclassical models—is the instability of the economy: how small disturbances can (because of the risk-averse behaviour of firms) lead to large changes in output and employment.

In this sense, their analysis is very much in the spirit of Kahn and Keynes, who looked for a multiplier process. We now recognize that an essential part of the Kahn–Keynes multiplier process is the rigidity of prices and wages. The Metzler–Samuelson accelerator model (Metzler 1941; Samuelson 1939) further emphasized the instability of the economy, but employed, in addition to the assumptions associated with the Kahn–Keynes multiplier (Kahn 1931; Keynes 1936), an investment accelerator, based on a fixed-coefficients technology of production, and a particular (and unconvincing) assumption of expectation formation. Greenwald and Stiglitz show how similar multiplier–accelerator phenomena can be obtained without assuming the price and wage rigidities of Kahn and Keynes and without making the strong assumption concerning technology and expectation formation that underlay the Samuelson–Metzler–Hicks analysis (Samuelson 1939; Metzler 1941; Hicks 1956). Their analysis is predicated solely on the (observed and explained) imperfections in equity markets, leading to risk-averse behaviour on the part of firms.

These are questions, however, which I cannot take up further in this paper. (See Stiglitz 1992.)

4.2 *The three markets and the three quandaries*

Another formulation stresses the central problems of interpreting phenomena in each of the three main markets of the economy, i.e. the labour, capital, and product markets.

(a) *The 'labour market quandary'*

We can state the labour market quandary in terms of the conventional demand and supply diagrams for labour. We observe large variations in employment with relatively little variation in real wages.[18] It is simply difficult to reconcile this with standard neoclassical markets always operating in equilibrium. Attempts to reconcile the facts with a market-clearing model take on two forms. The first requires that the supply schedule of labour is close to horizontal, combined with shocks to the demand curve for labour (Fig. 3.4). The hypothesis of a horizontal supply curve of labour seems inconsistent with all *microeconomic* studies of labour markets. Moreover, if individuals are really indifferent to working or not working, or content to work either 20 or 40 hours a week, why then the concern about unemployment? Why do the unemployed workers seem willing to wait hours in queues seeking jobs? Is it really the most enjoyable way to spend one's leisure?[19]

The second has shifts in the demand and supply curves for labour

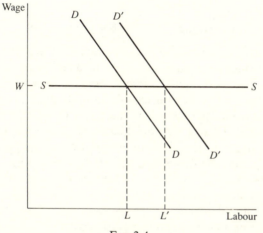

FIG. 3.4

[18] This is not the occasion to review the vast empirical literature on this question which developed subsequent to the work of Dunlop (1938) and Tarshis (1939), questioning the implication of Keynes's theory that real wages should rise in a recession. Though whether real wages increased or decreased may depend on what price deflator is used, it is clear that, at least in many industries, real product wages (which are relevant for the analysis of the *demand* for labour) decreased, and the average value of real product wages certainly did not increase to the extent predicted by Keynesian theory. Because of changes in the price of agricultural goods to industrial goods, it is likely that, for many workers, real consumer wages may have increased slightly in the Great Depression.

[19] Moreover, some of the recent attempts to come to terms with observed patterns of hours worked and employment seem particularly unconvincing. While it may well be the case that non-convexities either in production or work–leisure technologies (transportation costs) may account for the fact that, as labour demand is reduced, workers do not reduce the hours worked per day, or even per week, reasonable hypotheses concerning individual preferences lead in such situations to job rotation, rather than to prolonged unemployment, an observation that was made earlier in the context of the debate over the consequences of unemployment insurance in the implicit contract literature (see e.g. Stiglitz 1986).

which are just of the right magnitude to offset each other, so that the equilibrium real wage does not change much. The occurrence and persistence of this coincidence seems a weak reed on which to hang a theory, and the implied shifts in the supply curve seem implausible, even when doctored up to include intertemporal substitutability in labour supply.[20]

And whence the shocks to the demand curve for labour? In competitive theory, with price- and wage-taking firms, these shocks in the demand curve presumably represent changes in technology.[21] In the absence of wars, there are simply not the changes in technology that can account for shifts of the magnitude of those observed. Even technological revolutions as major as those associated with the transistor and computer take years, even decades, to have their effects diffuse through the economy.[22] We shall return to these issues in Section 5.2(d).

(b) The product market quandary: the magnitudes of the responses

I now come to the second quandary: how can we explain observed patterns of changes in output? We can divide the analysis of this problem into two parts. First, given that real product wages do not change very much, how can we explain the relatively large variations in output? Is it possible that the supply functions of firms change so much? Is it plausible that firms remain off their supply functions for long?

The second part of the quandary allows for the possibility of changes in wages and prices. While general equilibrium theory has taught us that there are relatively few general results on the stability of economic systems, the standard stories we present in price theory suggest that price adjustments dampen shocks. A shock to one sector, say an unexpected fall in demand, gets partly absorbed by a reduction in price, so that the actual reduction in quantity produced is smaller than the shift in the demand curve; price adjustments serve to dampen shocks. General equilibrium effects serve further to dampen the aggregate effect of any particular shock. Corresponding to a reduction in the demand curve facing one industry, there must be an increase in the demand

---

[20] Given the relatively small fluctuations in real interest rates and real wages during the period 1950–77, it is hard to see any large role for intertemporal substitution during that period. The varying cyclical movements in other periods make the intertemporal substitution hypothesis even more problematic.

[21] Elsewhere (Greenwald and Stiglitz 1987a) we present an alternative explanation, arising from certain imperfections in capital and futures markets.

[22] Taylor (1987) has presented other convincing arguments against the real business cycle. After observing the differences in the magnitudes of the fluctuations in Japan, Europe, and the USA, he asks why the technological shocks hitting the USA should be so much larger than those affecting Japan, or even Europe.

facing another. Thus, the aggregate effects of a shift in demand are likely to be small.

Yet we see many instances when what seems a small disturbance to the economy has large macroeconomic effects. The oil price shock provided the most recent example. Viewed as a negative shock to the aggregate production function for an oil-importing country such as the USA, the increases in the price of energy in 1973–4 should have had only a limited effect on the economy, much smaller than the observed effects.

Of course, traditional macro theory provides an explanation: it focuses on multipliers. But how do we obtain general equilibrium multipliers rather than dampeners?

I cannot here provide the answers to either of these questions. Let me simply assert that the New Keynesian theories, based on incomplete markets and imperfect information, do provide answers to both. (In conventional theory, these multipliers arise out of fixed prices; that is, once quantities become the locus of adjustment, shocks to one sector may have *multiplier* effects on the aggregate. Once one has constructed a theory explaining fixity of prices (wages, interest rates), as the efficiency wage theories and the credit-rationing theories we have constructed do, then it is easy to show that there may be these multiplier responses to disturbances.)

(c) The capital market quandary: the role of money and credit

The classical dichotomy argued that money should have no real effects. Recent work on perfect capital markets has extended and refined those conclusions: public financial policy should, in a world of perfect markets, be irrelevant (Stiglitz 1988; Barro 1974). Yet there is considerable evidence that monetary policy does have effects. Volker made a difference. The monetary authorities may be unable to bring us out of a recession, but they can spin the economy into one. Why is this? What is the mechanism by which monetary policy works?

Nominal price and wage rigidities provide the easy answer. But how do we explain these rigidities? Money illusion? But this seems to put the burden on irrationality, and with irrationality one can explain almost anything. Staggered contracts? This explains momentary wage rigidities, of a month's duration; but as contracts come up for negotiation, the 'free' contracts should prove freely flexible. Besides, what is 'relevant' is *price* rigidities, and one needs to explain why contracts are not indexed in such a way as to remove most or all of the effects of monetary policy.

Some versions of New Keynesian economics have addressed these questions directly, and have produced several theories of nominal rigidities (see Stiglitz 1985; Greenwald and Stiglitz 1989*a*).

4.3 *The stylized facts*

Beyond these broad issues, a good macroeconomic theory must address, or at least be consistent with, the important aspects of the economy's fluctuations. I cannot provide here a full range of the kinds of phenomenon for which I think a good macro theory needs to provide an interpretation, but let me just mention a few.

One of the reasons that it is critical for a good macroeconomic theory to explain key aspects of the *patterns* of fluctuations is that much of our concern over these fluctuations arises from the fact that their impact is borne disproportionately by certain sectors and certain groups of individuals. If credit markets were perfect, and if the impact of cyclical fluctuations were uniform, then none of the postwar recessions would have had much of an effect on lifetime incomes (utility), and even the Great Depression would have reduced lifetime incomes by little more than the cumulative effects of technical progress increase it.

1. Perhaps the most important issue is the explanation of unemployment, of the failure of wages to adjust to clear the labour market.[23] But beyond that, a good macroeconomic theory must explain (*a*) why there are lay-offs rather than work-sharing (including the absence of job rotation); and (*b*) why, at least in the USA unemployment is concentrated in certain groups.

In posing the problem this way, I have taken a stand on what to a few economists may seem a controversial issue: Is there any unemployment, and in particular, is there any involuntary unemployment? All economists would agree that there are variations in the level of *employment*, and that there are variations in the demographics that describe those people in the labour force who, at any given moment, could be gainfully employed but are not. The task of isolating and understanding the reasons for such variations, I believe, will bear much more fruit than debating or redefining such concepts as 'unemployment', 'voluntary unemployment', and 'involuntary unemployment'.[24]

[23] This parallels the first quandary discussed in the previous subsection.

[24] At the analytic level, the recent research of labour and other markets with imperfect information, including the efficiency wage theories, have established that (*a*) market equilibrium may not be (constrained)-Pareto-efficient—i.e., there exist government interventions which, while respecting the limitations on information and other restrictions facing markets, can make all individuals better off (see Greenwald and Stiglitz 1986, 1988*a*); and (*b*) individuals with no, or only slight, differences in observable characteristics may receive markedly different treatments, including markedly different levels of expected utility. Some individuals may be employed at high-paying jobs, while observationally similar, or even identical, individuals may have to choose between waiting for a good job, remaining unemployed in the interim, or accepting a much lower-paying job. The fact that it may be rational for an individual to remain unemployed rather than accept a low-paying job (See Ma and Weiss 1990; Greenwald and Stiglitz 1987*a*)—and in this sense the unemployment is voluntary—does not make the pain of unemployment any the less, and does not mean that there are not government actions that would improve welfare.

2. The theory must explain the cyclical patterns of inventory movements (inventories do not seem to provide the buffer role suggested by neoclassical doctrine cf. Blinder 1986): as well as the cyclical patterns of investment in machines, buildings (commercial, residential) and research and development (R and D).

3. The theory must explain the failure of prices to move over the cycle anywhere close to the way that competitive theory (or even monopoly theory with constant elasticity demand curves) would have predicted (cf. Hall 1988). The fact that among the sectors exhibiting the greatest cyclical movements are some with considerable price flexibility (construction) raises doubts about the central role sometimes assigned to fixed-price assumptions; and the fact that unemployment arises in economies experiencing considerable inflation where the constraints on downward movements in wages and prices would not seem to be binding, again raises questions about the central role of nominal price rigidities.[25]

4. The theory must also explain the 'time'-series properties of the aggregate series, the facts that there are marked fluctuations in output and employment, and that there is serial correlation.

5. The Labour Market Quandary

In this final section, I want to illustrate the approach of New Keynesian economics by examining the labour market quandary, discussed earlier. Recent years have seen the growth of several alternative explanations. I describe and comment briefly on each of these.

(a) The implicit contract theory

This argues that observed real wages have little to do with current economic activity. Elsewhere, I (and others) have provided criticisms both of the simpler versions of that theory and of the more refined attempts to extract from that theory a theory of unemployment. (See e.g. Azariadis and Stiglitz 1983; Newbery and Stiglitz 1987; or Stiglitz 1986.)

The most telling criticisms of the theory are that (a) while it may

---

[25] This list of the 'stylized facts' which a good theory should explain is not meant to be exhaustive. A good theory should also come to terms with observed patterns of serial correlations and cross-correlations of the variables. There are other 'stylized facts' about which there is less agreement. Views, for instance, concerning the direction and significance of movements in real interest rates depend on whether one calculates the rate by taking, say, nominal short-term interest rates and subtracting reported expected rates of inflation, or subtracting the actual rate of inflation.

provide an explanation of wage rigidity, it does not provide an explanation of unemployment; and (b) in particular, it does not provide an
explanation of either the form or the pattern of unemployment.[26]

We note further that that theory suggests that one looks to new hires
and spot labour markets to observe what is happening to 'shadow'
wages; and I suspect that if one does so the first quandary becomes
more striking: real product wages in these markets undoubtedly fall in
recessions more than observed average real wages.

(b) Efficiency wage and related theories

These theories argue that equilibrium may be consistent with high and
varying levels of unemployment.

Elsewhere (for a survey, see Stiglitz 1986, 1987c; Yellen 1984) I have
argued that the efficiency wage theories provide at least part of the
explanation for non-market-clearing.[27] These theories hold that the
productivity of the firm's workers depends (in part) on the wages paid.
Reducing wages below some critical level actually increases labour costs.
Hence if, at the efficiency wage, i.e. the wage at which labour costs are
minimized, there is an excess supply of workers, firms will still not lower
their wages, as conventional supply and demand analysis would have
suggested; for to do so would actually lower firms' profits. Several
alternative explanations for why productivity might depend on wages
have been explored—wages affect the mix of applicants (the adverse
selection effect), the incentive of workers to work hard, and labour
turnover. Efficiency may also be affected by morale concerns or by
nutritional considerations. The different theories have somewhat different implications. Still, the major consequence is the same for all the
variants: the possible existence of equilibrium unemployment.[28]

(c) Disequilibrium theories

In these theories wages do fall in the presence of unemployment, but
unemployment can persist none the less because prices fall simultaneously. Thus, it is the *decentralized* adjustment mechanism that is to
blame for the persistence of unemployment. Some twenty five years
ago, Solow and I (Solow and Stiglitz 1968) explored this possibility. An

---

[26] An exception is the version of implicit contract theory combining it with search and
efficiency wages (Arnott et al. 1988).

[27] Insider–outsider theory (Lindbeck and Snower 1989) focuses, in particular, on the
rigidity in wages for new hires.

[28] Elsewhere, I have also argued that these theories provide a much more convincing
explanation of the other labour market phenomena to be explained than, say, the implicit
contract theories (Stiglitz 1986, 1987c), although models combining elements of both may
eventually prove fruitful (Arnott et al. 1988).

important difference between our work and much of the subsequent fixed-price literature (besides the explicit formulation of the dynamics of adjustment) arose from our conviction that real balance effects simply were quantitatively of insufficient importance to play a first-order effect in the analysis of short-run equilibrium. That is why we postulated that proportional reductions in wages and prices would leave the aggregate demand curve (relatively) unaffected.[29]

It is, in fact, quite likely that a theory combining efficiency wage considerations and disequilibrium dynamics can account for the observed patterns in labour markets. Efficiency wage theory argues that wages are chosen to maximize (the expected utility of) profits. Accordingly, in the absence of uncertainty, a small change in the economic environment would normally necessitate a small change in wages; and the loss of expected profits from failing to respond would be small (Akerlof and Yellen 1985). The firm knows (or has views about) the consequences of its maintaining its current wage policy (say wage rate). There is however greater (subjective) uncertainty about the consequences of any change in wage policy; it must judge not only how its workers, and potential workers, might respond, but also how its competitors (both in the labour and the product market) will respond. As a result, the optimal policy, the one that maximizes the expected utility of profits (given the risk aversion of firms, or the firm's managers), may entail maintaining the firm's wage policy. This explains why firms may adjust wages slowly, or not at all, to changes in economic environment. The interdependence among wages, to which efficiency wage theory gives rise, argues further that, given that other firms have not changed their wages, or have changed their wages only very little, the wage that maximizes expected profits will not change, or will not change very much. Thus, while the earlier Solow–Stiglitz model postulated that wage adjustments might be slow, efficiency wage theory, combined with firms' risk aversion, provides an explanation for why those adjustments are likely to be slow (or non-existent).[30] (Elsewhere, we have provided an explanation for why firms should, in fact, behave in a risk-averse manner.[31])

---

[29] Actually, it seemed equally plausible that a detailed examination of the short-run effect of price adjustments would show that these exacerbated the problem rather than alleviating it; that is, if individuals or firms extrapolated a fall in price, they might be led to reduce their consumption and investment. Neary and I (1982) and Grandmont (1983) showed that this might in fact be the case.

[30] Staggered contract theory can be thought of as a particular formulation of, or explanation of, slow wage adjustments. But note that the fact that contracts are long-lived does not by itself provide much of an explanation for unemployment, unless accompanied by, say, efficiency wage considerations. For, as contracts come up for negotiation, wages on the flexible margin should adjust, to absorb all workers willing to work.

[31] The ideas summarized in this last paragraph have been developed more extensively and formally by Greenwald and Stiglitz (1989a). I have deliberately been somewhat vague about how a wage policy is defined, e.g. whether it represents a constant nominal wage, a

(d) Imperfect competition (unions)

The presence of imperfect competition in the labour market provides an explanation of why workers do not sell all the labour that they would like to *at the going wage*. But in the USA less than a fifth of the labour force in the private sector is in unions. At most, unions can explain why some workers get paid more than others—alone, they cannot explain unemployment. (Indeed, such theories cannot explain the variability of employment at a fixed real consumption wage unless accompanied either simultaneously by shocks to preferences, or by one of the other considerations which have been raised here.)

(e) Insider–outsider theory

Much of the specific knowledge of a firm lies in its current workers. New workers have to be trained, and the training is done largely by old workers. Thus, in most firms new workers cannot simply replace older workers, particularly without the 'consent' of the old workers; and the old workers are unlikely to give that consent. The fact that insiders and outsiders are not perfect substitutes gives insiders considerable bargaining power within the firm; alternatively, we can view the problem of management as paying a high enough wage to insiders—and having a form of commitment that they will continue to pay the high wage—to motivate them to train the new hires well. Thus, insider–outsider theory can be viewed as combining elements of imperfect competition in the labour market with efficiency wage concerns. Note, too, that what is relevant for a hiring decision (as in the next theory to be described) is the lifetime wage of the worker; his willingness to accept a low wage today does not necessarily mean that, once he becomes an insider, he will not demand a higher wage. Thus, workers find it difficult to commit themselves to a low lifetime wage; in effect, they cannot lower their wages.

(f) Employment as an investment decision

To the extent that there are fixed costs associated with hiring, training, and firing workers, the decision to hire workers is an investment

constant real wage, or a constant relative wage. In fact, in some versions of efficiency wage theory (Stiglitz 1985) there exist Nash equilibria in which nominal wages are rigid—all firms, believing that other firms are keeping their nominal wages fixed, find it optimal to keep their own wages fixed—and other equilibria in which real wages are fixed. In Greenwald and Stiglitz (1989a) we present a general theory of adjustment, in which what is entailed by 'maintaining the current policy' is explicitly defined within the context of the firm's problem of maximizing its expected utility of profits. We argue there that the uncertainties associated with changing wage policies are such as to make wage rigidities (as opposed to rigidities in other decision variables) particularly likely.

decision. Workers and firms can be thought of as having to decide when to make such an investment. They must compare the stream of returns they obtain as a result of making the decision at different times, evaluating the cost of capital at the appropriate shadow price for the period in which the investment is made. If, as we have argued elsewhere, there is capital-rationing, the lifetime wage that workers would have to be willing to accept to make firms willing to make the investment during recessionary periods may be much lower than if the investment decision is postponed to better times.[32,33]

6. Summary

New Keynesian economics can be viewed as a dynamic research programme. It seeks to understand the causes of imperfections in the labour, capital, and product markets, their macroeconomic consequences, and, on the basis of this, to derive policy prescriptions. Various variants of the school emphasize various imperfections. But the differences among the various strands are less important than the similarity of their underlying view of the economy. In most cases the explanations are not mutually exclusive. The debate is over the *relative* importance of various explanations.

The conformity of a theory to the basic qualitative facts of the economy seems to be the first hurdle to which any theory should be subjected. If it fails to meet that test, there is little to be gained from the sophisticated testing of one or two of its implications, for in the end, as I have emphasized, a theory must be judged by the consistency of all of its implications with the facts. The New Keynesian theories pass, or, perhaps I should say more modestly, show the promises of passing, that hurdle.

To conclude: the theory is still at a rudimentary stage. There are more qualitative implications to be drawn from it, to be judged against the empirical evidence. There are refinements to the theory: among

[32] This argument is developed in greater detail in Greenwald and Stiglitz (1987a). Note that, if firms can discriminate between old and new workers, the workers who choose to remain unemployed because of the low wage offer are, in a sense, voluntarily unemployed. On the other hand, if firms cannot discriminate between old and new workers (a hypothesis for which insider–outsider theory provides some justification, as does standard efficiency wage theory, focusing on morale considerations), then the firm will not be willing to hire workers at the going wage, and workers are, in this sense, involuntarily unemployed.

[33] One might ask, Couldn't workers absorb some of the risk of firms, by making their pay contingent on the performance of the firm? This makes workers in effect equity-holders, and the standard arguments for why equity markets are imperfect apply.

these are the development of a more formal dynamics, and the
integration of the important lessons to be drawn from other lines of
research in macroeconomics of the past quarter-century.[34] At the same
time, I hope that quantitative testing, both of the various pieces of the
model and of the model as a whole, will not only show that it provides a
superior model to alternatives, but will also provide further insights
leading to further refinements of the theory. It is an exciting research
programme, and one that I hope some readers will be persuaded to join.

References

ABEL, ANDREW (1982). 'Dynamic Effects of Permanent and Temporary Tax
Policies in a q Model of Investment'. *Journal of Monetary Economics*, 9:
353–73.

AKERLOF, GEORGE, and STIGLITZ, J. E. (1966). 'Investment and Wages',
Econometrica, 34, suppl.: 118.

—— and YELLEN, J. (1985). 'A Near-Rational Model of the Business Cycle with
Wage and Price Inertia'. *Quarterly Journal of Economics*, 100, suppl.: 823–38.

ARNOTT, RICHARD, HOSIOS, ARTHUR, and STIGLITZ, J. E. (1988). 'Implicit
Contracts, Labor Mobility and Unemployment'. *American Economic Review*,
78: 1046–66.

AZARIADIS, C., and STIGLITZ, J. E. (1983). 'Implicit Contracts and Fixed Price
Equilibria'. *Quarterly Journal of Economics*, 98, suppl.: 1–22.

BARRO, ROBERT J. (1974). 'Are Government Bonds Net Wealth?' *Journal of
Political Economy*, 82: 1095–117.

—— and GROSSMAN, H. I. (1971). 'A General Disequilibrium Model of Income
and Employment'. *American Economic Review*, 61: 82–93.

BENASSY, JEAN-PASCAL (1975). 'Neo-Keynesian Disequilibrium Theory in a
Monetary Economy'. *Review of Economic Studies*, 42: 503–23.

—— (1982). *The Economics of Market Disequilibrium*. New York: Academic
Press.

BLINDER, ALAN S. (1986). 'Can the Production Smoothing Model of Inventory
Behavior Be Saved?' *Quarterly Journal of Economics*, 101: 431–54.

DEBREU, G. (1974). 'Excess Demand Functions', *Journal of Mathematical
Economics*, 1: 15–21.

DUNLOP, J. T. (1938). 'The Movement of Real and Money Wage Rates'.
Economic Journal, 48: 413–34.

FRIEDMAN, MILTON (1968). 'The Role of Monetary Policy'. *American Economic
Review*, 58: 1–17.

GALE, IAN, and STIGLITZ, J. E. (1989). 'The Informational Content of Initial

---

[34] I have referred to some of these, such as implicit contract and insider–outsider
theory, earlier. My contention then was that these theories, by themselves, provided
inadequate explanation of the central questions at issue.

Public Offerings'. *Journal of Finance*, 44: 469–78.

GRANDMONT, JEAN M. (1983). *Money and Value: A Reconsideration of Classical and Neoclassical Monetary Theories*, Econometric Society, Monograph no. 5. Cambridge University Press.

——(1985) 'On Endogenous Competitive Business Cycles'. *Econometrica*, 53: 995–1046.

GREENWALD, BRUCE, and STIGLITZ, J. E. (1986). 'Externalities in Economies with Imperfect Information and Incomplete Markets', *Quarterly Journal of Economics*, 101: 229–64.

—— ——(1987a). 'Imperfect Information, Credit Markets and Unemployment'. *European Economic Review*, 31: 444–56.

—— ——(1987b). 'Keynesian, New Keynesian and New Classical Economics'. *Oxford Economic Papers*, 39: 119–33. Subsequently reprinted in P. J. N. Sinclair (ed.), *Price, Quantities, and Expectations*, Oxford University Press, 1987, pp. 119–33.

—— ——(1988a). 'Pareto Inefficiency of Market Economies: Search and Efficiency Wage Models'. *American Economic Review Papers and Proceedings*, 78: 351–5.

—— ——(1988b). 'Examining Alternative Macroeconomic Theories'. *Brookings Papers on Economic Activity*, no. 1: 207–70.

—— ——(1988c). 'Money, Imperfect Information and Economic Fluctuations'. In Meir Kohn and S. C. Tsiang (eds.), *Finance Constraints, Expectations, and Macroeconomics*. Oxford University Press, pp. 141–65.

—— ——(1988d). 'Information, Finance Constraints and Business Fluctuations'. [*Proceedings of Taipei*] *Symposium on Monetary Theory*. Beijing: Institute of Economics, Academia Sinica.

—— ——(1988e). 'Imperfect Information, Finance Constraints, and Business Fluctuations'. In Meir Kohn and S. C. Tsaing (eds.), *Finance Constraints, Expectations, and Macroeconomics*, Oxford University Press, pp. 103–40.

—— ——(1989a). 'Toward a Theory of Rigidities'. *American Economic Review*, 79: 364–9.

—— ——(1989b). 'Impact of Changing Tax Environment on Investments and Productivity'. *Journal of Accounting, Auditing and Finance*.

—— ——(1990a). 'Financial Market Imperfections and Productivity Growth'. *Journal of Economic Behavior and Organization*, 13: 321–45.

—— ——(1990b). 'Macroeconomic Models with Equity and Credit Rationing'. In R. Glenn Hubbard (ed.), *Information, Capital Markets and Investments*. Chicago: University of Chicago Press.

—— ——(1990c). 'Asymmetric Information and the New Theory of the Firm: Financial Constraints and Risk Behavior'. *American Economic Review*, 80: 160–5.

—— ——(forthcoming a). 'Financial Market Imperfections and Business Cycles'. *Quarterly Journal of Economics*. (NBER Working Paper no. 2494, 1988.)

—— ——(forthcoming b). 'Information, Finance and Markets: The Architecture of Allocative Mechanisms'. *Journal of Industrial and Corporate Change*. (Paper presented at the International Conference on the History of the Enterprise, Terni, Italy, September 1991.)

——— and WEISS, ANDREW (1984). 'Informational Imperfections in the Capital Markets and Macro-economic Fluctuations'. *American Economic Review*, 74: 194–9.

GROSSMAN, S., and STIGLITZ, J. E. (1976). 'Information and Competitive Price Systems'. *American Economic Review*, 66: 246–53.

——— (1980). 'On the Impossibility of Informationally Efficient Markets'. *American Economic Review*, 70: 393–408. Subsequently reprinted in S. Bhattacharya and G. Constantinides (eds.), *Financial Markets and Incomplete Information: Frontiers of Modern Financial Theory*, ii. Totowa, NJ: Rowman and Littlefield, 1989, pp. 123–36.

HALL, ROBERT E. (1988). 'Intertemporal Substitution in Consumption'. *Journal of Political Economy*, 96: 921–47.

HICKS, JOHN R. (1956). *A Contribution to the Theory of the Trade Cycle*. Oxford: Clarendon Press.

KAHN, RICHARD F. (1931). 'The Relation of Home Investment to Unemployment'. *Economic Journal*, 41: 173–98.

KEYNES, JOHN MAYNARD (1936). *The General Theory of Employment, Interest and Money*. London: Macmillan.

LINDBECK, ASSAR, and SNOWER, DENNIS J. (1989). *The Insider–Outsider Theory of Employment and Unemployment*. Cambridge, Mass.: MIT Press.

MA, ALBERT, and WEISS, ANDREW (1990). 'A Signalling Theory of Unemployment', Mimeo, Boston University.

MALINVAUD, EDMOND (1977). *The Theory of Unemployment Reconsidered*. New York: Basil Blackwell.

MANTEL, R. (1974). 'On the Characterization of Aggregate Excess Demand'. *Journal of Economic Theory*, 7: 348–53.

METZLER, L. A. (1941). 'The Nature and Stability of Inventory Cycles'. *Review of Economics and Statistics*, 23: 138–49.

MYERS, S. C., and MAJLUF, N. S. (1984). 'Corporate Financing and Investment Decisions when Firms Have Information that Investors Do Not'. *Journal of Financial Economics*, 11: 187–221.

NEARY, P., and STIGLITZ, J. E. (1982). 'Expectations, Asset Accumulation and the Real-Balance Effect'. Paper presented at Dublin meeting of the Econometric Society, September.

NEWBERY, DAVID, and STIGLITZ, J. E. (1981). *The Theory of Commodity Price Stabilization*. Oxford University Press.

——— (1987). 'Wage Rigidity, Implicit Contracts, Unemployment and Economic Efficiency'. *Economic Journal*, 97: 416–30.

PATINKIN, DONALD (1965). *Theory, Interest and Prices*. New York: Harper and Row.

SAMUELSON, PAUL A. (1939). 'Interaction between the Multiplier Analysis and the Principle of Acceleration'. *Review of Economics and Statistics*, 21: 75–8.

——— (1963). *Foundations of Economic Analysis*. Cambridge, Mass.: Harvard University Press.

SOLOW, R. (1957). 'Technical Change and the Aggregate Production Function'. *Review of Economics and Statistics*, 39: 312–20.

——— and STIGLITZ, J. E. (1968). 'Output, Employment and Wages in the Short Run'. *Quarterly Journal of Economics*, 72: 537–60.

SONNENSCHEIN, H. (1972). 'Market Excess Demand Functions'. *Econometrica*, 40: 549–63.

—— (1973). 'Do Walras' Identity and Continuity Characterize the Class of Community Excess Demand Functions?' *Journal of Economic Theory*, 6: 345–54.

STIGLITZ, JOSEPH E. (1982*a*). 'Information and Captial Markets', In William F. Sharpe and Cathryn Cootner (eds.), *Financial Economics: Essays in Honor of Paul Cootner*. Prentice Hall, pp. 118–58.

—— (1982*b*). 'The Inefficiency of the Stock Market Equilibrium'. *Review of Economic Studies*, 49: 241–61.

—— (1985). 'Equilibrium Wage Distribution'. *Economic Journal*, 95: 595–618.

—— (1986). 'Theories of Wage Rigidities'. In James L. Butkiewicz, Kenneth J. Koford, and Jeffrey B. Miller (eds.), *Keynes' Economic Legacy: Contemporary Economic Theories*. New York: Praeger, pp. 153–206.

—— (1987*a*). 'Technological Change, Sunk Costs, and Competition'. *Brookings Papers on Economic Activity*, 3 (Special issue on Microeconomics, ed. M. N. Baily and C. Winston): 883–947.

—— (1987*b*). 'On the Microeconomics of Technical Progress'. In Jorge M. Katz (ed.), *Technology Generation in Latin American Manufacturing Industries*. London: Macmillan, pp. 56–77.

—— (1987*c*). 'The Causes and Consequences of the Dependence of Quality on Prices'. *Journal of Economic Literature*, 25: 1–47.

—— (1988). 'On the Relevance or Irrelevance of Public Financial Policy'. In *The Economics of Public Debt*, Proceedings of the 1986 International Economic Association meeting. London: Macmillan, pp. 41–76.

—— (1990). 'Whither Socialism? Perspectives from the Economics of Information'. Wicksell Lectures, presented in Stockholm, May 1990.

—— (1991). 'The Invisible Hand and Modern Welfare Economics'. In D. Vines and A. Stevenson (eds.), *Information, Strategy and Public Policy*. Oxford: Basil Blackwell.

—— (1992). 'Capital Markets and Economic Fluctuations in Capitalist Economies'. Marshall lecture prepared for the European Economic Association Annual Meeting, Cambridge, UK, August 1991. In *European Economic Review* (forthcoming). North-Holland.

—— and WEISS, ANDREW (1978). 'Credit Rationing in Markets with Imperfect Information'. *American Economic Review*, 71: 393–410.

—— —— (1983*a*). 'Alternate Approaches to the Analysis of Markets with Asymmetric Information'. *American Economic Review*, 73: 246–9.

—— —— (1983*b*). 'Incentive Effects of Termination: Applications to the Credit and Labor Markets'. *American Economic Review*, 72: 912–27.

—— —— (1986). 'Credit Rationing and Collateral'. In Jeremy Edwards, Julian Franks, Colin Mayer, and Stephen Schaefer (eds.), *Recent Developments in Corporate Finance*. New York: Cambridge University Press, pp. 101–35.

—— —— (1987*a*). 'Macro-economic Equilibrium and Credit Rationing'. NBER Working Paper no. 2164, February 1987. (Forthcoming, *Oxford Economic Papers*.)

—— —— (1987*b*). 'Credit Rationing with Many Borrowers'. *American Economic Review*, 77: 228–31.

——— —— (1990*a*). 'Credit Rationing and Its Implications for Macro-Economics'. Working Paper.

——— —— (1990*b*) 'Banks as Social Accountants and Screening Devices and the General Theory of Credit Rationing'. In A. Courakis and C. Goodhart (eds.), *Essays in Monetary Economics in Honor of Sir John Hicks*. Oxford University Press.

TARSHIS, L. (1939). 'Changes in Real and Money Wage Rates'. *Economic Journal*, 49: 150–4.

TAYLOR, JOHN B. (1987). 'Differences in Economic Fluctuations in Japan, the United States and Europe'. Mimeo, Stanford University.

YELLEN, JANET (1984). 'Efficiency Wage Models of Unemployment'. *American Economic Review*, 74: 200–5.

4

Notes on the Non-Walrasian Approach to Macroeconomics

JOAQUIM SILVESTRE

1. Basic Ideas

1.1. *Three influences*

The non-Walrasian approach to macroeconomics is exemplified by the recent book by Benassy (1986) as well as by the econometrics described in Quandt (1988).[1] It was born in the early 1970s at the confluence of three theoretical lines.

The first line originated in was the attempt, by Clower (1965, 1967) and Leijonhufvud (1967, 1968), to clarify 'the purely formal differences, if any, between Keynes and the Classics' (Clower 1965: 103). It put forward some of the fundamental notions of the non-Walrasian approach by emphasizing the importance of quantity signals and the monetary character of transactions. This in turn evidenced the problem of co-ordination across markets and led to the modelling of quantity-constrained choice and the principle of effective demand.

The second line is exemplified by the suggestion of the fixprice method by Hicks (1965) and the literature on price dynamics in Walrasian general equilibrium. The possibility of slow adjustment of prices motivated the need for focusing on out-of-equilibrium trans-actions. It led to the formulation of the spillover effects by Patinkin (1956). Moreover, the (at the time) shocking results by Scarf (1960) and Gale (1963) on the instability of the Walras–Samuelson price *tâtonnement* motivated the study of non-*tâtonnement* processes, which at first

The author acknowledges helpful comments by J.-P. Benassy. The usual caveat applies.

[1] Other representative work includes Benassy (1978, 1983, 1984*a*, 1987*b*, 1990); Böhm (1989); Müller (1983) and Silvester (1987). See Benassy (1984*b*); Cuddington *et al.* (1984); Dixit and Norman (1980); and Neary (1980) for extensions to open economies. Economet-ric issues are discussed in Gourieroux *et al.* (1980); Laffont (1985); Lambert (1988); Quandt (1982); Quandt and Rosen (1988); Rudebusch (1987); and Sneessens (1981). Applications to centrally planned economies are found in Portes (1981); Portes *et al.* (1984); and Portes and Winter (1977, 1980).

sight appeared to converge under more general conditions. The formulation of out-of-equilibrium transactions in the non-*tâtonnement* literature prefigured some aspects of non-Walrasian analysis: the voluntary trade condition of non-Walrasian analysis reflects Negishi's (1961) and Uzawa's (1962) emphasis on utility-increasing trading paths, and the 'Hahn condition' (Hahn and Negishi 1962) anticipates the other basic assumption of non-Walrasian analysis, namely the absence of frictions. (See also Negishi 1962: 664; and Arrow and Hahn 1971: ch. 13.)

The third line was the analysis of imperfect competition in general equilibrium, pioneered by Negishi (1960–1). It gave for the first time a rigorous answer to the question of the compatibility among the decisions of firms that have price-making power in distinct but interdependent markets, a question that Cournot (1838) raised but left unsolved. Negishi's approach significantly influenced the early non-Walrasian literature (e.g. Benassy 1973: ch. 5, 1976, 1977; Grandmont and Laroque 1976). More recent work has evidenced various connections between the non-Walrasian approach and imperfect competition (see Section 4 below).

1.2. *Out-of-equilibrium transactions and the relevant market signals*

At a Walrasian equilibrium the quantity plans of price-taking agents are compatible and jointly realized. But the Walrasian model says nothing about the determination of quantities at disequilibrium prices: states where prices fail to equilibrate supply and demand are uninteresting from the Walrasian viewpoint. Yet the logic of the Walrasian method demands that such a neglect of disequilibrium states be dynamically justified. After all, the reason for disregarding disequilibrium states is not that they cannot appear but that, as soon as they do appear, market dynamics quickly lead the economy away from them and towards a Walrasian equilibrium. Thus, somewhat paradoxically, in order to justify the irrelevance of disequilibrium states, one must study what happens there; one must have a theory of the behaviour of the economy in disequilibrium.

The *tâtonnement* process of Walras and Samuelson offers a first approach, according to which the price of a commodity rises when the Walrasian excess demand for it is positive and drops when it is negative. Because Walrasian excess demands reflect plans made by price-taking, quantity-unconstrained economic agents, the approach presupposes that nothing is traded out of equilibrium, i.e., that prices are quoted out of equilibrium but no transactions occur. Thus, strictly speaking, it applies only to special institutions, as auctions where trade is delayed until supply equals demand. Three questions must be addressed as soon as one admits disequilibrium trading.

1. How are out-of-equilibrium transactions determined? Because the plans to buy and sell based on the price-taking hypothesis will be mutually incompatible, realized transactions must involve rationing of some sort.
2. Given that Walrasian excess demands are irrelevant under rationing, what are the 'relevant market signals' when trade occurs at non-Walrasian prices?[2] In other words, what are the laws of motion of prices? This in turn leads to the third question.
3. Can there be stationary non-Walrasian prices? That is, can there be prices that fail to equate supply and demand in each market but do not induce pressures for change in any market?

The first question was largely avoided before the development of the non-Walrasian literature, and no insight was offered beyond the suggestions implicit in the non-*tâtonnement* processes. The second question became the object of lively debate. Patinkin (1956) observed that the rationing of demand in one market may 'spill over' and increase the demand for a substitute product. In general, he suggested, a price may change as a result of excess demand for another good, and the market signal that governs the change of a price depends, in principle, on the vector of excess demands in all markets. Negishi (1965) and Clower (1965) objected to the imprecision of Patinkin's formulation and in particular to the possibility of obtaining a zero signal from a non-zero vector of excess demands. Clower's own contribution was the definition of 'effective demands', derived at the individual level from an income-constrained maximization programme that he called the 'dual decision hypothesis'. The formulation allowed Clower to justify Keynes's 'fundamental psychological law' of the consumption function in choice-theoretic terms. Moreover, it offered an unambiguous notion of 'relevant market signal', namely, excess effective demand.

Clower (1965) suggested an affirmative answer to the third question. Indeed, he seemed to view a state of Keynesian unemployment as one where the market signals fail to induce a change. For instance, one of his conclusions was that 'chronic factor unemployment at substantially unchanging levels of real income and output may be consistent with Keynesian economics even if all prices are flexible'; although he cautions that 'this problem has yet to be investigated within the context of a Keynesian model of market price formation'.

---

[2] Curiously, the non-*tâtonnement* literature neglected this point and persisted in taking Walrasian excess demands as the market signal that directs the change in price, even when transactions are carried out at disequilibrium prices.

The non-Walrasian literature answered the three questions. Question 1 is addressed from three approaches: that of Benassy (1973, 1975a, 1976), generalizing Barro and Grossman (1971, 1974, 1976) and Grossman (1971, 1972); that of Drèze (1975); and that of Malinvaud and Younès (1977a,b) and Younès (1970, 1975). The three approaches differ in form and motivation, but they turn out to be equivalent under certain conditions (see Silvestre 1978a, 1982a, 1983): they are particularly equivalent for the model of Section 2.1 below.

Question 2 is directly addressed in the work of Barro and Grossman and Benassy. Benassy (1973, 1975a, 1977) offers a coherent notion of market signal for economies with an arbitrary number of markets and agents by defining excess effective demand in a multi-market economy that transacts out of equilibrium.[3]

The answer to question 3 turns out to be a qualified 'no'.[4] Disequilibrium price dynamics failed to support the just mentioned conjecture of Clower. States of unemployment, in particular, display excess effective supply of labour, and thus a downward market pressure on wages. It is true that lowering wages will not, by itself, reduce unemployment of the Keynesian type. But in the Keynesian regime either there is excess effective supply of output, or else the output market is balanced, in which case a decrease in wages will lead to excess effective supply of output. Downward pressures on prices develop in either case. If prices and wages are free to fall, therefore, a state of general excess effective supply will be temporary.

1.3. *Markets in monetary economies*

Walrasian economics concerns the operation of perfectly competitive markets. Yet it leaves the very notion of 'market' undefined, as evidenced by its failure to provide a clear answer to the question, How many markets are there? Benassy (1986: 14) notes that Walras (1874) contemplated a market for each pair of goods, where traders can exchange one of the goods against the other one in a particular market. (This yields $n(n-1)/2$ markets in an economy with n goods.) The language of modern texts is ambiguous. Sometimes it suggests one

---

[3] See Eckalbar (1980), Honkapohja (1979), Honkapohja and Ito (1983), Laroque (1978, 1981), Mukherji (1990) and Veendorp (1975) for non-Walrasian price dynamics. The models of Drèze and Younès do not directly address this question, but they embody suggestions on the classification of disequilibrium regimes: see Silvestre (1978b, 1982a, 1983). Some subtleties in the definition of excess effective demand in general production contexts, including cases with interfirm trade, are discussed in Silvestre (1982b, 1983).

[4] The qualification is needed because, strictly speaking, zero signals may be generated by some full-employment situations where firms are simultaneously constrained in the input and output markets. See Silvestre (1986: sect. 3.3.1) for a discussion of this case.

market for each good;[5] on other occasions it suggests a single, central-ized clearing-house where agents do not trade among themselves, but each trader transacts commodity bundles of any composition with the coordinating centre. In any event, as Debreu (1959: 28) asserts, 'it is assumed that the economy works without the help of a good serving as medium of exchange'.

The non-Walrasian approach adopts a monetary view of the market institutions, following the suggestion of Clower (1967) that *money buys goods and goods buy money, but goods do not buy goods*. Clower (1967) first emphasizes that there may in principle be different exchange institutions with alternative elementary transactions. One such institu-tion is the barter economy, which agrees with the just mentioned view of Walras. It has $(n - 1)n/2$ 'trading posts', one for each pair of commodities, and it allows for any good to be directly exchanged against any other good. The second institution, that of a monetary economy, uses a particular good as money, and admits only elementary trans-actions between money and another good. Thus, there are $n - 1$ markets in a monetary economy with n goods. The monetary institution captures the typical exchange relations in a decentralized, mature economy.[6]

1.4. *The indirect utility of money and expectations*

The non-Walrasian approach views the money balances that agents hold at the end of the period as a store of value for future consumption. It assumes that future markets are not open (see Benassy, 1973, 1975*a*, 1982, 1986, 1990; Grandmont, 1977, 1983, 1987): agents must form expectations about the future state of the economy when deciding on the money balances to carry over. The expectations cover future prices and wages, and also future quantities (say, future GNP or future quantity constraints) and, in the case of agents with market power, future demand and supply curves.[7]

A consumer cares about present and future consumption. But her decision variables are present consumption and the money balances to be carried into the future. The consumer's decision can thus be viewed as the maximization of preferences defined on present consumption and

---

[5] For instance, Arrow and Hahn (1971: ch. 2, sect. 5) and the popular book by Varian (1984: 190) seem to indicate that there is a market for each good, and that there are 'transactions' in each market, but they do not specify what is exchanged against what.

[6] See also Benassy (1975*b*, 1986) and Malinvaud and Younès (1977*a,b*) for more detailed discussions.

[7] See Benassy (1973, 1975*a*) and, in particular Benassy (1990: sect. 6) for a discussion on the role of expected quantity constraints.

money balances, given her expectations. Such preferences are represented by an indirect utility function, with money balances, expected
prices, and expected quantity constraints as arguments. As Benassy
(1990: sect. 6) shows, even when the consumer anticipates future
quantity constraints, her indirect utility function is homogeneous of
degree 0 in money balances and expected future prices. Of course,
expectations will typically be influenced by current prices and current
quantity constraints. But, unless expected prices and wages always
coincide with the present ones (i.e. unless 'expectations are unit-
elastic'), the homogeneity with respect to money balances and current
prices and wages will not obtain.

The non-Walrasian approach accommodates many rules of expectation
formation. In particular, it is consistent with perfect foresight or with
the assumption that, in Muth's (1961) words, 'expectations, since they
are informed predictions of future events, are essentially the same as the
predictions of the relevant economic theory' (see Neary and Stiglitz
1983, and Benassy 1986: ch. 13). Because the 'relevant economic theory'
is not always Walrasian, one should distinguish, as Tobin (1980) did,
between perfect foresight or 'rational expectations' and the instantaneous equilibration of the Walrasian supply and demand for all
commodities.

2. Transactions in the Non-Walrasian Model

2.1. *A simple prototype*

Many features of the non-Walrasian approach can be illustrated in a
simplified version of the three-good model for a closed economy at a
given time period, studied by Barro and Grossman (1971, 1976) and
further elaborated by Benassy (1978, 1982, 1986), Hildenbrand and
Hildenbrand (1978), Malinvaud (1977), and Muellbauer and Portes
(1978), among others. The simplifications include the following: (1)
there is money but not bonds; (2) expectations of future prices, wages,
and quantity signals depend only on current prices and wages; (3) all
firms are identical; (4) consumers have homothetic preferences; and (5)
the supply of labour is fixed. The simplifications are by no means
essential. Indeed, non-Walrasian analysis covers general economies with
many commodities, firms, and consumers under the standard assumptions of general equilibrium theory (see Benassy 1973, 1975a, 1976;
Drèze 1975). Many versions of the three-good model assume a flexible
labour supply (see Barro and Grossman 1971, 1974, 1976; Benassy 1973,
1978, 1990; Malinvaud 1977). Some versions include a market for bonds,
which makes them directly comparable with the usual *IS–LM* model

(see Barro and Grossman 1976; Benassy 1983: 1986: ch. 6). Indeed, the latter characterizes three types of allocations that correspond to three textbook versions of the $IS-LM$ model by taking the view that the bond market always clears and that prices and wages are flexible upwards.

Readers may consult the mentioned literature for richer models. It suffices here to consider three goods, namely money, output, and labour, denoted respectively by M, Y, and L. Money is the numeraire: its supply is fixed at $\bar{M}$ units. The demand for money refers to the desired money balances at the end of the period. As discussed in Section 1.4 above, money balances indirectly yield utility. There are $\bar{L}$ units of labour initially available in the economy and supplied inelastically. Labour produces output according to the production function $Y = f(L)$. There are two markets: the labour market, with (nominal) wage w, and the output market, with price p. There is one firm and N consumers who have the same expectations and the same utility function.[8] It will be written $U(Y, M, p, w)$, where p and w appear as arguments because they may influence the expectations of future prices, wages, and quantity constraints. Assume that the utility function is homothetic in Y and M.[9] This makes aggregate demand independent of the distribution of wealth among consumers (i.e. the initial endowments of money and labour, and the shares in the profits of the firm).

Define the marginal rate of substitution $V'(Y, p, w) = (\partial U/\partial Y)/(\partial U/\partial M)$, with derivatives evaluated at $(Y/N, \bar{M}/N, p, w)$, or at any vector of the form $(\lambda Y, \lambda\bar{M}, p, w)$ for $\lambda > 0$. The marginal cost at Y is $w(f^{-1})'(Y)$, and the full-employment output is $\bar{Y} = f(\bar{L})$. The out-of-equilibrium level of output, named 'fixprice output', is defined as follows.

DEFINITION. The level of output Y is a *fixprice output for the price–wage pair* (p, w) if: (i) $Y \leqslant \bar{Y}$; (ii) $p \leqslant V'(Y, p, w)$; (iii) $p \geqslant w(f^{-1})'(Y)$; and (iv) at least one of (i)–(iii) is an equality.

Condition (i) requires output not to exceed the full-employment level. Condition (ii) means that a consumer at a vector multiple of $(Y, \bar{M})$ cannot gain by buying less output at the going price: it is a condition of 'voluntary trading' for a consumer.[10] The price cannot be lower than the marginal cost by condition (iii): it is a condition of 'voluntary trading' for the firm; i.e., profits cannot be increased by selling less at the going

---

[8] The one-firm assumption is inessential as long as all firms are identical and always produce the same amount.

[9] This assumption is, in particular, satisfied if the utility function is homothetic in output and 'real money balances', i.e. balances deflated by a price index.

[10] All consumers end up at a (possible different) scalar multiple of $(Y, \bar{M})$ if output under excess demand is rationed in proportion to wealth or demand (see Silvestre 1988).

price. Finally, at least one of the weak inequalities must be an equality: this is the condition of frictionless markets.

Figure 4.1 partitions the (p, w) plane according to which of the three possible equalities determines output (solid lines). In the full-employment region, $Y = \bar{Y}$; in the Keynesian region, $p = V'(Y, p, w)$; and in the classical (or full-capacity) region, $p = w(f^{-1})'(Y)$. In the boundaries between regions, the two relevant equalities hold. At the Walrasian point (p^c, w^c), all three equalities hold. There is unemployment outside the full-employment region. The dashed lines are iso-employment loci, with the arrows indicating the directions of increasing employment.

The labour market is in excess supply outside the full-employment region, and in excess demand in its interior. The output market is in excess supply in the interior of the Keynesian region, and in excess demand in the interior of the classical and full-employment regions. At the Walrasian point both markets are balanced. In the Keynesian region, the condition for determination of output, $p = V'(Y, p, w)$, can be rewritten as follows. The homotheticity of U implies that demand for output is a function of (p, w) and aggregate wealth I^D of the form $h(p, w)I^D$, where the function $h(p, w)$ satisfies the marginal equality $(\partial U/\partial Y)/(\partial U/\partial M) = p$ whenever (Y, M) is a multiple of $[h(p, w),$

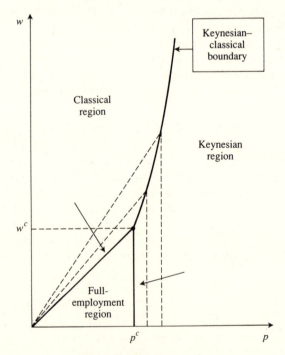

Fig. 4.1. The three regions

$1 - ph(p, w)]$. By setting $I^D = \bar{M} + pY$, we obtain the effective demand for output $C(Y) = h(p, w)(\bar{M} + pY)$. This is the textbook consumption function, with marginal propensity to consume equal to $h(p, w) < 1$. The satisfaction of effective demand requires that $Y = C(Y)$; i.e. $Y/\bar{M} = h(p, w)/[1 - ph(p, w)]$, which by the above marginal equality implies that $p = V'(Y, p, w)$.

2.2. The balanced-budget multiplier under fixed prices and wages

The supply condition 'price = marginal cost' determines the level of output in the classical region: only an increase in the price or a decrease in the wage can alleviate unemployment there. But in the Keynesian region the unemployment problem is on the demand side, because private demand does not suffice to generate full employment. A decrease in the price will certainly increase demand and employment, and, because prices exceed marginal costs, a competitive market for output will exert a downward pressure on prices. But such pressure may be insufficient to increase employment fast enough. Could government expenditure reduce unemployment?

Consider first the extreme case where (1) government expenditures do not directly affect private demand,[11] and (2) prices and wages adjust so slowly that we can safely assume them fixed. Let the spending pro-gramme of the government lead to an eventual purchase of g units of the produced good, which purchase ends up being totally financed by income or wealth taxes; i.e., the government balances its budget and there is neither government debt nor money creation. Then $I^D = \bar{M} + pY - pg$. Total demand for output, including private and public, becomes $h(p, w)(\bar{M} + pY - pg) + g$. But the requirement that demand be satisfied means that the expression must equal the quantity produced, Y. Therefore

$$Y = h(p, w)(\bar{M} + pY - pg) + g,$$

i.e.

$$Y[1 - ph(p, w)] = h(p, w)\bar{M} - ph(p, w)g + g,$$

i.e.

$$Y = b(p, w)\bar{M} + g,$$

where $b(p, w) = h(p, w)/[1 - ph(p, w)]$; i.e. as long as prices do not

---

[11] A model with heterogeneous produced goods is better suited to justify this assumption (see Bailey 1962; and Silvestre, forthcoming).

change, total output has increased by the exact amount bought by the government. This is the traditional Keynesian result: the balanced-budget multiplier of government spending is 1.

2.3. *The balanced-budget multiplier under fixed wages and flexible prices*

The preceding analysis assumes that prices and wages fail to equilibrate supply and demand before government spending, and stay fixed. Of course, under the opposite view that supply and demand are always equal, full employment prevails both before and after government spending; i.e., the multiplier is 0. An intermediate postulate may on occasion be more realistic: wages do not adjust, but prices adjust rapidly to balance supply and demand in the output market; i.e., both when the government does nothing and when it engages in fiscal policy, the output market automatically equilibrates without affecting wages.[12] In other words, the economy is always on the Keynesian–classical boundary of Fig. 4.1. What then would be the multiplier of government expenditure? It turns out that under some natural conditions it is still positive, but less than 1 (see Benassy 1986). Indeed, if the price increases as a result of the additional demand, then the quantity produced must increase in order to preserve the equality 'price = marginal cost' at an unchanged wage, and the equality must be satisfied at any point on the Keynesian–classical boundary. But a price increase will depress private demand and partially counteract the original expansion.

3. Normative Analysis

3.1. *Voluntary and efficient allocations are Walrasian*

The meaning of 'Pareto efficiency' is the usual one: a feasible allocation is Pareto-efficient if it is not dominated by another feasible allocation. The word 'feasible' denotes physical possibility, determined by the given technology and resources of the economy, but independent of property rights, markets, or prices.

Suppose that a price vector is given and that all trade must respect the budget constraints determined by it.[13] Assume moreover that the given price vector fails to equilibrate Walrasian demand and supply. Is

---

[12] This seems to be the view in Keynes (1936).
[13] Prices enter in both sides of the budget constraint; wealth in particular depends on prices through the valuation of profit income and resource sales.

efficiency impossible? The answer is no. One may well have Pareto efficiency with trading at false prices. The Edgeworth box of Fig. 4.2 provides an illustration. Point W is the Walrasian allocation from the initial endowment point $\bar{X}$. The corresponding Walrasian equilibrium price vector is p^*, yielding the budget constraint that goes through points $\bar{X}$ and W. But suppose now that trade must take place at the disequilibrium price vector p^D, and that both traders must respect the budget constraints depicted by the line through $\bar{X}$, A, and B. This is in principle compatible with efficiency: point B is efficient (it is on the contract curve) and all budget constraints are satisfied there.[14]

But point B violates the condition of voluntary trade in the sense that trader 1 would rather transact a smaller amount, namely A, at such prices. In other words, trader 1's marginal benefit from trading is negative at point B. This suggests that it is the combination of disequilibrium prices and the voluntariness of trade that prevents inefficiency.

Indeed, if one insists that all trade must respect the budget constraints and be both voluntary and efficient, then only Walrasian allocations qualify. This is true for economies with any number of commodities,

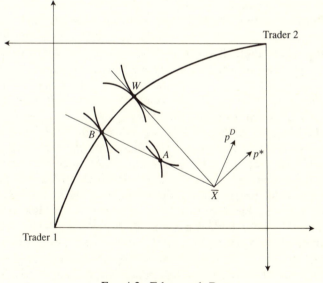

FIG. 4.2. Edgeworth Box
Point B is efficient, but not voluntary;
Point A is voluntary, but not efficient.

[14] See Balasko (1979), Keiding (1981) and Polterovich (1990) for a general treatment of allocations of this kind.

consumers, and firms, as long as all functions are differentiable and the allocation is interior (see Silvestre 1985). Because the non-Walrasian approach postulates the voluntariness of trade, the allocations that it singles out at disequilibrium prices will be typically inefficient. States of unemployment, in particular, are typically non-Walrasian and, thus, inefficient. Moreover, as Jacobsen and Schultz (forthcoming) show, starting from any unemployment situation with voluntary trades, it is possible to induce Pareto improvement by means of an increase in employment.

3.2. *Problems of co-ordination across markets*

The non-Walrasian approach sees each market as an efficient device for bringing together the sellers and buyers of a commodity, contrary to, say, the literature on search and transaction costs, which emphasizes the possibility of co-ordination difficulties within a market (see e.g. Diamond 1982; Howitt 1985). The non-Walrasian view emphasizes instead the problems of co-ordination problems across markets—say, between a labour market and the market for an output. (See, in particular, Clower 1965; and Leijonhufvud 1968, 1973, 1981: ch. 7, 1987.)

The problems of co-ordination across markets under disequilibrium trading may generate inefficiencies beyond those illustrated in the Edgeworth box of Fig. 4.2, to which we return. The non-Walrasian approach predicts that, at the disequilibrium prices, p^D, the quantities transacted will lead to point A. They yield an allocation that cannot be improved upon while respecting the budget constraints: a movement from A towards B may benefit trader 2 but it will hurt trader 1, whereas a movement from A towards $\bar{X}$ will be detrimental to both traders. Following Uzawa (1962), Benassy (1973), and Younès (1970, 1975), let us say that point A is p^{D-} *efficient* or *efficient relative to p^D*. In general, given an $(n-1)$-dimensional price vector p (normalized with money as numeraire), we say that a (physically) feasible allocation is p efficient if all traders satisfy their budget constraints at p, and the allocation is not Pareto-dominated by another feasible allocation where all traders satisfy their budget constraints at p.[15] As Clower (1965) and Leijonhufvud (1968) suggested, and as Benassy (1973, 1978, 1982) formalized, states of Keynesian unemployment will typically fail to satisfy this condition. The resulting inefficiency relative to allocations that satisfy the budget constraints can be viewed as a failure to co-ordinate the labour and output markets, because it would conceivably

---

[15] This is what Drèze and Müller (1980) call 'efficiency at the second level'.

disappear under a scheme for centralized exchange.[16] We explore the issue in more detail.

3.3. *Efficiency relative to given prices and wages*

Consider a model like the one discussed in Section 2.1 above, but where, in principle, consumers may be different and have non-homothetic preferences. Denote by $Z(p, w)$ the set of feasible allocations that satisfy the budget constraints at the price–wage pair (p, w). In accordance with our previous definition, an allocation in $Z(p, w)$ will be called (p, w)-efficient if it is not dominated by another allocation in $Z(p, w)$. We ask, Given (p, w), what allocations are (p, w)-efficient? The answer turns out to depend on the specification of the consumption sector. We study a few illustrative cases.

Consider first the single-consumer case (or the case with many identical, equally treated consumers). A feasible allocation is now a triple (Y, M, L) (interpreted as quantities of output, money, and labour input) such that $Y = f(L)$ and $M = \bar{M}$. It is easy to see that any feasible allocation satisfies the budget constraint for any price–wage pair; i.e. for any (p, w), $Z(p, w)$ coincides with the set of feasible allocations, because we always have that

$$\text{Expenditure} := pY + M = \bar{M} + wL + pf(L) - wL := \text{wealth.}$$

Hence (p, w)-efficiency is equivalent to Pareto efficiency; i.e. the only (p, w)-efficient allocation is $(f(\bar{L}), \bar{M}, \bar{L})$. It follows that a fixprice allocation is (p, w)-efficient if and only if (p, w) is in the full-employment region.[17] The (p, w)-inefficiency of Keynesian unemployment reflects, as noted above, a co-ordination problem between the labour and output markets. That of classical unemployment, on the contrary, stems from the divergence between the interests of the profit-maximizing firm and those of the consumer.

Consider next the case of two consumers, a worker who receives no profits and a shareholder who cannot work. Write the money endowments of the worker and the shareholder as $\bar{M}_L$ and $\bar{M}_S$ respectively. Assume that the shareholder wants only money. Now the interests of

---

[16] One can think that a barter institution where labour is directly exchanged for output could also serve as a co-ordinating device. This is true in our simple example, but in more general situations the lack of 'mutual coincidence of wants' will create co-ordination problems among barter markets as well, see Benassy (1975b, 1982: esp. appendix M) for a complete discussion.

[17] Were the labour supply variable (and under interiority and differentiability), the Walrasian allocation(s) would be the only (p, w)-efficient one(s) (by 'Voluntary and efficient allocations are Walrasian.')

the shareholder coincide with those of the firm; hence the reason why allocations of classical unemployment failed to be (p, w)-efficient in the previous case no longer applies. Indeed, it turns out that a fixprice allocation is (p, w)-efficient if and only if (p, w) does not belong to the interior of the Keynesian region. See Proposition 1 in the Appendix.

Last, consider the case where both the worker and the shareholder are interested in output and in money. In turns out that here, as in the previous case, fixprice allocations in the full-employment region or in the Keynesian–classical boundary are (p, w)-efficient, whereas those in the interior of the Keynesian region are not. But for the interior of the classical region the answer is now more complex: (p, w)-efficiency obtains there if and only if the shareholder is not constrained in his demand for output. Intuitively, the interests of a constrained shareholder diverge again from those of the firm. Proposition 2 in the Appendix presents a formal statement and proof.

3.4. *Undominated price–wage pairs*

A possible scenario for the fixity of prices and wages is their negotiation by representatives of business and labour, after which they are taken as given by individual firms and workers, and a fixprice allocation emerges. Presumably, the resulting agreement on prices and wages will reach a point in the relevant utility possibility curve, in the sense that any movement away from them would make somebody worse off. We call price–wage pairs that satisfy this condition *undominated*. By the first fundamental theorem by welfare economics, the prices and wages of a Walrasian equilibrium are undominated. Are there other undominated prices and wages? Note that the question has a different character from the (p, w)-efficiency discussed in the previous sections. There, the comparison was between alternative allocations at a given price–wage pair, whereas here we compare alternative price–wage pairs.

The results depend on the rationing of employment, that is, on whether the unemployment burden falls uniformly on workers or whether some are laid off whereas others experience no rationing (see Silvestre 1988, 1989). The model is that of Section 2.1 with the understanding that expectations of future prices, wages, and quantity constraints are rigid, i.e., formed in the past and unaffected by present conditions.

Consider first the case where the rationing of unemployment is uniform, so that all workers receive equal treatment. It is shown in Silvestre (1988) that, under some conditions, there exist prices and wages that generate unemployment and are undominated. This requires that the market for output be balanced, i.e. that the price–wage pair be in the Keynesian–classical boundary. Moreover, it also requires some assumptions on the data of the economy, namely that workers have initially low money balances, and that there be little substitution between present and future consumption. The last condition rules out Cobb–Douglas utility, but it admits some forms of CES utility functions.

The non-uniform rationing of employment typically expands the set of undominated price–wage pairs to include a band of the Keynesian region adjoining the Keynesian–classical boundary (see Silvestre 1989).

3.5. *Undominated wages*

A second group of papers, represented by Jacobsen and Schultz (1990, 1991), consider dynamic extensions of the analysis for the uniform rationing case. Instead of adopting the temporary viewpoint, they view the economy as unfolding along an infinite sequence of periods. They postulate, on the other hand, that the market for output is balanced, so that the economy is always on the Keynesian–classical boundary, as was assumed in Section 2.3 above. Workers and shareholders are aware of the dependence of price on wages implied by the balance in the output market. The question is again whether there are undominated wages that generate unemployment.

Jacobsen and Schultz (1990) observe that, in a dynamic economy, a person's money holdings at the beginning of a period are her final holdings at the end of the previous period. Given the wage rate, this defines a dynamic process. The authors endogenize such money holdings by considering their stationary values, which, together with the price of output, clearly depend on the wage. One can say that the representatives of workers and shareholders adopt the 'long-run' view and disregard short-term fluctuations in individual money holdings. It turns out that the set of undominated wages is, again, quite large, and that the possibility of wages that are undominated and generate unemployment depends again on the parameters of the economy. Contrary to the model discussed in the previous section, such wages can now appear under Cobb–Douglas preferences, as long as there is disutility of labour.

An extension to economies with overlapping generations is provided by Jacobsen and Schultz (1991). This makes it possible to define utility directly on future consumption and prices, rather than on money balances. The analysis focuses on sequences that are stationary in the sense that the market values for prices and wages are constant over time and coincide with their expected values. Again, wages that are undominated and generate unemployment appear for some values of the parameters. It should be noted that the initial money holdings of young people are zero. Thus, both this model and the previous one offer justifications of unemployment wages unrelated to the initial money holdings of workers, contrary to the case discussed in Section 3.4 above.

There is, in general, a continuum of undominated wages. On the other hand, as noted above, the study of undominated wages is motivated by the instances where wages are the outcome of negotiation by representatives of business and labour. This justifies studying whether particular solutions to the negotiation problem yield unemployment for some values of the parameters that define the economy. An affirmative answer is offered in Jacobsen and Schultz (1989, 1990) for the Nash bargaining solution.

4. Market Power

4.1. *Non-Walrasian allocations and market power*

The previous sections have focused on the out-of-equilibrium behaviour of markets that are Walrasian when in equilibrium. The maintained hypothesis has been that, at least at equilibrium, all firms and consumers are price-takers; i.e., they face horizontal demand curves for the commodities they sell and horizontal supply curves for the commodities they buy. But price-taking plans are mutually inconsistent out of equilibrium, so the price-taking hypothesis has to be somehow modified there. For instance, out-of-equilibrium behaviour can be formalized as constrained maximization, where the constraints include prices and quantities, both treated parametrically.[18]

Of course, other equilibrium notions adopt the viewpoint that market participants fail to behave as price-takers even at equilibrium. A well developed body of theory, initiated by Cournot (1838) and enriched by the contributions of Chamberlin (1933), Negishi (1960–1), and Robinson (1933), among others, views some economic agents as having market power, i.e. as facing non horizontal demand and supply curves. The compatibility of rational plans still defines equilibrium. Here 'rational' denotes the maximization of utility or profits subject to the market conditions, which are described by the demand and supply curves that the economic agent faces. But because some of the demand and supply curves are not horizontal, the resulting equilibrium, whether monopolistic, oligopolistic, imperfectly competitive, or monopolistically competitive, differs from the Walrasian one. The general equilibrium analysis of economies with market power was pioneered by Negishi (1960–1), and

---

[18] This is precisely Drèze's (1975) formulation. As noted before, the formulation of Benassy (1973, 1975a, 1976), and to some extent that of Malinvaud and Younès (1977a,b) and Younès (1975), can also be reinterpreted in these terms (see Silvestre 1978a, 1982a, 1983).

has more recently generated important insights into macroeconomic issues. Benassy (1987a, 1990: sect. 8), for instance, analyses the effectiveness of policy measures when prices are endogenously determined by the behaviour of price-making firms. Parallel results are obtained in a somewhat different context by Blanchard and Kiyotaki (1987).[19] I emphasize that these are equilibrium models: they comtemplate trade only at the (monopolistically competitive) equilibrium.

The market power view departs from the fixprice method in a fundamental manner, because it provides a theory for both quantities and prices, while the fixprice method is, by its very nature, unsuited to explain the variables that it takes as fixed, such as prices and wages. But, from its beginnings, the non-Walrasian approach has indicated various conceptual links between market power and disequilibrium trading. Some of these are discussed in the following sections.

4.2. Price adjustment without an auctioneer

Arrow (1959) observed that the appearance of, say, excess demand in a hitherto Walrasian market gives temporary monopoly power to sellers.[20] Thus, the out-of-equilibrium behaviour of an otherwise Walrasian economy is perhaps better understood as temporary price-setting instead of price-taking and rationing. But then, as Benassy (1987b: 861) notes, 'quantity signals must be a fundamental part of the competitive process in a truly decentralized economy. Indeed, it is the inability to sell as much as they want that leads suppliers to propose, or to accept from other agents, a lower price, and, conversely it is the inability to buy as much as they want that leads demanders to propose, or accept, a higher price.'

One could follow this approach to construct a non-*tâtonnement* process of adjustment to the Walrasian equilibrium. Informally, transactions occur at disequilibrium prices. This creates, say, excess supply in a market. A firm then perceives its sales opportunities as in Fig. 4.3, with a quantity bound y^* derived from the constraints that it has experienced. Selling above the quantity bound requires lowering the price. As long as this perceived demand curve is smooth and the current

---

[19] See Silvestre (forthcoming) for a survey of this line of work.

[20] In Arrow's (1959: 26) words, 'suppose we have a situation which conforms in all aspects of homogeneity of output and multiplicity of firms to the usual concept of perfect competition, but in which the aggregate supply forthcoming at the "market" price exceeds the demand at that price. Then the individual firm cannot sell all it wishes to at the market price; i.e. when supply and demand do not balance, even in an objectively competitive market, the individual firms are in a position of monopolists as far as the imperfect elasticity of demand for their products is concerned.'

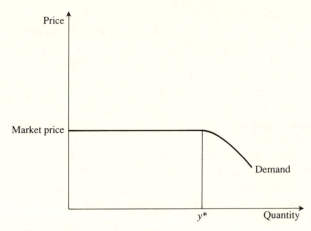

FIG. 4.3. Demand perceptions by a constrained seller

price exceeds the marginal cost, the firm would have incentives to lower its prices. So a lower price will appear. The process could then continue until the Walrasian equilibrium is established. Arrow's suggestion has failed to generate explicit price dynamics where agents on the short side of the market exploit their temporary monopoly power; but see Fisher (1970, 1972, 1983, 1987) and also Hahn (1982: sect. 4) for related ideas.

4.3. *The persistence of disequilibrium states*

As just mentioned, a firm facing the demand conditions reflected in Fig. 4.3 will lower its price, because the demand curve is locally flat as the state-of-the-market point y^* and the demand price is higher than the marginal cost. But if, following the tradition pioneered by Sweezy (1939), we postulate a kink at y^*, then it may well be that the right-hand-side marginal revenue is lower than the marginal cost, so that maximal profits are achieved at y^* (see Fig. 4.4). Thus, a situation of Walrasian disequilibrium is supported by a model that admits price flexibility. Work in this line includes Hahn (1977, 1978), John (1985), and Negishi (1974, 1976, 1977, 1979).

4.4. *The observational equivalence between fixprice and market power allocations*

The fixprice and the market power views are often 'observationally equivalent' in the sense that a given data set of prices and quantities can

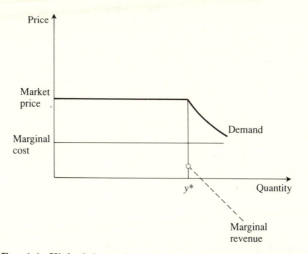

Fig. 4.4. Kinked demand perceptions by a constrained seller

be explained by either view. Consider Fig. 4.5, which depicts a market with given demand curve and a given number of firms, and where average costs are identical across firms and independent of quantity, i.e. equal to marginal costs. Suppose that point A on the demand curve is observed; i.e., demand is satisfied but prices are higher than marginal costs. This is, from the Walrasian viewpoint, an out-of-equilibrium state. The price is above its Walrasian equilibrium level and generates excess supply because firms, subject to quantity constraints, would like to sell more at the going price. Alternatively, point A may well be an oligopolistic equilibrium where all firms face downward-sloping demand curves and choose a point on them for which marginal cost equals marginal revenue, and thus with the price higher than marginal cost. Despite having chosen the price, our oligopolistic firms are quantity-constrained to the extent that they would like to sell more *at the going price*.[21] This fact, now well understood, is rather general. John (1985) shows that any Walrasian short-run allocation can be viewed as a Cournotian equilibrium for some specification of the demand and supply curves faced by economic agents. On the other hand, the results in Benassy (1982), Madden (1983), Silvestre (1986), and Madden and Silvestre (1991, 1992) show that, under some conditions, a market power equilibrium satisfies the definition of a fixprice allocation.

---

[21] Readers are referred to Weitzman's (1984: 6–9) colourful description of the contrasting appearances of a car salesroom, geared to attract buyers, and the working area in the back of the dealership, not designed to attract new workers.

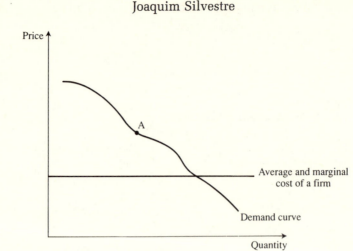

FIG. 4.5. Point *A* may result from excess supply or from an imperfectly competitive equilibrium

Indeed, some real-life examples of price rigidities and quantity rationing can be viewed as the implementation of an imperfectly competitive equilibrium. Administered or regulated prices, for instance, sometimes reflect the market power of sellers or buyers. The government may fix the price of a commodity at a level higher than that of marginal cost. An individual firm then takes such a price as given and faces a quantity constraint. But if the market is deregulated, *laissez-faire* may result in an oligopolistic equilibrium not too different from the previous position. A second example motivates the discussion in Sections 3.4–5 above. Consider price–wage agreements resulting from negotiations, perhaps sponsored by a government agency, between representatives of business and labour. Individual firms or workers then take prices and wages as given and they are rationed. But the resulting allocation may actually be implementing an oligopolistic equilibrium where unions have market power in the labour market whereas firms have power in the market for produced goods.

In general, the agent that is 'rationed' from the fixprice viewpoint is the one with market power in the imperfectly competitive model. The different regimes of disequilibrium can then be interpreted as different combinations of market power (see Benassy 1978; Silvestre 1986). For instance, the Keynesian region of Fig. 4.1 above corresponds to oligopoly in both the output and the labour market: firms have market power in selling output, whereas workers have market power in selling labour. The classical region, on the contrary, corresponds to oligopsony in the output market and oligopoly in the labour market; i.e. workers have market power in selling labour and consumers have market power in buying output. Finally, the full-employment region corresponds to oligopsony in both markets. The Keynesian region becomes the relevant one to the extent that oligopsony in the output market is infrequent.

4.5. *Non*-tâtonnement *in imperfectly competitive models*

A seller with market power chooses the price and the quantity simultaneously by selecting a point on the demand curve for its product. Partial equilibrium models just take such a demand curve to be a primitive datum of the economy; but in more general models the demand for a product should be derived from more fundamental data on preferences and technology. This task faces two challenges. First, there is the conceptual one of defining the 'objective' demand curve faced by firm j. To what extent are other things equal when firm j changes its price? Do other firms change theirs? Or perhaps other firms keep their prices unaltered but change the quantities supplied in order to accommodate the changes in demand generated by j's move? What if accommodating such changes generates negative profits? If other firms fail to serve the new quantity, does this unsatisfied demand spill over firm j's? This conceptual issue, addressed in Benassy (1988), will be discussed in a moment. But even if the meaning of the 'objective demand function' is unambiguous, it will typically be a complex mapping involving many parameters. As Benassy (1987*b*: 861) notes, 'it will require quite heroic assumptions on the computational ability and information available to price setters to assume that they know the "true" demand function (i.e. the true functional form) with the true parameters'.

Benassy (1973, 1976, 1982, 1987*a*) formulates a learning process by which firms acquire information on their demand curve. It is based on the Bushaw–Clower (1957) and Negishi (1960–1) 'perceived demand curve' approach. One can visualize a *tâtonnement* process in discrete time. At the beginning of each period, firms set their prices based on imperfect knowledge of demand conditions. Thus, markets may not clear, and a fixprice allocation is established for the period. The observed state of the market offers information by which the firm revises its estimate of the demand function, which in turn affects the decision on the price for the following period. One should note that the convergence properties of this process have not been studied.

4.6. *The objective-demand approach to price-setting*

As just noted, the definition of the 'objective demand curve' faced by price-setting firms is a non-trivial task, because the prices and quantities decided by different agents are interdependent; such a definition must, in any event, introduce assumptions about the strategic interaction among firms. Several approaches are present in the literature. Gabsewicz and Vial (1972) adopt Cournot's strategic assumption, whereas Marshak and Selten (1972) and Nikaido (1975) follow Bertrand's; i.e. they postulate that firm j takes as given all prices except for the ones under j's control.

Benassy (1988) presents a concept of objective demand, *à la* Bertrand, that builds on the notion of a fixprice equilibrium. The motivation has been alluded to under the previous heading: quantity magnitudes must enter the demand function faced by firm j not only through the process of income formation but also because, if firm j changes its price and the other firms do not change theirs, the other firms may find that satisfying demand is unprofitable or even technologically unfeasible. Thus, firm j cannot assume that the demand addressed to other firms will always be satisfied: on the contrary, it must consider how the rationing in other markets spills over the demand for j's product. Benassy's (1988) approach incorporates all these quantity interdependences. Formally, it defines objective demand by the mapping that assigns to each economy-wide price vector the set quantity signals corresponding to a fixprice equilibrium.[22] Benassy (1988) also offers a simple existence proof for the resulting (non-cooperative) equilibrium concept.

4.7. *Imperfect rationality and menu costs*

Some work in what has been called the 'new Keynesian' literature, as surveyed by Rotemberg (1987), Fischer (1988), and Blanchard (1990), aims at rationalizing price rigidities. Like the fixprice literature, it focuses on a status quo where prices fail to adjust to changing conditions; it does not explain why this particular status quo, one in a continuum of equally plausible situations, happens to appear, but it tries to explain why these agents decide not to adjust prices once they find themselves there. As a result, one obtains an explanation for observed price rigidity or stickiness (see Rotemberg 1982*a,b*; Rotemberg and Saloner 1986, 1987).

When observing the higher demand caused by an increase in the money supply, why would imperfectly competitive firms want to keep prices fixed? Two related explanations are offered: (1) the monopolist is

---

[22] This mapping is single-valued if a rationing scheme and constraint perception function are postulated (see Benassy 1975*a*, 1976, 1978) and if the Schulz (1983) conditions are satisfied.

less than 100 per cent rational (Akerlof and Yellen 1985); and (2) changing prices is costly: there are 'menu costs' (see Mankiw 1985; Blanchard and Kiyotaki 1987). The argument in either case is that, because marginal profits are zero at the profit-maximizing price p^M, small deviations from it will cause a negligible profit loss. For a given cost of adjusting prices (or a given degree of irrationality), there is an ε such that the economy can get stuck at any price in the interval $(p^M - \varepsilon,\ p^M + \varepsilon)$; i.e. around any imperfectly competitive equilibrium of the economy there will be a continuum of status quo where the economy can possibly get stuck. Thus, this approach shares the basic indeterminacy of the fixprice analysis.

5. Weitzman's Share Economy

5.1. *The Model*

Weitzman (1983, 1984, 1985) proposes an economy-wide reform in the way workers are paid: instead of a fixed wage per hour, workers should be paid a fixed share in the revenue (or a combination of both). Weitzman claims that the 'share' economy has the same long-run features as the present 'wage' economy, but that, in contrast with it, the share economy maintains full employment during the short-run adjustment to shocks.

Weitzman distinguishes between the short run and the long run as follows. In the long run, both prices and wage contracts are flexible; in the short run, prices are flexible whereas wage contracts are not. Thus, Weitzman's short run is similar to the situations considered in Sections 2.3 and 3.5 above. The aim of the following sections is to discuss Weitzman's claim both under his 'short-run' assumption and, in the spirit of most of this chapter, under the alternative short-run assumption that both prices and wage contracts are rigid. The analysis of the Weitzman model under price rigidity follows Saldanha (1987).

Consider the following simplified model.[23] There are Q firms that produce output using labour. Assume that labour is in fixed supply $\bar{L}$ so that, at a symmetric full-employment allocation, each firm will use $L^* = \bar{L}/Q$ units of labour. Each firm's revenue is a given function $R(L)$ of the labour that it employs. The formulation covers perfect competition: $R(L)$ equals $pf(L)$, where p is the market price that a competitive

---

[23] Weitzman presents first the basic argument in a simple setup with only output and labour (Weitzman 1983, 1984). He then carries out more detailed comparative statics in a model with output, labour, and money (1985). He emphasizes the imperfectly competitive character of real-life market economies, but his proposal is also applicable to price-taking firms.

firm takes as given, and $f(L)$ is the amount of output that L units of labour can produce with the available technology. Or perhaps the firm is a monopolistic competitor and $R(L)$ takes into account the downward-sloping demand curve faced by the firm. Assume that R is increasing.

A firm pays its workers according to a *per-worker compensation schedule* $\gamma(L, r)$, where L is the number of workers employed and r is the revenue obtained by the firm. Admissible compensation schedules are on occasion restricted to be of a particular type or system. For instance, a 'pure-wage' compensation schedule is of the form $\gamma(L, r) = w$; i.e. the compensation does not depend on revenue. As another example, a 'pure-share' compensation schedule is of the form $\gamma(L, r) = \lambda r/L$; i.e., the total compensation to workers is a given fraction of revenue. Linearly combining the two types yields the particularly interesting 'two-part' schedule $\gamma(L, r) = (1 - \lambda)\omega + \lambda(r/L)$, where ω and λ are positive parameters. A given family of admissible compensation schedules will be called a *compensation system*. As a first instance, compensation schedules are restricted to be of the 'pure wage' type in the 'wage-compensation system', also called the 'wage economy'. The alternative system proposed by Weitzman is the 'share-compensation system' or 'share economy' where both pure-share schedules and two-part schedules are admitted.

Compensation schedules and the amount of labour employed by each firm are endogenously determined in the long run. But $R(L)$ suffers a shock in Weitzman's short run: a firm can then change L, but it must stick to the payment schedule determined in the long run.

A long-run equilibrium relative to a given compensation system requires full employment. It also requires each firm to choose a compensation schedule γ among those in the compensation system, and a level of employment in order to maximize profits subject to the condition that the compensation per worker be no lower than the 'going rate' w^*. Formally, a (symmetric) long-run Weitzman equilibrium for a given compensation system Γ is a tuple of payment schedules $(\gamma_1^*, \ldots, \gamma_Q^*)$ and a going rate w^* such that, for $i = 1, \ldots, Q$, (γ_i^*, L^*) maximizes $R(L) - \gamma_i(L, R(L))L$ subject to $\gamma_i \in \Gamma$, and $\gamma_i(L, R(L)) \geq w^*$.[24]

It turns out that, as long as the compensation system Γ permits enough flexibility, all compensation systems have the same long-run equilibria.[25] Figures 4.6 and 4.7 illustrate the fact. The curve $R'(L)$ is

---

[24] It may be possible to construct a Bertrand-type game, as suggested in Weitzman (1983: 771, n. 2), where the strategies are payment schedules and quantities of labour demanded, with Nash equilibria which satisfy the conditions of a Weitzman long-run equilibrium.

[25] To be precise, define a compensation system Γ to be *flexible* if, given an arbitrary amount of labour $\bar{L}$ and an arbitrary going rate $\bar{w}$, there exists an admissible compensation schedule $\gamma \, \varepsilon \, \Gamma$ such that $\gamma(\bar{L}, R(\bar{L})) = \bar{w}$. It is easy to see that the pure-wage system is

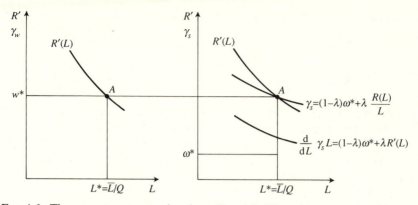

FIG. 4.6. The wage economy in the   FIG. 4.7. The share economy in the
          long run   long run

the same in both. It is decreasing, indicating that $R(L)$ is a concave
function. Figure 4.6 illustrates the wage economy. The long-run equilibrium wage is $w^* = R'(L^*)$, which coincides with the average and
marginal expenditures on labour. Figure 4.7 represents a share economy
with a two-part compensation scheme. The two parameters ω and λ give
one degree of freedom. One can, for instance, arbitrarily choose a value
for λ no higher than $L^*R'(L^*)/R(L^*)$, an expression less than 1
because of the concavity of R. Then the long-run equilibrium value of ω
is

$$\omega^* = \frac{L^*R'(L^*) - \lambda R(L^*)}{(1 - \lambda)L^*}, \tag{1}$$

a non-negative expression by the inequality imposed on λ. Moreover,
and again by the concavity of R,

$$\omega^* < \frac{L^*R'(L^*) - \lambda R'(L^*)L^*}{(1 - \lambda)L^*} = R'(L^*). \tag{2}$$

Average expenditure is now $\gamma_s = (1 - \lambda)\omega^* + \lambda(R(L)/L)$, which at L^*

flexible, as is a pure-share system or a two-part system where no constraints are imposed
on ω or λ. The precise statement of the fact is: *if R is differentiable and $(\gamma_1^*, \ldots, \gamma_Q^*, w^*)$*
is a long-run Weitzman equilibrium for Γ, where Γ is a flexible compensation system, then
$w^* = \gamma_i^*(L^*, R(L^*)) = R'(L^*)$, *for* $i = 1, \ldots, Q$. *Proof*: First, for all i, $\gamma_i^*(L^*, R(L^*))$
$= w^*$, because the completeness of Γ allows the firm to choose γ_i so that the constraint
'$\gamma_i(L^*, R(L^*)) \geq w^*$' holds with equality. Second, we claim that L^* maximizes
$R(L) - w^*L$. Suppose not. Then there exists a $\tilde{L}$ such that $R(\tilde{L}) - w^*\tilde{L} > R(L^*)$
$- w^*L^* = R(L^*) - \gamma_i^*(L^*, R(L^*))L^*$. But again, because Γ is flexible, there exists a $\tilde{\gamma}$ in
Γ such that $\tilde{\gamma}(\tilde{L}, R(\tilde{L})) = w^*$. Hence $R(\tilde{L}) - \tilde{\gamma}(\tilde{L}, R(\tilde{L}))\tilde{L} = R(\tilde{L}) - w^*\tilde{L} > R(L^*)$
$- \gamma_i^*(L^*, R(L^*))L^*$, contradicting the hypothesis that (γ_i^*, L^*) maximizes profits s.t. $\gamma_i \varepsilon$
Γ and $\gamma_i(L, R(L)) \geq w^*$. Hence, L^* maximizes $R(L) - w^*L$, which, since L^* is positive
and R is differentiable, implies that $R'(L^*) = w^*$. $\square$

becomes $\gamma_s(L^*, R(L^*)) = R'(L^*) = w^*$, the same as in the wage economy.[26]

5.2. The share economy under fixed wage-contracts and flexible prices

As Weitzman argues, the share economy performs better in the short run, because after an adverse shock on the revenue function the share economy maintains full employment. Figures 4.8 and 4.9 illustrate this fact. An adverse shock lowers the revenue function to $\bar{R}(L)$. Figure 4.8 depicts the wage economy. The payment per worker remains at $\gamma_w(L, r) = w^*$, which forces firms to lay off workers until employment drops to L_w, where $w^* = \bar{R}'(L_w)$. The movement from A to B depicts the change from the long-run state before the shock to Weitzman's short-run situation after the shock. If we assume a permanent shock, then eventually a new long-run state, represented by point C, will emerge, and it will yield a (long-run) average payment per worker equal to $\bar{R}(L^*)$.

Figure 4.9 depicts the two-part share economy for the same shock in the revenue function. The compensation per worker becomes, after the shock, $\gamma_s(L, \bar{R}(L)) = (1 - \lambda)\omega^* + \lambda(\bar{R}(L)/L$, lower than what it was for the revenue function $R(L)$. The (net) profit function is now $\bar{R}(L) - (1 - \lambda)\omega^* L - \lambda\bar{R}(L) = (1 - \lambda)(\bar{R}(L) - \omega^* L)$.   As   long   as

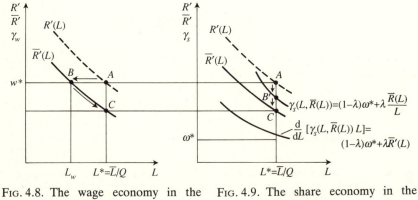

FIG. 4.8. The wage economy in the short run   FIG. 4.9. The share economy in the short run
$(\bar{R}'(L^*) > \omega^*)$

---

[26] Differentiating the expression for the average expenditure with respect to L, we obtain $\lambda(R'(L)L - R(L))/L^2$, a negative expression because of the concavity of R. Thus, the average expenditure on labour is decreasing, which in turn implies that the marginal expenditure is below the average one, as depicted in Fig. 4.7 and 4.9.

$\bar{R}'(L^*)$ *is still higher than* ω^*, the marginal net profit of the firm is positive at L^*, and thus the firm has no incentive to lay off workers. Point B' is the one reached in the short run, with full employment and a lower compensation per worker. If the shock is permanent, then the parameter ω will eventually adjust to its new long-run equilibrium value $[L^*\bar{R}'(L^*) - \lambda\bar{R}(L^*)]/[(1 - \lambda)L^*]$. This is point C in Fig. 4.9.[27] Full employment has been maintained throughout the process.

What if $\omega^* > \bar{R}'(L^*)$? Then the share firm maximizes $(1 - \lambda)(\bar{R}(L) - \omega L)$ by choosing L_s such that $\bar{R}'(L_s) = \omega^*$. In other words, *when the share firm contemplates the profitability of selling an additional unit of output (or, equivalently, hiring an extra worker), it views ω exactly as a firm in the wage economy would view w.* Hence the aggregate demand for labour in the share economy when ω equals, say, 13 coincides with the demand for labour in the 'wage' economy when w is 13.

5.3. *The share economy under fixed prices*

The superiority of the share economy depends on the instantaneous adjustment of prices. If prices adjust slowly to the changing conditions, then the analysis has to be modified. Let the short run be defined to mean that both the compensation scheme and prices are fixed. Saldanha (1987) shows that a share economy still maintains full employment after a technology shock but fails to do so if faced with a shock in demand. Saldanha's point can be illustrated as follows. Consider an economy with labour, output, and money as in Section 2 above but with rigid expectations. An adverse shock in demand is a change in preferences that lowers the demand for output at any given price and wealth. Let the technology be represented by an inverse production function βY^α, and consider shocks to the parameter β: productivity deteriorates when β increases.

As just noted, when the firm contemplates the profitability of selling an additional unit of output (or, equivalently, hiring an extra worker), it views ω exactly as it viewed w in the 'wage' economy. Therefore, the regions of satisfied and unsatisfied demand and of price greater than or equal to marginal cost are as in Fig. 4.1 if the fixed component ω of the payment schedule is measured along the vertical axis. (See the solid boundaries in Fig. 4.10.)

---

[27] Figure 4.9 depicts point B' above C, but it could be the other way. One has B' above C if $(1 - \lambda)\omega^* + \lambda(\bar{R}(L^*)/L^* > (1 - \lambda)\omega' + \lambda(\bar{R}(L^*)/L^*$, where ω' is the new long-run value, given by (1) when $\bar{R}$ and $\bar{R}'$ replace R and R'. But one can have $\omega' > \omega^*$ if the term 'λ times average revenue' drops more than marginal revenue. Short-run compensation would then fall below the new long-run value.

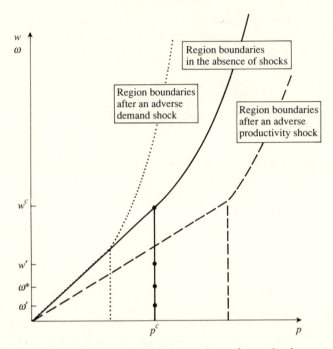

FIG. 4.10. The map of the three regions after a shock

Assume that the long-run equilibrium is Walrasian, i.e., that it yields an average compensation of w^c and a price of p^c both in the wage economy and in the share economy. Adverse shocks change the map of regions as indicated in Fig. 4.10 (see Malinvaud 1977; Silvestre 1986). Assume that p, w, λ, and ω are at their long-run values p^c, w^c, λ and ω^* before the shock, and that they stay there after it. An adverse shock in productivity leads the wage economy into classical unemployment, since (p^c, w^c) is now in the interior of the classical region, enclosed by the dashed boundaries. But the shock keeps the share economy in full employment, since (p^c, ω^*) remains in the full-employment region. An adverse shock in demand, however, generates Keynesian unemployment of the same magnitude in the wage economy and in the share economy as long as prices stay at p^c, because both (p^c, w^c) and (p^c, ω^*) are now in the interior of the Keynesian region.

The output market has so far been assumed to be competitive rather than imperfectly competitive. One can show that, if the output market is imperfectly competitive (and the labour market is perfectly competitive), then the long-run wage w' will be lower than the perfectly competitive wage w^c of Fig. 4.1, and the long-run ω' of a share economy with given share parameter λ will be lower than w' (see Fig. 4.10). Qualitatively, the effect of shocks under price rigidity will be the same whether it is a share or a 'wage' economy: in either case, an adverse productivity shock will lead to the full-employment region and an adverse demand shock leads to Keynesian unemployment. Figure 4.11 summarizes the short-run effects of adverse shocks in the wage and share economies for the alternative specifications of flexible prices when firms are oligopolistic (as in Weitzman 1985) and fixed prices when firms are price-takers (as in Saldanha 1987). For the sake of completeness, the figure adds the case of flexible prices and fixed wage contracts with price-taking firms (as in Sections 2.3 and 3.5 above) and that of fixed prices and wage contracts when firms have monopoly power (as in Section 4.7 above). We observe that the share reform never hurts, and it is advantageous in some cases.

	Adverse shock in productivity		Adverse shock in demand	
	Fixed prices	Flexible prices	Fixed prices	Flexible prices
Firms are price-takers	**Superior** • Share economy: Full employment • Wage economy: classical unemployment (Saldanha 1987)	**Equivalent or superior** • Share economy: full employment	**Equivalent** • Keynesian unemployment in either economy (Saldanha 1987)	**Superior** • Share economy: full employment • Wage economy: unemployment at the Keynesian–classical boundary
Firms have market power	**Equivalent** • Full employment in either economy	**Superior** • Share economy: full employment • Wage economy: Keynesian unemployment (Weitzman 1985)	**Equivalent** • Keynesian unemployment in either economy	**Superior** • Share economy: full employment • Wage economy: Keynesian unemployment (Weitzman 1985)

FIG. 4.11. When wage contracts are fixed, is the share economy superior?

Appendix

Postulate a three-good model with two consumers: one, the worker, is endowed with $\bar{L}$ units of labour, $\bar{M}_L$ units of money, and receives no profits from the firm. Writing Y_L for his consumption of output and M_L for his final money holdings, the worker's utility function is denoted $U_L(Y_L, M_L)$. The other consumer, the shareholder, owns $\bar{M}_S$ units of money but no labour, and receives all the profits of the firm. His utility function is denoted $U_S(Y_S, M_S)$, in obvious notation. The arguments (p, w) have been omitted because they are constant in this Appendix.

Our first proposition considers the case where the shareholder cares only about money. The fixprice output for (p, w) is determined as in Section 2.1 above, except that $V'(Y, p, w)$ is now the marginal rate of substitution evaluated at $(Y, \bar{M}_L + wf^{-1}(Y) - pY)$, the vector assigned to the worker. This vector and the one assigned to the shareholder, namely $(0, \bar{M}_S + pY - w\text{-}f^{-1}(Y))$, constitute the *fixprice allocation for (p, w)*.

> PROPOSITION 1. If $U_S(Y_S, M_S) = M_S$, $U_L(Y_L, M_L)$ is strictly increasing and differentiable, and f is strictly concave and differentiable, then a fixprice allocation is (p, w)-efficient if and only if (p, w) does not belong to the interior of the Keynesian region.

Proof. First, a feasible allocation is defined by (Y, M_L, M_S) (the consumption of output by the worker equals Y) where $Y \leqslant \bar{Y}$ and $M_L + M_S = \bar{M}_L + \bar{M}_S$. It follows that a feasible allocation is Pareto efficient if and only if $Y = \bar{Y}$. Thus, fixprice allocations (for any (p, w)) in the full-employment region (boundaries included) are (p, w) efficient.

Second, a feasible allocation satisfies the budget constraints at (p, w) if and only if:

$$pY + M_L = wf^{-1}(Y) + \bar{M}_L;$$

i.e.

$$M_L = \phi(Y) := \bar{M}_L - [pY - wf^{-1}(Y)].$$

The graph of $\phi(Y)$ is the heavy curve in Fig. 4.A1. Its minimum, at point C, corresponds to the unique maximizer of profits, i.e. the point where the equation $p = w(f^{-1})'(Y)$ is satisfied. If (p, w) happens to belong to the classical region, then point C is the vector assigned to the worker. If, on the contrary, (p, w) belongs to the interior of the Keynesian region (which entails unemployment, i.e. $Y < \bar{Y}$), then the consumption vector of the worker is a point like K (where $p > w(f^{-1})'(Y)$).

Let (p, w) belong to the classical region (including in particular the Keynesian–classical boundary), and, thus, let the worker's vector be point C in the figure. Respecting the budget constraint at the given prices means considering points on the $M_L = \phi(Y)$ curve. But any other point on the curve has a vertical coordinate higher than C (since the curve attains its unique minimum there); i.e. M_L is larger, and hence M_S must be smaller. It follows that a fixprice allocation in the classical region is (p, w) efficient.

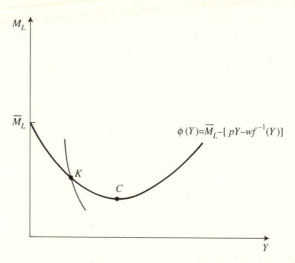

Fɪɢ. 4.A1. The curve $M_L = \phi(Y)$ is the locus of points that satisfy the budget constraint at the given prices and wages

Third, let (p, w) belong to the interior of the Keynesian region; i.e. the worker's vector is a point like K in the figure. We now check that the worker's indifference curve going through K is steeper than the $M_L = \phi(Y)$ curve, as depicted. Because demand is satisfied in the Keynesian region, the (absolute value of the) slope of indifference curve is p, greater than $p - w(f^{-1})'(Y)$, the (absolute value of the) slope of the $M_L = \phi(Y)$ curve. Hence movements along the $M_L = \phi(Y)$ curve to the right of K will improve the welfare of the worker. Moreover, since the ϕ curve is decreasing there, they entail a lower M_L, and thus a higher M_S. By increasing output (which is possible because there is unemployment), therefore, one can increase the utilities of both the worker and the shareholder without violating the budget constraints. It follows that a fixprice allocation in the interior of the Keynesian region is (p, w) inefficient. □

Consider next the case where the utility functions of both the worker and the shareholder are strictly increasing in both arguments. Postulate that the utility functions are differentiable and strictly concave. Note that a feasible allocation is described by a vector (Y_L, Y_S, M_L, M_S), where $M_L + M_S = \bar{M}_L + \bar{M}_S$, and $Y \leq \bar{Y}$, where we define $Y := Y_L + Y_S$, and that a feasible allocation satisfies the budget constraints at (p, w) if and only if:

$$pY_S + M_S = pY - wf^{-1}(Y) + \bar{M}_S.$$

The definition of fixprice allocation is a little more complex here. For $J = L, S$, define $V'_J(Y_J, M_J) = (\partial U_J/\partial Y_J)/\partial U_J/\partial M_J)$, with derivatives evaluated at (Y_J, M_J). Then the feasible allocation (Y_L, Y_S, M_L, M_S) that satisfies the budget constraints at (p, w) is a *fixprice allocation for* (p, w) if, writing $Y = Y_L + Y_S$, (i) $Y \leq \bar{Y}$; (ii) $p \geq w(f^{-1})'$ (Y); (iii) $p \leq V'_J(Y_J, M_J)$ for $J = L$, S; (iv) condition (i) or condition (ii) or condition (iii) holds with equality (or equalities). We say that the *shareholder is constrained in the output market* if $p < V'_S(Y_S, M_S)$. The definitions of the Keynesian, classical, and full-employment regions are straightforward extensions of the former ones. It is understood that the statements of the following lemmas postulate the just mentioned assumptions on the utility functions.

LEMMA 1. Consider a fixprice allocation for (p, w). An allocation that dominates it and belongs to $Z(p, w)$ must entail a higher level of output.

Proof. Let $(Y_L + \Delta Y_L, \ Y_S + \Delta Y_S, \ M_L + \Delta M_L, M_S + \Delta M_S)$ be an allocation that dominates the original one. Write also $\Delta Y := \Delta Y_L + \Delta Y_S$ and $\Delta L = f^{-1}(Y + \Delta Y) - f^{-1}(Y)$. The utility levels at the new allocation cannot be lower than at the original one. Therefore, by strict concavity,

$$\Delta Y_L \neq 0 \text{ implies that } V'_L \Delta Y_L + \Delta M_L > 0,$$

$$\Delta Y_S \neq 0 \text{ implies that } V'_S \Delta Y_S + \Delta M_S > 0, \qquad \text{(A1)}$$

and, because $\Delta M_L + \Delta M_S = 0$, the utility improvement implies that ΔY_L or ΔY_S (or both) is non zero.

Assume, by way of contradiction, that $\Delta Y \leq O$. This implies that $\Delta L \leq 0$ and, because marginal profits are non-negative at Y and the profit function is concave, that $p\Delta Y - w\Delta L \leq 0$. From the budget constraints, we obtain

$$p\Delta Y_L + \Delta M_L = w\Delta L \leq 0,$$

$$p\Delta Y_S + \Delta M_S = p\Delta Y - w\Delta L \leq 0. \qquad \text{(A2)}$$

Let $\Delta Y_L \neq 0$. Then from (A1), $V'_L \Delta Y_L + \Delta M_L > 0$, and from (A2), $0 \geq p\Delta Y_L + \Delta M_L$; i.e., $(V'_L - p)\Delta Y_L > 0$, and because $(V'_L - p) \geq 0$, by voluntariness, it follows that $\Delta Y_L > 0$. The same argument proves that if $\Delta Y_S \neq 0$ then $\Delta Y_S > 0$. Hence, $\Delta Y = \Delta Y_L + \Delta Y_S > 0$, a contradiction. $\square$

LEMMA 2. A fixprice allocation for (p, w), where $p = w(f^{-1})'(Y)$, and where the shareholder is unconstrained in the output market, is (p, w)-efficient.

Proof. By Lemma 1, only increases in output deserve consideration. But if output is increased at a point where $p = (f^{-1})'(Y)$, profits will decrease, and hence, from the budget constraint of the shareholder, $p\Delta Y_S + \Delta M_S < 0$. Because the shareholder is unconstrained in the output market, $p = V'_S$; i.e. $V'_S \Delta Y_S + \Delta M_S < 0$; i.e., the utility of the shareholder will decrease. $\square$

LEMMA 3. A fixprice allocation in the interior of the classical region and where the shareholder is constrained in the output market is (p, w)-inefficient.

Proof. In the interior of the classical region $Y + \Delta Y \leq \bar{Y}$ for ΔY positive and small enough. Because the shareholder is constrained in the output market, $V'_S > p = \lim_{\Delta Y \to 0} w\Delta L/\Delta Y$. Thus, for ΔY positive and small enough, $w\Delta L/\Delta Y < V'_S$ and $U_S(Y_S + \Delta Y, M_S - w\Delta L) > U_S(Y_S, M_S)$. Moreover, the shareholder's budget constraint is satisfied when $\Delta Y_S = \Delta Y > 0$ and $\Delta M_S = -w\Delta L$. So is that of the worker when $\Delta Y > 0$, $\Delta Y_L = 0$, and $\Delta M_L = w\Delta L > 0$, and clearly her utility is higher at $(Y_L, M_L + w\Delta L)$ than at (Y_L, M_L). $\square$

LEMMA 4. A fixprice allocation in the interior of the Keynesian region is (p, w)-inefficient.

Proof. Marginal profits are positive and there is unemployment. Thus, for ΔY positive and small enough, $p\Delta Y - w\Delta L > 0$ and $Y + \Delta Y \leq \bar{Y}$. Consider such a ΔY and define: $\Delta M_S = \Delta M_L = 0$; $\Delta Y_L = (w/p)\Delta L > 0$; and $\Delta Y_S = \Delta Y - \Delta Y_L > 0$. It is clear that both budget constraints are satisfied and that both utilities increase. □

PROPOSITION 2. Assume that the utility functions $U_L(Y_L, M_L)$ and $U_S(Y_S, M_S)$ are differentiable, strictly increasing in both arguments and strictly concave. Then:

(i) Fixprice allocations in the full employment region or in the Keynesian–classical boundary are (p, w)-efficient.

(ii) Fixprice allocations in the interior of the Keynesian region are (p, w)-inefficient.

(iii) A fixprice allocation in the interior of the classical region is (p, w)-efficient if and only if the shareholder is unconstrained in the output market.

Proof. It follows from Lemma 1 that any fixprice allocation in the full-employment region is (p, w)-efficient. Lemma 2 shows that fixprice allocations in the Keynesian–classical boundary are (p, w)-efficient. This proves (i). Lemmas 2 and 3 prove (iii). Lemma 4 proves (ii). □

References

AKERLOF, G. and YELLEN, J. (1985). 'A Near-Rational Model of the Business Cycle with Wage and Price Inertia'. *Quarterly Journal of Economics*, 100: 823–38.

ARROW, K. J. (1959). 'Towards a Theory of Price Adjustment'. In M. Abramovitz (ed.), *The Allocation of Economic Resources*. Stanford University Press.

——and HAHN, F. H. (1971). *General Competitive Analysis*. San Francisco: Holden Day.

BAILEY, M. J. (1962). *National Income and the Price Level*. New York: McGraw-Hill.

BALASKO, Y. (1979). 'Budget-Constrained Pareto-Efficient Allocations'. *Journal of Economic Theory*, 21: 359–79.

BARRO, R. J. and GROSSMAN, H. I (1971). 'A General Equilibrium Model of Income and Employment'. *American Economic Review*, 61: 82–93.

————(1974). 'Suppressed Inflation and the Supply Multiplier'. *Review of Economic Studies*, 41: 87–104.

————(1976). *Money, Employment and Inflation*. Cambridge University Press.

BENASSY, J.-P. (1973). 'Disequilibrium Theory'. Ph.D. dissertation and Working Paper no. IP-185, University of California at Berkeley.

—— (1975*a*). 'Neo-Keynesian Disequilibrium Theory in a Monetary Economy'. *Review of Economic Studies*. 42: 503–23.

—— (1975*b*). 'Disequilibrium Exchange in Barter and Monetary Economies'. *Economic Inquiry*, 13: 131–56.

—— (1976). 'The Disequilibrium Approach to Monopolistic Price Setting and General Monopolistic Equilibrium'. *Review of Economic Studies*, 43: 69–81.

—— (1977). 'On Quantity Signals and the Foundations of Effective Demand Theory'. *Scandinavian Journal of Economics*, 79: 147–68.

—— (1978). 'A NeoKeynesian Model of Price and Quantity Determination in Disequilibrium'. In G. Schwödiauer (ed.), *Equilibrium and Disequilibrium in Economic Theory*. Boston: Reidel.

—— (1982). *The Economics of Market Disequilibrium*. New York: Academic Press.

—— (1983). 'The Three Regimes of the *IS–LM* Model: A Non-Walrasian Analysis'. *European Economic Review*, 23: 1–18.

—— (1984*a*). 'A Non-Walrasian Model of the Business Cycle'. *Journal of Economic Behavior and Organization*, 5: 77–89.

—— (1984*b*). 'Tariffs and Pareto Optimality in International Trade: The Case of Unemployment'. *European Economic Review*, 26: 261–76.

—— (1986). *Macroeconomics: An Introduction to the Non-Walrasian Approach*. New York: Academic Press.

—— (1987*a*). 'Imperfect Competition, Unemployment and Policy'. *European Economic Review*, 31: 417–26.

—— (1987*b*). 'Disequilibrium Analysis'. In J. Eatwell, M. Milgate, and P. Newman (eds.), *The New Palgrave: A Dictionary of Economics*. London: Macmillan

—— (1988). 'The Objective Demand Curve in General Equilibrium with Price Makers', *Economic Journal*, suppl. 98: 37–49.

—— (1990). 'Non-Walrasian Equilibria, Money and Macroeconomics'. In F. H. Hahn and B. Friedman (eds.), *Handbook of Monetary Economics*. Amsterdam: North-Holland.

BLANCHARD, O. J. (1990). 'Why Does Money Affect Output? A Survey'. In F. H. Hahn and B. Friedman (eds.), *Handbook of Monetary Economics*. Amsterdam: North-Holland.

—— and KIYOTAKI, N. (1987). 'Monopolistic Competition and the Effects of Aggregate Demand'. *American Economic Review*. 77: 647–66.

BÖHM, V. (1989). *Disequilibrium and Macroeconomics*. Oxford: Basil Blackwell.

BUSHAW, D. W. and CLOWER, R. W. (1957). *Introduction to Mathematical Economics*. Homewoods, Illinois: Richard D. Irwin.

CHAMBERLIN, E. H. (1933). *The Theory of Monopolistic Competition*. Cambridge, Mass.: Harvard University Press.

CLOWER, R. W. (1965). 'The Keynesian Counter-revolution: a Theoretical Appraisal'. In F. H. Hahn and F. P. R. Brechling (eds.), *The Theory of Interest Rates*. London: Macmillan. Reprinted in R. W. Clower (ed.), *Monetary Theory: Selected Readings*. Harmondsworth: Penguin, 1969.

—— (1967). 'A Reconsideration of the Foundations of Monetary Theory'. *Western Economic Journal*, 6: 1–9. Reprinted in R. W. Clower (ed.), *Monetary Theory: Selected Readings*. Harmondsworth: Penguin, 1969.

Cournot, A. A. (1838). *Recherches sur les principes mathématiques de la théorie des richesses*. Paris: Librairie des sciences politiques et sociales, M. Rivière et Cie.

Cuddington, J. T., Johansson, P. O., and Logfren, K. G. (1984). *Disequilibrium Macroeconomics in Open Economies*. Oxford: Basil Blackwell.

Debreu, G. (1959). *Theory of Value: An Axiomatic Analysis of Economic Equilibrium*. New York: John Wiley.

Diamond, P. A. (1982). 'Aggregate Demand Management in Search Equilibrium'. *Journal of Political Economy*, 90: 881–94.

Dixit, A. and Norman, V. (1980). *Theory of International Trade*. Cambridge University Press.

Drèze, J. (1975). 'Existence of an Exchange Equilibrium under Price Rigidities'. *International Economic Review*, 16: 301–20.

—— and Müller, H. (1980). 'Optimality Properties of Rationing Schemes'. *Journal of Economic Theory*, 23: 131–49.

Eckalbar, J. C. (1980). 'The Stability of Non-Walrasian Processes: Two Examples'. *Econometrica*, 48: 371–86.

Fischer, S. (1988). 'Recent Developments in Macroeconomics'. *Economic Journal*, 98: 294–339.

Fisher, F. (1970). 'Quasi-Competitive Price Adjustment by Individual Firms: a Preliminary Paper'. *Journal of Economic Theory*, 2: 195–206.

—— (1972). 'On Price Adjustment without an Auctioneer'. *Review of Economic Studies*, 39: 1–19.

—— (1983). *Disequilibrium Foundations of Equilibrium Economics*. Cambridge University Press.

—— (1987). 'Adjustment Processes and Stability'. In J. Eatwell, M. Milgate, and P. Newman (eds.), *The New Palgrave: A Dictionary of Economics*. London: Macmillan.

Gabsewicz, J. J. and Vial, J. P. (1972). 'Oligopoly à la Cournot in General Equilibrium Analysis'. *Journal of Economic Theory*, 4: 381–400.

Gale, D. (1963). 'A Note on Global Instability of Competitive Equilibrium'. *Naval Research Logistics Quarterly*, 10: 81–7.

Gourieroux, C., Laffont, J.-J., and Monfort, A. (1980). 'Disequilibrium Econometrics in Simultaneous Equations Systems'. *Econometrica*, 48: 75–96.

Grandmont, J.-M. (1977). 'Temporary General Equilibrium Theory'. *Econometrica*, 45: 535–72.

—— (1983). *Money and Value: A Reconsideration of Classical and Neoclassical Monetary Theories*. Cambridge University Press.

—— (1987). 'Temporary Equilibrium'. In J. Eatwell, M. Milgate, and P. Newman (eds.), *The New Palgrave: A Dictionary of Economics*. London: Macmillan.

—— and Laroque, G. (1976). 'On Temporary Keynesian Equilibria'. *Review of Economic Studies*, 43: 53–67.

Grossman, H. I. (1971). 'Money, Interest and Prices in Market Disequilibrium'. *Journal of Political Economy*, 79: 943–61.

—— (1972). 'A Choice Theoretic Model of an Income-Investment Accelerator'. *American Economic Review*, 62: 630–41.

Hahn, F. H. (1977). 'Exercises in Conjectural Equilibria'. *Scandinavian Journal of Economics*, 79: 210–24.

——(1978). 'On Non-Walrasian Equilibria'. *Review of Economic Studies*, 45: 1–17.

——(1982). 'Stability'. In K. J. Arrow and M. D. Intriligator (eds.), *Handbook of Mathematical Economics*, ii. Amsterdam: North-Holland.

——and NEGISHI, T. (1962). 'A Theorem on Non-*Tâtonnement* Stability'. *Econometrica*, 30: 463–9.

HICKS, J. R. (1965). *Capital and Growth*. Oxford University Press.

HILDENBRAND, K. and HILDENBRAND, W. (1978). 'On Keynesian Equilibrium with Unemployment and Quantity Rationing'. *Journal of Economic Theory*, 18: 255–77.

HONKAPOHJA, S. (1979). 'On the Dynamics of Disequilibrium in a Macro Model with Flexible Wages and Prices'. In M. Aoki and A. Marzollo (eds.), *New Trends in Dynamic System Theory and Economics*. New York: Academic Press.

——and ITO, T. (1983). 'Stability with Regime Switching'. *Journal of Economic Theory*, 29: 22–48.

HOWITT, P. (1985). 'Transaction Costs in the Theory of Unemployment'. *American Economic Review*, 75: 88–100.

JACOBSEN, H. J. and SCHULTZ, C. (1989). 'Wage Bargaining and Unemployment in a General Equilibrium Model'. Discussion Paper no. 89–01, Institute of Economics, University of Copenhagen.

————(1990). 'A General Equilibrium, Macro Model with Wage Bargaining'. *Scandinavian Journal of Economics*, 92: 379–98.

————(1991). 'Undominated Wage Rates in a Unionized, Overlapping-Generations Economy'. *European Economic Review* 35(6): 1255–75.

————(forthcoming). 'Decreasing Unemployment Increases Welfare'. Scandinavian Journal of Economics.

JOHN, R. (1985). 'A Remark on Conjectural Equilibria'. *Scandinavian Journal of Economics*, 87: 137–41.

KEIDING, H. (1981). 'Existence of Budget-Constrained Pareto-Efficient Allocations'. *Journal of Economic Theory*, 24: 393–7.

KEYNES, J. M. (1936). *The General Theory of Employment, Interest and Money*. London: Macmillan.

LAFFONT, J. J. (1985). 'Fixprice Models: A Survey of Recent Empirical Work'. In K. J. Arrow and S. Honkapohja (eds.), *Frontiers of Economics*. Oxford: Basil Blackwell.

LAMBERT, J.-P. (1988). *Disequilibrium Macroeconomic Models: Theory and Estimation of Rationing Models Using Business Survey Data*. Cambridge University Press.

LAROQUE, G. (1978). 'On the Dynamics of Disequilibrium: A Simple Remark'. *Review of Economic Studies*, 45: 273–8.

——(1981). 'Stable Spillovers among Substitutes: A Comment'. *Review of Economic Studies*, 48: 335–61.

LEIJONHUFVUD, A. (1967). 'Keynes and the Classics: A Suggested Interpretation'. *American Economic Review*, 57: 401–10.

——(1968). *On Keynesian Economics and the Economics of Keynes*. Oxford University Press.

—— (1973). 'Effective Demand Failures'. *Swedish Journal of Economics*, 75: 27–58.

—— (1981). *Information and Coordination: Essays in Macroeconomic Theory*. Oxford University Press.

—— (1987). 'Natural Rate and Market Rate'. In J. Eatwell, M. Milgate, and P. Newman (eds.), *The New Palgrave: A Dictionary of Economics*. London: Macmillan.

MADDEN, P. (1983). 'Keynesian Unemployment as a Nash Equilibrium with Endogenous Price-Wage Setting'. *Economics Letters*, 12: 109–14.

—— and SILVESTRE, J. (1991). 'Imperfect Competition and Fixprice Equilibria when Goods are Gross Substitutes', *Scandinavian Journal of Economics* 93(4): 479–94 1992.

—— —— (1992). 'Imperfect Competition and Fixprice Equilibria under Consumer Aggregation and Net Substitutes', *Scandinavian Journal of Economics* 94(1): 103–11.

MALINVAUD, E. (1977). *The Theory of Unemployment Reconsidered*. Oxford: Basil Blackwell.

—— and YOUNÈS, Y. (1977*a*). 'Some New Concepts for the Microeconomic Foundations of Macroeconomics'. In G. Harcourt (ed.), *The Microeconomic Foundations of Macroeconomics*. London: Macmillan.

—— —— (1977*b*). 'Une nouvelle formulation générale pour l'étude de certains fondements microéconomiques de la macroéconomie'. *Cahiers du Séminaire d'Économétrie*, pp. 63–109. Paris: CNRS.

MANKIW, N. G. (1985). 'Small Menu Costs and Large Business Cycles: A Macroeconomic Model of Monopoly'. *Quarterly Journal of Economics*, 100: 529–39.

MARCHAK, T. and SELTEN, R. (1972). *General Equilibrium with Price-Making Firms*, Lecture Notes in Economics and Mathematical Systems, Berlin: Springer-Verlag.

MUELLBAUER, J. and PORTES, R. (1978). 'Macroeconomic Models with Quantity Rationing'. *Economic Journal*, 88: 788–821.

MUKHERJI, A. (1990). *Walrasian and Non-Walrasian Equilibria: An Introduction to General Equilibrium Analysis*, Oxford: Clarendon Press.

MÜLLER, H. (1983). *Fiscal Policies in a General Equilibrium Model with Persistent Unemployment*, Lecture Notes in Economics and Mathematical Systems, vol. 216. Berlin: Springer-Verlag.

MUTH, J. F. (1961). 'Rational Expectations and the Theory of Price Movements'. *Econometrica*, 29: 315–35.

NEARY, J. P. (1980). 'Nontraded Goods and the Balance of Trade in a Neo-Keynesian Temporary Equilibrium'. *Quarterly Journal of Economics*, 95: 403–30.

—— and STIGLITZ, J. E. (1983). 'Towards a Reconstruction of Keynesian Economics: Expectations and Constrained Equilibria'. *Quarterly Journal of Economics*, 98: 199–228.

NEGISHI, T. (1960–1). 'Monopolistic Competition and General Equilibrium'. *Review of Economic Studies*, 28: 196–201.

—— (1961). 'On the Formation of Prices'. *International Economic Review*, 2: 122–6.

—— (1962). 'The Stability of a Competitive Economy: A Survey Article'. *Econometrica*, 30: 635–69.

—— (1965). 'The Market-Clearing Processes in a Monetary Economy'. In F. H. Hahn and F. P. R. Brechling (eds.), *The Theory of Interest Rates*. London: Macmillan.

—— (1974). 'Involuntary Unemployment and Market Imperfection'. *Economic Studies Quarterly*, 25: 32–41.

—— (1976). 'Unemployment, Inflation and the Microfoundations of Macroeconomics'. In M. J. Artis and A. R. Nobay (eds.), *Essays in Economic Analysis: Proceedings of the 1975 AUTE Conference*. Cambridge University Press.

—— (1977). 'Existence of an Under-Employment Equilibrium'. In G. Schwödiauer (ed.), *Equilibrium and Disequilibrium in Economic Theory*. Boston: Reidel.

—— (1979). *Microeconomic Foundations of Keynesian Macroeconomics*. Amsterdam: North-Holland.

NIKAIDO, H. (1975). *Monopolistic Competition and Effective Demand*. Princeton University Press.

PATINKIN, D. (1956). *Money, Interest and Prices*. Evanston, Ill.: Row Peterson.

POLTEROVICH, V. M. (1990). 'Equilibrated States and Optimal Allocations of Resources under Rigid Prices', *Journal of Mathematical Economics*, 19: 255–68.

PORTES, R. (1981). 'Macroeconomic Equilibrium and Disequilibrium in Centrally Planned Economies'. *Economic Inquiry*, 19: 559–78.

—— and WINTER, D. (1977). 'The Supply of Consumption Goods in Centrally Planned Economies'. *Journal of Comparative Economics*, 1: 351–65.

—— —— (1980). 'Disequilibrium Estimates for Consumption Goods Markets in Centrally Planned Economies'. *Review of Economic Studies*, 47: 137–59.

—— QUANDT, R. E., WINTER, D., and YEO, S. (1984). 'Planning the Consumption Goods Market: Preliminary Estimates for Poland, 1955–1980'. In P. Malgrange and P. A. Muet (eds.), *Contemporary Macroeconomic Modelling*. Oxford: Basil Blackwell.

QUANDT, R. E. (1982). 'Econometric Disequilibrium Models'. *Econometric Reviews*, 1: 1–63.

—— (1988). *The Econometrics of Disequilibrium*. Oxford: Basil Blackwell.

—— and ROSEN, H. S. (1988). *The Conflict between Equilibrium and Disequilibrium Theories: The Case of the US Labor Market*. Kalamazoo, Mich.: W. E. Upjohn Institute for Employment Research.

ROBINSON, J. (1933). *The Economics of Imperfect Competition*. London: Macmillan.

ROTEMBERG, J. (1982a). 'Monopolistic Price Adjustment and Aggregate Output'. *Review of Economic Studies*, 49: 517–31.

—— (1982b). 'Sticky Prices in the United States'. *Journal of Political Economy*, 90: 1187–211.

—— (1987). 'The New Keynesian Microfoundations'. In S. Fischer (ed.), *NBER Macroeconomics Annual 1987*. Cambridge, Mass.: National Bureau of Economic Research and MIT Press.

—— and SALONER, G. (1986). 'A Supergame Theoretic Model of Price Wars'. *American Economic Review*, 76: 390–407.

———— (1987). 'The Relative Rigidity of Monopoly Price'. *American Economic Review*, 77: 917–26.

RUDEBUSCH, G. D. (1987). *The Estimation of Disequilibrium Models with Regime Classification Information*, Lecture Notes in Economics and Mathematical Systems, vol. 288. Berlin: Springer-Verlag.

SALDANHA, F. (1987). 'The Share Economy in the Short Run'. Unpublished paper, University of Arizona.

SCARF, H. (1960). 'Some Examples of Global Instability of Competitive Equilibrium'. *International Economic Review*, 1: 157–72.

SCHULZ, N. (1983). 'On the Global Uniqueness of Fix-price Equilibria'. *Econometrica*, 51: 47–68.

SILVESTRE, J. (1978a) 'Fixprice Analysis: A Synopsis of Three Solution Concepts'. Working Paper no. IP-270, University of California at Berkeley.

———— (1978b). 'Fixprice Analysis: The Classification of Disequilibrium Regimes'. Working Paper no. IP-271, University of California at Berkeley.

———— (1982a). 'Fixprice Analysis in Exchange Economies'. *Journal of Economic Theory*, 26: 28–58.

———— (1982b). 'Ambiguities in the Sign of Excess Effective Demand by Firms'. *Review of Economic Studies*, 49: 645–51.

———— (1983). 'Fixprice Analysis in Productive Economies'. *Journal of Economic Theory*, 30: 401–9.

———— (1985). 'Voluntary and Efficient Allocations are Walrasian'. *Econometrica*, 53: 807–16.

———— (1986). 'The Elements of Fixprice Microeconomics'. In L. Samuelson (ed.), *Microeconomic Theory*. Boston: Kluwer Nijhoff.

———— (1987). 'Fixprice Models.' In J. Eatwell, M. Milgate and P. Newman (eds.), *The New Palgrave: A Dictionary of Economics*. London: Macmillan.

———— (1988). 'Undominated Prices in the Three Good Model'. *European Economic Review*, 32: 161–78.

———— (1989). 'Who Benefits from Unemployment?' In G. Feiwel (ed.), *The Economics of Imperfect Competition: Joan Robinson and Beyond*. London: Macmillan.

———— (forthcoming). 'The Market Power Foundations of Macroeconomic Policy', *Journal of Economic Literature*.

SNEESSENS, H. (1981). *Theory and Estimation of Macroeconomic Rationing Models*. Lecture Notes in Economics and Mathematical Systems, vol. 191. Berlin: Springer-Verlag.

SWEEZY, P. M. (1939). 'Demand under Conditions of Oligopoly'. *Journal of Political Economy*, 47: 568–73.

TOBIN, J. (1980). *Asset Accumulation and Economic Activity*. Oxford: Basil Blackwell.

UZAWA, H. (1962). 'On the Stability of Edgeworth's Barter Process'. *Econometrica*, 29: 617–31.

VARIAN, H. (1984). *Microeconomic Analysis*, 2nd ed. New York: W. W. Norton.

VEENDORP, E. C. H. (1975). 'Stable Spillovers among Substitutes'. *Review of Economic Studies*, 42: 445–56.

WALRAS, L. (1874). *Éléments d'économie politique pure*. Lausanne: L. Corbaz.

WEITZMAN, M. L. (1983). 'Some Macroeconomic Implications of Alternative Compensation Systems'. *Economic Journal*, 93: 763–83.

——(1984). *The Share Economy: Conquering Stagflation*. Cambridge, Mass.: Harvard University Press.

——(1985). 'The Simple Macroeconomics of Profit Sharing'. *American Economic Review*, 75: 937–53.

YOUNÈS, Y. (1970). 'Sur les notions d'équilibre et de déséquilibre utilisées dans les modèles décrivant l'évolution d'une économie capitaliste'. Mimeo, CE-PREMAP, Paris.

——(1975). 'On the Role of Money in the Process of Exchange and the Existence of a Non-Walrasian Equilibrium'. *Review of Economic Studies*, 42: 489–501.

PART II

The Rational Expectations Controversy

5

Expectations in Macroeconomics and the Rational Expectations Debate

EDMUND S. PHELPS

Before there could be rational expectations in macroeconomic models, there first had to be expectations. So it is natural to begin with a brief review of the way expectations have been introduced into the supply block of macroeconomic models.

1. Injection of Expectations into Macro Models

The earliest papers explicitly introducing expectations into the wage–price, or supply, block of a macro model appeared in a volume of papers from a 1969 conference, *Microeconomic Foundations of Employment and Inflation Theory* (Phelps *et al.* 1970). These papers dealt predominantly with the case of synchronous wage- and price-setting by all firms, either continuously or periodically; the case of staggered wage-setting, discussed informally in my own contribution in Phelps *et al.* (1970), was not to receive attention until several years later.

Typically, there is derived a wage-setting equation or a price-setting equation or, as in the general case illustrated below, a simultaneous system in both equations. Letting P denote the nominal price level, W the nominal wage level, M the velocity-adjusted money supply, N the current employment level, J the level of productivity, and x a vector of state variables, we might have

$$
\begin{aligned}
P &= \varepsilon^P(W^e, P^e, M^e; J^e, N_{-1}, x) \\
&= \varepsilon^P(W^e/P^e, 1, M^e/P^e; J^e, N_{-1}, x)P^e \\
W &= \varepsilon^W(W^e, P^e, M^e; J^e, N_{-1}, x) \\
&= \varepsilon^W(W^e/P^e, 1, M^e/P^e; J^e, N_{-1}, x)W^e.
\end{aligned}
\tag{1}
$$

Equivalently, letting v^e denote W^e/P^e and m^e denote M^e/P^e,

$$\log P - \log P_{-1} = \varepsilon^P(v^e, m^e; J^e, N_{-1}, x) + \log P^e - \log P_{-1}$$
(1a)

$$\log W - \log W_{-1} = \varepsilon^W(v^e, m^e; J^e, N_{-1}, x) + \log W^e - \log W_{-1}.$$
(1b)

Inevitably, the function on the right-hand side of each of these latter two equations will remind us of excess-demand functions in Walrasian economics; but the analogy is of limited interest and may be misleading.

A number of terms appearing in this context are not used in uniform ways, unfortunately, so one must define one's terms.

Equilibrium in the product market occurs if and only if the price expected by everyone to prevail in that market is realized; similarly, labour-market equilibrium means that expectations of the wage are satisfied. In terms of the above system, then,

$$P = P^e$$
(2a)

$$W = W^e.$$
(2b)

In a stochastic model we would want $EP = P^e$ and $EW = W^e$, where E is the expected value operator. The spirit of these definitions does not really require a monetary economy, since equity shares (or any other real asset) could serve, however awkwardly, as the numeraire instead of money. General equilibrium, or its poor half-brother macroequilibrium, requires the foregoing equilibrium conditions plus some sort of capital-market equilibrium condition and a condition for monetary equilibrium, conditions I will be taking for granted in what follows. I have the impression that Myrdal, Hayek, Hicks, Harrod, Lindahl, and many other figures in the development of equilibrium theory in monetary and non-monetary economies used the term 'equilibrium' in this expectational sense (though Hicks, for example, was not totally consistent). My essay on equilibrium for the *New Palgrave* has the citations (Phelps 1987).

It should be commented that equilibrium in the above sense is orthogonal, as they say, to market-clearing. In some models equilibrium implies market-clearing (for if there were not clearing there would be surprises), but not in all models—not in so-called efficiency wage models, for example; and market-clearing does not imply equilibrium—not in the 'island parable' type of model, for example.

The rational expectations premise (REP) posits that the economy systematically exhibits equilibrium. As implied above, equilibrium is a condition on v^e and m^e such that

$$\epsilon^P(v^e, m^e) = 0, \qquad \epsilon^W(v^e, m^e) = 0$$
(3)

given the circumstances summarized by J^e, N_{-1}, and x. The rational expectations premise asserts that equilibrium holds in all circumstances (abstracting from any learning that may first be needed). Hence REP says

$$\epsilon^P(v^e, m^e) = 0, \qquad \epsilon^W(v^e, m^e) = 0, \tag{4}$$

for all J^e, N_{-1}, and x. This envisions a populace of agents with a knowledge possibly far exceeding what may be known when the economy is following a particular equilibrium path for which its history has prepared it.

Most macro models reduce the dimensionality of the problem by either of two familiar simplifications. One is to suppose that the price level is determined currently with output—for example, price is set equal to marginal cost—rather than predetermined at the beginning of the period, so that only the wage dynamics remain. The second device is to suppose that the wage level is determined currently—for example, the nominal wage is adjusted in proportion to the revealed price level—so that only the price dynamics remain. Then the above two-equation system is replaced by a single equation such as

$$P = \Pi(P^e, M^e; J^e, N_{-1}, x) \tag{1'}$$

or, in the log-linear case,

$$p = \beta p^e + \gamma x_{-1} + u. \tag{1''}$$

In the 'island parable' and 'customer market' stories, to take two examples, p is the average of the prices being set for the current period, and p^e is the average of the forecasts of this average price; these models give $\beta > 0$. In Marshall's model of price and quantity in the next harvest, p is the actual price and p^e is the forecast at planting time of the harvest price; here $\beta < 0$.

A final remark. After the expectational revolution struck macroeconomic theory, and spawned numerous micro–macro models of the economy, there was a bifurcation of economists into the New Classical school and what has come (inevitably) to be known as the New Keynesian school. The hallmark of the latter is the feature of non-synchronous price-setting or wage-setting or both; those economists who have done recent work on co-ordination problems and non-convergence to equilibrium are working in the Old Keynesian tradition, not the new, for better or worse. As it has turned out, most of the models of non-synchronous price/wage-setting have employed the REP—though they would not have been less new if they had not. Thus, the recent controversy over the rational expectations premise is not fundamentally a conflict between the New Keynesian and the New Classical schools: it would be more apt to regard it as a schism within the Keynesian family

between New and Old Keynesians, though no less heartfelt just because
the substantive goals are shared.

2. Issues in the Rational Expectations Controversy

I am going to take up three issues that are a part of the rational
expectations controversy.

1. Is REP applicable to a disinflation/inflation game between the public
   and the government (or the central bank)?
2. Is REP applicable when there is a game going on between one
   branch of government and another?
3. Does everyone learn to make the RE forecast if posited to process
   local information optimally—that is, in a way that a qualitative
   understanding of the economics of the economy would permit and
   encourage?

2.1 *Inflation/disinflation games*

The dynamic programming model of optimal inflation in Phelps (1967),
for example, presumed that adaptive expectations was the best the
public could do when faced with a government seeking to pursue a
(so-to-speak) scientific approach to inflation. Like everyone else, I used
the Cagan–Nerlove equation,

$$d\pi^e/dt = \beta(\pi - \pi^e), \qquad \beta > 0.$$

There was shown to be a steady-state equilibrium, displaying some
constant inflation rate $\hat{\pi} > 0$ that would be currently expected all the
time; but the approach to that equilibrium involved learning—learning
through trial and a string of one-signed errors. Taylor (1975) recast the
argument in statistical Bayesian terms. Obviously, this economy is not in
a rational expectations equilibrium: it has not managed even to hit upon
the equilibrium path from the particular initial givens, let alone to
acquire the ability to find its equilibrium way from every possibly
disturbed initial position.

The Kreps–Wilson type of model was first used in the inflation
context by Backus and Driffill (1985). There is uncertainty about the
objective of one of the players, namely the government in the present
context; and that player's reputation for having a certain objective is a
function of its past record. The best known model of this kind is
perhaps that by Barro (1986), which has been altered a little and
rendered into a continuous-time version by Andersen and Risager
(1987). In that model there is a reputation variable, α, that is the

estimated probability, based on past experience, that the government is a non-inflation-preferring type, and since the inflation-preferring type of government—it prefers $\widetilde{\pi}$—may be motivated to pretend that it is of the other type, the public also assigns a probability $\widetilde{p}$ that, if the government is inflation-preferring, it will none the less 'play' zero inflation. The expected inflation rate is

$$\pi^e = (1 - \alpha)(1 - \widetilde{p})\,\widetilde{\pi}.$$

It is shown that α obeys a differential equation,

$$d\alpha/dt = \{\alpha/[\alpha + (1 - \alpha)\widetilde{p}]\} - \alpha,$$

which might suggest that the expected inflation rate is likewise described by a differential equation in adaptive-expectations style. But Andersen and Risager show that $\widetilde{p}$ follows a compensating motion so as to keep the expected inflation rate constant, following the arrival of a new government of unknown type. What happens is that the expected inflation rate jumps down immediately to a new plateau if previously the economy was in the hands of a proven inflation-preferring regime; if the government prefers $\widetilde{\pi}$, there is a point at which it cashes in its accumulated reputation and switches to inflation, while if it prefers no inflation, there will arrive a critical point at which its failure to cash in convinces the public that it is indeed of that type π^e and drops discontinuously to 0. The broad message is therefore the same as in the adaptive-expectations formulation: seeing is believing, so there will have to be a prolonged episode of actual inflation below expectations and output depressed as a result until expectations are finally brought into line with the government's policy preferences. The abruptness with which expectations of inflation finally fall into line is a detail, and perhaps one could smooth that adjustment by requiring that people be heterogeneous with regard to some feature—perhaps risk aversion—affecting their behaviour (but not their estimates of reputation and of the above probability).

Is REP present here and, if so, what is the gain? One may say that it is a rational expectations model if the subjective estimate of the probability $\widetilde{p}$ is the correct one, which means that it is right on average over random samples of economies experiencing new governments engaged in disinflation. The benefit is that the REP makes explicit that the policies chosen by the two types of government do not rest on a posited tendency of people to underestimate or overestimate reputation, etc.—not because they don't, but because the analyst would feel unable to explain why it should be assumed that they have any such systematic tendency. It is less clear that this benefit outweighs the cost of having to deal with so complex a model. (But in any case, there is no going back now to a mechanical formulation.)

2.2 *Games exhibiting a policy impasse*

Economists have discussed the macro effects of several intra-govern-
mental 'games' in recent years.

1. Parkin (1976) argued that a depression can occur when policy
instruments are steadily on an unsustainable setting. It is understood
that the policies must adjust, but it is not yet resolved just what
adjustment will be made. Parkin argues that the hedging against a range
of outcomes may be depressionary even if, once the decision is made,
prices and wages will respond so as to return the economy to the
'natural rate'.

2. The so-called 'peso problem', credited to Milton Friedman, points
to the depressing effect of the expectation that the currency will be
devalued but with an unknown lag because the consensus for a devaluation or the decision as to the size of the devaluation has not been
achieved. The risk that a devaluation will occur, as represented in the
sequence of conditional probabilities $\tilde{p}_s$ that it will first occur s periods
hence, will cause the price level to be elevated this period in anticipation of the chance of higher export demand and the resulting elevation
of the prices of competitors, and this elevation in relation to the money
supply will cause expenditure and employment to be depressed.

3. More recently, various economists have speculated about the
effects of the impasse between Reagan Republicans, who have
demanded that the budgetary deficit be reduced by means of expenditure cuts, and Democrats in Congress, who seek a more balanced
budget through an increase of some tax rates. Some have seen the
impasse as having an expansionary influence on employment, in anticipation of a future drop of Tobin's q when the impasse is overcome,
while others see it as prompting excessive prices and wages in anticipation of an explosion of the money supply as continuing debt absorption
raises prohibitively the cost of bond finance.

Are these phenomena amenable to the rational expectations approach? Keynes, in an oft-quoted piece, declared that the intrinsic
uncertainty surrounding future policy conflicts and actions, both
domestic and international, ruled out the possibility that the economy's
trajectory could be deemed an equilibrium one (Keynes 1937). *A
fortiori*, such uncertainty would seem to rule out rational expectations
equilibrium—that is, an equilibrium path from every possible initial state
corresponding to every possible initial disturbance. Friedman likewise
declared, at a Stanford NBER conference (around 1976), that 'rational
expectations does not apply' to the peso problem. On the other side of
this question, evidently, are those model-builders who assume, implicitly

or explicitly, that the public has got the $\bar{p}$s right—that the public, in reacting to the historical sample of such problems, neither overestimates nor underestimates the likelihood of each sort of outcome—and who therefore call their solution the 'rational expectations equilibrium'. Perhaps we can agree that the latter practice is a case of poetic licence. These policy impasses are not repetitive data-points from some well defined and known-to-be-unchanging population. The big impasses seem unique to most of us—*sui generis*, in a word—which is why they get into the textbooks. I can understand, however, that it is in some way illuminating, or anyway interesting, to use the REP here, even though it is not well founded and is apt to be unreliable and misleading. But the REP religionists have no basis for claiming here that theirs is the only true faith.

2.3 *The game of simultaneous and atomistic learning*

Let me introduce this last section with an epigraph:

> If you can keep your RE forecast function when, all about you, men are losing theirs . . .

Added verse for If, by Rudyard Kipling

Consider an 'island parable' kind of economy in which all the agents know the correct specification, or form, of the economy, the price equation of which is

$$y_t = \beta(_{t-1}y_t^e) + \gamma x_{t-1} + u_t,$$

where y_t is the actual price level and $_{t-1}y_t^e$ is the average (subjective) expectation at the end of period $t - 1$. There is incomplete information in that, of the disturbances in the u term, the disturbances occurring in locality i are observed only by agents producing there:

$$x_{t-1}^{(i)} = x_{t-1} + \epsilon_i.$$

If every agent could observe $_{t-1}y_t^e$, the agents, each running a regression each period, could converge to the rational expectations forecasting function, as Townsend (1978) showed. But here, the agents cannot observe this average-opinion variable.

It has been shown by Roman Frydman (1982) that, if the agents make use of their knowledge of the model's specification, their estimations will fail to converge to the rational expectations forecasting function. If all the agents by luck started operating with the RE forecasting function, the ordinary chance disturbances would immediately begin drawing them away from that function. Frydman was careful in his paper not to imply that agents, by some fortunately chosen arational process, would not gravitate to the RE forecasting rule—a process in which, in apparent contradiction to their understanding of the model, they do not attempt to take into account their estimates of how the expectations of others are being revised with experience.

A number of authors have studied *arational* 'learning' in the past few years, among them Bray and Savin (1986), Fourgeaud *et al.* (1986), and Marcet and Sargent (Chapter 6 below). In the first case, however, there is no heterogeneity of information, and in all cases the learning is not *rational* in the sense that the agent uses his understanding of the influence of the learning of others during his own learning.

In a new paper by Frydman (1987), there is a model in which group 1 observes only y_{t-1} and z_{t-1}, and group 2 observes only y_{t-1} and w_{t-1}. In the interpretation that Frydman presses, group 2 does not feel it worth while to dig up what group 1 likes to examine, and similarly for group 1, as they have differently specified models of the fundamentals of the economy. (Here a group does not attempt to update its forecast of the expectations function of the other group because it does not have their data-set.) Let me dispense with setting down the results in equational form. It suffices to say that, under a not-uncommon restriction, both of two groups' forecasting functions will converge; correspondingly, these will be in a stochastic steady state.

It will not surprise readers that this steady state is not the rational expectations equilibrium; the latter would require in the present context that all agents believe in and 'practise' the same model. More interesting is the point that the resulting steady-state forecasting functions of each of the groups are not correct—in the sense of being the best possible— relative to the group's observation set. Yet, although the outcome is not true equilibrium behaviour, in the sense of correct expectations or even correct expectations relative to observation sets, this stochastic steady state might be called a Hahn-equilibrium, since the (somewhat naive) groups are not led, once they have reached the associated forecasting functions, to improve or otherwise change their forecasting functions. (But this 'settling down' of expectations is a sort of physicist's notion of equilibrium, which I do not find very congenial.)

3. Concluding Remarks

By way of closing this brief introductory survey, I would say that the rational expectations view of the motion of the economy has to come to grips with two problems: one is *learning*, and the other—a logically prior problem—is, *learning what?* In the real world agents have diverse models, so the individual agent must learn not only the parameters that would exist if all shared his beliefs about the model, but also the parameters that enter because other agents have other views. This observation is an obvious corollary of sunspot theory: if everyone else believes, you had better believe too (see e.g. Shell 1987).

A more general premise than REP, then, is that each agent thinks not only in terms of the forces that are for him the fundamental and exogenous factors determining the economy's current outcome, but also in terms of his estimate of the expectations of others with regard to these or other forces. In principle, one gets Keynes's 'infinite regress', which he sought to dramatize with the curious newspaper beauty contest that he had noticed. The 'algebra' of this infinite regress, worked out for a simple problem about inflation and disinflation, is set down in my paper for the Frydman–Phelps volume (Phelps 1983).

I realized somewhat later that this perceived heterogeneity of beliefs perhaps provides the explanation for what seems to be a rather general, though not necessarily perfectly general, phenomenon: when a shock occurs, there is typically an underreaction to it at first, then a series of 'after shocks' as the full nature and magnitude of the shock finally registers over the whole of the market. The evidence suggesting this thesis is discussed in a survey paper of mine for a 1986 Spoleto conference (Phelps 1986).

When I was beginning to venture this sort of criticism of REP—that the individual agent knows that some of the others conceive of the economy (or the polity) as working differently—the best I could do was to point to the absence of an agreed-upon political science on which to predict future policies and, in economics, to the division of economists between Keynesian, monetarist, and supply-side persuasions; I was not very sure how much weight the point would carry. I realize now that there are several more theoretical perspectives. Macroeconomics these days is virtually balkanized, though passports are issued. So there is an element of farce when, collectively, we work with all these different theories and yet posit rational expectations as if there were only one model.

The fact that the rational expectations premise is unsatisfactory is not sufficient to drive it out of use, only to prolong the life-span (at least in certain settings) of older (and also unsatisfactory) premises. Rational expectations will be retired only when there is agreed to be a better idea. Somewhere down the road, one imagines, there *is* a better idea waiting to be discovered and developed.

References

ANDERSEN, TORBEN M., and RISAGER OLE, (1987). 'Reputation and Rational Expectations'. Institute for International Economic Studies, University of

Stockholm. Seminar Paper no. 378, March.

BACKUS, D., and DRIFFILL, J. (1985) 'Inflation and Reputation'. *American Economic Review*, 75: 530–8.

BARRO, ROBERT J. (1986). 'Reputation in a Model of Monetary Policy'. *Journal of Monetary Economics*, 17: 3–20.

BRAY, M. M., and SAVIN, N. E. (1986). 'Rational Expectations Equilibria, Learning, and Model Specification'. *Econometrica*, 54: 1129–60.

FOURGEAUD, C., GOURIEROUX, C., and PRADEL, J. (1986). 'Learning Procedures and Convergence to Rationality'. *Econometrica*, 54: 845–68.

FRYDMAN, ROMAN (1982). 'Toward an Understanding of Market Processes: Individual Expectations, Learning and Convergence to Rational Expectations Equilibrium'. *American Economic Review*, 72: 652–68.

——(1987). 'Diversity of Information, Least Squares Learning Rules, and Market Behavior'. Unpublished paper, New York University, Department of Economics, September.

KEYNES, J. M. (1937). 'The General Theory of Employment'. *Quarterly Journal of Economics*. 51: 209–23.

PARKIN, MICHAEL (1976). 'Persistent Depression and "Stagflation" as Consequences of Rational Expectations and Inconsistent Policies'. Mimeo, University of Western Ontario, October. Reprinted in E. S. Phelps (ed.), *Recent Developments in Macroeconomics*, i. Aldershot: Edward Elgar Publishing, 1991.

PHELPS, EDMUND S. (1967). 'Phillips Curves, Expectations of Inflation, and Optimal Unemployment over Time'. *Economica*, 34: 254–81.

——(1968). 'Money Wage Dynamics and Labor Market Equilibrium'. *Journal of Political Economy*, 76: 678–711.

——(1983). 'The Trouble with Rational Expectations and the Problem of Inflation Stabilization'. In R. Frydman and E. S. Phelps (eds.), *Individual Forecasting and Aggregate Outcomes: 'Rational Expectations' Examined*. Cambridge University Press.

——(1986). 'Recent Studies of Speculative Markets in the Controversy over Rational Expectations'. European University Institute Working Paper; French trans., 'Marches spéculatifs et anticipations rationnelles', *Revue Française d'Économie*, 2 (1987).

——(1987). 'Equilibrium', in *The New Palgrave: A Dictionary of Economics*. London: Macmillan.

——*et al.* (1970). *Microeconomic Foundations of Employment and Inflation Theory*. New York: W. W. Norton.

SHELL, KARL (1987). 'Sunspot Equilibrium', in *The New Palgrave: A Dictionary of Economics*. London: Macmillan.

TAYLOR, JOHN B. (1975). 'Monetary Policy during a Transition to Rational Expectations'. *Journal of Political Economy*, 81: 1009–21.

TOWNSEND, ROBERT M. (1978). 'Market Anticipations, Rational Expectations and Bayesian Analysis'. *International Economic Review*, 19: 481–94.

6

The Convergence of Vector Autoregressions to Rational Expectations Equilibria

ALBERT MARCET and THOMAS J. SARGENT

1. Introduction

In economic affairs, the way that the future unfolds from the past depends partly on how people expect it to unfold from the past. Economic systems can thus be described as self-referential, because outcomes depend partly on what people expect those outcomes to be. This self-referential aspect of economic systems gives rise to enormous theoretical problems of indeterminacy (i.e. multiple equilibria) when people's expectations are left as 'free variables' that are not restricted by economic theory. To fight that threat of indeterminacy, economists have embraced the hypothesis of rational expectations. This hypothesis instructs us to focus only on outcomes and systems of beliefs that are consistent with one another, allowing for whatever differences between outcomes and beliefs can be attributed to uncertainty and limited information.

A rational expectations equilibrium is a fixed point of a particular mapping from beliefs to outcomes. When agents have an arbitrarily given set of beliefs about the laws of motion of the economy, their behaviour causes the actual laws of motion to be determined. We can think of people's behaviour collectively as inducing a mapping from their believed laws of motion to the actual laws of motion for the economy. A rational expectations equilibrium is a fixed point of that mapping, which is a set of beliefs about laws of motion that is consistent with realized outcomes.

Much work in economic theory and rational expectations econometrics simply assumes that the economy is described by a rational

Thomas Sargent's research was financed by a grant from the National Science Foundation to the University of Minnesota, NSF/SES8508935.

expectations equilibrium. This type of work is silent on the question of how the economy could have arrived at such a situation in which beliefs are consistent with outcomes. That is, the theory is silent about how agents might learn to have correct beliefs if they had started with beliefs that are wrong. Recently, a number of researchers have begun studying this 'learning' problem. One reason for studying the problem is that the notion of a rational expectations equilibrium would be a more attractive one if there were plausible and undemanding learning schemes which would drive the system towards a rational expectations equilibrium. A second reason for studying learning theories—one emphasized in the work of George Evans—is that, even though it restricts systems of beliefs, the concept of rational expectations is often not restrictive enough to prevent a multiplicity of equilibria from occurring. That is, for some economic environments, there can occur multiple systems of beliefs that are consistent with outcomes. One use of a learning theory that converges to a rational expectations equilibrium would be to select which of several equilibria might be expected to prevail in practice because learning schemes are attracted towards them and repelled from others.

Margaret Bray (1982, 1983), Bray and Savin (1986), and Fourgeaud *et al*. (1986) have studied the learning problem in environments that can be described by particular linear rational expectations equilibria. They relax the assumption of rational expectations and instead assume that agents must learn about some aspect of the environment through the sequential application of linear least squares. Each of these authors displays technical conditions under which their systems converge almost surely to a rational expectations equilibrium.

This paper summarizes and applies some of our research on least-squares learning mechanisms in the context of linear rational expecta-tions models with private information.[1] We model the agents in the economy as forming beliefs by fitting vector autoregressions. Each period, the agents add the latest observations and update their vector autoregressions. They use these updated vector autoregressions to form forecasts that influence decisions that they make, which in turn influence the motion of variables in the economy. We study conditions under which such an economy converges to a rational expectations equili-brium.

Studying the convergence of least-squares estimators in setups like ours involves technical difficulties because these setups involve depar-tures from the standard assumptions used in time-series econometrics to deliver convergence. Under standard conditions maintained in econo-

---

[1] This work is contained in four papers by Marcet and Sargent (1988, 1989*a*, 1989*b*, 1989*c*).

metrics (e.g. covariance stationarity, and ergodicity of the stochastic process for which the vector autoregression is being estimated), least-squares estimators of vector autoregressions are known to converge strongly. Such convergence results fail to cover the cases that we want to study, because in our systems agents' learning behaviour causes the stochastic process being learned about to be non-stationary. In effect, agents are shooting at (learning about) a moving target, rather than the fixed target assumed in the standard econometric setting. This feature is what has made convergence results difficult to attain.

In self-referential linear models, the least-squares estimators of vector autoregressions follow a complicated stochastic difference equation whose limiting behaviour we want to analyse. By building on technical results of Lennart Ljung (1977), it can be shown that the limiting behaviour of this stochastic difference equation is described by a much simpler ordinary differential equation.[2] The differential equation involves the operator mapping perceived laws of motion into actual laws of motion, which appears in the work of DeCanio (1979) and Evans (1983, 1985). Using this approach, one immediately obtains Margaret Bray's (1982) result that the only possible limit points of least-squares learning schemes are rational expectations equilibria. Further, the local stability of least-squares learning schemes about a rational expectations equilibrium can be determined by studying the stability of the associated differential equation at the rational expectations equilibrium.

We apply our results to three models that have appeared in the literature. These examples illustrate the power of the differential equation approach to shorten and unify proofs of convergence that have appeared in the literature. The differential equation approach also permits a unified interpretation of apparently diverse results in terms of the character of the operator mapping perceived to actual laws of motion. We first study a model of Margaret Bray, and show how our methods can be used to represent and somewhat strengthen her results. Next we study a model that we have created by modifying a model contributed by Roman Frydman. Under our modifications, the model converges strongly to a rational expectations equilibrium. The third model is a private-information version of a hyperinflation or stock price model. The rational expectations version of this model has many equilibria, all but one of which exhibit a 'speculative bubble'. Our results suggest that the equilibria with bubbles will not be attractors under our learning scheme.

---

[2] The ordinary differential equations approach is described and applied by Ljung and Soderstrom (1983) and Goodwin and Sin (1983). Margaritis (1985) gave an early application of the approach in economics. Woodford (1986) applies some of Ljung's methods to a nonlinear dynamic model. Also see Kushner and Clark (1978) and Robbins and Monro (1951).

2. The Model and a Convergence Proposition[3]

This section describes the technical results obtained by Marcet and Sargent (1989b), where we study the convergence of a system driven by the behaviour of two types of differentially informed agents, each of whom is learning through the sequential application of linear least squares. That distinct agents are differentially informed creates the situation that for each class of agent there are hidden state variables.[4] Our setup is as follows.

There is an ($n \times 1$) state vector z_t. We let z_{it} be an $n_i \times 1$ subvector, where $1 \le n_i \le n$, for $i = a$, b, c, d. There are two types of agents, types a and b, who observe $z_{at} = e_a z_t$ and $z_{bt} = e_b z_t$, respectively, possibly distinct subvectors of z_t. Agents of type j want to predict future value of possibly distinct subvectors $z_{k(j)} = e_{k(j)} z_t$, where $k(a) = c$ and $k(b) = d$, and to use the current observation on z_{jt} in order to form those predictions. The selection matrices e_a, e_b, e_c, e_d are constant through time. There is an economic model which maps beliefs of agents a and b into actual outcomes in the following way. If the beliefs of agents of type a and type b were given by the time-invariant rules,

$$E^*(z_{ct}|z_{at-1}) = \beta_a\, z_{at-1}$$
$$E^*(z_{dt}|z_{bt-1}) = \beta_b\, z_{bt-1} \qquad \text{for all } t, \tag{1}$$

then the actual law of motion of z_t would be given by

$$z_t = T(\beta)z_{t-1} + V(\beta)\epsilon_t \tag{2}$$

where ϵ_t is an ($m \times 1$)-vector white noise, $\beta = (\beta_a, \beta_b)$, and T and V are operators that map matrices comformable to the objects they operate upon. A particular economic model will determine the operators T and V. In subsequent sections, we describe several economic models and display the operators T and V that are associated with them.

We will work in regions of the parameter space β for which (2) implies that z_t is a covariance stationary stochastic process. For this purpose, we define the following set:

$$D_s = \{\beta | \text{the operators } T(\beta) \text{ and } V(\beta) \text{ are}$$
$$\text{well defined, and the eigenvalues of } T(\beta) \text{ are}$$
$$\text{less than unity in modulus}\}.$$

For $\beta \in D_s$, (2) generates a covariance stationary stochastic process, for which the second-moment matrix $Ez_t z_t'$ is well defined. Letting

---

[3] This section parallels and elaborates on the first section of Marcet and Sargent (1989b).

[4] Note that the models of Bray and Savin (1986) and of Fourgeaud *et al.* (1986) do not have hidden state variables.

$M_z(\beta) = Ez_t z'_t$, this moment matrix can be computed as the solution of the discrete Lyapunov equation,

$$M_z(\beta) = T(\beta)M_z(\beta)T(\beta)' + V(\beta)\Omega V(\beta)',$$

where $\Omega = E\epsilon_t \epsilon'_t$. We use the following notation for some submatrices of $Ez_t z'_t$:

$$M_{z_j}(\beta) = Ez_{jt} z'_{jt}, \qquad j = a, b$$

$$M_{z_j,z}(\beta) = Ez_{jt} z'_t, \qquad j = a, b. \tag{3}$$

In general, each of these moment matrices is a function of β.

If the actual law of motion for z_t is (2), then it can be calculated that the linear least-squares projection of $z_{k(j)t}$ on z_{jt-1} is given by

$$\hat{E}(z_{k(j)t}|z_{jt-1}) = S_j(\beta)z_{jt-1}, \tag{4}$$

where

$$S_j(\beta) = e_{k(j)}T(\beta)[M_{z_j}(\beta)^{-1}M_{z_j,z}(\beta)]', \qquad \text{for } j = a, b. \tag{5}$$

The operators $S_j(\beta)$ map the perceptions $\beta = (\beta_a, \beta_b)$ into the projection coefficients (in the linear least-squares sense), $S_a(\beta)$, $S_b(\beta)$. Let us define $S(\beta) = [S_a(\beta), S_b(\beta)]$.

We now advance the following.

DEFINITION. A rational expectations equilibrium with asymmetric private information occurs when perceptions in (1) are given by a matrix $\beta = (\beta_a, \beta_b)$ that satisfies

$$\beta_f \equiv [\beta_{af}, \beta_{bf}] = [S_a(\beta_f), S_b(\beta_f)] = S(\beta_f).$$

Thus, a rational expectations equilibrium is a fixed point of the mapping S. Notice that this concept of a rational expectations equilibrium is relative to the fixed information sets z_{at-1} and z_{bt-1} specified by the model-builder.

We now describe the model of learning. The learning scheme is a recursive version of least squares, modified to permit agents to disregard observations that threaten to drive the estimates outside of some pre-specified sets; $D_{1j}, j = a, b$. These pre-specified sets play an important role in governing the global convergence of the least-squares estimators. For $j = a, b$, we let $\{\alpha_{jt}\}$ be a positive, non-decreasing sequence with $\lim_{t\to\infty}\alpha_{jt} = 1$. Beliefs of agents of type $j(= a, b)$ evolve according to the following scheme. Define $\bar{\beta}_{jt}$ and $\bar{R}_{jt}$ by

$$\bar{\beta}'_{jt} = \beta'_{jt-1} + (\alpha_{jt-1}/t)R_{jt-1}^{-1}\{z_{jt-2}[z_{k(j)t-1} - \beta'_{jt-1}z_{jt-2}]'\}$$

$$\bar{R}_{jt} = R_{jt-1} + (\alpha_{jt-1}/t)(z_{jt-1}z'_{jt-1} - R_{jt-1}/\alpha_{jt-1}). \tag{6a}$$

Agent j specifies two sets D_{2j} and $D_{1j}, j = a, b$. Let $D_{2j} \subset D_{1j} \subset \mathbb{R}^{n_{k(j)} \times (n_j)^3}, j = a, b$. The algorithm generating beliefs at t is then

$$(\beta_{jt}, R_{jt}) = \begin{cases} (\bar{\beta}_{jt}, \bar{R}_{jt}) & \text{if} \quad (\bar{\beta}_{jt}, \bar{R}_{jt}) \in D_{1j} \\ \text{some value in } D_{2j} & \text{if} \quad (\bar{\beta}_{jt}, \bar{R}_{jt}) \notin D_{1j}. \end{cases} \tag{6b}$$

Equations (6b) define a 'projection facility' whose function is to keep beliefs (β_{jt}, R_{jt}) within the set D_{1j}. Two distinct sets, D_{1j} and D_{2j}, are used in defining the projection facility in order properly to invoke some technical arguments made by Ljung (1977). In practice, we shall be free to choose D_{2j} to be a set contained within, but arbitrarily close to, D_{1j}. In the applications below, we shall always think of D_{2j} as being arbitrarily close to D_{1j}, and thus will focus our attention on specification of the sets D_{1j}.[5]

If $D_{2j} = D_{1j} = \mathbb{R}^{n_{k(j)} \times (n_j)^2}$, then the 'projection facility' on the second branch of (6b) is never invoked, and with suitable initial conditions, (6a, b) simply becomes a recursive version of weighted least squares:

$$\beta_{jt} = \left(\sum_{i=1}^{t-1} \alpha_{ji} z_{ji-1} z'_{jt-1} \right)^{-1} \left(\sum_{i=1}^{t-1} \alpha_{ji} z_{ji-1} z'_{k(j)i} \right).$$

In the special case that $\{\alpha_{jt}\} = \{1\}$, the above formula is just ordinary least squares. In cases in which a nontrivial projection facility is specified by choosing D_{1j} to be a proper subset of $\mathbb{R}^{n_{k(j)} \times (n_j)^3}$, it is natural to set 'some point in D_{2j}' in (6b) equal to $(\beta_{jt'}, R_{jt'})$, where t' is the last time that $(\beta_{jt'}, R_{jt'}) \in D_{2j}$. With D_{2j} set arbitrarily close to D_{1j}, (6a, b) then amounts to least squares adjusted sequentially to ignore observations that threaten to drive (β_{jt}, R_{jt}) outside of the set D_{1j}. When the sequence $\{\alpha_{jt}\}$ is chosen to be strictly increasing, it leads to adjusting the least-squares algorithm to weight more recent observations more heavily. (The condition that $\lim_{t \to \infty} \alpha_{jt} = 1$ restricts the eventual rate of forgetting in a way sufficient to permit convergence of β_{jt} within the system to be studied below.)

The sets D_{1j} and D_{2j} will play important roles in one part of the proposition to be stated below. One role of the sets D_{1j} and D_{2j} can be to force the learning algorithm to remain the set D_s defined above.

We assume that, when agents are learning according to (6a, b), the actual law of motion is determined by substituting $\beta_t = (\beta_{at}, \beta_{bt})$ from (6a, b) for β on the right-hand side of (2):

$$z_t = T(\beta_{t-1})z_{t-1} + V(\beta_{t-1})\epsilon_t. \tag{7}$$

The system that we want to study is (6a, b) and (7). Equation (7) indicates the sense in which agents' process of learning influences the

---

[5] Ljung and Soderstrom (1983) frequently proceed in this way, specifying a projection facility in terms of a single set.

actual law of motion of the system. Agents' learning behaviour evidently causes the z_t process to be non-stationary. This property of the z_t process implies that the recursive estimation scheme $(6a, b)$, which could be rationalized as being optimal only in a constant coefficient environment, is in general a suboptimal way of learning for this class of environments. Our model is thus an irrational model of learning, a point emphasized by Bray and Savin (1986) and Bray and Kreps (1987).

We want to study $(6a, b)$–(7), which is a complicated system of stochastic difference equations. We shall use the method of Ljung (1977), whose approach is to find an ordinary differential equation that is associated with $(6a, b)$–(7) in the sense that the limiting behaviour of $(6a, b)$–(7) is described by that differential equation. It turns out that associated with the system of stochastic difference equations $(6a, b)$ and (7) is the following ordinary differential equation:

$$\frac{d}{dt}\begin{bmatrix} \beta_a \\ \beta_b \\ R_a \\ R_b \end{bmatrix} = \begin{bmatrix} R_a^{-1} M_{z_a}(\beta)[S_a(\beta) - \beta_a]' \\ R_b^{-1} M_{z_b}(\beta)[S_b(\beta) - \beta_b]' \\ M_{z_a}(\beta) - R_a \\ M_{z_b}(\beta) - R_b \end{bmatrix}. \tag{8}$$

Defining $R = (R_a, R_b)$, we can represent (8) in the vector form:

$$\frac{d}{dt}\begin{pmatrix} \text{col}(\beta) \\ \text{col}(R) \end{pmatrix} = g(\beta, R),$$

where $\text{col}(\beta)$ is a vector obtained by stacking columns of β on top of each other, and $\text{col}(R)$ is a vector obtained by stacking columns of R on top of one another. In the interest of studying the linear approximations that govern the local behaviour of (8), we define

$$h(\beta, R) = \frac{d}{d(\text{col}\,\beta, \text{col}\,R)'}\, g(\beta, R).$$

Let $\{(\beta(t), R(t))\}_{t \in [0, \infty)}$ denote the trajectories of (8). We define the set D_A to be the domain of attraction of the fixed point (β_f, R_f) of (8), which we assume to be unique. That is, D_A consists of the set of $(\beta(0), R(0))$ such that, when $(\beta(0), R(0)) \in D_A$, (8) implies $\lim_{t \to \infty}(\beta(t), R(t)) = (\beta_f, R_f)$.

We use a set of six assumptions about system (6)–(7) which are described in the Appendix. Among these, the first five are in the nature of regularity conditions which are easy to verify and are typically satisfied for the kinds of applications we have encountered. Assumption (A1), which states that S has a unique fixed point, could be relaxed to permit multiple fixed point; then our propositions would transform in a readily seen way to statements about each fixed point of $S(\beta)$.

Assumption (A6) can be considerably more difficult to verify than (A1)–(A5), as we discuss below. This assumption is used in only the first part of our four-part proposition. For this first part, we also use the following additional assumption.

ASSUMPTION A7. For $j = a, b$, assume that D_{2j} is closed, that D_{1j} is open and bounded, and that $\beta \in D_s$ for all $(\beta_a, R_a, \beta_b, R_b) \in D_{1a} \times D_{1b}$. Assume that the trajectories of (8) with initial conditions $(\beta_a(0), R_a(0), \beta_b(0), R_b(0)) \in D_{2a} \times D_{2b}$ never leave a closed subset of $D_{1a} \times D_{1b}$.

We now state the following.

PROPOSITION 1. Assume that (β_t, R_t, z_t) are determined by (6a, b), (7). Assume that (A1), (A2), (A3), (A4), and (A5) are satisfied.

(i) Assume also that (A6) and (A7) are satisfied and that $D_{1a} \times D_{1b} \subset D_A$, where D_A is the domain of attraction of (β_f, R_f) in (8). Then

$$P[\beta_t \to \beta_f] = 1.$$

(ii) Let $\hat{\beta} \neq \beta_f$, and assume that $M_{z_j}(\hat{\beta})$ is positive definite for $j = a, b$. Then

$$P[\beta_t \to \hat{\beta}] = 0.$$

(iii) If $h(R_f, \beta_f)$ has one or more eigenvalues with strictly positive real part, then

$$P[\beta_t \to \beta_f] = 0.$$

(iv) $h(\beta_f, R_f)$ has $(n_a)^2 + (n_b)^2$ repeated eigenvalues of -1. The remaining eigenvalues are the same as those of the following derivative matrix:

$$(\partial/\partial\beta) \begin{bmatrix} \text{col}\,[S_a(\beta) - \beta_a] \\ \text{col}\,[S_b(\beta) - \beta_b] \end{bmatrix} \Bigg|_{\beta = \beta_f}$$

This concludes the proposition.

Statement (i) asserts that sufficient conditions for $\beta_t \to \beta_f$ almost surely as $t \to \infty$ are that the set $D_{1a} \times D_{1b}$ generated in the projection facility be contained in D_A, and that, at (and close to) the boundary of $D_{1a} \times D_{1b}$, the differential equation (8) has trajectories that point towards the interior of $D_{1a} \times D_{1b}$. The situation described in part (i) is depicted in Fig. 6.1. Ljung (1977), Ljung and Soderstrom (1983), and Marcet and Sargent (1989a) describe what can happen when some of the trajectories of (8) point outside $D_{1a} \times D_{1b}$ at the boundary of $D_{1a} \times D_{1b}$. Statement (ii) asserts that the only candidate (β, R) as limit-points of the learning scheme are rational expectations equilibria. Statement (iii) asserts sufficient conditions for non-convergence of the learning scheme. Statement (iv) implies that everything can be learned

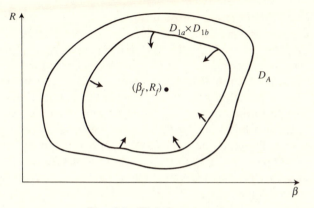

FIG. 6.1. Global convergence

The set D_A is the domain of attraction of the fixed point (β_f, R_f) of equation (8). The set $(D_{1a} \times D_{1b})$ determines the projection facility defined in (6b). When the trajectories of (8) point inward along the boundary of $D_{1a} \times D_{1b}$, and when $D_{1a} \times D_{1b}$ is inside D_A, then β_t converges almost surely to β_f.

about the local stability of the learning scheme by studying the differential equation,

$$\frac{d}{dt}\begin{pmatrix} \beta_a \\ \beta_b \end{pmatrix} = \begin{bmatrix} S_a(\beta) - \beta_a \\ S_b(\beta) - \beta_b \end{bmatrix} = S(\beta) - \beta. \tag{9}$$

Proposition 1 can be proved by retracing the steps used to prove propositions 1, 2, and 3 of Marcet and Sargent (1989a). Here we confine ourselves to relating an heuristic account of the mechanism underlying the proposition. This account is obtained simply by adapting the heuristic account of Ljung (1977) and Ljung and Soderstrom (1983) to our setting. In order to conserve notation, we describe only the special case of model (6a, b), (7) that emerges when we set $z_{at} = z_{bt}$, $z_{ct} = z_{dt}$, $\alpha_{at} = \alpha_{bt}$, $\beta_{at} = \beta_{bt}$, $R_{at} = R_{bt}$. This is an interesting special case, of which the model of Bray analysed in Section 3 and the model of hyperinflation analysed in Section 5 are further special cases. With the preceding special settings, the model is one in which there are homogeneous expectations but hidden state variables. For this special case, the trajectory of ordinary differential equation (8) is fully determined by the smaller ordinary differential equation,

$$\frac{d}{dt}\begin{pmatrix} \beta'_a \\ R_a \end{pmatrix} = \begin{matrix} R_a^{-1} M_{z_a}(\beta)[S_a(\beta) - \beta_a]' \\ M_{z_a}(\beta) - R_a, \end{matrix} \tag{10}$$

where it is understood that $\beta = (\beta_a, \beta_a)$. It will be obvious how, with some proliferation of notation, the following heuristic account would work for the model (6a, b), (7) without the restriction to homogeneous expectations.

Here is how the heuristic account of Ljung (1977) and Ljung and Soderstrom (1983) applies to our system. As t becomes large, the values of β_{at} and R_{at} determined by $(6a, b)$ and (7) change very little from $t - 1$ to t. This is partly a result of the regularity conditions imposed in assumption (A4), which require that $\alpha_{at-1}/t \to 0$ as $t \to \infty$. However, while (β_{at}, R_{at}) is changing very little, z_t given by (7) continues to vary quite a bit, owing to the imposition of the random shocks ϵ_t. Since β_{at} is not changing much while the z_t are, for large t the movement over long stretches of time of $(6a, b)$ and (7) is well approximated by the system that emerges when we replace α_{jt} by 1 and the terms in brackets on the right-hand side of $(6a)$ and (7) with their expected values, evaluated at the (nearly) fixed values $\beta_{at-1} = \tilde{\beta}_a$, $R_{at-1} = \tilde{R}_a$:

$$\beta'_{at} = \beta'_{at-1} + \frac{1}{t} \tilde{R}_a^{-1}[M_{z_a,z}(\tilde{\beta}_a)T(\tilde{\beta}_a)'e'_c - M_{z_a}(\tilde{\beta}_a)\tilde{\beta}'_a]$$

$$R_{at} = R_{at-1} + \frac{1}{t}[M_{z_a}(\tilde{\beta}_a) - \tilde{R}_a].$$

Using the definition of $S_a(\beta)$ in (3) and the approximation $\tilde{\beta}_a = \beta_{at-1}$ and $\tilde{R}_a = R_{at-1}$, the above equations become

$$\beta'_{at} = \beta'_{at-1} + \frac{1}{t} R_{at-1}^{-1} M_{z_a}(\beta_{at-1})[S(\beta_{at-1}) - \beta_{at-1}]'$$

$$R_{at} = R_{at-1} + \frac{1}{t}[M_{z_a}(\beta_{at-1}) - R_{at-1}]. \tag{11}$$

Equation (11) can be recognized as Euler's method for solving the ordinary differential equation (10) where the step size is $1/t$. Thus, for large t, the algorithms $(6a, b)$ and (7) provide a way of solving the differential equation (10). This suggests that the limiting behaviour of $(6a, b)$–(7) is governed by the trajectories of the associated differential equation (10). This concludes our transcription of the heuristic account of Ljung (1977) and Ljung and Soderstrom (1983).

The proof of the key parts of proposition 1 in effect involves verifying formally the approximations used in the various steps of the preceding heuristic argument. We refer the reader to Ljung (1977) and to Marcet and Sargent (1989a) for the proof. Partly as an aid to extending the proofs in Marcet and Sargent (1989a) to the present environment, we now briefly describe precisely the sense in which the model of Marcet and Sargent (1989a) is a special case of the present model.

We again work with the special case of the model that emerges when we set $a = b$, $c = d$, $e_c = e_d$, $\beta_a = \beta_b$, $R_a = R_b$. In the context of this special case, we use the following partitions of z_t:

$$z_t = \begin{bmatrix} z_{ct} \\ z_{ct}^c \end{bmatrix} = \begin{bmatrix} z_{at}^c \\ z_{at} \end{bmatrix},$$

where z_{ct}^c includes variables in z_t not in z_{ct}, and z_{at}^c includes variables in z_t not in z_{at}. Partitioning $T(\beta)$ conformably with the above partitions permits us to represent (2) in the form

$$\begin{bmatrix} z_{ct} \\ z_{ct}^c \end{bmatrix} = \begin{bmatrix} T_{11}(\beta) & T_{12}(\beta) \\ T_{21}(\beta) & T_{22}(\beta) \end{bmatrix} \begin{bmatrix} z_{at-1}^c \\ z_{at-1} \end{bmatrix} + V(\beta)\epsilon_t.$$

Using these partitions, it is possible to represent (5) as

$$S_a(\beta) = \begin{bmatrix} I_{n_c} & 0 \end{bmatrix} \begin{bmatrix} T_{11}(\beta) & T_{12}(\beta) \\ T_{21}(\beta) & T_{22}(\beta) \end{bmatrix} \begin{bmatrix} M_{z_a z_a}{}^c(\beta)' M_{z_a}(\beta)^{-1} \\ I_{n_a} \end{bmatrix}, (12)$$

where I_{n_j} is the $n_j \times n_j$ identity matrix. In (12), the matrix $M_{z_a z_a}{}^c(\beta)' M_{z_a}(\beta)^{-1} = \gamma'$, where $\hat{E} z_{at}^c | z_{at} = \gamma z_{at}$ is the linear least-squares projection of z_{at}^c on z_{at}. Representation (12) shows the way in which e_c, $T(\beta)$, and the regression coefficient γ of excluded on included variables interact to compose $S_a(\beta)$.

Marcet and Sargent (1989a) restricted themselves to analysing the further special case of the present model, which emerges when (12) can be written with

$$T_{11} \equiv 0, \tag{13}$$

so that the perceived law of motion $E^*(z_{ct}|z_{at-1})$ omits no variables from z_t which the actual law of motion would imply belonged in the regression of z_{ct} on z_t. In this special case, in which from agents' point of view there are no hidden state variables, (12) simplifies to

$$S_a(\beta) = T_{12}(\beta),$$

and the differential equations (8) and (9) simplify to those studied by Marcet and Sargent (with the notation $T_{12}(\beta)$ matching the notation $T(\beta)$ in Marcet and Sargent 1989a, and with $T_{11}(\beta)$ being 0, and $[T_{21}(\beta), T_{22}(\beta)] = A(\beta)$ in Marcet and Sargent 1989a).

Marcet and Sargent (1989a) describe a variety of models in the literature which satisfy the no-hidden-states assumption (13). The models described in subsequent sections of this paper all violate that assumption. It bears emphasizing that, when (13) is violated, the concept of a limited-information, rational expectations equilibrium used in this paper makes the equilibrium depend on the model-builder's specification of the information sets z_{at}, z_{bt}. In models with sufficiently rich dynamic structures, in specifying z_{at} and z_{bt} the model-builder will be inducing a concept of equilibrium which depends on his truncating lag distributions in specifying (1). For example, the equilibrium described in Section 5 and in Marcet and Sargent (1989b) are sensitive to such truncation. Truncations are unavoidable so long as one stays with a finite-dimensional z_t vector. Sargent (1989) suggests a modification of structures (1) and (2) which in effect permits agents to condition on an infinite number of past values of the variables in their information sets.

3. A Model of Bray

This section applies proposition 1 to the model of Margaret Bray (1982). Although there are differentially informed agents in Bray's model, the model fits into the framework of Section 2 with the special settings $\beta_a = \beta_b$, $z_{at} = z_{bt}$, $e_c = e_d$, $R_a = R_b$. We confirm a conjecture of Bray concerning the necessity of the stability condition that she discovered.

There are N_u uninformed traders and N_i informed traders. Let (r_t, s_t) be a sequence of independently and identically distributed random (2×1) vectors which obey a bivariate normal distribution.[6] Here r_t denotes the return on an asset, and s_t denotes the exogenous supply of the asset. Informed agents observe s_t at t, while uninformed agents only observe p_t, the price of the asset. Informed agents know all the moments of the model, while uninformed agents do not, and use a linear least-squares learning scheme to decide their demand. Each informed trader's demand is given by

$$\theta_i[E(r_t|s_t) - p_t], \qquad \theta_i > 0,$$

where $E(r_t|s_t)$ is the mathematical expectation of r_t conditional on s_t. Each uninformed agent's demand is given by

$$\theta_u[E_{t-1}^*(r_t|p_t) - p_t], \qquad \theta_u > 0,$$

where $E_{t-1}^*(r_t|p_t) = a_{t-1} + b_{t-1}p_t$, and (a_{t-1}, b_{t-1}) are obtained from a least-squares regression of r_s on p_s for $s = 1, \ldots, t-1$. The equilibrium price at t is determined by equating supply and demand for the asset:

$$N_i\theta_i[E(r_t|s_t) - p_t] + N_u\theta_u[a_{t-1} + b_{t-1}p_t - p_t] = s_t.$$

We map this model into the setting of Section 2. We define

$$z_t = \begin{bmatrix} r_t \\ r_{t-1} \\ r_{t-2} \\ s_t \\ p_{t-1} \\ 1 \end{bmatrix}; \qquad \epsilon_t = \begin{bmatrix} r_t - E(r_t) \\ s_t - E(s_t) \end{bmatrix}; \qquad \beta_t = (a_{t-1}, b_{t-1})$$

$$z_{ct} = r_{t-2}; \qquad z_{at} = \begin{bmatrix} 1 \\ p_{t-1} \end{bmatrix}; \qquad \beta = (a, b).$$

---

[6] In Bray's (1982) notation, we assume that the information set $I_t = s_t$. Expanding I_t to include additional variables would modify the analytics in the text in only trivial ways. The state vector z_t would simply have to be extended to include the additional components of I_t.

The actual law of motion of z_t is given by

$$
z_t = \begin{bmatrix} r_t \\ r_{t-1} \\ r_{t-2} \\ s_t \\ p_{t-1} \\ 1 \end{bmatrix} = \begin{bmatrix} 0, & 0, & 0, & 0, & 0, & Er_t \\ 1, & 0, & 0, & 0, & 0, & 0 \\ 0, & 1, & 0, & 0, & 0, & 0 \\ 0, & 0, & 0, & 0, & 0, & Es_t \\ 0, & 0, & 0, & T^{54}(\beta_t), & 0, & T^{56}(\beta_t) \\ 0, & 0, & 0, & 0, & 0, & 1 \end{bmatrix}
$$

$$
\times \begin{bmatrix} r_{t-1} \\ r_{t-2} \\ r_{t-3} \\ s_{t-1} \\ p_{t-2} \\ 1 \end{bmatrix} + V(\beta_t)\epsilon_t, \tag{14}
$$

where, letting $\rho = \mathrm{cov}\,(r_t, s_t)/\mathrm{var}\,(s_t)$,

$$
T^{54}(\beta) = \frac{N_i\theta_i\rho - 1}{N_u\theta_u(1 - b) + N_i\theta_i}
$$

$$
T^{56}(\beta) = \frac{N_u\theta_u a + N_i\theta_i[E(r_t) - E(s_t)\rho]}{N_u\theta_u(1 - b) + N_i\theta_i},
$$

where $V(\cdot)$ is a constant function such that $V^{11}(\cdot) \equiv V^{42}(\cdot) \equiv 1$ and the rest of the elements of V are equal to 0. Note that the operator $T(\beta)$ is not well defined at points (a, b) for which $b = 1 + (N_i\theta_i)/(N_u\theta_u)$. Thus, for this model, the set D_s defined in Section 2 excludes such points. To invoke part (i) of our proposition, a nontrivial projection facility (6b) must be used.

Following Bray, define the random variable $x_t = [N_i\theta_i E(r_t|s_t) - s_t]$. Then calculations on (14) show that[7]

$$
S(a, b) = [E(r_t) - kE(x_t)/(N_u\theta_u) - ka, \; k(N_i\theta_i + N_u\theta_u)/N_u\theta_u - kb], \tag{15}
$$

where, as in Bray, $k = N_u\theta_u/[N_i\theta_i - 1/\rho]$.

---

[7] The mapping S can be derived from formula (5). Alternatively, it can be found directly by computing the linear projection of z_{ct} on z_{at-1} for fixed beliefs β, and letting $S(\beta)$ be the coefficients multiplying z_{at-1} in this projection. For Bray's model this method is probably the most convenient: fix $\beta = (a, b)$; then, using $p_t = T^{56}(\beta) + T^{54}(\beta)s_t$, we have

$$
\begin{aligned}
E(r_t|p_t) &= E(r_t) - \rho\,E(s_t) - \rho\,T^{56}(\beta)/T^{54}(\beta) + \rho\,p_t/T^{54}(\beta) \\
&= \{E(r_t) - k[N_i\theta_i E(r_t) - E(s_t)]/N_u\theta_u - k\,a\} \\
&\quad + \{k(N_i\theta_i + N_u\theta_u)(1 - b)/N_u\theta_u\}pt \\
&= S_1(\beta) + S_2(\beta)p_t.
\end{aligned}
$$

It is readily verified that the fixed point $(a^*, b^*) = S(a^*, b^*)$ is given by Bray's formulas (3.10), (3.11). Differentiating the right-hand side of (15) and evaluating at (a^*, b^*) gives

$$\left.\frac{\partial[S(a, b) - (a, b)]}{\partial(a, b)}\right|_{\substack{a=a^* \\ b=b^*}} = \begin{bmatrix} -k - 1, & 0 \\ 0, & -k - 1 \end{bmatrix}, \qquad (16)$$

which has a repeated eigenvalue of $(-k - 1)$. Using parts (i), (iii), and (iv) of proposition 1, we can establish that the learning model is locally stable if and only if $k > -1$.[8] Whether or not this inequality is satisfied will depend on the values of the parameters of the model. Using (15), when $Es_t = Er_t = 0$, the unstable region of the parameter space can be deduced to be the shaded region depicted in Fig. 6.2, namely:

- If $1/\rho < 0$, then the stability region includes all $(N_i\theta_i, N_u\theta_u) \in R_+^2$.
- If $1/\rho > 0$, then the stability region includes all $(N_i\theta_i, N_u\theta_u)$ satisfying $0 < N_i\theta_i < 1/\rho$, and $N_u\theta_u + N_i\theta_i > 1/\rho$.

We note that, given any pair (θ_i, θ_u), any $1/\rho > 0$, and any positive ratio N_i/N_u of informed to uninformed agents, there exists an absolute number of traders $N_u + N_i$ sufficiently small to guarantee local stability of the learning mechanism. Under the same conditions, there also exists a number of traders sufficiently large to guarantee local stability.

Notice that all of our results are local, being based on the parts of proposition 1 that depend on an analysis of the 'small' ordinary differential equation (9). Parts (i) and (iv) of the proposition assure us

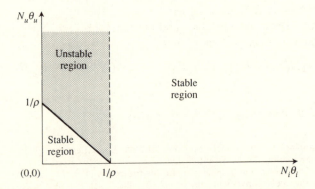

$N_u\theta_u$

Unstable region

Stable region

$1/\rho$

Stable region

(0,0) $1/\rho$ $N_i\theta_i$

FIG. 6.2. Stability region of parameter space for Bray's model

---

[8] For Bray's model, as well as the models of Sections 4 and 5, it is straightforward to verify that assumptions (A1)–(A5) are satisfied. Assumption (A6) is satisfied since, if D_1 is bounded, $|p_t| < K_1 + K_2|s_t|$ for some constants K_1, K_2. Normality of s_t then implies (A6).

that there exists some nontrivial choice of set D_{1a} under which almost sure convergence obtains, but are silent about how large that set can be. To get a stronger result, the 'larger' ordinary differential equation (8) must be analysed, and in particular its trajectories must be verified to point towards the interior of D_{1a} at points on the boundary of D_{1a}. For a model as complicated as Bray's, in which z_{at} involves endogenous variables and the $S(\beta)$ operator involves a nontrivial operator $M_{z_a}(\beta)^{-1} M_{z_a z_c}(\beta)'$, it is difficult to carry out this analysis analytically. Numerical techniques, like those illustrated for Townsend's model by Sargent (1991), could be used.

Note that assertion (iii) of proposition 1 confirms the conjecture about conditions for non-convergence made by Bray (1982).

4. Convergence in a Version of Frydman's Model

We briefly study least squares learning in a variant of a model due to Roman Frydman (1982). We alter the learning scheme relative to the one used by Frydman, but retain the economic structure contributed by him. The resulting model provides a useful technical contrast to Bray's, it being much easier to obtain global convergence results because agents are regressing on exogenous variables.

There are n competitive firms indexed by $i = 1, \ldots, n$. Demand for the firms' output is given by

$$p_t = a - b \sum_{i=1}^{n} y_{it} + u_t, \qquad a, b > 0,$$

where y_{it} is output of the ith firm, and u_t is an independently and identically distributed disturbance distributed $N(0, \sigma_u^2)$. Firm i's cost function at t is given by

$$C(y_{it}) = (1/2s)(y_{it})^2 + k_{it}y_{it} + C_f,$$

where C_f and s are positive constants and k_{it} is a random variable given by

$$k_{it} = \alpha_t + \epsilon_{it}, \qquad \text{for all } i, t,$$

where α and ϵ_i are independently and identically distributed with $\alpha_t \sim N(0, \sigma_\alpha^2)$ and $\epsilon_{it} \sim N(0, \sigma_\epsilon^2)$.

Firm i observes k_{it} at time t, but not p_t at t. The firm observes a history of $\{p_s, k_{is}\}$ for $s = 0, \ldots, t - 1$, and forms an expectation of p_t at time t according to

$$E^*(p_t | k_{it}) = \beta_{1t}^i + \beta_{2t}^i k_{it}, \qquad i = 1, \ldots, n$$

where $(\beta_{1t}^i, \beta_{2t}^i)$ are least-squares regression coefficients based on

$\{p_s, k_{is}\}$, $s = 0, \ldots, t - 1$. Firm i's output at t is given by $s[E^*(p_t|k_{it}) - k_{it}]$. The equilibrium price at t is determined from

$$p_t = a - bs \sum_{i=1}^{n} [E^*(p_t|k_{it}) - k_{it}] + u_t.$$

We show how the system behaves for the case $n = 2$. To map this model into the setup of Section 2, define

$$z_t = \begin{bmatrix} k_{1t} \\ k_{2t} \\ p_{t-1} \\ 1 \end{bmatrix}, \qquad \epsilon_t = \begin{bmatrix} \epsilon_{1t} \\ \epsilon_{2t} \\ \alpha_t \\ u_{t-1} \end{bmatrix}$$

$$z_{ct} = z_{dt} = p_{t-1}; \qquad z_{at} = k_{1t}; \qquad z_{bt} = k_{2t}.$$

The transition law corresponding to (2) is readily verified to be

$$z_t = \begin{bmatrix} 0, & 0, & 0, & 0 \\ 0, & 0, & 0, & 0 \\ T_{31}(\beta), & T_{32}(\beta), & 0, & T_{34}(\beta) \\ 0, & 0, & 0, & 1 \end{bmatrix} z_{t-1} + V(\beta)\epsilon_t,$$

where $V(\cdot)$ is a constant function, with zeroes everywhere except for elements V_{11}, V_{13}, V_{22}, V_{23}, V_{34}, which are unity; and where

$$T_{31}(\beta) = -bs(\beta_2^1 - 1)$$

$$T_{32}(\beta) = -bs(\beta_2^2 - 1)$$

$$T_{34}(\beta) = (a - bs)(\beta_1^1 + \beta_1^2).$$

It follows that

$$\begin{bmatrix} S_a(\beta) \\ S_b(\beta) \end{bmatrix} = \begin{bmatrix} a - bs(\beta_1^1 + \beta_1^2), & -bs[\beta_2^1 - 1 + (\beta_2^2 - 1)\gamma] \\ a - bs(\beta_1^1 + \beta_1^2), & -bs[(\beta_2^1 - 1)\gamma + \beta_2^2 - 1] \end{bmatrix},$$

where $\gamma = \sigma_\alpha^2/(\sigma_\alpha^2 + \sigma_\epsilon^2)$. Notice that $0 < \gamma < 1$. The rational expectations equilibrium is given by

$$\beta_{1f}^1 = \beta_{1f}^2 = a/(1 + 2bs)$$

$$\beta_{2f}^1 = \beta_{2f}^2 = bs(1 + \gamma)/[1 + bs(1 + \gamma)].$$

Evaluating the derivative of

$$\mathrm{col}\begin{bmatrix} S_a(\beta) - \beta_a \\ S_b(\beta) - \beta_b \end{bmatrix}$$

with respect to β at $\beta = \beta_f$, we obtain

$$\begin{bmatrix} -(bs + 1), & 0, & -bs, & 0 \\ 0, & -(bs + 1), & 0, & -bs\gamma \\ -bs, & 0, & -(bs + 1), & 0 \\ 0, & -bs\gamma, & 0, & -(bs + 1) \end{bmatrix}.$$

The eigenvalues of this matrix are[9]

$$[-(1 + 2bs), -1, -bs(1 + \gamma) - 1, -bs(1 - \gamma) -1].$$

Since $b > 0$, the eigenvalues are all less than 0, and, by proposition 1(iv), the associated differential equation (9) is locally stable. Furthermore, a version of corollary 2 of Marcet and Sargent (1989a) implies that proposition 1(i) applies with sets D_{1a}, D_{1b} chosen as

$$D_{1a} = \{(\beta_a, R_a)|\|\beta_a - \beta_{af}| < K_a\}$$
$$D_{1b} = \{(\beta_b, R_b)|\|\beta_b - \beta_{bf}| < K_b\},$$

for arbitrarily large positive constants K_a and K_b. This means that, for arbitrarily large sets D_{1a} and D_{1b} in the projection facilities (6b), proposition 1(i) holds. Thus, we get a strong global convergence result for this model, in contrast to Bray's model, in which a much more difficult analysis would have to be used to achieve such a result. The reason things are simpler in the current model depends on the fact that, since k_{jt} is exogenous for each j, $M_{z_j}(\beta)$ is independent of β for $j = a, b$, making S linear and corollary 2 of Marcet and Sargent (1989a) applicable.

It is evident how the analysis of this section could be extended to handle larger values of n.

5. Cagan's Hyperinflation Model and 'Bubbles'

This section applies proposition 1 to study a version of Cagan's hyperinflation model with a restricted information set. We analyse the ordinary differential equation (9) and display a set D_{1a} for which proposition 1(i) applies. We also describe some of the insights that (9) seems to yield about this model even for (β, R) pairs lying outside the set D_s defined in Section 2.

Consider the model

$$y_t = \lambda E^*(y_{t+1}|y_t) + x_t + v_t$$

$$x_t = \rho x_{t-1} + u_t, \tag{17}$$

where $|\rho|, |\lambda| < 1$; $Eu_t = Ev_t = Eu_s v_t = 0$ for all t, s, $Eu_t^2 = \sigma_u^2$, $Ev_t^2 =$

---

[9] The matrix of eigenvectors is

$$\begin{bmatrix} 1, & -1, & 0, & 0 \\ 0, & 0, & 1, & -1 \\ 1, & 1, & 0, & 0 \\ 0, & 0, & 1, & 1 \end{bmatrix}.$$

$\sigma_v^2 > 0$. The processes u_t and v_t are assumed serially uncorrelated.[10] Agents are restricted to forming expectations about future y on the basis of one lagged value of y. We study a learning version of the model in which

$$E^*(y_{t+1}|y_t) = \beta_t y_t, \tag{18}$$

where β_t is the least-squares estimator of the regression of y_s on y_{s-1} based on data for dates $s = 1, \ldots, t - 1$.

This model falls within the setting of Section 2, with $\beta_a = \beta_b$, $R_a = R_b$, $z_{at} = z_{bt} = z_{ct} = z_{dt}$. Define

$$z_t = \begin{bmatrix} y_t \\ x_t \end{bmatrix}; \qquad z_{at} = z_{bt} = y_t; \qquad \epsilon_t = \begin{bmatrix} u_t \\ v_t \end{bmatrix}.$$

The model can be represented by

$$\begin{bmatrix} y_t \\ x_t \end{bmatrix} = \begin{bmatrix} 0, & \rho/(1 - \lambda\beta_t) \\ 0, & \rho \end{bmatrix} \begin{bmatrix} y_{t-1} \\ x_{t-1} \end{bmatrix}$$

$$+ \begin{bmatrix} 1/(1 - \lambda\beta_t), & 1/(1 - \lambda\beta_t) \\ 1, & 0 \end{bmatrix} \begin{bmatrix} u_t \\ v_t \end{bmatrix}. \tag{19}$$

It can be verified from (19) that

$$M_{z_a,z}(\beta) = E \begin{bmatrix} y_t \\ x_t \end{bmatrix} y_t = \begin{bmatrix} \dfrac{\sigma_x^2 + \sigma_v^2}{(1 - \lambda\beta)^2} \\ \dfrac{\sigma_x^2}{1 - \lambda\beta} \end{bmatrix}$$

$$M_{z_a}(\beta) = E(y_t)^2 = \dfrac{\sigma_x^2 + \sigma_v^2}{(1 - \lambda\beta)^2}, \tag{20}$$

where $\sigma_x^2 = \sigma_u^2/(1 - \rho^2)$. Using the definition of $T(\beta)$ associated with (19) and formulas (20), we have that

$$S(\beta) = \rho\sigma_x^2/(\sigma_x^2 + \sigma_v^2).$$

A stationary rational expectations equilibrium is determined by

$$\beta_f = \frac{\rho\sigma_x^2}{\sigma_x^2 + \sigma_v^2} \quad \text{and} \quad R_f = \frac{\sigma_x^2 + \sigma_v^2}{(1 - \lambda\beta_f)^2} \tag{21}$$

Corresponding to (8), we have the associated differential equation

---

[10] This model is a version of one used by Shiller (1981) and LeRoy and Porter (1982), where y_t is interpreted as the price of a stock and x_t is its dividend. It is also Sargent and Wallace's (1973) version of Cagan's (1956) model of hyperinflation, with y_t representing the log of the price level and x_t the log of the money supply.

$$\left(\frac{d}{dt}\right)\begin{bmatrix} \beta \\ R \end{bmatrix} = \begin{bmatrix} R^{-1}[K_1 - \beta K_2]/(1 - \lambda\beta)^2 \\ K_2/(1 - \lambda\beta)^2 - R \end{bmatrix}, \tag{22}$$

where $K_1 = \rho\sigma_x^2$ and $K_2 = \sigma_x^2 + \sigma_v^2$. Corresponding to (9), we have

$$\left(\frac{d}{dt}\right)\beta = \frac{\rho\sigma_x^2}{\sigma_v^2 + \sigma_x^2} - \beta. \tag{23}$$

Examination of 23 reveals that it is locally stable about the fixed point β_f. Therefore, by proposition 1(iv), (22) is also locally stable about (β_f, R_f). More can be inferred about (22) from Fig. 6.3, which displays the phase diagram in the (β, R) plane, and Fig. 6.4, which displays some trajectories of (22). Note the vertical line at λ^{-1}, a value of β at which there is a singularity of the right-hand side of (22). Trajectories originating on the right-hand side of this vertical line can never cross

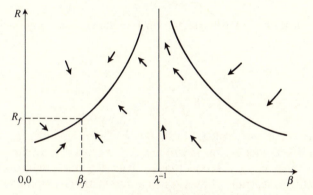

FIG. 6.3. Phase diagram of the ordinary differential equation associated with the hyperinflation model

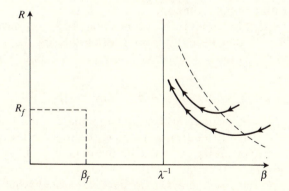

FIG. 6.4. Some trajectories of the ordinary differential equation associated with the hyperinflation model that start to the right of the singularity at λ^{-1}

this line, and so cannot converge to (β_f, R_f). The phase diagram informs us that trajectories starting from $\beta(0) > \lambda^{-1}$ and $R(0) > 0$ have $\lim_{t\to\infty}(\beta t), R(t)) = (\lambda^{-1}, +\infty)$.

The singularity on the right-hand side of (22) has an interpretation in terms of 'bubbles'. The solutions of the model (17) under rational expectations and no learning, where agents' information set is extended to include x_t at t, are given by

$$y_t = \frac{x_t}{1 - \lambda\rho} + c_t\lambda^{-t} + v_t,$$

where c_t is any martingale. The term $c_t\lambda^{-t}$ is called a 'bubble'. Note that one martingale is the process $c_t = c^{-t}x_t$ for any constant c. Thus, one rational expectations equilibrium with a bubble is given by

$$y_t = \frac{x_t}{1 - \lambda\rho} + c(\rho\lambda)^{-t}x_t + v_t,$$

for any constant $c \neq 0$. It can be verified that, along any such solution with $c \neq 0$,

$$\lim_{t\to\infty} \hat{E}(y_{t+1}|y_t) = \lambda^{-1}y_t$$

$$\lim_{t\to\infty} \frac{1}{t} \sum_{s=0}^{t} y_s^2 = +\infty.$$

Thus, the singularity of (22) at $\beta = \lambda^{-1}$ corresponds to a 'bubble' solution of the model. In specifying that agents form expectations by regressing y_{t+1} on y_t, it seems that we have left open the possibility that the model with learning converges to a non-stationary 'bubble'. We shall discuss this possibility below, and shall argue informally that the learning system is unlikely to converge to a bubble solution, even though the differential equation (22) does converge to values of (β, R) associated with a bubble solution.

To satisfy the hypotheses of proposition 1(i), we have to use a projection facility that keeps β_t from crossing the singular value λ^{-1}. A set that works is formed by selecting two real numbers $\bar{\epsilon} > 0$, $K > 0$ and defining

$$D_{1a} = \{(\beta, R)|\beta < \lambda^{-1} - \bar{\epsilon} \quad \text{and} \quad |\beta - \beta_f| < K\}.$$

For such a D_{1a} set, with K arbitrarily large and $\bar{\epsilon} > 0$ arbitrarily small, assumption (A7) is satisfied; in particular, the trajectories of (22) point towards the interior of D_{1a} at points on the boundary of D_{1a}. With such a D_{1a}, proposition 1(i) applies for this model.

With the preceding statement, we have exhausted what we can say about global convergence of our model on the basis of proposition 1. However, this is not the end of the matter because proposition 1(i) states sufficient, but not necessary, conditions for global convergence of the learning scheme. What would occur if there is no projection facility (i.e. if $D_{1a} = \mathbb{R}^2$), so that β can exceed λ^{-1}? We can gain some additional understanding about the behaviour of the system when β exceeds λ^{-1} by studying for large t how closely the recursive algorithm (6) keeps to the trajectories of (22). (Notice that the heuristic argument of Ljung cited above applies in the region for which $\beta_t > \lambda^{-1}$, breaking down only at the point $\beta = \lambda^{-1}$.) We have simulated (17)–(18) many times to address this issue, starting the simulations with $\beta > \lambda^{-1}$ and using normally distributed and orthogonal pseudo-random numbers for v_t and u_t in (17)–(18). We started the simulations at a large value for t, to make system (17)–(18) mimic (22) well from the beginning of our simulations. We used no projection facility. From every one of these simulations, the following pattern emerged. So long as β_t stayed far enough to the right of the singularity of (22) at λ^{-1}, the simulations traced out paths that mimicked the trajectories of (22). However, for β_t close to λ^{-1}, the stochastic version of 'Euler's method' that (17)–(18) constitutes turns out to be a bad one for solving differential equation (22). In particular, for every simulation that we generated, (β_t, R_t) stayed close to trajectories of (22) until β_t approached λ^{-1} so closely that eventually β_t dropped below λ^{-1}. After this event occurred, (β_t, R_t) in each case seemed to follow trajectories of (22) for $\beta < \lambda^{-1}$, with (β_t, R_t) approaching the fixed point (β_f, R_f).

Figure 6.5 reports one representative simulation in which we set initial conditions in order to start the system to the right of the singularity at $\beta = \lambda^{-1}$. We set $\lambda = 0.5$, $\rho = 0.5$ $Eu_t^2 = Ev_t^2 = 1$, $\beta_{t_0} = 2.4$ and $R_{t_0} = 58.3333$. This choice of (β_{t_0}, R_{t_0}) sets $\beta_{t_0} > \lambda^{-1}$ and sets R at a value satisfying $(d/dt)R = 0$ in (22). We set the initial time t_0 equal to 10,000 in order to make the differential equation system (22) well approximate the stochastic system (17)–(18) that we are simulating. (Recall the role that a large value of t plays in the heuristic argument reported in Section 2.) The results of a simulation of 20,000 periods are reported in Fig. 10.4. Except for very close to the singularity at λ^{-1} (= 2), the behaviour of the simulated system (17)–(18) clings close to the trajectories of (22).

Here is our interpretation of these simulations. With no operative projection facility, the learning mechanism has a recursive representation of the form

$$\theta_{t+1} = \theta_t + (1/t)Q(z_t, \theta_t), \tag{24}$$

where $\theta_t = (\beta_t, R_t)$. This is a stochastic version of Euler's method for solving the differential equation $(d/dt)\theta = f(\theta) \equiv E\, Q(z_t, \theta)$, namely,

$$\bar{\theta}_{t+1} = \bar{\theta}_t + (1/t)f(\bar{\theta}_t). \tag{25}$$

Now given the behaviour of the function f associated with (22) in a neighbourhood of $\beta = \lambda^{-1}$, the linear nature of the approximation involved in using (24) to mimic $(d/dt)\theta = f(\theta)$ is disastrous, because it involves taking a step of positive length along a straight line that crosses λ^{-1} (see Fig. 6.5). The small variation arising from randomness in $Q(z_t, \theta_t)$ makes it even more likely that eventually (β_t, R_t) will jump over the vertical line at λ^{-1} into the region $(-\infty, \lambda^{-1})$, which is in the domain of attraction of (β_f, R_f). Once inside this region, all of the simulations we computed again stuck close to the trajectories of (22).

We also computed trajectories of the ordinary differential equation (22) using both Euler's method and the Runge–Kutta method. In all cases, when the trajectory was started out to the right of λ^{-1}, the trajectory crossed λ^{-1} and converged to (β_f, R_f). This illustrates how the inability of the learning algorithm to converge to a bubble non-stationary equilibrium is associated with the numerical properties of methods like Euler's for recovering the non-stationary solutions of (22).

In summary, even though trajectories of the associated differential equation cannot cross the vertical line through λ^{-1}, the random difference equation (6) for (β_t, R_t) *can* cross λ^{-1} from above, and always did

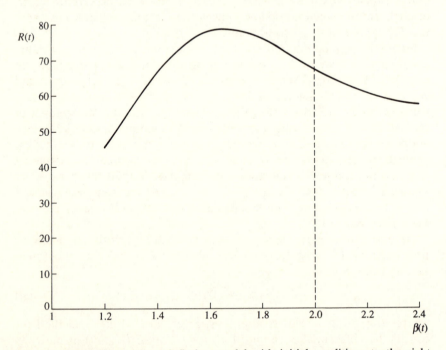

FIG. 6.5. Simulation of hyperinflation model with initial conditions to the right of the singularity at $\lambda^{-1} = 2$ (20,000 observations)

so in our simulations. Our analysis fails to prove that (β_t, R_t) from (17)–(18) cannot converge to the bubble solution $(\lambda^{-1}, +\infty)$, but it does indicate the existence of forces impeding convergence to such a solution.[11,12]

6. Conclusions

This paper has described the limiting behaviour of a class of self-referential systems in which differentially and imperfectly informed agents affect the motion of the system through their learning by least squares. We have described the senses in which the limiting behaviour of the system is governed by a particular ordinary differential equation. We have displayed some examples of rational expectations equilibria in which the learning schemes converge to a rational expectations equilibrium (Bray's model for some parameter settings, Frydman's model, and the hyperinflation model). We have also encountered cases in which the learning scheme does not produce convergences to a rational expectations equilibrium (Bray's model for some parameter settings) and some rational expectations equlibria from which the learning scheme is repelled (the bubbles equilibria of the hyperinflation model). These results all obtain in environments that satisfy Margaret Bray's theorem that, if the learning scheme converges, it must converge to a rational expectations equilibrium.

A remarkable feature of these results is how often a least-squares learning scheme performs well in eventually settling down to a rational expectations equilibrium. In fact, either the least-squares learning scheme or the ordinary differential equation associated with it can suggest effective algorithms for *computing* a rational expectations equilibrium for applied work.

When we encounter the strong sort of convergence to a rational expectations equilibrium embodied in much of the literature we have surveyed, one reaction might be that we analysts have chosen to make the learners 'too smart', and that the convergence results are the consequence of our choice. After all, although sequential application of linear least squares to vector autoregression is *not* rational for these

---

[11] The failure of our simulations to converge to $\beta = \lambda^{-1}$ is related to the numerical problems that arise in solving systems of Euler equations or Hamiltonian equations 'forward' in time on a computer. In these settings, once one gets close to the optimum, very small rounding errors propel the system away from the optimum solution.

[12] The presence of the random variable z_t in (25) means that in our system there can be a positive probability that β_t jumps back above λ^{-1} from below. For example, with normally distributed (u_t, v_t) in (17), even though remote, such an event has positive probability. This possibility would complicate the task of proving the conjecture that $P[\beta_t \to \lambda^{-1}] = 0$, which the behaviour of our simulations might suggest.

environments (again, see Bray and Kreps 1987), it is still a pretty sophisticated method. Further, in the setups that appear in this literature, the agents are typically supposed to be quite smart about all aspects of their decision making *except* their forecasting decisions. For example, agents typically are assumed to use the correct intertemporal marginal conditions. In effect, agents are supposed to be using state-of-the-art 'adaptive control' techniques (see e.g. Goodwin and Sin 1983).

The next frontier in the study of learning in self-referential systems is to study the consequences of withdrawing from agents some of the knowledge that has been attributed to them in the least-squares learning literature. The literature on genetic algorithms in artificial intelligence is a good source of ideas on how to proceed (see e.g. Holland 1975).

Appendix

We state six assumptions that we make about system $(6a, b)$–(7).

ASSUMPTION A1. The operator S has a unique fixed point $\beta_f = S(\beta_f)$ which satisfies $\beta_f \in D_s$.

ASSUMPTION A2. For $\beta \in D_s$, T is twice differentiable and V has one derivative.

ASSUMPTION A3. The covariance matrices $M_{z_j} (\beta_f)$ are non-singular for $j = a, b$.

ASSUMPTION A4. For $j = a, b$ and for all t, $\alpha_{jt} > 0$; α_{jt} is increasing in t; $\alpha_{jt} \to 1$ as $t \to \infty$; and

$$\limsup_{t \to \infty} t |\alpha_{jt} - \alpha_{jt-1}| = K_j < \infty, \qquad j = a, b.$$

ASSUMPTION A5. The vector ϵ_t consists of m stationary random variables; ϵ_t is serially independent. Further, $E|\epsilon_{it}|^p < \infty$ for all $p > 1$, all $i = 1, \ldots, m$.

ASSUMPTION A6. There exists a subset Ω_0 of the sample space with $P(\Omega_0) = 1$, four random variables $C_a(\omega)$, $C_b(\omega)$, $G_a(\omega)$, $G_b(\omega)$, and a subsequence $\{t_h(\omega)\}$ for which

$$|z_{jt_h}(\omega)| < C_j(\omega) \qquad j = a, b$$

$$|R_{jt_h}(\omega)| < G_j(\omega) \qquad j = a, b$$

for all $\omega \in \Omega_0$ and all $h = 1, 2, \ldots$.

References

BRAY, MARGARET (1982). 'Learning, Estimation, and the Stability of Rational Expectations'. *Journal of Economic Theory*, 26: 318–39.

—— (1983). 'Convergence to Rational Expectations Equilibrium'. In R. Frydman and E. S. Phelps (eds.), *Individual Forecasts and Aggregate Outcomes*. Cambridge University Press.

—— and KREPS, DAVID M. (1987). 'Rational Learning and Rational Expectations'. In George Feiwel (ed.), *Arrow and the Ascent of Modern Economic Theory*. New York University Press, pp. 597–625.

—— and SAVIN, N. E. (1986). 'Rational Expectations Equilibria, Learning and Model Specification'. *Econometrica*, 54: 1129–60.

CAGAN, P. (1956). 'The Monetary Dynamics of Hyperinflation'. In M. Friedman (ed.), *Studies in the Quantity Theory of Money*. University of Chicago Press.

DeCANIO, STEPHEN J. (1979). 'Rational Expectations and Learning from Experience'. *Quarterly Journal of Economics*, 93: 47–57.

EVANS, GEORGE (1983). 'The Stability of Rational Expectations in Macroeconomic Models'. In R. Frydman and E. S. Phelps (eds.), *Individual Forecasting and Aggregate Outcomes*. Cambridge University Press.

—— (1985). 'Expectational Stability and the Multiple Equilibria Problem in Linear Rational Expectations Models'. *Quarterly Journal of Economics*, 100: 1217–34.

FOURGEAUD, C., GOURIEROUX, C., and PRADEL, J. (1986). 'Learning Procedure and Convergence to Rationality'. *Econometrica*, 54: 845–68.

FRYDMAN, R. (1982). 'Towards an Understanding of Market Processes'. *American Economic Review*, 72: 652–68.

GOODWIN, G. C., and SIN, K. S. (1983). *Adaptive Filtering Prediction and Control*. Englewood Cliffs, NJ: Prentice-Hall.

HOLLAND, J. H. (1975). *Adaptation in Natural and Artificial Systems*. Ann Arbor: University of Michigan Press.

KUSHNER, H. J., and CLARK, D. S. (1978). *Stochastic Approximation Methods for Constrained and Unconstrained Systems*. New York: Springer-Verlag.

LeROY, S., and PORTER, R. (1982). 'The Present Value Relation: Tests Based on Implied Variance Bounds'. *Econometrica*, 49: 555–74.

LJUNG, L. (1977). 'Analysis of Recursive Stochastic Algorithms'. *IEEE Transactions of Automatic Control*, AC-22: 551–7.

—— and SODERSTROM, T. (1983). *Theory and Practice of Recursive Identification*. Cambridge, Mass.: MIT Press.

MARCET, ALBERT, and SARGENT, THOMAS J. (1988). 'The Fate of Systems with Adaptive Expectations'. *American Economic Review*, Papers and Proceedings, 78: 168–72.

—— —— (1989a). 'Convergence of Least Squares Learning Mechanisms in Self Referential Linear Stochastic Models'. *Journal of Economic Theory*, 48: 337–68.

—— —— (1989b). 'Convergence of Least Squares Learning in Environments with Hidden State Variables and Private Information'. *Journal of Political Economy*, 97: 1306–22.

—— —— (1989c). 'Least Squares Learning and the Dynamics of Hyperinflation'. In William Barnett, John Geweke, and Karl Shell (eds.), *Chaos, Complexity, and Sunspots*. Cambridge University Press.

MARGARITIS, DIMITRIS (1985). 'Strong Convergence of Least Squares Learning to Rational Expectations'. Working Paper, Univeristy of British Columbia.

ROBBINS, J., and MONRO, S. (1951). 'A Stochastic Approximation Method'. *Annals of Mathematical Statistics*, 22: 400–7.

SARGENT, T. J. (1979). *Macroeconomic Theory*. New York: Academic Press.

——(1991). 'Equilibrium with Signal Extraction from Endogenous Variables'. *Journal of Economic Dynamics and Control*, 15: 245–74.

——and WALLACE, N. (1973). 'Rational Expectations and the Dynamics of Hyperinflation'. *International Economic Review*, 14: 59–82.

SHILLER, R. (1981). 'Do Stock Prices Move Too Much to be Justified by Subsequent Dividends?' *American Economic Review*, 71: 421–36.

TOWNSEND, R. M. (1983). 'Forecasting the Forecasts of Others'. *Journal of Political Economy*, 91: 546–88.

WOODFORD, MICHAEL (1986). 'Learning to Believe in Sunspots'. C. V. Starr Center Working Paper no. 86–16, New York University, June.

PART III

Economic Fluctuations: Endogenous *v.* Exogenous Explanations

7

Real Business Cycle Theories

BENNETT T. McCALLUM

1. Introduction

The main objective of this chapter is to present a balanced evaluation of the 'real business cycle' approach to macroeconomic analysis, an evaluation that recognizes both strengths and weaknesses. In the end, however, my overall position is somewhat sceptical concerning the adequacy of the approach. Consequently, the paper has two additional objectives: to present an alternative perspective concerning the state of macroeconomic knowledge, and to outline a strategy for monetary and fiscal policy that is appropriate given existing knowledge.[1]

2. Real Business Cycle Theory

Real business cycle (RBC) analysis got its main impetus from the innovative paper of Kydland and Prescott (1982), while other notable contributions have been made by Long and Plosser (1983), King and Plosser (1984), Kydland (1984), and Prescott (1986).[2] The work involves an application of the equilibrium approach to business cycle analysis. More specifically, it is an outgrowth of the 'monetary misperception' models of Lucas (1972) and Barro (1981), but with emphasis given to propagation mechanisms and to the role of real shocks as a major source of fluctuations. The first of these two features does not involve any departure from the 'monetary misperceptions' line of work but is instead an extension that brings in one aspect of cyclical phenomena that Lucas (1972) abstracted from only for the sake of simplicity. Whether the second feature involves a departure depends on which of two positions the RBC analysis is understood to represent: that technology shocks are

---

[1] The next two sections of this exposition amount to a revised and condensed version of McCallum (1989), while Section 4 draws upon McCallum (1988*a*).

[2] More recent items of note include Kydland and Prescott (1986), Parkin (1988), King *et al.* (1988), Evans (1989), Shapiro (1987), Rudebusch (1988), Blanchard and Quah (1988), Christiano and Eichenbaum (1988), and Hercovitz and Sampson (1986).

an important source of fluctuations, or that they are the *only* important source. It is unclear which of these RBC writers have intended.

The best way to begin my description of the RBC approach is by way of a prototype model. The model economy is one with many similar households, each of which seeks at time t to maximize an objective function of the following form, where c_t is consumption and l_t is leisure during period t, while $E_t(\ )$ denotes the conditional expectation based on full period-t information:

$$E_t[u(c_t, l_t) + \beta u(c_{t+1}, l_{t+1}) + \beta^2 u(c_{t+2}, l_{t+2}) + \dots], \qquad (1)$$

where β is a discount factor satisfying $0 < \beta < 1$ and u is taken to be increasing in each argument and 'well behaved'. By appropriate choice of units, we can write $l_t = 1 - n_t$, where n_t is labour expended by the household during t.

On the production side, each household is assumed to have access to a technology that is represented by a production function, $y_t = z_t f(n_t^d, k_t^d)$, that is homogeneous of degree 1 and well behaved. The inputs of labour and capital, n_t^d and k_t^d, are potentially different from n_t and k_t (where the latter is capital owned by the household at the start of period t). A critical component of the production function is the random variable z_t, which is a stochastic index of the current state of technology. Fluctuations in z_t represent technology shocks, which are assumed to be generated by a Markov process—so the probability distribution of z_t may depend on z_{t-1} but not on other variables.

The model economy also has competitive rental markets for labour and capital, with real prices w_t and q_t, as well as for output. Thus the household's budget constraint for period t is

$$k_{t+1} + c_t = z_t f(n_t^d, k_t^d) + (1 - \delta)k_t - w_t(n_t^d - n_t) - q_t(k_t^d - k_t),$$
$$(2)$$

and similar constraints pertain as well for periods $t + j$, $j = 1, 2, \dots$.

Maximization of (1) subject to this sequence of constraints gives the following conditions for optimal choices on the part of the household, with $j = 0, 1, 2, \dots$:

$$E_t u_1(c_{t+j}, 1 - n_{t+j}) - E_t \lambda_{t+j} = 0 \qquad (3a)$$

$$E_t u_2(c_{t+j}, 1 - n_{t+j}) - E_t \lambda_{t+j} w_{t+j} = 0 \qquad (3b)$$

$$E_t z_{t+j} f_1(n_{t+j}^d, k_{t+j}^d) - E_t w_{t+j} = 0 \qquad (3c)$$

$$E_t z_{t+j} f_2(n_{t+j}^d, k_{t+j}^d) - E_t q_{t+j} = 0 \qquad (3d)$$

$$- E_t \lambda_{t+j} + E_t \beta \lambda_{t+j+1}[z_{t+j+1} f_2(n_{t+j+1}^d, k_{t+j+1}^d) + 1 - \delta] = 0. \qquad (3e)$$

In addition, there is a transversality condition:

$$\lim_{j \to \infty} E_t \beta^{j-1} \lambda_{t+j} k_{t+j+1}^d = 0. \tag{4}$$

Under the stipulated assumptions, equations (2), (3), and (4) are necessary and sufficient for a maximum of (1). Thus, if (4) is satisfied, (2) and (3) govern the household's choices of sequences for c_{t+j}, n_{t+j}, n_{t+j}^d, k_{t+j}, k_{t+j}^d, and λ_{t+j}.

Moving from the household's problem to the competitive market equilibrium, we note that the latter requires that $\Sigma n_t^d = \Sigma n_t$ and $\Sigma k_t^d = \Sigma k_t$, where the sums are over all households. But with similar households, that implies $n_t^d = n_t$ and $k_t^d = k_t$. Thus, we conclude that the economy's per capita variables c_t, k_t, n_t, and λ_t evolve according to the following conditions ($t = 1, 2, \ldots$):

$$c_t + k_{t+1} = z_t f(n_t, k_t) + (1 - \delta) k_t \tag{5}$$

$$u_1(c_t, 1 - n_t) - \lambda_t = 0 \tag{6}$$

$$u_2(c_t, 1 - n_t) = \lambda_t z_t f_1(n_t, k_t) \tag{7}$$

$$\lambda_t = E_t \beta \lambda_{t+1} [z_{t+1} f_2(n_{t+1}, k_{t+1}) + 1 - \delta]. \tag{8}$$

With u, f, and the distribution of z_t well behaved, there is one solution to these equations that satisfies (4).[3]

In fact, since z_t is generated by a Markov process, the only relevant state variables at t are k_t and z_t, and solutions for the main variables are of the form

$$k_{t+1} = k(k_t, z_t) \tag{9}$$

$$c_t = c(k_t, z_t) \tag{10}$$

$$n_t = n(k_t, z_t), \tag{11}$$

where k, c, and n are continuous functions. But while these expressions are simple in appearance, there are very few specifications for u and f that will permit explicit solutions to be found. I will mention one shortly, but first there is an issue that warrants brief mention.

In particular, it will be noted that the foregoing exposition has not taken the approach, common in the RBC literature, of finding a Pareto optimum and then assuming that the market equilibrium matches that solution. That approach is not taken here so as to avoid creating the impression that RBC models are necessarily ones in which Pareto optimality obtains, for this is not the case. The approach is also applicable, for example, to economies in which there are distorting taxes that finance government purchases. In fact, if government purchases and tax rules are constant over time, the solutions would still be of the form shown in (9)–(11).

---

[3] References to proofs are given in McCallum (1989) and Prescott (1986).

It might also be noted that in our example we would get the same equilibrium if we assumed that there was not a market in capital services but instead a loan market, in which one-period bonds were sold at a price of $1/(1 + r_t)$ and redeemed at unity. This loan market, like the capital rental market, would be inactive in equilibrium.

Now let us consider the special case mentioned above that permits an explicit solution. This case features complete depreciation during the period ($\delta = 1$) and the following utility and production functions:

$$u(c_t, 1 - n_t) = \theta \log c_t + (1 - \theta) \log (1 - n_t) \qquad 0 < \theta < 1 \qquad (12)$$

$$z_t f(n_t, k_t) = z_t n_t^\alpha k_t^{1-\alpha}. \qquad\qquad\qquad 0 < \alpha < 1. \quad (13)$$

With that specification, it turns out that employment does not vary:

$$n_t = \frac{\alpha\theta}{\alpha\theta + (1 - \theta)[1 - \beta(1 - \alpha)]} \equiv n. \qquad (14)$$

Furthermore, the following expressions are obtained:

$$k_{t+1} = (1 - \alpha)\beta(n^\alpha z_t k_t^{1-\alpha}) \qquad (15)$$

$$c_t = [1 - (1 - \alpha)\beta](n^\alpha z_t k_t^{1-\alpha}). \qquad (16)$$

Thus from (15) it is readily determined that

$$\log k_{t+1} = \phi_0 + (1 - \alpha) \log k_t + \log z_t. \qquad (17)$$

Assuming then that $\log z_t$ is autoregressive of order 1,[4]

$$\log z_t = \rho \log z_{t-1} + \varepsilon_t, \qquad (18)$$

where ε_t is white noise, we have that

$$\log k_{t+1} = \phi_0(1 - \rho) + (1 - \alpha + \rho) \log k_t - (1 - \alpha)\rho \log k_{t-1} + \varepsilon_t. \qquad (19)$$

Furthermore, this second-order autoregressive structure also pertains to $\log c_t$. That result is of interest because detrended quarterly US data series for (the logs of) consumption and other aggregate quantities are, in fact, well described by second-order autoregressive processes.

There is another important way in which this extremely simple special-case example matches actual US data, namely, by having markedly pro-cyclical behaviour of 'labour productivity', i.e., output per manhour. That feature is notable since most traditional theories, which attribute cycles to demand fluctuations, suggest that labour productivity will be counter-cyclical.

---

[4] Here we suppose that units have been chosen to make the mean value of $\log z_t$ equal to zero.

The special-case model has a constant employment level n_t, however, and implies that consumption and investment have the same degree of variability in percentage terms. As those two properties are sharply inconsistent with the facts, the RBC programme has from the first relied upon more complex structural specifications. With these, the possibility of an explicit solution is lost, so most RBC workers have (following Kydland and Prescott 1982) used stochastic simulations to deduce the cyclical properties of their numerically specified models. Support for the models is provided to the extent that their cyclical properties are similar to those reflected in actual data.

Tables 5.1 and 5.2 summarize some prominent results. In each of these tables the figures in the first column pertain to actual US quarterly postwar data, seasonally adjusted and detrended (or 'smoothed') by a particular method proposed by Hodrick and Prescott (1980). Although the Kydland–Prescott (1982) study came first chronologically, it is useful to begin the comparison with a simpler model described by Hansen (1985). In fact, this 'basic' model is like the special-case example described above except that the depreciation rate is realistic: $\delta = 0.025$. The other parameter values, chosen on the basis of steady-state and microeconomic consideration, are $\theta = 0.33$, $\alpha = 0.64$, $\beta = 0.99$, and $\rho = 0.95$.[5]

TABLE 5.1. *Standard deviations of percentage departures from trend*

Variable	US economy[a]	Basic model[b]	Kydland– Prescott[c]	Hansen model[b]
Output	1.76	1.76[d]	1.76[d]	1.76[d]
Consumption	1.29[e]	0.55	0.44	0.51
Investment	8.60[f]	5.53	5.40	5.71
Capital stock	0.63	0.47	0.46	0.47
Hours	1.66	0.91	1.21	1.35
Productivity	1.18	0.89	0.70	0.50

[a] Quarterly data, 1955(3)–1984(1), seasonally adjusted. *Source*: Hansen (1985).
[b] *Source*: Hansen (1985).
[c] *Source*: Prescott (1986).
[d] Shock variance set to provide match of output variation with actual data.
[e] This figure pertains to GNP-account consumption expenditures, which include expenditures on durable goods. For expenditure on non-durable goods and services the figures are about 1.2 and 0.6, respectively, so the relevant number for comparison is about 0.9.
[f] For fixed investment, the figure is approximately 5.3.

[5] Actually, both Hansen (1985) and Kydland and Prescott (1982) use $z_t = $ constant $+ 0.95 z_{t-1} + \varepsilon_t$, rather than the log-linear expression (18).

TABLE 5.2. *Contemporaneous correlations with output (departures from trend)*

Variable	US economy	Basic model	Kydland–Prescott	Hansen model
Consumption	0.85	0.89	0.85	0.87
Investment	0.92	0.99	0.88	0.99
Capital stock	0.04	0.06	0.02	0.05
Hours	0.76	0.98	0.95	0.98
Productivity	0.42	0.98	0.86	0.87

Notes: see Table 5.1.

Table 5.1 reports measures of the cyclical variability of the main variables. It should be noted that these are only relative magnitudes; i.e., they are based on values of the shock variance σ_ε^2 that are chosen to make the standard deviation of output match the actual (detrended) figure for each model; the plausibility of these σ_ε^2 will be discussed in Section 3 below. Comparison of the first two columns of the table shows that Hansen's basic model has relative variability properties that match the US data surprisingly well, especially when it is noted that for consumption services the actual figure is 0.6 and for fixed investment it is 5.3. (These series correspond to the model's variables better than to total consumption and investment.) Only for manhours employment is the relative variability far from the actual. In Table 5.2, moreover, we see a generally good correspondence between the basic model and reality in terms of contemporaneous correlations of other variables with output, though the model's productivity–output correlation is too high.

The third column in each of the tables pertains to the Kydland–Prescott (1982) model, which is more complex than the basic model in several respects, including gestation lags in the investment process and preferences that are not separable in the intertemporal dimension. These features lead to a bit more variability in manhours. The fourth column is for a model of Hansen's in which households are paid for agreeing to work either full-time (with a specified probability) or not at all. Again, this feature increases the variability of manhours; that improvement is offset, however, by a reduction in the variability of labour productivity.

While there are some significant discrepancies, in general the comparisons in Tables 5.1 and 5.2 are impressively supportive of the RBC approach. There are important issues, however, and other types of evidence, that must be considered. In the next section we turn to a critical evaluation of the RBC approach.

3. Evaluation

The first issue to be considered is whether the variance of ε_t that is required for the variance of output (relative to trend) to match that observed in actuality is of a plausible magnitude. The values of σ_ε that are assumed in the construction of Tables 5.1 and 5.2 are about 0.0093 for the basic model, 0.0090 for the Kydland–Prescott model, and 0.0071 for Hansen's all-or-nothing model. So the question is, What is the standard deviation of actual quarterly aggregate technology shocks in the US economy? Prescott (1986) has attempted to develop an answer as follows. Assume that the production function is of the Cobb–Douglas form (13) with labour-share parameter α equal to 0.75. Then find the residuals implied by US quarterly data and the relation

$$\Delta \log y_t = \text{constant} + 0.75\Delta \log n_t + 0.25\Delta \log k_t + \Delta \log z_t. \quad (20)$$

If the technology shock processes were

$$\log z_t = \log z_{t-1} + \varepsilon_t, \quad (21)$$

then the variance of residuals from (20) would provide an estimate of σ_ε^2. It is not entirely clear why Prescott uses the log-linear form for (21) but not in his simulation results, or why he uses $\rho = 1.0$ here and 0.95 in his model. But Evans (1989) has verified that these approximations are not seriously misleading. Using a weighted manhours series for n_t, Prescott (1986) obtains a raw estimate for σ_ε of 0.012, which he adjusts downward in a manner that would be appropriate under some assumptions regarding measurement error. Prescott's adjusted estimate is $\hat{\sigma}_\varepsilon = 0.0076$, which is reasonably close to the values utilized in Tables 5.1 and 5.2. In that sense, the requisite shock variance is not implausible.

   McCallum (1989) suggests that there are reasons to believe that the foregoing procedure will systematically overestimate σ_ε. If (20) were a regression relationship, then misspecification of the production function would tend to generate misleadingly large values of the residual variance. Since Prescott did not use least-squares regression to estimate the parameters of (20), this analogy is imperfect—but not misleading. The kind of misspecification suggested in McCallum (1989) is omitted variables reflecting dynamic adjustment costs. This argument would imply that lagged values of $\Delta \log n_t$ or $\Delta \log y_t$ should enter the relationship and perhaps make a large difference in the estimated value of σ_ε. But Evans (1989) has found that the neglect of dynamics is not as important as I had anticipated. That neglect might inflate $\hat{\sigma}_\varepsilon$ by 20–30 per cent, but not by an order of magnitude. A different type of omitted variable might be the quantity of imported raw materials, e.g., oil. That possibility will be discussed below.

A second fundamental issue concerns the *nature* of the unobserved random effects that the RBC literature refers to as 'technology shocks'. If the interpretation is that these are truly technological disturbances, then it is difficult to understand how there could be so much variability at the aggregate level. Different goods are produced by means of different technological processes, after all, so most scientific or engineering advances should pertain to only a few of them. Shocks in different sectors should presumably be nearly independent, so the economy-wide level of variability should be small in comparison to that of any single industry. If there were 10,000 processes, for example, then the aggregate σ_ε would be only 1/100 as large as for a typical industry.

A different interpretation is that the ε_t terms are more like terms-of-trade disturbances, such as the price of imported oil. But this alternative interpretation implies that quite a different type of empirical analysis would be appropriate for evaluation of the RBC approach. Observations are available on oil prices, for example, so there is no need to treat their changes as unobservable. Similar comments would apply, moreover, if the ε_t shocks were interpreted as pertaining to fiscal policy. The point of this discussion is that it matters what interpretation is given to Prescott's residuals. Under some interpretations one might want to proceed in quite a different fashion from that utilized in the RBC literature to date.

Much attention has been given in the existing literature to issues regarding shock-variance magnitudes and the variability of manhours. Other aspects of data analogous to those of Tables 5.1 and 5.2 have, by contrast, been seriously neglected. One such aspect—mentioned by Kydland and Prescott (1982: 1366) and McCallum (1989: 31) but not explored elsewhere—concerns correlations between output and (average labour) productivity at various leads and lags. Consider the following values for corr (y_t, v_{t+s}), where $v_t \equiv y_t/n_t$ denotes productivity:

	$s = -2$	$s = -1$	$s = 0$	$s = 1$	$s = 2$
Kydland–Prescott model	0.37	0.68	0.90	0.59	0.55
US economy	0.60	0.51	0.34	−0.04	−0.28

Clearly, there is a sharp divergence between model and actuality with regard to correlations between output and subsequent productivity levels. This divergence might possibly provide the basis for discriminating between the RBC model and alternatives. One competing possibility is the rather 'Keynesian' notion that output fluctuations are primarily demand-induced, with employment then determined by the production function but with gradual adjustments of the type often termed 'labour-hoarding'. Suppose, to illustrate, that output conforms to the process

$$y_t = ay_{t+1} - e_t, \quad 0 < a < 1 \tag{22}$$

where e_t is white noise, and that employment is given by

$$n_t = by_t + (1 - b)y_{t-1}. \quad 0 < b < 1 \tag{23}$$

Then it follows that $Ey_t v_t = (1 - a)(1 - b)\sigma_y^2$ is positive, that $Ey_t v_{t-1} = a(1 - b)(1 - a)\sigma_y^2$ is positive, and that $Ey_{t-1}v_t = (1 - b)(a - 1)\sigma_y^2$ is negative, which qualitatively matches the US data.

The main RBC literature has also been lacking in its attention to price variables—real interest rates and wages. It should be noted that the models referred to in Table 5.2 have the implication that the real wage is very strongly correlated with output; this follows since the Cobb–Douglas production function has equal marginal and average products of labour. In the US economy, by contrast, the comparable correlation is positive but very small. This counterfactual implication of the prototype RBC models has very recently been stressed by Christiano and Eichenbaum (1988).

Now let us turn to evidence of a different type. A natural sort of empirical approach would involve time-series studies designed to test the notion that monetary policy shocks have no significant effect on output or other aggregate quantity variables. At first glance it seems that this RBC property would be easy to test: all real variables should be block-exogenous to all nominal variables, so no nominal variable should Granger-cause real variables. But it turns out—as shown by Litterman and Weiss (1985), King (1986), and Eichenbaum and Singleton (1986)—that from a practical perspective this implication is only apparent, because it may not hold if there are variables that agents respond to but are not observed by the econometrician.

Some notable time-series evidence has recently been developed, however, by Evans (1989), who focuses on the production function residuals used as estimates of technology shocks by Prescott (1986). If these shocks were truly technological in nature, they should be uninfluenced by all nominal variables. Evans finds, however, that Prescott's residuals are Granger-caused by money growth rates and other nominal variables in a variety of time-series specifications. This finding is inconsistent with the hypothesis that Prescott's residuals truly reflect exogenous technology shocks.

Two additional types of evidence relating to RBC theory are discussed in McCallum (1986). The first of these is Sims's (1980) demonstration that money stock innovations, in small VAR systems, have little explanatory power for output measures when a nominal interest rate is included in the system. An interpretation that has been influential is that these money stock innovations represent surprise actions by the monetary authority—i.e. the Federal Reserve Board—suggesting that monetary policy actions are unimportant for output movements. But that interpretation is highly questionable. Suppose that the Fed implements its policy by manipulating nominal interest rates. Then interest rate innovations will reflect monetary policy surprises more accurately than will money stock innovations. And US monetary policy has in fact been implemented primarily by means of interest rate instruments throughout the postwar era.[6] So it is simply a *non sequitur* to conclude that monetary policy has been unimportant for output fluctuations. Indeed, the considerable explanatory power provided by the interest rate innovations in Sims's study suggests just the opposite.

The other line of argument is that initiated by Nelson and Plosser (1982), who argue (1) that univariate time-series processes for output and other real variables possess unit-autoregressive roots, and (2) that this implies that monetary influences are small. Step 1 is questioned in McCallum (1986) and in many recent papers, while step 2 has been shown to be unjustified by West (1988).

In light of the foregoing evaluation, it seems appropriate to conclude that RBC analysis has been valuable in terms of methodological development and has been useful as a reminder that a large component of real fluctuations is probably attributable to neither monetary nor fiscal policy actions. But there are several reasons to suspect that the typical RBC model does not provide an accurate picture of actual cyclical phenomena, and there is little reason to believe that monetary and fiscal policy actions have been of insignificant importance.

4. Macroeconomic Knowledge and Policy

The remainder of this paper will be devoted to more general issues regarding cyclical fluctuations and stabilization policy. Besides the RBC model, the other New Classical model of the cycle—and of the effects of aggregate demand on real output and employment—is the Lucas–Barro model, which features monetary misperceptions as the source of a nominal-to-real linkage. This model, however, has become widely regarded as inapplicable to today's developed economies, principally because sellers have too much information to permit the type of confusion that is required by Lucas's (1972) theory to occur. Actual sellers, that is, know whether economy-wide aggregate demand is currently high, low, or normal.

Keynesian models, by contrast, feature effects of aggregate demand on output that arise because of some form of nominal price stickiness—

[6] Some readers may find this statement surprising, in light of the policy 'experiment' of 1979–82. A detailed justification is provided in McCallum (1985).

i.e. slow adjustment of prices or wages to revised demand conditions. Now it can certainly be argued that there is no necessary incompatibility of sluggish price adjustments with the equilibrium approach to cyclical analysis promoted by Lucas and other New Classical analysts. It is conceivable, that is, that someone could construct a model that endogenously explains the slow adjustment of prices as a rational choice made by individual agents, optimizing in light of their own objectives and constraints. But there is a major problem with this strategy that has not yet been overcome. In particular, it is *nominal* price stickiness that is required in the foregoing story, whereas optimizing taste and technology analysis proceeds in terms of *real* (relative) prices. So most attempts to date have been directed towards explanation of the wrong phenomenon.

In any event, up until now there has been no model developed of sticky nominal prices, and consequent demand effects on output, that satisfies the methodological criteria of the equilibrium approach. A third possibility is provided by basically empirical models of slow price adjustments—i.e., econometric 'Phillips curves' or 'wage–price sectors'. But regarding these, the equilibrium approach position is that, unless a price adjustment equation is satisfactorily rationalized in terms of optimal choices by individuals acting in light of their own objectives and constraints, such an equation will probably not be structural. Instead, it will be likely to shift with demand policy changes—as stressed by Lucas (1976). So any model that incorporates such an equation cannot be relied upon for policy design.

The Keynesian response to this critique is to contend that, in reality, prices do not adjust promptly for a variety of complicated strategic and semi-institutional reasons that are not readily amenable to taste-and-technology analysis. But it is better (according to the Keynesian argument) to use a poorly rationalized but empirically justifiable price adjustment relation than to pretend—counterfactually—that prices adjust promptly. An estimated model including such a relation will fit the data better and might be usable for policy analysis.

It is hard to keep from having considerable sympathy for this suggestion. A poor price adjustment relation should be better than none—or, more precisely, than an extreme version adopted a priori. But it is also hard to escape the Lucas critique: How can one know that a relation will not shift sharply if one does not understand its nature? These conflicting points of view pose a genuine dilemma. Finding a way out is the central task of macroeconomists concerned with stabilization policy.

In a number of papers[7] I have described what seems to be a

[7] See especially McCallum (1988*b*).

reasonably satisfactory way of coping with the dilemma. The strategy begins by accepting the idea that the nature of price adjustment mechanisms—and thus the connection between nominal and real variables—is poorly understood. There is no compelling basis for the selection of any one model and no good prospect for a better situation in the near future. So the best way to proceed is to design a policy strategy that does not rely sensitively on any particular formulation— i.e., one that is insensitive to model specification.

But the strategy in question does incorporate one bit of critical macroeconomic knowledge that we possess: knowledge that, on a very long-term basis, output is approximately independent of the growth rate of nominal variables. Also, it seems to be the case that cyclical fluctuations in nominal demand and output are positively related. In the postwar USA, for example, quarterly growth rates of nominal GNP and real GNP have a simple correlation in excess of 0.80. So a policy that kept nominal GNP growing smoothly at a steady rate equal to the long-run rate of output growth should yield approximately zero inflation over any long span of time and might also help to reduce cyclical fluctuations. It would almost certainly prevent terribly severe recessions; the Great Depression would never have occurred if nominal GNP had been kept on a steady 3 per cent per year growth path, to take a figure that is roughly appropriate for the USA.

The strategy under discussion does not, however, consist merely of the adoption of a target path for nominal GNP. Equally essential is the proposed mechanism for achieving that path. In this regard, it is important to specify an operational rule, i.e., one that pertains to a directly controllable instrument rather than a more remote variable such as the money stock. In addition, the rule should be designed in a manner that does not rely upon the absence of regulatory and technological change in the payments and financial industries. And, most importantly, the rule should be one that is robust to model specification.

In recent work (McCallum 1988b) I have developed in quantitative terms a rule for US monetary policy based on the foregoing considerations. The rule dictates quarterly settings for the monetary base that are designed to keep nominal GNP close to a path that grows steadily at the rate of 3 per cent per year.[8] It does not rely on any specific model of the economy or on any details regarding the financial system: all it presumes is that an increase in the growth rate of the monetary base tends to have a stimulative effect on nominal GNP. Defining $b_t = $ log of monetary base (for quarter t), $x_t = $ log of nominal GNP, and x_t^* target-path values of x_t, the rule is as follows:

[8] Here it is being assumed that 3% is the long-term average annual growth rate of real GNP. It would be a simple matter to utilize a different figure or even to adopt a formula for periodic re-estimation of this rate.

$$\Delta b_t = 0.00739 - (1/16)(x_{t-1} - x_{t-17} - b_{t-1} + b_{t-17})$$
$$+ 0.25(x_{t-1}^* - x_{t-1}). \tag{24}$$

Here the constant term is simply a 3 per cent annual growth rate expressed in quarterly logarithmic units, while the second term subtracts from this the average growth rate of base velocity over the previous four years. Finally, the third term adds a gentle adjustment in response to cyclical departures of GNP from its target path.

To determine whether this rule would in fact keep nominal GNP close to the desired growth path, one must experiment with the economy or with a model. The former possibility is too expensive and the latter is hampered by the absence of any reliable or agreed-upon model. Consequently, my method of investigating the issue has been to determine whether the rule performs well in a wide variety of *different* models. To be specific, McCallum (1988*b*) reports the rule's performance with eleven models of nominal GNP determination: two atheoretic regressions involving Δx_t and Δb_t; six vector-autoregression systems; and three small 'structural' models designed to represent three theoretical positions concerning the aggregate-supply or Phillips-curve mechanism.[9] Using each model, simulations for 1954–85 are conducted with policy rule (24) incorporated to generate values for Δb_t. These simulations begin with actual conditions prevailing in the USA at the start of 1954 and proceed with shocks fed into the system in each simulated quarter, the shock estimates being residuals from the relations estimated in the various models. Alternative values were tried in place of the 0.25 adjustment coefficient appearing in the third term of (24).

In all eleven models, the behaviour of the rule is highly satisfactory. It serves, that is, to keep x_t close to x_t^* over the 128 simulated periods, with root-mean-square deviation values of about 0.020–0.025. Thus, the simulation experiments suggest that, if it had been followed, policy rule (24) would have kept nominal GNP close to a steady 3 per cent growth path over the period 1954–85, despite the various shocks—including those reflecting financial industry turmoil—that actually occurred.

Some classically oriented economists have suggested that the objective of stabilizing nominal GNP is less attractive than that of stabilizing the price level. Barro (1986: 35), for example, has noted that achievement of a smooth target path for nominal GNP 'must mean that the monetary authority does less good a job of stabilizing the overall price level'. But, according to classical flexible-price theories, there will be no effect of automatic policy rules on the cyclical behaviour of real variables. It should consequently be a matter of indifference to a flexible-price

---

[9] The last three models represent RBC and 'monetary misperception' theories, plus a more Keynesian alternative featuring Phillips-type wage adjustments and markup pricing.

theorist whether nominal GNP or the price level is smoothed cyclically, so long as the same inflation rate is generated on average. Thus, RBC proponents in particular have no basis for objection to rule (24). This rule might prove superior to direct price level stabilization, moreover, if price level stickiness is of empirical importance.[10] A fiscal policy counterpart would have government purchases chosen for allocative and distributional reasons, with tax rates set so as to yield budget balance on average over the cycle. Progressive or proportional tax schedules would, of course, result in automatic-stabilizer responses that tend to promote the smooth growth of nominal GNP. Together, this type of monetary and fiscal package would virtually eliminate inflation, avoid policy surprises that could be destabilizing, and perhaps contribute a bit to the dampening of real cyclical fluctuations.

References

BARRO, ROBERT J. (1981). 'The Equilibrium Approach to Business Cycles'. In his *Money, Expectations, and Business Cycles*. New York: Academic Press.
—— (1986). 'Recent Developments in the Theory of Rules versus Discretion'. *Economic Journal*, 96 (Suppl.): 23–37.
BLANCHARD, OLIVIER J. and QUAH, DANNY (1988). 'The Dynamic Effects of Aggregate Demand and Supply Disturbances'. NBER Working Paper no. 2737, October.
CHRISTIANO, LAWRENCE J. and EICHENBAUM, MARTIN (1988). 'Is Theory Really Ahead of Measurement? Current Real Business Cycle Theories and Aggregate Labor Market Fluctuations'. Working Paper, Federal Reserve Bank of Minneapolis, September.
EICHENBAUM, MARTIN and SINGLETON, KENNETH J. (1986). 'Do Equilibrium Real Business Cycle Theories Explain Postwar US Business Cycles?' *NBER Macroeconomics Annual 1986*. Cambridge, Mass.: MIT Press.
EVANS, CHARLES (1989). 'Using Measured Productivity Shocks to Test a Real Business Cycle Model'. Ph.D. thesis, Carnegie Mellon University.
HANSEN, GARY D. (1985). 'Indivisible Labor and the Business Cycle'. *Journal of Monetary Economics*, 16: 309–27.
HERCOVITZ, ZVI and SAMPSON, M. (1986). 'Growth and Employment Fluctuations'. Working Paper, University of Western Ontario.

---

[10] With price stickiness, stabilization of prices and nominal GNP would have different consequences for the cyclical behaviour of real variables. Which of the two would be superior depends upon many aspects of the macroeconomic structure, including static supply and demand elasticities, the precise mechanism of price stickiness that prevails, the relative variances of different shocks, and serial correlation properties of these shocks. Thus, it is not possible to develop an airtight case for the superiority of either of these objectives.

HODRICK, ROBERT J. and PRESCOTT, EDWARD C. (1980). 'Post-war US Business Cycles: An Empirical Investigation'. Working Paper, Carnegie Mellon University.

KING, ROBERT G. (1986). 'Money and Business Cycles: Comments on Bernanke and Related Literature'. *Carnegie–Rochester Conference Series on Public Policy*, 25: 101–16.

—— and PLOSSER, CHARLES I. (1984). 'Money, Credit, and Prices in a Real Business Cycle'. *American Economic Review*, 74: 363–80.

—— —— and REBELO, SERGIO T. (1988). 'Production, Growth, and Business Cycles, I and II'. *Journal of Monetary Economics*, 21: 195–232 and 309–41.

KYDLAND, FINN E. (1984). 'Labor Force Heterogeneity and the Business Cycle'. *Carnegie–Rochester Conference Series on Public Policy*, 21: 173–208.

—— and PRESCOTT, EDWARD C. (1982). 'Time to Build and Aggregate Fluctuations'. *Econometrica*, 50: 1345–70.

—— —— (1986). 'The Workweek of Capital and its Cyclical Implications'. Working Paper, Federal Reserve Bank of Minneapolis.

LITTERMAN, ROBERT B. and WEISS, LAWRENCE (1985). 'Money, Real Interest Rates, and Output: A Reinterpretation of Postwar US Data'. *Econometrica*, 53: 129–56.

LONG, JOHN B. and PLOSSER, CHARLES I. (1983). 'Real Business Cycles'. *Journal of Political Economy*, 91: 39–69.

LUCAS, ROBERT E. JUN. (1972). 'Expectations and the Neutrality of Money'. *Journal of Economic Theory*, 4: 103–24.

—— (1976). 'Econometric Policy Evaluation: A Critique'. *Carnegie–Rochester Conference Series on Public Policy*, 1: 19–46.

McCALLUM, BENNETT T. (1985). 'On Consequences and Criticisms of Monetary Targeting'. *Journal of Money, Credit, and Banking*, 17: 570–97.

—— (1986). 'On "Real" and "Sticky Price" Theories of the Business Cycle'. *Journal of Money, Credit, and Banking*, 18: 397–414.

—— (1988a). 'Postwar Developments in Business Cycle Theory: A Moderately Classical Perspective'. *Journal of Money, Credit, and Banking*, 20: 459–71.

—— (1988b). 'Robustness Properties of a Rule for Monetary Policy'. *Carnegie–Rochester Conference Series on Public Policy*, 29: 173–204.

—— (1989). 'Real Business Cycle Models'. In Robert J. Barro (ed.), *Modern Business Cycle Theory*. Cambridge, Mass.: Harvard University Press.

NELSON, CHARLES R. and PLOSSER, CHARLES I. (1982). 'Trends and Random Walks in Macroeconomic Time Series'. *Journal of Monetary Economics*, 10: 139–62.

PARKIN, MICHAEL (1988). 'A Method for Determining whether Parameters in Aggregative Models are Structural'. *Carnegie–Rochester Conference Series on Public Policy*, 29: 215–52.

PRESCOTT, EDWARD C. (1986). 'Theory Ahead of Business Cycle Measurement'. *Carnegie–Rochester Conference Series on Public Policy*, 25: 11–44.

RUDEBUSCH, GLENN D. (1988). 'Are Productivity Fluctuations Due to Real Supply Shocks?' *Economic Letters*, 27: 327–31.

SHAPIRO, MATTHEW D. (1987). 'Are Cyclical Fluctuations in Productivity Due More to Supply Shocks or Demand Shocks?' *American Economic Review*, 77: 118–24.

Sims, Christopher A. (1980). 'Comparison of Interwar and Postwar Business Cycles'. *American Economic Review*, 70: 250–7.

West, Kenneth D. (1988). 'On the Interpretation of Near Random-Walk Behaviour in GNP'. *American Economic Review*, 78: 202–9.

8

Equilibrium Models of Endogenous Fluctuations: An Introduction

MICHAEL WOODFORD

1. Introduction

Recently there has been a revival of interest in endogenous models of economic fluctuations—in models according to which fluctuations could continue to occur even in the absence of exogenous fluctuations in any of the external determinants of the economic environment, such as consumer tastes or the state of technology. One of the most important features of this recent literature has been careful attention to the consequences of optimizing behaviour on the part of economic agents, and of a state of competitive equilibrium between the various producers and consumers in the economy, for the possibility of endogenous fluctuations. It is this question of the possibility of endogenous *equilibrium* fluctuations with which I am concerned here. (For other classes of economic models characterized by endogenous fluctuations, see Lorenz (1989) or Chapters 9 and 10 below.)

I will begin by clarifying what is meant by endogenous fluctuations, and contrasting two rather different kinds of models of endogenous fluctuations: those in which equilibrium is determinate but unstable, and 'sunspot' models. In Section 3 I discuss some of the reasons why purely exogenous models of the source of economic fluctuations have been so popular in modern theorizing, and argue that the grounds for dismissal of endogenous models a priori are not so strong as the tenacity of this methodological prejudice might suggest. Finally, in Section 4 I consider the extent to which methodological commitments to explaining fluctuations in terms of optimizing behaviour and competitive equilibrium can justify an exclusive emphasis upon exogenous-shock models. I argue that

This paper has been improved substantially thanks to discussions with Michele Boldrin, Roger Guesnerie, David Laidler, Tom Sargent, and José Scheinkman. Research referred to here was supported by the National Science Foundation.

the most plausible models of endogenous fluctuations depend crucially upon the existence of 'market failures' of one kind or another, but that this need not imply that the endogenous-cycle hypothesis is inconsistent with a belief in the rationality of economic actors.

2. Endogenous versus Exogenous Explanations of Economic Fluctuations: Preliminary Distinctions and Examples

By *exogenous-shock models* of economic fluctuations I mean models in which equilibrium is determinate and intrinsically stable, so that in the absence of continuing exogenous shocks the economy would tend towards a steady state, but because of exogenous shocks a stationary pattern of fluctuations is observed. Such models of economic fluctuations are quite familiar—so familiar, indeed, that many readers may wonder how an explanation of economic fluctuations could be of any other kind. Typologies of business cycle theories—for example those that classify theories according to the dominant type of 'impulse' assumed on the one hand and the nature of the 'propagation mechanism' posited on the other—take for granted this general structure of explanation. All of the leading current equilibrium business cycle theories are of this kind, but the textbook 'Keynesian' and 'monetarist' models are of this kind as well, as are the econometric models inspired by them, if one accepts the conventional identification of residuals in the various equations with exogenous shocks to fundamentals (of perhaps an unspecified nature). Models of this kind include both theories that attribute aggregate instability mainly to variations in government policy, and theories that attribute it mainly to variations in private-sector behaviour (interpreted as originating in variations in tastes or technological possibilities).

But this structure of explanation is not the only logical possibility, and I argue below that it is not the only possibility consistent with economic theory. I will also argue that, if aggregate fluctuations could be shown to be endogenous to some important degree, this would be of considerable importance. Before addressing the reasons for interest in the endogenous-cycle hypothesis, however, it is useful to clarify exactly what is meant by it.

A simple definition might characterize endogenous models of economic fluctuations as ones in which persistent fluctuations occur despite an absence of variation in exogenous economic 'fundamentals' such as tastes and technology and government policies. This is indeed a property of the theoretical models that are usually thought of as examples of endogenous-cycle theories. But it is not an adequate definition from the point of view of explaining what is thought to be interesting about such theoretical examples. For the point of contention between proponents of exogenous and endogenous theories cannot be whether or not exogenous shocks in fact occur. Anyone must recognize that the aggregate economy is significantly affected by events that must be viewed as largely exogenous to the economic process itself—political events for example, but also the random timing of technological innovations. Hence we must be able to define endogenous fluctuations in such a way that the hypothesis does not deny this obvious fact.

A more careful definition requires a slightly more formal description. Let an economic model consist of a description of the evolution over time of variables of four sorts: exogenous 'fundamental' variables, to be denoted x_t; predetermined endogenous variables k_t; non-predetermined endogenous variables p_t; and 'sunspot' variables s_t. All of these may be supposed to be vector quantities, taking values in sets X, K, P, and S respectively. (A given model might not involve state variables of all these types, but that can be dealt with by assuming, for example, that the set K consists of a single point.) The 'fundamental' variables are exogenous variables (i.e., the evolution of x_t is described by a stationary Markov process on X, independent of the histories of the other state variables, and regarded as external to the economic process that is being modelled), whose values affect the economic relations determining the endogenous variables. The 'sunspot' variables are also exogenous, but their values do not have any effect upon the economic relations determining the endogenous variables. As is discussed further below, the possibility that endogenous variables might none the less take different values depending upon the state s_t may be taken to represent the role of arbitrary revisions of expectations as an autonomous source of instability in the economy. The predetermined endogenous variables k_t are determined completely by period $t-1$, so that their values must be unaffected by the realization of either x_t (period t changes in fundamentals) or s_t (period t revisions of expectations). The values of the non-predetermined variables p_t may depend upon the realization of either x_t or s_t.

A description of the economy's evolution consists of a specification of the histories of the endogenous variables, given any possible history of realizations of the exogenous variables, i.e., a sequence of functions

$$p_t = \pi_t(x_t, s_t, x_{t-1}, s_{t-1}, \ldots, x_0, s_0, k_0)$$

$$k_{t+1} = \kappa_{t+1}(x_t, s_t, x_{t-1}, s_{t-1}, \ldots, x_0, s_0, k_0)$$

for $t = 0, 1, 2, \ldots$ I will suppose that the equilibrium conditions take the form

$$k_{t+1} = g(x_t, k_t, p_t, \mu_t(p_{t+1})) \tag{1}$$

$$f(x_t, k_t, p_t, \mu_t(p_{t+1})) = 0, \tag{2}$$

where f is a vector-valued function of the same dimension as p_t, g is a vector-valued function of the same dimension as k_t, and $\mu_t(p_{t+1})$ denotes the probability distribution of possible values for p_{t+1}, given information available at time t.

Equation (1) indicates the determination of the predetermined variables for period $t + 1$ as a function of the economy's state in period t, including period t expectations regarding the future. An example of such a relation might be the determination of the capital stock in period $t + 1$ by an investment decision in period t, which depends upon period t prices, interest rates, and so on, as well as expectations regarding the future values of such variables. A probability distribution for k_{t+1} is not included among the arguments of g, because the value of k_{t+1} can be known with certainty at time t, and because in writing the condition in this form I have solved for k_{t+1}. A probability distribution for x_{t+1} is not included among the arguments of g, because, given the Markov process on X, this probability distribution is completely determined by the value of x_t. Equation (2) represents the determination of the non-predetermined variables p_t as a function of the predetermined period t state variables, the current state of exogenous fundamentals, and expectations. The variables p_t are defined only implicitly by (2), because the sort of equilibrium condition one has in mind (e.g. an equation stating that supply equals demand, to determine period t prices) may in general have multiple solutions for given values of the other variables; the values of predetermined variables are by contrast necessarily uniquely defined, if the set of state variables is made large enough (e.g., in the case of determination of the period $t + 1$ capital stock, if the list of period t endogenous variables includes the level of investment in period t). A probability distribution for k_{t+1} is not included among the arguments of f, because this can be written as a function of the other arguments using (1); and again, a probability distribution for x_{t+1} is not included because it can be written as a function of x_t. Neither current nor future values of the sunspot variables enter as arguments of either f or g—this is what makes them 'sunspot' variables rather than 'fundamentals'.

We will be concerned with the set of sequences of functions $\{\pi_t, \kappa_{t+1}\}$, for $t = 0, 1, 2, \ldots$, that satisfy (1) and (2) for all possible histories of realizations of the exogenous variables $\{x_t, s_t\}$ for $t = 0, 1, 2, \ldots$, given an initial condition k_0 for the predetermined endogenous variables. Let this be referred to as the *equilibrium set* $E(k_0)$. In the case of greatest interest, the equilibrium set is non-empty for all k_0 in the set K; this would generally be considered a minimal requirement for an internally consistent model. But equilibrium need not be unique.

Now the point of view that underlies the conventional methodological preference for exogenous shock models of fluctuations can be stated, I believe, in terms of two general propositions regarding the structure of the equilibrium set. The two propositions are related, and I will refer to both of them as determinacy theses; but it is important to realize that they are logically distinct, and indeed, the literature concerned with alternatives to exogenous-shock models can on the whole be divided into two parts, depending upon which determinacy thesis is being challenged.

THE GLOBAL WEAK DETERMINACY THESIS. The equilibrium values of (k_{t+1}, p_t) at any point in time t depend upon the history of realizations of the exogenous states up to that time, and upon the initial condition, only in so far as these affect the equilibrium conditions (1) and (2) for periods t or later. As a consequence, any equilibrium can be described by a pair of functions

$$p_t = \pi(x_t, k_t) \tag{3}$$

$$k_{t+1} = \kappa(x_t, k_t) \tag{4}$$

which furthermore have the property that, if (x^1, k^1) and (x^2, k^2) are such that $f(x^1, k^1, p, \mu) = f(x^2, k^2, p, \mu)$ and $g(x^1, k^1, p, \mu) = g(x^2, k^2, p, \mu)$ for all p in P and for μ any probability measure on P, and such that the distribution of possible values for x_{t+1} conditional upon x_t is the same when $x_t = x^1$ as when $x_t = x^2$, then $\pi(x^1, k^1) = \pi(x^2, k^2)$ and $\kappa(x^1, k^1) = \kappa(x^2, k^2)$. That is, there is no dependence upon 'irrelevant' components either of exogenous state variables or of predetermined endogenous state variables.

According to this proposition, the realizations of sunspot states can have no effect upon the equilibrium evolution of the endogenous variables, because the sunspot states have no effect upon the equilibrium conditions (1) or (2); and the history of realizations $(x_0, x_1, \ldots, x_t)$ and the initial condition k_0 affect the determination of (k_{t+1}, p_t) only through the sufficient statistics (x_t, k_t), which quantities may affect (k_{t+1}, p_t) because they may enter the equilibrium conditions (1) and (2) for period t, and because x_t may give information about the future values of fundamentals as well. Note also that the proposition implies that π and κ are time-invariant functions; for dependence upon time would be like dependence upon a sunspot state, given the time invariance of conditions (1) and (2).

The reason for the appeal of this determinacy thesis is simple. These properties of the solution follow immediately from our assumptions regarding the form of the equilibrium conditions if one supposes that equilibrium is unique for each k_0. The reasoning is straightforward. If equilibrium is unique, there exist unique equilibrium functions $\pi_0(x_0, s_0, k_0)$ and $\kappa_1(x_0, s_0, k_0)$. Furthermore, since the restrictions upon the sequences $\{k_{t+1}, p_t\}$ implied by equilibrium conditions (1)–(2) are the same regardless of the value of s_0, the unique equilibrium values for p_0 and k_1 must be independent of s_0, allowing us to define functions

$$\pi(x, k) = \pi_0(x, s, k)$$

$$\kappa(x, k) = \kappa_1(x, s, k).$$

And the recursive form of the equilibrium conditions (1)–(2) implies that, if the sequences $\{k_{t+1}, p_t\}$ for $t \geq 0$ are an equilibrium for initial condition k_0 and exogenous shocks $\{x_t\}$, then the sequences $\{k'_{t+1}, p'_t\}$ must be an equilibrium for initial condition k'_0 and exogenous shocks $\{x'_t\}$, where

$$k'_{t+1} = k_{t+2}$$

$$p'_t = p_{t+1}$$

$$x'_t = x_{t+1}$$

$$k'_0 = k_1.$$

It then follows, from the uniqueness of the equilibrium with initial condition k'_0, that one must have

$$\pi_1(x_1, s_1, x_0, s_0, k_0) = \pi(x_1, \kappa(x_0, k_0))$$

$$\kappa_2(x_1, s_1, x_0, s_0, k_0) = \kappa(x_1, \kappa(x_0, k_0)).$$

The argument proceeds in the same way for subsequent periods, so that the equilibrium must be of the form (3)–(4).

Uniqueness of equilibrium is often assumed, even though as noted above this need not follow from the definition given of equilibrium.[1] But the determinacy thesis is often assumed even when equilibrium is not assumed to be unique—indeed, even in the case of models where non-uniqueness can be shown to be possible. This is revealed by the fact that many authors choose a formalism with which to describe equilibria in their model that assumes the existence of a representation of the form (3)–(4); see e.g. Lucas and Stokey (1987).

Another tacit assumption of much analysis is the following.

---

[1] To be more precise, it is often argued that, if equilibrium is not unique, the definition of equilibrium must be supplemented by an additional 'selection criterion' that selects one equilibrium for each model specification and initial condition. The argument just given then explains why the principle of global weak determinacy often plays a central role in proposed selection criteria, such as McCallum's (1983) concept of the 'minimum state variable solution' for linear rational expectations models, or the 'Markov equilibrium' refinement for stationary dynamic games (Maskin and Tirole 1989).

THE ASYMPTOTIC STRONG DETERMINACY THESIS. Eventually, the equilibrium values of (k_{t+1}, p_t) depend only upon the realizations of the exogenous fundamentals $\{x_s\}$ for $s \leq t$; that is, the initial condition k_0 will have no effect upon the equilibrium values far enough in the future. Formally, for any initial condition k_0 and for any sequence of exogenous shocks $\{x_0, x_{-1}, x_{-2}, \ldots\}$, the sequences $\{k_s', p_s'\}$ defined recursively by

$$k_s'(0) = k_0$$

$$k_s'(n) = \kappa(x_{n-s}, k_s'(n-1)), \qquad 1 \leq n \leq s$$

$$k_s' = k_s'(s), \qquad\qquad s \geq 1$$

$$p_s' = \pi(x_0, k_s'(s-1)), \qquad s \geq 1,$$

converge to values (k^*, p^*) as s goes to infinity, which limiting values may depend upon the sequence $\{x_0, x_{-1}, x_{-2}, \ldots\}$ but are independent of k_0.[2]

The idea behind this proposition is that recursive substitution of expression (4) into itself ought to yield a sequence of representations

$$k_{t+1} = \kappa(x_t, k_t)$$

$$= \kappa(x_t, \kappa(x_{t-1}, k_{t-1}))$$

$$= \kappa(x_t, \kappa(x_{t-1}, \kappa(x_{t-2}, k_{t-2})))$$

$$= \ldots,$$

that converges eventually to a representation

$$k_{t+1} = \kappa^*(x_t, x_{t-1}, x_{t-2}, \ldots),$$

in which k_{t+1} is written as a function of a possibly infinite history of previous exogenous shocks, with lagged endogenous variables completely eliminated. The existence of such a representation also allows p_t to be written as a function of a possibly infinite history of previous exogenous shocks alone; i.e.,

$$p_t = \pi^*(x_t, x_{t-1}, x_{t-2}, \ldots)$$

$$= \pi(x_t, \kappa^*(x_{t-1}, x_{t-2}, \ldots)).$$

These functions κ^* and π^* then describe the limits (k^*, p^*) referred to in the above statement.

---

[2] In this statement I am assuming the validity of the representation (3)–(4), since I am mainly interested in the consequences of asymptotic strong determinacy when conjoined with global weak determinacy; but, strictly speaking, it is logically possible to assert asymptotic strong determinacy while denying the global weak determinacy thesis, in which case one would allow (k^*, p^*) to depend upon the history of realizations of all exogenous state variables, including sunspot variables.

One reason for the intuitive appeal of such a postulate is probably familiarity with the properties of linear systems (which are often assumed to provide an adequate approximation for purposes of quantitative investigations of equilibrium models of economic fluctuations). For suppose that the function κ is linear, i.e. that one can write $\kappa(x, k) = Ax + Bk$ for some matrices A and B. Suppose furthermore that the exogenous shocks to fundamentals satisfy some uniform bound $|x_t| \leq \bar{x} < \infty$, and that the equilibrium dynamics are such that a bounded sequence of exogenous shocks to fundamentals implies bounded fluctuations in the endogenous variables, i.e., that the matrix B has all eigenvalues with modulus less than 1. Then recursive substitution of the kind described is possible and yields

$$\kappa^*(x_t, x_{t-1}, x_{t-2}, \ldots) = \sum_{j=0}^{\infty} B^j A x_{t-j}$$

Now the theses of global weak determinacy and asymptotic strong determinacy together clearly imply that persistent fluctuations in the endogenous variables must be explained by fluctuations in the exogenous fundamentals. For suppose that there were no variation in fundamentals. Then any equilibrium would have to be described by a pair of functions

$$p_t = \pi(k_t) \tag{5}$$

$$k_{t+1} = \kappa(k_t) \tag{6}$$

and the function κ would have to have the property that the limit

$$\lim_{n \to \infty} \kappa^n(k_0) = k^*$$

exists and is independent of k_0. But this would imply that k_t must asymptotically converge to the constant value k^*, and that p_t must asymptotically converge to the constant value $p^* = \pi(k^*)$. Hence fluctuations in the endogenous state variables must eventually die out. It follows that a continuing pattern of fluctuations must be explained in terms of continuing shocks to fundamentals.

On the other hand, it should be clear at this point that one might wish to deny this conclusion—to assert the possibility of endogenous fluctuations—without one's being committed to a belief that there are in fact no exogenous variations in fundamentals. For one might wish to challenge one or both of the determinacy theses, both of which remain strong restrictions (and the denial of either of which is logically possible) even in the case of stochastic variation in fundamentals. And an obvious way of demonstrating that one or the other of these propositions need not be true of well-posed economic models is to exhibit examples of well-posed models with the property that, even if fundamentals are

assumed to be constant, equilibria characterized by persistent fluctuations exists. This is what I take to be the point of the theoretical
literature on endogenous-cycle models. The challenge posed to orthodox
business cycle theory is not the suggestion that perhaps fluctuations in
fundamentals are unimportant, but rather the suggestion that one or
both of the determinacy theses might be too restrictive. And one might
refer broadly to all models of fluctuations inconsistent with either of
these theses as 'endogenous' explanations.

The isolation of two distinct determinacy theses indicates that models
of fluctuations might be 'endogenous' in either of two distinct senses: (1)
a model might contradict the thesis of asymptotic strong determinacy
while possibly remaining consistent with the thesis of global weak
determinacy, or (2) it might contradict the latter while possibly remaining consistent with the former. And indeed, there exist to some extent
two distinct classes of endogenous models of fluctuations, in so far as
most examples in the literature are constructed in order to challenge one
of the determinacy theses or the other.

On the one hand, there are models of *determinate but unstable
dynamics*. In such models, equilibria have a representation of the form
(3)–(4), but differing initial conditions k_0 will imply different dynamic
paths which will fail to converge even far in the future. For example, in
the absence of shocks to fundamentals, a model may imply deterministic
equilibrium dynamics of the form (6); but it may be the case that all of
the steady-state equilibria, i.e. all of the vectors k^* that are fixed points
of the map κ in (6), are unstable because the derivative matrix $D\kappa(k^*)$
in each case has one or more eigenvalues of modulus greater than 1. In
such a case, the dynamics will not converge asymptotically to a steady
state, for almost all initial conditions: instead, the dynamics may
converge to a deterministic periodic orbit, or even to a chaotic attractor,
in which case bounded but aperiodic fluctuations continue for ever. Such
models are consistent with the thesis of global weak determinacy, but
contradict asymptotic strong determinacy.

Examples of this kind include the optimal growth models considered
by Benhabib and Nishimura (1979, 1985) and Boldrin and Montrucchio
(1986), among others. The simplest example in which complex dynamics
are possible is a two-sector growth model (capital and exogenously
supplied labour are used to produce both the capital good and a
consumption good) with a population of identical infinite-lived consumers with stationary recursive preferences. In such a model, because of
the first welfare theorem, an intertemporal competitive equilibrium must
maximize the utility of the representative consumer subject to the
constraints imposed by the technology and the initial capital stock. As a
consequence, there must be a unique equilibrium for each value of the
initial capital stock (k_0, if we let the scalar k_t denote the quantity of

capital brought into period t), and this equilibrium will be independent of the realizations of any extraneous sunspot variables, since the equivalent optimal planning problem does not involve them. Hence the global weak determinacy thesis is valid for this kind of model. The equilibrium dynamics for the capital stock can be described by a first-order difference equation of the form (6), where $\kappa(k)$ denotes the optimal production of capital goods in a period, plus undepreciated capital goods remaining at the end of that period, as a function of the capital stock carried into that period. But whether or not global asymptotic determinacy obtains depends upon the form of the map κ.

It can be shown, under relatively weak assumptions concerning the decreasing returns to additional capital inputs given the fixed exogenous labour supply, that the map κ must be such that, for any k_t above a critical value $\bar{k}$, $\kappa(k_t) < k_t$. As a result, the dynamics for the capital stock will eventually be confined to the bounded interval $[0, \bar{k}]$. But this alone does not imply convergence. Under additional assumptions—for example a one-sector technology (i.e., the production technologies for the capital good and the consumption good are identical) and preferences for the representative consumer that are additively separable over time—one can show that κ must be a monotonically increasing function, with a unique fixed point $k^* > 0$, and $\kappa(k)$ greater or less than k according to whether k is less than or greater than k^*. In this case, k_t must converge asymptotically to k^* for all initial conditions $k_0 > 0$. But, as was first shown by Benhabib and Nishimura (1985), and is further developed by Boldrin (1989), in the case of a general two-sector technology, κ need not be a monotonically increasing function. If, for some range of capital stocks k_t, the optimal production programme involves a sufficiently higher capital–labour ratio in the consumption goods sector, κ will be a decreasing function of k_t; and if it is sharply enough decreasing near the steady-state capital stock (specifically, if $\kappa'(k^*) < -1$), the dynamics near the steady state will be unstable, so that, except under fortuitous conditions, k_t will not remain near k^* asymptotically. If the relative capital intensity of the consumption goods sector increases as the overall ratio of capital to labour in the economy increases, then κ can be a hump-shaped function of the kind shown in Fig. 8.1. If the hump is steep enough quite complicated dynamics are possible—indeed, the asymptotic dynamics may be 'chaotic'.[3]

As a contrasting case, there are also models of fluctuations arising from *self-fulfilling expectations*, often referred to as 'sunspot' equilibria.[4]

---

[3] For a simple discussion of how a hump-shaped map can have this consequence, see May (1976). For further examples of economic models resulting in dynamics of this sort, see Boldrin and Woodford (1990).

[4] The term is due to Cass and Shell (1983). The first general equilibrium example is due to Shell (1977), although the indeterminacy of intertemporal equilibrium pointing to the

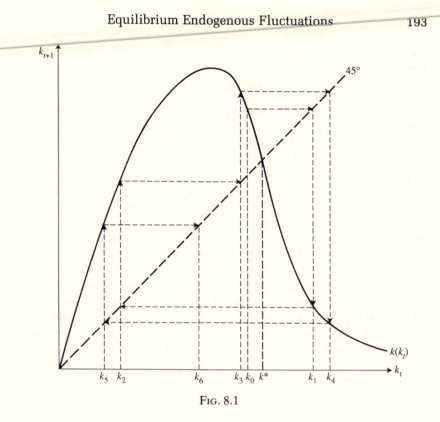

FIG. 8.1

Probably the best-known example is the overlapping-generations model of fiat money, studied by Azariadis (1981), Azariadis and Guesnerie (1982, 1986), and many subsequent authors. In this model there is no predetermined state variable k_t. The level of money prices p_t in each period is determined by an equilibrium condition of the form

$$f(p_t, \mu(p_{t+1})) = 0. \tag{7}$$

Here I have taken as given a non-stochastic path for the money supply, and assumed that there exist no other exogenous shocks to fundamentals either. Equation (7) indicates that expectations regarding the period $t + 1$ price level (and hence the real returns to holding money) affect desired money holdings in period t, and so the period t price level that equates the supply of and demand for real balances. Any stochastic process for $\{p_t\}$ that satisfies (7) represents a rational expectations equilibrium for such an economy.

possibility of purely 'speculative' fluctuations was discussed as early as Samuelson (1957), and the indeterminacy of rational expectations equilibrium in *ad hoc* macroeconomic models was much discussed in the 1970s (see e.g. Shiller 1978).

Even if we restrict attention to deterministic equilibria ('perfect foresight' equilibria), i.e., sequences of prices $\{p_t\}$ satisfying

$$f(p_t, p_{t+1}) = 0, \tag{8}$$

equilibrium may be indeterminate. For there is nothing to determine what the initial price level p_0 must be, except expectations about p_1. The price level p_0 might be anything in a certain interval of values, if appropriate expectations regarding p_1 exist. The equilibrium value of p_1 could similarly be anything in a certain interval of values, given appropriate expectations regarding p_2, and so on. To verify that many different values of p_0 are equally consistent with 'perfect foresight' equilibrium, one must show that each of them can be justified by a sequence of expected future price levels extending into the indefinite future. This can easily occur. For example, in the overlapping genera-tions model, money is the only way in which wealth can be transferred from the first to the second period of life. As a result, an increase in the expected price level in the second period of life may increase rather than decrease the real money balances desired by the young agents, if the income effect of changes in the expected return on savings out-weighs the substitution effect. If the income effect is sufficiently strong, the graph of pairs (p_t, p_{t+1}) satisfying (8) may be sharply backward-bending, as shown in Fig. 8.2.[5] The case drawn is that in which

$$f_2(p^*, p^*)/f_1(p^*, p^*) > 1. \tag{9}$$

A sequence of values $\{p_t\}$ of the kind shown is a 'perfect foresight' equilibrium, as is the steady state $p_t = p^*$ for all t. It will be observed that a similar construction is possible starting from any p_0 close enough to p^*. In this sense 'perfect foresight' equilibrium is indeterminate; each such sequence represents an equilibrium that can occur only if it is expected to.

Such indeterminacy also creates the possibility of equilibrium fluctu-ations in response to events ('sunspots') that do not change economic fundamentals. Consider a sunspot variable s_t that follows a two-state Markov chain, where $0 < q_{ij} < 1$ is the probability that state i is followed by state j, for $i, j = 1, 2$, and consider the possibility of an equilibrium in which $p_t = p_i$ whenever $s_t = i$, for $i = 1, 2$. The numbers (p_1, p_2) describe a rational expectations equilibrium if and only if the induced stochastic process for $\{p_t\}$ satisfies (7), i.e. if

$$f(p_i, \{p_1, p_2; q_{i1}\}) = 0, \qquad i = 1, 2, \tag{10}$$

where $\{p, p'; q\}$ denotes the probability distribution in which the value

---

[5] Here I have graphed this function with the inverse price level on the axes, so that the graph indicates the demand for real balances (on the horizontal axis) as a function of the expected real value of money in the following period (on the vertical axis).

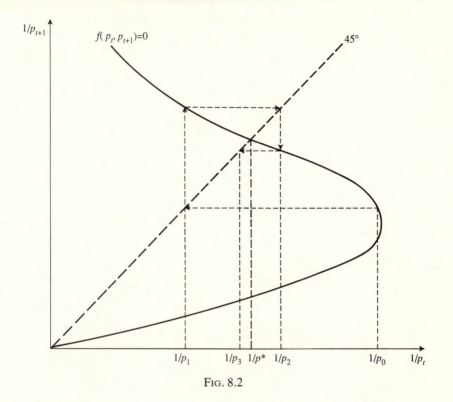

FIG. 8.2

p occurs with probability q and the value p' with probability $1 - q$. Given the transition probabilities $\{q_{ij}\}$, (10) is a set of two equations for the two variables (p_1, p_2). One solution is $p_1 = p_2 = p^*$, the deterministic steady-state equilibrium, but there may also be solutions with $p_1 \neq p_2$, in which case the price level depends upon the realization of the sunspot variable. In such a case the sunspot realization affects p_t through its effect upon expectations regarding the distribution $\mu(p_{t+1})$, which change in expectations is rational if people will continue to change their expectations in response to the sunspot realizations in the future. Thus, the belief that the sunspot variable indicates something that makes it appropriate to change one's expectations is self-fulfilling. The possibility of self-fulfilling revisions of expectations of this sort is clearly closely related to the indeterminacy of equilibrium just demonstrated for the deterministic case.[6]

The formal possibility of sunspot equilibria as solutions to (10) is illustrated by Fig. 8.3. Here the two equations in (10) are graphed; the

---

[6] For further discussion of this relationship, see Woodford (1984, 1986c).

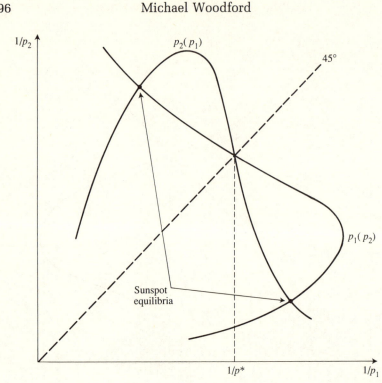

$$\text{FIG. 8.3}$$

intersections of the two curves represent rational expectations equilibria. The figure is drawn for the case of preferences and endowments like those that give rise to Fig. 8.2, and a sunspot process with q_{11} and q_{22} both small positive quantities. Because q_{12} is near 1, the first equation (10) gives p_1 as a function of p_2, where the function is similar to the one that gives p_t as a function of p_{t+1} in Fig. 8.2. (In Fig. 8.3, this graph is labelled $p_1(p_2)$.) Because q_{21} is near 1, the second equation in (10) gives p_2 as a similar function of p_1. (In Fig. 8.3 this graph is labelled $p_2(p_1)$.) The same condition discussed earlier—the demand for real balances being a sufficiently sharply decreasing function of the real return on money—makes the two curves cross at (p^{*-1}, p^{*-1}) in the directions shown. This crossing condition, together with the fact that desired real balances do not grow without bound as the expected return on money is made lower, then guarantees the existence of at least two off-diagonal intersections between the two curves, as shown.

   The Azariadis–Guesnerie construction, just discussed, depends upon strong income effects, so that the demand for real balances can be a sharply decreasing function of the expected return to holding money. While this is a theoretical possibility in the overlapping generations model, it is much more difficult for it to occur when the possibility of substituting between money and other assets is admitted, and it is not consistent with observed experience of the effects of inflation on money demand. It is accordingly perhaps useful to point out that, even in the sort of simple model just considered, the existence of sunspot equilibria does not depend upon this effect. Even when desired real balances are monotonically increasing in expected return (monotonically decreasing in expected inflation), it is still true that many values of p_t are consistent with equilibrium, given appropriate expectations regarding p_{t+1} and so on, and sunspot equilibria are often possible.

Chiappori and Guesnerie (1988) consider sunspot equilibria of the following form. Suppose that the sunspot variable is a countably infinite Markov chain, with a state space corresponding to the (positive and negative) integers, and suppose that, if the sunspot state is i in period t, in period $t + 1$ it will be $i - 1$ with probability $\frac{1}{2}$ and $i + 1$ with probability $\frac{1}{2}$. Consider again the possibility of equilibria in which $p_t = p_i$ whenever the sunspot state is i, for some fixed sequence of price levels (p_i) where i ranges over the positive and negative integers. A sequence (p_i) represents a rational expectations equilibrium if and only if

$$f(p_i, \{p_{i-1}, p_{i+1}; \tfrac{1}{2}\}) = 0, \tag{11}$$

for $i = \ldots, -2, -1, 0, 1, 2, \ldots$ Solutions to (11) can be analysed in the same fashion as the trajectories of a discrete-time dynamical system. If the left-hand side is monotonic in all three (say, decreasing in p_i and increasing in both p_{i-1} and p_{i+1}, as occurs if substitution effects outweigh income effects), then we can solve for p_{i+1} as a function of (p_{i-1}, p_i), and for p_{i-1} as a function of (p_i, p_{i+1}). Then, given any point (p_i, p_{i+1}) in the domain on which these maps are defined, we can define a 'forward' mapping that takes such a point to (p_{i+1}, p_{i+2}), and a 'backward' mapping that takes it to (p_{i-1}, p_i). We then wish to study the itineraries of points in the plane under repeated applications of these mappings. If we are able to apply both mappings an unlimited number of times (so as to define a complete 'trajectory') without reaching a point where prices become negative or where the mapping ceases to be defined, then we obtain a sequence (p_i) that represents a rational expectations equilibrium. One such solution is the sequence $p_i = p^*$ for all i; this fixed point of the 'dynamical' system defined by (11) corresponds to the monetary steady state. But there may be 'trajectories' other than fixed points that can be continued for ever as well, and these correspond to sunspot equilibria.

Chiappori and Guesnerie show that the dynamics in the plane induced by the 'forward' mapping can easily look like those shown in Fig. 8.4. (Again, I have graphed the inverse price level on the two axes.) Here

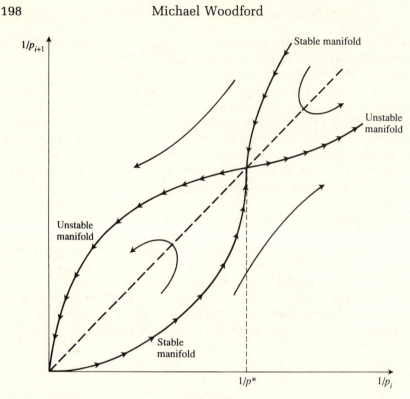

FIG. 8.4

the solid lines with arrows superimposed represent the stable and
unstable manifolds of the fixed point (p^{*-1}, p^{*-1}).[7] Now consider a
point (p_1^{-1}, p_2^{-1}) somewhere on the segment of the stable manifold that
connects $(0, 0)$ to (p^{*-1}, p^{*-1}). Applying the 'forward' and 'backward'
maps repeatedly to this point, one generates a sequence of values (p_i)
such that, for all i, (p_i^{-1}, p_{i+1}^{-1}) lies on that same segment of the stable
manifold, and such that

$$p^* < \ldots < p_{i+2} < p_{i+1} < p_i < p_{i-1} < p_{i-2} < \ldots < \infty.$$

This describes a sunspot equilibrium in which the price level fluctuates
for ever between p^* and infinity; the fluctuations are not transient, in
the sense that every state i is eventually visited infinitely often, with
probability 1. When the sunspot state changes from i to $i + 1$, the price
level falls, because the expected price level in the future falls, increasing
the current demand for real money balances through the standard

---

[7] Note that $(0, 0)$ is another fixed point, representing the deterministic equilibrium in
which money is not valued in any period because it is not expected to be valued in the
future.

Cagan–Bresciani–Turroni effect of inflation expectations on money demand. Again, the belief that the sunspot realizations will affect the price level in this way is self-fulfilling.[8]

These two types of models of endogenous fluctuations are different in some important respects. One is that sunspot equilibria are inherently stochastic. Hence the attempt to distinguish empirically between whether economic time series are 'genuinely random' or not (see e.g. Brock 1986) cannot be relevant to distinguishing between exogenous-shock theories and endogenous theories of economic fluctuations.[9]

Another difference is the extent to which nonlinearities are essential to the possibility of endogenous fluctuations of the two sorts. As indicated above, the asymptotic strong determinacy thesis is very generally true of linear systems of equilibrium conditions, assuming that global weak determinacy obtains and that equilibrium fluctuations do not grow without bound. Hence nonlinearities in the equilibrium conditions are crucial to the possibility of endogenous fluctuations of the kind that I have called 'determinate but unstable', and in the case of most examples in the literature (in particular the more interesting examples, which are those of chaotic dynamics) the nonlinearities must be quite severe. For example, in the case of one-dimensional dynamics of the kind illustrated in Fig. 8.1, it is necessary for the function κ to go from having a slope greater than 1 for low values of k to having a slope less than -1 for high values of k. Global weak determinacy is not, on the contrary, an especially general property even of linear models, and the features of the equilibrium conditions associated with the Azariadis–Guesnerie model that allow sunspot equilibria to exist have mostly to do with the derivatives of the functions involved (in particular, of the function f in (7)) near the steady-state values of the arguments.[10] For

---

[8] A similar construction is possible using points on the unstable manifold or, indeed, many other points in the plane that lie on 'trajectories' that can be extended arbitrarily in both directions, as is discussed by Chiappori and Guesnerie.

[9] For reasons explained above, the distinction between random and deterministic time series is not even an appropriate way of trying to distinguish what I have called 'determinate but unstable' dynamics from the dynamics associated with a pure exogenous-shock model.

[10] This may seem paradoxical, given that Azariadis and Guesnerie (1986) establish that the existence of a two-period deterministic cycle is necessary and sufficient for the existence of the two-state Markov equilibria, and the existence of deterministic cycles is dependent upon nonlinearity in the generic case, as just argued. None the less, a *sufficient* condition for the existence of the two-state Markov equilibria is (9), as shown by Azariadis (1981), and this condition does not involve any nonlinear aspects of the function f; (9) is both necessary and sufficient for the existence of sunspot equilibria that remain for ever near the steady-state equilibrium, as shown by Woodford (1986c). Furthermore, together with the boundary assumptions on the behaviour of f made by Azariadis and Guesnerie (which imply nonlinearity, at least at extreme values of the arguments), (9) is also a sufficient condition for the existence of a period 2 deterministic cycle. On the other hand, (9) is sufficient for the existence of two Markov equilibria even in the absence of the boundary conditions just referred to.

suppose that (7) were exactly linear, i.e. that it took the form

$$f_1(p_t - p^*) + f_2 E_t(p_{t+1} - p^*) = 0, \tag{12}$$

and suppose also that, in accordance with (9), the constant coefficients are such that $f_2/f_1 > 1$. Then, if $\{s_t\}$ is a sequence of independent random variables with mean zero, one class of solutions to (12) in which the sunspot realizations affect the price level would be

$$p_t = p^* + c\sum_{j=0}^{\infty}(f_1/f_2)^j s_{t-j},$$

where $c \neq 0$ is an arbitrary constant. (If the random variables $\{s_t\}$ are uniformly bounded, then the infinite sum in this expression is always well defined.)

Because sunspot equilibria are perfectly consistent with linearity, it will often be convenient to use linear methods, just as in the case of the familiar exogenous-shock models, both in theoretical analyses of the predicted character of economic fluctuations and in empirical testing of the implications of the models. This is a great advantage over the models of determinate but unstable dynamics, as it allows for the analysis and testing of more sophisticated (and so, possibly, more realistic) versions of the models. Finally, it should be observed that tests for nonlinearity in the laws governing the evolution of observed economic time series (see references below at footnote 13) have no clear connection with the issue of whether observed fluctuations are exogenous or endogenous in character, any more than do the tests for genuine randomness, in so far as one important class of models of endogenous fluctuations does not depend upon nonlinearity.

The degree to which these two types of models of endogenous fluctuations are qualitatively dissimilar has probably been obscured by the fact that the overlapping-generations model of fiat money, with a backward-bending demand for real money balances as shown in Fig. 8.2, has been much discussed as a leading example both of sunspot equilibria (Azariadis and Guesnerie) and of deterministic equilibrium cycles (Grandmont 1985). It will be observed that the mapping in Fig. 8.2 is the same as that in Fig. 8.1, but with the axes reversed. That is, the function that gives the demand for real balances as a function of the expected real value of money in the next period is the same sort of hump-shaped function that gives k_{t+1} as a function of k_t in the growth model of Benhabib and Nishimura. Accordingly, similar methods can be used (see Grandmont) to show that, if the hump is steep enough, the 'backward perfect foresight dynamics' of the overlapping-generations model will be characterized by an unstable steady state, the existence of deterministic equilibrium cycles, and even the existence of chaotic equilibrium trajectories.

But this should not be taken to mean that the mechanisms giving rise to sunspot equilibria on the one hand, and the sort of endogenous deterministic cycles studied by authors such as Benhabib and Nishimura on the other, are essentially the same. For in fact, the Grandmont example has little in common with the main literature on deterministic cycles.[11] The 'backward perfect foresight dynamics' are simply not the dynamics of interest, and the Grandmont example does not really have dynamical properties similar to those of models where a hump-shaped map describes the evolution of a predetermined state variable. In the overlapping generations model, there is not anything that fixes the price level at some future date (the way that an initial capital stock is given by history in the Benhabib–Nishimura model), so that one would be interested in deriving the consequences of that expectation for the price level in previous periods. And even if there were, one would not be interested in tracing the consequences of that expectation into the indefinite past (in the way that one solves a growth model forward into the indefinite future), so that one would not be interested in the asymptotic consequences of repeated iteration of the 'backward perfect foresight dynamics' map (such as whether the dynamics asymptotically approach a fixed point or a cycle, or instead are for ever aperiodic). In the case of the forward dynamics of a predetermined state variable, the existence of chaotic dynamics is interesting because it indicates that the time series generated could be very irregular even in the absence of exogenous shocks—indeed, could closely resemble a truly stochastic time series. But the existence of chaotic 'backward perfect foresight dynamics' in the overlapping generations model is not of similar interest. No such construction is needed to demonstrate that irregular or apparently stochastic equilibrium dynamics is possible in that model. Even setting aside the possibility of sunspot equilibria, it will be observed from Fig. 8.2 that a given equilibrium price level p_t can often be equally well justified by two different expectations regarding p_{t+1}, and so the *forward* perfect foresight dynamics, being often not uniquely defined, plainly allow for very irregular trajectories, since a very complex rule may be used to determine which value of p_{t+1} occurs following each time that p_t takes such a value.

The Grandmont analysis does suffice to demonstrate the possibility of deterministic cycles of all periods, since the existence of deterministic cycles in the backward dynamics is equivalent to the existence of such cycles in the forward dynamics. But as I have argued above, it is not really the possibility of deterministic cycles in the absence of exogenous shocks that is the important feature of models such as that of Benhabib and Nishimura, but rather, the fact that the equilibrium dynamics are

---

[11] For further discussion, see Boldrin and Woodford (1990).

determinate but unstable, a property not true of the Grandmont example. In my view the overlapping generations model illustrates the possibility of endogenous equilibrium fluctuations as a result of the indeterminacy of rational expectations equilibrium, and the deterministic cycles studied by Grandmont are best understood as simply degenerate, limiting cases of finite-state Markovian sunspot equilibria of the kind studied by Azariadis and Guesnerie. The sort of determinate cycles exhibited by Benhabib and Nishimura represent a distinct type of endogenous fluctuation.

3. The Revival of Interest in the Endogenous-Cycle Hypothesis

In this section I wish to consider some of the reasons for the current revival of interest in endogenous models of economic fluctuations. There are two broad issues to be addressed. First, what are the reasons for the widespread methodological presumption in favour of exogenous-shock models, and why do some now find them less compelling? And second, what is especially interesting about endogenous explanations as a class, so that the question of whether or not economic fluctuations have an endogenous component should be worthy of discussion, quite apart from a consideration of the merits of any particular endogenous theory? I take up these issues in sequence. Because, as explained above, the literature on endogenous-cycle models consists largely of two rather different types of models—the models of determinate but unstable dynamics on the one hand, and the models of sunspot equilibria or self-fulfilling expectations on the other—I will discuss the revival of interest in each of these two modelling strategies separately.

The idea that economic fluctuations might be due to intrinsically unstable dynamics of the market system is not new. Indeed, the earliest formal models of business cycles were largely of this type, including most notably the business cycle models proposed by John Hicks, Nicholas Kaldor, and Richard Goodwin. In all of these models, given initial conditions determine a unique time path for the economy, but the stationary equilibrium growth path for the economy is unstable. Deviations from this stationary path reinforce themselves, leading to explosive movement away from it; however, eventually these are contained by 'floors and ceilings', such as shortages of productive factors on the up-side or technological limits to the speed at which the capital stock can be decreased on the down-side, resulting in repetitive bounded fluctuations. As explained above, the nonlinearity of the dynamical laws proposed by these theorists plays a crucial role in allowing for endogenous deterministic cycles (and also, although this was not realized until recently, for chaotic dynamics).

By the late 1950s, however, this way of attempting to model aggregate fluctuations had largely fallen out of favour, the dominant approach having become instead the Slutsky–Frisch–Tinbergen methodology of exogenous stochastic 'impulses' that are transformed into a characteristic pattern of oscillations through the filtering properties of the economy's 'propagation mechanism'. There were probably two main reasons for the overwhelming popularity of the latter methodology, apart from whatever comfort may have been provided by a vision of the market process as fundamentally self-stabilizing.

First of all, as explained earlier, models of determinate but intrinsically unstable dynamics are essentially nonlinear. But the linear specifications that were possible in the case of the exogenous-shock models were extremely convenient, both from an analytical point of view (the properties of nonlinear differential or difference equations could be studied only in special cases, as when Goodwin was able to demonstrate a formal analogy between a particular business cycle model and the Van der Pol oscillator) and from the point of view of empirical testing (linear regression techniques were well understood, tractable ways of estimating nonlinear models much less so).

Second, the endogenous-cycle hypothesis was thought to have been empirically refuted. Actual business cycles, it was easily shown, are far from being regular periodic motions.[12] The spectrum, for example, of an aggregate time series (such as real GNP) typically exhibits no pronounced peaks, let alone actual spikes at certain frequencies, as one would expect in the case of exact deterministic cycles. Yet the analytical treatment of the endogenous-cycle models had been directed entirely towards the demonstration that nonlinear deterministic relationships could give rise to exactly repetitive deterministic cycles. Furthermore, econometric models began to be estimated which, when simulated with repeated exogenous stochastic shocks, produced data that in many respects resembled actual aggregate time series, but which when simulated without the exogenous shocks indicated convergence to a steady state (Adelman and Adelman 1959). Demonstrations of this kind appeared to show that the true structural relations implied an intrinsically stable economy, with business cycles being observed only because of the constant occurrence of exogenous shocks.

Both of these sorts of considerations have less force today than they

---

[12] At the workshop, Sir John Hicks indicated that this had been the main reason for his own loss of interest in the hypothesis of endogenous cycles after the 1950s. He attributed the downfall of the endogenous models to the availability in the postwar period of better time-series data on economic aggregates.

must have seemed to have around 1960. For one thing, advances in the mathematics of dynamical systems, in the econometrics of nonlinear models, and, above all, in computational capacity make both the analysis and the estimation of nonlinear models much more tractable. It is certainly still true that linear models are much simpler to handle; and, if one wants to allow complicated lag structures not much constrained by an a priori theory, as advocated by the currently popular vector-autoregression methodology, linear models alone easily provide one with a set of free parameters whose number is quite large compared with the size of typical macroeconomic data-sets, so that nonlinear specifications might be ignored on principle in order to lessen the danger of 'over-fitting'. None the less, it is clearly possible to imagine a demonstration that a nonlinear specification allows for an improvement in fit that more than justifies the inclusion of the additional free parameters; and indeed, a number of recent studies of this kind have been able to reject the null hypothesis of linearity in formal econometric tests.[13] It is also certainly possible to test particular nonlinear specifications that might be suggested on theoretical grounds.

Also, from the point of view of analysis of theoretical models, linear dynamics continue to be vastly simpler to analyse. Particularly in the case of chaotic dynamics, a reasonably complete mathematical theory exists only for relatively simple classes of dynamic systems, such as first-order nonlinear difference equations. This continues to severely constrain the modelling assumptions of theorists who wish to be able to provide analytical results regarding the conditions under which equilibrium dynamics should be chaotic, a handicap that becomes critical when one wishes to compare the assumptions and predictions of such models with actual data. (The problem is not quite as bad in the case of analytical results regarding the existence of deterministic cycles, since some of the techniques used here, such as the Hopf bifurcation theorem, can equally well be applied to systems of arbitrarily high order; but here one cannot hope for success in modelling actual fluctuations in anything but an extremely rough sense, since actual fluctuations are plainly not close to being exactly repetitive.) Probably the development of models of this kind that would even allow the question of empirical adequacy to be seriously engaged will require a shift to greater emphasis upon numerical solution techniques for particular parameter values chosen to be roughly realistic, as opposed to analytical results; such a shift has already taken place in work in the equilibrium business cycle theory of the conventional (exogenous-shock) sort.

---

[13] Some examples are Neftci (1984), Hinich and Patterson (1985), Ashley and Patterson (1987), Hammour (1988*b*), and the work cited in fn. 15 below.

In addition to making the investigation of nonlinear models more tractable, recent mathematical advances have shown that the simple empirical 'refutations' of the endogenous-cycle hypothesis referred to above do not prove as much as they might have seemed to. The mere fact that a particular statistical model is judged to 'fit' the data, in the sense of coming close to a correct prediction of a few sample moments, does not mean that some very different model, outside the class of models considered by the estimation strategy being used, would not in fact describe the data much better. John Blatt (1978) showed that, when a linear autoregressive model was fitted to periodic data generated by simulation of the Hicks nonlinear cycle model, the parameter estimates implied a stable second-order autoregressive process for output, perturbed by stochastic shocks (of the kind that is in fact obtained from autoregressions of US GNP data), despite the fact that the exact nonlinear model generating the data involved intrinsically unstable dynamics. It is now understood that deterministic dynamical systems can generate chaotic dynamics that can look very irregular and can have autocorrelation functions and spectra that exactly mimic those of a 'stable' linear stochastic model, such as a stationary AR(1) model (Sakai and Tokumaru 1980).[14] Indeed, a nonlinear deterministic model can generate chaotic data that, as far as the complete autocorrelation function is concerned (the only moments of the data with which linear econometric techniques are concerned), look like perfect 'white noise'— not merely a stable model, but one with no persistence of fluctuations at all.

In order to meet the challenge posed by Blatt's demonstration and similar exercises, new techniques for the analysis of economic time series are necessary. A start has been made on this problem by William Brock and co-workers,[15] who have developed a set of tests (based upon previous work by physicists) that can in principle distinguish data generated by deterministic models quite generally (including deterministic chaos) from data that are 'genuinely stochastic'. None of the results yet obtained provide anything that could be called even a strong suggestion of the existence of deterministic chaos, although several economic times series have been found to exhibit important nonlinear structure.

[14] Nor are the types of dynamics required for this in any way inconsistent with economic theory. Brock and Chamberlain (1985) show that spectra of this kind can be associated with the sort of nonlinear dynamics implied by an intertemporal general equilibrium model. Boldrin and Montrucchio (1986) show that this is true even of the dynamics associated with an optimal growth model.

[15] This literature begins with Brock (1986). Other important contributors include William Barnett, Dee Dechert, David Hsieh, Blake LeBaron, James Ramsey, Chera Sayers, and Jose Scheinkman. For recent surveys of these contributions, see Brock (1988) and Scheinkman (1990).

The question of real interest, of course, is not whether the data are truly deterministic as opposed to stochastic (again, we know the economy's evolution is not deterministic, at least not if we restrict our set of state variables to any relatively small set of purely 'economic' variables), nor whether they exhibit some kind of nonlinearity (why should the true laws of motion be exactly linear, even if the economy is very stable in the absence of exogenous shocks?). What we would like to know is whether there seems to be nonlinearity of the particular sort associated with models in which the economy would exhibit an endogenous tendency to fluctuate even in the absence of exogenous shocks, despite the fact that in reality there are also perturbations arising from such shocks. Most of the tests for nonlinearity proposed so far are not designed to answer this question.

Indeed, it is not clear that the question can be answered by purely statistical (i.e. atheoretical) methods. For example, one might think that estimating threshold autoregressive models (as proposed by Hammour 1988b), in which the coefficients of a piecewise linear model are allowed to take different values in different regions of the state space, would allow one to test for the existence of unstable dynamics near the economy's steady-state growth path together with stable dynamics in the case of sufficiently large deviations from the steady state. But the mere discovery that the best-fitting autoregressive model, in the case of data from periods when the economy is near its long-run trend path, involves 'unstable' coefficients does not prove that the data are generated by a process involving intrinsically unstable dynamics. The fact that the conditional expectation of some state variable x_{t+1}, given an observed value for x_t, is a function of x_t with slope greater than 1 does not imply that an exogenous shock that perturbs the value of x_t must cause an even larger change in the value of x_{t+1}, so that the effect of the initial perturbation propagates explosively until nonlinearities ('floors and ceilings') succeed in containing it. The extreme sensitivity of the conditional expectation (that would show up as a large coefficient in the threshold autoregression) might simply be because (under the process that happens to be generating the observed data) the value of x_t conveys information about some unobserved exogenous fundamental state variable that is strongly persistent and whose value in period $t + 1$ will have an important causal effect upon x_{t+1}; and it happens that, in the range of values for x_t under consideration, small differences in x_t imply large changes in the conditional expectation of the unobserved fundamental state. The dynamics for x_t in the absence of variation in the unobserved fundamental state need not be unstable, nor need it be the case that any other perturbations to the value of x_t would not be quickly damped. For this reason, it seems unlikely to me that much progress can be made in assessing the empirical validity of the hypothesis of intrinsically unstable dynamics, except by investigating particular nonlinear specifications implied by a particular theoretical model. Progress thus depends upon better understanding of the theoretical conditions under which endogenous fluctuations can occur, and in particular upon an extension of our theoretical understanding to much more flexible specifications, using numerical solution techniques as suggested above.

The hypothesis that endogenous fluctuations result from self-fulfilling fluctuations is also not really new, although its incorporation into formal models of economic dynamics dates only since the 'rational expectations' revolution of the 1970s. A long tradition of attempts to explain recurrent cyclical fluctuations in business activity assigned a central role to shifts in the 'degree of optimism' or 'confidence' on the part of economic actors—changes in outlook that were not required by any objective change in economic circumstances. Writers who assigned an important role to expectations as an autonomous causal factor include John Stuart Mill, John Mills, Alfred and Mary Marshall, Frederick Lavington and Arthur Pigou. The culmination of this tradition was, of course, the *General Theory* of John Maynard Keynes, in which aggregate fluctuations are argued to be driven mainly by fluctuations in investment spending, which in turn is volatile largely because of its sensitivity to volatile expectations, the 'animal spirits' of entrepreneurs.

Changes in expectations have not, however, been assigned so large a role in the explanation of business fluctuations in the period since Keynes wrote. There are probably several reasons for this. For one, in the postwar heyday of positivist social science, there was an evident reluctance to appeal to 'subjective' factors. Thus, Alvin Hansen (1964; 288) writes approvingly of Tugan-Baranovsky's rejection of an important role for expectational factors. 'In the end it is cold objective facts that control, not simply psychological moods of optimism and pessimism. The hour of reckoning comes sooner or later.'

Perhaps more crucially, the main object of macroeconomic modelling came to be the identification of stable quantitative relationships between measurable economic variables, through econometric means; the logic of rational choice was still considered to be useful in determining what sorts of econometric specifications were likely to be useful, but the interpretability of the asserted relationships was of secondary importance to their consistency with the statistical evidence. From this point of view, it mattered little whether or not investment demand fluctuated mainly in response to arbitrary changes in expectations. If the changes in expectations could not be independently measured, they would simply show up as a residual in the investment equation, and the interpretation of such residuals was not important except in so far as one could find ways of reducing the residual variance by introducing additional regressors.

More recent developments, however, leave us less reason to dismiss the hypothesis of expectational instability as uninteresting even in principle. On the one hand, Lucas (1976) has forcefully argued that it is vital to model explicitly the role of expectations in the equations of one's model, rather than regarding as 'structural' the way in which variables that affect people's expectations are found to enter in one's regressions, because a change in policy regime should change the way that expectations respond to those variables and hence the coefficients in the regression. But once one begins modelling expectations explicitly in this way, it becomes reasonable to ask whether changes in expectations unrelated to shifts in economic 'fundamentals' are not among the ultimate sources of variability in economic activity. Indeed, modelling expectations as 'rational', i.e., as consistent with the actual relationships between variables determined by those same people's behaviour, and hence as endogenous, directs attention to this possibility.

There has also doubtless been a fear that free use of the hypothesis of expectational instability makes things too easy—any event, it might be argued, can be 'explained' after the fact by positing an arbitrary shift in expectations, but nothing can be predicted in advance. This is an understandable concern, but it is unfair to the earlier literature on expectational instability. Changes in expectations were not invoked simply as a *deus ex machina*, allowing the analyst to evade any responsibility for narrative continuity in his account of economic events. On the contrary, there is frequently an insistence upon the extent to which a change in expectations, once begun, produces effects that confirm and strengthen that very belief. Lavington, for example, writes that an initial increase in the confidence of some producers, 'whether or not this confidence is justified', leads to actions that are themselves 'a real cause of increased confidence on the part of many other producers', so that a boom results (1921: 171–2). In other words, changes in beliefs become important in generating fluctuations in circumstances in which they tend to be *self-fulfilling*. Accordingly, this literature emphasizes the role of particular economic structures in creating the conditions under which revisions of expectations can become self-fulfilling, and gives detailed discussions of the particular sequence of events consequent upon such a trajectory once the initial perturbation from the economy's stationary state occurs. While little attempt is made to predict why the initial triggering event occurs or even what sort of event it must be, there are many predictions about the typical course of a 'business cycle' and about the kind of economies that should be subject to instability of that sort.

The view that expectations ought not to be assigned any independent explanatory role is sometimes thought to follow from the rational expectations hypothesis; for it is assumed that, if expectations change in the absence of any change in economic 'fundamentals', they must be biased. But in fact, it is possible even in a rational expectations equilibrium for expectations to change in response to a random event that does not affect fundamentals; the very fact that people change their expectations and hence their actions in response to the event can make it rational to change one's forecast when it occurs. This is what is meant by a 'sunspot equilibrium'; in the previous section I have shown how such equilibria can be possible. In grounding the possibility of a causal role for revisions of expectations upon an underlying indeterminacy of rational expectations, the modern literature again formalizes a theme of the older writers, as represented in particular by Keynes's comparison of the stock market to a beauty contest (1936: 154–8).

Some have argued that economic models with multiple equilibria should be judged unsatisfactory for that very reason, and so should be either assumed not to describe the world, or supplemented by a selection criterion which picks out a unique equilibrium, or at least a more restricted class of equilibria, that presumably will not involve any fluctuations in response to sunspot variables. The principle that I have above called the 'global weak determinacy thesis' is simply the most generally accepted element of such a criterion. Behind such a proposal is the idea that ruling out such equilibria a priori imposes more discipline upon the process of economic explanation, by establishing a tighter link between assumptions about underlying structure and the predictions generated about aggregate fluctuations. But such reasoning is hardly persuasive. First, it is undesirable to rely upon an arbitrary selection principle that has no interpretation in terms of a causal mechanism the realism of which could be independently verified. A causal analysis of how equilibrium expectations might arise (involving an explicit model of how people learn from their experience) can in some cases indicate that expectations should converge upon an equilibrium in which sunspot events affect people's expectations (Woodford 1990). I have shown that, in the case of the model economy of Azariadis and Guesnerie discussed earlier, if people use a particular plausible algorithm as a way of determining how useful the sunspot state is to them in forecasting the rate of return on holding money, then, in the case of certain kinds of preferences, the deterministic steady-state equilibrium is unstable under the learning dynamics, which converge to one of the Markovian sunspot equilibria with probability 1 (see Woodford 1990).

But even more crucially, it is unfair to characterize reliance upon a multiplicity of rational expectations equilibria as making the predictions of economic theory too general, if the alternative strategy for explaining aggregate fluctuations is to assume continual random shifts in preferences and/or technology as needed in order to account for the fluctuations. Indeed, the latter approach allows the theorist many more degrees of freedom in explaining observed patterns of variation than does the one I argue for here. For only under certain conditions will sunspot equilibria be possible, while one can always obtain fluctuating equilibria if one posits fluctuating fundamentals; and, in so far as one is free to assume any statistical properties one likes for the fluctuating fundamentals, the range of possible types of equilibrium fluctuations that are consistent with a given basic model becomes very large. The predictions of a sunspot model for the character of equilibrium fluctuations can be quite specific, despite the existence of a large set of equilibria. For example, all rational expectations equilibria of the Azariadis–Guesnerie model, and not just the finite-state Markov solutions discussed above, must satisfy equation (7), which is a testable restriction upon the stochastic process followed by the price level. In the case of any equilibrium involving fluctuations that are small enough in amplitude for the nonlinear aspects of (7) to be relatively unimportant, (7) is essentially a specification of the degree of serial correlation of the price level. The model also makes precise predictions regarding the co-movement of the price level and the real allocation of resources; in the case of a more complex model with more state variables, the number of such predictions regarding the co-movement of state variables that must hold in any sunspot equilibrium can be quite large.[16]

Another general ground for reluctance to consider models with multiple equilibria is the feeling that in such models determinate predictions about the consequences of policy interventions are not possible, so that economic theory ceases to provide any guidance for policy. It is true that the same sort of economic structures that allow for sunspot equilibria will render indeterminate the response to many kinds of policy changes, and this even if one neglects to consider the possibility of sunspot equilibria, as Roger Farmer and I (Farmer and Woodford 1984) have shown previously. But this does not mean that such a model makes no useful predictions about policy choices. For it remains possible to distinguish between policy regimes or institutional arrangements that allow for sunspot equilibria and those that do not, and the choice of policies or institutions of the latter sort, in order to rule out one possible source of aggregate instability, may itself be an appropriate object of public policy. That interesting discriminations of this sort among policy regimes can be made is demonstrated in Woodford (1988b). (See also Grandmont 1986.)

Still, some may ask, Why should the question of whether observed aggregate fluctuations are to some extent endogenous matter? Of course, all will agree that a more accurate model of economic fluctu-

---

[16] For examples of the predictions that sunspot models generate about the character of fluctuations, see Woodford (1988a, 1991).

ations would be useful, and methodological blinders that prevent one from discovering the true structure are obviously undesirable. But this does not explain why the endogenous or exogenous origin of fluctuations should be a question of interest in itself, apart from the interest that there might be in arguing for some particular model that happens to explain fluctuations as endogenous. Indeed, it might be argued that endogenous and exogenous explanations considered as general categories cannot be regarded as different for any practical purposes, owing to the substantial continuity that exists between the two categories. Not much can follow from the claim that an economy fluctuates in response to random events that are true sunspot variables—in the sense of having no effect whatsoever on fundamentals—as opposed to its fluctuating in response to events that represent changes of negligible size in fundamentals.[17] Nor can much follow from the claim that global asymptotic determinacy does not hold for an economy, and so that the effect of initial conditions on the endogenous state variables remains non-negligible for ever—instead of eventually dying out, as claimed by the determinacy thesis, but with an extremely slow rate of decay.

But these are not really adequate reasons for ignoring the possibility of endogenous fluctuations. The simple fact that the boundary between the different categories of explanations that would be most relevant is not susceptible of clear definition does not mean that models that represent 'ideal types' of the endogenous category are not useful in demonstrating what would be meant by an explanation of that kind and under what circumstances it would be possible. And it is possible to speak of relatively general implications of the hypothesis of endogenous instability that make the question of interest even when framed so generally.

For one, it can be stated with reasonable generality that an endogenous explanation of aggregate fluctuations implies that they are inefficient and so undesirable. The general argument is that, under the usual modelling assumptions of strictly concave production sets and utility functions, fluctuations in the allocation of resources that occur other than as a response to fluctuations in either tastes or technological possibilities must reduce expected utility compared with a steadier growth path. More precise results along this line are discussed in the next section. It is shown there that the claim just made is subject to a

---

[17] Indeed, one can show that, when sunspot equilibria exist, the equilibrium response to small shocks to fundamentals is also indeterminate, and that among the possible rational expectations equilibria are equilibria in which the endogenous-state variables respond very strongly, despite the fact that the change in fundamentals is very small. Such 'over-response' to a change in fundamentals would be observationally indistinguishable from a sunspot equilibrium. See Farmer and Woodford (1984), Woodford (1986c: theorem 2); and Chiappori and Guesnerie (1988).

number of qualifications; one can construct theoretical examples, both of sunspot equilibria and of determinate but unstable equilibrium dynamics, in which the equilibria are Pareto-optimal. None the less, it is argued that the cases of most likely practical relevance under which endogenous fluctuations of either sort are possible are conditions under which the fluctuating equilibria are inefficient (and can occur only because of some kind of market failure). Nor is it by any means the case that exogenous-shock models must imply that fluctuations are not a problem: the mere fact that exogenous shocks to fundamentals imply that *some* response would be efficient does not mean that the one that actually occurs must be. None the less, this is a property of at least the currently most popular class of exogenous-shock models (real business cycle models), which is not surprising, given the general predilection of economists to be led from a basic commitment to an explanation in terms of optimization and equilibrium into the assumption of a perfect system of competitive markets, except in cases where the phenomenon to be explained is clearly incompatible with such an assumption.

Second, endogenous explanations as a class result in a presumption that in principle there ought to exist policy interventions that can suppress or at least significantly reduce the fluctuations, without requiring a radical alteration of the structure of the economy and, in particular, without having to cure the underlying market failures (arising from private information, say, or increasing returns) that allow the inefficient fluctuations to occur in equilibrium in the first place. In the case of exogenous shocks, policy interventions can affect the nature of the fluctuations that occur in response to the shocks, but it is hard to prevent fluctuations of one sort or another from occurring. If the fluctuations are purely endogenous, then there is no reason why the economy could not follow a completely steady path, and the modifications required to get this to happen might be minimal. For example, in the case of sunspot equilibria, there will typically also exist equilibria in which there are no fluctuations in response to the sunspot variables; one simply needs to design a policy regime that prevents the occurrence of the sunspot equilibria and leaves the non-fluctuating equilibrium or equilibria as the only possibility. The type of intervention needed may be a credible commitment to intervene only if fluctuations were to arise, which will never have to be acted upon in equilibrium.[18] In the case of determinate but unstable dynamics, elimination of the endogenous cycles requires only that the feedback loop that sustains them be weakened to the point where the cycles cease to be self-sustaining, and not that the nature of any of the causal links in the chain that creates

---

[18] For an example of stabilization policy of this kind, see Woodford (1986a).

the cycles be completely changed. Thus, in the case of the dynamics represented by Fig. 8.1, an intervention that changed the shape of the hump to make it a bit less steep would succeed in rendering stable the deterministic steady state; it is not necessary to transform the dynamics to the extent that they are no longer described by a hump-shaped map. The issue of stabilization policy will not be discussed in the case of any of the examples of endogenous cycle models that are sketched here, both because of space limitations and because of the foolishness of talking too much about the policy prescriptions that might be drawn from models whose empirical relevance has not yet been established. But the fact that models of the general class discussed here could well have consequences for policy analysis that are different from those associated with more conventional models remains an important reason for being interested in the question of those models' logical coherence and empirical adequacy.

4. The Consistency of Endogenous Fluctuations with Optimizing Behaviour

In discussing reasons for neglect of the hypothesis of endogenous fluctuations in the previous section, I have set aside what is perhaps the most serious objection to this general class of explanations. This is the view that the possibility of endogenous fluctuations can be ignored, not because of a special methodological commitment to the determinacy theses, but as a consequence of more basic methodological commitments—specifically, commitments to explaining economic phenomena in terms of optimizing behaviour and competitive equilibrium. If it can be shown that economic models founded upon these postulates necessarily satisfy the determinacy theses, then there is no need to argue for them as independent modelling principles.

The examples presented in Section 2 already have demonstrated that no really strong claim of this kind is tenable, since the economies described are ones in which all agents maximize their expected utility, all agents have rational expectations, and all markets are perfectly competitive and clear at all times. None the less, sufficiently restricted versions of this claim are actually true. Some may feel that these suffice to create a presumption against the empirical relevance of the endogenous-cycle hypothesis. I wish instead to emphasize that these results show the extent to which endogenous fluctuations, if they do occur, are likely to be connected with the failure of an ideal system of competitive markets to exist.

One important general result of this kind is the following:

THE SUNSPOT IRRELEVANCE THEOREM. Suppose that the economy is perfectly competitive and that the standard conditions required to prove the efficiency of competitive equilibrium (no externalities, no distorting taxes, etc.) are satisfied. In particular, suppose that there exist only a finite number of distinct consumer types, and suppose that there exists a complete set of Arrow–Debreu contingent-claims markets, including markets for securities contingent upon all possible realizations of the sunspot variables. Finally, suppose that production sets are convex (no increasing returns) and that consumers' von Neumann–Morgenstern utility functions are strictly concave (consumers are risk-averse). Then no rational expectations equilibria involve fluctuations in the allocation of resources, or fluctuations in the relative prices of any goods, in response to the realization of the sunspot variables.

The basic idea behind this result was first demonstrated by Cass and Shell (1983). The result has been extended by Balasko (1984), and a thorough discussion is given in Guesnerie and Laffont (1988). The basic idea is that, under the conditions assumed, a rational expectations equilibrium is equivalent to an Arrow–Debreu equilibrium, and involves a Pareto optimal allocation of resources. But no allocation of resources that depends upon the sunspot state can be Pareto optimal (given that preferences, technology, and endowments are independent of the sunspot state). For, if an allocation that fluctuates in response to the sunspot state is feasible, then there exists another allocation that is not contingent upon the sunspot state (e.g., in each state take the allocation that is the probability-weighted average of the allocations previously specified for the various sunspot states), that is also feasible (because of convexity of the production sets), and that gives a higher expected utility to all consumers whose allocation previously depended upon the sunspot state (because of strict concavity of the utility functions). Hence no sunspot-contingent allocation can be an equilibrium allocation. But then, relative prices of goods cannot differ across sunspot states either, in so far as in a competitive equilibrium these relative prices must correspond to marginal rates of substitution in consumption and marginal rates of transformation in production, which will not differ if the allocation of resources does not.

This strong result might appear to justify the view described above, according to which sunspot fluctuations are simply inconsistent with rational expectations equilibrium, when the full consequences of optimization and equilibrium are properly taken into account. But the irrelevance theorem contains many qualifications, which indicate ways in which self-fulfilling expectations may be a source of economic fluctuations, even granting the postulates of optimization, rational expectations, and equilibrium.

For one, the 'averaged' allocation referred to above need not be feasible if there are indivisibilities, non-convex adjustment costs, or increasing returns to scale: in such cases, a randomized allocation (where the randomization is independent of any variation in fundamentals) can be efficient,[19] and as a result might be associated with a competitive equilibrium even under circumstances under which equilibrium would have to be efficient. Second, if consumers' utility functions are not strictly concave, then the 'averaged' allocation need not be a Pareto improvement over the sunspot allocation, and so again there might be a Pareto-optimal sunspot equilibrium. Guesnerie and Laffont (1988) exhibit an example of this kind, based upon locally 'risk-loving' behaviour of the Friedman–Savage sort, in which the sunspot equilibrium Pareto-dominates the unique non-sunspot equilibrium. And third, an equilibrium may not be Pareto-optimal, because of any of a variety of sorts of violations of the conditions under which it is possible to prove the first welfare theorem. As a result, an equilibrium allocation might involve fluctuations in response to sunspot realizations.

One reason why a competitive equilibrium might not be Pareto optimal is the absence of a complete set of Arrow–Debreu markets for contingent commodities. Here it is important to note that, if one allows for equilibria in which prices and supply and demand behaviour may be contingent upon sunspot variables, then the first welfare theorem requires, among other things, a complete set of markets for securities contingent upon all possible realizations of the sunspot variables. Even if there exists a complete set of frictionless markets in all other senses, so that an equilibrium not contingent on the sunspot states would necessarily be Pareto optimal, if there do not exist markets for insurance against sunspot risk, in which all consumers who will ever exist can trade prior to the realization of any of the sunspot states, then there might also exist inefficient sunspot equilibria. Given the large number of types of random signals that might conceivably serve to co-ordinate shifts in people's expectations, it is not implausible to suppose that a complete set of such markets do not in fact exist, in which case the irrelevance theorem is of no practical significance.

The sunspot equilibria in the Azariadis–Guesnerie model referred to in Section 2 are of this kind.[20] They cease to be possible if markets for

[19] Hence the use of 'lotteries' to support efficient allocations in generalizations of the notion of Arrow–Debreu equilibrium to economies with non-convexities, e.g. Rogerson (1988). The relation of this idea to the literature on sunspot equilibria is developed explicitly in recent work by Karl Shell and Randy Wright.

[20] Strictly speaking, this is not a model in which rational expectations equilibrium, even when not contingent upon sunspot states, must be Pareto optimal, as discussed below. But monetary equilibria in which the value of money is for ever bounded away from zero are necessarily Pareto optimal (Balasko and Shell 1980), if not contingent upon sunspot states,

insurance against sunspot realizations are introduced. To see why, it is necessary to understand more fully the microeconomic foundations of the demand for money in the model considered by Azariadis and Guesnerie. In this model, each consumer lives for two consecutive periods, and acquires money (the only asset) by selling goods in the first period of life, holds the money until the second period of life, and then uses it to purchase goods. Each consumer's preferences over consumption are additively separable between the two periods of life. The demand for real balances in a given period is then just the desired saving by young consumers in that period; this depends upon the expected real return on savings, which in turn depends upon the rate of inflation. Now suppose that there were also a complete set of markets for securities that paid off in the event of different sunspot histories, which securities are all in zero net supply. Suppose that all consumers who will ever consume in any period have an opportunity to trade in these securities before the realization of any of the sunspot states, and that they trade so as to maximize their expected utility, taking into account what their consumption will be in the event of each of the possible sunspot histories, and with common (correct) expectations regarding the probability with which the different sunspot histories will occur and what the consequences of each will be for market prices. It is then impossible that a rational expectations equilibrium could involve a different allocation of resources in a given period in the case of different sunspot states. For if it did, then in one state the consumption of the old would have to be higher than in another, while the consumption of the young would have to be correspondingly lower, given that endowments cannot depend upon the sunspot state.[21] But then, given strict concavity of the consumers' von Neumann–Morgenstern utility functions, the marginal utility of consumption by the old must be lower in the first state than in the second, while the marginal utility of the young is higher in that state. This is inconsistent with rational expectations equilibrium

and the Azariadis–Guesnerie sunspot equilibria have this property. Furthermore, as is shown in Woodford (1984), sunspot equilibria of the same kind exist under exactly analogous conditions in an overlapping-generations model in which the store of value ('land') pays a constant positive real dividend, unlike the fiat money considered by Azariadis and Guesnerie. In the case of the economy with 'land', dynamic inefficiency is impossible, and competitive equilibrium is necessarily Pareto optimal if not contingent upon sunspot states. None the less, inefficient sunspot equilibria can exist, if markets do not exist in which all agents can insure against the sunspot realizations.

[21] The argument here assumes an exchange economy where the total available supply is simply given by consumers' aggregate endowment. But a similar argument is possible if one allows for variation in endogenous labour supply across sunspot states, as in Azariadis (1981); then, instead of the *goods* consumed by the young being lower in the first state, it is their consumption of *leisure*; but the argument proceeds in the same way.

in the case of insurance markets against sunspot risk, since that would require the ratio of marginal utilities between the two states to be the same for all consumers who consume in both states, i.e. equal to the relative price of contingent claims to consumption in the two states divided by the relative probability of the two states occurring (upon which probability both types of consumers must agree at the time of the trading in the contingent claims).

There are several possible defences of the relevance of the Azariadis–Guesnerie sunspot equilibria despite this result. One is to observe that all sorts of random events could play the role of the sunspot states, so that, even if there were trading in claims contingent upon some of them, one could still have sunspot equilibria in which the allocation of resources fluctuated in response to other events, against which insurance was not possible. This line of argument is developed by Azariadis (1981) and Azariadis and Guesnerie (1982). It is not entirely convincing, however. After all, as noted in Woodford (1990), the existence of a sunspot equilibrium requires a great degree of co-ordination by agents as to what signals will be interpreted in what way. As a result, the fact that the existence of an Azariadis–Guesnerie sunspot equilibrium would create a profit opportunity for those who were to introduce a new type of contingent security, the introduction of which would then prevent the equilibrium fluctuations, is no trivial problem; for it is not clear how easily co-ordination upon some new, as yet uninsurable, sunspot event could arise. Furthermore, it is not true that a large number of types of securities must be traded in order to rule out the Azariadis–Guesnerie sunspot equilibria; the existence of securities contingent upon the price level would suffice.

Another defence of these equilibria is to point out that trading in securities contingent upon the sunspot states is consistent with the existence of the sunspot equilibria, if trading is possible only by consumers who are 'alive' at the time of the trading (i.e. who consume in that period). For in the Azariadis–Guesnerie model, each consumer lives for only two consecutive periods. Thus, the only types of consumers who would care to insure against sunspot risk in period t are the consumers who consume in periods $t - 1$ and t, and those who consume in periods t and $t + 1$; and of these, only the former are 'alive' in any period prior to the realization of the period t sunspot state. But if all consumers in a given generation have the same preferences and endowments (as assumed by Azariadis and Guesnerie), then trading in period $t - 1$ in securities contingent upon the period t sunspot state by members of the generation that consumes in periods $t - 1$ and t will result in market-clearing securities prices such that no consumer's consumption allocation is any different because of the existence of the markets for contingent securities.[22] This resolution, however, is convincing only under the literal interpretation of the Azariadis–Guesnerie model as referring to consumers whose actual life-spans are only two periods. An interpretation of this model of fiat money (and the associated possibility of sunspot equilibria) that I prefer is one according to which it represents an economy of long-lived consumers who are, however, constrained in their ability to borrow every other period, owing to periodic fluctuations in either their endowments or their taste for consumption.[23] In this interpretation, the motivation for the restriction upon trading in the sunspot-contingent securities by the other type of consumers disappears.

The best response to the objection that introduction of trading in contingent claims removes the possibility of sunspot equilibria in the Azariadis–Guesnerie model is to observe that this result is rather special to that model; many other examples of sunspot equilibria do not depend upon the non-existence of or restrictions upon participation in markets for insurance against sunspot risk. For sunspot equilibria can fail to be Pareto optimal for many reasons other than the absence of opportunity for trade of that sort. There are many kinds of models in which equilibrium is not, or at least need not be, Pareto optimal, even when sunspot equilibria are not considered. In these same kinds of models, inefficient sunspot equilibria may be possible, as conditions assumed by the irrelevance theorem do not hold. In some of these cases, the

---

[22] Tom Sargent has suggested the following interpretation of this result. One may suppose that consumers do not insure against sunspot risk by trading in contingent securities at any time before their first period of 'life' because consumers 'born' in the same period but subsequent to different histories of sunspot realizations are distinct individuals who do not desire to pool their risk *ex ante*. Under this interpretation, an alternative allocation of resources should be considered to be 'Pareto-improving' only if the expected utility of no consumer type is reduced, where consumers 'born' subsequent to distinct sunspot histories are treated as distinct types, and where the expected utility of each type is measured as of the first period in which that consumer type consumes. With this considerably weakened criterion for Pareto optimality, the argument sketched above according to which sunspot fluctuations cannot be Pareto optimal does not work, and indeed, the Azariadis–Guesnerie sunspot equilibria are Pareto optimal. This interpretation is of some relevance to the issue discussed at the end of Section 3, of whether sunspot fluctuations are necessarily inefficient and hence undesirable. Since, however, the Azariadis–Guesnerie example of sunspot equilibria does not seem to me to be the type of example of greatest potential macroeconomic relevance, I will not discuss further the desirability of this interpretation of that example.

[23] See Townsend (1980), Woodford (1986b), or Sargent (1987: Ch. 6). This interpretation has the advantage of providing a theory of the demand for fiat money that does not require assumptions that imply the possibility of a dynamically inefficient equilibrium even in the presence of perfect intertemporal markets, regarding which see below. For example, this sort of monetary theory is consistent with an assumption of Barro-type bequest links between generations, or the existence of 'land', as long as the use of 'land' as a means of payment is assumed to involve sufficiently large transaction costs as to continue to allow the borrowing constraints to bind periodically. On the possibility of sunspot equilibria in a monetary economy of this kind, see Woodford (1988a).

introduction of markets for insurance against sunspot risk has no effect whatsoever upon the existence or character of the sunspot equilibria.

For example, equilibrium need not be Pareto optimal in overlapping generations models, despite the absence of any restrictions upon trading by any consumer types, because of the existence of an infinite sequence of distinct consumer types.[24] And it can be shown (Cass and Shell 1989) that sunspot equilibria are possible in overlapping generations models, even with *ex ante* trading in claims contingent upon the sunspot history by all consumer types who will ever consume, (1) if one allows for preferences that are not additively separable between periods, so that the above impossibility argument does not go through, and (2) if one considers equilibria with a 'dynamically inefficient' allocation of resources (arising from a real rate of return that is on average lower than the growth rate of endowments), unlike the allocations associated with the Azariadis–Guesnerie equilibria. There are many reasons, however, for doubting that the theoretical possibility of dynamic inefficiency in economies with a complete set of perfectly competitive markets is empirically realistic. These may relate either to a belief that at least some positive fraction of the economy's endowment is at all times under the control of 'dynastic' families who, because of bequest linkages, behave like infinite-horizon maximizers, as argued by Barro (1974), or to a belief that assets exist that are sufficiently productive that a finite equilibrium value for those assets implies a finite value for the economy's aggregate endowment as well. (One might think that actual land has the properties of the ideal 'land' referred to above, or, more plausibly, that physical capital in advanced economies is too productive to be consistent with a dynamically inefficient equilibrium allocation, as argued by Abel *et al.* 1989.) Hence this does not seem to me the most persuasive reason for the possible existence of sunspot equilibria.

More relevant, in my view, is the fact that price signals may fail to guide the economy to an efficient allocation of resources in the event of any of a number of types of 'market failures'. I will limit my attention here to some of the types of market failures that have been given frequent attention in macroeconomic modelling, for reasons unrelated to an interest in the possibility of sunspot equilibrium. Three broad classes

---

[24] The existence in the case of equilibrium prices of a well-defined budget constraint for each consumer type need not imply a well-defined value for the economy's aggregate endowment, if the number of consumer types is not finite, so that the standard proof of the first welfare theorem is invalid. This explains the reference to a finite number of consumer types in the statement above of the sunspot irrelevance theorem. A first welfare theorem can, however, be proved for some classes of economies with an infinite sequence of consumer types—e.g. if there exists 'land' of the kind mentioned above, or if some finite number of consumer types have a total endowment that is more than some positive fraction of the economy's aggregate endowment in all periods. The sunspot irrelevance theorem can be extended to all such cases.

of deviations from the idealized competitive model come to mind. First, there are the types of imperfect financial intermediation that make possible a role for intrinsically valueless fiat money (even in a world where dynamic inefficiency would not exist in the case of perfect frictionless markets), or that may explain the apparent importance of disruptions of financial intermediation in generating recessions and depressions. Second, there are models of rigid money prices together with associated non-price rationing of goods in some markets, often invoked to explain the non-neutrality of variations in the money supply, and the role of variations in aggregate demand more generally, in generating temporary fluctuations in the level of economic activity. And third, there are increasing returns to scale in production, arising either from externalities between firms who individually face decreasing returns (the 'thick market' externalities discussed by Diamond 1982, Howitt and McAfee 1988, and Hall 1989 or the technological spillovers discussed by Murphy *et al.* 1988), or from increasing returns at the firm level, combined (in order for equilibrium to exist) with imperfect competition between firms, of a kind that have often been invoked to explain observed cyclical variations in productivity (Murphy *et al.* 1989), as well as certain facts about long-run growth (Romer 1986). All three types of imperfections are known to be possible sources of sunspot equilibria. What is more, all three may result in sunspot equilibria even in representative consumer economies, i.e., in economies in which all consumers are assumed to be identical, infinite-lived Barro 'dynasties'. Examples of the latter sort are plainly not dependent upon assumptions about whether or not there is trading in securities contingent upon sunspot realizations. For, given that all traders have identical circumstances, trading in such securities simply results in market clearing at securities prices such that no trader wishes either to buy or sell the securities in question, and as a result equilibrium behaviour is unaffected by the existence of the markets for these securities. For this reason, I will emphasize here only the representative-consumer examples of these types.

A representative-consumer variant of an economy in which financial constraints create a role for valued fiat money (even under circumstances under which dynamic inefficiency would not exist in the case of perfect markets) is the cash-in-advance economy considered by Lucas and Stokey (1987), among others. Here again, an equilibrium condition of the form (7) is obtained, although the microeconomic foundations of the condition are different. The demand for real money balances (and hence the equilibrium price level) in period t depends upon the extent to which consumers desire in that period to purchase cash goods as opposed to credit goods; the optimal trade-off between the two kinds of purchases depends upon the expected price level in period $t + 1$ as well as the price level in period t, in so far as credit goods will be purchased in period t to the point where the value of a marginal unit of currency in period $t + 1$ is equal to the value of the marginal quantity of credit goods that could have been purchased in period t by promising to pay that amount at the beginning of period $t + 1$. Again, the sort of situation depicted in Figs. 6.2 and 6.3 is possible, for the right kind of utility function. Indeed, Woodford (1988a) shows that, in the case where the representative consumer's utility function is additively separable between periods and between cash and credit goods within each period, there is an exact formal correspondence between the equilibrium conditions of the Azariadis–Guesnerie model and those of the Lucas–Stokey model, with 'consumption of cash goods' ('credit goods') taking the place of 'consumption by old consumers' ('young consumers') in each period, and with the endowment of the representative consumer each period (which can be transformed into either cash or credit goods) taking the place of the endowment of the young consumers each period (some of which is consumed by them and some by the old). As a result, the conditions known to allow the existence of sunspot equilibria in the Azariadis–Guesnerie model can be immediately translated into the context of the Lucas–Stokey model (roughly, the utility function for cash goods consumption must be sufficiently strongly concave near the level of consumption associated with the monetary steady state).[25]

In this case, however, the introduction of trading in securities contingent upon the history of sunspot realizations does not affect the conditions for the existence of sunspot equilibria. Following Lucas and Stokey, we can introduce securities trading by supposing that in each period there is first a securities market sub-period, then a goods market sub-period, with cash goods purchased in the second sub-period having to be paid for with money held at the end of the first sub-period (possibly acquired by selling securities), and with securities purchased in the first sub-period of period t paying off (or being able to be traded again) in the first sub-period of the period $t + 1$. In equilibrium, the ratio of marginal utilities of cash goods consumption in two sunspot states in period t will have to equal the ratio of the money price level in the two states times the relative price in the period $t - 1$ securities market sub-period of securities paying off contingent claims to money (payable in the first sub-period of period t) in the two states, divided by the relative probability of occurrence of the two states (given information at the time of securities trading in period $t - 1$). But the ratio of marginal utilities of credit goods need not equal this, if the cash-in-advance constraint binds in one or more of the states, since the shadow price on the cash-in-advance constraint may be different in the different sunspot states. Hence the previous argument for the impossibility of sunspot equilibria with insurance against sunspot risk does not go through. Indeed, because of the assumption of a representative consumer, there is no change whatever in the conditions for the existence of, or in the predicted character of, the sunspot equilibria.[26]

Woodford (1991) demonstrates the possibility of sunspot equilibria in an economy with perfect financial intermediation, but in which output prices are rigid in money terms, so that variations in aggregate demand induce a change in equilibrium supply, despite the fact that marginal costs must vary relative to price.[27] In this economy, the existence of the rigid price and rationing in the product market results in an equilibrium level of output y_t that (in the absence of shocks to fundamentals) will be given by

$$y_t = f(i_{t-1}, i_t), \tag{13}$$

where i_t denotes investment in period t. Here past investment (which equals the period t capital stock, assuming complete depreciation each period[28]) enters through the effect of the capital stock and hence capacity upon equilibrium supply, while the current investment enters through the 'multiplier' effect of current investment spending upon aggregate demand. The returns, r_t per unit of capital in period t, depend upon the amount of capital in place and the level of output that ends up being produced. Substituting (13) into this relationship allows one to write

$$r_t = g(i_{t-1}, i_t). \tag{14}$$

Finally, owing to the special form of preferences assumed for the representative consumer, it can be shown that in equilibrium the expected real return on all assets must always equal a constant r^*. As a result, the level of investment chosen in equilibrium in period t will be that level that results in an expected return on capital in the following period that is exactly equal to this desired return, so that

$$E_t[g(i_t, i_{t+1})] = r^*. \tag{15}$$

[26] Other examples of economies with infinite-lived consumers in which financial constraints result in the possibility of sunspot equilibria are discussed in Woodford (1988a). Indeterminacy of equilibrium, endogenous cycles, and sunspot equilibria in representative consumer monetary economies of the Sidrauski–Brock variety are discussed in Matsuyama (1989a, b).

[27] This example was originally introduced in the lecture notes for this workshop, but the presentation here has been greatly condensed owing to space limitations.

[28] Complete depreciation is in no way essential to the logic of this example. The same analysis applies if in each equation one replaces i_t by the capital stock chosen for period $t + 1$. I have used the notation i_t only to make it clear that this is a non-predetermined endogenous state variable determined in period t.

Condition (15) indicates how equilibrium investment in period t is determined by expectations regarding investment (and hence aggregate demand) in period $t + 1$. This is an equilibrium condition of the same form as (7), and can be analysed in a similar manner. Any stochastic process for $\{i_t\}$ that satisfies (15) at all times (and stays within certain bounds assumed in deriving (15)) represents a rational expectations equilibrium; a fluctuating solution represents an equilibrium in which investment spending fluctuates in response to self-fulfilling expectations, and results in fluctuations in economic activity through (13). Stationary fluctuating solutions to (15) exist, including finite-state Markov process equilibria of the kind discussed by Azariadis and Guesnerie, if both the 'multiplier' effect of i_t on y_t and the 'accelerator' effect of expectations regarding y_{t+1} on i_t are sufficiently strong.[29]

Indeterminacy of rational expectations equilibrium and the possibility of sunspot equilibria in dynamic models with increasing returns and/or externalities have been discussed by a number of recent authors (Hammour 1988a; Spear 1988; Murphy *et al.* 1988; Kehoe *et al.* 1989; Matsuyama 1991). A slight modification of a standard one-sector growth model with a representative consumer can illustrate this possibility. Let $Y(K)$ denote aggregate output, net of depreciation, when the aggregate capital stock is K, and let $R(K)$ denote the gross real return per unit of capital under the same circumstances. Then if consumers are all identical and seek to maximize an infinite discounted sum of utilities, $\sum_{t=0}^{\infty}\beta^t u(C_t)$, where $0 < \beta < 1$ and u is an increasing concave function, intertemporal optimization requires a consumption plan satisfying

$$u'(C_t) = \beta R(K_{t+1})E_t[u'(C_{t+1})], \tag{16}$$

together with a transversality condition. The resulting evolution of the aggregate capital stock will then be given by

$$K_{t+1} = Y(K_t) - C_t. \tag{17}$$

Any stochastic processes for $\{K_t, C_t\}$ satisfying (16) and (17) for a given initial condition K_0, and with both variables for ever bounded (so that the transversality condition is also satisfied) will constitute a rational expectations equilibrium.

Now there will typically exist a steady-state equilibrium for such an economy, namely a pair (K^*, C^*) such that, if $K_0 = K^*$, then a possible equilibrium is $C_t = C^*$, $K_t = K^*$, for all t. These quantities will satisfy the equations $R(K^*) = \beta^{-1}$, $C^* = Y(K^*) - K^*$. Under the assumptions that $R'(K^*) \neq 0$, $Y'(K^*) \neq 1$, it can be shown that, in the

---

[29] Other types of market imperfections which allow fluctuations in aggregate demand for produced goods to result in fluctuations in equilibrium labour demand, such as the oligopolistic model of Rotemberg and Woodford (1989), also allow sunspot equilibria to exist under certain conditions.

case of any equilibrium in which C_t and K_t remain sufficiently near to the steady-state values in all periods, the equilibrium is well approximated by a solution to the following linear approximation to the system (16)–(17):

$$
\begin{bmatrix} E_t[C_{t+1} - C^*] \\ K_{t+1} - K^* \end{bmatrix} = \begin{bmatrix} 1 - BR' & BR'Y' \\ -1 & Y' \end{bmatrix} \begin{bmatrix} C_t - C^* \\ K_t - K^* \end{bmatrix}, \quad (18)
$$

where $B = -\beta u'(C^*)/u''(C^*)$, and the derivatives R' and Y' are evaluated at K^*. It can be shown furthermore (Woodford 1986c[30]) that

1. In the case where one eigenvalue of the matrix in (18) is real with modulus less than 1, and one is real with modulus greater than 1—the case of 'saddlepoint stability' or 'exact determinacy'—there is a unique rational expectations equilibrium in which the state variables remain for ever near the steady-state values for each choice of K_0 sufficiently near K^*, and this equilibrium is in all cases described by the same pair of functions $C_t = \gamma(K_t)$, $K_{t+1} = \kappa(K_t)$, so that a representation of the form (5)–(6) exists. Furthermore, the functions γ and κ are such that in all cases this equilibrium converges asymptotically to the steady-state values of the state variables. Hence both determinacy theses are valid for this class of equilibria, and no equilibria involving endogenous fluctuations are possible, at least near the steady-state values of the state variables.
2. In the case where both eigenvalues of the matrix in (18) have modulus less than 1—the case of 'indeterminacy'—there exists a large set of rational expectations equilibria for each choice of K_0 sufficiently near K^*, in which the values of the state variables remain for ever near their steady-state values, including a large set of stationary sunspot equilibria, where the stationarity of the latter stochastic processes implies that the sunspot fluctuations do not die down in amplitude asymptotically.
3. In the case where both eigenvalues of the matrix in (18) have modulus greater than 1—the case of 'instability'—then, for each choice of K_0 sufficiently near K^*, with $K_0 \neq K^*$, there exists no equilibrium in which the state variables remain for ever near their steady-state values. In addition, it follows that for most initial conditions there exist no equilibria converging asymptotically to the steady-state values of the state variables, so that in this case the thesis of global asymptotic determinacy must be invalid.

Finally, it can be seen that in the present example, assuming that $Y' > 0$, case 1 occurs if $R' < 0$, case 2 occurs if $R' > 0$ and $Y' < 1$, and case 3 occurs if $R' > 0$ and $Y' > 1$.

---

[30] See also Woodford (1984) for a more elementary discussion of this classification of local dynamics.

Now in the standard neoclassical growth model, $Y(K) = F(K)$, the production function shared by all firms, and under the standard assumption of decreasing returns to scale, or equivalently constant returns with a fixed factor (inelastically supplied labour), one must have $F'' < 0$. The real rate of return in equilibrium is furthermore given by the marginal product of capital, $R(K) = F'(K)$. From this it follows that at the steady-state equilibrium $Y' = R = \beta^{-1} > 1$ and $R' = F'' < 0$, so that only case 1 is possible. (Since we have already shown in Section 2 that in this model both determinacy theses hold not just locally but globally, this must be the case.)

But increasing returns and externalities and/or imperfect competition permit other possibilities. I will discuss here the case of external increasing returns because of its simplicity, but Hammour (1988a) shows that similar possibilities arise in the case of increasing returns internal to the firm combined with imperfect competition. Suppose that a given firm's production function is $y = F(k, K)$, where k is the capital used by that firm and K is the aggregate capital stock. Then the first-order condition for optimal capital accumulation by each firm is $R = F_1(K, K)$, so that $R(K)$ is no longer the derivative of $Y(K) = F(K, K)$. If $F_2 < 0$ (which Hammour interprets as a congestion externality), it is possible to have $Y' < 1$ at the steady state despite the fact that one must have $R = \beta^{-1} > 1$.[31] And the second-order condition for optimal capital accumulation is $F_{11} < 0$, which no longer implies that one must have $R' < 0$. If one has external increasing returns despite decreasing returns for the individual firm, one may have $R' > 0$.[32] Hence all three cases are in general possible, and in particular case 2 is possible, in which case sunspot equilibria exist in which fluctuations of the consumption and capital accumulation paths continue to occur for ever in response to arbitrary random events.[33] Kehoe et al. (1989) show that similar effects

[31] Imperfect competition can also drive a wedge between the real rate of return and the marginal product of capital. For example, excess capacity due to Chamberlinian competition between firms could also result in $R > Y'$.

[32] Alternatively, $R' > 0$ may result from increasing returns at the firm level, with an interior optimum existing for the capital accumulation decision of the firm despite $F_{11} > 0$, owing to the fact that firms face downward-sloping demand curves.

[33] Equilibrium may be indeterminate and sunspot equilibria may exist even when the local dynamics are not 'indeterminate' in the sense of case 2. For example, even in the case of type 3 local dynamics, all 'perfect foresight' equilibria beginning near the steady state may diverge from the steady state and be attracted to an invariant circle that is 'stable' in the sense of having a stable manifold that includes all points near it. In such a case, 'perfect foresight' equilibrium is indeterminate and sunspot equilibria exist; see the discussion of the Diamond model in Woodford (1984). Hammour shows how examples of this kind can be constructed for a continuous time variant of this model using the Hopf bifurcation theorem; similar techniques (see e.g. Reichlin 1986) are available in the discrete-time case. Similar cycles, with a similar implication for indeterminacy and sunspot equilibria, are shown to be a possible consequence of the externalities and increasing returns associated with a search technology for matching trading partners in Diamond and Fudenberg (1989).

can result from the presence of distorting taxes in a growth model. In all of these examples, because they involve representative consumers, the existence of sunspot equilibria is independent of assumptions regarding the existence of contingent claims markets.

The sort of endogenous fluctuations that we have identified with determinate but unstable equilibrium dynamics are also inconsistent with assumptions of optimization and equilibrium, in at least certain special cases that are not so special as to be completely without interest. The case that has been most studied is that of deterministic optimal growth models, which is to say perfectly competitive representative consumer economies with decreasing-returns-to-scale technologies. I have already shown in Section 2 that, in the case of a one-sector technology and additively separable preferences for the representative consumer, the thesis of global asymptotic determinacy is valid, ruling out determinate but unstable dynamics. I have also already indicated that, on the other hand, deterministic equilibrium cycles and chaotic equilibrium dynamics are possible in the case of optimal growth models with multi-sector technologies. But even in the case of relatively general multi-sector technologies, strong conclusions are possible concerning asymptotic dynamics if the representative consumer does not discount future consumption very much.

Consider an n-sector growth model, in which n distinct capital goods in addition to one or more consumption goods are produced using those same n capital goods together with fixed factors such as inelastically supplied labour. Let $V(k_t, k_{t+1})$ denote the maximum possible level of single-period utility of consumption in period t by the representative consumer that is technologically feasible, given a vector of capital stocks k_t to use along with the fixed factors, and given that at least a vector k_{t+1} of capital goods must be produced. This function is defined on a set D of $2n$-vectors (k_t, k_{t+1}) that represent technologically feasible possibilities for the evolution of the capital stocks. Then, because competitive equilibrium must maximize the welfare of the representative consumer, given an initial vector of capital stocks k_0, the unique equilibrium allocation of resources corresponds to the sequence of capital stocks $\{k_t\}$ that maximizes $\sum_{t=0}^{\infty} \beta^t V(k_t, k_{t+1})$ subject to the constraint that $(k_t, k_{t+1}) \in D$ for all t, and given the initial condition k_0. The following result is of particular interest.

THE TURNPIKE THEOREM. Let V be increasing in its first vector of arguments, decreasing in its second vector of arguments, and strictly concave, and let D be convex and compact. Then, for given V and D, there exists a discount factor $\bar{\beta} < 1$ such that, if the discount factor of the representative consumer lies in the interval $\bar{\beta} < \beta < 1$, the equilibrium dynamics are such that

$$\lim_{t \to \infty} k_t = k^*$$

where k^* is the steady-state capital stock, regardless of the value of k_0.

This version of the theorem is due to Scheinkman (1976); related theorems were first proved for continuous-time optimal growth models by McKenzie and Rockafellar (see McKenzie 1986). This result establishes a sense in which, if one believes that the case of greatest empirical relevance is that in which consumers do not discount the future very much, the thesis of asymptotic global determinacy is a consequence of equilibrium theory, even for multi-sector economies. While the proof of the result involves many technicalities, the intuition is reasonably simple. A perpetually fluctuating path for the vector of capital stocks does not achieve as high an average value of the strictly concave objective function V as does a constant vector of capital stocks which is near the long-run average vector in the fluctuating case. Hence, in order to maximize the long-run average value of V, one would eventually move the vector of capital stocks to the value that maximizes $V(k, k)$ and keep it there, regardless of the initial condition. In the case where one is maximizing a discounted sum, the initial condition matters, but if the discounting is sufficiently weak it is still optimal to move the vector of capital stocks asymptotically towards a constant vector, the value of which involves a correction for the value of β.

Despite the strength of this result, it is worth emphasizing that there are still many ways in which endogenous fluctuations can occur in an optimal growth model. One is to suppose that the rate of time discount is simply greater than is consistent with the turnpike property. Indeed, Boldrin and Montrucchio (1986) prove an 'anti-turnpike' result, according to which any twice differentiable function κ mapping an n-dimensional compact, convex set into itself corresponds to the equilibrium dynamics generated by some n-sector optimal growth model satisfying the Scheinkman conditions, assuming that the discount factor can be chosen arbitrarily in the interval $0 < \beta < 1$. It should also be noted that the theorem says only that some $\bar{\beta} < 1$ exists for given V and D; this does not mean that for β arbitrarily close to 1 one cannot find a V and D satisfying the Scheinkman conditions for which the turnpike property would not hold: one simply needs to find a V and D for which $\bar{\beta}$ is even higher. (For further discussion of why this is possible, see Boldrin and Woodford 1990.[34])

---

[34] Benhabib and Rustichini (1989) show how to construct explicit examples of continuous-time models with two capital goods sectors and a consumption sector (all Cobb–Douglas with constant returns) using the two capital goods and inelastically supplied labour, in which equilibrium limit cycles exist, for rates of time preference arbitrarily close

Finally, it should be noted that a $\bar{\beta} < 1$ need not exist if V is not strictly concave. While concavity is a standard assumption (albeit not the only case of possible empirical interest, as discussed above), strict concavity is a bit more special. In particular, in the case of a multi-sector technology with constant returns to scale, strict concavity does not hold in general, even though there are diminishing returns to capital in the sense that all sectors require a fixed factor, as long as the number of distinct capital goods exceeds the number of fixed factors, or the number of capital goods is as large as the number of fixed factors and utility is linear in consumption. This is the basis of a famous counter-example due to Weitzman (reported in Samuelson 1973). Of course, strict concavity can be achieved in any such example by introducing even a very small amount of decreasing returns to scale; but if the perturbation is small, the turnpike property will hold only for very low rates of time preference. Hence it is not clear how empirically unrealistic are the technology and preference specifications needed for endogenous cycles in optimal growth models.

None the less, the known examples of really complex endogenous fluctuations in optimal growth models, i.e. the examples of chaotic dynamics,[35] involve what seem to be extremely high rates of time preference. Furthermore, the reliance upon complications that become possible only in the case of multi-sector technologies may not be of practical relevance for business cycle theory, given that the kind of fluctuations one seeks to explain typically involve a large degree of co-movement between different types of investment, rather than cyclical variations in the type of capital goods that are accumulated. Accordingly, a more important qualification to the turnpike theorem may be that, like the sunspot irrelevance theorem, it has little relevance once one admits the existence of market imperfections of any of a variety of kinds.

All of the market imperfections just discussed in connection with sunspot equilibria are also conditions that can result in failure of the

---

to the rate of depreciation of capital. These examples do not satisfy the strict concavity condition needed for the turnpike theorem, for the reason discussed immediately below. None the less, perturbations of these examples that make V strictly concave and preserve the limit cycles, while keeping the rate of time preference within a neighbourhood of desired size of the depreciation rate, should be possible.

[35] These are of greater interest than the examples of deterministic cycles, not only because observed aggregate fluctuations are not close to being exactly repetitive, but also because many of the examples of deterministic cycles simply establish the possibility of a bifurcation creating a deterministic cycle of very small amplitude in a neighbourhood of the steady state. The examples of chaos necessarily involve fluctuations of a larger amplitude in so far as a greater degree of nonlinearity in the dynamics is required.

turnpike property.[36] I will here discuss only a very simple example, which shows how determinate but unstable dynamics, including possibly chaotic dynamics, can arise in a growth model with a simple one-sector technology, and even in the case of arbitrarily low rates of time preference on the part of all consumers, if one abandons the assumption of complete financial markets.

Consider again the one-sector growth model of Section 2, but now suppose that there are two types of infinite-lived consumers, 'entrepreneurs', who alone are able to invest in capital, hire labour, and organize production, and 'workers', who alone supply labour. (Some sort of consumer heterogeneity must be introduced, or financial markets have no effect upon equilibrium.[37]) The assumption that consumers are heterogeneous does not in itself allow for more complex dynamics, if there are complete financial markets; for in that case a competitive equilibrium still must maximize a weighted sum of the utilities of consumption of the two consumer types.[38] But suppose also that entrepreneurs are unable to finance investment other than out of their own funds, owing to adverse selection or moral hazard problems.[39] Then the capital stock k_{t+1} carried into period $t + 1$ can never be larger than the wealth of the entrepreneurs, which in turn can never be larger than the gross returns to the existing capital stock, $k_t F'(k_t)$, where $F(k)$ denotes aggregate production given a capital stock k and the exogenous labour supply. Now if F is a sufficiently concave function (i.e. if there is not too much factor substitutability in production), $kF'(k)$ is decreasing in k, for large k. As a result, large values of k_t will result in conditions that force k_{t+1} to be low. One case that is particularly simple to analyse is that in which the entrepreneurs have logarithmic utility, so that they consume exactly a fraction $(1 - \beta)$ of their wealth each period, regard-

---

[36] See Boldrin and Woodford (1990). The models discussed above in which financial constraints result in a role for fiat money obviously allow for deterministic equilibria that cycle for ever, given that they can generate price-level dynamics that exactly replicate those of the Grandmont (1985) model. However, these are not examples of determinate but unstable dynamics: the equilibrium cycles are a manifestation of the indeterminacy of equilibrium, and equilibria converging to the steady state generally exist among others. The Hammour (1988a) example of deterministic motion on an invariant cycle, discussed in fn. 33 above, is also necessarily associated with indeterminacy of equilibrium, but this case does to some extent involve intrinsically unstable dynamics, in so far as, for almost all initial conditions, there are no equilibria converging to the steady state.

[37] Bewley (1986) shows how deterministic equilibrium cycles may be possible in a model with two infinite-lived consumer types when no borrowing and lending are possible, where the heterogeneity has to do with the timing of the consumers' endowments.

[38] Bewley (1982) and Yano (1984) provide turnpike theorems for economies with multiple consumer types.

[39] Greenwald and Stiglitz (1988) argue for the importance of financial constraints of this kind in the generation and propagation of aggregate fluctuations. The generalized model discussed below, in which non-contingent debt contracts are possible but not securities contingent upon firm-specific risk, coincides closely with their analysis.

less of the expected return on savings. Then the capital stock evolves
according to

$$k_{t+1} = \beta k_t F'(k_t).$$

In the event that F is sufficiently concave, this map has a graph of the
kind shown in Fig. 8.1, and can result in an unstable steady state and in
equilibrium paths that converge to a deterministic cycle or are even
chaotic. The conditions for this to occur in no way depend upon a low
value of β for the entrepreneurs; indeed, for a given production function
F, raising β makes the hump in Fig. 8.1 steeper, making the steady
state more unstable and allowing more complex fluctuations. Nor do
they have anything to do with the rate of time preference of the
workers.

In Woodford (1989) this example is extended to allow for endogenous
labour supply and a competitive market for debt issued by entrepreneurs
and held by workers. Complete financial markets still do not exist if one
assumes the existence of film-specific productivity shocks, which have no
effect upon aggregate production possibilities because of the existence of
a continuum of firms with independent shocks, and which cannot be
insured against because their realization is private information. That is,
entrepreneurs can finance investment by issuing straight debt securities,
but cannot issue securities contingent upon the uncertain events that will
affect the return upon that investment. Insolvency risk then limits the
extent to which entrepreneurs are willing to leverage themselves in
order to invest in physical capital, even when the expected return on
capital exceeds the real rate of return at which they can borrow. As a
result, entrepreneurial wealth continues to be an important determinant
of the level of investment, making unstable dynamics possible in a
similar way.

My overall conclusion about the two types of models of endogenous
fluctuations is roughly the same. The most plausible conditions under
which either sunspot equilibria or determinate but unstable dynamics
can occur would seem to be conditions under which such equilibria are
possible only because of market imperfections. As a result, endogenous
fluctuations of these kinds, if they occur, will indicate an inefficient
phenomenon and a flaw in the functioning of the competitive mechanism, even if it does not follow from that that an intervention that
succeeds in eliminating the endogenous fluctuations must necessarily
bring about an improvement. On the other hand, it is important to note
that equilibria of these kinds can result from a variety of kinds of
market imperfections that are often argued to be of importance for
macroeconomics, and that, once these imperfections are granted, the
existence of the endogenous fluctuations is fully consistent with optimizing behaviour, rational expectations, and equilibrium. Whether these

theoretical possibilities are of any practical importance in explaining aggregate fluctuations will, of course, depend upon the construction of examples that are not only logically coherent, but whose assumptions (including quantitative assumptions about parameter values) are empirically realistic and whose predictions match actual time series.[40]

References

ABEL, A. B., MANKIW, N. G., SUMMERS, L. H., and ZECKHAUSER, R. J. (1989). 'Assessing Dynamic Efficiency: Theory and Evidence'. *Review of Economic Studies*, 56: 1–20.

ADELMAN, I., and ADELMAN, F. L. (1959). 'The Dynamic Properties of the Klein–Goldberger Model'. *Econometrica*, 27: 596–625.

ASHLEY, R. A., and PATTERSON, D. M. (1987). 'Linear versus Nonlinear Macroeconomies: A Statistical Test'. Unpublished paper, Virginia Polytechnic Institute, January.

AZARIADIS, C. (1981). 'Self-Fulfilling Prophecies'. *Journal of Economic Theory*, 25: 380–96.

—— and GUESNERIE R. (1982). 'Prophéties créatrices et persistance des théories'. *Revue économique*, 33: 787–806.

—— —— (1986). 'Sunspots and Cycles'. *Review of Economic Studies*, 53: 725–36.

BALASKO, Y. (1984). 'Extrinsic Uncertainty Revisited'. *Journal of Economic Theory*, 31: 203–10.

—— and SHELL, K. (1980). 'The Overlapping Generations Model, I: The Case of Pure Exchange without Money'. *Journal of Economic Theory*, 23: 307–22.

BARRO, R. (1974). 'Are Government Bonds Net Wealth?' *Journal of Political Economy*, 82: 1095–118.

BENHABIB, J., and NISHIMURA, K. (1979). 'The Hopf Bifurcation and the Existence and Stability of Closed Orbits in Multisector Models of Optimal Economic Growth'. *Journal of Economic Theory*, 21: 421–44.

—— —— (1985). 'Competitive Equilibrium Cycles'. *Journal of Economic Theory*, 35: 284–306.

—— and RUSTICHINI, A. (1989). 'Equilibrium Cycling with Small Discounting: A Note'. Unpublished paper, New York University, May.

BEWLEY, T. (1982). 'An Integration of Equilibrium Theory and Turnpike Theory'. *Journal of Mathematical Economics*, 10: 233–68.

—— (1986). 'Dynamic Implications of the Form of the Budget Constraint'. In H. F. Sonnenschein (ed.), *Models of Economic Dynamics*. New York: Springer-Verlag.

---

[40] For crude but illustrative examples of discussion of the empirical realism of the parameter values required for endogenous fluctuations to exist, and comparison of quantitative properties of the predicted fluctuations to actual business cycles, see Woodford (1988*a*, 1991).

BLATT, J. M. (1978). 'On the Econometric Approach to Business-Cycle Analysis'. *Oxford Economic Papers*, 30: 292–300.

BOLDRIN, M. (1989). 'Paths of Optimal Accumulation in Two-Sector Models'. In W. A. Barnett, J. Geweke, and K. Shell (eds.), *Economic Complexity: Chaos, Sunspots, Bubbles, and Nonlinearity*. Cambridge University Press.

—— and MONTRUCCHIO, L. (1986). 'On the Indeterminacy of Capital Accumulation Paths'. *Journal of Economic Theory*, 40: 26–39.

—— and WOODFORD, M. (1990). 'Equilibrium Models Displaying Endogenous Fluctuations and Chaos: A Survey'. *Journal of Monetary Economics*, 25: 189–222.

BROCK, W. A. (1986). 'Distinguishing Random and Deterministic Systems: Abridged Version'. *Journal of Economic Theory*, 40: 168–95.

—— (1988). 'Nonlinearities and Complex Dynamics in Economics and Finance'. In P. Anderson, K. Arrow, and D. Pines (eds.), *The Economy as an Evolving Complex System*. Reading, Mass.: Addison-Wesley.

—— and CHAMBERLAIN, G. (1985). 'Spectral Analysis Cannot Tell a Macro-Econometrician Whether his Time Series Came from a Stochastic Economy or from a Deterministic Economy'. SSRI Working Paper no. 8419, University of Wisconsin at Madison, November.

CASS, D., and SHELL, K. (1983). 'Do Sunspots Matter?' *Journal of Political Economy*, 91: 193–227.

—— —— (1989). 'Sunspot Equilibrium in an Overlapping Generations Economy with an Idealized Contingent-Claims Market'. In W. A. Barnett, J. Geweke, and K. Shell (eds.), *Economic Complexity: Chaos, Sunspots, Bubbles, and Nonlinearity*. Cambridge University Press.

CHIAPPORI, P.-A., and GUESNERIE, R. (1988). 'Self-Fulfilling Theories: The Sunspot Connection'. Unpublished paper, École des Hautes Études en Sciences Sociales, Paris.

DIAMOND, P. A. (1982). 'Aggregate Demand Management in Search Equilibrium'. *Journal of Political Economy*, 90: 881–94.

—— and FUDENBERG, D. (1989). 'An Example of Rational Expectations Business Cycles in Search Equilibrium'. *Journal of Political Economy*, 97: 606–19.

FARMER, R. E. A., and WOODFORD, M. (1984). 'Self-Fulfilling Prophecies and the Business Cycle'. CARESS Working Paper no. 84-12, University of Pennsylvania, April. Published in Spanish translation in *Cuadernos Economicos de ICE [Madrid]*, no. 35, 1987.

GRANDMONT, J.-M. (1985). 'On Endogenous Competitive Business Cycles'. *Econometrica*, 53: 995–1046.

—— (1986). 'Stabilizing Competitive Business Cycles'. *Journal of Economic Theory*, 40: 57–76.

GREENWALD, B. C., and STIGLITZ, J. E. (1988). 'Imperfect Information, Financial Constraints, and Business Fluctuations'. In M. Kohn and S.-C. Tsiang (eds.), *Finance Constraints, Expectations, and Macroeconomics*. Oxford University Press.

GUESNERIE, R., and LAFFONT, J.-J. (1988). 'Notes on Sunspot Equilibria in Finite Economies'. In *Volume en l'honneur d'Edmond Malinvaud*. Paris: Economica–EHESS (English edn. forthcoming: MIT Press, Cambridge, Mass.).

HALL, R. E. (1989). *Temporal Agglomeration*. NBER Working Paper no. 3143, October.

HAMMOUR, M. (1988*a*). 'Increasing Returns and Endogenous Business Cycles'. Unpublished paper, Massachusetts Institute of Technology, October.

—— (1988*b*). 'Are Business Cycles Exogenous?' Unpublished paper, Massachusetts Institute of Technology, November.

HANSEN, A. H. (1964). *Business Cycles and National Income*, expanded edn. New York: W. W. Norton. First published 1951.

HINICH, M. J., and PATTERSON, D. M. (1985). 'Evidence of Nonlinearity in Daily Stock Returns'. *Journal of Business and Economic Statistics*, 3: 69–77.

HOWITT, P., and MCAFEE, R. P. (1988). 'Stability of Equilibria with Trade Externalities'. *Quarterly Journal of Economics*, 103: 261–77.

KEHOE, T. J., LEVINE, D. K., and ROMER, P. M. (1989). 'Characterizing Equilibria of Models with Externalities and Taxes as Solutions to Optimization Problems'. Unpublished paper, Federal Reserve Bank of Minneapolis, April.

KEYNES, J. M. (1936). *The General Theory of Employment, Interest, and Money*. London: Macmillan.

LAVINGTON, F. (1921). *The English Capital Market*. London: Methuen.

LORENZ, H. W. (1989). *Nonlinear Dynamical Economics and Chaotic Motions*. Berlin: Springer-Verlag.

LUCAS, R. E., JUN. (1976). 'Econometric Policy Evaluation: A Critique'. *Carnegie-Rochester Conference Series on Public Policy*, 1: 19–46.

—— and STOKEY, N. L. (1987). 'Money and Interest in a Cash-in-Advance Economy'. *Econometrica*, 55: 491–514.

MCCALLUM, B. T. (1983). 'On Non-uniqueness in Rational Expectations Models: An Attempt at Perspective'. *Journal of Monetary Economics*, 11: 139–68.

MCKENZIE, L. W. (1986). 'Optimal Economic Growth, Turnpike Theorems, and Comparative Dynamics'. In K. J. Arrow and M. D. Intriligator (eds.), *Handbook of Mathematical Economics*, iii. Amsterdam: North-Holland.

MASKIN, E., and TIROLE, J. (1989). 'Markov Equilibrium'. Unpublished paper, Harvard University.

MATSUYAMA, K. (1989*a*). 'Endogenous Price Fluctuations in an Optimizing Model of a Monetary Economy'. CMSEMS Discussion Paper no. 825, Northwestern University, March. Forthcoming, *Econometrica*.

—— (1989*b*). 'Serial Correlation of Sunspot Equilibria (Rational Bubbles) in Two Popular Models of Monetary Economies'. CMSEMS Discussion Paper no. 827, Northwestern University, July.

—— (1991). 'Increasing Returns, Industrialization, and Indeterminacy of Equilibrium'. *Quarterly Journal of Economics*, 106: 617–50.

MAY, R. B. (1976). 'Simple Mathematical Models with Very Complicated Dynamics'. *Nature*, 261: 459–67.

MURPHY, K. M., SHLEIFER, A., and VISHNY, R. W. (1988). 'Increasing Returns, Durables, and Economic Fluctuations'. Unpublished paper, University of Chicago, October.

———— (1989). 'Building Blocks of Market Clearing Business Cycle Models'. In S. Fischer (ed.), *NBER Macroeconomics Annual 1989*. Cambridge, Mass.: MIT Press.

NEFTCI, S. N. (1984). 'Are Economic Time-Series Asymmetric Over the Business Cycle?' *Journal of Political Economy*, 92: 307–28.

REICHLIN, P. (1986). 'Equilibrium Cycles in an Overlapping Generations Economy with Production'. *Journal of Economic Theory*, 40: 89–102.

ROGERSON, R. (1988). 'Indivisible Labor, Lotteries, and Equilibrium'. *Journal of Monetary Economics*, 21: 3–16.

ROMER, P. (1986). 'Increasing Returns and Long Term Growth'. *Journal of Political Economy*, 94: 1002–37.

ROTEMBERG, J., and WOODFORD, M. (1989). 'Oligopolistic Pricing and the Effects of Aggregate Demand on Economic Activity'. NBER Working Paper no. 3206, December.

SAKAI, H., and TOKUMARU, H. (1980). 'Autocorrelations of a Certain Chaos'. *IEEE Transactions in Acoustics, Speech, and Signal Processing*, 28: 588–90.

SAMUELSON, P. A. (1957). 'Intertemporal Price Equilibrium: A Prologue to the Theory of Speculation'. *Weltwirtschaftliches Archiv*, 79: 181–219.

—— (1973). 'Optimality of Profit, Including Prices under Ideal Planning'. *Proceedings of the National Academy of Sciences* [USA], 70: 2109–11.

SARGENT, T. J. (1987). *Dynamic Macroeconomic Theory*. Cambridge, Mass.: Harvard University Press.

SCHEINKMAN, J. A. (1976). 'On Optimal Steady States of *n*-Sector Growth Models when Utility is Discounted'. *Journal of Economic Theory*, 12: 11–30.

—— (1990). 'Nonlinearities in Economic Dynamics'. *Economic Journal*, 100: 33–48 (Conference Issue).

SHELL, K. (1977). 'Monnaie et allocation intertemporelle'. Mimeo, Seminaire de E. Malinvaud, Paris, November.

SHILLER, R. J. (1978). 'Rational Expectations and the Dynamic Structure of Macroeconomic Models'. *Journal of Monetary Economics*, 4: 1–44.

SPEAR, S. E. (1988). 'Growth, Externalities, and Sunspots'. Unpublished paper, Carnegie Mellon University, May.

TOWNSEND, R. M. (1980). 'Models of Money with Spatially Separated Agents'. In J. H. Kareken and N. Wallace (eds.), *Models of Monetary Economies*. Minneapolis: Federal Reserve Bank of Minneapolis.

WOODFORD, M. (1984). 'Indeterminacy of Equilibrium in the Overlapping Generations Model: A Survey'. Unpublished paper, Columbia University, May.

—— (1986a). 'Stationary Sunspot Equilibria in a Finance Constrained Economy'. *Journal of Economic Theory*, 40: 128–37.

—— (1986b). 'Asset Bubbles and Fiat Money'. Unpublished paper, University of Chicago, August.

—— (1986c). 'Stationary Sunspot Equilibria: The Case of Small Fluctuations around a Deterministic Steady State'. Unpublished paper, September.

—— (1987). 'Three Questions about Sunspot Equilibria as an Explanation of Economic Fluctuations'. *American Economic Review*, 77: 938–42.

—— (1988a). 'Expectations, Finance, and Aggregate Instability'. In M. Kohn and S.-C. Tsiang (eds.), *Finance Constraints, Expectations, and Macroeconomics*. Oxford University Press.

—— (1988b). 'Monetary Policy and Price Level Determinacy in a Cash-in-Advance Economy'. Unpublished paper, University of Chicago, December.

—— (1989). 'Imperfect Financial Intermediation and Complex Dynamics'. In

W. A. Barnett, J. Geweke, and K. Shell (eds.), *Economic Complexity: Chaos, Sunspots, Bubbles, and Nonlinearity*. Cambridge University Press.

—— (1990). 'Learning to Believe in Sunspots'. *Econometrica*, 58: 277–307.

—— (1991). 'Self-Fulfilling Expectations and Fluctuations in Aggregate Demand'. In N. G. Mankiw and D. Romer (eds.), *New Keynesian Macroeconomics*. Cambridge, Mass.: MIT Press.

YANO, M. (1984). 'The Turnpike of Dynamic General Equilibrium Paths and its Insensitivity to Initial Conditions'. *Journal of Mathematical Economics*, 13: 235–54.

9

Nonlinear Economic Dynamics and Chaos: An Introduction

RICHARD M. GOODWIN and
PIER MARIO PACINI

1. Introduction

The purpose of this chapter is to offer readers some guidelines through the intricate and ever growing literature on the theoretical and applicative aspects of chaotic dynamical systems. More specific issues concerning chaotic fluctuations in growth theory and the relation between chaos and expectations are discussed elsewhere in this book by Day and Lin (Chapter 10) and by Woodford (Chapter 8); here we analyse the formal bulk of the theory of chaos and its main general implications for both theory and policy. We then examine the ramifications that deterministic chaos is undertaking in various fields of economic theory, trying to show the most common routes through which chaotic dynamics is arrived at. The discussion tries to support the following views:

1. Deterministic chaos represents a radical change of perspective in the explanation of fluctuations and irregularities observed in economic time series. It has huge implications for both theory and policy.
2. Deterministic chaotic systems are to be taken seriously; their occurrence is a possibility that theory cannot rule out and a hypothesis that, in several instances, empirical tests have not rejected.
3. In many cases, observable chaos is not a generic property; often, special conditions must be imposed to obtain chaos that must be carefully accounted for and which require attention in drawing conclusions.

The paper is organized as follows. Some background information is provided in Section 2. The basic mathematical tools are then presented in Section 3. More specific aspects are dealt with in Section 4, where we analyse the significance of chaotic systems and some of their general implications in economics. Sections 5 and 6 introduce specific applications in macroeconomics and microeconomics respectively. The survey of the literature is driven by a grouping criterion based on modelling strategies. Each class will be further dissected according to the economic mechanisms or economic conditions that are analysed. Finally, Section 7 introduces some statistical techniques devised to detect the presence of nonlinear deterministic structures in economic time series. Technicalities are avoided as much as possible, with reference to quoted papers for details.

2. Some Background to Dynamic Economic Theory

It is a well-known fact that economic time series arrive in a very complicated form; data, though following broadly recognizable patterns, show peaks and troughs that alternate irregularly in both size and time. Typical examples are the time series of exchange rates and stock returns: they are characterized by volatility of variables, absence of regular patterns, and unpredictability of future values. To explain and mimic such behaviour, basically two theoretical hypotheses have been set forth: the exogenous and the endogenous explanations of cyclical fluctuations. These two approaches originate from completely different visions of the working of the economic system and are rooted in the different views that economists have of the strength with which the market mechanism operates to stabilize the economy.

The exogenous approach (EXO in the following), which started with Frisch (1933) and was recently reinvigorated by the New Classical school, tries to build a theory of economic fluctuations on the basis of an equilibrium premise: the market is seen as a stabilizing mechanism and, in absence of extraneous perturbations, the economy regulates itself towards an equilibrium determined by market fundamentals (endowments, preferences, technology). Therefore, the origin of observed fluctuations lies in the optimal response of rational agents to the exogenous stochastic perturbations affecting the basic characteristics of the economy. With respect to the two examples of exchange rates and stock returns, their volatility is nothing more than the market response to the unpredictable 'news' continually hitting the economy (see Dornbusch 1976). When these processes are simulated, bounded irregular oscillations are generated and the method has a certain success in mimicking some of the features of aggregate time series. What emerges, clearly, is the attempt to incorporate 'cyclical phenomena into the system of economic equilibrium, with which they are in apparent contradiction', in line with Hayek's original programme; however, there is a clear trade-off between the descriptive and the explanatory power of this theory, given its basic inability to explain the exogenous forcing stochastic process.

An opposite view was taken by the endogenous approach. Starting from a basic rejection of the equilibrium and stability paradigm, it tries to highlight the endogenous sources of cyclical movements and identify some internal mechanisms of the economy as responsible for the observed fluctuations. Several attempts followed one another: the oldest one represented the dynamics of some relevant variable by a simple linear one-lag scheme $y_{t+1} = \alpha y_t$. But this scheme is rather unsuited to represent fluctuations; as is well known, a linear first-order difference equation generates only four types of structurally stable motions around the equilibrium $y_t = 0$: (1) monotonic stability $(0 < \alpha < 1)$, (2) stable oscillations $(-1 < \alpha < 0)$, (3) monotonic instability $(1 > \alpha)$, and (4) unstable oscillations $(-1 > \alpha)$. The possibility of fluctuations is linked with the very particular (structurally unstable) case in which $\alpha = -1$. More robust explanations required a different modelling, and three ways were open: (1) to increase the order of the governing difference equation (Samuelson 1939); (2) to maintain the simple linearity assumption superimposing a well-behaved periodic movement of some autonomous variable that fluctuates, leading other magnitudes (e.g. Samuelson 1947); (3) to drop the linearity assumption, resorting to mechanisms such as the presence of bounds to expansion and recession (Hicks 1950), the investment behaviour (Kaldor 1940, Goodwin 1951), etc., that produce nonlinearities in the system (see also Kalecki 1935). Following any displacement from equilibrium, such nonlinearities drive the economy towards a self-perpetuating, periodic trajectory. The limit of these nonlinear representations was that they could not explain the irregularities of the time paths observed in the real world: indeed, they were able at most to drive the system towards regular periodic motions which did not fit the complexity of the observed time series.

Recent years have seen the rise of a mathematical technology, *chaos theory*, which is able to reproduce the 'statistical' aspects of economic time series within the framework of nonlinear deterministic difference/differential equations, thus providing new strength for the endogenous approach. In a sense to be made precise later, chaos theory concerns the study of dynamical systems that generate bounded, never converging, oscillations with an irregularity of behaviour very similar to the one produced by a stochastic process. In this view, also, the complexities of economic time series receive an endogenous explanation and are traced back to the strong nonlinearities that can pervade the economic system.

In the next section the formal tools of chaos are examined. The mathematical apparatus is tackled first, since we regard the understanding of the mathematical techniques as essential to an understanding of the strength and limits of many economic applications.

3. Basic Mathematical Tools

Notwithstanding the common agreement on the notion of 'chaotic behaviour', there is not a commonly accepted formal definition of chaos.

In this section we will give different definitions, trying to capture that same notion of complexity. Choosing one or other of them is not a simple matter of formal taste, but may have implications for the subject we are going to study. For the sake of simplicity, we deliberately confine the discussion to the simplest possible formal setting, i.e. one-dimensional discrete systems.[1]

3.1. *Mono-dimensional systems: definitions and preliminary results*

It is common practice to start the formal study of chaos with the analysis of the quadratic difference equation[2]

$$y_{t+1} = \alpha y_t(1 - y_t) = g_\alpha(y_t), \qquad y_t \in [0, 1], \ \alpha \in [0, 4] \qquad (1)$$

The phase diagram of (1) (i.e. the graph of g_α on $[0, 1]$) is the familiar unimodal map and is represented in Fig. 9.1 for different values of α (the tuning or control parameter). For every α, g_α is a continuous map

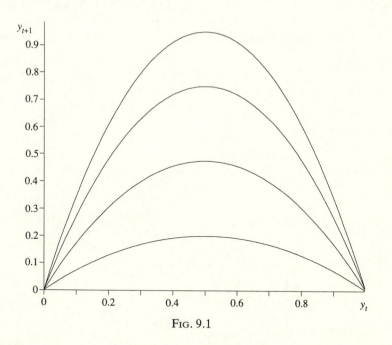

FIG. 9.1

---

[1] Similar properties for continuous-time models require at least three dimensions. Interested readers are urged to consult Sparrow (1982), Guckenheimer and Holmes (1983), Devaney (1987).

[2] Many results extend without modifications to more general schemes $y_{t+1} = f_w(t_t)$ where $y_t \in [a, b] \subset \mathbb{R}$ and $f_w: [a, b] \rightarrow [a, b]$ is a continuous self-map parameterized by w. A sufficient (but not necessary) condition usually imposed on f_w is that its phase diagram is *single-peaked*.

from a compact interval into itself and hence has at least a fixed point y^*: we call y^* a (steady-state) equilibrium of (1). It is easily checked that 0 is an equilibrium for all α.

In the following definitions, we will denote by $g_\alpha^{(k)}(y_t)$ the kth iterate of (1), defined recursively as $g_\alpha^{(k)}(y_t) = g \circ g_\alpha^{(k-1)}(y_t)$:

> DEFINITION 1. The *orbit* (or *trajectory*) of y_t is the set of points $\{y_t, y_{t+1}, y_{t+2}, \ldots\} = \{y_t, g_\alpha(y_t), g_\alpha^{(2)}(y_t), \ldots\}$.

> DEFINITION 2. An orbit of y_t is *periodic of order k* or (1) has a *cycle of order k* if the set $\{y_t, y_{t+1}, y_{t+2}, \ldots\}$ is finite and has cardinality k.

Any y_{t+i}, $0 \le i \le k - 1$, on a cycle of period k is a fixed point of $g_\alpha^{(k)}$.

In order to understand how chaos emerges, we study the dynamics of this simple system for different values of the control parameter α. It is easily verified that for $\alpha \in [0, 1]$, $A^* = 0$ is the only equilibrium of (1) and that for $\alpha \in [0, 1)$ it is (monotonically) stable since $dg_\alpha(y)/dy|_{A^*} = \alpha$. As α increases beyond 1, A^* loses stability, but a new positive fixed point B^* appears at the intersection of the phase diagram and the 45° line, as Fig. 9.2 shows. Point B^* and the derivative of g_α at B^* are given as functions of the parameter by the following expressions:

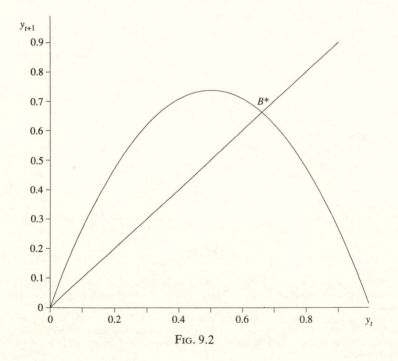

FIG. 9.2

$$B^* = \frac{\alpha - 1}{\alpha}; \qquad \frac{dg_\alpha}{dy}\bigg|_{B^*} = (2 - \alpha).$$

Therefore, for $\alpha \in (1, 3]$, there are two different equilibria: A^*, which is repelling, and B^*, which is stable and is approached by monotonically convergent trajectories for $1 < \alpha < 2$ and damped oscillations for $2 < \alpha < 3$.

As α exceeds 3, the fixed point B^* also loses stability since $(2 - \alpha) < -1$. However, the nonlinearity of g_α prevents the unbounded divergence of trajectories; they remain trapped in the square $[0, 1] \times [0, 1]$ and converge to a cycle that is initially of period 2. The following discussion will briefly describe how this happens. Let us take the function $g_\alpha^{(2)}$, i.e. the second iterate of g_α, and the associated dynamic equation

$$y_{t+2} = g_\alpha^{(2)}(y_t) = \alpha^2 y_t(1 - y_t)(\alpha y_t^2 - \alpha y_t + 1). \qquad (2)$$

This is again a nonlinear system, and we can pursue the same analysis as before studying its dynamic behaviour as α varies. For $\alpha \in [0, 3]$ the dynamics of (2) follows that of (1), namely: as $\alpha \in [0, 1]$, the only equilibrium of $g_\alpha^{(2)}$ is $A^* = 0$, which is monotonically stable since

$$\frac{dg_\alpha^{(2)}(y)}{dy}\bigg|_{A^*} = \left[\frac{dg_\alpha(y)}{dy}\right]^2 = \alpha^2 \leqslant 1.$$

As α increases beyond 1, A^* becomes unstable and the trajectories of (2) are attracted by the fixed point $B^* = (\alpha - 1)/\alpha$ where the slope of phase diagram is $(2 - \alpha)^2$. This equilibrium is stable until $\alpha \leqslant 3$. Beyond that value B^* loses attractivity, but two new fixed points (see Fig. 9.3) emerge that have no counterpart in the original equation (1). They are given by the points

$$C^* = \frac{\sqrt{(\alpha + 1)}[\sqrt{(\alpha + 1)} - \sqrt{(\alpha - 3)}]}{2\alpha};$$

$$D^* = \frac{\sqrt{\alpha + 1}[\sqrt{(\alpha + 1)} + \sqrt{(\alpha - 3)}]}{2\alpha}.$$

For values of α between 3 and 3.45, the slope of the phase diagram at both C^* and D^* decreases monotonically from 1 to -1, thus implying that each of them locally attracts the dynamics of (2). With respect to system (1), we observe the following fact: as B^* becomes unstable, the trajectories escape from it and diverge towards the pair of points C^* and D^*. Any one of them is unstable since $dg_\alpha(y)/dy$ at both C^* and D^* is greater than 1 in absolute value, so that the trajectories, once in C^* (D^* resp.) are initially repelled. However, the dynamics of the first-order system is to be consistent with the dynamics of the second-order system (2), which finds in C^* (D^* resp.) a locally stable equilibrium; therefore,

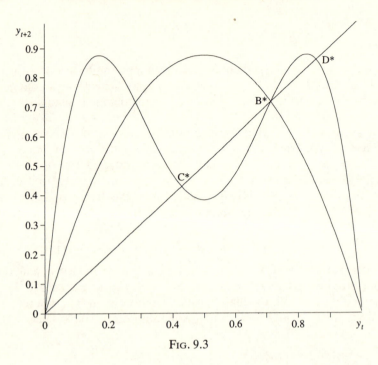

FIG. 9.3

after having moved away from C^* (D^* resp.) in the first step, trajectories come back to it in the second, thus making the dynamics of the second-order system stable with respect to C^* (D^* resp.), as required. Summarizing, when α increases beyond 3, the trajectories of system (1) no longer converge to the fixed point $(\alpha - 1)/\alpha$ (which is still present), but start oscillating in the set $\{C^*, D^*\}$, giving rise to a stable periodic point of order 2 for g_α. In this case the system is said to undergo a *Flip bifurcation* (see Guckenheimer and Holmes 1983). The same story can be repeated over and over again and the situation is pictured in Fig. 9.4, where dotted lines represent unstable equilibria. As α increases beyond 3.45, the cycle of period 2 becomes unstable and each of the two periodic points bifurcates in a new pair of points, giving rise to the set $\{E^*, F^*, G^*, H^*\}$; it forms a periodic orbit of order 4 which is stable for a small interval of the parameter α (*window of stability* of the four-period cycle).

Following this route, we generate a period doubling cascade of bifurcations, in which higher and higher periodic orbits are superimposed to existing ones with windows of stability of decreasing amplitude. In particular, the following theorem proves that the increase in the period of the observed cycles follows an orderly structure: higher-period cycles are associated with higher values of the tuning parameter:

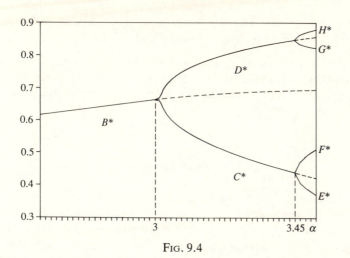

Fɪɢ. 9.4

Theorem 1. (Collet and Eckmann 1980; Grandmont 1984.) Consider the family of maps g_α and the system defined by (1):

(i) Let α_j^* be the first value of the parameter α for which a stable cycle of period 2^j obtains for $j > 1$. Then the sequence α_j^* increases with j and converges to some value $\alpha_\infty^* < 4$ as j tends to $+\infty$. For each a in $[0, \alpha_\infty^*)$, all cycles of the map g_α have a period that is a power of 2 or are fixed points.

(ii) If stable cycles of period 2^j and 2^k, $k > j + 1$, occur respectively for the values α_j and α_k in $[0, \alpha_\infty^*)$, then a stable cycle of period 2^i with $k > i > j$ must appear for some values α_i in the open interval (α_j, α_k).

The above theorem makes precise the notion of continuous transition to turbulence: increases in α drive the system towards regions of increasing complexity (*Landau scenario*). Theorem 1 is complemented by the following very important theorem which ascertains that, whenever a given period is present in the motion of the system, all the lower-order periodic motions are also present at the same time:

Theorem 2. (Šarkovskii 1964; Stefan 1977). Consider the following ordering of integers:

$$1 < 2 < 4 < 8 < \ldots < 2^m < \ldots$$
$$< 2 \times 3 < 2 \times 5 < 2 \times 7 < \ldots$$
$$\vdots$$
$$< 2^n \times 3 < 2^n \times 5 < 2^n \times 7 < \ldots$$
$$\vdots$$
$$\ldots < 7 < 5 < 3.$$

If the continuous map g_α: $[0, 1] \to [0, 1]$ has a cycle of order k, then it has a cycle of every period k', for $k' < k$.

Theorem 2 receives an immediate illustration in Fig. 9.4: the first periods in the Šarkovskii ordering (consisting of the power of 2 in increasing order) correspond to the sequence of Flip bifurcations described above.

3.2. Definitions of chaos

So far, we have shown the presence of periodic motions of any order. Though mortal agents could well assimilate very long period cycles with chaotic trajectories, from the strictly formal point of view, the notion of truly chaotic maps is characterized by some features that are not captured by cyclical motions, namely: (1) absence of periodicity, and (2) absence of stability. To capture these aspects, several definitions have been proposed, each of them highlighting some particular features inherent (1) and (2).

(a) Topological chaos (chaos in the Li–Yorke sense)

The following definition of chaos has been often used in applications:

DEFINITION 3. A map g_α: $[0, 1] \to [0, 1]$ is *chaotic* if there is an uncountable subset $S \subset [0, 1]$ such that:

(i) For every x and y in S, $x \neq y$,

$$\limsup_{n \to \infty} \|g_\alpha^{(n)}(x) - g_\alpha^{(n)}(y)\| > 0$$

$$\liminf_{n \to \infty} \|g_\alpha^{(n)}(x) - g_\alpha^{(n)}(y)\| = 0;$$

(ii) For every x in S and y periodic,

$$\limsup_{n \to \infty} \|g_\alpha^{(n)}(x) - g_\alpha^{(n)}(y)\| > 0.$$

Part (i) of the definition accounts for an essential feature of turbulence: chaotic trajectories starting from two points in S will get arbitrarily close and then will separate again as time goes on: neither of them attracts the other. Part (ii) excludes any asymptotic convergence to periodic orbits; i.e., no point in S lies in the *basin of attraction* of any cycle. The task of the theory is then to show under what conditions the map g_α is chaotic. Li and Yorke (1975) first proved that, if g_α has a cycle of period 3 (stable or unstable), then it is chaotic. (*Period 3 implies chaos.*) This result can be generalized to:

THEOREM 3. (Grandmont 1987). If the map g_α has a cycle of a period that is not a power of 2, then g_α is chaotic.

Despite its formal interest, the above result is rather weak from the practical point of view: it does not exclude that the chaotic set S be of (Lebesgue) measure 0, so that almost all trajectories are attracted by a stable cycle. For example, system (1) is often chaotic in the interval $(\alpha_\infty^*, 4]$, but S may be a null set; i.e., there is a zero probability of finding a chaotic trajectory by a random choice of initial conditions. In these cases, the chaotic behaviour may be essentially unobservable (see Section 4 below).

(b) Sensitive dependence on initial conditions

In order to cope with this measure-theoretic weakness, an alternative definition of chaos has been suggested in which trajectories are classified as chaotic if they exhibit *sensitive dependence on initial conditions* (SDIC) for some tangible set of initial conditions. SDIC is here defined as follows:

DEFINITION 4. A map g_α is said to have SDIC if there exists a subset $S \subset [0, 1]$ having positive Lebesgue measure such that, for every x in S and every neighbourhood U of x, there is a y in U, $x \neq y$, such that[3]

$$\lim_{n \to \infty} \sup \|g_\alpha^{(n)}(x) - g_\alpha^{(n)}(y)\| > 0$$

$$\lim_{n \to \infty} \inf \|g_\alpha^{(n)}(x) - g_\alpha^{(n)}(y)\| = 0.$$

Intuitively, SDIC means that, for any small change δy_0 in the initial condition y_0, the corresponding change $\delta y_t = g_\alpha^{(t)}(y_0 + \delta y_0) - g_\alpha^{(t)}(y_0)$ of $y_t = g_\alpha^{(t)}(y_0)$ evolves irregularly with t and eventually becomes large when t becomes large. When SDIC occurs any notion of continuity is lost; under the repeated action of g_α, close initial conditions do not produce similar forward behaviours and their orbits can be regarded as fairly independent sequences. If such a case is verified, for all practical purposes, the dynamics of (1) defies computations; measurement errors or computer roundings provide continuous 'shocks' to the system that, accumulating, make the forecasting of future behaviour an almost impossible task. Parallel to the case of topological chaos, conditions are sought to establish when a system exhibits SDIC. As a first result, we can determine when SDIC is *not* present:

---

[3] Besides the absence of something like Def. 3(ii), Def. 4 differs from Def. 3 since, apart from S being of positive Lebesgue measure, it requires also the possibility to choose x and y arbitrarily close.

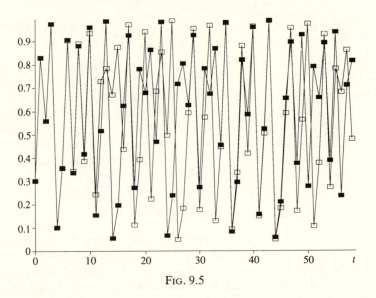

FIG. 9.5

THEOREM 4. (Collet and Eckmann 1980.) If g_α has a stable periodic orbit of period k, the map g_α has no sensitivity on initial conditions.

Positive results require a mathematical apparatus that exceeds our purposes, and we refer to Collet and Eckmann (1980: Section II.7). For the simple case of equation (1), we can show that there are values of the parameter for which no stable periodic orbit exists and hence for which SDIC prevails:

THEOREM 5. Consider the family of maps g_α. Then,
(i) for any α in $[0, \alpha_\infty^*)$, the map g_α has a (unique) stable periodic orbit;
(ii) There is an uncountable set of values of α in $[\alpha_\infty^*, 4]$ for which g_α has no stable periodic orbit: this set has positive Lebesgue measure.

3.3. Strange attractors and ergodic measures

Some other mathematical concepts have been proposed to capture the idea of complexity, namely *strange attractors* and *absolutely continuous invariant ergodic measures* (ACIEM). The mathematical technology required for their formal discussion is rather advanced, so only the basic ideas and results will be dealt with.

(a) Strange attractors

Attractor sets, and strange attractors in particular, play an important role in chaotic dynamics. To illustrate the idea of strange attractors, one has to start with the notion of *limiting set*, i.e. the collection of the cluster points of an orbit $\{y_t\}_{t=0}^{\infty}$. A limiting set is an *attractor* if orbits, emanating from nearby initial conditions, are trapped in the limit by that set and move in or near it for ever. The generally accepted conjecture is that the complexity (*strangeness*) of the attractor increases with its dimension: more precisely, low-dimensional attractors are generically[4] regular (fixed points, limit cycles), but higher-dimensional attractors 'tend not to be smooth surfaces like spheres and tori but rather to have a very complicated, infinitely many-layered structure' (Lanford 1981). Trajectories within a strange attractor may have a very complicated behaviour looking like noisily periodic motions and exhibiting SDIC. In this way, a strange attractor combines the two aspects of being strange, in the sense that within it the kind of behaviour as chaotic trajectories is reproduced, of being an attractor and hence an empirically relevant object.

From the more formal point of view, a strange attractor for a system $x_{t+1} = f(x_t)$ is defined as a subset Ω of the state space with the following properties (see Lanford 1981 and Guckenheimer and Holmes 1983 for further discussion):

1. Ω is *invariant*.[5]
2. There is an open neighbourhood $U \supset \Omega$ of *positive Lebesgue measure* such that $f^{(k)}(U) \subset U$ for all $k > 0$ and such that $f^{(k)}(U)$ shrinks down to Ω as $k \to \infty$.
3. The orbit of f on Ω is *recurrent* and *indecomposable*. 'Recurrent' means that no subset of Ω is initially visited and then left for ever by the trajectory of the system; 'indecomposable' means that Ω cannot be split into two closed non-overlapping invariant pieces.

Notwithstanding that the presence and importance of strange attractors is increasingly acknowledged,[6] there is not a commonly agreed and general classification of strange attractors in $\mathbb{R}^n$. Some examples of them will be encountered in economic applications.

---

[4] We refer here to the concept of topological genericity, defined and discussed in Sect. 4.1 below.

[5] A set Ω is *invariant* if it is the collection of the points x that remain in Ω under all forward and backward iterates of f.

[6] See Guckenheimer and Holmes (1983) for results and sufficient conditions, Sparrow (1982) and Abraham and Shaw (1983) for examples and illustrations.

(b) Absolutely continuous invariant ergodic measures

When we pass to the study of systems possessing ACIEM, we implicitly assume a different definition of chaos based on a measure-theoretic notion of randomness in ergodic systems. The basic motivation to this approach is as follows. If a system is chaotic, its trajectories wander in a compact region, following an apparently random process; given their complexity, an analytical description is almost impossible, but some relevant properties can be summarized by means of their statistical asymptotic distributions over the range of f. In other words, given a one-dimensional discrete chaotic system $y_{t+1} = f(y_t)$, one interprets the iterates f^n as the realizations of a data-generating process f on D and computes the frequency distribution of the iterates of f as n become large. When the system generated by f possesses an ACIEM, we have the striking result that, in the limit, those frequency distributions can be described by a non-degenerate probability measure with support over an invariant set for f of positive Lebesgue measure. Therefore, chaotic systems may display nice statistical regularities after all. To see that this is the case when the system generated by f possesses an ACIEM, we recall some basic definitions:

> DEFINITION 5. A probability measure μ on D is *invariant* if $\mu(B) = \mu(f^{-1}(B))$, for any $B \subset D$.

> DEFINITION 6. A probability measure μ on D is *ergodic* if $f(B) = B$ implies $\mu(B) = 1$ or $\mu(B) = 0$.

> DEFINITION 7. A probability measure μ on D is *absolutely continuous* with respect to the Lebesgue measure λ if μ has a density which is integrable with respect to λ.

Suppose that μ is invariant; this means that f neither 'expands' nor 'contracts' the measure of any set B. If μ is also ergodic, its support cannot be decomposed by f into two disjoint invariant subsets of positive measure. These two properties together imply that f wanders evenly on the whole support of μ, and if absolute continuity holds, the Lebesgue measure of this set is positive; as desired, the wandering region of f has positive measure. Some other properties are also of interest: the *ergodic mean*, i.e. $\lim_{n \to \infty}(1/n)\sum_{i=0}^{n} f^{(i)}(x_0)$, and the *ergodic mean sojourn time* in any set B, i.e. $\lim_{m \to \infty}(1/m)\sum_{i=0}^{n}\chi(f^{(i)}(x_0), B)$,[7] exist and are well defined for μ—almost all x_0. In addition, if μ is ergodic such ergodic means can be made independent of x_0; in particular $\lim_{n \to \infty}(1/n)\sum_{i=0}^{n}\chi(f^{(i)}(x_0), B) = \mu(B)$. In words, the probability of finding the trajectory of f visiting any

---

[7] The function $\chi(x, X)$ is the step function defined as $\chi(x, X) = 1$ if $x \in X$, and $\chi(x, X) = 0$ if $x \notin X$.

desired, however small, subset of the chaotic attractor is equal to its μ-measure.

4. Prominence and Implications of Chaotic Dynamics

With this set of tools, we can come closer to our subject. We have seen (and we will see, in Sections 5 and 6 below) that chaos theory provides an alternative to the explanation of fluctuations based on exogenous shocks. Now we address another question: Is it a significant alternative, where the term 'significant' stands for 'strong enough', not to be destroyed by small perturbations? In other words, suppose we have a one-dimensional, one-parameter dynamical system $y_{t+1} = f_\alpha(y_t)$ which describes the law of evolution of an economic variable y_t: what are the chances that an arbitrary orbit $\{y_t, y_{t+1}, y_{t+2}, \ldots\}$ generated by this model will be a chaotic one? In answering this question, we have to deal with two possible sources of 'small perturbations':

1. perturbations of the value of the controlling parameter;
2. perturbations of the initial states.

The first of these induces the question, Is chaos structurally stable? This will be dealt with in Section 4.1. The second induces another question: Are there sufficiently many initial conditions giving rise to chaotic trajectories to say that chaos is observable? This will be dealt with in Section 4.2. Both questions have implications for economic modelling.

4.1. *Robustness of aperiodic dynamics*

The question of structural stability is usually thought to have implications for model building purposes: 'Due to measurement uncertainties, etc., a model ... is valuable only if its qualitative properties do not change with perturbations' (Guckenheimer and Holmes 1983: 259). That is to say, goodness of model, robustness of its qualitative properties and genericity of its qualitative behaviour are all regarded as similar (stability dogma). However, when the problem of robustness is posed with respect to systems that are chaotic in the sense of Definitions 3 and 4, one has to face a preliminary question of definition regarding the concept of genericity that we adopt. Indeed, there is a 'tension between two different notions of genericity (topological genericity and measure theoretic genericity) when trying to assess the relative frequency of chaotic motion' (Grandmont 1987). According to the topological point of view, there exists a (yet unproved) conjecture that for some families of maps f_α, the set of values of the parameter for which stable cycles occur is open and dense, so that chaos can be considered rare and structurally unstable. On the other hand, it has been proved (Collet and Eckmann 1980; Jacobson 1981) that, for a large class of maps, chaotic trajectories exist for a set of values of the parameter α that has a positive Lebesgue measure (see also Theorem 5(ii)), so that, beyond a positive probability of stable periodic motions, there is also a non-zero probability of ergodic and mixing behaviour (i.e. SDIC). Also, for the alternative definitions of chaos (i.e. ACIEM and strange attractors), the question of structural stability is a delicate subject, although examples have been found of systems that are robust to small variations of the tuning parameter (see Guckenheimer and Holmes 1983; Abraham and Shaw 1983). However, to the best of our knowledge, there are no examples of dynamical systems that are chaotic for all values of the parameter.[8]

These observations make chaos theory both weak and attractive at the same time. From the theoretical point of view, we have seen that obtaining chaotic regimes is not an easy task: may occur for small subsets of the parameter space and the imposition of special, though not improbable, values of the control parameter requires careful explanations and confronts us with the interesting problem of checking whether the parameter values for which chaotic systems obtain fit the ranges of values established by empirical works. On the other hand, from the practical point of view, the values of the governing parameters are to be estimated from past observations and hence are subject to measurement errors. Since such small errors may suffice to displace the system from the chaotic regime, it implies that simulations conducted by means of the estimated model may use a structure that is 'qualitatively different' from the true data-generating process. In this case, future simulated behaviour will be completely different from the one effectively observed, thus offering a possible explanation of the often observed failure of the medium–long-term predictions.

4.2. Observability of aperiodic dynamics

The problem we are concerned with here is whether and to what extent the presence of chaos depends on the choice of initial conditions, i.e.

---

[8] There is an alternative way of dealing with the problem, namely to restrict and redefine the class of properties that we are interested in when we analyse the structural stability of chaotic systems: cf. Guckenheimer and Holmes (1983: Sect. 5.4) for a discussion of this point.

the problem of 'observable–unobservable', 'thick–thin' chaos (see Grandmont 1984; Malese and Transrue 1986, 1987; Day 1986; Day and Shaffer 1987). The issue is particularly evident in the case of the topological definition of chaos: the Li–Yorke theorem (and similar ones) cannot rule out the possibility that the set S of chaotic initial conditions is of Lebesgue measure 0 (thin or unobservable chaos); and indeed, this is the case for our system (1). If this situation holds, proving the existence of the scrambled set, and hence of chaos, may become a speculative discussion; from the practical point of view, most trajectories are attracted by stable cycles and there is no sensitivity to initial conditions. Moreover, even if the system happens to move chaotically, any policy intervention affecting only the state of the system suffices to reduce the volatility of variables setting them down to regular motions. This is to be interpreted as a warning against unwarranted statements such as that the existence of a cycle of period 3 implies chaotic behaviour, as some economic applications seem to suggest (see Day 1982, 1983; Benhabib and Day 1980, 1982). Some cases are known in which the possibility of a scrambled set of positive and even full measure has been proved,[9] but this seems to be linked with non-trivial situations (piece-wise linear or piece-wise smooth systems, i.e. switching regimes) whose presence is also to be carefully justified. As already mentioned in Section 3.2 above, the alternative route of assimilating cycles with very long-period to chaotic trajectories is to be taken carefully. The suggested assimilation rests on our giving up some peculiar characteristics of chaotic trajectories: think of the differences in the results of policy simulations assuming the system on a cyclical but stable motion or in a truly chaotic regime with strong SDIC.

The fragility of chaotic models is less pronounced when we adopt alternative definitions of chaos, namely the notion of ACIEM (see Day and Shaffer 1987; Day and Kim 1987) or strange attractors with a basin of attraction of positive measure (see Montrucchio 1984; Lorenz 1987a, b; Goodwin 1989). In these cases, a random choice of initial conditions is not bound to sweep away the complex erratic behaviour of the system, so that chaotic dynamics should be 'observable'. However, they do not get rid of the following observation: the study of chaotic systems poses serious problems concerning initial conditions; arbitrary choices of initial conditions are not uninfluential with respect to the behaviour we are going to generate. This validates an old claim that a 'detailed theory predicting plausible values of the initial conditions is essential' (Haavelmo 1954), against a common practice followed in time-series modelling.

---

[9] The classical example is the *tent map*: $T(x) = \begin{cases} 2x & 0 \le \frac{1}{2} \\ 2(1-x) & \frac{1}{2} \le 1 \end{cases}$.

4.3. *Implications of chaotic systems*

The discussion in Sections 4.1 and 4.2 suggests that chaotic dynamics is a delicate mechanism and its use to interpret real events is subject to some restrictions that the theory itself poses. In what follows we do not consider such restrictions, and proceed *as if* the system were in a chaotic regime, with a set of chaotic initial conditions of positive measure which is sufficiently great compared with our purposes and measurements. Under these conditions, the application of chaos theory to economics will be shown to be fruitful of far-reaching implications. Starting at a very general level, some of them are here discussed and grouped under four headings:

1. inability to forecast perfectly;
2. inability to fine-tune;
3. persistence of temporary disturbances;
4. necessity of structural policy intervention.[10]

(a) *Inability to forecast perfectly*

The inability of forecasting when the economy is in a chaotic regime is imputable to two basic reasons: sudden qualitative breaks in the time path, and sensitive dependence on initial conditions (see Baumol and Quandt 1985; Baumol 1986, 1987; Baumol and Benhabib 1989). As to the first, a peculiar characteristic of chaotic trajectories is 'their propensity to introduce sharp and unheralded qualitative breaks in time paths'. Figure 9.6 illustrates the point. A regime of damping oscillations followed by a steady state seems to prevail up to point E^*. No forecasting technique based on extrapolation from past observed data could have predicted the sudden drop that occurred at E^*. A similar behaviour is observed by De Grauwe and Vansanten (1990) in simulating a dynamic model of exchange-rate determination: 'Sequences of relatively stable cyclic behaviour are sometimes suddenly interrupted as if the system were subjected to large exogenous shocks.' The same applies to the variability of chaotic sequences: these are characterized by

---

[10] There is a whole class of implications for econometric work. The theory of deterministic chaos is in clear contrast with the usual procedure of decomposing time series in a trend, a cycle, and random shocks that maintain the observed irregularities. Some empirical procedures coherent with the deterministic approach are examined in Sect. 7. Here, however, we abstract from such methodological considerations as, for example, how the concept of rationality should be redefined in an environment that can never be known, given its complexity, or the meaning of *negligible frictions* in models in which the introduction of any disturbance, however small, is able to destroy important properties (see Spear 1989). These are still open fields, and even a simple introduction would take us too far.

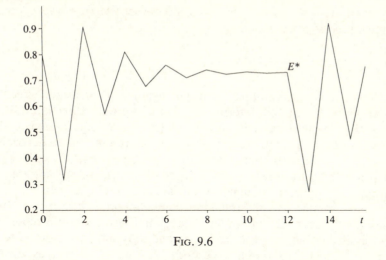

FIG. 9.6

non-stationarity in variance, *as if* the generating model were subject to exogenous structural changes. Without exact knowledge of the dynamics of the system, such changes were unpredictable.

Another source of unpredictability is SDIC. If the system exhibits SDIC, two trajectories, no matter how close they start, present a positive rate of divergence and after a while are completely independent of one another: in other words, we lose information about the system as time goes by, and we are not able to predict its future states unless that they are dispersed over the whole domain of definition (see Shaw 1981). It is clear that the unavoidable measurement errors and precision rounding in computer calculations are equivalent to changes in initial conditions, so that the system shifts among different trajectories, and after a while simulations produce values of the variables that have nothing to do with the values produced by the true model. Predictability of future realizations requires an exact knowledge of the law of evolution and of the state of the system and an infinite precision in computational devices, all of which seem to exceed human and techno-logical capabilities, especially in the social sciences.

Consequently, whenever chaotic regimes prevail, learning procedures based on observations are bound to fail in driving towards a correct perception of future events; what can be done, at most, is to learn the asymptotic probability distribution of future events that exists if the dynamics of the underlying system possesses an ACIEM. However, in this case also, confident forecasts cannot exceed the short run. More elaborate prediction techniques, suited for a nonlinear environment, have been proposed (see Farmer and Sidorowich 1987). However, their eventual success is again limited to the short run.[11]

(b) Inability to fine-tune

The impossibility of fine-tuning can be regarded as a further effect of the presence of SDIC. Interpreted in the forward direction, SDIC produces the effects seen in subsection (a) above. Interpreted in the backward direction, SDIC simply says that we are not able to determine which are the past (present resp.) states that give rise to well determined present (future resp.) states. In other words, we are not able to fine-tune the initial conditions of the system to obtain some desired state. An example can illustrate the point. Suppose that $w_{t+1} = f(w_t)$ represents the correctly known law of evolution of wealth of a representative individual, and that at time t an authority has to act on w_t (e.g. taxation) in order to obtain a desired value w^*_{t+T}, T periods ahead, $T \geq 1$. Were the system not chaotic, the knowledge of f would have allowed the backward reconstruction of the values of w in t that produce w^*_{t+T}. But in presence of SDIC, this backward procedure is bound to reconstruct present values of wealth (and hence a tax policy) that, when left to their own evolution, produce huge discrepancies from targets. Therefore, the inaccuracy of available measurement technologies, and the limited resolution with which events can be analysed, make any attempt to fine-tune likely to obtain undesired effects; the design of policy rules to achieve a target in the future has to face a huge problem of knowledge concerning the state of the system and the impact of the policy to be taken. A fortiori, this is valid when the achievement of the target depends on the co-ordination of several actors; in the presence of deterministic chaos, co-ordination must be perfect, and any trembling-hand equilibrium is bound to produce undesired effects in the evolution of the system.

(c) Persistence of temporary disturbances

One of the primary tenets of the EXO approach is that, in absence of other sources of disturbance, exogenous shocks are dampened out and absorbed by the system that recovers its equilibrium position. Therefore, if an intervention has to have permanent effects, it must be permanent. However, this is not the case when we are in presence of chaotic systems exhibiting SDIC; temporary disturbances are amplified by the

---

[11] These considerations highlight the difficulty that agents can encounter in forming rational expectations when the system is in a chaotic regime.

subsequent dynamic evolution and tend to have permanent effects, since they alter substantially the complete future history of the system. In the above-mentioned model of exchange-rate determination, De Grauwe and Vansanten (1990) observe: 'One temporary shock changes the path the exchange rate will follow around the equilibrium for the indefinite future. This result stands in contrast with traditional exchange-rate models that typically predict that temporary shocks only lead to temporary movements in the exchange rate.' Since the system never forgets its past, actions of the 'hit and run' type must also take into account all possible strong distortionary effects in the future.

(d) Necessity of structural policy intervention

The above arguments offer a direct justification for this last point: if an economy is found to operate in a chaotic regime, policy intervention acting only on the state of the system may succeed in affecting the actual time paths but not their qualitative features. 'If irregular fluctuations depend on the structure of the system, rather than on external disturbances, intervention to eliminate or reduce them will have to change the system rather than shield it from shocks' (Medio 1987). In other words, structural intervention is required to promote changes in the value of the governing parameters if stabilization is required. This is in striking contrast with much of the recent policy debate centred around the feasibility and optimality of interventions affecting the level of state variables (e.g. money stocks) leaving unaltered the structural relations of the economy.

5. Applications in Macroeconomics

Models offering a deterministic explanation of the erratic behaviour of economic aggregates are classified according to two more general approaches to macroeconomics: the macrodynamic approach and the intertemporal maximization approach. Given their distinguishing characteristics, they will be analysed separately in Sections 5.1 and 5.2, respectively. The former is more fragmented and diversified, so after a brief survey of the main research directions, a flavour of how it works is given by developing a version of a classical growth model. The opportunity is also taken to discuss some further technical points of chaos and to show possible extensions to the continuous-time case. In the second approach, some lines of reasoning are more clearly distinguished and will be discussed in a unified context.

5.1. *The macrodynamic approach*

By the macrodynamic approach, we mean the descriptive approach in which an aggregate economy is modelled as a set of dynamic equations that are not derived from an underlying optimization process. The 'strategy' followed by this class of models consists in reformulating well-known models in such a way that, under suitable conditions, chaotic movements of variables cannot be ruled out. Such a strategy is pursued following two routes, which we term the formally applicative modelling approach and the interactionist approach.

(a) Formally applicative models

A typical model in this class works with a highly aggregative structure which, after suitable manipulations, is shown to produce a one-lag, one-variable dynamic equation representing the law of evolution of the relevant economic aggregate (GNP, capital stock, inventory levels, productive capacity, etc....). Then conditions on the behavioural relations of the models are imposed in order to obtain that the 'dynamic data-generating process' follows (a form of) the unimodal law studied in Section 3.1. Finally, it is shown that, for appropriate values of the parameters, the nonlinearities of the model are strengthened enough to obtain the possibility of chaos. This sequence of manipulations and subsequent restrictions on the basic relations of the model is justified in several and often *ad hoc* ways. For example, Stutzer (1980) shows that chaos is present in a discrete version of Haavelmo's (1954) growth model for appropriate values of the parameters, given the combined nonlinearity of the production and labour demand functions. Pohjola (1981) examines a discrete version of Goodwin's (1967) growth cycle model and introduces a further degree of nonlinearity through the introduction of a nonlinear reaction of aggregate income distribution to variations in the employment rate, which can be thought of as the result of a bargaining over real wage rates in which wage levels depend positively but nonlinearly on the employment rate. Similarly, Simonovitz (1982) shows the possibility of chaotic behaviour in the dynamics of a non-Walrasian model; such possibility emerges from the nonlinear dependence of production and employment on inventories when the latter are used as buffers to satisfy demand. Neoclassical growth models *à la* Solow have been extensively studied, and sufficient conditions for chaotic dynamics have been found by suitably restricting the production function and/or making the saving propensity dependent on the capital–labour ratio (Day 1982), or else by assuming that the elasticity of consumption depends positively on wealth, thus obtaining proportionately higher consumption–wealth ratios in a capital-rich society and higher savings–wealth ratios when low-wage, capital-scarce periods come in (Benhabib and Day 1980).

(b) Interaction models

A different attitude is taken by what has been termed the interactionist approach. Rather than working with one-variable aggregative models, this approach envisages an economy disaggregated in at least two sectors. Provided that the economy is not in a steady state and that sectors are linked by intersectoral exchanges, the oscillations that each of them independently experiences interfere with those of the others, providing shocks that are exogenous to the receiving sector but endogenous in an economy-wide perspective. The dynamic behaviour of the resulting coupled system may be characterized by an irregular cyclical motion described in terms of a strange attractor.[12] This is essentially the idea behind Lorenz (1987a), in which three sectors oscillate independently in terms of their own levels of output and capital. Were the system decoupled, this would be the end of the story; however, if markets are interdependent and each sector produces a positive demand for goods delivered by the other sectors, any intersectoral trade can be interpreted as a perturbation of the stable independent cyclical trajectories, and the overall result is the possible presence of a strange attractor in the dynamics of the coupled system. The same reasoning holds when different sectors are substituted by different national economies; in this case, international trade is the vehicle of perturbations, thus obtaining the possibility of chaotic movements (see Lorenz 1987b; Puu 1987). The same flavour inspires models such as Goodwin's (1989), which is a two-variable model representing output and capacity. Output is expanded whenever demand exceeds supply and capacity is expanded whenever output exceeds capacity, but the rates of adjustment are different, being higher for output and lower for capacity, so that the former becomes a fast variable and the latter a slow variable. Unbounded expansion of the economy is prevented by imposing full employment as an upper bound; this implies also that cyclical fluctuations are obtained. However, the lags with which the slow variable follows the fluctuations of the fast variable affect and perturb the motion of the former, thus giving rise to a (*ring*) strange attractor.

---

[12] The mathematical technology used to arrive at these results is that of coupled oscillators systems, for which we refer to Lorenz (1989: Sect. 4.2.3).

5.2. An application to the classical von Neumann model

As a further illustration of the macro-behavioural approach, and in order to present some interesting results, we now develop a violently simplified version of classical von Neumann growth model (1937). Two cases are analysed. In the first we assume a constant rate of growth of labour productivity; this case is analysed in discrete terms. Subsequently, the possibility of endogenous variations in productive capacity will be considered in a continuous-time reformulation of the same model.

(a) Constant labour productivity growth

In this case oscillations will be shown to exist, since the real wage may rise more or less rapidly than productivity, yielding either a rising or falling unit labour cost; this in turn will alter the growth rate of output and employment, thus producing fluctuations. The model works as follows. The von Neumann n-dimensional model is reduced to a single dimension and represented by means of the following equation, in which the variable q stands for the output level:

$$q^{t+1} = (\alpha^t + u^{t+1})^{-1} q^t \tag{3}$$

where $u^{t+1} = \alpha_l^{t+1} w^{t+1}$ represents unit labour cost. Let $v^t = \alpha_l^t q^t / N^t$ represent the degree of employment in period t, given population N^t. We assume that the real wage w^t depends positively on the degree of employment v^t according to

$$\frac{\Delta w^t}{w^t} = f(v^t) = b\left(\frac{1}{1 - v^t} - c\right), \qquad b > 0,\ c \geq 0, \tag{4}$$

where b is a parameter determining the sensitivity of real wage to employment, and $f(v^t)$ produces an infinite rate of increase of real wage for $v^t = 1$. By the definition of u^{t+1} and using (4), we obtain

$$\frac{\Delta u^t}{u^t} = \frac{\alpha^{t+1} w^{t+1} - \alpha^t w^t}{\alpha^t w^t} = \frac{\alpha^{t+1}(1 + f(v^t)) - \alpha^t}{\alpha^t}$$

$$= (1 + g_\alpha)(1 + f(v^t)) - 1$$

from which

$$u^{t+1} = (1 + g_\alpha)\left[1 + b\left(\frac{1}{1 - v^t} - c\right)\right] u^t, \tag{5}$$

where $g_\alpha = \Delta \alpha^t / \alpha^t$. Defining $g_N = \Delta N^t / N^t$ and taking into account (3), similar calculations for v^t give

$$v^{t+1} = \frac{1 + g_\alpha}{1 + g_N}(\alpha + u^{t+1}) v^t \tag{6}$$

For reasonable values of the parameters, the solutions of the system formed by equations (3), (5), and (6), are shown in Figs. 9.7 and 9.8. Evidently, the solutions for u and v are mildly erratic with q growing unsteadily. If this model is elaborated to produce an asymptotically stable equilibrium motion, the phase portrait will result in a series of points lying not on a smooth curve, but within a closed, bounded, annular region. This occurs because we have a system that is unstable around its fixed point (equilibrium steady-state growth) and hence will grow in its amplitude of oscillations, but which is stable in its outer region and will experience diminishing amplitude there. A high employment rate v^t means a high growth rate of wage cost, and low v^t means

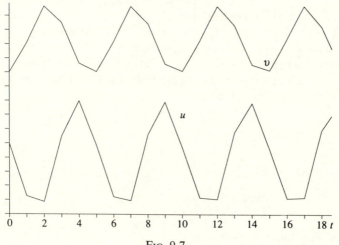

FIG. 9.7

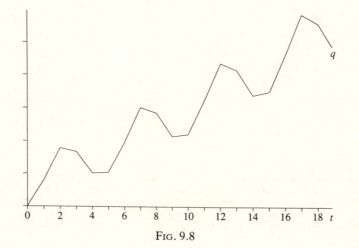

FIG. 9.8

a low one. A high growth rate of wages means a deceleration of growth
and leads to a decline in the employment rate; the resulting low v^t
means a low growth rate of wages and restores growth and ultimately
brings us back to a high v^t. To exemplify such a discrete-time-limit
cycle, one can simulate the following pair of equations in dimensionless
form, which give the essence of the behaviour:

$$v^{t+1} = \alpha v^t (1 - u^t - v^t),$$

$$u^{t+1} = \alpha u^t v^t,$$

where α is the unique parameter open to choice. Figure 9.9 shows the
solution of the above system for $\alpha = 3.1$: it approaches a closed annular
band. An enlarged section of the set of limiting points is reproduced in
Fig. 9.10 to make it evident that the points do not lie on any simple
smooth curve. Consequently, the resulting time series of u^t and v^t are
not strictly periodic, only quasi-periodic.[13] Figure 9.11 simulates the
same model when the parameter α is further increased up to 4: a typical
example of a strange attractor is then obtained, in which the behaviour
of u^t and v^t is absolutely erratic.

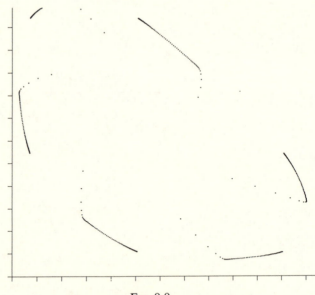

Fig. 9.9

[13] Simulations reveal another remarkable aspect of discrete-time-limit cycles. The
approach to the limit set is not asymptotic in the same sense as for continuous-time
models. Proceeding in discrete steps, it may and often does join the limit set in finite, not
infinite, time. Also, it may leap over the annular region and only subsequently expand to
join the limit set. Once in the limiting band, it appears to be constrained to remain in the
limit set.

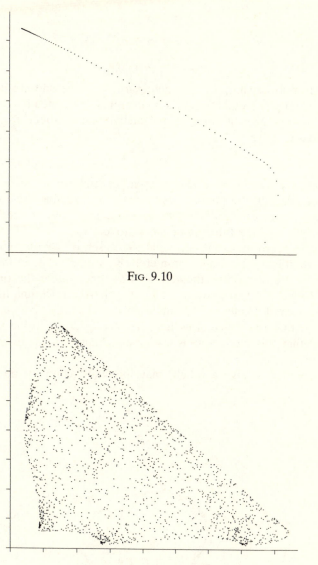

FIG. 9.10

FIG. 9.11

(b) Endogenous variations in a continuous time model

To come closer to economic reality, it is useful to formulate the above model in continuous time, in the form of the well-known *Rössler band*. In the simplest, dimensionless form, with u as the unit cost of labour, v as the employment ratio, and z as a dynamically variable control parameter representing productive capacity, one has:

$$\dot{v} = -u - z$$

$$\dot{u} = +v + az$$

$$\dot{z} = +b + z(v - c).$$

Being of opposite sign, v and u necessarily oscillate and are in deviation from a fixed-point equilibrium, which represents a steady-state growth, given constant growth rates of productivity and labour force. Setting $z(0)$ equal to 0,

$$\ddot{v} - a\dot{v} + v = 0.$$

If $a < 0$, the result is a stable cycle asymptotic to steady growth. However, with all the parameters positive, an unstable cycle occurs. As v grows and becomes greater than c, $\dot{z}$ becomes positive; $z(t)$ ceases to be negligible and the full system is operative.

The aim is to illustrate the gradual onset of chaotic solutions by period doubling, as one parameter is varied. Therefore, we set $a = b = 0.20$ and observe the solutions as functions of the parameter c alone. With $c = 2.1$, the result is a limit cycle (the thick line in Fig. 9.12) which is asymptotically stable but in an unusual way. We can see from the figure that the trajectories jump from outside to inside the boundary, and that this limit cycle is an annular band, similar to the discrete time case.

It is possible to give a rough, plausible explanation of the economic

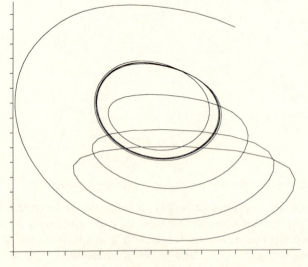

FIG. 9.12

meaning of the Rössler band. It is clear that u and v can produce an unstable cycle with realistic values of the parameters. If, as a result of expansive behaviour, real wages and investment expand more rapidly than output, the system will produce a decrease in the employment rate, leading to a deceleration and subsequent decline. The succeeding cycle will exhibit a different period and amplitude. In Fig. 9.13 ($c = 3.1$) two periods and two amplitudes coexist and the aspect of band is made even clearer, the band consisting of similar but not identical cycles. These evident band widths are the initial hint of aperiodic and chaotic behaviour.

For higher values of c, the number of bands increases markedly (Fig. 9.14). The trajectories implode inward, so that if c is increased to 5.7 (Fig. 9.15) true chaos is present, with the ensemble of almost periodic bands occupying most of the limit set. This obviously produces a chaotic time series, some indication of which is given in Fig. 9.16 for four successive 15-year periods. Without independent knowledge, one cannot extract the model from the time series, nor can one predict. Thus, though the end state seems quite bizarre, we have arrived there step by step, which helps to lessen the 'strangeness' of the attractor. The varying of a single parameter illustrates the astonishing generalization of stable equilibrium from a fixed point to a fixed motion and finally to a whole bounded region of non-wandering, non-repeating motions.

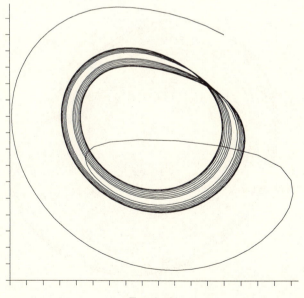

Fig. 9.13

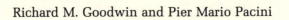

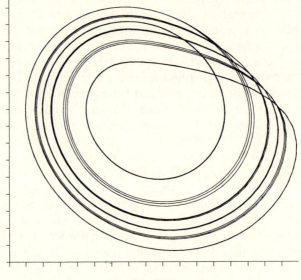

Fɪɢ. 9.14

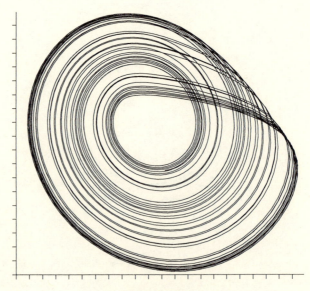

Fɪɢ. 9.15

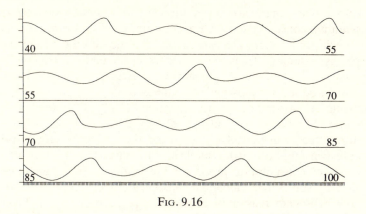

40   55

55   70

70   85

85   100

FIG. 9.16

5.3. *The intertemporal maximization approach*

Works within this approach adopt a different research strategy: they derive the relevant behavioural relationships from the principle of optimization and show that rationality, maximization and market-clearing are not sufficient to support the equilibrium paradigm and methodology, but, in general, allow intertemporal substitution effects, in either the consumption or the production sector or both, which can be regarded as the true sources of instability. For the sake of presentation, we distinguish two lines of research: general equilibrium overlapping-generations models (subsection (*a*) below) and optimal growth models (subsection (*b*)).

(*a*) *General equilibrium overlapping-generations models*

The objective of this class of models is to challenge the basic premise of the EXO approach that the economy is asymptotically stable around the equilibrium (trend) in absence of exogenous shocks. Instead, they offer counter-examples showing that

a competitive monetary economy of which the environment is stationary may undergo persistent and large deterministic fluctuations under *laissez faire*; that these cyclical fluctuations may displace moreover the sort of correlation that recent Classical macroeconomic models have thought to incorporate, even under complete information, without having to make the *ad hoc* assumption that cycles are due to exogenous shocks. (Grandmont 1985: 996)

To give the main ideas and results of this approach, we assume the simple structure of an exchange economy, with one good only, in which there is an infinite sequence of overlapping generations and a stationary population. Consumers are supposed identical so that we can take a representative consumer for each generation; he lives for two periods so that in each period there are two agents, the old and the young. Perfect foresight is assumed. Each consumer receives endowments ω_y^t when young and ω_o^{t+1} when old. The behavioural assumption is that the young consumer in period t chooses his lifetime consumption pattern (c_y^t, c_o^{t+1}) maximizing a two-period utility function $U(c_y^t, c_o^{t+1})$ subject to an intertemporal budget constraint $c_o^{t+1}/\rho^t + c_y^t = \omega_o^{t+1}/\rho^t + \omega_y^t$ where ρ^t is the interest factor in period t (measuring the exchange rate of present for future consumption). An equilibrium for this economy is a sequence $\{c_y^t, \rho^t\}_{t=0}^{\infty}$ of consumption levels for the young and of interest factors such that c_y^t solves the individual maximization problem given ρ^t and given the aggregate feasibility constraint $c_y^t + c_o^t = \omega_y^t + \omega_o^t$. From the first-order conditions for individual maximization, we have that the equilibrium interest factor in period t, ρ^t, is equal to the marginal rate of substitution between the two consumptions: i.e., $\rho^t = U_y/U_o$ where $U_s = \partial U/\partial c_s$, $s = y, o$.

Depending on individual preferences, intergenerational exchanges may take place in each period, giving rise to two possible situations: the young consumer may be either a net borrower or a net saver (the classical and the Samuelsonian cases, respectively, according to Gale's (1973) terminology). Provided that enough regularity conditions on $U(\cdot, \cdot)$ are satisfied, the equilibrium sequence $\{c_y^t\}_{t=0}^{\infty}$ can be thought of as generated by a deterministic dynamical system: in the classical case it takes the form of a forward dynamical system $c_y^{t+1} = f(c_y^t)$, whose dynamical properties have been investigated by Benhabib and Day (1982); in the Samuelsonian case the equilibrium sequence must be represented in an alternative way. Indeed, a dynamical system such as the previous one would not be always well defined, since cases may arise (as it can be checked in Fig. 9.19 below) in which a given present consumption is compatible with multiple future consumption patterns (and corresponding interest factors). To cope with these possibilities, the analysis is pursued in terms of a backward dynamical system $c_y^t = g(c_y^{t+1})$, which has been studied by Grandmont (1985).

Benhabib and Day (1982) suggest that a potential source of erraticism in the sequence of consumption choices lies in the strong mutual dependence between present consumption and the rate at which agents are ready to substitute present for future consumption. In the following theorem $\rho(\hat{c})$ stands for the interest factor, corresponding to a level of consumption equal to $\hat{c}$.

THEOREM 7. Suppose the utility function satisfies the following *sufficient substitutability condition* (SSC): there exists a level of consumption $\hat{c} > \omega_y$ such that

1. $\alpha_1 = \rho(\hat{c}) > 1$

2. $\alpha_2 = \rho[\alpha_1\hat{c} + (1 - \alpha_1)\omega_y] > 1$

3. $0 < \alpha_3 = \rho\alpha_1\alpha_2[\alpha_1\alpha_2 + (1 - \alpha_1\alpha_2)\omega_y] < 1$.

Then the difference system $c_y^{t+1} = f(c_y^t)$ is chaotic.

The restriction imposed by SSC is illustrated in Fig. 9.17, where $\rho(c)$ is related to the corresponding level of present consumption. The SSC condition implies that at low levels of consumption the interest factor is very high (consumers are ready to sacrifice a lot of future consumption for a small increase in present consumption), but that this decreases substantially when consumption increases. This implies a strong restriction on the utility functions, imposing a sufficient degree of concavity to make the marginal rates of substitution vary considerably with consumption. By means of an intuitive argument, it is possible to show that, under SSC, the dynamics of consumption may exhibit a three-period cycle. In Fig. 9.18, the thick line represents the individual offer curve and the $-45°$ line the locus of feasible transformations of present for future consumption. Suppose that the interest factor ruling in period t is at the very high level α_1. Then the young generation in period t finances a (small) excess demand in period t $(c^0 - \omega_y)$ at the expense of a big real excess supply in the next period; this means that the new young generation has a greater amount of consumption available than

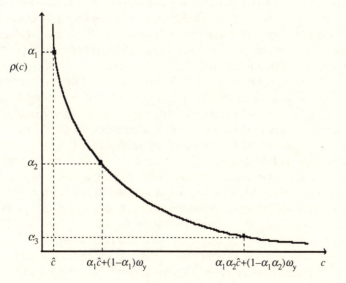

Fig. 9.17

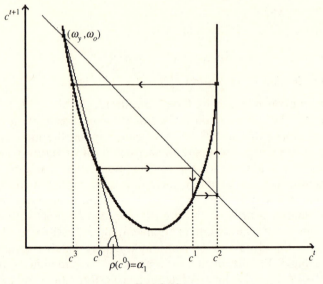

FIG. 9.18

the previous young generation, since $\omega_y + \rho_o(\omega_y - c_y^o) > c_y^o$. To consume this amount as present consumption, the second generation is ready to expand its old-age excess supply (compared with the one of the first generation) at a decreased interest factor. Now, the available consumption facing the third young generation (initial endowments plus excess supply of the second generation in its old age) is even greater, and is accepted only at a negative interest rate. (The marginal utility of present consumption is now lower than the marginal utility of future consumption.) This means that the excess supply of the third generation in its old age is positive but small, so that the fourth generation has available a low level of consumption, thus restoring an interest factor higher than the one in the original situation. When this 're-switching' of consumption levels and interest rates is obtained, the Li–Yorke theorem can be invoked to show the presence of aperiodic orbits.

Grandmont (1985) pursues the same kind of analysis in the case in which the young consumer is a net saver, having a negative net demand and lending to the old. The key to the model is the understanding that nothing prevents lifetime demands from being affected by 'perverse' income effects, which destabilize the behaviour of the consumption sequence to such a degree that even chaos may be obtained. To see this, one can follow the usual procedure and decompose the changes in the optimal consumption patterns, deriving from variations in the interest factor ρ, in income and substitution effects; with respect to future consumption, a rise in ρ produces a net increase because of the intertemporal substitution effect (in a two-good case the cross-substitution effects are always positive) and because overall income is now higher (normality is assumed). With respect to present consumption, the intertemporal substitution effect induces a net decrease, but the increase in overall income makes the variation in present consumption ambiguous. This case is shown in Fig. 9.19, where an offer curve is drawn as function of ρ: when the income effect dominates substitution (points on the offer curve above S), a rise in real interest rate may result in an increase in both present and future consumption.[14] Whenever this last situation emerges, and nothing in the preference structure or in the maximization process prevents it, the conditions verify for the presence of chaotic dynamics in consumption patterns. To see how this can happen, imagine that the interest rate ruling at t is ρ^{*t}; this implies that the young person in period t plans to consume $c_y^t(\rho^{*t})$. The market feasibility condition for period t, $c_y^t(\rho^{*t}) + c_o^t(\rho^{t-1}) = \omega_y^t + \omega_o^t$, implies that the interest rate in $t-1$ had to be ρ^{*t-1}. The same reasoning can be reiterated backward and a cycle of period 3 is easily shown to exist, thus producing the sufficient formal conditions for chaos.

These models have been objected to, since the possibility of chaos seems to rest on the fact that agents optimize over a time horizon that is

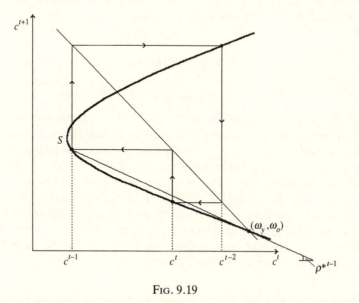

F$_{\text{IG}}$. 9.19

---

[14] Grandmont (1985: 1002) shows that this case emerges whenever the indirect utility function is concave enough with respect to future wealth.

shorter than the period of the generated cycle; this subverts the empirical observation that commonly experienced cycles occur over a period considerably shorter than the individual planning horizon. One could then think that models with market-clearing and infinitely lived agents who optimize over the infinite future cannot produce chaotic movements (see Epstein 1987). The study of optimal growth models in a neoclassical context also tries to cope with this question.

(b) Optimal growth models

This class of models seems to confirm the previous conjecture: when the horizon of maximization is extended to infinity, persistent cycles and chaotic fluctuations can occur only if the future is discounted enough to prevent agents from perceiving advantageous intertemporal exchange opportunities.[15] In other words, it is possible to obtain fluctuations and chaos in models of intertemporal optimization only at the expense of introducing substantial obstructions to the stabilizing intertemporal smoothing behaviour of far-seeing agents.

Boldrin and Montrucchio (1986) first reached this conclusion, showing that an infinite-horizon maximization problem can give rise to any sort of dynamical behaviour and even chaos, provided a condition in the form of strong impatience in maximization is imposed (see also Benhabib et al. 1987). Their model is a typical neoclassical model of accumulation in which a social planner solves a discounted maximization problem,

$$\max \sum_{t=0}^{\infty} \delta^t V(k_t, k_{t+1}) \tag{P}$$

$$\text{s.t. } (k_t, k_{t+1}) \in T, \qquad k_0 \text{ given,}$$

where k_t is capital stock in period t, T is a technology set, and $\delta \in (0, 1)$ represent a discount factor used to weight future values of the aggregate welfare function V. The solution to this optimization problem is a sequence of feasible capital stocks $\{k_t\}_{t=0}^{\infty}$, which, under mild conditions, is expressible in terms of the successive iterates of a policy function τ_δ; i.e., $k_{t+1} = \tau_\delta(k_t)$ (see e.g. Boldrin 1989: 238).

Boldrin and Montrucchio propose to perform the following exercise: suppose we have an arbitrary chaotic policy function τ_δ^c: is it possible to reconstruct an optimal accumulation problem (P) whose solution is exactly τ_δ^c? The following theorem provides a positive answer.

---

[15] As an extreme case one can take cases of *myopia*, i.e. maximization over a finite horizon in an infinite-horizon model. Montrucchio (1982) showed that in this case the dynamics of the system is compatible with cycles of any order and with aperiodic trajectories.

THEOREM 8. There exists a discount parameter $\delta^c \in (0, 1)$, the value of which depends on τ_δ^c, such that for every fixed $0 \leq \delta \leq \delta^c$ we can construct a return function $V_\delta(k_t, k_{t+1})$ with the following property: the optimal policy function solving (P) under feasibility constraints and with $V = V_\delta$ is the map τ_δ^c.

The value of δ^c can be calculated and in general is very small, so that the theorem reads as an anti-turnpike theorem. Whereas for values of δ close to 1 we have monotonic convergence to a fixed point of τ_δ, at the other end of the range of possible variation, where the future is very poorly valued, almost all behaviours are possible.

Following this result, one could wonder whether complexity is uniquely imputable to such purely subjective elements as the individual under-valuation of future returns. Benhabib and Nishimura (1985), Deneckere and Pelikan (1986), and Benhabib et al. (1987) provide a unified line of research according to which the coupling of subjective elements and technological factors can also be responsible for oscillations and even for aperiodic movements in a two-sector growth model.[16] The argument can be sketched as follows. Suppose we have a two-sector economy, one sector producing a consumption good c_t and the other an investment good k_{t+1} to be used next period. Consumption and investment goods can be produced from capital and labour without lags: $c_t = f(k_t^c, l_t^c)$, $k_{t+1} = g(k_t^k, l_t^k)$. An optimal capital accumulation problem is posed by maximizing an intertemporal discounted aggregate utility function subject to technological and feasibility constraints; i.e.,

$$\max_{l_t^c, l_t^k, k_t^c, k_t^k} \sum_{t=0}^{\infty} \delta^t U(c_t)$$

$$\text{s.t.} \quad c_t \leq f(k_t^c, l_t^c)$$

$$k_{t+1} \leq g(k_t^k, l_t^k)$$

$$l_t^c + l_t^k \leq L$$

$$k_t^c + k_t^k \leq k_t, \qquad k_0 \text{ given.}$$

This optimization problem can be shown to be equivalent to the following problem (P'), which has the same formulation as problem (P) above; i.e.,

$$\max \sum_{t=0}^{\infty} \delta^t W(k_t, k_{t+1}) \qquad \text{(P')}$$

$$\text{s.t.} \quad (k_t, k_{t+1}) \in T, \qquad k_0 \text{ given,}$$

[16] In another context, Woodford (1989) provides an example in which subjective discounting is not the only cause of chaotic movements. In particular, working with a model in which future financial markets are involved, he shows that 'complex dynamics can occur . . . in the case of economies that lack the complete set of competitive markets' assumed in standard models.

where $W(\cdot, \cdot)$ represents now a consumption possibility frontier describing a trade-off between present consumption and future capital for every given stock of present capital. Solving problem (P′), we obtain a policy function θ_δ that, for any given value of present capital, returns the optimal value of future capital; its characteristics depend on δ. It is possible to single out two significant values of δ (see McKenzie 1986):

1. There exists a δ^- such that, for all $\delta \leqslant \delta^-$, $\theta_\delta \equiv 0$.
2. There exists a δ^+, $\delta^- < \delta^+ < 1$, such that, for all $\delta > \delta^+$, θ_δ has a globally stable fixed point.

When δ belongs to the interval (δ^-, δ^+), the sequence of k_t generated by θ_δ presents the most interesting dynamical aspects: Benhabib and Nishimura (1985) showed that, for $\delta \in (\delta^-, \delta^+)$, the dynamics of the capital accumulation path depends on the sign of $W_{12} = \partial^2 W/\partial x \partial y$: $W_{12} > 0$ produces monotonic convergence to a steady state, while $W_{12} < 0$ implies the existence of a periodic point of order 2 for the policy function.[17] Therefore, more complex phenomena can be expected when W_{12} changes sign on the relevant domain. General conditions on the utility and production functions that produce these reversals are as yet unknown. The unique exception is studied by Deneckere and Pelikan by means of a numerical example, in which the consumption possibility frontier $W(\cdot, \cdot)$ takes a very particular form (see Deneckere and Pelikan 1986: 17). Though particular, however, this example suggests that the mixed effects of moderately low discounting and technological substitution may result in an erratic sequence of capital stocks.[18]

As a way of concluding, one can say that the basic message of these models is that nothing in the purely neoclassical structure—not preferences, nor technology, nor the principle of maximization—is strong enough to justify the unqualified adoption of the equilibrium paradigm. Macro relations derived from optimization are not restricted enough to rule out fluctuations and complexities.

6. Applications to Microeconomics

It is commonly reckoned that chaotic behaviour should naturally arise in a micro setting, given the complexities deriving from the interpersonal

---

[17] Indeed, if W_{12} is negative, an increase in k_t decreases the marginal benefit of k_{t+1} and hence the optimal adjustment is to decrease k_{t+1}.

[18] This also offers support to an interesting conjecture proposed by Dechert (1984), suggesting a positive correlation between 'optimizing behaviour' and monotonicity of capital accumulation paths in one-dimensional growth models. This is indeed valid in so far as the one-dimensional case is concerned; if chaos is to be incorporated in models of optimization, we need at least to resort to two-sector models and to intertemporal substitution effects.

relations of a multitude of selfish agents, and given the few restrictions that the principle of rational choice imposes on the generated functions (demand, supply, reaction, etc.). However, this conjecture has to face the difficulty of finding sensible sufficient conditions for chaos in the multi-dimensional case. And indeed, the state of the literature reflects this difficulty: on one side, we have strong negative results asserting that the presence of chaotic dynamics is a possibility that cannot be ruled out on the sole basis of rationality and perfectly informed maximization of preferences; on the other hand, once we want to explain in detail how chaotic behaviour and individual decision processes are related, i.e. once sufficient conditions are looked for, some other 'external' rule—passive adherence to some rule of thumb, time dependence of preferences, interpersonal effects, imitation, etc.—must be added to the process of maximization over financial and technological constraints.

According to these considerations, we distinguish works in this area in two classes. The first class of models (Section 6.1) tries to show that, in well-known theoretic frameworks, chaotic behaviour cannot be ruled out under standard assumptions (non-impossibility results). The second class of models (Section 6.2) is concerned primarily with the study of sufficient conditions for chaos in micro models.

6.1. Non-impossibility results

These models follow an approach very close to the one taken by Boldrin and Montrucchio (1986), examined in Section 5.3, and concerns two main fields of applications: the dynamics of general equilibrium, and dynamic duopoly games.

(a) General equilibrium theory

A sequence of papers study the global behaviour of the trajectories generated by the Walrasian process of price revision (Saari and Urenko 1984; Saari 1985a, b); they obtain the rather negative result that, apart from not being stable, Walrasian *tâtonnement* is also compatible with chaotic dynamics. To illustrate the point, let a pure exchange economy be given, with prices in the unitary simplex; the *tâtonnement* process of price adjustment is given by

$$p_{t+1} = p_t + M(z(p_t), Dz(p_t)), \tag{7}$$

where $z(\cdot)$ is the vector of market excess demand functions, $Dz(\cdot)$ is their Jacobian, and M is a smooth function that determines the incremental change of p_t on the basis of the knowledge of $z(\cdot)$ and $Dz(\cdot)$. (The equilibrium condition is $M(0, \cdot) = 0$.) The excess demand function for every commodity $z_j(p)$ is chosen in the set $\mathbb{F}$ of continuous functions satisfying $z_j > 0$ if $p_j = 0$ and $z_j < 0$ if $p_j = 1$. The vector of excess demand functions satisfies Walras's law. Movements of p are confined to the price simplex by the hypothesis that values greater than 1 (smaller than 0 resp.) are identified with 1 (0 resp.). The final result is as follows:

> THEOREM 9. There does not exist a mechanism M of the type given in (7) which is globally convergent for every z in $\mathbb{F}$. Moreover, let there be given an aperiodic sequence of prices $s = \{p_t, p_{t+1}, p_{t+2}, \ldots\}$; then, for any M, there exists an open set of functions C such that
> (i) $C \subset \mathbb{F}$;
> (ii) if $z \in C$ then there is an open set of initial conditions for which s is the trajectory given by (7).

The result is even stronger when the mechanism M is of the form $M(z(p))$, as it would be commonly required. These findings can be seen as particular implications for the present case of the basic result of Sonnenschein (1972, 1973), Debreu (1974), and Mantell (1976) concerning the failure of general equilibrium theory to impose restrictions on aggregate excess demand functions except for continuity and Walras's law; these restrictions, however, are compatible with both regular fluctuations and chaotic dynamics.

(b) Dynamic duopoly games

Dana and Montrucchio (1986, 1987) (see also Rand 1976) are much in the same spirit; they argue that, in a dynamic duopoly game in which agents move sequentially, we are always able to find a description of the problem that supports whichever sequence of moves we can construct, even a chaotic one. More precisely, they examine an infinite-horizon dynamic duopoly game between two firms, 1 and 2; each firm, $i = 1, 2$, maximizes a discounted sum of profits $\sum_{t=1}^{\infty} \delta^{t-1} \pi_i(x_1^t, x_2^t)$ which is a function of its own and its opposer's actions chosen in the respective sets X_1^t, X_2^t. Players are supposed to move alternately: firm 1 chooses an action in period t and commits itself to that action in period $(t + 1)$, in which firm 2 is to make its move, and so on. In equilibrium, agents' behaviour is represented by a pair $(r_{1\delta}, r_{2\delta})$ of reaction functions forming a *Markov perfect equilibrium*,[19] in which $r_{1\delta}$ is the optimal policy function for the first player, given that player 2 is henceforth committed to $r_{2\delta}$ (and vice versa). A sequence of pairs of moves

---

[19] The concept of Markov perfect equilibrium corresponds to a perfect equilibrium with stationary Markovian strategies. It has been introduced and developed by Maskin and Tirole (1983, 1985).

$\{(x_1^t, x_2^t)\}_{t=1}^{\infty}$ is constructed in the following way. Choose a player, e.g. firm 2, to make the first move in period 0, x_2^0, to which it is committed also in period 1. Then in period 1, firm 1 computes $x_1^1 = r_{1\delta}(x_0^2)$, thus obtaining the pair of moves for period 1 $(x_1^1, x_2^1) = (r_{1\delta}(x_2^0), x_2^0)$. In the second period, firm 1 sticks to $r_{1\delta}(x_2^0)$, while firm 2 chooses $x_2^2 = r_{2\delta}(r_{1\delta}(x_2^0))$, thus obtaining the second period pair $(x_1^2, x_2^2) \equiv [r_{1\delta}(x_2^0), r_{2\delta}(r_{1\delta}(x_2^0))]$, and so on. This sequence of moves can be described in terms of a Cournot map $\Phi_\delta(\cdot, \cdot)$ such that $(x_1^{t+1}, x_2^{t+1}) = \Phi_\delta^{(t)}(r_{1\delta}(x_2^0), x_2^0)$. The question is then, Is it possible for the dynamical system Φ_δ to be a chaotic one? The following theorem provides a positive answer; it is possible to obtain arbitrary reaction functions and hence also a chaotic Φ_δ, as solutions of a suitably posed maximization problem:

> THEOREM 10 (Dana and Montrucchio 1986). Let $r_1: X_1 \to X_2, r_2:$ $X_2 \to X_1$ be any pair of continuous functions. Let δ^* be fixed in $(0, 1)$. There exist continuous payoffs π_1, π_2 such that (r_1, r_2) is a Markov perfect equilibrium for the associated duopoly game when the discount factor equals δ^*. Moreover, if r_1 and r_2 are twice differentiable $\pi_1(\cdot, x_2)$ and $\pi_2(x_1, \cdot)$ can be chosen strictly concave for δ small enough.

Parallel to our results in subsection (a) above, if intertemporal smoothing is prevented and optimization cannot take into account the whole future, any kind of dynamics can be generated.

6.2. Sufficient conditions for chaos

The strategy followed to find sufficient conditions for chaotic behaviour consists in either restricting directly the results of the optimization process (demand and supply functions), or in imposing qualifications on the objective to be maximized. An example of the first solution is offered by the extensive literature on the cobweb model examined in subsection (a) below. Examples of the second solution are studied in subsections (b) and (c), in which the possibility of erratic sequences of choices is traced back to the preference structure. They depart from the standard description of static preferences and find sufficient conditions in either the history dependence or the environment dependence that preferences may exhibit.

(a) The dynamics of the cobweb model

It is well know that, in so far as the demand and supply are monotonic functions of prices, only simple movements (monotonic convergence to or divergence from a steady state or a regular cycle) are possible. However, when supply (Artstein 1983) or demand (Goodwin 1988) is made sufficiently non-monotonic, virtually any kind of behaviour in prices and quantities can be expected. Suggestions have been made to justify such behaviours of demand and supply functions, resorting either to the presence of some naivety in the formation of expectations (Artstein 1983; Shaffer 1984), or to the myopic way in which agents form their decisions (Montrucchio 1982); as an example, the supply function in Fig. 9.20 has been justified on the presumption that, when prices fall below a certain level, agents fear a further decline and increase the quantity supplied.

As was the case in a macro setting, this recourse to side-conditions seems to suggest that, if chaos is to be present, we have to introduce some 'imperfections' limiting individual abilities to forecast and optimize. Once these obstacles are removed, and the purest environment of perfect information, rational expectations, and infinite calculating abilities is restored, complexities are bound to disappear. This is indeed the implication of works such as Shaffer (1984) and Holmes and Manning (1988), in which, if naivety in expectations is abandoned (e.g. towards consistent conjectures), or if agents are attributed long memory, the resulting dynamics converges to a long-run equilibrium.

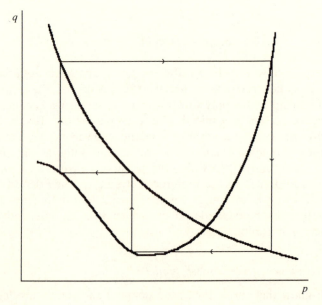

Fɪɢ. 9.20

(b) History-dependent preferences

Benhabib and Day (1981) examine the case in which tastes depend endogenously on past choices. The subject has been explored by Hammond (1976), showing that the dynamic sequence of choices converges to a long-run stationary choice if an *acyclicity* condition is imposed on preferences, i.e. 'a requirement that prevents the selection of a feasible choice at a given time that was previously rejected'. Removing such an acyclicity condition is the main argument for the proof of the possible existence of chaotic sequences of choices. Indeed, Benhabib and Day examine situations in which a certain choice, previously preferred and then rejected, may recur after some other possibilities have been experienced. In particular, they examine the case in which preferences are *tricyclic*. To define tricyclicity of preferences, some notation is in order. Let X be a consumption set and B a budget set for a given vector of prices, and $U(y, x)$ a utility function representing preferences on X and giving the utility of a consumption vector y in X after a vector x has been experienced; finally, let $P(x) = \{y | y \in X, U(y, x) \geqq \max_{\varepsilon \in B} U(z, x)\}$ and $P(A) = \bigcup_{x \in A} P(x)$. Then:

> DEFINITION. The preferences represented by $U(\cdot, \cdot)$ are tricyclic if there is some set $A \subset X$ such that
> (i) $A \cap P(A) = \varnothing$ and
> (ii) $A \cup P(A) \subset P(P(A) \cap B)$.

Therefore preferences are tricyclic if there is a set of consumption alternatives, $A \subset B$, that, once experienced, give rise to a set of no-worse-off alternatives, $P(A)$, that has an empty intersection with A itself; however, both A and the elements of $P(A) \cap B$ are parts of the set of alternatives in B that give the highest utility, after any element in $P(A)$ has been experienced.

Assuming tricyclicity of preferences, Benhabib and Day prove that the associated choice function, $x_{t+1} = C(x_t)$, giving the individual choice in period $t + 1$ after x_t has been experienced, is tricyclic, in the sense that there is a set A in B such that

(i) $A \cap C(A) = \varnothing$ and
(ii) $A \cup C(A) \subset C(C(A) \cap B)$.

Then the possibility of chaotic sequences of choices is proved by the application of Diamond's theorem (see the Appendix to this chapter). As is the case for many applications encountered so far, the theorem does not guarantee the existence of chaotic set S of initial conditions of positive Lebesgue measure, so that the possibility of existence of chaotic trajectories does not suffice for the assertion that they are the observed objects of the model.

(c) Context-dependent preferences

Granovetter and Soong (1986) arrive at the same result, introducing interpersonal effects that may influence individual preferences and demands. Interpersonal effects exist because consumption may be a signal of status or may result from imitative behaviour, or even from rational behaviour when the usefulness or quality of a good increases (or decreases) with the number of people consuming it. (Two examples are personal computers and crowded skiing-tracks.) Whenever such external effects play a role, average market demand in a certain period may depend on the average market consumption in the previous period; multiple equilibria may exist, and it cannot be excluded that the phase diagram exhibits the well-known unimodal shape, thus being able to produce an irregular sequence of choices. The typical case in which such oscillations obtain is when consumption is encouraged by a low level of market demand and discouraged when the latter is very high (see Fig. 9.21). However, this is not the general situation: Iannaccone (1989) shows that such cases obtain either when agents are poorly informed or when the utility functions are of a very particular form. This observation introduces in the present context the same kind of distinctions and observations that Shaffer (1984) and Holmes and Manning (1988) introduced with respect to the cobweb model previously seen.[20]

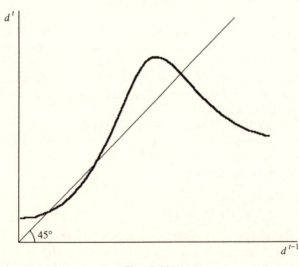

FIG. 9.21

[20] A variety of other examples can be found in the literature, ranging from static duopoly (Shaffer 1984) to the dynamics of expenditure of private industry in R and D (Baumol and Wolff 1983), to bargaining models of various kinds. See Baumol and Benhabib (1989) for a more extensive discussion.

7. Testing for Chaos

So far, we have outlined a theoretically consistent argument that, both in premises and in implications, points in a direction opposite to the EXO approach. The crucial question then is, What view does evidence favour? Or, more correctly, Is it possible to ascertain whether non-linearities are at least partly responsible for the observed variability of actual economic data? This suggestive aspect of chaos theory is still in its infancy and hence suffers from the lack of any systematization. For the sake of presentation, we first introduce some analytical techniques that have been devised to cope with this problem; then some limitations to their applicability are discussed and a few empirical applications are mentioned.

7.1. *Detecting deterministic chaos*

Linear time-series methods (spectral analysis and autocovariance functions) have gained a good success in distinguishing between periodic and aperiodic time series but have substantially failed in discriminating between chaotic and random sequences (see Lorenz 1989: Sect. 5). Both random and chaotic trajectories have similar power spectra: 'the behaviour of a chaotic time path . . . was contrasted with one that followed an uncomplicated deterministic regime that was subject to substantial random disturbances of moderately low probability. Spectral analysis then yielded very similar results for the chaotic series and the series subject to random disturbances' (Baumol and Benhabib 1989). In particular cases, chaotic systems generate sequences in which the auto-correlation at any lag is 0 so that they look exactly like white noise (see Sakai and Tokumaru 1980). In other words, according to standard procedures, there is a substantial observational equivalence between sequences of data subject to random disturbances or generated by a model that is perfectly deterministic but chaotic.

Therefore, some empirical and statistical procedures have been proposed to bypass this observational equivalence and to test the hypothesis of deterministic systems against the one of a system subject to truly random shocks. They are briefly reviewed here.[21]

---

[21] The presentation here is necessarily excursionary. The technically interested reader is referred to the following more comprehensive works: Barnett and Chen (1988*b*); Barnett and Choi (1989); Brock (1986); Brock and Dechert (1988); Brock and Malliaris (1989); Brock and Sayers (1988); Grassberger and Procaccia (1983); Lorenz (1989); Scheinkman (1990).

(a) Fitting the phase diagram

Suppose we have an economic time series $\{y_t\}_{t=0}^{\tau}$ and that it shows cyclical irregularities. The first immediate test—to detect whether it has been generated by random or chaotic influences—proceeds by taking the observed data and seeing whether a generating difference equation, or its phase diagram, can be fitted from those data. So, for example, one can set forth the hypothesis that the data-generating process is $y_{t+1} = \alpha_t y_t (1 - y_t)$: were it correct, and given the absence of any random disturbance, plotting each y_{t+i+1} against y_{t+1}, $i = 0, \ldots, \tau - 1$, should perfectly reconstruct the well-known hill-shaped phase diagram. However, such a procedure is rather naive and has several shortcomings (see Baumol 1986; Baumol and Benhabib 1989; Brock and Malliaris 1989). The underlying system may have a very complicated and probably unknown lag structure with an unknown number of variables: if the structure of the model is not correctly specified, the test can reject the hypothesis of a deterministic system in face of a truly chaotic data-generating process. More important is the fact that often we observe not the variables of the system but a function of them, i.e. $y_t = h(x_t)$, $x_t \in \mathbb{R}^n$. The reconstruction of the dynamics of the system in terms of its representations y_t may be at least misleading, and poses problems of identification, any value of y_t being in principle compatible with many values of x_t.

(b) Takens's embedding theorem

More promising tests are associated with two types of quantities related to invariant sets: correlation dimension, and Liapunov exponents (see Takens 1980, 1985; Brock and Dechert 1988; Brock 1986). They have a common root in the *embedding theorem* (see Takens 1980), which is a central tool for the numerical study of chaotic systems. A simplification of it can be given as follows. Suppose that the 'true data-generating process' of the variables defining the economy is given by $x_{t+1} = f(x_t)$, $x_t \in \mathbb{R}^n$, and that we are interested in one of them, say x^i. However, neither f nor the complete set of variables x is known, but only some measurements y_t of the variable x_t^i are available and these are given by a measurement apparatus $h(\cdot)$; i.e., $y_t = h(x_t)$. Then the problem is: is it possible to derive useful information about the dynamical system $f(x_t)$, given the sequence of observations $\{y_t\}_{t=0}^{\tau}$? Takens's embedding theorem provides a positive answer in the following way. Take an m-history z_t from $\{y_t\}_{t=0}^{\tau}$ defined as an m-vector of consecutive observations from $\{y_t\}_{t=0}^{\tau}$; i.e., $z_t = (y_{t+m}, y_{t+m-1}, \ldots, y_t)$;[22] then consider the sequence of m-histories

[22] One could also take the backward orientation, $z_t = (y_t, y_{t-1}, \ldots, y_{t-m+1})$, without affecting the results.

$\{z_t\}_{t=0}^{\tau-m}$ and imagine that it is generated by a dynamical system $z_{t+1} = g(z_t)$. The theorem proves that, provided m is large enough, and provided g and h are smooth functions, the attractors (if any) of g and f have the same properties. In particular, this implies that, if g has a strange attractor, the same holds true for the original system in x_t. Therefore, one can check the sequence of m-histories to detect relevant properties—namely, the correlation dimension and the largest Liapunov exponent.

(c) Correlation dimension

As to the correlation dimension, its definition is given by the following formal statement where Ω is an invariant set of the m-dimensional system generated by g:

DEFINITION 6. (Takens 1980; Brock 1986.) The correlation dimension γ of (g, Ω) is given by (when the limits below exist)

$$C(\varepsilon) = \lim_{N \to \infty} \{(z_i, z_j)|//z_i - z_j// < \varepsilon, \qquad 1 \leq i, j \leq N\}/N^2$$

$$\gamma = \lim_{\varepsilon \to 0} \frac{\ln C(\varepsilon)}{\ln \varepsilon}$$

where $z_i \equiv g^{(i)}(z_0)$, $i = 1, 2, \ldots$; $z_j \equiv g^{(j)}(z_0)$, $j = 1, 2, \ldots$.

Roughly speaking, γ is an average measure of the relative dispersion of the points of the trajectory generated by g (see Lorenz 1989 and Barnett and Choi 1989 for more complete discussions); the higher it is, the less the trajectory is concentrated on an attractor. It is clearly related to the concept of entropy rate in the language of stochastic processes (see Papoulis 1984) and tightly linked with the notion of *Kolmogorov entropy* (see Eckmann and Ruelle 1985; Lorenz 1989). Accordingly, it can be thought of as a measure of the degree of uncertainty about future realizations of the process $g^{(n)}$: it grows to infinity for stochastic processes and settles down to finite values for chaotic but deterministic processes. More precise results are available that impose bounds to the magnitude of correlation dimension (see Brock and Dechert 1988):

(A) If Ω is an m-dimensional closed attractor that possesses an invariant measure, then $\gamma \leq n$ generically and is independent of m, for m large enough.
(B) If there is noise in data of positive variance, then $\gamma = m$ almost surely, for $m > 2n + 1$. In general, it may be infinite.

(A) and (B) imply that the test for chaos corresponds to the test of the hypothesis that f has an attractor whose dimension is small compared with the length of z and independent of the number of lags used in forming z.[23] An example can be given with reference to equation (1): the dimension of the attractor of the system increases from 0 (fixed points, low period cycles) to 0.5 for $\alpha \sim 3.56994 \ldots$ and 1 for $\alpha = 4$ when the whole phase diagram (a one-dimensional curve) is visited by the generated trajectories. Were there any noise, there would be a whole scatter of points around the hill shape, covering a two-dimensional region.

(d) Liapunov exponents

The concept of Liapunov exponents constitutes the generalization to forward orbits of the eigenvalues of $D_{z^*}g$ at a fixed point equilibrium z^* of g and has been introduced to detect the presence of SDIC (see Collet and Eckmann 1980; Brock and Malliaris 1989; Lorenz 1989). The formal definition is given by[24]

$$L_i = \lim_{n \to \infty} \frac{1}{n} \sum_{j=1}^{n} \log \|D_g(z_{j-1})v_i\| = \lim_{n \to \infty} \frac{1}{n} \log \|D_g^{(n-1)}(z_0)v_i\|,$$

where D denotes derivatives and v_i is a direction vector in the ith direction. Intuitively, Liapunov exponents measure, up to a linear approximation, the average rate of separation between two nearby trajectories. Clearly, there are as many Liapunov exponents as the number of elements in z; if they all are negative the system is stable, but if at least one of them is positive, then forward orbits starting from close initial conditions will diverge 'on average' at an exponential rate given by the same Liapunov exponent. Provided that the system does not explode, this in turn implies that the distance between the two trajectories expands and contracts arbitrarily, well capturing the notion of SDIC and giving evidence that we are in the presence of an attractor continually deformed and stretched by the iterated application of g. Therefore, the test of non-randomness consists just in showing the positiveness of the largest Liapunov exponent associated with the time series under study.

7.2. Quality of testing procedures

The procedures to test for chaos described in the previous section are essentially non-parametric. As Barnett and Choi (1989) argue, non-

---

[23] A theory concerning the asymptotic distribution of statistics based on measures of correlation dimension has been recently developed. Interested readers are referred to Brock *et al.* (1987) and Scheinkman (1990).

[24] It is easily checked that, whenever z is a fixed point or a periodic point of order k, the Liapunov exponents are simply the logarithm of the Eigen values of $Dg^{(k)}(z)$.

parametric chaotic inference possesses uniquely interesting capabilities that have no counterpart in the standard econometric approach. One of them is implicit in the computation of the correlation dimension, by which

we are able to compute a lower bound to the dimension of the state space. This inference is especially interesting because in all sciences, including economics, there is a natural interest in determining the simplest theory (perhaps *à la* Milton Friedman's methodology of positive economics) that can explain the data. The Grassberger–Procaccia algorithm does indeed produce a lower bound to the complexity (dimensionality) needed to explain the data; therefore the objective of that algorithm clearly is important in economics. (Barnett and Choi 1989: 154–5)

However, these procedures and the conclusions that might be drawn from them suffer limitations deriving from the quality of data:

1. Testing procedures examined in Section 7.1 above are based on Takens's embedding theorem and hence require the construction of fairly long sequences of m-histories from available data. This implies that the original time series has to be extremely long, a requirement that can be hardly satisfied in economics, given the shortness of available time series.

2. Suggested procedures essentially test the absence of noise, but noise may derive from the very process of aggregation over both goods and economic agents. As an example, 'most governmental data are produced from Laspeyres or Paasche indexes, which are only first-order approximations to the true aggregation-theoretic aggregate. The resulting second-order remainder terms could possibly produce a troublesome amount of noise for the nonlinear inference procedure' (Barnett and Choi 1989: 154–5).

3. Similarly, noise is present not only in data, but in the dynamics itself: it is rather implausible to think that strictly deterministic systems are the sole components that generate observed time series. A certain amount of noise is unavoidable so that the data-generating process becomes $x_{t+1} = f(x_t) + \varepsilon(x_t)$ where $\varepsilon(x_t)$ is a noise with a known probability distribution (*noisy chaos*).[25]

Observations (1)–(3) are at the heart of the partial unsuccess of the empirical tests: evidence for chaos is not uncontroversial, and the common situation is that the presence of chaos and nonlinearities in time series, though not rejected, receives scanty support.[26] We select

[25] Ben-Mizrachi *et al.* (1984), and Atten and Caputto (1985), have proposed methods to analyse these mixed cases and find when the deterministic components prevail on the random elements.

[26] This weakness of evidence receives different interpretations: while opposers take the occasion to reject the whole theory, some supporters (see in particular Brock and Sayers 1988; Brock and Malliaris 1989) give arguments ascribing this ambiguity to the weakness of available testing techniques.

two areas that are good examples of the state of the art. We refer to quoted works for technical discussions.

(a) GNP time series

Studies that have examined GNP data for different countries have rejected the hypothesis of deterministic chaos, and accepted that of a linear trend buffeted by noise (e.g. an AR(2) process for detrended real GNP). The deterministic hypothesis has been rejected by Brock and Sayers (1988) for postwar US quarterly data, by Frank and Stengos (1988) for Canadian GNP data, by Frank *et al.* (1988) for UK–Italian–German–Japanese GNP data starting from the mid-1960s, and by Scheinkman and LeBaron (1989a) for real per capita GNP data over 1870–1986. In contrast with these results, some related series reveal the presence of nonlinearities, for example the monthly growth rates of US industry production (Scheinkman and LeBaron 1989a) and the civilian employment rate and the unemployment rate for US data in the postwar period (Brock and Sayers 1988).

(b) Financial markets

In capital markets theory, the stochastic approach, in the form of Martingale models (see Fama 1970; LeRoy 1989), has gained a considerable success at both the theoretical and the empirical level. However, Scheinkman and LeBaron (1989b) have proved the presence of nonlinearities in a fairly long time series of US daily stock return rates. The same conclusion is reached by Hinich and Patterson (1989) with observations taken at smaller time intervals (15 minutes). However, this conclusion cannot be extended to even smaller time intervals, when errors in measurements are bound to dominate.[27]

8. Conclusions

We have gone through this rather lengthy discussion of mathematical tools and economic implications and applications of chaos theory with the following question in mind: Is this merely a storm in a mathematical teacup, or does it offer the occasion for serious applications in economics? We have tried to promote a positive attitude towards it and to show that there are good grounds for application in economics just as there has been in the natural sciences and meteorology, where it started from.

---

[27] Other studies concerning the presence of chaos in *Divisa* monetary aggregates have been done by Barnett and Chen (1986, 1988a) with positive results.

We have tried also to highlight the difficulties and limitations of the same mathematical apparatus, in order to prevent ourselves from drawing hasty conclusions and generalizations. The most solid conclusion, however, is that the adoption of the deterministic viewpoint does not serve the purpose merely of a formal re-edition of consolidated results, but constitutes and provokes a completely alternative way of theorizing and making empirical works.

However, there is still a good deal of work to be done to construct a scenario that goes beyond disparate, *ad hoc* applications and to find plausible and testable conditions. This is the big challenge that faces the theory of chaotic deterministic fluctuations. A stimulating challenge, especially if one thinks that the strength of chaos theory lies just where the *alternative*, the probabilistic analysis, drew its confines, i.e. in the attempt to give an endogenous consistent explanation of that part of behaviour that was banished as an unexplainable error or an unpredictable shock.

Appendix: Extensions to Higher Dimensions

Some results valid for the one-dimensional system (1) have been generalized to the n-dimensional case (see Collet and Eckmann 1980; Devaney 1987). These extensions, though unable to reconstruct a complete scenario like the period-doubling cascade of bifurcations, provide sufficient conditions for the existence of a chaotic set S of initial conditions for an n-dimensional dynamical system $x_{t+1} = f(x_t)$. An example is given by the extension to the multi-dimensional case of the Li–Yorke theorem, 'Period 3 implies chaos', as follows:

THEOREM 11 (Diamond 1976). Let A be a set in $\mathbb{R}^n$ and suppose $f \colon A \to \mathbb{R}^n$ to be continuous. Assume that there is a non-empty compact set X in A, satisfying

(c1) $X \cup f(X) \subseteq f^{(2)}(X) \subset A$,
(c2) $X \cap f(X) = \varnothing$.

Then

(1) for every $k = 1, 2, \ldots$, there is in A a k-period set,
(2) there is an accountable set S in A which contains no periodic set and for which
   (i) $f(S) \subset S$;
   (ii) for distinct points p, q in S
   $$\limsup_{k \to \infty} \|f^{(k)}(p) - f^{(k)}(q)\| > 0;$$
   (iii) for every p in S and periodic set P in A, for all q in p,
   $$\limsup_{k \to \infty} \|f^{(k)}(p) - f^{(k)}(q)\| > 0;$$

Similar results for sufficient conditions are obtained by Marotto (1978, 1979) via the introduction of the snap-back repeller (an unstable fixed point which is traversed after some time by the trajectory of the system). All these results illustrate that there are cases in which an unstable fixed point does not necessarily mean unbounded divergence or convergence to regular oscillations; but the system may fluctuate erratically, $f(\cdot)$ being chaotic in the Li–Yorke sense. In a more abstract setting, other results have been obtained by Ruelle and Takens (1971), Smale (1980), Guckenheimer and Holmes (1983), Devaney (1987) (see also May 1976 for further references). Their application is however yet to come.

References

ABRAHAM, R. H., and SHAW, C. D. (1983). *Dynamics: The Geometry of Behaviour*. Santa Cruz, Cal.: Aerial Press.

ARTSTEIN, Z. (1983). 'Irregular Cobweb Dynamics'. *Economic Letters*, 11: 15–17.

ATTEN, P., and CAPUTTO, J. C. (1985). 'Estimation expérimentale de dimension d'attracteurs et d'entropie'. In M. Cosnrad and C. Mira (eds.), *Traitement numérique des attracteurs étranges*. Grenoble: Conference Proceedings.

BARNETT, W. A., and CHEN, P. (1986). 'Economic Theory as a Generator of Measurable Attractors'. In I. Prigogine and M. Sanglier (eds.), *Laws of Nature and Human Conduct: Specificities and Unifying Themes*. Brussels: GORDES, pp. 209–24.

——— (1988a). 'The Aggregation-theoretic Monetary Aggregates are Chaotic and Have Strange Attractors: An Econometric Application of Mathematical Chaos'. In W. A. Barnett, E. Berndt, and H. White (eds.), *Dynamic Econometric Modelling*. Cambridge University Press, pp. 199–246.

——— (1988b). 'Deterministic Chaos and Fractal Attractors as Tools for Nonparametric Dynamical Econometric Inference'. *Mathematical Computer Modeling*, 10: 275–96.

—— and CHOI, S. S. (1989). 'Comparison between the Conventional Econometric Approach to Structural Inference and the Nonparametric Chaotic Attractor Approach'. In W. A. Barnett, J. Geweke, and K. Shell (eds.), *Economic Complexity: Chaos, Sunspots, Bubbles and Nonlinearity*. Cambridge University Press, pp. 141–212.

BAUMOL, W. J. (1986). 'Unpredictability, Pseudorandomness, and Military–Civilian Budget Interactions'. *Rivista Internazionale di Scienze Economiche e Commerciali*, 4: 297–318.

—— (1987). 'The Chaos Phenomenon: A Nightmare for Forecaster'. *LSE Quarterly* I: 99–114.

—— and BENHABIB, J. (1989). 'Chaos: Significance, Mechanism, and Economic Applications'. *Journal of Economic Perspectives*, 3: 77–105.

—— and QUANDT, R. E. (1985). 'Chaos Models and their Implications for Forecasting'. *Eastern Economic Journal*, 11: 3–15.

—— and WOLFF, E. N. (1983). 'Feedback from Productivity Growth to R&D'. *Scandinavian Journal of Economics*, 85: 147–57.

BENHABIB, J., and DAY, R. H. (1980). 'Erratic Accumulation'. *Economic Letters*, 23: 261–6.

—— —— (1981). 'Rational Choice and Erratic Behaviour'. *Review of Economic Studies*, 48: 459–72.

—— —— (1982). 'A Characterization of Erratic Dynamics in the Overlapping Generation Models'. *Journal of Economic Dynamics and Control*, 4: 37–55.

—— and NISHIMURA, K. (1985). 'Competitive Equilibrium Cycles'. *Journal of Economic Theory*, 35: 284–306.

—— MAJUMDAR, M., and NISHIMURA, K. (1987). 'Global Equilibrium Dynamics with Stationary Recursive Preferences'. *Journal of Economic Behaviour and Organization*, 8: 429–52.

BEN-MIZRACHI, A., PROCACCIA, I., and GRASSBERGER, P. (1984). 'Characterization of Experimental (Noisy) Strange Attractors'. *Physical Review*, 29: 26–39.

BOLDRIN, M. (1989). 'Paths of Optimal Accumulation in Two-Sector Models'. In W. A. Barnett, J. Geweke and K. Shell (eds.), *Economic Complexity: Chaos, Sunspots, Bubbles, and Nonlinearity*. Cambridge University Press, pp. 231–52.

—— and MONTRUCCHIO, L. (1986). 'On the Indeterminacy of the Capital Accumulation Paths'. *Journal of Economic Theory*, 40: 26–39.

BROCK, W. E. (1986). 'Distinguishing Random and Deterministic Systems: Abridged Version'. *Journal of Economic Theory*, 40: 168–95.

—— and DECHERT, W. D. (1988). 'Theorems on Distinguishing Deterministic and Random Systems'. In W. A. Barnett, E. Berndt, and H. White (eds.), *Dynamic Econometric Modeling*. Cambridge University Press, pp. 247–68.

—— and MALLIARIS, A. G. (1989). *Differential Equations, Stability and Chaos in Dynamical Economics*. Amsterdam: North-Holland.

—— and SAYERS, C. L. (1988). 'Is the Business Cycle Characterized by Deterministic Chaos?' *Journal of Monetary Economics*, 22: 71–90.

—— DECHERT W. D., and SCHEINKMAN, J. A. (1987). 'A Test for Independence Based on the Correlation Dimension'. Working Paper, Department of Economics, University of Winsconsin, Madison.

COLLET, P., and ECKMANN, J. P. (1980). *Iterated Maps on the Interval as Dynamical System*. Boston: Birkhaüser.

DANA, R. A., and MONTRUCCHIO L. (1986). 'Dynamic Complexity in Duopoly Games'. *Journal of Economic Theory*, 40: 40–56.

—— —— (1987). 'On Rational Dynamic Strategies in Infinite Horizon Models where Agents Discount the Future'. *Journal of Economic Behaviour and Organization*, 8: 497–511.

DAY, R. H. (1982). 'Irregular Growth Cycles'. *American Economic Review*, 72: 406–14.

—— (1983). 'The Emergence of Chaos from Classical Economic Growth'. *Quarterly Journal of Economics*, 98: 201–13.

—— (1986). 'Unscrambling the Concept of Chaos Through Thick and Thin: Reply'. *Quarterly Journal of Economics*, 101: 424–5.

—— and KIM, K. H. (1987). 'A Note on Non-Periodic Demoeconomic Fluctuations with Positive Measure'. *Economic Letters*, 23: 251–6.

—— and SHAFFER, W. (1987). 'Ergodic Fluctuations in Deterministic Economic

Models'. *Journal of Economic Behaviour and Organizations*, 8: 339–61.

DEBREU, G. (1974). 'Excess Demand Functions'. *Journal of Mathematical Economics*, 1: 15–23.

DECHERT, D. W. (1984). 'Does Optimal Growth Preclude Chaos? A Theorem on Monotonicity'. *Zeitschrift für Nationalökonomie*, 44: 57–61.

DE GRAUWE, P., and VANSANTEN, K. (1990). 'Deterministic Chaos in the Foreign Exchange Market'. CEPR Discussion Paper no. 370.

DENECKERE, R., and PELIKAN, S. (1986). 'Competitive Chaos'. *Journal of Economic Theory*, 40: 13–25.

DEVANEY, R. L. (1987). *An Introduction to Chaotic Dynamical Systems*. Menlo Park, NY: Benjamin Press.

DIAMOND, P. (1976). 'Chaotic Behaviour of Systems of Difference Equations'. *International Journal of Systems Science*, 7: 953–6.

DORNBUSCH, R. (1976). 'Expectations and Exchange Rate Dynamics'. *Journal of Political Economy*, 84: 1161–76.

ECKMANN, J. P., and RUELLE, D. (1985). 'Ergodic Theory of Chaos and Strange Attractors'. *Reviews of Modern Physics*, 57: 617–56.

EPSTEIN, L. G. (1987). 'The Global Stability of Efficient Intertemporal Allocations'. *Econometrica*, 55: 329–56.

FAMA, E. (1970). 'Efficient Capital Markets: A Review of Theory and Empirical Work'. *Journal of Finance*, 25: 383–417.

FARMER, J. D., and SIDOROWICH, J. J. (1987). 'Predicting Chaotic Time Series'. Mimeo, Los Alamos National Laboratories.

FRANK, M., and STENGOS, T. (1988). 'The Stability of Canadian Macroeconomic Data as Measured by the Largest Lyaponov Exponent'. *Economic Letters*, 27: 11–14.

—— GENCAY, R., and STENGOS, T. (1988). 'International Chaos'. *European Economic Review*, 32: 1569–84.

FRISCH, R. (1933). 'Propagation Problems and Impulse Problems in Dynamic Economics'. In *Economic Essays in Honour of Gustav Cassel*. London: Allen & Unwin.

GALE, D. (1973). 'Pure Exchange Equilibrium of Dynamic Economic Models'. *Journal of Economic Theory*, 6: 12–36.

GOODWIN, R. M. (1951). 'The Non-linear Accelerator and the Persistence of Business Cycles'. *Econometrica*, 19: 1–17.

—— (1967). 'A Growth Cycle'. In C. H. Feinstein (ed.), *Socialism, Capitalism and Economic Growth*. Cambridge University Press, pp. 54–8.

—— (1988). 'Chaotic Economic Dynamics'. EUI Working Paper no. 88/357.

—— (1989). 'An Irregular Asymmetric Oscillator, or the Discrete Charm of Erraticism'. In R. M. Goodwin, *Essays in Nonlinear Economic Dynamics*. Frankfurt: P. Lang.

GRANDMONT, J. M. (1984). 'Periodic and Aperiodic Behaviour in Discrete One-Dimensional Dynamical Systems'. CEPREMAP Working Paper no. 8317.

—— (1985). 'On Endogenous Competitive Business Cycles'. *Econometrica*, 53: 995–1045.

—— (1987). 'Nonlinear Difference Equations Bifurcations and Chaos: an Introduction'. IMSSS–Economics Lecture Notes Series, no. 5.

GRANOVETTER, M., and SOONG, R. (1986). 'Threshold Models of Interpersonal

Effects in Consumer Demand'. *Journal of Economic Behaviour and Organization*, 7: 83–99.

GRASSBERGER, P., and PROCACCIA, I. (1983). 'Measuring the Strangeness of Strange Attractors'. *Physica*, 90: 189–208.

GUCKENHEIMER, J., and HOLMES, P. (1983). *NonLinear Oscillations, Dynamical Systems, and Bifurcations of Vector Fields*. New York: Springer Verlag.

HAAVELMO, T. (1954). *A Study in the Theory of Economic Evolution*. Amsterdam: North-Holland.

HAMMOND, P. J. (1976). 'Endogenous Tastes and Stable Long Run Choices'. *Journal of Economic Theory*, 13: 329–40.

HICKS, J. R. (1950). *A Contribution to the Theory of the Trade Cycle*. Oxford University Press.

HINICH, M. J., and PATTERSON, D. M. (1989). Evidence of Nonlinearity in the Trade-by-Trade Stock Market Return Generating Process'. In W. A. Barnett, J. Geweke, and K. Shell (eds.), *Economic Complexity, Chaos, Sunspots, Bubbles and Nonlinearity*. Cambridge University Press, pp. 383–409.

HOLMES, J. M., and MANNING, R. (1988). 'Memory and the Market Stability: the Case of the Cobweb'. *Economic Letters*, 28: 1–7.

IANNACCONE, L. R. (1989). 'Bandwagons and the Threat of Chaos: Interpersonal Effects Revisited'. *Journal of Economic Behaviour and Organization*, 11: 431–2.

JACOBSON, M. V. (1981). 'Absolutely Continuous Invariant Measures for One-Parameter Families of One-Dimensional Maps'. *Communications of Mathematical Physics*, 81: 39–88.

KALDOR, N. (1940). 'A Model of the Trade Cycle'. *Economic Journal*, 50: 78–92.

KALECKI, M. (1935). 'A Macroeconomic Theory of Business Cycle'. *Econometrica*, 3: 327–44.

LANFORD, O. E. (1981). 'Strange Attractors and Turbulence'. In H. L. Swinney and J. P. Gollub (eds.), *Hydrodynamic Instabilities and the Transition to Turbulence*. Berlin: Springer-Verlag, pp. 7–26.

LEROY, S. F. (1989). 'Efficient Capital Markets and Martingales'. *Journal of Economic Literature*, 27: 1583–1622.

LI, T., and YORKE, J. A. (1975). 'Period Three Implies Chaos'. *American Mathematical Monthly*, 82: 985–92.

LORENZ, H. W. (1987a). 'Strange Attractors in a Multisectoral Business Cycle Model'. *Journal of Economic Behaviour and Organization*, 8: 397–411.

—— (1987b). 'International Trade and the Possible Occurrence of Chaos'. *Economic Letters*, 23: 135–8.

—— (1989). *Nonlinear Dynamical Economics and Chaotic Motion*. Berlin: Springer-Verlag.

MALESE, F., and TRANSUE, W. (1986). 'Unscrambling Chaos through Thick and Thin'. *Quarterly Journal of Economics*, 101: 419–23.

—— —— (1987). 'Unscrambling Chaos through Thick and Thin: An Explanation'. *Quarterly Journal of Economics*, 102: 425–6.

MANTELL, R. (1976). 'Homothetic Preferences and Community Excess Demand Functions'. *Journal of Economic Theory*, 12: 197–201.

MAROTTO, F. R. (1978). 'Snap-Back Repellers Imply Chaos'. *Journal of*

Mathematical Analysis and Applications, 63: 199–223.

—— (1979), 'Perturbations of Stable and Chaotic Difference Equations'. *Journal of Mathematical Analysis and Applications*, 72: 716–29.

MASKIN, E., and TIROLE, J. (1983). 'A Theory of Dynamic Oligopoly Competition with Large Fixed Costs'. Paris: CERAS.

———— (1985). 'A Theory of Dynamic Oligopoly, II: Price Competition'. Working Paper no. 373, MIT, Cambridge, Mass.

MAY, R. M. (1976). 'Simple Mathematical Models with Very Complicated Dynamics'. *Nature*, no. 261: 459–67.

MCKENZIE, L. (1986). 'Optimal Economic Growth and Turnpike Theorems'. In K. J. Arrow and M. Intriligator (eds.), *Handbook of Mathematical Economics*, iii. Amsterdam: North-Holland, Chapter 26.

MEDIO, A. (1987). 'Advances in the Analysis of Economic Dynamic Systems: Introduction'. *Journal of Economic Behaviour and Organization*, 8: 333–7.

MONTRUCCHIO, L. (1982). 'Chaotic Dynamics in Economics'. *Institute of Mathematics Publications No. 45*, Turin Polytechnic.

—— (1984). 'Optimal Decision over Time and Strange Attractors'. Report no. 9, Department of Mathematics, Turin Polytechnic.

PAPOULIS, A. (1984). *Probability, Random Variables and Stochastic Processes*. Singapore: McGraw-Hill.

POHJOLA, M. T. (1981). 'Stable, Cyclic and Chaotic Growth: The Dynamics of a Discrete-Time Version of Goodwin's Growth Cycle Model'. *Zeitschrift für Nationalökonomie*, 41: 27–38.

PUU, T. (1987). 'Complex Dynamics in Continuous Models of the Business Cycle'. In D. Batten, J. Casti, and B. Johansson (eds.), *Economic Evolution and Structural Change*. Berlin: Springer-Verlag.

RAND, D. (1976). 'Exotic Phenomena in Games and Duopoly Models'. *Journal of Mathematical Economics*, 5: 173–84.

RUELLE, D., and TAKENS, F. (1971). 'On the Nature of Turbulence'. *Communications of Mathematical Physics*, 20: 167–92.

SAARI, D. G. (1985*a*). 'Iterative Price Mechanisms'. *Econometrica*, 53: 1117–32.

—— (1985*b*). 'Price Dynamics, Social Choice, Voting Methods, Probability and Chaos'. In C. D. Aliprandis, O. Burkinshaw, and N. J. Rothman (eds.), *Advances in Equilibrium Theory*. Berlin: Springer-Verlag, pp. 276–97.

—— and URENKO, J. B. (1984). 'Newton's Method, Circle Maps and Chaotic Motions'. *American Mathematical Monthly*, 91: 3–17.

SAKAI, H., and TOKUMARU, H. (1980). 'Autocorrelation of a Certain Chaos'. *IEEE Transactions Acoustics, Speech Signal and Processes*, 6: 588–90.

SAMUELSON, P. A. (1939). 'Interactions between the Multiplier Analysis and the Principle of Acceleration'. *Review of Economic Statistics*, 21: 75–8.

—— (1947), *Foundation of Economic Analysis*. Cambridge, Mass.: Harvard University Press.

ŠARKOVSKII, A. N. (1964). 'Coexistence of Cycles of a Continuous Map of a Line into Itself'. *Ukrainskii Matematičeskii Žurnal*, 16: 61–71.

SCHEINKMAN, J. A. (1990). 'Nonlinearities in Economic Dynamics'. *Economic Journal*, 100: 33–48.

—— and LEBARON, B. (1989*a*). 'Nonlinear Dynamics and GNP Data'. In W. A. Barnett, J. Geweke, and K. Shell (eds.), *Economic Complexity: Chaos,*

Sunspots, Bubbles and Nonlinearity. Cambridge University Press, pp. 213–27.

—— —— (1989*b*). 'Nonlinear Dynamics and Stock Returns'. *Journal of Business*, 62: 311–37.

SHAFFER, S. (1984). 'Chaos, Naïveté and Consistent Conjectures'. *Economic Letters*, 14: 155–62.

SHAW, R. S. (1981). 'Strange Attractors, Chaotic Behaviour, and Information Flow'. *Zeitschrift für Naturforschung*, 36: 80.

SIMONOVITS, A. (1982). 'Buffer Stocks and Naive Expectations in a Non-Walrasian Dynamic Macro-Model: Stability, Cyclicity and Chaos'. *Scandinavian Journal of Economics*, 84: 571–81.

SMALE, S. (1980). *The Mathematics of Time: Essays in Dynamical Systems, Economic Processes and Related Topics*. New York: Springer-Verlag.

SONNENSCHEIN, H. (1972). 'Market Excess Demand Functions'. *Econometrica*, 40: 549–63.

—— (1973). 'The Utility Hypothesis and the Market Demand Theory'. *Western Economic Journal*, 11: 404–10.

SPARROW, C. (1982). *The Lorenz Equation: Bifurcations, Chaos, and Strange Attractors*. Berlin: Springer-Verlag.

SPEAR, S. E. (1989). 'When are Small Frictions Negligible?' In W. A. Barnett, J. Geweke, and K. Shell (eds.), *Economic Complexity: Chaos, Sunspots, Bubbles, and Nonlinearity*. Cambridge University Press, pp. 291–308.

STEFAN, P. (1977). 'A Theorem of Šarkovskii on the Existence of Periodic Orbits of Continuous Endomorphisms of the Real Line'. *Communications of Mathematical Physics*, 54: 237–48.

STUTZER, M. J. (1980). 'Chaotic Dynamics and Bifurcation in a Macro Model'. *Journal of Economic Dynamics and Control*, 2: 353–76.

TAKENS, F. (1980). 'Detecting Strange Attractors in Turbulence'. In D. Rand and L. Young (eds.), *Dynamical Systems and Turbulence*. Berlin: Springer-Verlag, pp. 366–82.

—— (1985). 'Distinguishing Deterministic and Random Systems'. In G. Borenblatt, G. Jooss, and D. Joseph (eds.), *NonLinear Dynamics and Turbulence*. Boston: Pitman, pp. 315–33.

VON NEUMANN, J. (1937). 'Über ein Ökonomisches Gleichung-System und eine Verall-gemeinerung des Brouwerschen Fixpunktsatzes'. In K. Menger (ed.), *Ergebnisse eines Mathematischen Kolloquiums*; translated as 'A Model of General Economic Equilibrium', *Review of Economic Studies*, 13: 1–9 (1945–6).

WOODFORD, M. (1989). 'Imperfect Financial Intermediation and Complex Dynamics'. In W. A. Barnett, J. Geweke, and K. Shell (eds.), *Economic Complexity: Chaos, Sunspots, Bubbles, and Nonlinearity*. Cambridge University Press, pp. 309–34.

10

An Adaptive, Neoclassical Model of Growth Fluctuations

RICHARD H. DAY and TZONG-YAU LIN

> The development of the real gross national product of a country does not follow a smooth path but shows irregularities . . .
>
> Erik Lundberg, *Instability and Economic Growth*

1. Introduction

We reconsider the standard neoclassical growth theory with the following modification: we suppose that agents maximize period after period (as time unfolds) with respect to present consumption and an indefinite future of sustainable consumption on the basis of adaptive expectations. Depending on the parameters of time preference and productivity, the resulting trajectories can but need not converge to an optimal steady state. They may exhibit cycles or fluctuate erratically, perhaps never reaching equilibrium, thus providing a deterministic model of the real business cycle which can generate irregular trajectories without the imposition of random shocks.

When this happens, phenomena that bear a resemblance to the real world occur. After some periods of growth, equilibrium capacity is exceeded and the real rates of return and investment decline; when capacity falls, the marginal productivity of capital recovers, investment increases, and output expands. Real interest rates, output, and capacity correspondingly oscillate, and expectations always overestimate or underestimate the real rate of return. In its extreme form, there can occur periods of excess capacity in which aggregate capital stock is allowed to decay before a new period of growth sets in. The situation is roughly like that of the relatively long cycles that occur in very durable goods industries such as office buildings, mining activity, heavy manufacturing, petroleum refining capacity, and electric power production.

After providing some historical background on nonlinear business cycle theory in Section 2, equilibrium theory is briefly reviewed in Section 3; then our model is presented in Section 4. Some numerical experiments are shown in Section 5 which illustrate irregular cycles; in this case the long-run behaviour of capital and the expected rate of return converge to 'strange attractors' which, because of their non-periodic, Kantor set nature, cannot be represented in any finite way, yet have a definite structure, complex and apparently fractile in character. A stability analysis is presented in Section 6. In Section 7 the special case of naive expectations is analysed, and in Section 8 a bifurcation analysis is summarized which shows how the qualitative dynamics change when the various parameters are varied. The statistical dynamics of the model are also briefly considered. Section 9 compares the results of the optimal and adaptive versions of the neoclassical model and concludes with a brief comment on some methodological issues that call for attention.

2. Some Background

Nonlinear business cycle theory may have had its origin in Leontief's (1934) more or less definitive analysis of cobweb cycles in competitive markets with production lags, Samuelson's (1941) early discussions of stability, and especially the models of Hicks (1951) and Kaldor (1949), in which nonlinearity was not assumed away but was made the centre-piece of the analysis. These early studies were followed by the brilliant papers of Goodwin, who perceived the germ of a profound new insight: that intrinsic causal relationships, completely deterministic and with no intervening exogenous shocks, could behave in a non-periodic manner, one that would be irregular and unpredictable in nature! But this work, though prescient and quite sophisticated, did not yet carry the analysis of intrinsic irregularity very far. The seed had been cast, but its germination and flowering awaited a later season (see Goodwin 1982).

Interest in cycles, which had been so active through the 1950s, actually began to wane as the 'golden Keynesian era' of the 1960s wore on. Growth in actual GNP persisted. The dominant 'stylized fact' seemed no longer to be the unstable nature of capitalism, with its intermittent undulations of unemployment and inflation, but rather its capacity to generate growth. Quite understandably, most economists abandoned the task of explaining business fluctuations. They shifted to explaining trends in output, capital accumulation, and productivity using new developments in applied mathematics, in particular optimal control theory and Bellman's dynamic programming, which made it possible to extend the idea of a competitive equilibrium to that of a growing economy.

Then, in the wake of the first really substantial downturn in economic activity of the postwar era (1972–4), the business cycle re-emerged as a

major field of study. It is hardly surprising that the tools of analysis used
to study optimal growth were turned to the task involved. So arrived the
equilibrium business cycle theory. Robert Lucas's (1975) seminal introduction to the approach stimulated a considerable body of subsequent
work, culminating in texts by Sargeant (1987), the collection of essays
edited by Barro (1989), and several recent review articles, e.g. McCallum (1989) and Stockman (1988). The theoretical motivation was to
solve Hayek's 'crucial problem' of incorporating cyclical phenomena into
the system of economic equilibrium theory (see Lucas 1977).

In this theory, (1) agents' behaviours are based on an optimizing
response to their economic environment; (2) agents are assumed to
incorporate complete knowledge of the probabilistic structure of this
environment in forming expectations; and (3) prices and quantities at
each point in time are determined in competitive equilibrium. In Lucas's
version money is neutral; the equations of motion are linear and, in the
absence of shocks, stable so that fluctuations are propagated by random
impulses in essentially the manner described already in 1934 by Frisch.
Lucas associated the random impulses with money shock incurred by
active monetary policy. Later studies emphasized shocks in tastes and
especially in technology. The nature of aggregate time-series data are
derived from the autoregressive structure assumed in the shock-generating process. In this way the full burden of explaining the irregularity of
the business cycle is placed on exogenous factors.[1]

In the meantime, an alternative explanation of erratic macroeconomic
fluctuations has been developed in the absence of exogenous shocks by
retaining nonlinearities in structural relations; an approach that has also
engendered a substantial literature, some of which has been reviewed in
Baumol and Benhabib (1987) and Boldrin (1988). (See also Grandmont
1987 and Medio 1987.) In the rebirth of nonlinear business cycle theory,
some quite different models have been used: the overlapping-generations model, the optimal growth theory, and a number of disequilibrium
macro models of the Keynesian genre.

We shall not attempt to review all these developments here. Rather,
we shall use the neoclassical growth model itself to illustrate a few of
the main concepts of nonlinear dynamic analysis in the context of
business cycle theory.

3. Optimal Growth

We begin with the fundamental expression for capital accumulation.

---

[1] Great stress, therefore, is placed on the theoretical specification of the stochastic-
shock-generating mechanism, a specification that is derived not from economic theory but,
as I understand it, from the character of time-series data of economic aggregates.

Suppose that capital goods wear out at a constant rate δ: we have

$$k_{t+1} = \frac{1}{1+n}[(1-\delta)k_t + y_t - c_t], \tag{1}$$

where $s_t = (y_t - c_t)$ is savings of the tth period, y_t is per capita income, c_t is consumption, and k_t is the capital stock, all in per capita terms. This is a market-clearing condition that equates savings with gross investment.

Let $y = f(k)$ be the production function and suppose that capital stocks cannot be consumed. Then we have the constraints

$$f(k_t) - c_t \geq 0, \qquad c_t \geq 0. \tag{2}$$

Now let $u(c_t)$ be the utility of consumption in period t. The utility of the entire consumption stream $c_t, c_{t+1}, \ldots,$ is

$$U(c_t, c_{t+1}, \ldots) = \sum_{i=t}^{\infty} \alpha^{i-t} u(c_i). \tag{3}$$

An *optimal intertemporal equilibrium growth path* emanating from a fixed capital–labour ratio k_t is a consumption stream $c_t, c_{t+1}, \ldots$ and a sequence of capital stocks $k_t, k_{t+1}, \ldots$ which maximizes (3) subject to (1) and (2) for $t, t+1, \ldots$. Let

$$V(k_t) := \max \sum_{i=t}^{\infty} \alpha^{i-t} u(c_i), \tag{4}$$

subject to (1) and (2) $t, t+1, \ldots$. Then, according to the principle of optimality,

$$V(k_t) = \max_{c_t, k_{t+1}} [u(c_t) + \alpha V(k_{t+1})] \tag{5}$$

subject to (1)–(2) or

$$V(k) = \max_{0 \leq c \leq f(k)} \{u(c) + \alpha V[(1-\delta)k + f(k) - c]\} \tag{6}$$

for any k. A function $c = h^*(k)$ that satisfies (6) for all $k > 0$ is called an *optimal strategy*. A sequence (c_n, k_n), $n = t, t+1, \ldots$ such that

$$c_n = h^*(k_n) \tag{7}$$

and satisfies (1) gives the optimal intertemporal equilibrium solution already defined.

It is well known that the optimal trajectories are monotonic, Pareto-optimal, and consistent; that is, a stream beginning at generation t will contain consumption levels for each generation that would be optimal in the above sense from the perspective of that generation when its turn comes. Moreover, all trajectories converge to a unique stationary state k^* such that

$$f(k^*) = (n + \delta)k^* \tag{8}$$

and

$$r^* = f'(k^*) = (1 + n)/\alpha - (1 - \delta). \tag{9}$$

This is the neoclassical core from which the contemporary real business cycle has evolved.[2] By adding random shocks to the function $f(\cdot)$ or to the utility function $u(\cdot)$, the model can propagate fluctuations in the manner alluded to in Section 2.

4. An Adaptive, Neoclassical Growth Model

The functional equation that embodies the principle of optimality is based on a backward recursion from the future to the present (equation (5)) which in turn is derived from a knowledge of how each successive state of the economy emerges from its predecessor (equation (1)). The optimal growth trajectory that it generates is supported by a sequence of competitive equilibrium prices, which if known by the agents will induce them to behave, period after period, in a manner consistent with the equilibrium consumption and capital stream (Stokey and Lucas 1989: Ch. 6). This, of course, requires that the pricing half of the dual quantity–value problem is already solved.

In the world as we know it expectations are seldom realized, adjustment occurs out of equilibrium, and intertemporal inefficiencies are perpetuated for considerable periods of time. It is not without interest, therefore, to consider a model of growth that reflects these conditions. To this end we reconsider the neoclassical model from an adaptive point of view.

Behaviour at each point in time is based on anticipations that depend on current experience, which in turn derives from the feedback effect of past production and capital accumulation. Expectations are not perfect but crudely proximate, and though they are adjusted in response to what actually happens, the trajectory of the system as a whole does not satisfy an optimality principle except (possibly) at a steady state. Technically, behaviour is generated by a forward rather than a backward recursion as in the case of optimal growth, and it is this property that is responsible for the emergence of cycles or chaos in the present theory. Despite the differences between the adaptive and equilibrium growth models, the relationships between them are of interest, and we comment on these below after explaining the implication of our own assumptions.

Adaptive expectations, on which the present analysis rests, has played

---

[2] See Stokey and Lucas (1989: Sect. 2.3) for a thorough exegesis.

a key role in dynamic modelling ever since Hicks's *Value and Capital* and was central to much subsequent macroeconometric work. It waned in the mid-1970s with the advent of the rational expectations hypothesis and the emergence of equilibrium business cycle theory. Recently, however, strong evidence supporting the empirical relevance of adaptive expectations has been found both in econometric studies and in laboratory experiments (Bergmann 1988; Smith *et al.* 1988; Sterman 1989; and Williams 1986). Its reconsideration in the context of business cycle theory would seem to be amply justified on this ground alone.

Two descriptive settings for the present theory can be imagined, one pertaining to the long run and one to the short run. In the case of long-run growth, consider the following highly simplified overlapping-generations framework for a private-ownership economy. Adults of a given generation are managers or workers to whom all proceeds of production are distributed in the form of wages or salary and dividends or real interest. They determine consumption and savings for themselves and their children, who, we assume, are being born at a constant relative rate n (as generally assumed in equilibrium growth theory). The savings are invested, and the capital stock that results, allowing for depreciation in the mean time, constitutes the endowment of the next generation of adults, that is, the bequest left by the parents who have passed away. As in other neoclassical growth models, it is assumed that the capital and labour markets clear.

If one is thinking instead of the short run, the story is essentially the same except that now, instead of a generation of, say, twenty-five years, we would be thinking of a much shorter period, say a year. Agents provide for the future as before by endowing themselves (and their families) with capital that can generate an expected flow of income, which can be allocated next period when the time comes. In either case, expectational errors can lead to over- or under-investment and a fluctuation in wages, interest, and per capita wealth.[3]

To formalize this notion, reconsider the intertemporal utility function (1) and suppose that, instead of an infinite stream in which consumption must be determined at each date, a two-period function,

$$u(c) + W(c^1), \tag{10}$$

is imagined in which the first term is the utility of current consumption as before, c^1 is a sustainable level of well-being in perpetuity, and $W(c^1)$ its utility to current decision-makers of this future potentiality under the assumption that their tastes (or those of their heirs) are constant. Under our assumptions,

---

[3] For the origin of this model, see Leontief (1958) and the subsequent analysis in Day (1969).

$$W(c^1) = \sum_{m=t+1}^{\infty} \alpha^{m-t} u(c^1) = \gamma u(c^1), \tag{11}$$

where $\gamma = \alpha/(1 - \alpha)$. We also assume that $u'(c) > 0$, $u''(c) < 0$.

The sustainable level of living to be provided by the bequest must account for the maintenance of the capital stock and the need to provide an endowment for net additions to the population, so

$$c^1 = y^1 - (n + \delta)k^1, \tag{12}$$

where the income anticipated for the next generation in terms of wages w^1 and dividends $r^1 k^1$ is

$$y^1 = w^1 + r^1 k^1. \tag{13}$$

The variable r^1 is the anticipated rate of return, and k^1 is the planned future capital stock. The latter, of course, depends on current savings, so that

$$k^1 = \frac{1}{1 + n} [y - c + (1 - \delta)k], \tag{14}$$

where y and k are current per capita means and capital stock, respectively. Define the anticipated and current net rates of return to be, respectively,

$$\rho^1 := \frac{r^1 - (n + \delta)}{1 + n}, \qquad \rho := \frac{r - (n + \delta)}{1 + n}. \tag{15}$$

Then, substituting (13) and (14) into (12), collecting terms, and using (15), we have the sustainable consumption level,

$$c^1 = w^1 + \rho^1 [y - c + (1 - \delta)k_t]. \tag{16}$$

The currently most preferred combination of present consumption and future sustainable consumption (c_t, c_t^1) maximizes (11) subject to (1)–(2) and (16). This is equivalent to maximizing

$$\mathcal{L} := u(c) + \gamma u\{w^1 + \rho^1 [y_t - c + (1 - \delta)k_t]\} + \pi(y_t - c), \tag{17}$$

with respect to c and the Lagrange on multiplier π. Given the properties of $u(\cdot)$, it is necessary and sufficient that

$$u'(c_t) = \gamma \rho^1 u'\{w^1 + \rho^1 [y_t - c_t + (1 - \delta)k_t]\}, \quad \pi = 0$$

$$\text{when } c_t < y_t, \tag{18}$$

and

$$\pi = u'(c_t) - \gamma \rho^1 u'\{w^1 + \rho^1 [y_t - c_t + (1 - \delta)k_t]\} > 0$$

$$\text{when } c_t = y_t. \tag{19}$$

When $c_t = y_t$ note that, as $u'(c) > 0$, all $c > 0$, (19) implies only that

$\rho^1 < u'/W'$, so that the net real rate of return can be positive and yet no savings occur. When this happens, increasing—or even just maintaining—the next generation's capital stock is not worth the sacrifice in current consumption. Certainly, when $\rho^1 < 0$, savings are zero and capital stock is allowed to decumulate.

As long as the anticipated rate ρ^1 is finite, there is always a positive solution that satisfies (18) or (19). It is a function of y_t, k_t, w^1, r^1, γ, and the parameters of u and is bounded by y_t; that is,

$$c_t = \begin{cases} c(y_t, k_t, r^1, w^1; \gamma) < y_t, & \rho^1 > 0 \\ y & \rho^1 \leqslant 0, \end{cases} \tag{20}$$

where $c(\cdot)$ is the unconstrained consumption function satisfying equation (18).

In line with our recognition that a given generation cannot foretell the future (or understand the mechanism that generates it), suppose that the current income and interest levels are used as a basis for the consumption–savings–bequest trade-off.

Let us adopt the usual form of adaptive expectations for the anticipated rate of return, but for simplicity let us suppose that the anticipated wage rate is formed naively. Then, denoting the anticipated rate of return by r_t^1, which the adults during period t anticipate will hold in period $t + 1$, and where $\mu \in (0, 1)$ is the adjustment coefficient that determines how much the expectations for the future are modified in the light of experience, we have

$$r_t^1 = r_{t-1}^1 + \mu(r_t - r_{t-1}^1) \tag{21}$$

and

$$w_t^1 = w_t. \tag{22}$$

By assumption, $w^1 = w_t = y_t - r_t k_t$. The anticipated *net* rate of return is $\rho^1 = [1/(1 + n)][r^1 - (n + \delta)]$ where r^1 is generated by (21). Using the production function, $y_t = f(k_t)$, in (21) and (22), we get instead of $c(\cdot)$ in (20) a function $g(k_t, r_t^1)$, so that consumption of the current generation is given by

$$c = \begin{cases} g(k, r^1), & r^1 > n + \delta \\ f(k), & r^1 \leqslant n + \delta \end{cases} \tag{23}$$

This equation is the temporarily optimal consumption 'strategy' that satisfies (18)–(19). Define

$$\psi^1(r_t^1, k_t) := \begin{cases} [1/(1 + n)][(1 - \delta)k_t + f(k_t) - g(k_t, r_t^1)], & r_t^1 > (n + \delta) \\ (1 - \delta/1 + n)k_t, & r_t^1 \leqslant (n + \delta) \end{cases}$$

$$\psi^2(r_t^1, k_t) := (1 - \mu)r_{t-1}^1 + \mu f'(k_t). \tag{24}$$

Then

$$k_{t+1} = \psi^1(r_t^1, k_t)$$
$$r_{t+1}^1 = \psi^2(r_t^1, k_t),$$

(25)

which, given the initial conditions (r_0^1, k_0), describe how per capita wealth and expectations evolve. A sequence $(r_n^1, k_n)_t^\infty$ satisfying (25) is a *suboptimal, temporary equilibrium trajectory* with initial condition (r_t^1, k_t). At each stage the agents determine their saving and investment behaviour optimally with respect to the succeeding period and the labour and goods markets clear. Expectations need not be realized, and in any case the agents have to decide anew, period after period, how to allocate their inherited endowments.

5. Standard Functional Forms

A hint of the possibilities can be obtained by using specific functional forms and particular parameter values. To this end, consider the following:

$$u(c) := \log c, \qquad W(c^1) := \gamma \log c^1, \qquad y = f(k) := Bk^\beta. \quad (26)$$

The unconstrained consumption function is

$$c(y, k, w^1, \rho^1) = \frac{1}{1 + \gamma} [w^1/\rho^1 + y + (1 - \delta)k]. \quad (27)$$

Given that $w^1 = w = (1 - \rho)y$, we find that the consumption function becomes

$$g(k, r^1) = \frac{1}{1 + \lambda} \left[(1 - \delta)k + Bk^\beta + \frac{(1 - \beta)Bk^\beta}{r^1 - (n + \delta)} \right]. \quad (28)$$

To get an idea of the possible long-run behaviour of the system, we have plotted the state variables (r_t^1, k_t) for $t = 301, \ldots, 650$ in Figs. 10.1 and 10.2 for the two examples in which the first 500 points have been discarded. Part (a) in each figure shows the numerical 'attractors' in the (r^1, k) space. Parts (b) and (c) show local enlargements of the small boxes in (a) and (b). They suggest that the local micro structure of the orbits resembles their global counterpart and has a fractile character like the famous Henon Attractor. Here, the phenomenon is found for a quite different map derived from totally different theoretical considerations.

6. Stability and Instability[4]

The locus of stationary states are pairs (r^1, k) such that $r^1 = \psi^1(r^1, k) = f'(k) = \beta B k^{\beta - 1}$. It forms a hyperbola in the (r^1, k) space shown in Fig. 10.3. The locus of stationary wealth values (stationary states must occur when savings are positive) are pairs (r^1, k) such that $k = \psi^2(r^1, k)$. This locus consists of two loci separated by the value of k, say k_∞, satisfying

$$\gamma - [(1 + \gamma)(1 + n) - \gamma(1 - \delta)] \frac{k}{y} = 0. \tag{29}$$

Let k_m be the unique capital–labour ratio satisfying $(n + \delta)k_m = f(k_m)$. This value is the upper bound of all possible solutions of the

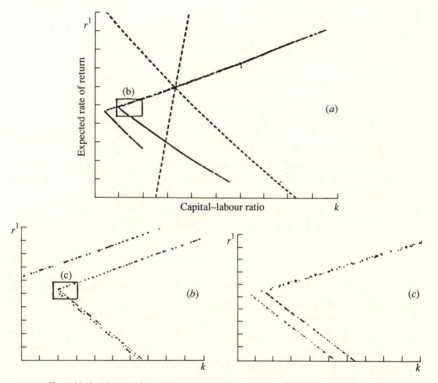

FIG. 10.1. An orbit on the phase plane with adaptive expectations
(a) The orbit of (r^1, k) pairs. The dashed lines are the loci of stationary expected rates and capital–labour ratios.
(b) An enlargement of box (b) in part (a)
(c) An enlargement of box (c) in part (b)

[4] This section is based on Lin (1988).

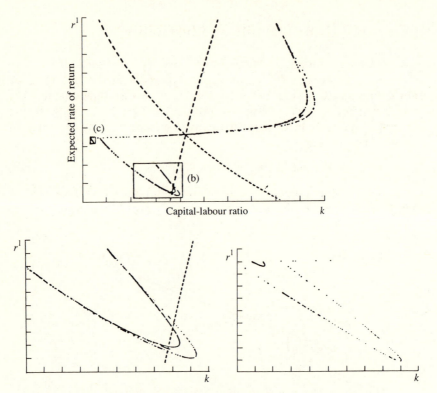

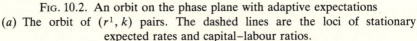

Fig. 10.2. An orbit on the phase plane with adaptive expectations
(*a*) The orbit of (r^1, k) pairs. The dashed lines are the loci of stationary
expected rates and capital–labour ratios.
(*b*) An enlargement of box (*b*) in part (*a*)
(*c*) An enlargement of box (*c*) in part (*a*)

system. Moreover, it can be shown that $k_m < k_\infty$. Therefore, only the
fixed point smaller than k_∞ is economically meaningful. These loci of
stationary values are shown in Fig. 8.3. As already indicated, only the
non-shaded area is germane. It is divided into four regions. Using
(36)–(37), the direction of local variations in each regime shown by the
arrows in the diagrams is derived from the expressions

$$\text{sign}\,[\psi^1(r^1, k) - r^1] \tag{30}$$

$$\text{sign}\,[\psi^2(r^1, k) - k]. \tag{31}$$

The question is, Do trajectories that begin anywhere away from $(\tilde{r}^1, \tilde{k})$
converge to their stationary state, or fluctuate indefinitely? To answer
this, define the implied map on R^2 to be

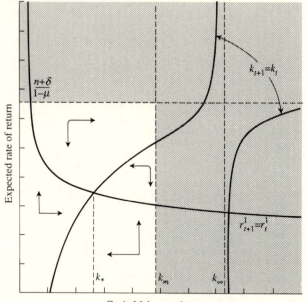

FIG. 10.3. Region of viable trajectories
The unshaded area is the viable region.

$$\psi(r^1, k) := \begin{pmatrix} \psi^1(r^1, k) - r^1 \\ \psi^2(r^1, k) - k \end{pmatrix}$$

and denote the associated matrix by $D\phi$. Then,

$$D\phi = \begin{bmatrix} \alpha_1 & \alpha_2 \\ \alpha_3 & \alpha_4 \end{bmatrix},$$

where

$$\alpha_1 \equiv \frac{\partial k_{t+1}}{\partial k_t}$$

$$= \frac{1}{1+\gamma} \left\{ \gamma \frac{r_t + 1 - \delta}{1+n} - \left[(1-\beta) \frac{r_t}{r_t - (n+\delta)} - \frac{w_t}{[r_t^1 - (n+\delta)]^2} \frac{\partial r_t^1}{\partial k_t} \right] \right\}$$

$$\alpha_2 \equiv \frac{\partial k_{t+1}}{\partial r_t^1} = \frac{1}{1+\lambda} \frac{w_t}{[r_t^1 - (n+\delta)]^2} \frac{\partial r_t^1}{\partial r_{t-1}^1}$$

$$\alpha_3 \equiv \frac{\partial r_t^1}{\partial k_t} = \mu f''(k_t)$$

$$\alpha_4 \equiv \frac{\partial r_t^1}{\partial r_{t-1}^1} = 1 - \mu.$$

The eigenvalues λ_1 and λ_2 can be obtained by solving the following polynomial:

$$\lambda^2 - \text{tr}(D\tilde{\phi})\lambda + \Delta(D\tilde{\phi}) = 0,$$

where $\text{tr}(D\tilde{\phi}) \equiv \tilde{\alpha}_1 + \tilde{\alpha}_4$ is the trace of $D\tilde{\phi}$ and $\Delta(D\tilde{\phi}) \equiv \tilde{\alpha}_1\tilde{\alpha}_4 - \tilde{\alpha}_2\tilde{\alpha}_3$ is the determinant evaluated at $(\tilde{k}, \tilde{r})$. Then

$$\lambda_{1,2} = \tfrac{1}{2}\big(\text{tr}(D\tilde{\phi}) \pm \sqrt{\{[\text{tr}(D\tilde{\phi})]^2 - 4\Delta(D\tilde{\phi})\}}\big)$$

gives the pair of eigenvalues. The steady state $\tilde{k}$ is then stable (unstable) if

$$\max\{|\lambda_1|,|\lambda_2|\} < 1 \qquad (> 1). \tag{32}$$

The eigenvalues are complex conjugates if $[\text{tr}(D\tilde{\phi})]^2 < 4\Delta(D\tilde{\phi})$, which is equivalent to

$$[\tilde{\alpha}_1 - (1 - \mu)]^2 < -4\tilde{\alpha}_2\tilde{\alpha}_3. \tag{33}$$

As the steady state,

$$\tilde{\alpha}_1 = a - \mu b,$$

$$\tilde{\alpha}_2\tilde{\alpha}_3 = -\mu(1 - \mu)b,$$

where

$$a = \left[1 - \frac{1-\beta}{1+\gamma}\left(1 + \gamma\frac{n+\delta}{1+n}\right)\right]\Big/(1 + \gamma), \tag{34}$$

$$b = \left[\frac{(1-\beta)^2}{\beta}\left(1 + \gamma\frac{n+\delta}{1+n}\right)^2\right]\Big/(1 + \gamma). \tag{35}$$

We can then express (33) as

$$H := H(\gamma, \beta, \mu, \eta, \delta) := [a - \mu b - (1 - \mu)]^2 - 4\mu(1 - \mu)b < 0. \tag{36}$$

Note that here a is always positive and less than 1, as is $(1 - \mu)a$. Therefore, if the system has a pair of complex eigenvalues, it has to be stable.

Next, let us see when the eigenvalues can be real. It is necessary and sufficient if the inequality sign in (36) is reversed. Rewrite (36) as

$$G(\mu) := H(\gamma, \beta, \mu, \eta, \delta) \equiv (1 + b)^2\mu^2 + 2(a - ab - 1 - b)\mu$$

$$+ (a - 1)^2 < 0, \tag{37}$$

which can be viewed as a polynomial in μ with coefficients in a and b. According to the fundamental theorem of algebra, there always exist solutions in the complex plane for which $G(\mu) = 0$. The solution of μ could be obtained from the following formula:

$$\mu = \frac{(1 + b + ab - a) \pm \sqrt{[(1 + b + ab - a)^2 - (1 + b)^2(1 - a)^2]}}{(1 + b)^2}.$$

(38)

Notice that the term under the square root can be written as $4ab(1 - a + b)$. Since $0 < a < 1$, μ can only be real. Furthermore, since $a < 1$, we get

$$ab < b(1 + b) \Rightarrow (1 + a)b < 2b + b^2 \Rightarrow 1 + (1 + a)b < (1 + b)^2,$$

and

$$1 + (1 + a)b - a = 1 + b + ab - a < (1 + b)^2.$$

Therefore

$$\frac{1 + b + ab - a}{(1 + b)^2} < 1,$$

and the solution of μ with a smaller value in (39) will be well defined; i.e., $\mu \in (0, 1)$. In other words, $G(\mu)$ would have a typical graph which is depicted in Fig. 10.4, where μ' and μ'' are indicated as points at which $G(\mu)$ intersects the μ-axis, and we can choose $\mu'' = \min\{1, \mu''\}$. Therefore, the eigenvalues may be real numbers for a given value of μ. There then should be an eigenvalue

$$\lambda = \frac{(a - \mu b + 1 - \mu) - \sqrt{\{[a - \mu b - (1 - \mu)]^2 - 4\mu(1 - \mu)b\}}}{2},$$

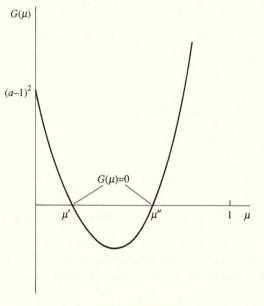

Fig. 10.4. The $G(\cdot)$

which is equal to -1 for some $\beta \in (0, 1)$. This is quite evident because, for a finite γ,

$$\lim_{\beta \to 0} b = \infty, \qquad \lim_{b \to \infty} \lambda = -\infty$$

$$\lim_{\beta \to 1} b = 0, \qquad \lim_{b \to 0} \lambda = 0.$$

This may be seen more clearly by investigating Fig. 10.5. It depicts contours for which $H(\cdot) = 0$ in the (β, μ)-plane given any γ, n, δ. The region above and below the contours has $H < 0$. Here the eigenvalues are complex conjugates; the system is therefore stable. Otherwise, $H > 0$ and the system may be unstable.

7. Naive Expectations[5]

When $\mu = 1$, adaptive expectations are called naive. In this special case rather complete global results can be given.

Using (16) together with (6) and (13)–(15) in (12), we find

$$c_t = \begin{cases} h(k), & \rho^1 > 0 \\ f(k), & \rho^1 \leq 0, \end{cases} \tag{39}$$

where

$$h(k) := c\left(f(k), k, \frac{f'(k) - (n + \delta)}{1 + n}, f(k) - f'(k)k\right). \tag{40}$$

Returning to (1), we obtain the difference equation

$$k_{t+1} = \theta(k_t) =$$

$$\begin{cases} \theta^s(k_t) := \dfrac{1}{1 + n} [(1 - \delta)k_t + f(k_t) - h(k_t)], & k_t \in K^s \\ \theta^d(k_t) := \dfrac{1 - \delta}{1 + n} k_t, & k_t \in K^d, \end{cases} \tag{41}$$

where

$$K^s := \{k | f'(k) > (n + \delta)\}, \qquad K^d := \{k | f'(k) \leq (n + \delta)\}. \tag{42}$$

Obviously, growth *may* occur in K^s, but, as $(1 - \delta)/(1 + n) < 1$, decay *must* occur in K^d. We would like to know what (if any) other kinds of developments can occur in such an economy.

---

[5] This section is based on Lin *et al.* (1989).

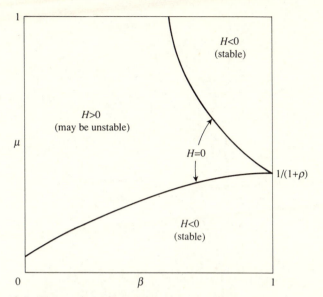

FIG. 10.5. Zones of stability and possible instability in the (β, μ)-space

Everything depends on the character of the map $\theta(\cdot)$. Given the concave nature of $f(\cdot)$, the latter can be determined if we know the profile of $h(\cdot)$. Indeed, the following can be established.

LEMMA. The consumption wealth function is monotonically increasing on $[0, k^0)$ where $f'(k^0) = n + \delta$. In addition, $h'(0) = h'(k^0) = \infty$ with $h(0) = 0$, $h(k)$ becomes unbounded as $k \to k^0$. Moreover, there exists a unique k, say $k^s < k^0$, where $f'(k^s) = n + \delta$ such that $h(k) < f(k)$, $k \in (0, k^s)$, $h(k^s) = f(k^s)$ and $h(k) > f(k)$, $k \in (k^s, k^0)$.

(See Fig. 10.6.)

Given this lemma, it is clear that in (42) $K^s = [0, k^s)$ and $K^d = [k^s, k^m]$. Next, note that trajectories are bounded. To see this, consider

$$k_{t+1} = M(k_t) := \frac{1}{1 + n} [(1 - \delta)k_t + f(k_t)]. \qquad (43)$$

The function $M(\cdot)$ is monotonically increasing, and as $c(k) > 0$ for all $k > 0$ have $k_{t+1} = \theta(k_t) \leq M(k_t)$ for all $k_t \geq 0$. From the Inada conditions and the intermediate value theorem, (43) has a fixpoint, k^m. Consequently, all trajectories with initial conditions $k \in K := (0, k^m)$ remain in K.

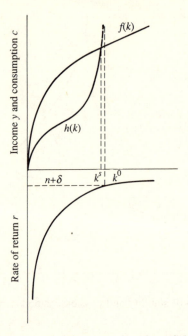

Fig. 10.6. Current consumption as a function of the capital stock

Now consider the existence of stationary solutions $\tilde{k}$ such that $\tilde{k} = \theta(\tilde{k})$. Clearly, zero is one such state; the trivial one. Suppose a nontrivial, positive $\tilde{k}$ exists. Because $(1 - \delta)/(1 + n) < 1$, it must occur on the positive savings phase of (20), so that

$$(n + \delta)\tilde{k} = f(\tilde{k}) - h(\tilde{k}). \tag{44}$$

That is, at a positive stationary state savings must first restore worn-out capital stock, then augment it sufficiently to endow net additions to the population. Obviously, therefore, $\tilde{k} \leqslant k^m$. Note that $h'(\cdot)$ behaves like $c_y[f' + (1 - \delta)]$, which becomes unbounded as k approaches zero. Consequently, close enough to 0, $\theta(k) > k$. The expression $\theta(k) < k$ is equivalent to $f(k) - h(k) < (n + \delta)k$. But we know that $f(k^s) = h(k^s)$, so the required inequality holds for all k close enough to k^s. Therefore, $\theta(k) - k$ changes signs on K, and this gives us the following.

PROPOSITION 1. For all initial conditions in $k \in K = [0, k^m)$ trajectories exist, their orbits belong to K, and there exists a unique, positive stationary state $\tilde{k} \in (0, k^s)$.

To determine if $\tilde{k}$ is stable or unstable, note that $\partial\theta(k^s)/\partial\gamma$ becomes unboundedly negative when γ gets large enough or small enough.

Suppose $\delta = n = 0$. Then, as these extremes are reached, $\tilde{k} = k^s$ becomes unstable from the left. By increasing δ and n slightly so that the slope of $\theta^d(k) = (1 - \delta)/(1 + n)$ is close enough to unity and $\tilde{k}$ is close enough to k^s, $\theta'(\tilde{k})$ will be strongly negative so that $\tilde{k}$ is unstable. Then, by choosing new values of δ and n so that $(1 - \delta)/(1 + n)$ is still closer to unity, we can ensure that $\theta'\{[(1 - \delta)/(1 + n)]k^s\}$ is negative enough so that, for some iterate p, $\theta^p(\cdot)$ is expensive (i.e., has a derivative everywhere greater than 1) on the trapping set $[(1 - \delta)/(1 + n)]K^s$, $\theta\{[(1 - \delta)/(1 + n)]k^s\}$. Arguing in this way, we arrive at the following.

PROPOSITION 2. If $n = \delta = 0$, there exists a $\gamma^1 > 0$ such that $\tilde{k}$ is stable (unstable) to the left and neutrally stable to the right for all $\gamma \leq \gamma^1$ ($\gamma > \gamma^1$). Given γ^1, for any $\gamma < \gamma^1$, there exists an ϵ, say ϵ^1, depending on γ such that $\tilde{k}$ is unstable (to the left and to the right) for each $\epsilon < \epsilon^1$ for all δ, n satisfying

$$1 - \epsilon < \frac{1 - \delta}{1 + n} < 1. \tag{45}$$

Given this γ^1, there exists a positive value of ϵ, say $\epsilon^2 < \epsilon^1$, such that the process is ergodic for all δ, n satisfying (29) for all $\epsilon < \epsilon^2$.

The ergodicity of proposition 2 means that the distribution of capital–labour ratios in any orbit $\omega(k)$ can be represented by a stable, absolutely continuous, invariant probability measure with positive densities being distributed over a set of finite intervals in k. Moreover, time averages of finite samples of values obey the central limit theorem. These interpretations are explained and illustrated in detail in Day and Shafer (1987). Actually, this proposition applies only to the situation that arises in Fig. 10.7(d). The profiles of $\theta(\cdot)$ (restricted to the trapping set) shown in parts (b) and (c) of the figure also arise and require a rather more intricate argument to obtain similar results. Day and Shafer (1987) go into these technical matters, which need not be elaborated further here.

8. The Example Revisited

We can enhance our understanding of the varied possibilities by considering further the example of Section 4. Using the functions specified in (21), it can be shown that

$$\theta'(k) = \frac{1}{1 + n} \left[\frac{\gamma}{1 + \gamma} (r + 1 - \delta) + \left(\frac{1}{(1 + n)(1 + \gamma)} \frac{w}{(1 + \gamma)} \frac{k}{\rho} \right) r \right], \tag{46}$$

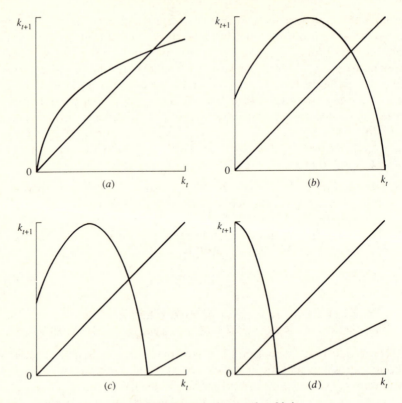

FIG. 10.7. Canonical maps for $\theta(\cdot)$
In (b), (c), and (d) the diagram is restricted to the trapping set where fluctuations are perpetuated.

where, it will be recalled, $r = f'$, $\rho = [r - (n + \delta)]/(1 + n)$, and $w = (1 - \beta)y$. It can also be shown that, as the positive stationary state $\tilde{k}$, the stationary net rate of return equals the reciprocal of the future weight γ,

$$\tilde{\rho} = \frac{1}{1 + n} [\tilde{r} - (n + \delta)] = \frac{1}{\gamma}, \tag{47}$$

where $\tilde{r} = f'(\tilde{k})$. Using this fact, we find that

$$\theta'(\tilde{k}) = 1 - \frac{(1 - \beta)\gamma^2}{(1 + n)^2(1 + \gamma)} \left[\frac{1 - \beta}{\beta} \tilde{r}^2 + \frac{(1 + n)}{\tilde{\rho}} \tilde{r} \right]. \tag{48}$$

As usual, local stability or instability is determined by the critical bifurcation point, $\theta'(\tilde{k}) = -1$. Rewrite this equation as

$$\frac{1 - \beta}{\beta} (\tilde{r})^2 + \frac{1 + n}{\gamma} \tilde{r} - 2 \frac{(1 + n)^2(1 + \gamma)}{(1 - \beta)\gamma^2} = 0.$$

This is a second-order polynomial in $\tilde{r}$, the largest root of which is given by

$$\tilde{r} = \frac{1}{2} \left\{ -\frac{1 + n}{\gamma} + \sqrt{\left[\left(\frac{1 + n}{\gamma}\right)^2 + \frac{8}{\beta} \frac{8(1 + n)^2(1 + \gamma)}{\gamma^2}\right]} \right\} \frac{1 - \beta}{\beta}.$$

Using equation (31), this equality is seen to be identical to

$$H(\gamma,\beta) := 1 + \frac{\gamma(n + \delta)}{1 + n} - \frac{-1 + \sqrt{[1 + 8(1 + \gamma)/\beta]}}{2} \frac{\beta}{1 - \beta} = 0.$$

(49)

The first term is constant for fixed γ, n, δ; the second term is a continuously increasing function of β whose value goes to 0 as β goes to 0, and infinity as β goes to 1. Consequently, for any given γ, $H(\gamma, \beta)$ changes sign as β increases from 0. Therefore, by the intermediate-value theorem, for each γ there exists a $\beta \in (0, 1)$, say β^u (depending on γ), such that $H(\gamma, \beta^u) = 0$ or, equivalently, such that $\theta'(\tilde{k}) = -1$.

PROPOSITION 3. For each $\gamma > 0$ there exists $\beta^u \in (0, 1)$ (depending on γ) such that $\theta'(\tilde{k}) = -1$ and such that $\tilde{k}$ is unstable (stable) whenever $\beta < \beta^u (\beta > \beta^u)$.

Proposition 3 states that points in the region *below* the $H(\gamma, \beta)$ curve give rise to an *unstable* steady state; and points *above* to a *stable* one. Moreover, in general, the smaller the capital share in output, the more likely the system is to be unstable. As (49) is independent of the scale factor B, the Hicks neutral technological change has a 'neutral' impact on stability. Figure 10.8 depicts several curves using various combinations of values of γ and β such that (49) holds for given different values of n and δ.

To see how complex the picture is, consider points P and P' in the diagram. For a pair of values close to a point like P, a sufficiently larger value of γ would tend to stabilize the system and vice versa. But this effect is reversed for points close to a point like P'! One may note that such an effect-reversal phenomenon cannot happen when $(n + \delta)/(1 + n) > \frac{3}{5}$. In this case, there are situations where an arbitrarily small value of the future weight γ does not suffice to ensure a globally stable steady state, a result in contrast with the literature on optimal growth (e.g. Benhabib and Nishimura 1979).

When $\tilde{k}$ is unstable, of course, fluctuations are perpetuated. As we have already seen, these can be periodic, converging to periodic cycles, or non-periodic and non-covergent to any periodic behaviour. Indeed, the argument conducted for the general model can be extended to the

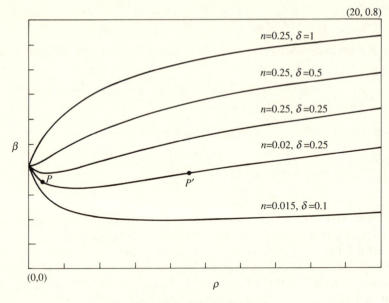

FIG. 10.8. Bifurcation loci

present case to obtain (for fixed n, δ) a sequence of functions, say $H^i(\gamma, \beta)$, $i = 2, \ldots$, giving loci of bifurcation points at which cycles of order 2, 4, $\ldots$ become unstable in the manner shown by one of us elsewhere for $n = 0$, $\delta = 0$ and capital non-fungible (Day 1969). Moreover, a function $H^e(\gamma, \beta)$ exists giving the locus of bifurcation points for γ and β below which fluctuations become ergodic. All of this requires some tedious calculations and is left to the ambitious reader to pursue further. The picture derived would be like that shown in Fig. 9(a).

It should be noticed that the selection of the values of parameters n and δ should be consistent with the length of period under consideration. They have something important to do with the likelihood of stability. Thus, Fig. 10.8 indicates that, other things being equal, the longer the time period and the larger n and δ are, the more likely it is that the system will display unstable behaviour.

An extensive bifurcation analysis of the model has been carried out in Lin et al. (forthcoming), which shows the emergence of cycles of ascending even and descending odd order and zones of 'thin' and 'thick' chaos. Also included is a discussion of behaviour for plausible parameter values. An example of these diagrams is shown in Fig. 10.9.

It is possible also to investigate the statistical dynamics; that is, the

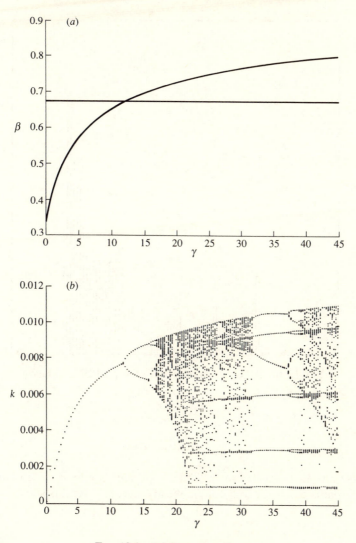

FIG. 10.9. A bifurcation diagram
(a) Stable–unstable parameter zones
(b) Bifurcation diagram along the line $\beta = 0.67$ in (a)

behaviour of the distribution of values of the endogenous variables as time passes and data accumulate. Under certain conditions (discussed in Day and Shafer 1986), numerical distribution histograms generated by the model converge to density functions which characterize the behaviour of the system 'in the long run'. An example is shown in Fig. 10.10.

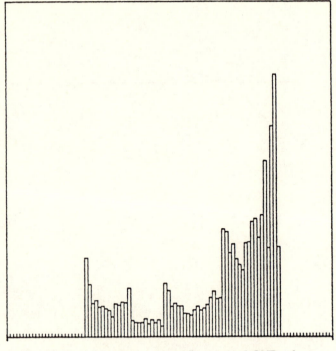

Fɪɢ. 10.10. A histogram of model-generated GNP values

9. Conclusions

In Section 3 it was observed that optimal competitive equilibrium growth paths converge to a unique steady state k^*. At this state,

$$f(k^*) - h^*(k^*) = (n + \delta)k^*$$

and

$$r^* = f'(k^*) = (1 + n)/\lambda - (1 - \delta)$$

(see Lin 1988: 8–11).

At a steady state of the adaptive neoclassical (ANC) model,

$$\tilde{r} = (1 + n)/\gamma + n + \delta.$$

Consequently, $\tilde{k} = k^*$ if and only if $r^* = \tilde{r}$; the implication is that the steady state of an ANC economy yields an intertemporally optimal growth path,

$$\gamma = \lambda/(1 - \lambda). \tag{50}$$

Off this path trajectories are suboptimal, but if the adaptive economy is stable, it converges to the optimal result. Then $h(k) \rightarrow h^*(k)$ as $k \rightarrow k^*$, and fluctuations can occur only if the economy is perturbed by exogenous shocks.

Setting aside infinite-horizon optimality, suppose that agents behave according to the recursive programming framework of the present model but that they possess perfect foresight; that is, they foresee r_{t+1} correctly at time t. Then it is easy to show that capital trajectories are monotonic and converge to $\tilde{k}$. If (50) holds, this value is the optimal steady state. Along such paths decisions are piecewise or temporarily optimal because expectations are fulfilled, but in general they are suboptimal from an intertemporal point of view because the choice at any time t is based on a single postulated consumption in perpetuity and not on a trajectory of consumption choices for each and every future period for ever (or, equivalently, on the optimal strategy $h^*(\cdot)$). In general, the Bellman equation will not be satisfied. Consequently, *in the adaptive theory* perfect foresight eliminates intrinsic fluctuations but does not guarantee optimality.

With perfect foresight, fluctuations could occur only in the presence of shocks. Without it they may or may not occur. If the economy is not stable, then each generation will continue to revise the sustainable consumption stream planned for its heirs, and an intrinsic real business cycle, possibly chaotic, will emerge, being driven by forecasting errors indefinitely.

Modelling fluctuations in the market economy using the theory of optimal growth has gradually come to dominate business cycle research. Certainly, it is a valid and interesting exercise to show, as various authors have done, that intertemporal equilibrium paths may oscillate in multi-sector models or in single-sector models if shocks are added. This does not mean, however, that such paths are good first approximations of empirical economic performance. Individuals, however intelligent, and nations, however well organized and planned, never calculate for an infinite horizon and cannot deduce optimal strategies for this complex world; forecasting is never perfect, nor are truly optimal strategies ever learned. Empirical evidence suggests that expectations might in fact be adaptive. Thus, the present model represents a small step in the direction of realism. That such a small step should open up a much wider range of possible behaviours, while still converging to the intertemporally optimal competitive equilibrium as a special case, seems to us to add much to its inherent interest and potential usefulness as a starting-point for further analysis. Whether it will restore a substantial scope for active counter-cyclical policy by the government is another question. Its answer would require an expansion of the model to incorporate monetary and fiscal instruments.

We agree that, if mistaken forecasts were easily correctable market imperfections, they would have been eliminated long ago. The fact that forecasting remains imperfect even with the advent of massive efforts to improve it demonstrates the point. Besides, why should we associate intertemporal disequilibrium with market imperfections anyway? The equilibrium business cycle school was motivated in part by a desire to remove the easily correctable market imperfections from the theory of cycles on grounds that rational agents would surely do so. But markets that do not exist cannot co-ordinate future behaviour. We should rather think of the market's primary role as facilitating decentralized exchange in disequilibrium, a function that radically lowers the social cost that would be incurred if exchanges out of equilibrium were outlawed, especially since an equilibrium might never come to pass. The results, of course, are non-optimal, but it is increasingly clear that they are still preferable to the centralized, non-market alternatives.

In closing, we observe that in econometric work it would be appropriate to add a shock term in the usual manner to account for all the variations in the data unexplained by the model. Then fluctuations would be caused by a mixture of intrinsic and extrinsic forces.

References

ANDO, A., and KENNICKELL, A. B. (1987). 'Life Cycle in Micro Data: United States and Japan'. In R. Dornbusch, S. Fischer, and J. Bossons (eds.), *Macroeconomics and Finance*. Cambridge, Mass.: MIT Press, pp. 159–223.

——and MODIGLIANI, F. (1963). 'The "Life Cycle" Hypothesis of Saving: Aggregate Implications and Tests'. *American Economic Review*, 53: 55–84.

BARRO, R. (1974). 'The Equilibrium Approach to Business Cycles'. In *Money, Expectations, and Business Cycles*. New York: Academic Press.

——(1989). *Modern Business Cycle Theory*. Cambridge, Mass.: Harvard University Press.

BAUMOL, WILLIAM J., and BENHABIB, JESS (1989). 'Chaos; Significance, Mechanism and Economic Applications'. *Journal of Economic Perspectives*, 3: 77–105.

BENHABIB, JESS, and DAY, RICHARD H. (1982). 'A Characterization of Erratic Dynamics in the Overlapping Generations Model'. *Journal of Economic Dynamics and Control*, 4: 37–55.

——and NISHIMURA, K. (1979). 'The Hopf-bifurcation and the Existence and Stability of Closed Orbits in Multisector Models of Optimal Economic Growth'. *Journal of Economic Theory*, 21: 412–21.

BERGMANN, BARBARA (1988). 'An Experiment on the Foundations of Expectations'. *Journal of Economic Behavior and Organization*, 9: 137–52.

BOLDRIN, MICHELE (1988). 'Persistent Oscillations and Chaos in Dynamic Economic Models: Notes for a Survey'. In P. Anderson, K. J. Arrow, and

D. Pines (eds.), *The Economy as an Evolving Complex System*. Reading, Mass.: Addison Wesley.

—— and MONTRUCCHIO, LUIGI (1986). 'Cyclic and Chaotic Behavior in Intertemporal Optimization Models'. *Mathematical Modelling*, 8: 627–700.

BUCCOLA, STEVEN T., and SMITH, VERNON (1987). 'Uncertainty and Partial Adjustment in Double Action Markets'. *Journal of Economic Behavior and Organization*, 8: 587–602.

DAY, RICHARD H. (1969). 'Flexible Utility and Myopic Expectations in Economic Growth'. *Oxford Economic Papers*, 21: 299–311.

—— (1982). 'Irregular Growth Cycles'. *American Economic Review*, 72: 406–14.

—— and SHAFER, WAYNE (1987). 'Ergodic Fluctuations in Deterministic Economic Models'. *Journal of Economic Behavior and Organization*, 8: 339–61.

DECHERT, W. D., and NISHIMURA, K. (1983). 'A Complete Characterization of Optimal Growth Paths in an Aggregated Model with a Non-concave Production Function'. *Journal of Economic Theory*, 31: 322–54.

FRIEDMAN, M. (1968). 'The Role of Monetary Policy'. *American Economic Review*, 58: 1–17.

GABISCH, GUENTER, and LORENZ, HANS-WALTER (1987). *Business Cycle Theory*. Berlin: Springer-Verlag.

GOODWIN, RICHARD (1982). *Essays in Economic Dynamics*. London: Macmillan.

GRANDMONT, J. M. (1987). *Nonlinear Economic Dynamics*. New York: Academic Press.

GUCKENHEIMER, J., and HOLMES, P. (1983). *Nonlinear Oscillations, Dynamical Systems and Bifurcation of Vector Fields*. New York: Springer-Verlag.

HARTL, R. F. (1987). 'A Simple Proof of the Monotonicity of the State Trajectories in Autonomous Control Problems'. *Journal of Economic Theory*, 41: 211–15.

HAYEK, F. A. (1933). *Monetary Theory and the Trade Cycle*. London: Jonathan Cape.

KOOPMANS, TJALLING C. (1964). 'On Flexibility of Future Preference'. In M. W. Shelley II and G. L. Bryan (eds.), *Human Judgements and Optimality*. Amsterdam: John Wiley. Also in *Scientific Papers of Tjalling C. Koopmans*, Berlin: Springer-Verlag, 1970, pp. 469–80.

—— (1965). 'On the Concept of Optimal Economic Growth'. In *The Econometric Approach to Development Planning*. Amsterdam: North Holland. Also in *Scientific Papers of Tjalling C. Koopmans*, Berlin: Springer-Verlag, 1970, pp. 485–519.

KYDLAND, F. E., and PRESCOTT, E. C. (1982). 'Time to Build and Aggregate Fluctuations'. *Econometrica*, 50: 1345–70.

LEONTIEF, WASSILY (1934). 'Verzögerte Angebotsanpassung und Partielles Gleichgewicht'. *Zeitschrift für Nationalökonomie*, 5: 670–6.

—— (1958). 'Theoretical Note on Time, Preference, Productivity of Capital, Stagnation and Economic Growth'. *American Economic Review*, 48: 105–11.

LIN, TZONG-YAU (1988). 'Studies of Economic Instability and Irregular Fluctuations in a One-Sector Real Growth Model'. Ph.D. dissertation, University of Southern California at Los Angeles.

—— TSE, RAYMOND, AND DAY, RICHARD H. (forthcoming). 'A Real Growth Cycle with Adaptive Expectations'. In Dimitri G. Papadimitrious (ed.),

Profits, Deficits and Instability. New York: Macmillan.

LUCAS, R. E. (1975). 'An Equilibrium Model of the Business Cycle'. *Journal of Political Economy*, 83: 1113–44.

—— (1977). 'Understanding Business Cycles'. In K. Brunner and A. H. Meltzer (eds.), *Stabilization and the Domestic and International Economy*. Amsterdam: North-Holland.

LUNDBERG, ERIK (1968). *Instability and Economic Growth*. New Haven, Conn.: Yale University Press.

MCCALLUM, BENNETT T. (1986). 'On "Real" and "Sticky-Price" Thunen of the Business Cycle'. *Journal of Money, Credit, and Banking*, 18: 397–414.

—— (1989). 'Real Business Cycle Models'. In Robert J. Barro (ed.), *Modern Business Cycle Theory*. Cambridge, Mass.: Harvard University Press.

MEDIO, ALFREDO (ed.) (1987). *Advances in the Analysis of Economic Dynamic Systems. Journal of Economic Behavior and Organization*, special issue, 8/3: 332–540. Amsterdam: North-Holland.

MODIGLIANI, F. (1987). 'Life Cycle, Individual Thrift, and the Wealth of Nations', Nobel Lecture 1985. In R. Dornbusch, S. Fischer, and J. Bossons (eds.), *Macroeconomics and Finance*. Cambridge, Mass.: MIT Press, pp. 1–28.

SAMUELSON, P. A. (1942). 'The Stability of Equilibrium: Linear and Nonlinear Systems'. *Econometrica*, 10: 1–25.

SARGEANT, THOMAS J. (1987). *Dynamic Macroeconomic Theory*. Cambridge, Mass.: Harvard University Press.

SCHINASI, G. J. (1982). 'Fluctuations in a Dynamic, Intermediate-Run *IS–LM* Model: Applications of the Poincaré–Bendixson Theorem'. *Journal of Economic Theory*, 28: 369–75.

SMITH, VERNON, SUCHAREK, GERRY and WILLIAMS, ARLINGTON, (1988). 'Bubbles, Crashes and Endogenous Expectation in Experimental Spot Asset Markets'. *Econometrica,* 56: 1119–51.

SOLOW, ROBERT M. (1956). 'Comments'. In R. Dornbusch, S. Fischer, and J. Bossons (eds.), *Macroeconomics and Finance*. Cambridge, Mass.: MIT Press, pp. 224–8.

STERMAN, JOHN (1989). 'Deterministic Chaos in an Experimental Economic System'. *Journal of Economic Behavior and Organization*, 12: 1–32.

STOCKMAN, ALAN C. (1988). 'Real Business Cycle Theory: A Guide, and Evaluation and New Directions'. *Economic Review*, 24: 24–47.

STOKEY, NANCY L., and LUCAS, ROBERT E. JUN. (1989). *Recursive Methods in Economic Dynamics*. Cambridge, Mass.: Harvard University Press.

WILLIAMS, ARLINGTON (1986). 'The Formations of Price Forecasts in Experimental Markets'. *Journal of Money, Credit, and Banking*, 19: 1–18.

PART IV

Wage Determination and Inflation

11

Synchronized Wage Determination and Macroeconomic Performance in Seven Large Countries

JOHN B. TAYLOR

1. Introduction

Wage responsiveness to supply and demand conditions differs substantially among different countries. For example, wages are considerably more responsive to labour demand and labour supply in Japan than in the USA, Canada, or European countries. This high responsiveness, along with a stable monetary policy that reacts promptly to changes in inflation, is one of the explanations for the more stable macroeconomic performance in Japan since the early 1970s compared with the USA or Europe (see Suzuki 1988).

An important empirical question for both macroeconomics and labour economics is whether these differences can be traced to differences in the degree of synchronization of wage decisions. High wage response in Japan is due to the Japanese Shunto system, in which many workers' wages are adjusted in synchronization in the spring or early summer of each year, or to other factors such as the bonus system, under which a large component (as much as 20–30 per cent) of earnings takes the form of a special bonus payment over and above the contracted money-wage rate. In theory, either of these factors could make money wages relatively more responsive to demand conditions in Japan than in other countries.

This paper was presented at the conference, 'Corporations and Labor Relations: An International Comparison', at the Ministry of International Trade and Industry, Tokyo, Japan, 9 January 1989. This research is supported by a grant from the National Science Foundation at the National Bureau of Economic Research and by the Center for Economic Policy Research at Stanford University. The research is part of a multicountry modelling project conducted at Stanford University. I am grateful to Andrew Levin for excellent research assistance on this project and in particular for formulating the modification of the staggered wage setting model to incorporate synchronization and for writing the computer programs that estimate these equations.

Synchronization of wage determination through the Japanese Shunto system tends to eliminate the overlapping or staggering of wage contracts, which can lead to relatively slow adjustment of the average money wage in a decentralized economy. Overlapping wage contracting is an especially important feature of US labour markets, but is also prevalent in France, Germany, Italy, and the UK. Hence synchronized wage-setting is a logical candidate for explaining relatively high wage responsiveness in Japan.

Bonus payments, if they are keyed to profits or sales, permit actual wage payments to adjust quickly to changes in the state of the economy. If profits drop off in a cyclical contraction, then money wages will automatically fall or at least will not increase as quickly as stated in the wage contracts. Bonus payments are not as large a share of earnings on average in the USA or Europe as in Japan. Hence the bonus system is another candidate for explaining the relatively high wage responsiveness in Japan. While, in theory, either synchronized wage-setting or the bonus system can explain the relatively high responsiveness of wages in Japan, the empirical significance of each has only recently begun to be studied. In one recent study (Taylor 1989), I examined the empirical significance of the bonus system and concluded that the empirical role of the bonus payments in increasing nominal wage flexibility for the Japanese economy as a whole is quite small. In practice, the bonus payments do not vary much as a fraction of total earnings in the Japanese economy, and the variation that does occur is only weakly related to the state of aggregate demand. More specifically, using simple regression techniques and aggregate wage data with and without the bonus and/or overtime payments, I concluded that the bonus system increases the degree of aggregate nominal wage flexibility in Japan by only about 20 per cent: from about five to six times that of the USA. In other words, even without the bonus system, nominal wages would be much more flexible in Japan than in the USA.

The purpose of this chapter is to examine the empirical significance of synchronized wage determination as a source of the difference in wage flexibility in different countries. I estimate empirical wage equations for Japan, the USA, Canada, France, Germany, Italy, and the UK. A novelty of these equations is that the degree of synchronization in Japan is taken into account according to a particular algebraic specification. The equations are fitted to quarterly data for the period 1972–86. By comparing the equations in the different countries, I endeavour to determine the empirical importance of synchronized wage determination for wage flexibility in Japan. The results indicate that synchronization does significantly affect the behaviour of aggregate wages in Japan compared with the other countries. Somewhat surprisingly, however, there are significant differences between the wage responsiveness in

Japan and that of the other countries which the synchronization *per se*, at least as modelled here, does not explain.

Most of the paper is devoted to explaining the model and the estimation results. In the next section I introduce the wage determination equations and explain how the degree of synchronization and its importance for aggregate nominal wage change can be estimated. I then report the estimates and discuss their implications.

2. Wage Determination Models in the Synchronized and Non-synchronized Cases

The starting point for wage determination in this paper is the staggered wage-setting model used in Taylor (1980). In the standard, non-synchronized version of this 1980 model, only a small fraction of workers have their contract wage rate changed in a given time period. The contract wage is assumed to be set to equal the expected average wage in the economy during the upcoming four quarters, plus an amount that depends on expected excess demand in the economy as measured by the deviations of actual GNP from trend GNP during the next four quarters. The crucial parameter to estimate in the model is the sensitivity of the wages to this future excess demand term.

In my 1980 paper, I made the simple theoretical assumption that 25 per cent of workers change wages each quarter with the wage being set for one year. This assumption seemed to work well as an approximation, in that certain general features of the dynamic behaviour of wages in the USA could be explained by the model. However, for detailed empirical work, whether wage-setting is synchronized or not, one needs to go beyond this simple approximation.

2.1. *Non-synchronized wage-setting with different contract lengths*

In the more general, but still non-synchronized, version of the model, not all workers are working under contracts that last the same number of quarters. The 'contract' wage is determined according to the following equations:

$$x_{it} = \pi_{i0} E w_{it} + \pi_{i1} E w_{it+1} + \pi_{i2} E w_{it+2} + \pi_{i3} E w_{it+3}$$
$$+ \alpha_i (\pi_{i0} E y_{it} + \pi_{i1} E y_{it+1} + \pi_{i2} E y_{it+2} + \pi_{i3} E y_{it+3}) + v_{it},$$

$$(1)$$

where x_i is the log of the contract wage in country i, w_i is the log of the average wage in country i, y_i is the output gap in country i, and v_i is a serially uncorrelated disturbance. The symbol E refers to the conditional expectations operator based on information through time t. All countries except Japan are assumed to have non-synchronized wage-setting, so the subscript represents either the USA, Canada, France, Germany, Italy, or the UK. (The synchronized case is considered below.) The aggregate wage is given by the equation

$$w_{it} = \pi_{i0}x_{it} + \pi_{i1}x_{it-1} + \pi_{i2}x_{it-2} + \pi_{i3}x_{it-3}. \qquad (2)$$

In previous empirical work (Taylor 1979), I estimated equations (1) and (2) using full-information maximum likelihood as part of a small but complete linear closed-economy model of the USA. A simpler approach is taken here.[1] An alternative scaled-down full-information method is used in which a simple autoregressive model describes the relationship between wages and demand—the 'aggregate demand' equation—as implied by the rest of the model. In other words, rather than estimate an entire aggregate demand model, a reduced-form relation between wages and output is estimated. In this reduced form, real GNP as a deviation from trend is assumed to depend on its own two lags and on the deviation of the average wage from a linear trend during the sample period 1973 (1)–1986 (4). (A break in the trend is also permitted, as described below.) Several variations on this same autoregressive equation were tried. The final 'aggregate demand' equation was

$$y_{it} = \beta_1 y_{it-1} + \beta_2 y_{it-2} + \beta_3 w_{it-1} + u_{it}, \qquad (3)$$

where u is a serially uncorrelated disturbance. The parameters of this equation were estimated jointly with (1) and (2) using maximum likelihood and observations on the average wage w in each country and the level of the output gap y in each country.[2] Because the initial values of the contract wages are unobservable and figure into the calculation of

---

[1] An even simpler approach—the instrumental variable approach, whereby the four future expected wages and four future output terms are replaced by their actual values and two-stage least-squares or Hansen's GMM estimator is applied—turned out to give values for the sensitivity parameter that were the wrong sign. In other words, high expected future output would lead to lower wages, a property that neither makes economic sense nor is compatible with the model being stable. Timing of expectations in the staggered wage-setting model is important for the implied behaviour of wages. Effectively, average wages today depend on expected past, current, and future wages, with a whole term structure of viewpoint dates. Replacing the expected values with their actuals—as in the Hansen method—ignores these different viewpoint dates, and it is likely that this is the source of the problem with these limited information methods as applied to this model.

[2] Evaluation of the likelihood function is straightforward once the model is solved. For the estimates reported in this paper, the model was solved by the extended path method of Fair and Taylor (1983).

the likelihood function, these values were estimated along with the other coefficients.

2.2. *Interpreting the estimated π-coefficients*

As described above, in the simple staggered-contract model of Taylor (1980), the π-parameters were set to equal 0.25 with the interpretation that 25 per cent of all workers sign contracts each quarter and that each contract lasts four quarters. We now must consider the interpretation of these parameters in the more general case. We seek an interpretation in terms of the distribution of workers by different lengths of contracts. This interpretation is also used when we consider synchronized contracting. Let

x_{jt} = average contract wage set in quarter t in contracts that are j quarters in length ($j = 1, \ldots, J$)

n_{jt} = number of workers affected by contract wage changes in quarter t in contracts that are j quarters in length ($j = 1, \ldots, J$)

f_{jt} = fraction of workers in quarter t affected by contract wage changes in quarter t in contracts that are j quarters in length ($j = 1, \ldots, J$)

a_{jt} = fraction of workers in the labour force in quarter t who have contracts of length j ($j = 1, \ldots, J$)

w_t = average wage in the economy in quarter t.

Then, by definition of f_{jt}, a_{jt}, and w_t, we have

$$f_{jt} = \frac{n_{jt}}{\sum\limits_{j=1}^{J} n_{jt}} \tag{4}$$

$$a_{jt} = \frac{\sum\limits_{s=0}^{j-1} n_{jt-s}}{\sum\limits_{j=1}^{J} \sum\limits_{s=0}^{j-1} n_{jt-s}} \tag{5}$$

$$w_t = \frac{\sum\limits_{j=1}^{J} \sum\limits_{s=0}^{j-1} n_{jt-s} x_{jt-s}}{\sum\limits_{j=1}^{J} \sum\limits_{s=0}^{j-1} n_{jt-s}} \tag{6}$$

If the distribution of workers by contract length is homogeneous over time ($n_{jt} = n_j$), and if the variation of average contract wages over contracts of different length is negligible ($x_{jt} = x_t$), then (6) reduces to

$$w_t = \frac{\sum\limits_{j=1}^{J} \sum\limits_{s=0}^{j-1} n_j x_{t-s}}{\sum\limits_{j=1}^{J} \sum\limits_{s=0}^{j-1} n_j}$$

$$= \frac{\sum\limits_{s=0}^{J-1} \sum\limits_{j=s+1}^{J} n_j x_{t-s}}{\sum\limits_{j=1}^{J} j n_j}$$

$$= \sum\limits_{s=0}^{J-1} \pi_s x_{t-s}, \tag{7}$$

where the π_s are defined as

$$\pi_s = \left(\sum\limits_{j=s}^{J-1} n_{j+1} \right) \left(\sum\limits_{j=1}^{J} j n_j \right)^{-1} \tag{8}$$

Note that the π-weights sum to 1 and are time-invariant. Hence the aggregate wage w_t is a fixed-coefficient moving average of the 'index' of contract wages x_t set in the recent past. The π-weights can also be written in terms of the $a_{jt} = a_j$. For example, when $J = 4$,

$$\pi_0 = a_1 + a_2/2 + a_3/3 + a_4/4 \tag{9}$$

$$\pi_1 = a_2/2 + a_3/3 + a_4/4 \tag{10}$$

$$\pi_2 = a_3/3 + a_4/4 \tag{11}$$

$$\pi_3 = a_4/4. \tag{12}$$

Some examples are useful for illustrating how the π-weights depend on the distribution of workers across contracts of different lengths. If all contracts are the same length, say four quarters, then $n_1 = n_2 = n_3 = 0$, and $\pi_0 = \pi_1 = \pi_2 = \pi_3 = 0.25$. This is the type of contract distribution used in the theoretical examination of staggered contracts presented in Taylor (1980). If the distribution of workers across contracts of different lengths in a given quarter is uniform up to four-quarter contracts, then $n_1 = n_2 = n_3 = n_4$ and the π-weights decline linearly: $\pi_0 = 0.4$, $\pi_1 = 0.3$, $\pi_2 = 0.2$, and $\pi_3 = 0.1$. Note that the distribution of workers across contracts can be recovered from the π-weights through the identities.

$$(\pi_{i-1} - \pi_i)\pi_0^{-1} = f_i, \qquad i = 1, 2, \ldots, J, \qquad (\pi_J = 0), \tag{13}$$

$$(\pi_{i-1} - \pi_i)i = a_i, \qquad i = 1, 2, \ldots, J \qquad (\pi_J = 0). \tag{14}$$

The π-weights, and hence this distribution of workers, are part of the economic structure to be estimated. In the estimation we can use assumptions about the a_i to impose constraints on the π_i. For example, we must have that $a_i > 0$ and that the a_i sum to 1. In addition, we impose $a_3 = 0$, which implies that $\pi_2 = \pi_3$. In other words, we assume that there are no three-quarter contracts.

Equation (7) describes how the aggregate wage w_t evolves from the index of contract wages x_t. Since the contracts that constitute this index will prevail for several quarters, workers and firms negotiating a contract wage will be concerned with the labour market conditions expected to prevail during the upcoming contract period. For example, those setting two-quarter contracts will be concerned with the going wage and the availability of workers during the next two quarters, while those setting four-quarter contracts must forecast these variables four quarters ahead. Moreover, in the process of forecasting future wages, these firms and workers will take account of contracts negotiated in the recent past since these will be part of the relative wage structure during part of the contract period. Equation (1) is thus a behavioural equation for the determination of the contract wage index which takes account of these factors.[3]

2.3. Synchronized wage-setting

The parameter a_{4t} measures the fraction of workers who sign contracts four quarters in length (annual contracts). If all contracts are annual, and if there is complete synchronization of annual wage contracts with all wage changes occurring in the second quarter, then $a_{1t} = a_{2t} = a_{3t} = 0$ and a_{4t} would equal 1 in the second quarter of each year and 0 in the other three quarters. According to equations (9)–(12), this would imply that the π-weights would have a seasonal pattern: in the second quarter of each year π_0 would equal 1 and $\pi_1 = \pi_2 = \pi_3 = 0$, implying that $w_t = x_t$ in the second quarter when the wage is changed. In the third quarter, then, $w_t = x_{t-1}$, so that $\pi_1 = 1$ with the other π-weights equal to 0. In the fourth quarter $w_t = x_{t-2}$, so that $\pi_2 = 1$ with the π-weights equal to 0, and in the first quarter $w_t = x_{t-3}$ so that $\pi_3 = 1$.

The contract wages determination equations would have a similar seasonal pattern. In the second quarter the contract wage $x_t = Ew_t + \alpha Ey_t$, which implies that $Ey_t = 0$. Wages would adjust in the second quarter so that excess demand, as measured by the output gap y_t, would be expected to be 0. In this sense, full synchronization would reduce the business cycle persistence of output fluctuations: in the second quarter of each year, real output would bounce back to the full-employment level.

---

[3] An alternative wage contracting equation can be derived in which the weights on the future wages and output levels are not the same as the π-weights.

Of course, even in the Japanese economy not all workers have wage adjustments in the second quarter. Some of the annual wage changes in the Shunto system occur in the summer quarter, and not all annual wage contracts are adjusted as part of the Shunto. Moreover, wages for some workers would change more frequently than once per year. Since the main purpose of this paper is to estimate the importance of the actual Shunto, a more general specification is required.

To allow for these possibilities, I estimate a seasonal pattern for the a_{4t} in Japan. Moreover, I do not impose the assumption that $a_1 = a_2 = 0$, although these fractions are assumed to be fixed constants in each quarter. As with the non-synchronized wage equations in the other countries, I assume that there are no three-quarter contracts $(a_3 = 0)$. The π-weights are then given by

$$\pi_{0i} = a_1 + a_2/2 + a_{4i-3}$$

$$\pi_{1i} = a_2/2 + a_{4i}$$

$$\pi_{2i} = a_{4i-1}$$

$$\pi_{3i} = a_{4i-2},$$

where the index i runs from the first quarter to the fourth quarter and a_{4i} has a seasonal pattern.

The π-weights are estimated with data on average contracted wages in Japan, excluding the bonus payments. (Overtime is included in the wage measure, but this is a fairly small percentage on average.) If the Shunto is an important element in the overall Japanese economy, then we would expect to estimate a value for a_{42} that is high (though not as high as 1) and a relatively low value for the other coefficients.

3. The Estimation Results

The estimation results for the synchronized case for Japan and the non-synchronized case for the other countries (USA, Canada, France, Germany, Italy, and UK) are tabulated in a compact form in Tables 11.1, 11.2, and 11.3. Table 11.1 reports the estimates of equations (1) and (2) along with the distribution of workers by contract length; Table 11.2 reports the results for the synchronized estimates in Japan; and Table 11.3 reports the results for the aggregate demand equation (3).

The maximum-likelihood approach gives generally sensible results for wage distributions in all the countries. The equations fit the data well, with relatively small standard errors and little serial correlation of the disturbances. However, for France, Italy, and the UK the fully uncon-strained maximum-likelihood estimates resulted in weights on the con-tract wages that declined very rapidly. For these three countries I chose

TABLE 11.1. *Estimated coefficients of wage equations (1) and (2)*

	USA	Canada	France	Germany	Italy	Japan	UK
α	0.0298	0.0541	0.0368	0.0393	0.1084	0.2965	0.0528
	(0.011)	(0.043)	(0.012)	(0.025)	(0.091)	(0.111)	(0.031)
π(0)	0.3270	0.4499	0.5117	0.5024	0.4991	*	0.5272
π(1)	0.2744	0.3173	0.2883	0.2892	0.3009	*	0.2728
	(0.015)	(0.033)	(0.024)	(0.029)	(0.028)		(0.029)
π(2)	0.1993	0.1164	0.1000	0.1042	0.1000	*	0.1000
	(0.013)	(0.045)		(0.045)			
π(3)	0.1993	0.1164	0.1000	0.1042	0.1000	*	0.1000
% annual	79.7	46.6	40.0	41.7	40.0	87.5	40.0
% semi-annual	15.0	40.2	37.7	37.0	40.2	0.7	34.6
% quarter	5.3	13.3	22.4	21.3	19.8	11.8	25.4
s.e.	0.0027	0.0091	0.0083	0.0061	0.0167	0.0157	0.0159
D–W	1.3	1.9	1.7	2.1	1.9	1.9	1.9
Sample	71.4	76.4	71.4	71.4	71.4	71.4	71.4
	86.4	86.4	86.2	86.3	86.3	86.3	Target
Shift	83.1	82.4	81.3	77.3	82.3	76.3	81.2
Initial conditions							
x(−1)	−0.4541	−0.4684	−1.2406	−0.7687	−1.3675	−0.8793	−1.3188
x(−2)	−0.4031	−0.3628	−1.2491	−0.5475	−1.6123	−1.1033	−1.3935
x(−3)	−0.3821	−0.2811	−1.1870	−0.6528	−1.7719	−1.0157	−1.3128

*Japanese estimates of π by quarter allowing for synchronization are shown in Table 11.2.

John B. Taylor

TABLE 11.2. *Estimated coefficients for Japan*

	Quarter			
	1	2	3	4
$\pi(0)$	0.1533	0.5414	0.3857	0.2815
$\pi(1)$	0.1633	0.0351	0.4232	0.2675
$\pi(2)$	0.2638	0.1597	0.0314	0.4196
$\pi(3)$	0.4196	0.2638	0.1597	0.0314
% of workers in quarter (a_{4i})	3	42	26	16

Notes to Tables 11.1 and 11.2

All equations were estimated with maximum likelihood. In France, Italy, and the UK the number of annual contracts were constrained to equal 40%, which is not significantly different from the unconstrained likelihood for these countries. The target shift is the quarter in which it is assumed that the central banks reduce their 'target' for wage inflation. Standard errors of the estimated coefficients are shown in parentheses. Using the formula that relates the percentage of contracts to the weights, the standard error of the estimated percentage annual contracts can be calculated. These are 5.2 percentage points for the USA, 18.2 percentage points for Canada, and 16.6 percentage points for Germany.

TABLE 11.3. *Estimated coefficients of the aggregate demand equation*

	USA	Canada	France	Germany	Italy	Japan	UK
$y(-1)$	1.24	1.14	1.26	0.64	0.96	1.05	0.80
$y(-2)$	−0.40	−0.33	−0.33	0.13	−0.14	−0.25	−0.02
$w(-1)$	−0.20	−0.17	−0.03	−0.30	−0.05	−0.06	−0.05

Note: These coefficients were estimated simultaneously with the coefficients of equations (1) and (2) using a maximum-likelihood technique described in the text.

a contract wage distribution close to that of the other European country (Germany) which is not statistically different from the maximum-likelihood estimate. This distribution entails 40 per cent annual contracts in France, Italy and the UK. With this exception, all the other estimates in the tables are the maximum-likelihood estimates.

Note that for all the countries the aggregate demand equations have a negative coefficient on the average wage. The coefficient is relatively large in the USA, Canada, and Germany and relatively small in France, Italy, Japan, and the UK. This negative coefficient is important, for it ensures that the model is stable. It corresponds to the aggregate demand curve (with the nominal wage rather than the price on the vertical axis) being downward-sloping: when the nominal wage rises, real output falls. This negative effect is influenced by monetary policy and reflects how accommodating the central bank is to inflation. High absolute values of this coefficient represent less accommodating policies.

In interpreting these aggregate demand equations, it is important to note that the implicit target rate of wage inflation is assumed to have shifted down in the late 1970s or early 1980s. The exact year is shown in Table 11.1. In other words, after the shift in the target rate of wage inflation, the central banks are assumed to have been willing to tolerate less inflation. According to the estimates in this table, Japan was the first of the seven countries to shift down its inflation target.

Focusing first on Japan, the estimates indicate that aggregate wages behave as if roughly 88 per cent of wage contracts in Japan are annual, 12 per cent are adjusted every quarter, and a negligible amount are adjusted every two quarters. The effect of the Shunto shows up clearly in the seasonal π-coefficients, which have the same general form as in the extreme case where all contracts are adjusted in the spring quarter. However, because some workers have more frequent wage adjustments, and because not all annual wage adjustments occur in the spring quarter, the coefficients do not have the exact 0–1 pattern. According to these estimates, aggregate wages in Japan adjust as if 42 per cent of workers have their wages changed in the spring quarter, 26 per cent in the summer quarter, 16 per cent in the autumn quarter, and 3 per cent in the winter quarter. This general pattern is what one would expect from the Shunto system.

Now compare these estimates with those in the other countries. Here it is assumed that wage-setting is non-synchronized so that the coefficients do not have a seasonal pattern. The coefficients for the other countries indicate that annual contracts are the most common length of contract. Wages in the USA behave as if about 80 per cent of workers have annual contracts; the fraction is smaller in Canada and Germany. Although some wage contracts, especially in the USA, Canada, and Italy, extend for more than one year, indexing in these longer contracts usually calls for adjustment in the second and third years.

4. The Importance of Synchronization for Wage Responsiveness in Japan

Overall, the results support the view that the Shunto system is an important part of aggregate wage behaviour in Japan. The significant seasonal pattern in the estimated parameters has a plausible interpretation in terms of the Shunto: most (88 per cent) workers have annual wage adjustments, and about half of these (or 42 per cent of all workers) have their wage adjustments in the second quarter during the spring. About 77 per cent of workers who have their wages adjusted annually receive the adjustments in the spring or summer quarters.

The analysis in Section 3 shows that such synchronization would make aggregate wages appear more flexible, in the sense that the aggregate wage would quickly adjust to eliminate excess demand or supply, and that cyclical fluctuations would be short-lived. This greater aggregate wage flexibility with synchronization compared with non-synchronization would occur even if the adjustment parameter α were the same.

However, it is important to note that the adjustment parameter is not the same in the different countries. In particular, the adjustment coefficient in Japan is much greater than in the other countries. As shown in the first row of Table 11.1, the Japanese coefficient is about six times greater than the average adjustment coefficient in the other countries. In other words, even if the estimated equations showed no synchronization effects in Japan, the individual contract wages would adjust more quickly than in other countries. It appears, therefore, that a significant part of the high aggregate wage responsiveness in Japan is not due to synchronization *per se*, as described in Section 2 above. Some other factor must be at work. As mentioned previously, the bonus payments do not appear to be responsive enough to make the difference.

Perhaps the most likely possibility is that the Shunto bargaining process itself makes the individual contract wage adjustments more responsive to demand and supply conditions. As part of the annual discussions between unions, firms, and the government, the rationale for wage changes, given alternative forecasts for the aggregate economy, could lead to a more flexible wage adjustment process.

5. Concluding Remarks

The purpose of this paper is to assess the role of synchronized wage-setting in explaining differences in wage flexibility in different countries. Using a new technique for estimating the effects of such synchronization with aggregate nominal wage data, the importance of synchronization in Japan compared with six other large industrialized economies clearly emerges. This synchronization would tend to make aggregate wages more flexible by eliminating much of the slow adjustment of average money wages resulting from overlapping contracts.

However, the synchronization effects leave much of the difference between aggregate nominal wage flexibility in Japan and other countries unexplained. Although the empirical results reported here are not decisive on other plausible explanations, one hypothesis is that the annual discussions surrounding the Shunto process itself lead to greater wage flexibility in Japan. Testing the validity of this hypothesis is an important task for future research.

Appendix: Data Sources for Aggregate Wage Data

USA	Hourly earning index, adjusted for overtime and inter-industry shifts CITIBASE, SA; base year = 1980
Canada	Hourly earnings in manufacturing OECD MEI, SA; base year = 1980
France	Hourly wage rates in manufacturing OECD MEI; base year = 1980
Germany	Hourly earnings index, all industries IMF IFS, NSA; base year = 1980. Seasonally adjusted using TSP
Italy	Hourly wage rates, all industries OECD MEI; base year = 1980. Pre-1983 data adjusted from manufacturing
Japan	Monthly contractual cash earnings, all industries IMF IFS, NSA; base year = 1980
UK	Average monthly earnings, all industries IMF IFS, SA; base year = 1980

Abbreviations

CITIBASE	Citibase Data Tape
IMF IFS	International Monetary Fund, International Financial Statistics
NSA	not seasonally adjusted
OECD MEI	Organization for Economic Co-operation and Development, Main Economic Indicators
SA	seasonally adjusted

References

FAIR, RAY, and TAYLOR, JOHN B. (1983). 'Solution and Maximum Likelihood Estimation of Dynamic Nonlinear Rational Expectations Models'. *Econo-*

metrica, 51: 1169–85.

SUZUKI, YOSHIO (1988). 'Japanese Monetary Policy under the Floating Exchange Rate Regime'. Conference on Japanese Financial Growth, 3–4 October, London.

TAYLOR, JOHN B. (1979). 'An Econometric Business Cycle Model with Rational Expectations: Some Estimation Results'. Unpublished paper.

—— (1980). 'Aggregate Dynamics and Staggered Contracts'. *Journal of Political Economy*, 88: 1–23.

—— (1989). 'Differences in Economic Fluctuations in Japan and the US: The Role of Nominal Rigidities'. *Journal of the Japanese and the International Economies*, 3: 127–44.

12

Notes on Very High Inflation and Stabilization

DANIEL HEYMANN

1. Introduction

Episodes of very high inflation are of interest for two reasons. First, from a practical viewpoint, they pose an immediate and serious policy problem: in the limit, controlling the inflationary process becomes a necessary condition for the economy to function at all. As a matter of fact, very high inflations (at annual rates of four digits, say) have been short-lived and in general have ended abruptly. Discussions of the subject have concentrated mainly on this transition, and on the policy design that may bring it about at an acceptable cost. This is indeed an important matter. But also, there remains the question of how to sustain a durable stabilization: recent experiences suggest that this can be as difficult, or more so, as producing a sharp, transitory disinflation.

Second, observations drawn from cases of extreme nominal instability can offer insights of a more general type. Part of the still active debate on expectations and their effect on price behaviour has been based on the stabilization of very high inflations. Equally interesting, but less studied, is the way in which economies operate when subject to large inflationary disturbances—how contracts are rewritten, pricing and payments practices evolve, and the like. One can hope to find there some clues about the role of monetary institutions, the 'resilience' of markets, and the ability of agents to make decisions with unreliable information, which may show features of the economy that remain hidden under more tranquil conditions.

Clearly, this is a broad subject. The following notes do not attempt to deal with it in much detail or depth, but present some general remarks about how high inflations develop, what adaptations economies undergo in these processes, and how to go about the design of stabilization policies. Although the comments are more or less general, some of

A preliminary version of these notes was presented at the Workshop on Alternative Approaches to Macroeconomics, Siena, November 1987: this paper follows the original with only minor additions and revisions.

them, for reasons of comparative advantage, are based on the Argentine experience.

2. The Development of High Inflation Processes

Economic behaviour varies noticeably depending on the degree of price instability, which can generally be proxied by the rate of inflation. Under price stability or moderate inflation, money performs most of its traditional 'functions'; at the other extreme, in hyperinflations, nominal assets—if they are at all in demand—have maturities of a few days; many prices become 'dollarized' (i.e. they are set with reference to a standard like the price of foreign currencies), and sometimes other assets are substituted for the domestic money as a means of payment in some transactions. In an intermediate range of 'high inflation', money still functions as a unit of account for everyday trade, but the maturity of nominal contracts is very short; although indexing and 'dollarization' develop, long-run markets shrink and sometimes disappear.

One of the most characteristic features of monetary instability is the shortening of planning horizons. This is reflected even in the way in which agents consider price measurements. In moderate inflations the rate of price growth is usually reported on an 'annual basis', but a 12-month span does not seem relevant for individuals in a high-inflation situation, where decisions are rapidly modified each time a new monthly observation of the price indices is available: in actual hyperinflations, monthly data are just a matter of statistical record, since prices and decisions in general are revised with much greater frequency.

We will refer here to a heterogeneous collection of episodes, including both 'high' and 'hyperinflations', that is, to cases ranging from inflation rates of 'only' 500 per cent per year (or near 15 per cent per month) to extremes where national currencies were close to being actually repudiated. In any event, these episodes have been relatively few, and bunched together in certain periods and groups of countries: the postwar big inflations and the Latin American and Israeli experiences in the 1980s are among the best-known examples.

This concentration of cases suggests the presence of some common element in the origin of such processes. Large government deficits are an obvious candidate for that role. Indeed, big inflations are generally associated with serious fiscal disorders, and often occur in countries in unsteady political conditions.

In the tradition initiated by Cagan (1956), monetary–fiscal models of high inflation start from a stable money demand function, where changes in the real interest rate are regarded as negligible in comparison with the movements in expected inflation and real income is considered exogenous. The price level is then derived by 'inverting' the portfolio balance condition, as a function of the money stock and expected inflation. In addition, it is generally assumed that, given the limited market for public debt typical of high-inflation economies, fiscal deficits are fully monetized. Thus, the money supply is driven by fiscal requirements: the central bank's role would be limited to creating money at a rate such that the real value of new currency issues equals the given gap between government spending and taxes. Inflation, then, would have a purely fiscal origin: its rate would depend on the size of the deficit and on price expectations, which influence the volume (and the rate of change) of real balances.

For many specifications of the money demand function, the size of the 'inflation tax' (i.e. the total value of the real depreciation of cash balances arising from inflation) has a maximum at a finite inflation rate. In those cases, if the deficit is positive but smaller than the maximum revenue of the inflation tax, there are two steady states where the government's budget constraint is satisfied at a constant inflation rate equal to expected inflation: in one equilibrium the inflation rate is (comparatively) low while real money demand is high, and in the 'bad' steady state it is the other way around. The dynamic stability of these equilibria has been much discussed in the literature (e.g. Bruno and Fischer 1985; Kiguel 1989): it turns out that the system's behaviour, starting from arbitrary initial conditions, depends on the way in which expectations are formed and on the existence (or not) of frictions in price adjustments or money demand.

Although some of these results are quite sensitive to the exact specification of the models,[1] they serve to point out that, in a strictly monetary–fiscal model, the rate of inflation depends crucially on the deficit, but is not uniquely determined by its value. The possibility that economies might get into 'high-inflation traps' has been raised in connection with the design of stabilization policies (Bruno 1985).

---

[1] This applies not only to the parameters of the model, but also to the precise way in which fiscal and monetary policies are represented. For example, in models with perfect foresight, where a given deficit is being monetized, the convergence to a 'high-inflation' steady state starting from arbitrary initial conditions between the two equilibria results from the fact that, in that region, the inflation tax revenue exceeds the given deficit: real money balances 'must' then fall to compensate for that excess. The stability properties can be different if it is assumed that the central bank is able to expand the money supply more rapidly than dictated by fiscal requirements. It may be noted, in addition, that alternative specifications of the money demand function can give rise to changes in the number of steady states: the usual Cagan function implies a monotonic decline in the inflation tax revenue at very high inflation rates, but this need not be the case with other functional forms. In fact, the behaviour of money demand near or in hyperinflation (i.e. for how long and to what extent the domestic money 'continues to hold' when it is heavily taxed) seems to remain an open question.

Monetary–fiscal theories clearly stress a central aspect of high-inflation processes. They do not, however, give a complete account of how prices are formed. A lively debate occurred in the 1920s between the fiscal explanation of the German inflation and the 'balance-of-payments' view. According to this second approach, the inflation resulted from an inconsistency of relative prices: the payment of reparations in foreign currencies implied a real devaluation, hence lower real wages; labour resistance to a reduction in real earnings meant that the relative price shift could take place only (if at all) at a very high inflation rate. In this view, the 'race' between wages and the exchange rate gave the monetary authorities no alternative but to validate the resulting inflation in a more or less passive way.

This early discussion (see e.g. Bresciani-Turroni 1937; Robinson 1938) bears some resemblance to more recent ones in Latin America. Authors who take a 'neo-structuralist' approach have stressed the influence of relative price changes on aggregate inflation when some prices (especially wages) are formed using backward-looking indexation rules:[2] in that case, upward movements in real flexprices, the exchange rate, or public-sector prices will produce permanent increases in the inflation rate (see e.g. Taylor 1983; Lopes 1984; Bresser and Nakano 1987). Contrary to the more traditional analysis, these authors regard inflation as an inertial phenomenon; changes in the price trend would be explained mostly by intersectoral shifts, while money and the fiscal deficit would have only a slight short-run effect on prices and, at most, an accommodative role.

Such theories are clearly incomplete, and can hardly provide a general interpretation of the various episodes of very high inflation, which show a large diversity regarding labour market institutions, the size of foreign trade disturbances, and the pattern of movements in relative prices. However, non-monetary modes of analysis serve to point to the lack of neutrality of inflationary processes and to features of price dynamics which do not come out in simple standard models.[3] Shocks to the balance of payments seem to have played an important role in the acceleration of inflation in Germany in the 1920s and, more recently, in Latin America after the debt crisis; indexation schemes are a usual

---

[2] The effects of indexing arrangements are discussed in Williamson (1985); see also Fischer (1986). Views differ regarding how strictly indexation rules are applied; for example, Frenkel (1984) presents evidence suggesting that, in the Argentine case, wage adjustments usually were linked to past price increases, except in the event of shocks that caused large, sudden shifts in the inflation rate.

[3] Even in models where the trend of the inflation rate is driven by the fiscal deficit, the short-run behaviour can depend very much on the features of price- and wage-setting. For instance, a permanent increase in the real prices changed by public enterprises, which may (through its fiscal effect) reduce the 'long-run' inflation, is likely to accelerate prices on impact (see Heymann and Canavese 1988).

characteristic of countries in high (but short of hyper-) inflation: they do cause inertia in price increases and propagate inflationary impulses.

On the other hand, fiscal deficits are not strictly exogenous. First, there are more or less mechanical effects: lags between tax assessment and payment make real revenues fall as the inflation rate rises (Olivera 1967; Tanzi 1977). In addition, price instability has other consequences on fiscal policies, since it greatly complicates the design of an enforceable budget and disturbs financial markets, thus reducing the demand for public debt.

However, it would be hard to argue that the crisis in government finances that is typical of high inflations is merely an endogenous response to rapidly rising prices. The question, then, is how and why deficits are driven to the point where they generate, or validate, very costly inflations. It is not generally the case that the fiscal troubles are taken lightly in high-inflation countries. In Germany, for example, one finds several instances of attempts to reform fiscal policies in the early 1920s—although they failed.[4] While, clearly, this experience does not necessarily extrapolate directly to other cases, the existence of political obstacles to a more or less consistent fiscal arrangement seems a quite general feature of very high-inflation episodes.

A growing literature analyses policy decisions as choices in a game between the authorities and private agents.[5] When applied to fiscal policies, this approach is useful in stressing that deficits are not just arbitrarily given, but result from a set of actions by individuals or groups acting with some purpose; it also serves to put into focus the role of institutions and of reputation effects, without which 'well-meaning' policies can easily be far from optimal.

However, optimizing, representative agent models do not appear to offer an accurate description of high inflations: the difficulties in doing away with the inflation tax do not come out clearly in a setting where the policy game is depicted as one between a single government agent, endowed with well defined preferences, facing a single private actor,

---

[4] See e.g. Maier (1975). In the 1920s, some French commentators (see Aglietta and Orléan 1982 for specific references) argued that the German hyperinflation was in a sense 'voluntary', and could be interpreted as a 'signal' to show the impossibility of making reparations transfer. German writers (e.g. Schacht 1927) strongly rejected that argument. In the Latin American case, there is no evidence that high inflation was 'engineered' in order to obtain relief on debt services. Yet, there is little doubt that the debt contributed much to increase government deficits and to accelerate inflation.

[5] See e.g. Kydland and Prescott (1977), Calvo (1978), Thompson (1981), Lucas and Stokey (1983), Barro and Gordon (1983a, b), Rogoff (1987), and Alesina and Tabellini (1987). Persson and Tabellini (1990) present a useful survey. Part of this literature models cases where it is assumed that policies are constrained by a short-run Phillips curve. However, it does not seem that high inflations are caused mainly by attempts to induce 'excessively high' levels of aggregate output. For this reason, the argument in the text concentrates on 'fiscal games'.

and where, consequently, all matters of income distribution within the private sector are ignored. Moreover, the picture of high inflations as equilibrium steady-state outcomes conflicts with some noticeable characteristics of those processes, such as the instability both of the rate of price growth and of economic policies. It does not look as if some countries choose once and for all to run high deficits by considering all the relevant costs: rather, those deficits seem to result from the play of a variety of pressures, which operate with different strengths at different moments. High inflations usually have quite eventful histories. In this connection, the analogy of inflation with a tax, while illuminating in some respects, is misleading in others. As has often been noted, inflation is a particularly flexible source of revenue, precisely because it is not explicitly legislated.[6] Inflation acts as a 'residual' way of financing expenditures, and governments rely on it especially when a predictable fiscal policy has not been defined. High inflation, then, would be a symptom not only of large deficits, but also of erratic policies and of the absence of systematic, more or less permanent, decisions on public spending and receipts. This observation suggests that high inflations are likely to happen in countries without well established fiscal institutions.

A common feature of high-inflation episodes, and also of hypers, is the importance of 'extraordinary' government expenditures: wars, reconstruction, reparations payments, or the servicing of a large foreign debt. It is not just a coincidence that, in Latin America, the debt crisis of the 1980s came together with a widespread acceleration of inflation throughout the region. Although by itself a large debt is not a necessary or sufficient condition for a fiscal crisis, it is without doubt a large contributing factor. Not only does it put direct pressure on government finances,[7] but it also makes it more difficult to define permanent policies (since the almost continuous debt negotiations create a high degree of uncertainty); and, given that 'belt tightening to pay the debt' is not usually a proposal that commands a great deal of support, it makes it harder to reach political agreement on the means to close the fiscal gap.

---

[6] Another common argument is that the inflation tax can be raised 'on the sly', because it is not perceived as clearly by those who pay it as a standard tax. It seems true that it may be difficult to attribute inflation to a given, well defined set of actions of the government or other agents ('repealing' the inflation tax is not equivalent to eliminating a given piece of legislation); however, it does not seem true that inflation is costless for the authorities. It is usually quite unpopular, and it is widely recognized that the burden of the inflation tax falls on low-income groups, who have a comparatively more difficult access to money substitutes.

[7] In some countries, much of what originally were private debts ended up as liabilities of the government, in a process that often implied large subsidies. This transfer, which occurred as a result of pressures from both the private debtors and the creditors, is probably one of the clearest examples of the ability of strong interest groups to extract concessions from the government in high-inflation economies.

Debt payments are one, particularly large, instance of the various claims that impinge on fiscal policies. But, of course, conflicting demands are not exclusive to unstable economies: everywhere, groups seek to get advantages for themselves. In order to have fiscal stability, there must be ways of making this conflict resolve into a consistent outcome, through some process that takes into account the costs and benefits ('political' as well as more narrowly economic) of alternative allocations.[8] Standard budget procedures are designed to do that. In principle, these procedures dictate that expenditures and receipts are to be decided in a comprehensive discussion that defines at the same time the value of individual items and that of the aggregate deficit; once the budget has been legislated, it is meant to function as a binding constraint on the actions that the executing authority might undertake. Such a procedure confronts groups with one another when they express their claims; it tends to reduce the costs of getting information about the demands of other groups, and of organizing possible coalitions among those that are likely to 'pay the bill' when a given set of agents receives a transfer. The legal status of the budget also makes it more difficult for groups to break an agreement by exerting direct pressure on the executive. Comprehensive budget negotiations do not seem to provide a recipe for a consistent fiscal policy, but they are likely to be very useful mechanisms for conducting the distributional game, since they make more or less transparent the burden that transfers to some agents impose on others (either through explicit taxation or through deficits), and they offer groups a relatively simple way to bargain so as to avoid outcomes with very large social costs.[9]

By the same token, in the absence of an enforced, explicit budget, groups are involved in a variety of bilateral negotiations with the fiscal authorities, which may themselves have their distributive bias. In this setting, groups have few incentives to limit their demands and apply all their strength to maximize the transfers in their favour of one type or another.[10] It is less likely that groups will enter into workable coalitions to oppose the transfers others receive if there are not institutionally

---

[8] Heymann et al. (1988) and Heymann and Navajas (1989a) present a discussion of this point in the context of the Argentine case.

[9] The specific way in which budget institutions are designed will of course influence the relative bargaining strength of different groups. The argument here emphasizes the ability (or lack of it) of budget mechanisms to deliver a consistent outcome (in particular, to avoid producing 'inefficiently high' deficits), rather than the precise distributional characteristics of that solution. Note, however, that a 'centralized' budget process is more likely to operate in the fashion described if the importance of off-budget items is relatively small; otherwise, deficits resulting from the legislative process lose relevance, which in turn affects the attitude of groups engaged in the bargaining.

[10] Budget constraints become 'soft', in Kornai's (1986) terminology.

defined forms to reduce the costs of expressing that opposition.[11] It is conceivable that government decisions may be taken in a way that internalizes the costs of financing a certain transfer. But, if fiscal policies are set by addressing bilaterally each specific claim, the pressure of groups goes in the same direction: they all try to increase the 'gross' transfers in their favour, without regard to the source of the funds. Under these conditions, the deficit can well be 'suboptimally' high; and it is also possible that, given the social costs of inflationary finance, most groups end up worse off after the game is played. For those in control of the government, the lack of a binding budget allows them some room to redistribute income according to their preferences, but it also makes unwelcome demands more difficult to refuse. When strong groups face the government one after the other, large deficits are particularly probable, regardless of the specific distributional objectives of the government. It may be significant, in this respect, that high inflations often take place during the decline of authoritarian regimes, or in new democracies that have not yet developed well functioning fiscal institutions.

Another common characteristic of high-inflation cases is the weakness of the tax systems, with a large number of taxes imposed on narrow bases (either by design, or because of widespread evasion) and taxes with high legislated rates but low effective revenues. Why, then, do some economies end up having tax systems that are highly distortionary while raising little revenue? One possibility is the existence of a 'technological' constraint (Aizenman 1985). This seems only a partial answer, since countries of very different degrees of development manage to finance the government without large deficits, while countries with similar real incomes can be quite diverse in the effectiveness of their tax organizations. It may be that distributive considerations also play a crucial part in determining whether an economy has or does not have an efficient tax 'machinery'.

Clearly, a general discussion of the conditions that make it possible to define and implement a given tax structure is well beyond the scope of these notes. It is conceivable, however, that in some circumstances distortionary taxes, particularly the inflation tax, face less opposition than a system with lower social costs. An efficient tax machinery can be a powerful instrument; some groups may strongly resist an effort to build such machinery (even if they realize that it may reduce the social costs of taxation) if they suspect that it could be used at some future

---

[11] The argument that the benefits of a given transfer are generally more concentrated than the costs is a common one. The suggestion here is that the dispersion of costs might be more or less important in determining the size of the transfers and of the overall deficit depending on the organization of the bargaining process that results in fiscal policies.

date to make large redistributions against them. Conversely, a tax system with high 'collection costs'[12] limits the size of possible redistributions. In this sense, tax systems can be expected to be less effective in economies where groups have enough power to block an improvement; and, at the same time, there is much uncertainty about the use that current or future governments would make of an efficient collection 'machinery' if they could choose according to their preferences. A workable tax reform that would dispense with the inflation tax would then require some sort of long-run agreement on the tax structure and on the order of magnitude of the rates that will be applied. But a settlement of this sort is not easily arranged.

It would seem, therefore, that the instability and disorder in fiscal policies characteristic of high-inflation economies derive in part from inflation itself, but in part from the play of various demands that the fiscal system is unable to reconcile consistently. Thus, the conditions that generate high inflations are likely to result in a quite unstable environment for economic decisions. As agents adapt to that environment, their economic behaviour changes in a number of ways that, in many cases, are unrelated to the high expected real cost of holding money balances.

3. Adaptations to Very High Inflation

It is often difficult to discriminate between the effects of erratic nominal prices *per se* and those of the 'real' instability that usually accompanies high inflation. If, in particular, the fiscal regime is such that both the aggregate deficit and the composition of government expenditures and receipts are very variable and relative prices are volatile, this creates both the potential for a high and unsteady inflation and uncertainty about future trading opportunities. Thus, agents have to adjust not only to a high rate of inflation tax, but also to an increase in the complexity of their decision problems.

The fact that real money demand falls with (anticipated) inflation is well documented. An erosion in the 'store of value' function of money is

---

[12] This expression is used here to indicate not only the direct resource costs of running a tax agency, but also the economic losses (including the effect on macro performance) that a government may impute to an attempt to increase revenue with the existing tax system. Note that the lack of a thick market for government debt can be linked to the effectiveness of the tax system: when existing taxes are very costly to increase, there may be incentives not only to raise income through the inflation tax but also to make the internal public debt a target for taxation of one type or another. The management of domestic debts—and the associated problems of time inconsistency and multiple equilibria—has received an increasing attention in the literature: see e.g. Alessina *et al.* (1989); Calvo (1988).

already observed in mild inflations, or even in stable economies as the menu of assets grows richer. In high inflation, people obviously try to limit their holdings of cash to very short periods. In hyperinflations there are a number of colourful examples of the effort to get rid of money in a matter of a few minutes. Even when these extremes are not reached, agents tend to keep their liquid assets in the form of foreign currencies or time deposits (often with maturities of only a few days) and sometimes devise elaborate schemes to synchronize payments and receipts. These practices clearly increase transaction costs, as stressed in the standard analysis.

Erratic inflation makes nominal contracting riskier. If this could be represented by a larger error term in the forecast of a well defined price index that could be observed contemporaneously, one might expect a generalized move to a commonly used form of indexing. Actually, it would then be difficult to rationalize the survival of nominal contracts even under mild price uncertainty. However, indexing does not appear capable of 'neutralizing' inflation, and the transition to indexing is gradual and incomplete.

The experience with indexation is varied (see Williamson 1985). In recent times, for example, Brazil and Israel had formal indexing rules for a large variety of contracts, while in Argentina in the mid-1980s this was not the case to the same extent. There, contracts like housing rentals were often adjusted by indexing to the CPI, and there is some evidence that wages were set using as a reference a backward-looking CPI formula (first at quarterly intervals, then monthly, as inflation accelerated). These formulae offer only a partial protection against shifts in the inflation rate when (as is usually the case) the CPI is calculated monthly and made available with some lag: the real value of indexed payments varies inversely with the difference between current and past inflation. The existence of those lags, moreover, makes indexing a poor way of adjusting very short-term contracts.

Although these mechanical problems of indexing are important, they do not exhaust the difficulties that high and variable inflation pose in arranging payments at future dates. In high inflations some markets thin out, or just disappear, while others 'open up'. In Argentina, for example, even if the CPI was a commonly used escalator, various other indexing clauses were applied; it would appear that this was not simply an enrichment of the set of available contingent contracts, but may have reflected the troubles agents had in finding an adequate proxy for 'the' inflation rate or in agreeing on a suitable denominator. Furthermore, the length of financial transactions generally falls: long-run credits (even indexed ones) become less common, while there remains a sizeable volume of nominal assets of very short maturity. Thus, high inflation does not merely induce a change in the form of contracts, keeping fixed the time structure of assets: instead, one observes an increased reluctance to make commitments for more than the immediate future,[13] which is not overcome by resorting to indexing. The survival of nominal contracts (and of backward-looking indexation), on the other hand, is an important characteristic that distinguishes high inflations from 'proper' hyperinflations, where practically all financial transactions are dollarized or based on similar mechanisms of almost contemporaneous escalation.

Hyperinflations and 'merely' high inflations differ from the more usual cases of moderate inflation also in the pricing practices observed. In hyperinflations, prices are eventually set with reference to a 'standard' like the exchange rate,[14] although this does not prevent significant disruptions in trading. In a less extreme case, like that of Argentina in the mid-1980s, some prices were quoted in dollars, but this remained limited to real estate and some durable goods, and in those instances dollar prices were not constant, but fluctuated (even if not proportionally) with the real exchange rate. It would seem, then, that 'dollar pricing' in such inflations serves mainly as a way to post a given price for a certain length of time in markets where buyers have a strong incentive to search (and where, often, the asset is to be purchased by drawing on savings in foreign currencies[15]), but does not imply the use of a strict 'dollar standard'. The prices of most goods are revised at frequent intervals, but by steps rather than continuously or (it would seem) through the application of a simple rule. Domestic money maintains its role as a unit of account, even with an inflation rate on the order of 1 per cent per day, and a general linkage of typical 'fixprices' to a 'flexprice' like the exchange rate does not take place.[16] A possible explanation would be that, except in the limit of enormously high inflations, the advantages of having prices fixed for some time in terms of the medium of exchange outweigh the costs of having non-synchronized and discrete price adjustments.

Very high inflation forces agents to adapt to rapid changes in the

---

[13] An increased 'demand for flexibility' may already appear in moderate inflations: see Leijonhufvud (1977).

[14] The evidence on wages is less clear but suggests that 'inertial', backward-looking behaviour eventually breaks down and is replaced by frequent adjustments based either on price forecasts or on some scheme of more or less contemporaneous indexing. See Schacht (1927) for anecdotal references to wage-setting in the German hyperinflation, which suggest that arranging labour contracts under very rapid inflation can be a quite costly and complicated matter.

[15] Capital flight is a commonly observed phenomenon in high-inflation economies (although its intensity varies from country to country); the fact that many people choose to keep a sizeable part of their portfolio in the form of foreign currencies seems to stem both from reluctance to hold assets within the country and from the uncertainty about the real return of alternative financial instruments.

[16] Dual exchange rate systems are common in high-inflation economies. In those cases, dollarization, when it happens, implies setting prices with references to the floating 'financial' (or parallel) exchange rate.

markets where they operate. Prices must still be set for some time and compared with one another in order to decide what quantities to buy or sell, but by the time a decision is reached, the original information is no longer relevant. Consumers have trouble distinguishing favourable from unfavourable offers; this reduces the effect of price competition. In some way or other, all firms and individuals have to engage in the task of guessing future price changes, but there is no easily available, well defined model to refer to. People anxiously watch the movements of some indicators like the exchange rate or some 'key' prices, although their interpretation is often not trivial at all. The additional time and effort spent in gathering and processing information does not seem to compensate for the increased difficulty in 'making sense' of data; in the end, price expectations become much less reliable. Under those circumstances, agents prefer to pursue flexible strategies and avoid commitments of any sort beyond very short horizons. When they do take a bet, the two sides of a transaction will often act on inconsistent beliefs: many trades in assets, for example, can originate in differences in price expectations rather than in real preferences or opportunities. One of the most characteristic images of very high inflation is that of generalized 'speculation', in which each individual gambles against the rest.

The position of policy-makers is no better. In the more extreme episodes, the very operation of the government is endangered as ordinary tax receipts fall drastically (given that the fiscal lag effect cannot be completely offset by reducing payment delays or by indexing), and the base of the inflationary tax is also much reduced. Even when this point of imminent paralysis is not reached, the ability to run effective policies is quite limited when the government cannot predict with any confidence the consequences of its decisions and the public perceives that it has lost control over the economy.

4. Disinflation Policies

High inflations typically stop abruptly. Disinflation becomes an all-or-nothing matter. A gradual strategy promises a long period of continued instability and may be endangered by expectations that the attempt is easily reversible. A long transition can imply costs in terms of economic performance and, probably also, constraints on the government's ability to define and execute policies.[17] This poses difficult questions regarding

[17] See Kiguel and Liviatan (1988) for a discussion of gradual programmes to deal with high inflations. Bruno (1985) argues that, under certain conditions, economies might be trapped near a high-inflation equilibrium; in addition to a correction in fiscal policies, a discrete initial shift in price expectations would then be required to move the system to a lower steady-state inflation. See also Bruno and Fischer (1985).

what makes governments willing and capable of producing a definite disinflation and, later, of sustaining that result.[18] In any case, actual stabilization programmes have been relatively complex sets of policy actions and announcements; the connections between their parts and the mechanisms through which they operate have been the subject of much discussion.

4.1. *Fiscal policies*

There is no doubt that a sustainable stabilization requires the reordering of government finances so as to get rid of the inflation tax; even a transitory disinflation seems to have little chance of succeeding without a correction in fiscal policies. In fact, with different instruments and different strengths, all disinflation programmes that achieved an effect on prices brought about a reduction in the deficit. An episodic fall in the gap between income and expenditure, however, is not equivalent to a durable fiscal reform: there are questions, also, regarding how fiscal policies act on prices and whether they should be complemented with other types of policies.

A well defined and influential view of the stabilization process regards a permanent (and publicly perceived as such) cut in the public-sector deficit as a necessary and sufficient condition for making the transition to low inflation: the government must show that it is able to generate a stream of revenues such that its present value covers the value of expected spending. This could be achieved through current and (credibly) announced future measures, and could be reinforced by institutional changes that clearly isolated the central bank from fiscal demands. Stabilization would occur mainly as a result of a sudden change in private expectations, triggered by a firm belief in the reform of the fiscal regime; as expectations adjust, actual inflation would come down without necessarily causing a fall in real output (Sargent 1982).

One of the indicators used in support of this view is the rise in real money demand, which is commonly observed in sharp disinflations. Although the increase in real balances is generally gradual, and does not always imply a return of real liquidity to the levels of the period before the big inflation, it does suggest a noticeable shift in expectations during those episodes. Still, it is less clear that the perception of a definite

---

[18] Flood and Garber (1980) have developed a model where very high inflation rates generate the expectation of a policy reform, given that the government has strong incentives to stabilize if the revenue from the inflation tax is tending to zero (see also La Haye 1985). In general, it seems true that the 'demand for stability' has been an important element in the transitions out of high inflation; this, however, leaves open the question of how governments were able to change their policies in order to satisfy that demand.

change in the fiscal regime is a necessary or sufficient condition to make a smooth initial transition out of high inflation.

There is, first, an ambiguity in the concept of credibility. Policy announcements are obviously meant as signals to the public that the authority has the purpose (and, implicitly, the ability) to execute some action. But the effect of such signals on expectations depends on how agents evaluate the chances of the actions being actually carried out, given their perceptions of the government's objectives and restrictions. Policy moves seem to be the outcome of quite complex interactions: often, individuals do not know, unanimously and for sure, whether to believe or not: rather, many people do not know *what* to believe. Especially when there has been a recent experience of unstable behaviour, it is likely that announcements of a big policy shift will be met with a variety of responses (many of them more or less 'reasonable') and that, while there might be an average effect on anticipations, these will not conform fully to the announcements, or change homogeneously across agents. In fact, there is mixed evidence regarding the strength of 'announcement effects' in disinflation episodes. In the German case of the 1920s, for example, there are indications that the credibility of the programme was not well established when it started, while measures that had no prospect of being sustainable managed to produce a short deflation some months before (Dornbusch 1987).

Clearly, presenting a well designed programme, with information about the future course of policies, greatly helps in making disinflation easier. Still, the process of designing, discussing, deciding, and starting to execute policies seems hard to compress in to a single instant, particularly when they are as far-ranging as a fiscal reform. In addition, coming from a high inflation the horizon of decisions is likely to stay short for some time, since the way in which the economy reacts to a stabilization programme is not easy to forecast with precision. This also applies for policy-makers: while disinflation probably requires a clear indication that there has been a change in behaviour, the announcement of a complete sequence of future measures seems too strict to be considered a necessary condition. Successful programmes were not always announced (and, possibly, designed) once and for all: some of them developed piecemeal, and were adjusted to address the problems that appeared. Stabilization appears to imply a sequence of actions at the right time and in the right direction, rather than a single, overall decision. Thus, it is likely that a disinflation programme will include transitory elements. The initial drop in the deficit might be based, in part, on more or less fragile measures. While announcements of future actions can produce a certain shift in the public's perceptions, credibility may be limited, and can depend on the observation both of actual policies and of the economy's reaction (Cukierman 1988).

4.2. *Fixing nominal variables*

The purely expectational view of disinflations makes strict assumptions about the reaction of prices: agents should revise their forecasts of the fiscal deficit and the future rate of monetary expansion; accordingly, they should change their estimate of the equilibrium inflation rate and judge that other agents are forming their expectations in the same way, and that they will all decide their actions based on those beliefs; the shift in expectations should then be reflected in actual price decisions. If there are explicit or implicit contracts that may propagate the previous high inflation rates into the future, they should be re-negotiated, and agents would have to feel confident that this will happen.

These conditions do not seem easy to satisfy, especially when they are all taken together. Agents can have different implicit models about the causation of prices: given an anticipated fall in the fiscal deficit, some individuals may not directly infer that inflation will actually come down. Even if agents agree on the 'fundamentals' that drive inflation, their conjectures about others' expectations will not necessarily match their equilibrium forecasts (Phelps 1983; Di Tata 1983). In order to produce a rapid disinflation, a large number of price decisions have to be revised simultaneously. This poses the question of what makes price-setters react in a co-ordinated fashion: doubts about how other agents will react can make some price-setters refuse to stop increasing their prices before they observe, or at least receive the definite signal, that most others have stabilized the prices under their respective management (Simonsen 1988).

In some circumstances, the stabilization of a narrow set of prices can serve as such a signal. This seems, in particular, the case of actual hyperinflations, where 'dollarization' has become a generalized practice: if the exchange rate remains stable, this would more or less immediately be transmitted to prices (Lopes 1984; Dornbusch 1987). The problem is different in situations where prices do not move on the basis of a dollar-like standard; then, there might remain residues of contractual inertia, and the anchoring of a single variable such as the exchange rate may be insufficient to induce price-setters to modify their decisions consistently so as to generate a smooth disinflation. In those instances, incomes policies may have a useful role in providing a 'multiple anchor' to ease the transition (see e.g. Dornbusch and Simonsen 1987).

The initial set of relative prices can have an important effect on the outcome of a disinflation attempt, especially when the programme includes measures of direct intervention on prices: if some variables are fixed too far from sustainable values, that may imply either residual inflationary pressures or shortages and supply disturbances. It is obviously impossible to identify an 'equilibrium' vector of relative prices,[19] particularly when there is a sudden policy shift, that will most probably change real supplies and demands. However, some judgement (based on necessarily vague criteria) has to be exercised in order to determine the initial value of 'macro' prices, like the exchange rate or the prices of public utilities, and to avoid large 'micro' distortions, if the policy is to serve as an effective co-ordinating device.[20] Also, there may be ways to deal with mechanical sources, of relative price variability, such as those derived from the de-synchronization of price and wage adjustments.[21]

Measures like price–wage ceilings can help in certain conditions to facilitate a rapid disinflation by providing a reference to workers and firms about how others can be expected to behave, and by making search easier for consumers. At the same time, it is clear that such policies are a possible complement, but definitely not a substitute, for a definite deceleration in nominal demand. In addition, direct controls overdetermine prices: the multiple anchoring provided by a freeze or a similar instrument is certainly a short-run instrument.[22] At some point, policies have to find a way to establish a more permanent system to regulate the price level on a sustainable path; this implies allowing market pressures to be reflected on prices. While recent experiences suggest that 'defreezing' can occur without large disturbances, maintaining a low inflation after an initial fall has proved to be a particularly difficult problem.

4.3. *Monetary policies and monetary reform*

Monetary policies during a sharp disinflation have to deal with a high degree of uncertainty regarding the change in money demand. Taking

[19] In 'proper' hyperinflations, the argument for the use of incomes policies is much weakened by the lack of more or less well defined prices in domestic currency. The Hungarian programme of 1946 did include a price freeze, but the starting prices had to be 'made' in an *ad hoc* way on the basis of prewar values (Bomberger and Makinen 1980, 1983).

[20] In this sense, the presence of large-scale price controls in the period of high inflation can pose a serious restriction on the use of incomes policies for the purpose of disinflation.

[21] For example, the Brazilian programme of 1986 included a system intended to 'homogenize' starting relative wages, as earnings in different sectors had previously been determined by non-simultaneous revisions at 6-month intervals (Lopes 1986).

[22] The overdetermination has costs, even in the short run. However, the alternative is to rely on the validity of some very specific hypothesis about price formation. When there is considerable 'model uncertainty' and the decision weighs heavily the objective of producing a definite effect on prices, it is more probable that more instruments will be used than is recommended by any particular theory. The argument is presented somewhat more formally in Heymann (1989).

for granted (as a necessary condition for a disinflation with any chance of being sustained) that fiscal requirements do not constrain monetary policies to an excessive expansion, it is generally difficult to identify precisely at what speed the money stock should be allowed to increase. This poses the risk of either creating pressures on prices or, alternatively, keeping the interest rate too high, with adverse consequences on real activity, and possibly also (to the extent that there is some amount of public debt that has to be rolled over) on public finances. Targeting the interest rate or the money stock, in any case, has uncertain results, given the lack of precise knowledge about the state of expectations: at the beginning of a disinflation programme it is often found that monetary policies concentrate on stabilizing the exchange rate.

But the problem of redefining the monetary regime extends beyond the management of the first phase of disinflation. The programmes that ended the post-First-World-War hyperinflations typically included as a key feature a reform that changed the rules under which the central bank was to operate. This meant, in general, limiting loans to the government to a predetermined nominal amount, and the *de facto* pegging of the exchange rate. The system (which in some cases involved a certain degree of foreign supervision) was clearly intended as a constraint on the monetization of budget deficits and, indirectly, on fiscal policies. It was not always the case, however, that the announcement of the separation of monetary from fiscal policies was received with full confidence: in Germany, for example, it took time to establish that the central bank could indeed keep its credits to the government within the established ceiling. In other cases (like that of the first stabilization attempt in Poland and, more dramatically, in an episode in China in 1948), money creation to finance deficits went much beyond the original limits (see Schacht 1927; Yeager *et al.* 1981; Chang 1958).

After some hyperinflations, policies had to deal with demands for compensation arising from the loss in real value of long-run nominal assets. In high inflations where there are still short-run contracts being written in nominal terms (or indexed with lags), the opposite problem can arise: avoiding large wealth redistributions from debtors to creditors when the inflation rate comes down suddenly and unexpectedly. A currency reform (although not strictly necessary for this purpose) can be useful to adjust contracts to a sudden drop in the inflation rate. The system applied in Argentina in 1985 (and, with some variants, also in Brazil in 1986) consisted in the creation of a new currency, with a 'conversion scale' that set a predetermined daily exchange rate between the new money and the old one (in which payments arranged before the reform were denominated). The conversion scale defined a depreciation of the old currency at a rate similar to the pre-reform inflation, so as to approximate the real value of payments to what it would have been under that inflation.[23]

It may be noted that the conversion mechanism implies a drastic change in the nominal value of pre-contracted payments in order to maintain their real value. This kind of intervention works in a 'neutral' way if prices do stabilize, at least approximately, and for a period comparable with the length of outstanding contracts[24]; it can be acceptable to the public if this condition is likely to be met.

4.4. *Foreign loans*

To the extent that exchange rate stabilization is a crucial element in disinflation, the chances of success are reinforced if the central bank has, and is known to have, sufficient holdings of foreign reserves. Foreign loans, or a reprogramming of the external debt, if this is large, can be important for that purpose. In fact, the European programmes after the First World War were supported by 'stabilization loans'. In the German case, in addition, an agreement on reparations was reached, although this happened some time after the disinflation had started. In more recent instances, the Israeli programme of 1985 had substantial foreign support (Garber 1988); this was absent in the Brazilian case of 1986. The 1985 programme in Argentina was followed by an agreement with the IMF and by negotiations with the foreign creditors, but the financing obtained covered only in part the interests on the debt.

5. The Problem of Stabilizing: Some Recent Experiences

Managing to induce an initial disinflation is clearly an important step towards stabilizing, but it can be far from sufficient. This has been

---

[23] The system resembles the 'blueback scheme' described in Leijonhufvud (1984); see also Heymann and Leijonhufvud (1989). Arida and Lara Resende (1985) have proposed a different mechanism, which relies on the issue of an 'indexed money' that would circulate along with the old currency for some period: the exchange rate between the two moneys would be market-determined. This last scheme has features in common with the experiment with indexed money in Hungary after the Second World War.

[24] The system applied in Argentina in 1985 pre-announced the conversion rate for only a limited period; the rate of depreciation of the old currency could then be adjusted to reflect the pre- and post-reform inflation differential. However, most of the existing nominal contracts were short-term, so that the resulting payments were made at the rates established at the moment of the reform itself. Many of the contracts to be converted had originated not long before the reform, during a period when the inflation rate had stayed fairly steady (although extremely high). This was important in making the scheme workable, even if it was obviously impossible to validate the (possibly incoherent) inflationary expectations entertained by the parts when they agreed on each contract.

shown quite dramatically in the recent experiences of Argentina, Bolivia, Brazil, and Israel, which started stabilization programmes in the mid-1980s.[25] In all four cases, the inflation rate dropped noticeably;[26] Israel and Bolivia were able to maintain a relatively low inflation (in the case of Bolivia, after a sharp, but transitory, acceleration that lasted a few months). By contrast, the Brazilian programme unravelled in less than one year. In Argentina, although the return to high inflation was less abrupt, successive attempts to stop the rising trend proved ineffective until, in the end, inflation surged in 1989, reaching a peak of 200 per cent per month.

These programmes differed not only in their actual performance, but also in the analysis behind the initial disinflation package. In particular, the design of the Cruzado Plan in Brazil assumed that inflation was mainly driven by inertia; consequently, it concentrated almost exclusively on incomes policies and on the treatment of outstanding contracts, and did not contemplate a fiscal correction.[27] In the opposite extreme, the Bolivian programme considered that, in the hyperinflationary situation it had to deal with, it was unnecessary to use price controls (Sachs 1986; Morales 1988): the disinflation strategy was to decelerate the rate of money growth through a sharp fiscal adjustment, in order to stabilize the exchange rate. The programmes of Israel and Argentina included both a general price–wage freeze and measures to cut the fiscal deficit.[28]

An indication that comes out clearly from the Brazilian case is that the anchoring of nominal variables cannot be a useful instrument except when it acts in support of a consistent aggregate demand management: otherwise, generalized shortages or unsustainable deficits in the balance of payments quickly lead again to open inflation. This does not mean,

---

[25] Bruno et al. (1988) includes a collection on these plans; see also Kiguel and Liviatan (1988), Helpman and Leiderman (1988), Blejer and Liviatan (1987), and Solimano (1989). In addition to the works cited in the text, other discussions of specific programmes can be found in Cardoso and Dornbusch (1987), Di Tella and Canavese (1988), Fischer (1987), Frenkel and Fanelli (1987), Gerchunoff and Bozalla (1987), Kiguel (1988), Machinea and Fanelli (1988), Rodríguez (1988). The hyperinflationary bursts of the late 1980s have motivated a 'new wave' of recent programmes in countries such as Argentina, Brazil, and Peru. The following discussion refers only to the earlier programmes.

[26] The rate of growth of the CPI in the 6 months before the start of the Bolivian programme had exceeded 50 per cent per month; it had been near 25 per cent per month in Argentina and around 14 per cent in Israel and Brazil. In the 9 months following the announcement of the programmes, the inflation rate fell to 7 per cent per month in Bolivia, 3 per cent in Argentina, and less than 2 per cent in Israel and Brazil.

[27] See Modiano (1988), Simonsen (1988), Macedo (1988). The Brazilian government had announced a new tax policy some time before. However, the budget deficit was larger than expected, as the programmed increase in receipts did not materialize and expenditures kept growing, in part because of the wage raises that were granted at the start of the plan.

[28] The Mexican programme of 1987 also combined a drastic fiscal adjustment with incomes policies, although these did not take the form of a freeze.

however, that incomes policies necessarily produce that result. In Argentina and Israel, although demand recovered in the disinflation phase, that did not generate widespread disturbances in supplies; rather, it would seem that the much smaller uncertainty about future prices encouraged consumers to search and stimulated competition, so that in more than a few instances market prices were lower than the ceilings.

Still, in every case, inflation was not negligible, even during the period in which freezes were nominally in effect or the exchange rate remained fixed. In fact, the persistence of a certain residual inflation seems almost unavoidable, especially because, in order to create confidence in the stability of the main anchors (such as the exchange rate), the programmes are likely to start by setting these variables at high real values; the reaction of other prices over time would imply a drift in the aggregate price level.[29]

One of the problems that a stabilization programme is likely to face at some point or other is how to prevent an early return of indexing practices which can propagate the residual inflation. This was not solved in Argentina: the inflation of around 3 per cent that was observed in the second half of 1985 soon became a floor for wage adjustments in the private sector and for price expectations. In Israel, by contrast, inflation moderated over time and (despite significant wage increases) later stabilized at a low level.

While the administration of the nominal anchors can play a part in maintaining a disinflation, what seems crucial is the behaviour of fiscal policies. High inflation lasting residues. Although money demand recovers when individuals anticipate a smaller rate of price growth, real balances will probably remain low (Piterman 1988; Ahumada 1989); in addition, the demand for public debt may not increase significantly before the experience of some time of stable performance restores the government's creditworthiness.[30] That is, in an incipient disinflation, the 'unpleasant monetarist arithmetic' (Sargent and Wallace 1981) would operate at high speed. Therefore, coming out of a high inflation, fiscal

---

[29] All the programmes considered, except one of Brazil, included an initial discrete devaluation. A high real exchange rate at the beginning of a disinflation programme is clearly a signal that the plan will not face immediate difficulties arising from balance-of-payments problems, but it also tends to generate an increase in foreign reserves, which gradually raises the money supply, if it is not offset by an equivalent fiscal surplus or a (potentially costly) sterilization through monetary instruments. For a given fiscal policy, then, there would be a trade-off between starting with a 'credible' exchange rate and accepting some inflation later. The recovery of the real prices of non-traded goods is a typical feature of disinflation episodes; in addition, there may be other upward adjustments as the initial set of 'micro' relative prices shifts to reflect market conditions.

[30] In countries with a large foreign debt, the expected size of the transfers associated with its service can also have a strong influence on the public's perception about the solvency of the governments.

policies have to be managed under strong restrictions: cash spending and receipts must be approximately balanced even over short periods.

The ways in which governments can produce a fiscal adjustment are obviously country-specific. In Israel, where the tax system had maintained its capacity to generate revenues, the drop in the deficit was achieved principally by reducing subsidies. Bolivia, by contrast, had practically no tax revenues at the end of its hyperinflation: the stabilization started with a sharp increase in the price of petrol (which is sold by a public company), while government salaries were frozen at very low real levels.[31] The Argentine programme relied on a variety of measures: an initial raise in public-sector prices, higher taxes on foreign trade, a forced loan linked to the income tax, and a fall in public investment and real wages.

It is clear that, at least in the cases of Argentina and Bolivia, the initial measures could restrict for some time the demands for monetary financing, but could not promise a sufficient fall in the normal value of the public deficit. In fact, at the end of 1985 the Bolivian programme faced a crisis, when the international price of tin (the country's main export) dropped suddenly and, at the same time, the government had to borrow from the central bank to cover its spending. The sudden jump of the inflation rate, to more than 30 per cent in a month, led to a tightening in fiscal policies (which included delaying payment to government employees), later consolidated through a tax reform and the approval of a budget that was enforced in nominal terms.[32] In Argentina no such crisis occurred, but neither did fiscal instruments strengthen: there was no definite change in the very distorted tax system, and spending decisions remained subject to strong pressures.

If the fiscal regime does not undergo a timely reform so as to make it consistent with a low inflation, macroeconomic policies are likely to be confronted with very difficult dilemmas. The Argentine experience suggests that running a moderately high inflation is hardly a feasible alternative once the attempt to induce a more or less clear cut stabilization has been abandoned. Contrary to many predictions at the time of the programme, the end of the freeze did not provoke a sudden de-compression of prices. However, in the following three years the inflation rate accelerated sharply, and also had wide swings. During some periods, nominal adjustments in the exchange rate and public-sector prices were slowed down in an attempt to anchor inflation; in others, the government's concern was to make these variables grow in real terms. Monetary policies showed similar oscillations, subject to an

---

[31] In addition, Bolivia maintained its moratorium on the services of the foreign debt.
[32] Morales (1988) stresses the importance of the legislated budget in limiting the demands on the Bolivian Treasury.

unpleasant trade-off: either to let the money supply expand at a rapid pace (when it was clear that demand was very sensitive to shifts in expectations) or to make the real interest rate rise sharply, which had a direct impact on public finances. In these cycles, the government was once again absorbed in the tasks of short-run management, and its ability to regulate the course of an increasingly volatile economy was severely weakened. The loss of control became evident in Argentina in 1989, after an incipient run on its reserves forced the central bank to stop intervening in the foreign exchange market, and as the election to be held in May of that year came closer, the government was left with practically no instruments against an explosive rise in inflation.

It would seem that stabilization implies little less than changing the form in which the economy functions. The required reforms can hardly be implemented in a single act, but without them a disinflation is easily reversible. Although the strategy to go about the initial transition may vary according to the case, and may involve the use of instruments of different types, the main problem is to find permanent means to finance the government. The specific content of the policies that are used for that purpose matters of course a great deal for resource allocation and income distribution. However, from the narrow point of view of stabilization, what counts is the consistency of fiscal management: doing without the inflation tax restricts the sequence of aggregate spending and receipts, but does not impose a particular structure to them. In any case, it is likely that a sustainable reduction of public deficits would imply in general changes in all of the 'margins' of taxation, expenditures, and (when applicable) foreign debt servicing. Also, institutions may need to be established or reinforced, so as to endow the fiscal regime with basic but important features, like systematic budget procedures or a working tax system.

Much of the discussion on stabilization policies has centred on the effects of the initial transition on aggregate output. The experience shows that it is possible to disinflate without serious contractionary consequences. If a programme gives sufficiently clear signals that prices will decelerate in a co-ordinated fashion, this can happen without a persistent pressure of excess supply. On the other hand, the inflation tax reduces consumption possibilities, especially of low-income groups; its reduction stimulates spending accordingly, so as to compensate for the fall in the government's deficit. A revival of short-term credit is another typical characteristic of abrupt disinflations. The effects on supply can be important after a very high inflation, when the degree of short-run uncertainty is so great that firms are reluctant to sell and to commit resources to production.

However, economies that have suffered a big inflation will not return at once to normal patterns of behaviour. Planning horizons are likely to remain short, and the recovery of capital markets does not happen at once: even in countries that have maintained a low inflation for some years, it is common to find that interest rates are much higher than in traditionally stable economies. Thus, it would be difficult to expect an early and strong response of private savings and investment. Also, often the fiscal adjustment implies at first a deterioration in the quality of public services, as investment is cut and real wages in the government are kept low. These transitory expedients have to be replaced with more solid instruments in order to make fiscal equilibrium compatible with some growth. Overcoming the effects of high inflation, then, requires important changes in the behaviour both of the public sector and of private individuals, even after prices have stopped rising rapidly; in this sense, the costs of economic instability seem to last beyond the disappearance of its more obvious symptoms.

References

AGLIETTA, M., and ORLÉAN, A. (1982). *La Violence de la monnaie*. Paris, PUF.

AHUMADA, H. (1989). 'Saldos Monetarios Reales e Inflación: Tests de Efectos Asimétricos usando Técnicas de Co-Integración (Argentina, 1971–1988).' Working Paper, CEMYB–Banco Central de la República Argentina.

AIZENMAN, J. (1985). 'Inflation, Tariffs and Tax Enforcement Costs'. Working Paper, no. 1712 NBER.

ALESINA, A., and TABELLINI, G. (1987). 'A Political Theory of Fiscal Deficits and Government Debt in a Democracy'. Working Paper no. 2308, NBER.

ARIDA, P., and LARA RESENDE, A. (1985). 'Inertial Inflation and Monetary Reform in Brazil'. In J. Williamson (ed.), *Inflation and Indexation: Argentina, Brazil and Israel*. Cambridge, Mass.: MIT Press.

BARRO, R., and GORDON, D. (1983*a*). 'A Positive Theory of Monetary Policy in a Natural Rate Model'. *Journal of Political Economy*, 91: 589–610.

—— and GORDON, D. (1983*b*). 'Rules, Discretion and Reputation in a Model of Monetary Policy'. *Journal of Monetary Economics*, 91: 101–22.

BLEJER, M., and LIVIATAN, N. (1987). 'Stabilization Strategies in Argentina and Israel'. Working Paper, IMF.

BOMBERGER, W., and MAKINEN, G. (1980). 'Indexation, Inflationary Finance and Hyperinflation: the 1945–1946 Hungarian Experience'. *Journal of Political Economy*, 88: 550–60.

———— (1983). 'The Hungarian Hyperinflation and Stabilization of 1945–1946'. *Journal of Political Economy*, 91: 801–24.

BRESCIANI-TURRONI, C. (1937). *The Economics of Inflation*. New York: Barnes & Noble.

BRESSER PEREIRA, L., and NAKANO, Y. (1987). *The Theory of Inertial Inflation*. Boulder, Colo.: Lynne Rienner.

BRUNO, M. (1985). 'Stabilization of the Israeli Economy: the Emergency Program in its Early Stage'. Mimeo, Jerusalem.

—— and FISCHER, S. (1985). 'Expectations and the High Inflation Trap'. Working Paper, MIT.

—— and PITERMAN, S. (1988). 'Israel's Stabilization: a Two Year Review'. In Bruno *et al.* (1988).

—— DI TELLA, G., DORNBUSCH, R., and FISCHER, S. (eds.) (1988). *Inflation Stabilization: The Experience of Israel, Argentina, Brazil, Bolivia and Mexico.* Cambridge, Mass.: MIT Press.

CAGAN, P. (1956). 'The Monetary Dynamics of Hyperinflation'. In M. Friedman (ed.), *Studies in the Quantity Theory of Money.* University of Chicago Press.

CALVO, G. (1978). 'On the Time Consistency of Optimal Policy in a Monetary Economy'. *Econometrica*, 46: 411–28.

CARDOSO, E., and DORNBUSCH, R. (1987). 'Brazil's Tropical Plan'. *American Economic Review*, 77: 288–92.

CHANG, K. (1958). *The Inflationary Spiral: The Experience of China, 1939–1950.* Cambridge, Mass.: MIT Press.

CUKIERMAN, A. (1988). 'The End of the Israeli Hyperinflation: an Experiment in Heterodox Stabilization'. In Bruno *et al.* (1988).

DI TATA, J. C. (1983). 'Expectations of Expectations and the Transitional Non-Neutrality of Fully Believed Systematic Monetary Policy'. In R. Frydman and E. Phelps (eds.), *Individual Forecasting and Aggregate Behaviour: Rational Expectations Considered.* New York: Cambridge University Press.

DI TELLA, G., and CANAVESE, A. (1988). 'Inflation Stabilization of Hyperinflation Avoidance? The Case of the Austral Plan in Argentina, 1985–87'. In Bruno *et al.* (1988).

DORNBUSCH, R. (1987). 'Stopping Hyperinflation: Lessons from the German Experience of the 1920s'. In S. Fischer (ed.), *Essays in Honor of Franco Modigliani.* Cambridge, Mass.: MIT Press.

—— and SIMONSEN, M. (1987). 'Inflation Stabilization with Income Policy Support'. Working Paper no. 2153, NBER.

FISCHER, S. (1986). *Indexing, Inflation and Economic Policy.* Cambridge, Mass.: MIT Press.

—— (1987). 'The Israeli Stabilization Program, 1985–86'. *American Economic Review*, 77: 275–8.

FLOOD, R., and GARBER, P. (1980). 'An Economic Theory of Monetary Reform'. *Journal of Political Economy*, 88: 24–58.

FRENKEL, R. (1984). 'Salarios Industriales e Inflación en el Periodo 1976–1982'. *Desarrollo Económico,* 24: 389–414.

—— and FANELLI, J. (1987). 'El Plan Austral un Año y Medio Después'. *Trimestre Económico*, 54: 75–132.

GARBER, P. (1988). 'Comment on Bruno-Piterman'. In Bruno *et al.* (1988).

GERCHUNOFF, P., and BOZALLA, C. (1987). 'Posibilidades y Limitaciones de un Programa Heterodoxo de Estabilización: el Caso Argentino'. Working Paper, Instituto Torcuato Di Tella, Buenos Aires.

HELPMAN, E., and LEIDERMAN, L. (1988). 'Stabilization in High Inflation Countries: Analytical Foundations and Recent Experiences'. *Carnegie-Rochester Conference Series in Public Policy*, 28: 9–84.

HEYMANN, D. (1986). *Tres Ensayos sobre Inflación y Politicas de Estabilización*. Buenos Aires: CEPAL.

—— (1987). 'The Austral Plan'. *American Economic Review*, 77: 284–7.

—— (1989). 'Decisiónes con Conocimiento Limitado'. Mimeo, Buenos Aires.

—— and CANAVESE, A. (1988). 'Tarifas Públicas y Déficit Fiscal: Compromisos entre Inflación de Corto y Largo Plazo'. Working Paper, Instituto Torcuato Di Tella, Buenos Aires.

—— and LEIJONHUFVUD, A. (1989). 'On the Use of Currency Reform in Inflation Stabilization'. Working Paper, European University Institute.

—— and NAVAJAS, F. (1989a). 'Conflicto Distributivo y Déficit Fiscal: Notas sobre la Experiencia Argentina'. Paper presented at a seminar on Structural Reforms and Macroeconomic Performance, CIEPLAN, Santiago de Chile.

—— —— (1989b). 'Fiscal Policies in High-Inflation Economies'. Paper presented at the conference of the International Institute of Public Finance, Buenos Aires.

—— —— and WARNES, I. (1988). 'Conflicto Distributivo y Déficit Fiscal: Algunos Juegos Inflacionarios', Working Paper, Instituto Torcuato Di Tella, Buenos Aires.

KIGUEL, M. (1988). 'Ups and Downs in Inflation: Argentina since the Austral Plan'. Working Paper, World Bank.

—— (1989). 'Budget Deficits, Stability and the Dynamics of Hyperinflation'. *Journal of Money, Credit and Banking*, 21: 148–57.

—— and LIVIATAN, N. (1988). 'Inflationary Rigidities and Orthodox Stabilization Policies: Lessons from Latin America'. *World Bank Economic Review*, 2: 273–98.

KORNAI, J. (1986). 'The Soft Budget Constraint'. *Kyklos*, 39: 3–46.

KYDLAND, F., and PRESCOTT, E. (1977). 'Rules rather than Discretion: the Inconsistency of Optimal Plans'. *Journal of Political Economy*, 85: 473–91.

LA HAYE, L. (1985). 'Inflation and Currency Reform'. *Journal of Political Economy*, 93: 537–60.

LEIJONHUFVUD, A. (1977). 'Costs and Consequences of Inflation'. In G. C. Harcourt (ed.), *The Microeconomic Foundations of Macroeconomics*. London: Macmillan.

—— (1984). 'Inflation and Economic Performance'. In B. Siegel (ed.), *Money in Crisis*. Cambridge, Mass.: Ballinger.

LOPES, F. (1985). 'Inflaçao Inercial, Hiperinflaçao e Desinflaçao: Notas e Conjecturas'. *Revista de Economia Politica*, 5: 135–51.

—— (1986). *Choque Heterodoxo, Combate à Inflaçao e Reforma Monetária*. Rio de Janeiro: Editora Campus.

LUCAS, R., and STOKEY, N. (1983). 'Optimal Fiscal and Monetary Policy in an Economy without Capital'. *Journal of Monetary Economics*, 12: 55–93.

MACEDO, R. (1988). 'Comments to Modiano and Simonsen'. In Bruno *et al.* (1988).

MACHINEA, J., and FANELLI, J. (1988). 'Stopping Hyperinflation: The Case of the Austral Plan in Argentina, 1985–87'. In Bruno *et al.* (1988).

MAIER, C. (1975). *Stabilization in France, Germany and Italy after World War I*. Princeton University Press.

MODIANO, E. (1988). 'The Cruzado First Attempt: the Brazilian Stabilization

Program of February 1986'. In Bruno *et al.* (1988).

MORALES, J. (1988). 'Inflation Stabilization in Bolivia'. In Bruno *et al.* (1988).

OBSTFELD, M., and ROGOFF, K. (1983). 'Speculative Hyperinflations in Maximizing Models: Can We Rule Them Out?' *Journal of Political Economy*, 91: 675–87.

OLIVERA, J. H. G. (1967). 'Money, Prices and Fiscal Lags: a Note on the Dynamics of Inflation'. *Banca Nazionale del Lavoro Quarterly Review*, 20: 258–67.

PERSSON, T., and TABELLINI, G. (1990). *Macroeconomic Policy, Credibility and Politics*. London: Harwood Academic Publishers.

PHELPS, E. (1983). 'The Trouble with Rational Expectations and the Problem of Inflation Stabilization'. In R. Frydman and E. Phelps (eds.), *Individual Forecasting and Aggregate Behaviour: Rational Expectations Considered*. New York: Cambridge University Press.

PITERMAN, S. (1988). 'The Irreversibility of the Relationship Between Inflation and Real Balances'. *Bank of Israel Review*, 60: 71–81.

ROBINSON, J. (1938). 'Review of the Economics of Inflation by C. Bresciani-Turroni'. *Economic Journal*, 48: 231–6.

RODRIGUEZ, C. (1988). 'Comment to Di Tella–Canavese and Machinea-Fanelli'. In Bruno *et al.* (1988).

ROGOFF, K. (1987). 'Reputational Constraints on Monetary Policy'. *Carnegie-Rochester Conference Series on Public Policy*, 26: 141–82.

SACHS, J. (1986). 'The Bolivian Hyperinflation and Stabilization'. Working Paper no. 2073, NBER.

SARGENT, T. (1982). 'The End of Four Big Inflations'. In R. Hall (ed.), *Inflation: Causes and Effects*. University of Chicago Press.

—— and WALLACE, N. (1981). 'Some Unpleasant Monetarist Arithmetic'. *Federal Reserve Bank of Minneapolis Quarterly Review*, 5: 1–17.

SCHACHT, H. (1972). *The Stabilization of the Mark*. London: Allen & Unwin.

SIMONSEN, M. (1988). 'Price Stabilization and Income Policies: Theory and the Brazilian Case Study'. In Bruno *et al.* (1988).

SOLIMANO, A. (1989). 'Inflation and the Costs of Stabilization: Historical Cases, Recent Experiences and Policy Lessons'. Working Paper, World Bank.

TANZI, V. (1977). 'Inflation, Lags in Collection and the Real Value of Tax Revenue'. *IMF Staff Papers*, 24: 154–67.

TAYLOR, L. (1983). *Structuralist Macroeconomics*. New York: Basic Books.

THOMPSON, E. (1981). 'Who Should Control the Money Supply'. *American Economic Review*, 71: 356–61.

WILLIAMSON, J. (ed.) (1985). *Inflation and Indexation: Argentina, Brazil and Israel*. Cambridge, Mass.: MIT Press.

YEAGER, L. *et al.* (1981). *Experiences with Stopping Inflation*. Washington, DC: American Enterprise Institute.

PART V

Empirical Evidence and Induction

13

Assessing Empirical Evidence in Macroeconometrics with an Application to Consumers' Expenditure in France

DAVID F. HENDRY

1. Introduction: Theories and Evidence

Scientific progress in any field depends on a complex interplay between theoretical analysis and empirical evidence, and economics is no exception. At each point in time, a wealthy background of both theoretical and empirical findings co-exists, so that potential new contributions can enter anywhere in the cycle, taking earlier outcomes as given. Most of the papers in this volume have focused on developing economic–theoretical models which seek to account for 'stylized facts' about the macroeconomy; this chapter concentrates instead on some of the data evidence available, and on its assessment.

Empirical evidence will be taken as direct sensory data or observations derived from sensory data—sometimes in very indirect ways as with, say, brain-scan tomography, or GNP. 'Facts' are items of empirical evidence that can be reliably replicated, yet depend only on very well established (often called lower-level) theories and measurement systems. Thus, while all evidence is 'theory-laden' in one sense, the relevant theories are not those under scrutiny in the same analysis but, rather, those that can be treated as part of the 'background knowledge base'. Of course, nothing precludes those low-level theories themselves being overturned at a later date, and thereby jeopardizing the interpretation of

I am grateful to the UK Economic and Social Research Council for the financial support of this research under grants B00220012, B01250024, and R000231184; to Adrian Neale for help in developing the recursive estimation procedures; to Carlo Favero for research assistance; and to Mike Clements, John Muellbauer, and Adrian Neale for helpful comments on earlier drafts of this paper. This is a revised and extended version of Hendry (1988c).

all consequent analyses; but such an outcome is an inevitable aspect of scientific research, independent of the subject matter of the science (physical or social).

The importance of distinguishing between the levels of the theories involved in any study is that the charge of 'measurement without theory' is essentially impossible, and at best could only relate to the low level of the theories used. Conversely, a data-based approach is feasible even in the social sciences since most of our evidence depends on low-level theories. While 'theory without measurement' is both feasible and all too common, the key issue is the optimum blend of theory and evidence, which is a matter of research efficiency, not of principle, dependent on the inherent usefulness of the existing highest-level theories. When that usefulness is great, research is best undertaken closely in line with theoretical predictions; but when extant theories are of little value (e.g. phlogiston), empirical research will contribute most when it relies only on lower levels of theory. In my opinion, the present state of advanced macroeconomic theory offers little to assist researchers seeking to understand how economies actually function, and a much greater emphasis on establishing whether there are empirical constancies and, if so, what they are, will currently yield greater dividends by fostering more relevant theories. As discussed in Hendry (1986), the credibility of a great proportion of empirical econometric evidence depends on the prior credibility of the theoretical model from which it was derived, so when the theory fails, so does most of the evidential basis. That is not common to other disciplines. (Electric lights would not go out if quantum mechanics was rejected.) Further, many theoretical advances in physical sciences follow after empirical discoveries (a recent example being high-temperature super-conductivity), but few do so in economics owing to the pre-eminence accorded to prior postulated theories. To reiterate, neither theory nor evidence can claim precedence in scientific progress, and their respective roles and contributions change over time.

A major methodological difficulty concerns how to proceed if the empirical and theoretical models are inconsistent (for example, if the empirical model has no long-run solution, or contains variables precluded by the theory, or if the coefficients have signs that are uninterpretable within the theoretical framework). If the model is rejected, the issue remains as to why the theory cannot explain the results of the model. If the model is not rejected, then the theory must be altered to avoid maintaining two contradictory propositions. In practice, either or both the model or the theory may be revised until apparent consistency is achieved. This aspect of model design will be investigated below.

Turning to the role of empirical evidence, its assessment raises complicated and evolving issues, irrespective of whether it is predominantly theory- or data-based, or the optimal mixture. We consider four main facets of that assessment.

First, econometrics is still such a young discipline that later developments do indeed overturn what were previously regarded as well established 'facts' by showing that the underlying implicit low-level theories of previous researchers were flawed. One example is the behaviour of the consumption–income ratio: when the variables in both numerator and denominator of a ratio are non-stationary and highly autocorrelated, its distribution is not well approximated by conventional central limit theorems based on assuming independent, identically distributed, random variables. Consequently, the believed long-run constancy of the consumption–income ratio, itself the basis for much theorizing about consumers' behaviour, becomes doubtful (see Kuznets 1946, and the reappraisal in Spanos 1989). Thus, it is unclear how much trust to place in earlier evidence which may be an artefact of invalid implicit assumptions: both theories and evidence merit only tentative acceptance (see Hendry and Richard 1982).

Second, since evidence does not speak for itself, some framework is essential in order to interpret any empirical claim. That comment applies equally well to the deep parameters of so-called structural models, to regression findings, to 'stylized facts', and to data graphs. For the first two it is widely accepted, but the last two are simply low-dimensional projections of high-dimensional phenomena. Thus, at the univariate (i.e. marginal) level, a set of stylized facts may be a reasonable summary of the salient features of the data (e.g. a savings rate of 10 per cent, or a real interest rate of 4 per cent), yet jointly they can be wholly inconsistent with the evidence (in that there is a negligible probability of observing the vector of stylized facts, given the joint distribution of the original data). Similarly, high or low simple (or partial) correlations implicit in graphs can neither prove nor disprove any but the most trivial conjecture, since mapping to a higher dimension can reverse the sign or totally remove an empirical correlation. Even salient features of graphs must be interpreted as *data* phenomena to be accounted for within the context of an acceptable model, but, as will be seen below, an encompassing approach offers a resolution of this conundrum (see e.g. Mizon and Richard 1986).

Third, data evidence summarized in empirical models is sometimes challenged as *data-mining*, connoting the outcome of a prejudiced search for supportive or corroborative evidence (see Leamer 1978, and Hendry *et al.* 1990*a*). Two aspects can usefully be distinguished: (1) Did the search deliberately ignore or camouflage anomalies and/or conflicting results? (2) Did the approach rely primarily on corroboration? The former is unscientific but is open to analysis by requiring the favoured model of any given study to account for all the results obtained within its purview (see Gilbert 1986). The latter raises a host of paradoxes of corroboration (see e.g. Caldwell 1982, and Ericsson and Hendry 1989), but can also be resolved by requiring encompassing (see Section 2).

Finally, many empirical models tend to be accompanied by a range of 'test statistics' reporting evidence which aims to assess their adequacy in characterizing the data. The role of such tests must be carefully appraised, given the ability of investigators to revise models iteratively in the light of any adverse evidence. Below, I shall distinguish between model design criteria (exhausting the available data evidence) and genuine tests in the Neyman–Pearson sense (based on previously unavailable evidence).

These four issues of the validity of earlier (or rival) findings, inter- preting salient data features, the status of empirical models, and the role of test statistics in evaluation, are among the more controversial in applied econometrics. Moreover, they are highly interdependent, since (for example) some of the worries pertinent to data-mining arise precisely because so-called tests can be made insignificant through simply revising the initially postulated model in the light of manifest misfits. Nevertheless, all four issues can be analysed, and even partially resolved, using a framework that builds on five major constructs:

1. Empirical models are reductions of a common data generation process (which need not be stationary) and are not numerically calibrated theoretical models.
2. Since the error processes on empirical models are derived via the reduction operations and are not autonomous in general, models are susceptible to *redesign* to achieve desired criteria, and test statistics used in that design process become part of the selection criteria.
3. Previous findings, data graphs, and even data-mined results all constitute part of the empirical evidence to be encompassed (or accounted for) by a successful model.
4. If constructs 1–3 hold, they must do so over the whole historical period, leading to an emphasis on recursive procedures.
5. Economics time series are generally non-stationary, which compli- cates the behaviour of statistics but makes it easier to detect inadequate models.

Section 2 describes these constructs in more detail, but a technical treatment is not offered here (see *inter alia* Hendry and Richard 1982, 1983, 1989; Spanos 1986; and Hendry 1987, 1989). Rather, the present focus is on expositing the concepts to reveal that, for example, data-mining entails important unencompassed data evidence; that genuine testing requires evidence unavailable at the modelling stage; that previous findings are interpretable despite being potentially invalid; and that recursive procedures are a vastly more powerful method of testing both models and conjectures than full-sample estimation alone.

Section 3 provides an illustration based on aggregate postwar quarterly consumers' expenditure in France. This example differs from that used at the conference in two important respects: the area of interest (consumption as against money demand), and the mode of analysis (paper reporting as against a live computer investigation which could resolve debates *in situ*). The latter change involves much the greatest loss (discussed in Hendry 1988*a*) but seems inevitable outside of a video medium. Section 4 concludes the paper.

2. The Econometric Background: Methodology and Technique

The process whereby good models of empirical phenomena are discovered depends on the brilliance, creativity, and ingenuity of individual investigators as much as on their methodology and technique (see Hendry 1987). The latter affect the efficiency of research and may even help generate valuable solutions, but they are impotent if isolated from good ideas of how to solve empirical puzzles. Conversely, any method, however unpromising in general, may stimulate a useful answer, and the history of the physical sciences generates many illustrations. (See the discussion in Mason (1962), noting for example the discovery of penicillin.) Precisely how new, improved, or insightful ideas develop remains an unresolved problem and has led some to question the role of methodology (see Chalmers 1982), but inappropriate methodology and unsound techniques can certainly vitiate the successful empirical implementation of otherwise excellent ideas, as we shall see below.

2.1. *Models as reductions*

Since the economic mechanism is too complicated to be precisely modelled, all empirical models must be simplifications and hence false, albeit some are much more useful than others. For a single economy (e.g. France) and historical epoch (e.g. the last quarter-century), empirical models share the basis of the common economic mechanism. For a given measurement system, all models must represent *reductions* of this underlying data generation process (DGP) (see Hendry and Richard 1982). Since the dependent variable is observed, the disturbance on any equation (i.e. the unexplained component) must be a derived and not an autonomous process, defined by the specification of the model and its associated estimation procedure. Consequently, error terms can be redesigned by model respecification to satisfy predefined criteria.

The model selection criteria regularly used in time-series econometrics include:

1. (*past data*) homoscedastic white-noise disturbances, which are an innovation against the available information and are approximately normally distributed;
2. (*present data*) weakly exogenous conditioning variables, which would comprise regressors in least squares, or instruments in instrumental variables methods;
3. (*future data*) parameters of interest, which are constant over relevantly long time periods and invariant across regimes;
4. (*theory information*) relationships that are consistent with the theoretical framework;
5. (*rival model information*) results which explain the findings of other models of the same phenomena and explain additional phenomena.

Since empirical models are different reductions of the common DGP, the structure of that DGP and the degree of reduction must interact to determine the extent to which any or all of these five criteria can be satisfied. It is possible to construct models that are adequate on all of these criteria (see e.g. the sequence of money demand models in Hendry 1979; Trundle 1982; Hendry 1985; and Hendry and Ericsson 1991). For some decisions, such as any single one of inference, forecasting, or policy analysis, satisfying a limited subset of the criteria may be adequate, but my own experience suggests that macro models are used for all sorts of decisions by a wide range of agencies and hence should satisfy all of the criteria, or should proceed only if accompanied by clearly stated caveats.

Criterion 1 is well established and will not be discussed any further here; criterion 3 is discussed in Section 2.4 below; criterion 4 was the subject of the previous section; and 5 will be analysed in Section 2.3, so only criterion 2 requires a more comprehensive treatment. Engle *et al.* (1983) analyse three distinct concepts of exogeneity which they call weak, strong, and super exogeneity. The first sustains conditional inference and requires that the parameters of interest in a conditional model can be efficiently analysed without specifying the marginal model for the potentially exogenous variables (the process determining the conditioning variables). They show that the absence of feedback from endogenous on to potentially *weakly exogenous* variables (which is the concept of Granger's 1969 'causality') is neither necessary nor sufficient for exogeneity, and they note that variables cannot be preclassified as exogenous or otherwise since their status depends on the parameters of interest and hence on the structure of the conditional model. Strong exogeneity is the conjunction of weak exogeneity and the absence of feedback, but again is a relationship between variables and parameters of interest, not an inherent property of variables. Strong exogeneity is necessary for conditional forecasting.

Finally, *super exogeneity* is weak exogeneity combined with the invariance of the parameters of interest to a class of interventions that alter the marginal model, so that the parameters of the conditional model remain constant under a regime change (see Frisch 1938; Haavelmo 1944; Lucas 1976; Aldrich 1989). Invariance is needed to sustain conditional policy analyses. For example, if agents' demand for wheat (and hence the price of wheat) depended on their rational expectations about the number of aurorae each year, and if the process generating the latter altered for some reason (a switch in the magnetic poles, say), then the number of aurorae would not be weakly exogenous and might not be super exogenous (depending on how well the expectations process was modelled), even though it was not influenced by economic activity. This relates the notion to the 'sunspot' models discussed in this volume. Engle and Hendry (1989) describe tests for super exogeneity; Hendry and Neale (1988) consider the relationship between encompassing and exogeneity and highlight its clarifying role in models involving expectations formation; Chong and Hendry (1986) consider systems evaluation using forecast encompassing; and Hendry (1988*b*) investigates the encompassing implications of feedback versus expectations formulations to reveal that the Lucas critique is potentially refutable as well as confirmable (see Breusch 1986, and Favero and Hendry 1989). Regime shifts are one class of non-stationarity that regularly reveal model inadequacies.

2.2. *Model design*

Each of the test criteria 1–5 listed above can be decomposed into a specific null hypothesis (such as homoscedasticity, serial independence, etc.), which then constitutes the basis for a test statistic. Most tests have the power to detect departures from their explicit null hypothesis against a range of alternative hypotheses. However, some tests may have no power when other misspecifications are present (called their *implicit null*: see Breusch 1986, and Mizon and Richard 1986). Consequently, rejecting a null against a specific alternative contains little information about what the best (or even an appropriate) alternative model reformulation might be.

A potentially more serious objection to testing arises precisely because empirical models are reductions of the economic mechanism: since disturbance processes are derived, and hence can be redesigned in the light of test information, test statistics can be made insignificant by construction. The regular use of autoregressive corrections to circumvent

evidence of residual autocorrelation is perhaps the best-known implementation of this possible difficulty. Since the correction procedure
adopted is deliberately selected to ensure that the test criterion will not
be significant after the respecification, such an outcome occurs *inde-*
pendently of the correctness of the selected solution. Thus, the test merely
reflects design adequacy, not model validity. This objection applies to all
within-sample tests which are used implicitly or explicitly as selection or
redesign criteria, and genuine testing requires fresh evidence against
which to check a model.

However, note that rejection on a test does entail model invalidity (or
a type I error). Moreover, if, after a sequence of 'problem corrections',
rejection is obtained on some other test (such as criterion 3), then the
entire modelling process must be discarded, since rejecting the predica-
ting assumptions implies that earlier inferences must have been incorrect. (For example, residual autocorrelation may have reflected a
structural break and could vanish once the break was appropriately
modelled.)

This last issue arises because of the nature of the research strategy
involved, namely, successive *generalizations* of a model in the light of
test outcomes (see e.g. Hendry 1979). The converse approach of first
testing the validity of an autoregressive error representation against a
general dynamic model does not suffer from this drawback as in
Sargan's (1980) 'common factor' approach (see Hendry and Mizon 1978,
and Hendry *et al.* 1984 for expositions), since the test outcome is not
independent of the correctness of the solution. However, a different
potential problem arises concerning the consequences of *repeated* testing, and this will be discussed below.

2.3. *Rival models*

Although rival models may be false, a good model should be able to
account for their results. This concept was called *encompassing* in
Davidson *et al.* (1978) and will receive more extensive discussion given
the many different approaches to macroeconomics discussed in this
volume (see Mizon 1984; Mizon and Richard 1986; and Hendry and
Richard 1989).

Consider two linear models, M_1 and M_2, of a variable y which are
reductions of a process M_4 whereby $\{y_t\}$ was generated. Let M_3 denote
the minimal linear model embedding M_1 and M_2, so that each of these
can be obtained by imposing a set of zero restrictions on M_3 but there
are no redundant or additional variables in M_3. The difficult, yet
essential, practical problems of standardizing M_1 and M_2 for common
measurements and definitions, historical time periods, functional forms,

and regressors are assumed to have been resolved.[1] Models need not share exogeneity assumptions, but an agreed set of identifying instruments must be available (see Ericsson 1983).

We seek to test whether either model M_1 or M_2 encompasses the other, that is, whether M_1 can account for the empirical findings of M_2 or vice versa. This involves checking whether the information in M_2 that is not already in M_1 adds to the explanation of M_1 (or conversely). Consequently, we need to test whether or not M_1 (M_2) is a significantly poor reduction of M_3. If the former reduction is valid, M_1 is said to parsimoniously encompass M_3, and we denote this by $M_1 \, \mathcal{E}_p \, M_3$ (see Hendry and Richard 1989). If M_1 and M_2 are genuinely different models, then in large samples both cannot parsimoniously encompass M_3. If $M_1 \, \mathcal{E}_p \, M_3$ but $M_2 \, \mathcal{E}_p^c \, M_3$ (i.e. does not encompass M_3), then M_1 must encompass M_2 and so M_2 is inferentially redundant. However, we did not assume that M_3 was valid relative to M_4, and hence $M_1 \, \mathcal{E}_p \, M_3$ is insufficient to allow us to conclude that M_1 is a valid reduction of M_4 even though M_1 can account for the behaviour of a non-nested rival M_2. Thus, criterion 5 is only a necessary condition for a valid model (failure to encompass entails rejection), and not a sufficient one (successful encompassing does not entail validity).

This limitation applies to all of the criteria, singly or jointly—they are only necessary and not sufficient for validity. Moreover, their insufficiency is the reason for the stress on comprehensive evaluation of empirical models.

Multiple criteria generally entail multiple tests, and a frequently expressed worry about repeated testing concerns the so-called 'pre-test' problem. (See Hendry *et al.* 1990*a* for a discussion.) If the DGP is given, but an investigator tests various null hypotheses about parameter values, then biased and (statistically) inadmissible estimates generally result, and these may have higher risk than unrestricted estimates. (See Trivedi 1984 for a general analysis.) However, the relevance to econometric practice of a framework based on a known DGP is not obvious, and omits consideration of the alternative problem of never discovering that the postulated model class might be entirely incorrect, which could have unbounded risk. Certainly, repeated testing needs to be formulated in a way that allows control over the size of the complete testing process (again supporting general to simple methods), and that size must decline as the sample increases to ensure a consistent test sequence (see White 1990); but, subject to these constraints, and to that of encompassing all of the existing evidence (as against using a scalar model selection

---

[1] These issues are far from trivial and are essential before comparisons can begin (see Davidson *et al.* 1978), but are not central to the principles under discussion.

criterion), rigorous testing offers a viable research tool. (See Hendry 1987 for further discussion.)

2.4. *Recursive estimation and testing*

Recursive estimation denotes sequentially updating estimates one observation at a time. The mathematical basis for recursive least-squares estimation was established over forty years ago (see Plackett 1950 and Terasvirta 1970; and for a brief history see Neale 1987), but its popularity seems to date more from G. D. A. Phillips and Harvey (1974) and Brown *et al.* (1975) (also see Dufour 1982). Given the vast increase in information produced by having $T - K - N$ coefficient estimates, standard errors, residual standard deviations, F-tests etc., rather than just one set (for T observations, K regressors, and $N > K$ initial values), graphical representation seems essential. As summary statistics at each admissible sample size T^*, PC-GIVE plots one-step-ahead forecast errors with $\pm$ twice the residual standard error at T^* shown on either side of the origin, coefficient estimates $\pm$ two standard errors, and parameter constancy tests scaled by their critical values; several such graphs are shown below. Note that recursive calculations add little to the computer-time cost over direct estimation, especially in relation to the additional information produced. (See Hendry and Neale 1987, and Hendry 1989 for further discussion.)

2.5. *Non-stationarity*

The final issue needing discussion is that of data non-stationarity, which crucially affects the distributions of estimators and tests. Conventionally, limiting distributions in econometrics have been predicated on weak stationarity in the DGP so that generalized martingale or mixing central limit theorems are applicable, leading to asymptotic normality of order $T^{-1/2}$ (i.e., $\sqrt{T}(\hat{\beta} - \beta)$ tends to a normal distribution, for an estimator $\hat{\beta}$ of β: see e.g. White 1984). In practice, autoregressive representations of economic time series seem to have roots close to unity and hence may be better approximated by integrated processes. One (overly) simple example is a random walk with drift:

$$x_t = \alpha + x_{t-1} + \epsilon_t \qquad \text{when } \epsilon_t \sim ID(0, \sigma^2), \tag{1}$$

so that (taking $x_0 = 0$)

$$x_t = \alpha t + \sum_{j=0}^{t} \epsilon_{t-j}, \tag{2}$$

and hence x_t is the cumulation of all past errors, whereas

$$\Delta x_t = \alpha + \epsilon_t, \tag{3}$$

which is mean-α white noise (if ϵ_t is). Processes like (3) are denoted $I(0)$ (non-integrated), and if differencing d times is needed to produce a non-integrated process whereas $d-1$ differencing is insufficient, then the variable is $I(d)$. Thus, $x_t \sim I(1)$ in (1).

If x_t is a vector of $I(1)$ processes, then in general any linear combination $\alpha'x_t \sim I(1)$ also. However, the integrated components may cancel in the combination so that $\alpha'x_t$ is $I(0)$, in which case the set is said to be cointegrated as in (say)

$$y_t = \alpha + \beta z_t + u_t \qquad \text{where } u_t \sim I(0). \tag{4}$$

(See Granger and Weiss 1983; Engle and Granger 1987; the special issue of the *Oxford Bulletin* 1986; and Banerjee *et al.* 1992.) Clearly, if $u_t \sim I(1)$, so y_t and z_t are not cointegrated, then $(y_t - \alpha - \beta z_t)$ can 'drift' anywhere (not having a constant mean and having a trending variance), and hence no long-run relationship exists between those series: this is the 'nonsense regressions' problem (see Yule 1926; Granger and Newbold 1974; P. C. B. Phillips 1987*b*). Thus, it is important to establish cointegration between the series involved.

In doing so, however, account must be taken of the fact that, since the series are $I(1)$, the underlying distributions are non-standard (see Stock 1987; P. C. B. Phillips 1987*a*, and Johansen 1988, *inter alia*). The most popular tests are due to Dickey and Fuller (1979, 1981) (the DF and ADF tests) and to Sargan and Bhargava (who tabulate critical values for the Durbin–Watson statistic testing for a unit root—the CRDW test): for a recent survey, see Dolado *et al.* (1990). In the ADF test, equation (4) is estimated over the full sample, $\hat{u}_t = y_t - \hat{\alpha} - \hat{\beta}z_t$ is calculated, and

$$\Delta \hat{u}_t = \lambda \hat{u}_{t-1} + \sum_1^n \gamma_j \Delta \hat{u}_{t-j} + e_t \tag{5}$$

is estimated in order to test $H_0: \lambda = 0$ (i.e. a unit root) against $H_1: \lambda < 0$ (i.e. cointegration with $u_t \sim I(0)$). The DF test has $n = 0$. In either case, under H_0, Δu_t is $I(0)$ and u_{t-1} is $I(1)$, so (5) is 'unbalanced' and the resulting distribution of $\hat{\lambda}$ is a Wiener process for which some tabulated critical values are reported in the Dickey–Fuller papers. If y_t and z_t are cointegrated, then they have an error correction representation; and conversely (see Davidson *et al.* 1978, and Granger 1986), although it remains to determine in which equation that error correction term occurs. If the direction of error correction is known (e.g. from u_{t-1} on to Δy_t), then unrestricted dynamic models of y_t seem usable from the outset both to establish cointegration and to model it (see Banerjee and Dolado 1987). If a given error correction term or cointegration vector occurs in more than one equation, that is sufficient to violate weak exogeneity, and leads to inefficient estimation of single equations (see P. C. B. Phillips and Loretan 1989).

2.6. *Concluding remarks*

While it is obviously possible for an ingenious investigator to reach useful conclusions despite an erroneous approach, the above analysis points up four general ideas.

First, be *explicit* about model design so that tests can be correctly interpreted as to when they are (one-off) tests and when they are selection criteria. Generally, only information that arrived after a model is in the public domain can be deemed an adequate basis for a test.

Second, since model (re)design is inevitable in practice, be *efficient* in model design: if residual autocorrelation will in fact prompt later serial correlation corrections, then allow longer lags from the outset of the exercise. This approach mimics the reduction concept described above for the derivation of models from the DGP during the process of modelling.

Third, be *rigorous* in testing: check a model against all of the criteria so that its strengths and weaknesses are known, rather than just hoping that the latter are absent. White (1990) presents a powerful analysis of the role of testing in modelling strategies which ensure the selection of an acceptable data representation. Anomalies that are discovered when modelling may be due to type I errors or may reflect inherent flaws, but time usually reveals which holds in macroeconomics, and neither problem can be studied if the anomalies are not known.

Finally, be *comprehensive* in evaluation. Alternative models also are reductions of the DGP and hence directly reflect different facets of the economic mechanism, leading to encompassing. Alternative samples may reveal parameter change, leading to recursive procedures.

We define a model to be *congruent* if it is consistent with all of the available evidence. Policy agencies generally require congruent models — that is, interpretable empirical representations of non-rejected theories that are not only well-fitting within sample, but also encompass the main rival explanations and have parameters that are relatively constant over time and also have proved reasonably invariant historically to the range of regime changes that actually occurred (and hence invariant to correlated components of changes likely to ensue). But that argument requires congruence to hold over sub-periods as well as the complete sample, supporting recursive estimation and testing of models and of theory-based claims.

An illustration should help clarify the application of these ideas.[2] At the conference, the presentation using PC-GIVE (see Hendry 1989) was live from the microcomputer, so that questions could be answered and doubts resolved (or confirmed!) instantly. Moreover, a vastly greater range of graphs could be shown than is feasible in a printed paper, allowing a sequential development of information and of approaches which cannot be replicated below. Much is lost in the translation to paper, but hopefully some of the flavour remains.

3. A Model of Aggregate Consumers' Expenditure in France

The data-set (kindly provided by INSEE) is quarterly, not seasonally, adjusted for the French economy over the period 1963(1)–1985(2). The focus is on aggregate real consumers' expenditure (C) in relation to aggregate real disposable income (Y). Such a bivariate relationship entails a vast reduction of: (1) micro information to aggregates; (2) information about alternative assets and their rates of return (financial, durables, housing, etc.); (3) public and private savings institutions (including pensions, insurance, etc.); (4) types of income (earnings, profits, rents, interest); and (5) the measurement of income and expenditure (e.g. adjusted for inflation: see Hendry and von Ungern-Sternberg 1981; including or excluding investment in consumer durables: see Patterson 1986).

Any observed predictive failures should be reviewed in the light of such reductions, especially those that are known to have altered (e.g. capital gains when stock prices surge or tumble: see Pesaran and Evans 1984; changes in capital rationing, etc: see Hendry et al. 1990b). Such issues often seem obvious in retrospect but are usually far from clear at the time, and a list of deliberate reductions can stimulate productive research improvements (e.g. inflation effects in the consumption function as in Davidson et al. 1978).

Figure 13.1 shows the behaviour of $c_t = \log c_t$ and $y_t = \log Y_t$ over time and Fig. 13.2 graphs their annual first differences, $\Delta_4 c_t = c_t - c_{t-4}$ and $\Delta_4 y_t = y_t - y_{t-4}$. The rate of inflation $(\Delta p_t = \Delta_1 \log P_t$ where P_t is the implicit deflator of C_t) is shown in Fig. 13.3 and the ratio of C to Y in Fig. 13.4 (using $c_t - y_t$). While C/Y has remained within the range 0.75–0.9, and hence C is highly correlated with Y, the ratio C/Y in France has nevertheless varied substantially over the last twenty-two

---

[2] The following example covers most of the issues for a macroeconomic relationship previously analysed in Hendry (1988c).

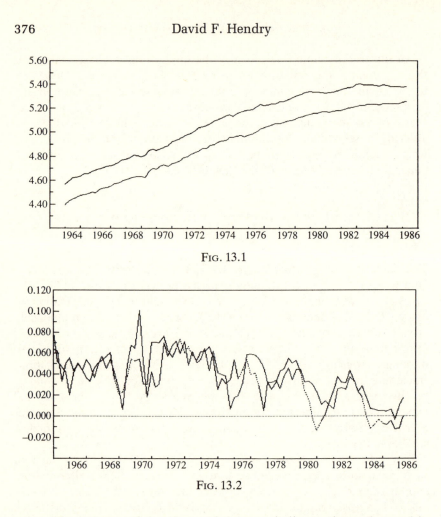

Fig. 13.1

Fig. 13.2

years. The patterns of Δc, Δy, and Δp are similar to those observed in the UK and USA, except perhaps for the apparent decline in $\mathrm{var}\,(\Delta y)$ over time.

The model seeks to explain the consumption–income ratio in terms of a long-run steady-state equilibrium solution of the form: $C/Y = f(g_y, \dot{p})$, where g_y is the growth rate of real income and $\dot{p}$ is the rate of inflation in steady state.[3] Such a long-run solution is consistent with the life-cycle hypothesis (see e.g. Deaton and Muellbauer 1980, and for a UK application see Hendry 1983), and the coefficients of g_y and $\dot{p}$

[3] This is related to the types of savings models reported at the INSEE conference on French Macro Modelling in December 1985. Thus, given its similarity to previously estimated models, the illustration is unlikely to contribute substantively to empirical econometrics, although some of the findings reported below differ from those embodied in any model described at the INSEE conference, and some of the tests do yield new information: see INSEE (1988).

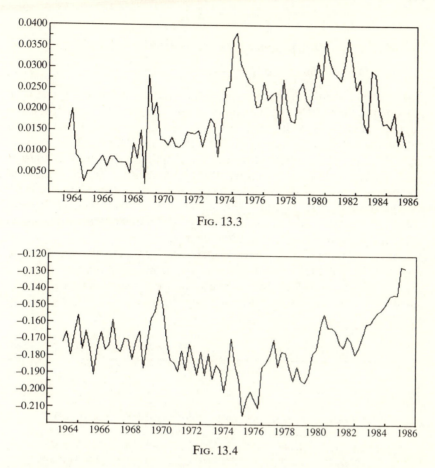

FIG. 13.3

FIG. 13.4

should correspond to the ratios of total assets and of liquid assets to income respectively, so that the coefficient of g_y should exceed that of $\dot{p}$ in absolute terms: both should be negative.

Previous research on savings in the main French macroeconometric systems, METRIC, DMS, and PROPAGE, suggested a role for labour demand and supply in modifying C/Y (owing to labour market rationing). The two variables considered were vacancies and unemployment, O and D respectively (for *offre* and *demand*), but since the former never proved important in the earlier study, I shall focus on D below.

I first estimate the static empirical analogue of the equilibrium solution noted above. From their graphs, and from testing for unit roots, c_t, y_t, Δp_t, and Δd_t all behave more like $I(1)$ than $I(0)$ or $I(2)$ variables. Thus, prior to the substantive modelling exercise, we test whether this set of variables is cointegrated. Figure 13.1 suggests that c and y might be, but using the whole sample information formally:

$$c_t = 1.02y_t - 0.14\Delta d_t - 0.64\Delta p_t - 0.27$$

$$T = 1963(2)-1985(2) \qquad R^2 = 0.997 \qquad \hat{\sigma} = 0.015$$

$$\text{DW} = 0.63 \qquad \text{ADF} = -2.2 \tag{6}$$

The evidence is mixed: the R^2 value, the unit coefficient on y_t, and the reasonably high CRDW statistic suggest cointegration, whereas the augmented Dickey–Fuller (ADF) test (using three lags to remove residual serial correlation) does not exceed the tabulated 5 per cent critical value. The coefficient on the levels feedback in the ADF test is -0.22, which is large and suggests that the inability to reject the null of no cointegration may just reflect a lack of test power (see Banerjee *et al.* 1986). In Table 13.1, once the dynamics are modelled, a similar feedback coefficient results, but the fit of the unrestricted model allows significant rejection of the null of no cointegration.

Static equations like (6) have sometimes been estimated in order to test theories. In that framework, the low DW statistic could reflect a myriad of ills, and certainly reveals that the estimated coefficients' standard errors are downward-biased: great care is needed in attempting

TABLE 13.1. *The unrestricted dynamic model estimates*

Variable/lag	0	1	2	3	4	Σ	F/[df]	CV
c	−1.000	0.460	0.166	0.399	−0.186	−0.161	36.5	2.51
	—	(0.120)	(0.110)	(0.099)	(0.096)	(0.074)	[4,65]	
y	0.242	0.146	−0.117	−0.019	−0.094	0.159	8.2	2.36
	(0.077)	(0.116)	(0.108)	(0.110)	(0.091)	(0.073)	[5,65]	
Δp	0.077	0.155	−0.225	—	—	−0.147	1.1	2.75
	(0.152)	(0.158)	(0.131)			(0.136)	[3,65]	
Δd	−0.057	−0.026	0.032	—	—	−0.051	6.5	2.75
	(0.019)	(0.020)	(0.018)			(0.024)	[3,65]	
Δo	0.0016	0.0075	−0.0072	—	—	0.002	0.7	2.75
	(0.0069)	(0.0069)	(0.0068)			(0.010)	[3,65]	
D68(2)	−0.021	0.027	—	—	—	0.006	8.6	3.14
	(0.007)	(0.009)				(0.011)	[2,65]	
Constant	−0.009	—	—	—	—	−0.009	0.2	3.99
	(0.02)					(0.026)	[1,65]	

$$T = 1964(1)-1985(2) \qquad R^2 = 0.9996 \qquad \hat{\sigma} = 0.00572$$
$$F(20,65) = 8260.3 \qquad \text{DW} = 2.05$$

$$\bar{c} = 4.93 \qquad \text{s.d.}(c) = 0.252 \qquad \text{SC} = -9.518 \qquad \eta_1(4, 61) = 1.6$$
$$\xi_2(2) = 0.93$$

$$\eta_3[4, 57] = 1.30 \qquad \eta_4(12, 53) = 1.32 \qquad \eta_5(38, 26) = 0.35 \qquad \eta_7[2, 63] = 0.03.$$

any inferences in models with autocorrelated disturbances since coefficients divided by standard errors do not have t-distributions under the null of a zero parameter, even for stationary data. Further, as discussed above, it is rarely valid in static models to assume that residual autocorrelation is error autoregression, and to impose a common factor on the dynamics by re-estimating with an autoregressive correction. Note that this also entails that the adjustment mean lag is imposed as zero, and is the same for all variables. If the autocorrelation parameter is close to unity, differencing is often assumed, although a unit common factor eliminates all long-run information in the data. Otherwise, if the series are cointegrated in levels, the long-run information in the data will be reflected whatever the lag structure, and hence that finding is interpretable without entailing the favouring of any given econometric specification as discussed in Section 2.

For the present data-set, a third-order autoregressive error is needed to leave white-noise residuals, and this generates the estimates

$$c_t = 0.459y_t - 0.079\Delta d_t + 0.280\Delta p_t + 3.175 + \hat{u}_t$$
$$\quad\quad (0.075) \quad\;\; (0.016) \quad\quad\;\; (0.149) \quad\quad (0.460)$$

$$\hat{u}_t = 0.523\hat{u}_{t-1} + 0.217\hat{u}_{t-2} + 0.245\hat{u}_{t-3}$$
$$\quad\quad (0.107) \quad\quad\;\; (0.120) \quad\quad\;\; (0.108)$$

$$(7)$$

$$T = 1963(2)-1985(2) \quad\quad \Sigma c^2 = 5.2025 \quad\quad \hat{\sigma} = 0.0072$$

$$\xi_2(2) = 0.24 \quad\quad \bar{c} = 4.92 \quad\quad \text{s.d.}(c) = 0.264$$

All of the autoregressive error coefficients are marginally and jointly significant, the roots of the error polynomial are 0.991 and $0.234 \pm 0.439i = (0.497^t)\cos\{2.06t + \theta\}$, and the residual correlogram reveals no further autocorrelation ($\xi_1(16) = 17.5$) where $\xi_i(k)$ denotes a $\chi^2(k)$, and the subscripts 1 and 2 relate to null hypotheses of white noise and normal residuals, respectively. There is a root of approximately unity in the residual autoregression (consistent with no cointegration) and if only a first-order error scheme is allowed, the autoregressive coefficient is 0.991. However, common factors in the static model (6) are not a valid representation of the data, since allowing third-order lags on all the variables nearly halves the residual sum of squares relative to (7), so the evidence in that equation is suspect. Despite the invalidity of the common-factor assumption, however, the residuals have been successfully redesigned to be approximately white noise but are not an innovation against the available information set. Note how the coefficient of y_t is less than 0.5, and so is interpretable as a short-run rather than a long-run effect, consistent with the autoregressive error acting as a difference operator.

Next, Table 13.1 reports the least-squares estimates of an unrestricted dynamic model relating c to y, Δd, Δp, and Δo with a dummy variable

$D68(2)$ equal to unity in 1968(2). $(\cdot)$ denotes an estimated standard error; $\bar{x}$ is the sample mean, and s.d. $(\cdot)$ the sample standard deviation; $\hat{\sigma}$ is the standard error of equation; Σ denotes the sum of coefficients in the lag polynomial; SC is the Schwarz criterion; F is the test of no effect from the complete set of variables; CV is the 5 per cent critical value of the associated F-test, and $\eta_i(\cdot)$ denotes an F-statistic. In the order reported, the tests relate to:

(a) residual autocorrelation of 4th order: $\eta_1(4, 61)$;
(b) non-normality as for (7) above (see Jarque and Bera 1982): $\xi_2(2)$;
(c) an ARCH error process of 4th order (see Engle 1982): $\eta_3(4, 57)$;
(d) parameter constancy on the last 12 observations (see Chow 1960): $\eta_4(12, 53)$;
(e) heteroscedasticity arising from the squares of the regressors: $\eta_5(38, 26)$;
(f) White's (1980) general heteroscedasticity statistic (not calculated in the table);
(g) the RESET statistic for the omitted square and cube of the fitted dependent variable (see Ramsey 1969): $\eta_7(2, 63)$.

The derived 'long-run' solution from the Table 13.1 model is given by

$$c_t = 0.991y_t - 0.916\Delta p_t - 0.317\Delta d_t + 0.012\Delta o_t + 0.037D68(2) - 0.055,$$
$$ (0.031) \quad (0.837) \quad\quad (0.171) \quad\quad (0.064) \quad\quad (0.074) \quad\quad\quad (0.157)$$

which is close to the directly estimated static model in (6) above. Various orthogonalizing transformations were carried out on the Table 13.1 model to create growth rates, the error correction term, and so on; then this (still unrestricted) equation was re-estimated, and variables with t-statistics less than 1.0 in absolute value, and negligible coefficients were sequentially eliminated. The eliminated block of 12 variables was tested by an overall F-test $(F_{64}^{12} = 0.6)$. This yielded the restricted model:

$$\Delta c_t = -0.145\Delta_2 c_{t-1} + 0.197\Delta c_{t-3} + 0.235\Delta y_t - 0.204\Delta p_{t-2} - 0.067\Delta d_t$$
$$ (0.071) \quad\quad\quad (0.060) \quad\quad\quad (0.094) \quad\quad\quad (0.084) \quad\quad\quad (0.015)$$

$$-0.020\Delta_1 D68(2)_t - 0.020 - 0.195(c-y)_{t-1} - 0.138\Delta_4(c-y)_{t-1}$$
$$(0.005) \quad\quad\quad (0.009) \quad (0.061) \quad\quad\quad\quad (0.052)$$

(8)

$$T = 1964(2){-}1985(2) \qquad R = 0.721 \qquad \hat{\sigma} = 0.00553$$
$$F(8, 76) = 24.58 \qquad (CV = 2.06)$$

$$DW = 2.252 \qquad \overline{\Delta c} = 0.0092 \qquad s.d.(\Delta c) = 0.00997$$
$$\eta_1(4, 72) = 1.32 \qquad \eta_1(8, 68) = 0.80$$

$$\xi_2(2) = 0.13 \qquad \eta_3(4, 68) = 1.90 \qquad \eta_4(40, 36) = 0.50$$
$$\eta_5(16, 59) = 1.58 \qquad \eta_6(27, 48) = 0.96$$

$$\eta_7[2, 74] = 0.6 \qquad SC = -10.04$$

Analyses of related models are presented in Davidson *et al.* (1978) and Meullbauer and Bover (1986). Figures 13.5 and 13.6 show actual outcomes of, and the fitted values from, equation (8) over the whole sample and with a forty-quarter 'forecast' sub-period. Given the marked change in the behaviour of C/Y around 1975 (see Fig. 13.4), the performance is acceptable, although there is some evidence of deterioration at the very end of the sample.

Most of the statistics recorded for Table 13.1 and equation (8) relate to design against the historical sample, that is, information set (*a*) above. The twelve observations and forty-period constancy tests are the only checks for (*c*), and no checks for (*b*), (*d*), or (*e*) are reported as yet. In terms of (*d*) first, the results are consistent with the error correction model in Davidson *et al.* (1978), although the actual lag structure is different, and the significance of Δd_t suggests that labour

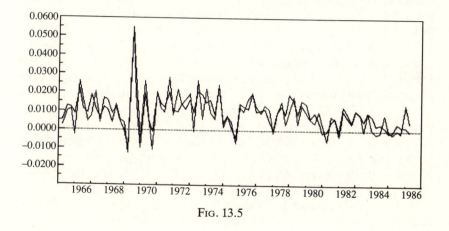

FIG. 13.5

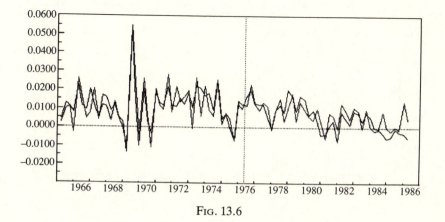

FIG. 13.6

market constraints may have been important in France. In a hypothetical dynamic steady state of constant (quarterly) growth rates, the model in (8) solves to (compare Hendry 1983)

$$\log \frac{C}{Y} = -0.10 - 4.4g_y - 1.06\dot{p} - 0.34g_d. \qquad (9)$$
$$\phantom{\log \frac{C}{Y} =} (0.02) \quad (1.2) \quad (0.41) \quad (0.11)$$

The solution is close to that in (6) or as derived from Table 13.1. The coefficients of g_y and $\dot{p}$ suggest (quarterly) total asset–income and liquid asset–income ratios of about 4.4 and 1.0, which are in a similar relationship to values found for the UK but are about four times as large. Overall, however, this design aspect seems acceptable.

Since solutions like (9) assume constant parameters, more checks on (c) are needed. Several authors have commented on the arbitrary nature of picking particular sub-samples for testing constancy (see e.g. Patterson 1986). For super-exogeneity, one would like to select periods where potential influences on parameters changed most—but this is more the task of the critics of a given model than of the proprietors! With the good graphical facilities available on modern microcomputers, the advantages of recursive estimation methods can be readily exploited, and Figs. 13.7 and 13.8 show plots for equation (8) of the complete sequence of 'break point' Chow tests and of the one-step residuals together with $0 \pm 2\hat{\sigma}_t$ $(t = 1969(3)-1985(2))$ where $\hat{\sigma}$ is the estimated equation standard error. The former are scaled at each point by the 5 per cent critical value of the associated F-distribution so that the significance line for a single test is unity: as yet, we do not have a 5 per cent overall test with reasonable power. Even so, both plots confirm the overall constancy, with the deterioration at the end of the sample being clear.

Finally, Figs. 13.9 and 13.10 show the sequences for the coefficient of Δy_t and $(c - y)_{t-1}$ (together with $\pm$ twice their estimated standard

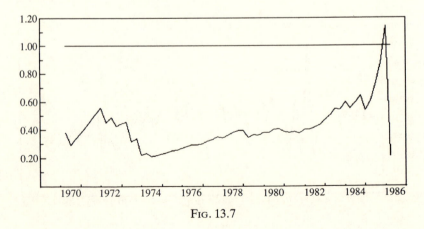

FIG. 13.7

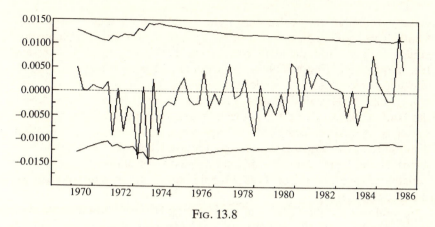

FIG. 13.8

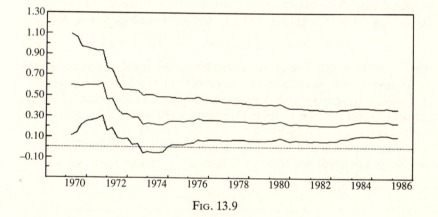

FIG. 13.9

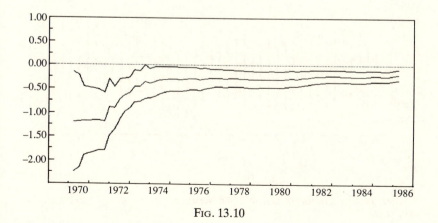

FIG. 13.10

errors). Initially, the coefficients trend slightly, then they remain constant. This later constancy argues against significant simultaneous-
equations bias since the data correlations have not remained constant
(see Favero and Hendry 1989). As evidence of such a claim, the forty
one-step forecasts for the static regression of $(c - y)_t$ on Δy_t, Δp_t, and
Δd_t in Fig. 13.11 show manifest predictive failure, despite the width of
the confidence bands (± 1.8 per cent when the unconditional standard
deviation is 1.5 per cent). Strictly speaking, however, if the equation
disturbances are autocorrelated, the reported confidence intervals are
incorrect and hence convey a misleading picture of parameter estimation
variability. (See Corsi et al. (1982) for this result summarized in terms of
the Chow test.)

Several tests of the validity of conditioning (b) are feasible, but these
are dependent on the validity and relevance of some other set of
variables to be used as instruments (which claim again has testable
implications). Re-estimating (8) using as instruments $(t, \Delta i_{t-1}, i_{t-2},$
$\Delta d_{t-1}, \Delta p_{t-1})$ with both Δy_t and Δd_t treated as endogenous yielded[4]

$$\hat{\sigma} = 0.56\% \qquad s = 0.64\% \qquad \xi_3(3) = 5.60,$$

where s is the residual standard deviation of the reduced form and $\xi_3(3)$
is Sargan's (1964) Wald test of the validity of the instruments (equivalent to testing parsimonious encompassing of the unrestricted by the
restricted reduced form). Thus (b) seems acceptable so far as it can be
tested here.

Testing for encompassing (i.e. against (e)) naturally involves using
previously reported models for this data-set, preferably corresponding to

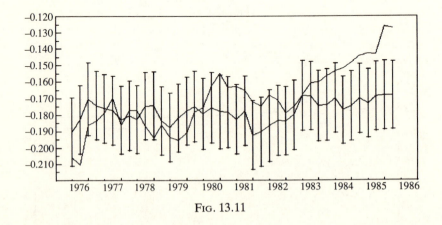

FIG. 13.11

---

[4] I is the level of investment; note that the irrelevance in (8) of Δd_{t-1} and Δp_{t-1} has
been pre-tested.

contending theoretical paradigms. Consider a hypothetical model M_2 in which Δc_t is explained by the set of lagged variables $(\Delta(d - o)_{t-1}, \Delta i_{t-1}, (i - y)_{t-1},$ and $i_{t-2})$ related to the earlier instruments. The encompassing F-test is equivalent to testing for the marginal significance of these added variables in (8), or for whether (8) parsimoniously encompasses the extended model of (8) plus the four additional regressors (see Hendry and Richard 1989). However, the tests that are due to Cox (1961) and Ericsson (1983) are not invariant to the presence of other variables from (8) in M_2. The encompassing test table produced by PC-GIVE is reproduced as Table 13.2. None of the statistics rejects M_1 against M_2, but all do the converse, although the latter is not too surprising given the design of M_1. The joint model had thirteen regressors and yielded $\hat{\sigma} = 0.56$ per cent. This evidence is against the hypothesis that, e.g., $\Delta(d - o)_{t-1}$ correctly models the labour market constraint on expenditure.

A more demanding contender for encompassing is provided by the rational expectations, permanent-income model of Hall (1978), in which it is argued that real consumption is a random walk. The data here are for (unadjusted) total consumers' expenditure, and as the dependent variable includes current expenditure on durables, direct tests are not feasible. Nevertheless, the base-line model that $\Delta c_t = v_t$ (where $\{v_t\}$ is a mean innovation process against lagged information) remains of interest. In an encompassing framework, two aspects are important:

1. whether or not the hypothesis is rejected on a test against lagged information;
2. whether the results so obtained can be explained by equation (8).

We take these issues in turn (compare Davidson and Hendry 1981).

1. A fourth-order autoregression in Δc_t (with a constant and $D68(2)$) yields a test for the significance of the lag set $(\Delta c_{t-1} \ldots \Delta c_{t-4})$ of $F(4, 79) = 3.85$ (5% CV = 2.49), whereas excluding $D68(2)$ yields $F(4, 80) = 3.18$. Adding $(\Delta y_{t-1} \ldots \Delta y_{t-3}, \Delta p_{t-1} \ldots \Delta p_{t-4}, \Delta d_{t-1} \ldots \Delta d_{t-2}, (c - y)_{t-1}, \Delta_4(c - y)_{t-1}, t, (d - o)_{t-2})$ results in $R^2 = 0.68$ and

TABLE 13.2. *Encompassing tests of equation (8) against lagged information*

M_1 v M_2	Form	Test	Form	M_2 v M_1
0.34	$N(0, 1)$	Cox (1961)	$N(0, 1)$	−79.5
−0.32	$N(0, 1)$	Ericsson IV (1983)	$N(0, 1)$	43.8
2.96	$\chi^2(4)$	Sargan (1964)	$\chi^2(9)$	59.2
0.73	$F(4, 72)$	Joint (see Dastoor 1983)	$F(9, 72)$	21.7

an F-test for no relation of $F(18, 66) = 7.92$. Reducing this unrestricted lagged representation as earlier for the Table 13.1 model, but now to establish the 'best' forecasting relationship, yields

$$\Delta c_t = \underset{(0.06)}{0.20\Delta^2 c_{t-3}} - \underset{(0.10)}{0.18\Delta y_{t-2}} - \underset{(0.05)}{0.20\Delta(p_{t-2} + p_{t-4})} - \underset{(0.05)}{0.22(c-y)_{t-1}}$$

$$\underset{(0.05)}{-0.08\Delta_4(c-y)_{t-1}} - \underset{(0.010)}{0.032\Delta D68(2)} - \underset{(0.008)}{0.020} \tag{10}$$

$T = 1964(2)-1986(2) \qquad R^2 = 0.64 \qquad \hat{\sigma} = 0.62\%$

$F(6, 78) = 23.3 \qquad \text{DW} = 2.25$

$\eta_1(4, 75) = 0.90 \qquad \xi_2(2) = 0.15 \qquad \eta_3(4, 71) = 1.07$

$\eta_5(10, 68) = 2.46 \qquad \eta_6(20, 58) = 1.97.$

In (10), since η_5 is significant, $(\cdot)$ denotes heteroscedastic-consistent standard errors (see White 1980, and MacKinnon and White 1985). No 'breakpoint' Chow test for any sub-period against 1985(2) is significant, and Fig. 13.12 shows the recursive estimates of the error correction coefficient (of $(c-y)_{t-1}$) over the available sample. The model in (10) is of potential interest for forecasting, and also demonstrates that the random walk hypothesis is strongly rejected.

2. The more substantive role of (10) is for testing the specification in (8), and doing so involves seeing if (8) can encompass (10). The test results are given in Table 13.3. It is unsurprising that M_3 fails to encompass M_1, given the latter's use of current data information and its better fit; it is more interesting that M_1 encompass M_3, so that the lagged variables in (10), which are absent from (8), fail to add to the explanation of (8), the joint model having $\hat{\sigma} = 0.55$ per cent.

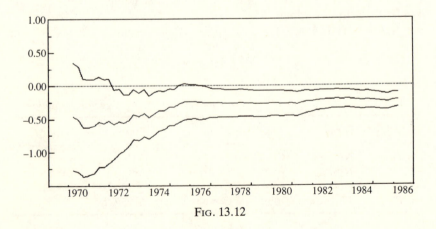

FIG. 13.12

TABLE 13.3. *Encompassing tests of equation (8) against equation (10)*

M_1 v M_3	Form	Test	Form	M_3 v M_1
0.09	$N(0, 1)$	Cox	$N(0, 1)$	−30.31
−0.08	$N(0, 1)$	Ericsson IV	$N(0, 1)$	15.81
4.07	$\chi^2(3)$	Sargan	$\chi^2(9)$	61.93
1.38	$F(3, 73)$	Joint	$F(9, 73)$	25.03

Given that (8) is (adequately) congruent with the evidence, we return to reinterpret the data graphs reported earlier. The parallel behaviour of c_t and y_t is attributed to their cointegration through the error correction $(c - y)_{t-1}$, whereas the downward-then-upward trend in that ratio (i.e. C/Y) is attributed to the behaviour of the inflation rate and labour market constraints. The large 'bump' in 1968 is not explained, however, but is removed by a $(+1, -1)$ indicator variable. Clearly, 1968 is an anomalous year: deleting the dummy for the quarters 1968(2)/(3) yields $F(1, 76) = 21.8$ and $\hat{\sigma}$ rises to 0.62 per cent, although the previously reported coefficients are not greatly altered. Historically, we cannot be surprised that the effects on expenditure of the social and political turbulence of 1968 are not easily modelled in a simple linear structure, but the same result clearly indicates room for better explanations in the future.

4. Conclusion

An expository study never merits a long conclusion, since little new material has been reported above, and a summary would miss the point altogether! The main themes meriting comment are that macroeconomic evidence can be rigorously evaluated; that congruent models are not an impossibility despite having more demanding requirements than are often sought; that encompassing offers a powerful and useful analytical framework; that microcomputers greatly facilitate empirical research; and that software developments are extending the evaluation frontier and enhancing research productivity at an exceptionally rapid rate.

References

ALDRICH, J. (1989). 'Autonomy'. *Oxford Economic Papers*, 41: 15–34.

BANERJEE, A., and DOLADO, J. (1988). 'Tests of the Life Cycle–Permanent

Income Hypothesis in the Presence of Random Walks: Asymptotic Theory and Small-Sample Interpretations'. *Oxford Economic Papers*, 40: 601–35.

—— —— GALBRAITH, J. K., and HENDRY, D. F. (1992). *Co-integration, Error-Correction, and the Econometric Analysis of Non-Stationary Data*. Oxford University Press.

—— —— HENDRY, D. F., and SMITH, G. (1986). 'Exploring Equilibrium Relationships in Econometrics through Static Models: Some Monte Carlo Evidence'. *Oxford Bulletin of Economics and Statistics*, 48, special issue: 253–77.

BREUSCH, T. S. (1986). 'Hypothesis Testing in Unidentified Models'. *Review of Economic Studies*, 53: 635–51.

BROWN, R. L., DURBIN, J., and EVANS, J. M. (1975). 'Techniques for Testing the Constancy of Regression Relationships over Time' (with discussion). *Journal of the Royal Statistical Society*, B, 37: 149–92.

CALDWELL, B. (1982). *Beyond Positivism: Economic Methodology in the Twentieth Century*. London: George Allen & Unwin.

CHALMERS, A. F. (1982). *What is this Thing Called Science?* Milton Keynes: Open University Press.

CHONG, Y. Y., and HENDRY, D. F. (1986). 'Econometric Evaluation of Linear Macro-Economic Models'. *Review of Economic Studies*, 53: 671–90.

CHOW, G. C. (1960). 'Tests of Equality between Sets of Coefficients in Two Linear Regressions'. *Econometrica*, 28: 591–605.

CORSI, P., POLLOCK, R. E., and PRAKKEN, J. C. (1982). 'The Chow Test in the Presence of Serially Correlated Errors'. In G. C. Chow and P. Corsi (eds.), *Evaluating the Reliability of Macro-Economic Models*. New York: John Wiley.

COX, D. R. (1961). 'Tests of Separate Families of Hypotheses'. *Proceedings of the Fourth Berkeley Symposium on Mathematical Statistics and Probability*, i: 105–23. Berkeley: University of California Press.

DASTOOR, N. K. (1983). 'Some Aspects of Testing Non-nested Hypotheses'. *Journal of Econometrics*, 21: 213–28.

DAVIDSON, J. E. H., and HENDRY, D. F. (1981). 'Interpreting Econometric Evidence: The Behaviour of Consumers' Expenditure in the UK'. *European Economic Review*, 16: 177–92.

—— —— SRBA, F., and YEO, S. (1978). 'Econometric Modelling of the Aggregate Time Series Relationship between Consumers' Expenditure and Income in the United Kingdom'. *Economic Journal*, 88: 661–92.

DEATON, A. S., and MUELLBAUER, J. N. J. (1980). *Economics and Consumer Behaviour*. Cambridge University Press.

DICKEY, D. A., and FULLER, W. A. (1979). 'Distribution of the Estimators for Autoregressive Time Series with a Unit Root'. *Journal of American Statistical Association*, 74: 427–31.

—— —— (1981). 'Likelihood Ratio Statistics for Autoregressive Time Series with a Unit Root'. *Econometrica*, 49: 1057–72.

DOLADO, J., JENKINSON, T., and SOSVILLA-RIVERO, S. (1990). 'Cointegration and Unit Roots'. *Journal of Economic Surveys*, 4: 249–73.

DUFOUR, J.-M. (1982). 'Recursive Stability Analysis of Linear Regression Relationships: An Exploratory Methodology'. *Journal of Econometrics*, 19: 31–76.

DURBIN, J., and WATSON, G. S. (1950). 'Testing for Serial Correlation in Least

Squares Regression: I'. *Biometrika*, 37: 409–28.

———— (1951). 'Testing for Serial Correlation in Least Squares Regression: II'. *Biometrika*, 38: 159–78.

ENGLE, R. F. (1982). 'Autoregressive Conditional Heteroscedasticity with Estimates of the Variance of United Kingdom Inflation'. *Econometrica*, 50: 987–1007.

—— and GRANGER, C. W. J. (1987). 'Co-Integration and Error Correction: Representation, Estimating and Testing'. *Econometrica*, 55: 251–76.

—— and HENDRY, D. F. (1989). 'Testing for Super Exogeneity and Invariance'. Discussion Paper no. 89–51, University of California at San Diego.

———— and RICHARD, J.-F. (1983). 'Exogeneity'. *Econometrica*, 51: 277–304.

ERICSSON, N. R. (1983). 'Asymptotic Properties of Instrumental Variables Statistics for Testing Non-nested Hypotheses'. *Review of Economic Studies*, 50: 287–304.

—— and HENDRY, D. F. (1989). 'Encompassing and Rational Expectations: How Sequential Corroboration Can Imply Refutation'. International Finance Discussion Paper no. 354, Board of Governors of the Federal System, Washington DC.

FAVERO, C., and HENDRY, D. F. (1989). 'Testing the Lucas Critique: A Review'. Mimeo, Nuffield College, Oxford.

FRISCH, R. (1938). 'Statistical versus Theoretical Relations in Economic Macrodynamics'. Mimeo, University of Oslo.

GILBERT, C. L. (1986). 'Professor Hendry's Econometric Methodology'. *Oxford Bulletin of Economics and Statistics*, 48: 283–307. Reprinted as Ch. 13 in C. W. J. Granger (ed.), *Modelling Economic Series: Readings in Econometric Methodology*. Oxford University Press.

GRANGER, C. W. J. (1969). 'Investigating Causal Relations by Econometric Models and Cross-Spectral Methods'. *Econometrica*, 37: 424–38.

—— (1986). 'Developments in the Study of Cointegrated Economic Variables'. *Oxford Bulletin of Economics and Statistics*, 48: 213–28.

—— and NEWBOLD, P. (1974). 'Spurious Regressions in Econometrics'. *Journal of Econometrics*, 2: 111–20.

—— and WEISS, A. A. (1983). 'Time-series Analysis of Error-Correction Models'. In S. Karlin, T. Amemiya, and L. A. Goodman (eds.), *Studies in Econometrics, Time Series, and Multivariate Statistics*. New York: Academic Press, pp. 255–78.

HAAVELMO, T. (1944). 'The Probability Approach in Econometrics'. *Econometrica*, 12: suppl.

HALL, R. E. (1978). 'Stochastic Implications of the Life-Cycle–Permanent Income Hypothesis: Theory and Evidence'. *Journal of Political Economy*, 86: 971–87.

HENDRY, D. F. (1979). 'Predictive Failure and Econometric Modelling in Macroeconomics: The Transactions Demand for Money'. Ch. 9 in P. Ormerod (ed.), *Economic Modelling*. London: Heinemann Educational Books, pp. 217–42.

—— (1983). 'Econometric Modelling: The Consumption Function in Retrospect'. *Scottish Journal of Political Economy*, 30: 193–220.

—— (1985). 'Monetary Economic Myth and Econometric Reality'. *Oxford*

Review of Economic Policy, 1: 72–84.

—— (1986). 'On the Credibility of Econometric Evidence'. Walras–Bowley Lecture, Meeting of the North American Econometric Society, 1986.

—— (1987). 'Econometric Methodology: A Personal Perspective'. Ch. 10 in T. F. Bewley (ed.), *Advances in Econometrics*. Cambridge University Press.

—— (1988a). 'Econometrics in Action'. *Empirica*, 2/87: 135–56.

—— (1988b). 'The Encompassing Implications of Feedback versus Feedforward Mechanisms in Econometrics'. *Oxford Economic Papers*, 40: 132–49.

—— (1988c). 'Some Foreign Observations on Macro-economic Model Evaluation at INSEE-DP'. In INSEE (1988).

—— (1989). *PC–GIVE: An Interactive Econometric Modelling System*. Oxford Institute of Economics and Statistics.

—— and ERICSSON, N. R. (1991). 'Modelling the Demand for Narrow Money in the United Kingdom and the United States'. *European Economic Review*, 35: 833–81.

—— and MIZON, G. E. (1978). 'Serial Correlation as a Convenient Simplification, not a Nuisance: A Comment on a Study of the Demand for Money by the Bank of England'. *Economic Journal*, 88: 549–63.

—— and NEALE, A. J. (1987). 'Monte Carlo Experimentation using PC-NAIVE'. *Advances in Econometrics*, 6: 91–125.

—— —— (1988). 'Interpreting Long-Run Equilibrium Solutions in Conventional Macro Models: A Comment'. *Economic Journal*, 98: 808–17.

—— and RICHARD, J.-F. (1982). 'On the Formulation of Empirical Models in Dynamic Econometrics'. *Journal of Econometrics*, 20: 3–33.

—— —— (1983). 'The Econometric Analysis of Economic Time Series'. *International Statistical Review*, 51: 111–63.

—— —— (1989). 'Recent Developments in the Theory of Encompassing'. In B. Cornet and H. Tulkens (eds.), *Contributions to Operations Research and Econometrics: The XXth Anniversary of CORE*. Cambridge, Mass.: MIT Press.

—— and VON UNGERN-STERNBERG, T. (1981). 'Liquidity and Inflation Effects on Consumers' Expenditure'. Ch. 9 in A. Deaton (ed.), *Essays in the Theory and Measurement of Consumers' Behaviour*. Cambridge University Press.

—— PAGAN, A. R., and SARGAN, J. D. (1984). 'Dynamic Specification'. Ch. 18 in Z. Griliches and M. D. Intriligator (eds.), *Handbook of Econometrics*, ii. Amsterdam: North-Holland.

—— LEAMER, E. E., and POIRIER, D. J. (1990a). 'The ET Dialogue: A Conversation on Econometric Methodology'. *Econometric Theory*, 6: 171–261.

—— MUELLBAUER, J. N. J., and MURPHY, A. (1990b). 'The Econometrics of DHSY'. Ch. 13 in J. D. Hey and D. Winch (eds.), *A Century of Economics*. Oxford: Basil Blackwell.

INSEE (1988). *Groupes D'études macroéconométriques concertées*. Paris: Institut National de la Statistique et des Études Économiques.

JARQUE, C. M., and BERA, A. K. (1980). 'Efficient Tests for Normality, Homoscedasticity and Serial Independence of Regression Residuals'. *Economics Letters*, 6: 255–9.

JOHANSEN, S. (1988). 'Statistical Analysis of Cointegration Vector'. *Journal of*

Economic Dynamics and Control, 12: 231–52.

KUZNETS, S. (1946). *National Income: A Summary of Findings*. New York: National Bureau of Economic Research.

LEAMER, E. E. (1978). *Specification Searches*. New York: John Wiley.

LUCAS, R. E. (1976). 'Econometric Policy Evaluation: A Critique' In K. Brunner and A. H. Meltzer (eds.), *The Phillips Curve and Labor Markets*, Carnegie–Rochester Conference Series on Public Policy, i. Amsterdam: North-Holland, pp. 19–36.

MACKINNON, J. G., and WHITE, H. (1985). 'Some Heteroscedastic Covariance Matrix Estimators with Improved Finite Sample Properties'. *Journal of Econometrics*, 29: 305–25.

MASON, S. F. (1962). *A History of the Sciences*. New York: Collier.

MIZON, G. E. (1984). 'The Encompassing Approach in Econometrics'. In D. F. Hendry and K. F. Wallis (eds.), *Econometrics and Quantitative Economics*. Oxford: Basil Blackwell, pp. 135–72.

—— and RICHARD, J.-F. (1986). 'The Encompassing Principle and its Application to Non-nested Hypothesis Tests'. *Econometrica*, 54: 657–78.

MUELLBAUER, J. N. J., and BOVER, O. (1986). 'Liquidity Constraints and Aggregation in the Consumption Function under Uncertainty'. Discussion Paper no. 12, Institute of Economics and Statistics, Oxford.

NEALE, A. J. (1987). 'Recursivity in Econometrics: An Historical Overview'. Mimeo, Nuffield College, Oxford.

Oxford Bulletin of Economics and Statistics (1986). Special issue: *Econometric Modelling with Cointegrated Variables*, 48.

PATTERSON, K. D. (1986). 'The Stability of Some Annual Consumption Functions'. *Oxford Economic Papers*, 38: 1–30.

PESARAN, M. H., and EVANS, R. A. (1984). 'Inflation, Capital Gains and UK Personal Savings: 1953–81'. *Economic Journal*, 94: 237–57.

PHILLIPS, G. D. A., and HARVEY, A. C. (1974). 'A Simple Test for Serial Correlation in Regression Analysis'. *Journal of the American Statistical Association*, 69: 935–9.

PHILLIPS, P. C. B. (1987a). 'Time Series Regression with a Unit Root'. *Econometrica*, 55: 277–301.

—— (1987b). 'Understanding Spurious Regressions in Econometrics'. *Journal of Econometrics*, 33: 311–40.

—— and LORETAN, M. (1989). 'Estimating Long Run Economic Equilibria'. Mimeo, Cowles Foundation, Yale University.

PLACKETT, R. L. (1950). 'Some Theorems in Least Squares'. *Biometrika*, 37: 149–57.

RAMSEY, J. B. (1969). 'Tests for Specification Errors in Classical Linear Least Squares Regression Analysis'. *Journal of the Royal Statistical Society*, B, 31: 350–71.

SARGAN, J. D. (1964). 'Wages and Prices in the United Kingdom: A Study in Econometric Methodology'. In P. E. Hart, G. Mills, and J. K. Whitaker (eds.), *Econometric Analysis for National Economic Planning*. London: Butterworths. Reprinted in D. F. Hendry and K. F. Wallis (eds.), *Econometrics and Quantitative Economics*. Oxford: Basil Blackwell.

—— (1980). 'Some Tests of Dynamic Specification for a Single Equation'.

Econometrica, 48: 879–97.

—— and BHARGAVA, A. (1983). 'Testing Residuals from Least Squares Regression for Being Generated by the Gaussian Random Walk'. *Econometrica*, 51: 153–74.

SPANOS, A. (1986). *Statistical Foundations of Econometric Modelling*. Cambridge University Press.

—— (1989). 'Early Empirical Findings on the Consumption Function, Stylized Facts or Fiction: A Retrospective View'. *Oxford Economic Papers*, 41: 150–69.

STOCK, J. H. (1987). 'Asymptotic Properties of Least Squares Estimators of Cointegrating Variables'. *Econometrica*, 55: 1035–56.

TERASVIRTA, T. (1970). *Step-wise Regression and Economic Forecasting*, Economic Studies Monograph no. 31. Helsinki: Finnish Economic Association.

TRIVEDI, P. K. (1984). 'Uncertain Prior Information and Distributed Lag Analysis'. In D. F. Hendry and K. F. Wallis (eds.), *Econometrics and Quantitative Economics*. Oxford: Basil Blackwell, pp. 173–210.

TRUNDLE, J. M. (1982). 'The Demand for M1 in the UK'. Mimeo, Bank of England.

WHITE, H. (1980). 'A Heteroscedastic-Consistent Covariance Matrix Estimator and a Direct Test for Heteroscedasticity'. *Econometrica*, 48: 817–38.

—— (1984). *Asymptotic Theory for Econometricians*. London: Academic Press.

—— (1990). 'A Consistent Model Selection'. Ch. 16 in C. W. J. Granger (ed.), *Modelling Economic Series: Readings in Econometric Methodology*. Oxford University Press.

YULE, G. U. (1926). 'Why Do We Sometimes Get Nonsense-Correlations between Time-Series? A Study in Sampling and the Nature of Time Series'. *Journal of the Royal Statistical Society*, 89: 1–64.

14

Causality and Economic Analysis: A Survey

ALESSANDRO VERCELLI

1. Introduction[1]

At the beginning of this century Russell declared that causality 'is a relic of a bygone age surviving, like monarchy, only because it is erroneously supposed to do no harm' (Russell 1913: 1). This prophecy of a rapid disappearance of causality in scientific language seemed correct for a few decades but collapsed altogether later on. After a period of disgrace—a period that began at the end of the last century and culminated in the 1930s and 1940s—causality had made a formidable comeback in the natural and social sciences, as well as in the philosophy of science. The wind changed direction so fast that in 1970 Suppes could observe that, 'contrary to the days when Russell wrote this essay, the words "causality" and "cause" are commonly and widely used by physicists in their most advanced work. There is scarcely an issue in *Physical Review* that does not contain at least one article using either "cause" or "causality" in its title' (Suppes 1970: 5). As for the social sciences, Granger recently observed that the 'Social Science Citation Index lists over 1000 papers with words such as "causal", "causation" or "causality" in their titles, and in a recent five-year period the Science Citation Index lists over 3000 such articles. Papers mentioning such words in the body of the paper, not in the title, are vastly more numerous' (Granger 1980: 332).

This is hardly surprising. Causality has to do with the basic architectural principles of the real world and of our knowledge of it. As Hume said many years ago, causal relations are the main 'ties of our thoughts; they are really to us the cement of the universe, and all the operations of the mind must, in a great measure, depend on them' (Hume 1938: 32). Others would contend that causation 'is not merely, as Hume says, *to us*, but also *in fact*, the cement of the universe' (Mackie 1974: 2).

[1] Sections 4, 5.2, 5.4, and the Appendix partially overlap with Sections 2, 4, and 5 of Vercelli (1990).

Of course, there are different architectural principles and styles. Granger observed that causality is clearly a topic in which individuals' tastes predominate since, 'unlike art, causality is a concept whose definition people know what they do not like but few know what they do like' (Granger 1980: 330). Notwithstanding its inherent ambiguity, scientists and philosophers seem particularly concerned to defend and propagate their own views of the concept, probably because it is profoundly entrenched in the epistemological and practical structures of adaptation to the real world. We may thus understand why methodological debates on causality often happen to be fiercer than those on substantive matters.

In this chapter, I will assume a completely different attitude. At this stage in the evolution of causal concepts, we have to understand, first of all, why causal intuitions differ so widely across disciplines, topics, and problems as well as among individuals. We thus need a thorough analysis of the philosophical, theoretical, and applicative scope of each serious notion of causality. The main aim of this paper is to apply this pluralist point of view to the causality concepts applied in economics.

After a cursory glance at causality concepts in the early stages of economics (Section 2), this survey begins in the early 1950s, when a sophisticated view of the role of causality in econometric models began to coalesce around the Cowles Commission. The debate focused first on deterministic versions of the causal concepts worked out by authors such as Simon and Wold (Section 3). During the early 1970s the debate turned towards probabilistic concepts of causality suggested in particular by Granger and Sims. I will consider first Keynes's conception of probabilistic causality—a conception that may be considered an important ancestor of modern conceptions of probabilistic causality (Section 4). I will then consider (in Section 5) the scope and limitations of Granger causality, a conception that is at the centre of the recent debates as far as economic and econometric models are concerned. Conclusions follow in Section 6. In the Appendix I will analyse analogies and differences between Keynes's and Granger's conceptions of causality, using as a bridge Suppes's theory of probabilistic causality, a theory that is very influential in the philosophy of science.

2. Historical Background

The evolution of causality concepts in economics has been intimately linked to the evolution of causality concepts in philosophy. I will briefly mention a few episodes in this parallel history without pretending to give a complete and/or analytical account.

The classical economists were profoundly influenced by Hume's regularist view of causality. (For a synthesis see Hume 1938.) Adam Smith, who was a close friend of Hume, suggested in the very title of his great book that economists should seek to discover the causes of economic phenomena. However, although Smith develops many causal arguments, he never suggests an explicit definition of causality. Nor does Ricardo, though in the *Principles* he employs the word 'cause' very often (at least twenty-six times in the first chapter, according to Garb 1964: 594). Still, we may detect a close link between the conception of causality adopted by classical economists and the regularist tradition initiated by Hume. In particular, J. S. Mill, the epigone of the classical school, made an important contribution to this tradition both in economics and in philosophy.

With the emergence of the neoclassical school, the 'romantic' criticism of causality also affected economics. According to this view, everything affects everything else. In particular, the general equilibrium approach fostered by Walras stresses general interdependence in contrast to asymmetric causality. Under the influence of this point of view, it became customary to attack explicitly the causalism or 'successivism' of Ricardo (which was also called the 'Ricardian vice'). This attitude remained widespread until recently. For instance, Knight maintained that in a so-called causal relationship we cannot see anything more than 'a functional relationship, the cause being the independent variable and the effect the dependent variable' (Knight 1956: 40, 94–5, 138–9). The prevailing view was often explicitly anti-causal, as witnessed by Robbins in his very influential essay: 'we no longer enquire concerning the cause determining variations of production and distribution. We enquire rather concerning the conditions of equilibrium of various economic "quantities" . . .' (Robbins 1935: 67). A similar attitude may be found, even more recently, in authors committed to the general equilibrium approach. For example, in his influential book *Money, Interest and Prices* Don Patinkin (1965) maintained that it is meaningless to speak of causal relations among dependent variables, and thus—generally speaking—among economic variables.[2]

However, the marginalist revolution did not expunge causality concepts from economics. The causal tradition somehow survived in the Marshallian and Wicksellian schools. Marshall and Wicksell remained open-minded towards causality, particularly in the macroeconomic arguments of their works. The Marshallian tradition was developed in a causal direction by Keynes who, in his *Treatise on Probability*, sketched a very original conception of probabilistic causality which he then

---

[2] In a general equilibrium approach such as that advocated by Patinkin, virtually all the economic variables are dependent variables.

applied to his economic works (see Section 4 below). The Wicksellian tradition was developed in a causal direction by the propounders of period analysis (see e.g. Lundberg 1964).

The post-Keynesian and post-Wicksellian causal approaches got mixed up in the methodological debate which, in the 1930s and 1940s, accompanied the first developments of econometrics. The first methodological assessment of econometrics was profoundly influenced by Scandinavian and Dutch scholars such as Tinbergen, Haavelmo, B. Hansen, and Wold. These scholars were combining the Wicksellian and Keynesian traditions, and thus were reasoning in terms of causal relations, in spite of the disrepute into which causality had fallen in orthodox economic theory. As a result, rapid development of econometrics from the 1930s onwards produced a revival of interest in causality concepts in economics. The sophisticated contributions of methodologists and econometricians such as Simon and Wold in the late 1940s and early 1950s also had an impact in other disciplines and contributed to the general come-back of causality in science and philosophy.

3. 'Cowles Causality': Simon and Wold

In recent decades, causality in economics has been discussed almost exclusively in relation to economic models. The most important seminal contributions were made in the early 1950s by Simon and Wold. Working independently, they developed a rigorous notion of causality for a class of models widely used in economic theory and econometrics, i.e. models involving the use of matrices. Simon's and Wold's concepts of causal order are very similar from the formal point of view, but differ substantially from the methodological point of view.

Simon's approach focuses almost exclusively on the epistemic relationship between 'cause' and 'effect' conceived as the order in which the solutions of a linear equation system must be computed. This order is completely determined when the system is recursive. Causal ordering in this view is thus related to a purely syntactic property of a mathematical system. This has been considered the main weakness of Simon's contribution (see e.g. Zellner 1979: 49).

However, this criticism is not altogether appropriate. Simon is fully aware that epistemic relations alone do not tell us anything about empirical causal relations unless we are able to detect some sort of correspondence between an epistemic relation and an empirical relation:

When we construct a model of the world, then to each property of the model that is invariant under 'trivial' transformations . . . there generally corresponds a property of the world the model describes . . . we have thus two notions of 'direction': the relations of points on a map, and the relations of cities on the globe. Similarly in the case of causality, we have a relation between variables in a mathematical model (the relation denoted by my term 'cause') and a relation in the real world between the phenomena denoted by these variables (the relation denoted by the common-sense term 'cause'). (Simon 1955: 194)

On several occasions Simon discussed the question of how to determine a correspondence between epistemic causality and empirical causality. The main criteria considered are as follows.

(a) *'Cosmological' assumptions*. One example is given by the so-called 'postulate of prepotence', according to which the behaviour of any system involving very large quantities of energy (e.g. the atmosphere) is practically independent of the behaviour of variables involving very much less energy (e.g. wheat growing).

(b) *Pragmatic assumptions*. Simon believes, for example, that, if we can associate with each epistemic 'cause' a specific power of intervention or 'direct control', we can provide the causal ordering with an operational basis (Simon 1953: 70).

(c) *Empirical assumptions*. An interesting suggestion, systematically developed in recent years by 'synergetics' (Haken 1983: 35–36), refers to the relative speeds of processes:

We can divide the variables, by rough criteria, in three classes:

1. Variables that have changed so slowly that they can be replaced by constants for the period under observation.
2. Variables that have adjusted so promptly that they are always close to (partial) equilibrium, hence their first derivatives are always close to zero. We can replace the first derivatives of these variables by zero in their equations (regarding them) as the dependent variables in the corresponding equations.
3. All other variables. We will retain their equations in canonical form.

Wold's conception of causal ordering is bolder than that of Simon: he defines the epistemic relation in a very similar manner but has much stronger convictions about the nature of the empirical relation and its correspondence with the epistemic relation. He thinks that only a fully recursive model is able to describe the underlying causal structure — which is considered to be firmly rooted in the stimulus–response behaviour of economic agents. An interdependent model is seen as the outcome of a mistaken specification, or of a derived specification justified by equilibrium assumptions and aggregation. Wold's conception of causality is explicitly 'manipulative', as is apparent from the following definition:

z is a cause of y if, by hypothesis, it is or 'would be' possible by *controlling* z indirectly to control y, at least stochastically. But it may or may not be possible by controlling y indirectly to control z. (Strotz and Wold 1960: 418)

I am not interested here in going deeper into the technical and philosophical differences between Simon, Wold, and the other authors who intervened in the debate in the 1950s and 1960s (Strotz, Orcutt, B. Hansen, etc.). However most of them shared a few basic ideas on causality. Among them I will stress particularly the following.

1. Causal order in the epistemic sense is given by the order of computation typical of recursive linear deterministic systems.
2. No causal statement with an operational content may be consistently entertained without theoretical a priori assumptions: 'the decision that a partial correlation is or is not spurious (does not or does indicate a causal ordering) can in general only be reached if a priori assumptions are made that certain other causal relations do not hold among the variables' (Simon 1954: 470).

Henceforth I will call this conception of causality, broadly speaking, 'Cowles causality', for it was typical of the Cowles Commission and of all the scholars around it who in the 1950s and 1960s provided the methodological foundations for classical econometrics.

Among the early criticisms of this conception of causality, the following can be mentioned.

1. It is at variance with the received conception accepted in the philosophy of science. This criticism is raised by Basmann, who believes that the 'classical' view is some sort of Laplacean determinism, as well as by Zellner, who believes that the classical concept is 'predictability according to a law' (Zellner 1979: 8). They are both wrong, because there is no such thing as a prevailing view on causality in the philosophy of science. Moreover, the two views considered classical by Basmann and Zellner are not equivalent (as Zellner contends) and are both rather old-fashioned.

2. Either the control experiment implied by Wold's definition can actually be implemented—which would be very restrictive—or 'impossible experiments' would be involved. According to Zellner, who quotes Jeffreys (1957: 8), the existence of a thing or the estimate of a quantity must not involve impossible experiments. However, Basmann himself, referring to his own conception of causality, made it clear that 'it is not necessary that such experiments be feasible; it is sufficient that they are not ruled out in principle' (Basmann 1963: 442).

3. The preference for recursive systems is arbitrarily and unduly restrictive: 'it is methodologically unsound to rule out, on a priori grounds alone, logically consistent laws that assume particular forms' (Zellner 1979: 30). This criticism is correct, provided that we substitute 'models' for 'laws'.[3] We should in particular recall that, if we want to

---

[3] There are strong doubts about the existence and reliability of economic laws. Kalecky found a particularly witty way of expressing this scepticism: 'Economics consists of

apply such a criterion to stochastic models, as was already clearly shown by Phillips (1956), we have to assume that errors satisfy fairly restrictive conditions as they must be neither mutually nor serially correlated (Malinvaud 1966: 613). Wold proved that we can always find a recursive system equivalent to any simultaneous-equations system (Wold and Juréen 1952: sect. 12.7), but equations of the derived recursive form do not generally have the same autonomy as the original structural equations (Malinvaud 1966: 614).

The identification of causal systems with recursive systems is certainly questionable, but, to be fair to the supporters of this conception of causality, we should briefly recall and reconstruct some of the deepest reasons lying behind their point of view. There are many reasons why they hold their particular opinion: statistical and econometric convenience, intuitive appeal, etc. The main reason is epistemological, and it might be labelled 'stimulus–response reductionism'. According to this view, the ultimate foundation of economic causality is rooted in the nexus, existing at the level of individual agents, between a stimulus received by a decision-maker and his response. This is either considered to be the 'true' causal relation underlying all the other derived relations (Orcutt 1952; Strotz 1960), or else it is considered to be at least a principle of intelligibility (Puu 1969). The principle is nothing but a corollary of methodological individualism interpreted from a behaviourist perspective. Unfortunately, it conflicts with another principle of intelligibility held by most mainstream economists: the principle that only equilibrium configurations are fully intelligible. (A classical version of this principle may be found in the work of Pareto, and a recent forceful restatement has been made by Lucas.) Equilibrium systems are typically characterized by symmetric relations among all the endogenous variables, and they are naturally represented in most cases by interdependent systems.[4] The debate about recursive versus interdependent systems which raged in the 1950s and 1960s was thus very much the expression of the conflict between two principles of intelligibility. A preference for recursive systems has often been the expression of a high level of attention paid to the role of disequilibrium processes (as in the Wicksellian and Keynesian schools), or else to the role of bounded rationality (as in the case of Simon). On the other hand, a preference for interdependent systems has often been the expression of a deep belief in substantive rationality.

theoretical laws which nobody has verified and of empirical laws which nobody can explain' (quoted in Steindl 1965: 18).

[4] As we have seen, an extreme view maintained by many supporters of the equilibrium approach is the conviction that it is meaningless to speak of causal relations among endogenous variables (Patinkin 1965).

4. Keynes's Theory of Probabilistic Causality

Proponents of Cowles causality did not exclude the possibility of working out probabilistic versions of causal concepts (see e.g. the references in Section 3 to Phillips and Malinvaud). However, the debate focused almost exclusively on deterministic versions. The same thing happened, in that period, in other sciences and in the philosophy of science itself. In all such disciplines, attention turned towards probabilistic causality only in the early 1970s. Economics and econometrics are not exceptions. Before going into the details of recent contributions to probabilistic causality, I will take a step back in time in order to analyse briefly one of the roots of modern theories of probabilistic causality, namely, Keynes's conception of causality.

In his economic contributions Keynes often employs a causal language, but in these writings he never clarifies the precise meaning of the causal concepts utilized. However, the issue is discussed in some detail in his *Treatise on Probability* (1921), where he worked out the foundations of his epistemological point of view. We find there a very interesting outline of a theory of probabilistic causality which in many respects anticipates the more mature and sophisticated recent theories (in particular that of Suppes 1970). Interpreters of Keynesian thought have neglected this link,[5] partly because they could not be acquainted with a fully fledged theory of probabilistic causality—something that is very recent. Keynesian causality has thus been interpreted as a version of deterministic causality close to that of Simon and Wold. The trouble is that Keynes explicitly judges deterministic causality to be not very useful, especially for the 'Moral Sciences':[6] 'One is led, almost inevitably, to use "cause" more widely than "sufficient cause" or than "necessary cause", because, the necessary causation of particulars by particulars being rarely apparent to us, the strict sense of the term has little utility' (Keynes 1921: 306).

Keynes feels the need for a much more comprehensive concept of causality than the traditional one. What is required is a concept of '*probable cause*, where there is no implication of necessity and where the antecedents will sometimes lead to particular consequents and sometimes will not' (p. 306). He is fully aware of the novelty and difficulties of this task, because 'a partial or possible cause involves ideas which are still obscure' (p. 182). The main problems arise from the conviction, then universally shared, that physical determinism could not

[5] An important exception is the excellent essay by Carabelli (1988), where Keynesian causality is correctly interpreted as probabilistic causality.

[6] Keynes classifies economics among the moral sciences, whose method is contrasted to that of the natural sciences: see e.g. Keynes (1971– , xiv, 300).

be questioned.[7] Keynes manages to get round the obstacle by introducing a crucial distinction between what he called '*causa essendi*', i.e. the ontological cause, which in the physical world must be conceived as deterministic, and what he called '*causa cognoscendi*', i.e. the epistemic cause, which may be conceived as probabilistic. He puts the main emphasis on the second concept, because

we wish to know whether knowledge of one fact throws light *of any kind* upon the likelihood of another. The theory of causality is only important because it is thought that by means of its assumptions light *can* be thrown by the experience of one phenomenon upon the expectation of another. (Keynes 1921: 308)

Ontological causality ('*causa essendi*') is interpreted as a limiting case of epistemic causality, whenever we have accurate enough knowledge of a certain set of phenomena to be able to individuate a necessary or sufficient cause. This is possible only if we are able to determine the nomic conditions K (expressed by proposition k), both formal and theoretical, and the existential conditions, both general L (expressed by proposition l) and hypothetical H (expressed by proposition h), which make the causal influence of an event on another sufficient or necessary.

The nexus between ontological and epistemic causality is clarified by Keynes through a sequence of formal definitions of causality, definitions which progressively relax the hypothesis of complete information. The starting-point is given by a definition of *causa essendi*:

(1) an event A is a sufficient cause of event B in conditions l, iff:
  (i) the proposition a describes an event A by referring to moments which are all prior to those referred to by proposition b in describing event B
  (ii) $b/akl = 1$ and $b/kl \neq 1$.

This definition is progressively restricted in relation to some further hypothetical existential knowledge, expressed by proposition h, leading to the definition of a *possible cause under conditions l*. A possible cause may be sufficient or necessary. For example, 'an event is a possible necessary cause of another, relative to given nomologic data, if circumstances can arise, not inconsistent with our existential data, in which the first event will be indispensable if the second is to occur' (Keynes 1921: 307).

The final, and weakest, definition is that of *causa cognoscendi*, which is conceived as a purely epistemic relation, one that does not necessarily imply a similar ontological relation. In this case, 'a and b may be any proposition whatever and are not limited as they were in the causal definitions' (p. 308). We may formulate the following definition:

---

[7] This depends very much on the fact that Keynes was writing before the quantum mechanics revolution (Keynes 1921: 106).

(2) an event *A*, described by proposition *a*, is a *causa cognoscendi* of event *B*, described by proposition *b*, relative to the background knowledge *hkl*, iff

$$b/ahkl \neq b/hkl.$$

Keynes stops here in the *Treatise* because the theory of epistemic causality ends up by overlapping with his theory of probability—since, after all, the essential relation according to Keynes is that of 'dependence for probability' or *causa cognoscendi* (p. 308). Still, I believe it is not improper to consider Keynes a forerunner of the modern theory of probabilistic causality (see the Appendix to this chapter).

5. Granger Probabilistic Causality

5.1. *Preview*

The causality concept worked out by Granger in the 1960s (Granger 1963, 1969), following a suggestion by Wiener (1958), has been and still is at the centre of a lively debate over the extent of its validity and its implications for economic theory.

The debate was initially provoked by the publication of an influential article by Sims (1972), who used Granger causality to argue that the money stock exerts a causal influence on nominal income and not vice versa. Granger causality rapidly became very popular with the New Classical economists (Lucas, Sargent, Barro, Prescott, etc.), partly because it was found to fit in well with the rational expectations approach.[8] This conception also became an important source of inspiration for the 'new econometrics', a partially new approach founded on time-series analysis 'without pretending to have too much a priori economic theory' (Sargent and Sims 1977; Sims 1979). An appraisal of the conception's epistemological legitimacy and its range of validity is thus very important.

The basic idea of Granger causality is very simple. Correlation between two stochastic variables is neither a sufficient nor a necessary condition for causality but undoubtedly gives us a legitimate reason for believing that some sort of causal connection may exist between them, unless we can show that the correlation is spurious. Moreover, if we assume that the cause must always precede the effect, we can ascertain empirically the direction of the causal nexus. The point of view that correlation plus a temporal lag individuate a causal relation is appealing because it seems that we could prove the existence and the direction of

---

[8] Lucas and Sargent explain why 'Granger causality is of natural interest for scholars of rational expectations', in the Introduction to Lucas and Sargent (1981: xxii–xxiv).

a causal relation through statistical methods only, without any explicit intervention of specific subject-matter theoretical hypotheses. The causal relation so ascertained would be useful, at least for prediction purposes, under the assumption—very common in empirical sciences—that the regularities underlying the correlation and the direction of the temporal lag will not change in the period to which the prediction refers. A conception of causality of this kind was used by Friedman and other monetarists in the 1960s in order to prove the typical monetarist assumption that money 'causes' income and not the other way round. However on that occasion Tobin and other Keynesian economists were able to show, through appropriate counter-examples, that the causal relation so detected was likely to be spurious under reasonable assumptions. This debate convinced most economists that '*post hoc ergo propter hoc*', as Tobin dubbed the monetarist view of causality, is a fallacy, since we cannot prove the existence of empirical causal relations without the explicit intervention of specific subject-matter causal hypotheses. Tobin thus confirmed in this debate one of the basic tenets of Cowles causality.

Granger causality is basically a sophisticated application to stochastic processes of the correlation-plus-lag point of view on causality. As Sims candidly recognized at the beginning of his seminal paper, his method of identifying causal direction 'does rest on a sophisticated version of the *post hoc ergo propter hoc* principle' (Sims 1972: 543). In this work Sims applies tests of Granger causality to the relation between money and income to bring new and more robust evidence in favour of the thesis that money causes income and not the other way round. He believed his arguments and tests to be robust enough to overcome the objections raised by Brainard and Tobin (1968) and Tobin (1970):

> the method is not easily fooled. Simple linear structures with reversed causality like the one put forth by Tobin cannot be constructed to give apparent money-to-GNP causality. Complicated structures like the one put forward by Brainard and Tobin in which both GNP and money are endogenous will, except under very special assumptions, yield a bivariate reduced form showing bidirectional causality. (Sims 1972: 543)

Sims's arguments and tests made a significant contribution to the popularity of Granger causality, a popularity that increased in the subsequent years, owing to the numerous interventions in the debate of both supporters and detractors. The main issue at stake is of course spuriousness. Granger, Sims, and other supporters maintain that:

1. spuriousness is extremely unlikely with Granger causality;
2. in any case, the likelihood of spuriousness may be settled empirically through appropriate tests, without the intervention of any specific subject-matter theoretical hypotheses.

Are they right in believing that Granger causality is a case of 'new wine in a new bottle', or is it rather a case of 'old wine in a revarnished old bottle'? I will try to answer this question in what follows.

5.2. *The definitions of Granger causality*

Granger develops his conception of causality through a succession of definitions which, not unlike that of Keynes, follow a downward path towards increasing uncertainty. In this case, however, such a procedure is justified by the intention to arrive at a definition of causality that is fully 'operative', i.e. amenable to empirical verification.

Let us assume that Y_n and X_{n+1} are two stochastic variables, Ω_n is a complete set of information available at time n, and F is a conditional distribution of X. The starting-point is the following definition:

DEFINITION 1. Y_n is a cause of X_{n+1} iff

$$F(X_{n+1}/\Omega_n) \neq F(X_{n+1}/\Omega_n - Y_n).$$

In other words, 'for causation to occur, the variable Y_n needs to have some unique information about what value X_{n+1} will take in the immediate future' (Granger 1980: 330).

In order to make this definition operative, Granger has to substitute for the complete information set Ω the incomplete information sets J_n, an information set actually available at time n, and J'_n for the information set J_n plus the past and present values of Y_n. We obtain the following definition:

DEFINITION 2. Y_n is a prima facie cause of X_{n+1} relative to the information set J'_n iff

$$F(X_{n+1}/J'_n) \neq F(X_{n+1}/J_n).$$

The use of incomplete information sets makes it necessary to introduce two qualifications which bring Granger's definition closer to that of Suppes:

1. A causal statement must be interpreted in relation to given background information.
2. Y_n is thus only a prima facie cause because we cannot exclude the possibility that adding new information might cause it to become spurious.

The definition is not yet operative because an empirical test should up to now refer to population attributes of X_{n+1}, which we cannot know.

Granger is thus compelled to be content with the first moment of the distribution, introducing the following definition:

DEFINITION 3. Y_n is a prima facie cause in mean of X_{n+1} relative to the information set J'_n iff

$$E(X_{n+1}/J'_n) \neq E(X_{n+1}/J_n).$$

In addition, Granger limits himself to point forecasts of X_{n+1} using a least-squares criterion. We may eventually express an operative definition of Granger causality, assuming that $\sigma^2(X_{n+1}/J_n)$ is the variance of the one-step-ahead forecast error of X_{n+1} given J_n:

DEFINITION 4. Y_n is a prima facie cause in mean of X_{n+1} relative to the information set J' iff

$$\sigma^2(X_{n+1}/J'_n) < \sigma^2(X_{n+1}/J_n).$$

In other words, knowledge of Y_n increases one's ability to forecast X_{n+1} in a least-squares sense, because it reduces the variance of forecast errors. Since much current economic and econometric practice is prediction-oriented, we may well understand why this definition, although very restrictive, has appealed to many. However, the definition actually tested is further restricted to linear predictors (Granger 1969: 429; 1980: 338), owing to the limitations of the available modelling and forecasting techniques:

DEFINITION 5. Y_n is a prima facie linear cause in mean of X_{n+1} relative to the information set J' iff definition 4 is applied to a class of linear predictors.

From now on, the term 'Granger causality' will stand for the concept stipulated in this last definition.

Before discussing the extent of validity of this concept, we must recall that its operational implementation is subject to further limitations. The principal ones are made explicit by Granger himself through the following axioms:

AXIOM A. 'The past and present may cause the future, but the future cannot cause the past' (Granger 1980: 330).

This axiom excludes not only backward causation, whose relevance is questionable, but also 'contemporaneous causation', which—as we have seen—is considered important by many economists.

AXIOM B. The information sets contain no redundant information (Granger 1980: 330).

This axiom is much more restrictive than it may at first appear. Redundant information could generate the erroneous conviction that a certain prima facie cause is spurious. This difficulty is particularly serious in economics, where time series often follow very similar fluctuating patterns.

AXIOM C. All causal relationships remain constant in direction through time (Granger 1980: 335).

This axiom has been considered very stringent by a few critics (see e.g. Zellner 1982: 314). However, Granger is right in pointing out that this assumption, though not literally true, is usual in causal inference and, indeed, in scientific inference in general. What should be considered much more disturbingly restrictive is the related hypothesis, routinely accepted in procedures used to test Granger causality: namely, that the series are jointly covariance-stationary. This assumption, according to Granger, is not strictly necessary for the definition of causality, but it is required for practical implementation. He admits that economic time series are often non-stationary, but he believes that they can be made stationary by transformations such as those suggested by Box and Cox (1964) and Box and Jenkins (1976). Unfortunately, it may be shown that these transformations do not preserve the causal properties of the original time series (see Conway *et al.* 1983: 17–23).

In addition, we have to emphasize that, as Granger himself stressed (1980), his definition of causality does not apply to single events, to deterministic processes, or to data not measurable on a cardinal scale.

5.3. *Sims's testing procedure*

Having considered the main definitions of Granger causality, we may now turn our attention to the testing procedures. Many tests have been suggested. Each one has been shown to have special problems and pitfalls. Since I am here interested only in the general strategy of the testing procedure, a procedure that is basically the same in all cases, I will consider only the test suggested by Sims (1972). It is the first and most popular test of Granger causality, and most of its shortcomings are common to all other tests.

In most tests, what is really tested is Granger non-causality. Sims (1972) was able to show that, in a regression of X on past, present, and future values of Y, the null hypothesis of absence of causality from X to Y is equivalent to all the coefficients on the future values of Y being equal to zero. Thus, Sims estimates a two-sided regression model and tests the hypothesis that all the coefficients for negative lags (i.e. for future values of Y) are zero. An analogous regression of Y on past and future X is then estimated to test the hypothesis that Y causes X.

From the very outset, the researcher applying this test is faced with two arbitrary decisions:

1. What is the appropriate order of the negative and positive lag polynomials?
2. Should the series be prefiltered and, if so, what filter is appropriate?

In fact, the error term will generally be serially correlated. While ordinary least squares may still yield consistent estimates, F-tests based on the estimated coefficients are invalid. Sims suggested prefiltering the X and Y series in the hope that this would reduce or eliminate the serial correlation problem. However, we have no guarantee that this result will be obtained. And, what is worse, the results of the tests are very sensitive to the choice of filter.

However, even if we consider the results of tests as non-arbitrary and non-ambiguous, we have still to interpret them before being allowed to refer them to the population variables. This is fully recognized by both Granger and Sims, who however play down the difficulties connected with the interpretation of results.

Let us assume that, as a result of a Sims test, the null hypothesis that X does not cause Y is rejected, while the null hypothesis that Y does not cause X is not rejected: then all we can say is that the results of the test are not inconsistent with the hypothesis that X is a *one-way prima facie linear cause in mean* of Y. We thus have no reason, for the time being, to believe that X is a genuine, or non-spurious, cause of Y. To do so, we have to analyse what empirical causal ordering is likely to have generated the result. If we were able to classify all the possible sources of spuriousness and were able to reject all of them, we could actually prove that X is a genuine Granger-cause of Y. Granger and Sims try hard to do this. They seem to believe that there is a limited number of sources of spuriousness and that their likelihood can be assessed a priori. They mention in particular the following sources.

1. A classical case of spurious causal ordering between X and Y arises when both variables are determined by a third variable. Sims tries to prove that this case is 'unlikely' with Granger causal orderings (Sims 1977*b*: 40). In theorems 2 and 3 of this work he provides two sets of alternative sufficient conditions for 'common cause' spuriousness, but he is unable to argue that these conditions, or their union, give the necessary conditions for this sort of spuriousness. Moreover, his theorems show only that *exact* spurious causal orderings of this kind are not very probable, while all we can infer from the data is that restrictions that define a causal ordering hold *approximately*. Therefore, Sims's and Granger's contention that this sort of spuriousness should be considered 'unlikely' for Granger causality is not convincing.

2. Another case of possible spuriousness considered by Granger (1980: 350) and seriously analysed by Sims (1977*b*: 39) is the case, apparently first suggested by Friedman, that, 'when a variable X is used

to control an objective variable Y, we may observe a spurious causal ordering from Y to X' (Sims 1977*b*: 38). Sims maintains that, if the optimal control problem is solved by policy-makers according to a larger time unit than applies to the fitted data, this sort of spuriousness should be considered unlikely. This argument is again far from conclusive, because it once more refers to exact spuriousness.

3. A third set of possible sources of spuriousness relates to the information set to which the tests are applied. The following instances are emphasized.

- Whenever there is a very large measurement error in one variable, and not in the other, this last will appear exogenous relative to the error-ridden variable (Sims 1977*b*: 35).
- Another obvious problem arises when the data are gathered with a frequency insufficient to 'capture' the causal influence (Granger 1980: 340).
- Further difficulties arise when the time at which a variable is recorded is different from the time at which the event relevant for the causal relation occurred (Granger 1980: 341).

Sims (1977*b*: 35) stresses that the first case is unlikely because it is true only for certain special structures in the measurement errors. The other two cases are also considered unlikely by Granger and Sims, but they do not provide arguments in favour of this thesis.

Tests of Granger causality are subject to further limitations. I will briefly mention a few of them.

1. The test suggested in Sims (1972) gives necessary conditions for Granger non-causality but not also sufficient conditions (see e.g. Jacobs *et al.* 1979: 401; Conway *et al.* 1983: 25).

2. Granger causality tests suffer from identification problems. A serious problem arises, for example, because samples are finite, whereas covariance-stationary processes are infinite in length; it is not possible to distinguish among processes of infinite duration on the basis of time-series of finite length without making strong arbitrary assumptions (see Conway *et al.* 1983: 22).

3. Any specification error, no matter how small, renders the causality tests uninterpretable. In fact, as has been observed, 'the smallest specification error will imply that a point null hypothesis will certainly be rejected, if the sample size is large enough. The usual cure for this problem is to test the composite hypothesis that a parameter is small rather than the point hypothesis that it is zero. In the case of (Granger) causality tests it is not possible to test the composite hypothesis because the model is not identified' (Jacobs *et al.* 1979: 401).

4. Granger himself has doubts about the usual tests for Granger causality (as summarized in theorem 2 of Pierce and Haugh 1977),

because they 'are just tests of goodness of fit, whereas the original definition requires evidence of improved forecasts' (Granger 1980: 348), and because 'the performance of these tests needs further investigations, either using statistical theory or Monte Carlo study, especially as some are suspected to be occasionally biased or to be lacking in power' (p. 347).

We can conclude this cursory description of the two-stage procedure for testing Granger causality with a cautionary note. It seems unsafe to claim too much of these testing procedures in view of the long chain of restrictive assumptions marking each step of the procedure for implementation of the tests, and in view of the fact, fully recognized by Granger and Sims, that the list of sources of spuriousness is not exhaustive.

5.4. *Granger causality: an appraisal*

Claims for the scope of Granger causality are sometimes very ambitious—at least, if we take literally some of the assertions made by Granger, Sims, and other supporters. Since, however, such assertions are intermixed with much more modest and cautious claims, we will distinguish between a strong version and a weak version of the claims, without trying to argue which one has really been entertained by whom. I will now summarize and discuss these claims and criticisms of them, distinguishing—somewhat arbitrarily—between claims referring to the definition regardless of the strength and persuasiveness of the actual testing procedures, and claims referring specifically to the testing procedures.

As regards the definition, we find a strong claim summarized in the following passage: 'While Granger's definition of causality does not cover every sense in which people use the notion of causality, and while tests for Granger causality have been misapplied and misinterpreted, Granger's definition does crystallize the central usage of the notion of causality as it was developed in scientific economics' (Sims 1979: 103). But we also find much more defensible claims, such as the following: 'so long as the need to be explicit about assumptions on residuals is kept in mind, the Granger method is a legitimate way to justify an exogeneity assumption' (Sims 1977*b*: 34).

Granger's definition of causality has been criticized first of all for terminological reasons. According to many critics, Granger does not really define a causal relation but rather something else. Unfortunately, the critics do not agree on what Granger's *definiendum* should be called, as shown by the following small sample of suggestions:

- Schwert (1979): 'incremental predictive content'
- Jacobs *et al.* (1979): 'informativeness'
- Conway *et al.* (1983): 'relative predictive efficiency'
- Spohn (1983): 'causal relevance'

Granger himself sometimes seems to be assailed by terminological doubts: 'possibly cause is too strong a term, or one too emotionally laden to be used. A better term might be *temporally related* but since cause is such a simple term we shall continue to use it' (Granger and Newbold 1977: 225). In any case, I think that Granger's rejection of this sort of criticism is reasonable:

it has been suggested that the name should not involve words like 'cause' or 'causality', as these words are too emotion-laden, involve too much preconception and have too long a history . . . Provided I define what I personally mean by causation, I can use the term . . . If others wanted to refer to my definition they can just call it 'Granger causality' to distinguish it from alternative definitions. (Granger 1980: 333)

This point of view is questioned by a few critics, who lament the inconsistency of Granger's definition with the 'philosophical definition'. According to Zellner, philosophers of science agree in defining causality as 'predictability according to a law'. He maintains that this notion may be traced back to Herschel (1831), and that it received its classical statement in Feigl (1953). However, the Herschel–Feigl definition is only a particular version of a prediction-oriented regularist theory, and not even one particularly entrenched in the recent philosophical debate.[9] In addition, the regularist theory is only one among many existing theories on causality entertained in the philosophical debate. We cannot even say that it is the most authoritative theory, and—what is worse—its influence has been steadily declining in recent decades. One of the theories that have recently gained a large audience is that of probabilistic causality, to which Granger's conception of causality may legitimately be related (see Appendix). There is no a priori reason to deny philosophical legitimacy to the notion of Granger causality.

However, the formal analogy conceals a profound difference. In all cases probabilistic causality is defined in relation to certain background information. But in other definitions (e.g. in Keynes's and Suppes's), background information encompasses a theoretical framework, while in Granger it includes only the past and present values of the relevant stochastic variables. The other peculiarities of Granger causality, such as the exclusive reference to events that have actually occurred, and hence

---

[9] Many recent versions of the regularist theory do not accept the thesis of the symmetry between explanation and prediction and are explanation-oriented rather than prediction-oriented (see e.g. Gärdenfors 1988).

not to types of events and to dispositional magnitudes, all arise from this inductivist point of view.

Supporters of Granger causality believe that it is the only conception of causality that is really operational. Pierce and Haugh, for example, note that 'it appears difficult to present an alternative definition for causality which can be tested empirically' (Pierce and Haugh 1977: 266). Granger and Sims concede that there are other notions of causality in economics that may be considered in some sense operational, but they contend that the validity of the tests based on them is conditional upon certain theoretical assumptions, so that we can never know whether a favourable or unfavourable result depends on the causal hypothesis or rather on the auxiliary theoretical hypotheses. Hence, in contrast to Granger causality, which is considered 'unconditional', i.e. independent of a priori theoretical assumptions, they call this sort of causality 'conditional'. For this reason they claim the superiority of Granger causality over alternative concepts of causality, including that of Simon and Wold.[10]

It is shown that, from the formal point of view, these two conceptions are strictly analogous,[11] and that the only significant difference is that defenders of Cowles causality always explicitly refer causal statements to a theoretical framework. It is moreover admitted that the range of applicability is broader in this second case, since Cowles causality also applies to deterministic variables and contemporaneous causation. If we could prove that the unconditionality claim is wrong, the superiority claim would in general be denied, if not reversed. This is what will be argued in the sequel.

Many empirical tests of Granger causality have been devised, and they have different advantages and disadvantages. However, they all have in common a two-stage procedure of implementation, as exemplified by the test suggested by Sims (1972) (see Section 5.2 above). In the first stage a few statistical tests are applied to data, and in the second stage the results of tests are interpreted. In the first stage the theoretical hypotheses are not clearly defined. It could be objected that any procedure of selection and manipulation of data already presupposes a theoretical point of view, even if only implicitly (see e.g. Blaug 1980: 14). Whatever one may think of this objection, in the second stage insuperable difficulties emerge. The crucial problem is to discriminate between genuine and spurious causes. This cannot be done without an

---

[10] Granger agrees with Sims (1977b), who 'has discussed the Simon and Wold approach and found it not operational in practice' (Granger 1980: 334).

[11] The two notions are very close in their epistemic structure, as they impose very similar a priori restrictions on a stochastic system (see Sims 1977b: 32; see also Geweke 1982, 1984). From the purely formal point of view, we may consider Granger causality as a dynamic analogue of the static notion of Wold.

explicit intervention of theoretical hypotheses. The supporters of
Granger causality believe that they can get round this obstacle. They
discuss a list of circumstances under which a prima facie cause is likely
to be spurious, in order to prove that all these circumstances are
extremely unlikely in the case of Granger causality. Unfortunately, this
strategy fails.

In particular, in order to exclude the possibility that we can find a
third variable that would make a prima facie cause spurious, it is
suggested that certain empirical tests be applied to all the variables that
might have this effect. This procedure is clearly unacceptable, unless we
make a sufficient number of a priori theoretical assumptions regarding
the behaviour of the economic system; otherwise the list of third
variables that could induce spuriousness would be virtually infinite.

More generally, we may observe that one cannot demonstrate the
exhaustiveness of any list of circumstances that might induce spuriousness. An a priori discussion of the likelihood of certain spuriousness-
inducing circumstances cannot substantially increase confidence in the
'genuineness' of a certain prima facie cause, unless one explicitly
declares his theoretical background. Thus, even Granger causality refers
implicitly to a certain theoretical conceptual framework. The only real
difference in this respect is that the theoretical hypotheses are made
explicit by Simon and Wold, while they remain implicit in the arguments
of Granger and Sims. The charge of presumption against the use of
Simon and Wold causality may thus be turned against an uncritical use
of Granger and Sims causality. What one really cannot do is to assert
the truth of a causal statement, 'pretending' that it is 'unconditional' to
any theoretical framework.

Supporters of Granger causality seem on many occasions to be
unaware of the well-known limits of inductive methods—limits that have
been clarified by the prestigious philosophical tradition stretching from
Hume to Popper and beyond. They apparently accept one or more of
the following mistaken axioms:

- Measurement is possible without theory.
- Correlation implies causation.
- *Post hoc ergo propter hoc.*

Each of these theses is at times provocatively entertained by the
supporters of Granger causality, perhaps in order to flaunt the novelty
of their conception, as if the new techniques of time series were by
themselves able to overcome the traditional methodological principles.
In so doing, they risk slipping into the pitfalls of 'operationism' and
'inductivism', long since rejected by the philosophy of science.

However, there is a second line of defence for Granger causality
which is less pretentious and more convincing. Granger causality is

considered particularly relevant for certain specific scientific aims. We can mention in particular the following (see e.g. Sims 1972, 1977*b*):

1. Granger causality is a necessary and sufficient condition for exogeneity, which in its turn is a necessary condition for efficient estimation.
2. Granger causality is a necessary and sufficient condition for optimal forecasts.
3. Granger causality is a necessary, though not sufficient, condition for economic policy (forecast and control).

Unfortunately, even these claims are exaggerated. Granger causality is a necessary but not sufficient condition for predicting the outcomes of processes that are not influenced by policy, or are in any case structurally stable; but it is neither a necessary nor a sufficient condition for correct estimation, nor for prediction and control of processes that are influenced by policy interventions, or are in any way structurally unstable (Engle *et al.* 1983).

We may thus conclude that Granger causality is not without relevance for a few well defined and circumscribed scientific aims. But the claim of its general superiority over alternative conceptions of causality is totally groundless.

6. Conclusions

We have seen that Keynes causality is probabilistic and in many ways anticipates the more recent and mature theory of Suppes. Granger's conception can in turn be interpreted as a particular version of Suppes causality. However, we have seen that, behind the formal analogies, profound philosophical divergences between Keynes and Granger are detectable. While Keynes, as well as supporters of Cowles causality (in particular Simon and Wold), insist that it is necessary to relate any causal statement to a well defined theoretical background, the supporters of Granger causality claim that their conception is superior precisely because of its alleged independence of theoretical hypotheses. This presumption has been shown to be completely groundless, although this does not exclude the utility of Granger causality for a few well defined scientific purposes. In particular, we have seen that it is a necessary, though not sufficient, condition for efficient predictions of the outcomes of processes that are not influenced by policy interventions, or are in any case structurally stable.

The preceding considerations are not without implications for the lively debate between new classical economists and Keynesian economists. All the claims of superiority based on the results of Granger causality tests are to be considered open to question, because they depend on a priori theoretical hypotheses which are not explicitly discussed in these contributions.

Appendix: Suppes's Probabilistic Causality

Probabilistic causality has occupied a central place in the philosophical debate on causality since the publication in 1970 of a monograph by Suppes which rapidly became a classic of epistemological literature. Thus, probabilistic causality has a very short history, though we could mention a few earlier seminal contributions which were completely neglected (Reichenbach 1956; Good 1961–2; and, as we have seen, Keynes 1921). This might at first seem quite surprising, because both ingredients of the concept have been on the stage of philosophical debate for a very long time (more than two millennia in the case of causality, and more than two centuries in the case of probability). This may be ascribed to the fact that causality and determinism were considered mutually inseparable until very recently, by which time the quantum physics revolution (which began in the 1920s) had had the time to percolate through into common wisdom, and probabilistic language (after Kolmogorov's axiomatization in 1933) had begun to acquire the sophistication needed to fit the subtleties of causal language.

It is rather early to attempt a full appraisal of the usefulness of probabilistic causality in disciplines such as economics. Work is needed to develop and adapt it to the specific requirements of economic analysis. Suppes's conception is particularly fruitful for this purpose, because its point of view is taxonomic rather than prescriptive.

The starting-point of his analysis is not, as it was typical in earlier literature, a stipulative definition of causality proposed as the paradigm for a correct use of the concept. All attempts in this direction proved rather unsuccessful because the range of application of each of these concepts was shown to be very narrow compared with the wide variety of meanings that may be found in scientific languages.

Suppes thus prefers to start from a 'weak' definition of causality, one that may be considered the 'least common denominator' of a wide variety of causal concepts. This is seen as a necessary premise for articulating the definition so that the ensuing causal analysis may evolve in diverse directions in order to fit the different characteristics of many subjects and languages. This approach agrees very well with a discipline such as economics, where causal intuitions are particularly varied and heterogeneous.

The starting-point is the concept of 'prima facie cause', which may be roughly defined as follows: 'An event B is a *prima facie* cause of an event A if and only if (i) B occurs earlier than A, (ii) the conditional probability of A occurring when B occurs is greater than the unconditional probability of A occurring' (Suppes 1984a: 48). In other words, the occurrence of event B increases the probability of the occurrence of event A. Prima facie causality is thus a necessary, though not a sufficient, condition for identifying a peculiar causal relation. Such a weak concept is unable to discriminate between 'genuine' causes and 'spurious' causes because even 'spurious' causes appear to increase the probability that the effect will occur.

In order to discuss this and the following problems, we must now introduce a slightly more precise definition of prima facie causality. Let us assume that A_t and $B_{t'}$ are events defined as 'subsets of all the possible outcomes', i.e. in the sense (introduced by Kolmogorov 1933) of the mathematical theory of probability. In addition, let us assume that the events are referred to a well defined instant of time. We may thus introduce the following definition:

> DEFINITION A1. B_t is a prima facie (potential) cause of $A_{t'}$, as regards the background information Z_t, iff
> (i) $P(B_t \cap Z_t) > 0$ and $t < t'$
> (ii) $P(A_{t'}/B_t \cap Z_t) > P(A_{t'}/Z_t)$

This definition is identical to that put forward by Suppes (1970) except for two specifications, implicit in Suppes, which are particularly relevant for what follows. First of all, we have stated explicitly that prima facie causality does not necessarily presuppose the actual occurrence of events. This allows a consistent utilization of Suppes causality within an explicit theoretical context, because the concept becomes applicable not only to single events but also to *types of events*, and not only to directly observable magnitudes but also to *dispositions*. As is generally agreed, types of events and dispositions are essential ingredients in any theoretical argument (see e.g. F. Suppe 1977).

We also stated explicitly from the very outset that in Suppes's approach any causal statement or inference is always relative to a corpus of information organized by theoretical hypotheses which we may define as 'background information'. This should be kept firmly in mind in order to understand the nexus linking the conceptions of causality of Suppes, Keynes, and Granger.

We are now in a position to analyse the distinction between genuine and spurious causes. Let us begin by considering a couple of examples. One of the favourite examples of a spurious cause, at least since Laplace, has been that of the barometer. The sudden shift of the barometer pointer is a prima facie cause of the storm that breaks out shortly afterwards, because the first event induces an upward revision of the probability of the second event. But the barometer shift is not a genuine cause of storm, for as everyone knows, both events are effects of a third cause, the drop in the atmospheric pressure. In other words, as soon as we take account of the common cause, the effect becomes stochastically independent of the spurious cause. In Reichenbach's terminology, the common cause *screens off* the prima facie stochastic influence of the spurious cause (Reichenbach 1956). This suggests the following definition:

> DEFINITION A2. B_t is a *spurious* cause of $A_{t'}$ iff
> (i) B_t is a prima facie cause of $A_{t'}$
> (ii) there is a $t'' < t$ and an event $C_{t''}$ such that
>
> $P(B_{t'} \cap C_{t''}) > 0$
>
> $P(A_{t'}/B_t \cap C_{t''}) = P(A_{t'}/C_{t''})$
>
> $P(A_{t'}/B_t \cap C_{t''}) \geqslant P(A_{t'}/B_t)$

The barometer's example might, because of its theoretical obviousness, obscure the crucial role played by the conceptual framework in any argument aimed at discriminating between spurious and genuine causes. An example drawn from economics may better illustrate this point. Both Keynes and the classical economists would readily have admitted that an increase in real wages above the full-employment level could be considered a prima facie cause of a reduction in employment. However, Keynes would have considered such a cause to be spurious, since both events would have been interpreted as joint effects of a reduction in effective demand; on the other hand, a classical economist, who rejected the principle of effective demand and accepted Say's law, would have considered such a cause to be genuine.

On these premises, Suppes was able to work out a very flexible concept of causality that may be applied in different empirical and theoretical contexts. I cannot survey here the interesting articulations, specifications, and developments of the concepts explored by Suppes and his followers, but shall only briefly recall two aspects which are particularly useful for the economic analysis.

First of all, Suppes defines deterministic causality as a particular instance of probabilistic causality:

DEFINITION A3. A_t is a sufficient cause of $B_{t'}$ iff
(i) A_t is a prima facie cause of $B_{t'}$
(ii) $P(B_{t'}/A_t) = 1$

Suppes causality may thus also be applied to deterministic causality.   In addition, Suppes causality also applies whenever probability is not measurable on a cardinal scale. This is particularly important in disciplines like economics, where these unhappy circumstances often prevail, as Keynes and many other economists have recognized. As Hicks recently maintained, in economics probabilities are in most cases only ordinal and often not even in a complete way (Hicks 1979: 115). Suppes's theory may be easily adapted to these cases by translating his quantitative theory into a qualitative one, following the suggestions put forward by Keynes (1921) and developed by Koopman (1940).

Suppes and Keynes.

Keynes's definition (1) may be easily translated into Suppes's language, setting $a = A_t$, $b = B_t$, $kl = K \cap L_t = Z_t$. This is possible because Suppes's events are strictly analogous to Keynes's propositions (see Vercelli, 1990: 230–231). Definition (1) is translated in the following way:

DEFINITION A4. A_t is a sufficient cause of $B_{t'}$ relative to $Z_t = K \cap \overset{\bullet}{L}_t$, iff
(i) $P(A_t \cap Z_t) > 0$ and $t < t'$
(ii) $P(B_{t'}/A_t \cap Z_t) = 1$ and $P(B_{t'}/Z_t) \neq 1$

Notice that A_t is a (potential) prima facie cause of $B_{t'}$ because (ii) implies that $P(B_{t'}/A_t \cap Z_t) > P(B_{t'}/Z_t)$. Keynes's definition (2) is thus strictly equivalent to Suppes's definition (A3).

Keynes then progressively weakens definition (2) by relaxing the conditions under which a concept of ontological causality may be defined. An intermediate step is, for example, the definition of a 'possible sufficient cause', when the background information Z_t includes a set H_t of existential hypotheses. The last step in this chain of definitions is that of the *causa cognoscendi*:

DEFINITION A5. A_t is a *causa cognoscendi* of $B_{t'}$ relative to Z_t iff
(i) $P(A_t \cap Z_t) > 0$
(ii) $P(B_{t'}/A_t \cap Z_t) \neq P(B_{t'}/Z_t)$

We may easily verify that a *causa cognoscendi*, which does not imply a necessary or sufficient nexus between cause and effect, corresponds to a (potential) prima facie cause as stated by Suppes in definition (A1), apart from the following two differences. (1) A temporal lag is not required. Keynes does not exclude the possibility of an epistemic cause contemporaneous with its effect. It is no wonder that contemporaneous causation may be found in his economic contributions. (2) A positive statistical relevance of the cause for the effect is not required. In other words, a cause might also reduce the probability of the occurrence of the effect (in which case the cause is 'negative' or inhibitory, as is admitted by Suppes himself, though this is not made explicit in the definition).

Suppes and Granger.

As we have seen, the range of applicability of Granger causality is much narrower than that of Suppes causality. We may further clarify the issue by translating into Suppes's language Granger's definition 2, which, as in Suppes, is the most general definition postulating incomplete information. Let assume that $A_{t'} = X_{n+1}$, $B_t = Y_n$, $Z_t = J_n$, $B_t \cap Z_t = J'_n$, and that both $A_{t'}$ and B_t occurred. Granger's definition 2 may thus be expressed in the following way:

DEFINITION A6. B_t is a prima facie Granger cause of $A_{t'}$ relative to background information Z_t iff
(i) $A_{t'}$ and B_t occur and $t < t'$
(ii) $P(A_{t'}/B_t \cap Z_t) \neq P(A_{t'}/Z_t)$

As we may easily verify by comparing (A6) with (A1), Granger causality appears as a particular case of Suppes causality.

References

BASMANN, R. L. (1963). 'The Causal Interpretation of Non-triangular Systems of Economic Relations'. *Econometrica*, 32: 439–48.
—— (1965). 'A note on the Statistical Testability of "Explicit Causal Chains" against the Class of "Interdependent" Models'. *Journal of the American Statistical Association*, 60: 1080–93.
BENTZEL, R., and HANSEN, B. (1954). 'On Recursiveness and Interdependency in Economic Models'. *Review of Economic Studies*, 22: 153–68.
BLAUG, M. (1980). *The Methodology of Economics*. Cambridge University Press.
BOX, G. E. P., and COX, D. R. (1964). 'An Analysis of Transformations'.

Journal of the Royal Statistical Society, B26: 211–43.

—— and JENKINS, G. M. (1976). *Time Series Analysis: Forecasting and Control*, 2nd edn. San Francisco: Holden Day.

BRAINARD, W., and TOBIN, J. (1968). 'Pitfalls of Financial Model Building'. *American Economic Review (Proc.)*, 58: 99–122.

BUNGE, M. (1982). 'The Revival of Causality'. In G. Fløistad (ed.), *Contemporary Philosophy*, ii. The Hague: Martinus Nijhoff, pp. 133–55.

CARABELLI, A. (1988). *On Keynes's Method*. London: Macmillan.

CONWAY, R. K., SWAMY, P. A. V. B., and YANAGIDA, J. F. (1983). 'The Impossibility of Causality Testing'. *Federal Reserve Board, Special Studies Papers*, no. 178.

ENGLE, R. F., HENDRY, D. F., and RICHARD, J.-F. (1983). 'Exogeneity'. *Econometrica*, 51: 277–304.

FEIGE, E., and PEARCE, D. K. (1979). 'The Casual Causal Relationship between Money and Income: Some Caveats for Time Series Analysis'. *Review of Economics and Statistics*, 61: 521–33.

FEIGL, H. (1953). 'Notes on Causality'. In H. Feigl and M. Brodbeck (eds.), *Readings in the Philosophy of Science*. New York: Appleton-Century-Crofts.

FRIEDMAN, M. (1961). 'The Lag in the Effect of Monetary Policy'. *Journal of Political Economy*, 69: 447–66.

GALAVOTTI, M. C., and GAMBETTA, G. (eds.) (1983). *Causalità e Modelli Probabilistici*. Bologna: CLUEB.

GARB, G. (1964). 'The Problem of Causality in Economics'. *Kyklos*, 17: 594–609.

GÄRDENFORS, P. (1988). *Knowledge in Flux: Modeling the Dynamics of Epistemic States*. Cambridge, Mass.: MIT Press.

GEWEKE, J. (1982). 'Causality, Exogeneity, and Inference'. In W. Hildenbrand (ed.), *Advances in Econometrics*. Cambridge University Press.

—— (1984). 'Inference and Causality in Economic Time Series Models'. In Z. Griliches and M. Intriligator (eds.), *Handbook of Econometrics*, ii. Amsterdam: North-Holland.

—— MEESE, R., and DENT, W. (1983). 'Comparing Alternative Tests of Causality in Temporal Systems: Analytic Results and Experimental Evidence'. *Journal of Econometrics*, 21: 161–94.

GOOD, I. J. (1961/2). 'A Causal Calculus I–II'. *British Journal for the Philosophy of Science*, 11: 305–18; 12: 43–51.

GOODWIN, R. M. (1947). 'Dynamical Coupling with Especial Reference to Markets Having Production Lags'. *Econometrica*, 5: 181–204.

GRANGER, C. W. J. (1963). 'Economic Processes Involving Feedback'. *Information and Control*, 6: 28–48.

—— (1969). 'Investigating Causal Relations by Econometric Models and Cross-spectral Methods'. *Econometrica*, 37: 424–38.

—— (1980). 'Testing for Causality: A Personal Viewpoint'. *Journal of Economic Dynamics and Control*, 2: 303–28.

—— and NEWBOLD, P. (1977). *Forecasting Economic Time Series*. New York: Academic Press.

HAKEN, H. (1983). *Advanced Synergetics*. Berlin: Springer.

HERSCHEL, J. F. W. (1831). *A Preliminary Discourse on the Study of Natural*

Philosophy. London: Longman.

HICKS, J. (1979). *Causality in Economics*. Oxford: Basil Blackwell.

HUME, D. (1938). *An Abstract of a Treatise of Human Nature*, ed. J. M. Keynes and P. Sraffa. Cambridge University Press.

JACOBS, R. L., LEAMER, E. E., and WARD, M. P. (1979). 'Difficulties with Testing for Causation'. *Economic Inquiry*, 17: 401–13.

JEFFREYS, H. (1957). *Theory of Probability*, 3rd rev. edn. Oxford University Press.

KEYNES, J. M. (1921). *A Treatise on Probability*. New York: Macmillan.

—— (1971–). *The Collected Writings of J. M. Keynes*, ed. D. E. Moggridge and E. Johnson. London: Macmillan.

KIM, J. (1973). 'Causation, Nomic Subsumption and the Concept of Event'. *Journal of Philosophy*, 70: 217–30.

KNIGHT, F. (1956). *On the History and Method of Economics*. University of Chicago Press.

KOLMOGOROV, A. N. (1933). *Grundbegriffe der Wahrscheinlichkeitsrechnung*. Berlin: Springer-Verlag. Engl. trans. *Foundations of the Theory of Probability*. New York: Chelsea, 1956.

KOOPMAN, B. O. (1940). 'The Bases of Probability'. *Bulletin of American Mathematical Society*, 46: 762–74.

LUCAS, R. E., and SARGENT, J. T. (eds.) (1981). *Rational Expectations and Econometric Practice*. London: Allen & Unwin.

LUNDBERG, E. (1964). *Studies in the Theory of Economic Expansion*. New York: Augustus M. Kelley.

LUNGHINI, G. *et al.* (1984). *La Scienza Impropria*. Milan: Angeli.

MACKIE, J. L. (1974). *The Cement of the Universe: A Study of Causation*. Oxford: Clarendon Press.

MALINVAUD, E. (1966). 'Pour une axiomatique de la causalité'. In H. Wold, *Model Building in the Human Sciences*. Monaco: Union Européenne d'Éditions.

MILL, J. S. (1848). *Principles of Political Economy, with Some of their Applications to Social Philosophy*. London: Longman, 1909 edn.

—— (1851). *A System of Logic*. London: Parker, 1951 edn.

ORCUTT, G. H. (1952). 'Actions, Consequences, and Causal Relations'. *Review of Economics and Statistics*, 34: 305–13.

PASINETTI, G. L. (1974). *Growth and Income Distribution: Essays in Economic Theory*. Cambridge University Press.

PATINKIN, D. (1965). *Money, Interest and Prices: An Integration of Monetary and Value Theory*, 2nd edn. New York: Harper and Row.

PHILLIPS, A. W. (1956). 'Some Notes on the Estimation of Time-Forms of Reactions in Interdependent Dynamic Systems'. *Economica*, 23: 99–113.

PIERCE, D. A. (1977). 'Relationships—and the Lack Thereof—Between Economic Time Series, with Special Reference to Money and Interest Rates'. *Journal of the American Statistical Association*, 72: 11–21.

—— and HAUGH, L. D. (1977). 'The Assessment and Detection of Causality in Temporal Systems'. *Journal of Econometrics*, 5: 265–93.

PUU, T. (1969). 'Causal versus Teleological Explanation in Economics'. *Swedish Journal of Economics*, 71: 111–26.

REICHENBACH, H. (1956). *The Direction of Time*. University of California Press at Berkeley.

RICARDO, D. (1817). *On the Principles of Political Economy and Taxation*. In P. Sraffa (ed.), *The Work and Correspondence of David Ricardo*. Cambridge University Press, 1970.

ROBBINS, L. (1935). *An Essay on the Nature and Significance of Economic Science*. London: Macmillan.

RUSSELL, B. (1913). 'On the Notion of Cause'. *Proceedings of the Aristotelian Society*, 13: 1–26.

SALMON, W. C. (1984). *Scientific Explanation and the Causal Structure of the World*. Princetown University Press.

SARGENT, T. J., and SIMS, C. A. (1977). 'Business Cycle Modelling without Pretending to Have Much a priori Economic Theory'. In Sims (1977a).

SCHWERT, G. W. (1979). 'Tests of Causality: The Message in the Innovations'. In K. Brunner and A. H. Meltzer (eds.), *Carnegie–Rochester Conference Series on Public Policy*, x. Amsterdam: North-Holland.

SIMON, H. A. (1952). 'On the Definition of the Causal Relation'. *Journal of Philosophy*, 49: 517–28.

——(1953). 'Causal Ordering and Identifiability'. In W. C. Hood and T. C. Koopmans (eds.), *Studies in Econometric Methods*. New York: John Wiley, pp. 49–74.

——(1954). 'Spurious Correlation: A Causal Interpretation'. *Journal of the American Statistical Association*, 49: 467–79.

——(1955). 'Causality and Econometrics: Comment'. *Econometrica*, 23: 193–5.

SIMS, C. A. (1972). 'Money, Income and Causality'. *American Economic Review*, 62: 540–52.

——(ed.) (1977a). *New Methods in Business Cycle Research*. Federal Reserve Bank of Minneapolis.

——(1977b). 'Exogeneity and Causal Ordering in Macroeconomic Models'. In Sims (1977a).

——(1979). 'Macroeconomics and Reality'. *Econometrica*: 48, 1–48.

SMITH, A. (1776). *An Inquiry into the Nature and Causes of the Wealth of Nations*. London: Methuen, 1961 edn.

SPOHN, W. (1983). 'Probabilistic Causality: From Hume via Suppes to Granger'. In Galavotti and Gambetta (1983).

STEINDL, J. (1965). *Random Processes and the Growth of Firms: A Study of the Pareto Law*. London: Griffin.

STROTZ, R. H. (1960). 'Interdependence as a Specification Error'. *Econometrica*, 28: 428–42.

—— and WOLD, H. (1960). 'Recursive vs. Non-Recursive Systems: An Attempt at Synthesis'. *Econometrica*, 28: 417–27.

SUPPE, F. (ed.) (1977). *The Structure of Scientific Theories*. Urbana, Ill.: University of Illinois Press.

SUPPES, P. (1970). *A Probabilistic Theory of Causality*. Amsterdam: North-Holland.

——(1984a). *La Logica del Probabile*. Bologna: CLUEB.

——(1984b). *Probabilistic Metaphysics*. Oxford: Basil Blackwell.

TOBIN, J. (1970). 'Money and Income: *Post Hoc* Ergo Propter Hoc?' *Quarterly*

Journal of Economics, 84: 301–17.

VELUPILLAI, K. (1982). 'Linear and Nonlinear Dynamics in Economics: The Contributions of Richard Goodwin'. *Economic Notes*, 10: 73–92.

VERCELLI, A. (1990). 'Probabilistic Causality and Economic Models: Suppes, Keynes, Granger'. In K. Velupillai (ed.), *Nonlinear and Multisectoral Macrodynamics*. London: Macmillan.

WIENER, N. (1958). 'The Theory of Prediction'. In E. F. Beckman (ed.), *Modern Mathematics for Engineers*, Series 1. New York: McGraw-Hill, Ch. 8.

WOLD, H. O. (1949). 'Statistical Estimation of Economic Relationships'. *Econometrica*, 17, Suppl.: 1–21.

—— (1954). 'Causality and Econometrics'. *Econometrica*, 22: 162–77.

—— (1960). 'A Generalization of Causal Chain Models'. *Econometrica*, 28: 443–63.

—— (1969). 'Mergers of Economics and Philosophy of Science'. *Synthèse*, 20: 427–82.

—— and JURÉEN, L. (1952). *Demand Analysis: A Study in Econometrics*. New York: John Wiley.

ZELLNER, A. (1979). 'Causality and Econometrics'. In K. Brunner and A. H. Meltzer (eds.), *Carnegie–Rochester Conference Series on Public Policy*, x. Amsterdam: North-Holland.

—— (1982). 'Comment' on J. Geweke, 'Measurement of Linear Dependence and Feedback between Multiple Time Series'. *Journal of the American Statistical Association*, 77: 313–14.

15

A New Approach to Economic Analysis: Computational Economics

SIRO LOMBARDINI

1. Introduction

Over the last forty years economic analysis has followed two opposing lines of approach. Along the first, economists have produced theoretical models in order to clarify logical relations for ideal economies. Sraffa's theory of value and distribution, neoclassical theories of economic growth, and the New Classical models are various instances of this kind of approach.

The second line of economic analysis is oriented towards the construction of econometric models, generally models that are more directly aimed at solving practical problems. The starting-point of this approach is the conviction that the principal goal of economic research is to make possible efficient forecasting, and that any model that proves to be successful in forecasting, by utilizing past observations, is also theoretically meaningful.

This chapter aims at envisaging a third line, which may offer new perspectives for a fruitful interaction between theorizing and empirical research. The argument is divided into three parts. In Section 2 I shall deal with some methodological problems that can help us in understanding the need for a more satisfactory interaction between theorizing and empirical research. In Section 3 I shall stress the limitations that theorizing in economics suffers because of the paradigm of equilibrium. In the final section I shall try to make a few suggestions about a third line of research labelled 'computational economics'.

2. Theory and Facts: Some Methodological Reflections

2.1. *Uncertainty and rationality*

Econometrics and historical research are conceived as two polar approaches to economic reality. The former aims at describing reality by a set of quantitative relations, deemed to visualize a set of possible states of the world; the latter aims at understanding a unique set of events which have already occurred.

However, in my opinion econometrics and historical research are not two independent, still less opposite, approaches. In both cases facts do not pre-exist theory, but are theory-dependent. In addition, *understanding*, which is the proper aim of historical research, is a prerequisite for all kinds of theorizing. In all research we have to face problems of meaning. The heuristic value of equilibrium theory, for instance, depends on the meaning of the word 'equilibrium'. Its meaning does not result uniquely from the formal definition.[1] Understanding is the primitive link between perceiving facts and thinking: it enables us to talk about facts.

Econometrics differs from historical research essentially because it is based explicitly on theoretical models, and its main purpose is the forecasting of future events. In econometrics past events are only the fuel required to make models work.

According to the traditional view, the purpose of scientific explanation is considered to be, essentially, the removal of uncertainty. This goal can be pursued inasmuch as it is assumed that 'the data of the experiments should rest ultimately on something that is perceptually certain and without any component of error' (Suppe 1977: 282). Such an assumption seemed reasonable after the discovery of celestial mechanics; it was no longer self-evident after the development of quantum theory. When we deal with matters of knowledge, we must accept the fact that 'real houses are always built on sand and never on rock' (Suppe 1977: 283).

Certainty can be associated with a psychological attitude: the agent aims at certainty about the results of the possible courses of action available to him. However, on closer scrutiny, certainty appears not as a prerequisite for, but as an obstacle to, rationality. In fact, in order to be rational, we must be sufficiently uncertain that we are willing to try new experiences and are able to learn by doing.

---

[1] The opposition that is assumed to exist between Sraffian and some Walras–Leontief models is based more on different conceptions of equilibrium than on different formal definitions and logical relations. (In fact, Sraffa did not like either the word 'equilibrium', or even the weaker term 'quasi-equilibrium' suggested by Joan Robinson.)

Thus, uncertainty is the essential context of critical reason. No assessment can be taken as definite. Indeterminacies may then result from the awareness that the explanation obtained is only partial.[2]

The problem of uncertainty is then twofold. It has both an objective and a subjective side. If we increase our information and obtain a better knowledge of the system with which we interact, we can say that we have decreased our uncertainty; in principle, other people who have the same information, and who start from the same initial conditions, should make a similar evaluation of the event. The concept of uncertainty can thus be given an objective meaning.[3]

In normative problems the subjective side of probability is unavoidable. Rational behaviour presupposes that all agents having the same goals, and given the same data, make the same choice. Reduction of uncertainty can be obtained by assigning subjective probabilities to the possible states of the world. Then optimization models can be applied to state the problem of rational choice.[4]

In econometrics, the probability approach is often a way of surmounting (of escaping?) the inadequacy of the information available, or of remedying the limitations of the model, being always a partial model. In framing the model for rational behaviour, probability has been considered the proper tool to remove uncertainty. Yet there are reasons for thinking that uncertainty cannot be completely removed by the notion of subjective probability: there is residual uncertainty arising from the fact that people cannot envisage all possible states of the world (Lombardini 1953, 1954).

Some removal of uncertainty has been considered a prerequisite for the formalization of rationality criteria. The definition of rationality is, in its turn, a pre-condition for posing the problem of the removal of uncertainty. This vicious logical circle has hardly received any attention

---

[2] Indeterminacy has a different meaning and raises different questions in quantum theory and in the physics of particles. There it reflects the impossibility of conceiving objects that exist in the qualities (dimensions) relevant to us, independently of our experimental techniques. I do not intend to discuss this conception of the possible results of scientific research and its associated philosophical problems. Suffice it to say that such a conception may offer a way of overcoming the juxtaposition between normative and descriptive analysis. For the methodological remarks I shall make in order to properly assess the new computational-economics approach, we can abide by the traditional conception.

[3] Objectivity is here conceived in a weaker sense—one that does not entail a principle of correspondence between ontological and logical relations. For a statement to be *objective*, it is sufficient that the relevant community has defined models and rules that can determine the situations in which different individuals make such statements independently from one another.

[4] Such a general model for rational behaviour reminds one of the probability approach to econometrics (see, in particular, Haavelmo 1944, and Marschak 1950). Yet probability has different meanings in the two applications, as I have tried to show in Lombardini (1992).

on the part of economists. In fact, while objective removal of uncertainty—as can be obtained through scientific progress—is to be considered positive (in normal conditions[5]), making subjective certainty
correspond to a well defined structure may entail certain ambiguities. In
the theory of general equilibrium, such a correspondence is made
between the normal state of the economy and the rational state. In
defining the normal (equilibrium) state, we assume a (market) mechanism running individual behaviours (the Walras auctioneer), while the
economy rationality is reduced to individuals' rationality.[6]

The notion of individual rationality may entail a tautology, as it
occurs with Popper's definition. According to Popper, 'individuals
always behave in the way that fits better to the situation in which they
find themselves' (Popper 1987: 145). In fact, Popper's principle of
rationality makes possible a coherent description of *any* behaviour.
Therefore, far from being the only acceptable notion of rationality,
Popper's is too weak a conception of rational behaviour. Why should
agents adapt themselves to situations rather than trying to adapt
situations to themselves? The Schumpeterian entrepreneur has no doubt
about this question.

On the contrary, if the principle of rationality is defined in such a way
as to integrate the choice problem into the problem of an objective
rational structure (which is the only scientifically intelligible one, according to the mechanistic paradigm), then the problem of choice vanishes.
The agent, being a rational individual, is compelled to act as theory says
he should act. Social activities can be predicted with much the same
certainty as we predict sun and moon eclipses.

2.2. *Theorizing and empirical research*

The first of the two lines of development of economic analysis mentioned in the first section is mainly concerned to corroborate the
correspondence between the objectively rational and thus scientifically
intelligible normal state and rational choice (with reference to individual
goals).

---

[5] Not in all cases. Let us suppose that scientific progress will enable us to predict the
occurrence of certain incurable diseases. Will an individual be better off if he is told that at
a certain age he will be struck by a disease of this kind? I would answer: no! In fact, in
such cases objective reduction of uncertainty may not help rationality.

[6] Such a reduction has been made by Pareto in his concept of 'optimality for' (and not
of) community. The link between the rationality criterion and the notion of normal
structure has been made very clear by the correspondence that has been logically proved to
exist between competitive market equilibria and Pareto optima (see Arrow and Hahn 1971:
183–8).

The second line, namely the empirical approach, is pragmatically oriented. It aims at increasing our knowledge of the actual working of the economic system, thus reducing objective uncertainty and facilitating behaviour that is rational. While we can build a theory that has no practical purpose, we can build no operational model in a theoretical vacuum.

First, as epistemologists are well aware, facts are theory-laden (see e.g. Suppe 1977: 141–2). In fact all empirical investigation presupposes at least some pre-analytical knowledge (see Lombardini 1982: 41–4). On the other hand, theory, as we have already noticed, emerges from a primitive link between facts (or at least psychological attitudes of the researcher) and thinking.

In addition, the naive empiricist approach presupposes something more than a theory. As Quine (1961: 37) reminds us, 'for all its a priori reasonableness, a boundary between analytical and synthetic statements simply has not been drawn. That there is such a distinction to be drawn at all is an empirical dogma of empiricists, a metaphysical article of faith.' Empirical significance is certainly an important feature of scientific research, but as Quine (1961: 42), once again, reminds us, 'the unit of empirical significance is the whole of science'.

In fact, we can have a twofold relation between theorizing and empirical research:

1. Analysis starts from empirical observations that enable us to arrive at 'stylized facts'. A theory is then searched for in order to explain the facts.
2. Analysis starts from the elaboration of a model that can be empirically tested (in such a way that parameters can be estimated).

The first approach can be contested, inasmuch as theorizing cannot be a by-product of manipulation of empirical data. As we have already remarked, some sort of theorizing is required in order to produce data.[7]

The starting-point of the second approach can never be pure theorizing. It is theorizing under the stimuli of concrete experiences, in particular of specific perceptions and/or data collections.

There are indeed two extreme views about the relationships between theorizing and empirical research. The first makes theorizing a by-product of empirical investigations; the second conceives of empirical investigation as being subsequent to theorizing, observation of facts being the tribunal deciding the validity of any theory.

If we accept the notion of causality proposed by Granger (1969)[8] —that is, if we think that causal relations can be established

---

[7] Moreover, stylized facts can be explained by different theories. Theories that can explain different stylized facts may not be congruent with one another.
[8] For a critical assessment of the notion, see Vercelli (1991).

through empirical observations—then stylized facts can be assumed to be theoretically relevant and the observation of facts can directly produce scientific statements. In fact, regression techniques are increasingly being used to ascertain whether changes in some variables or in some relations can be attributed to changes in others. Yet scientists should be aware that correlations can be spurious.

The second extreme view is Friedman's. Facts become relevant only when we want to test theories. If we adhere to an instrumentalist view of science, then we can accept Friedman's philosophy. If we share some of Popper's doubts about instrumentalism, then we cannot rely only on the tribunal of facts when assessing the validity of a theory.[9] Some reflections may be helpful at this point.

1. When we say that a theory has been empirically validated, what we really mean is that the *empirical model* associated with the theory has not been refuted by observations. Yet we must remember that a large number of models are compatible with any given theory. In fact, to obtain a model associated with a given theory, we need to make specific assumptions concerning the forms of the relations and the values of the parameters.[10]

2. Not all facts required to validate a theory can be obtained. The meaning of most economic concepts (like that of unemployment) varies with the theoretical context in which they are defined. Empirical data are often unreliable. In fact, most of them are collected for practical reasons, and these may not coincide with the scientist's needs.

3. Improvements to the model that are justified on theoretical grounds may make it less efficient as an empirical model. As much has been observed by Koopmans (1957: 194) with reference to the disaggregation of Leontief models.

4. Some regularities that can be empirically observed, and that apparently prove the validity of a given theory, may be produced by mechanisms that are unrelated to the phenomena that the theory is designed to explain. Suffice it to recall Slutzky's paper on 'The Summation of Random Causes as the Source of Cyclic Processes' (Slutzky 1937).

5. Empirical research is in general carried out in macroeconomic terms. Changes in the structure of aggregate variables may invalidate the theoretical model underlying the research (see Section 1.3).

[9] I am more inclined than Popper to accept instrumentalism as a method for the solution of practical problems. A large part of medical science has been built using this method, and yet it is certainly of some use in curing diseases. However, we must always bear in mind the limits of statements that are not grounded in theories that have proved to be capable of explaining a much larger set of possible facts.

[10] We can easily notice that for many theories, even if they are inconsistent with one another, it is possible to build specific models (possibly by changing trends and distributed lags) that can be empirically validated on the basis of specific sets of data.

All these observations suggest that theory and facts are mutually
linked in a very complex way.

2.3. *The aggregation problem*

In macroeconomic models the variables are aggregate variables. Aggregation raises quite a few technical problems, problems that have been
extensively analysed by various authors.[11] It needs to be emphasized
that in macroeconomic models interdependence between individuals'
objective functions, together with the interaction between agents' behaviours,[12] are generally disregarded. Even if we rule out such interaction,
the lack of homogeneity of certain structural coefficients of individual
relations (such as those reflecting individuals' tastes) deprives the
aggregate relation of some of the properties that have been obtained for
the individual relations.[13]

To explain individual behaviour, we also need to assume some error
correction mechanism. As Lippi (1985) has shown, the form of the
global relation expressing the error correction mechanism is different
from that of the micro relations from which the former is logically
derived. In general, it is much more complex. When we turn to
aggregate analysis, some factors that affect individuals' behaviour in one
period only are capable of influencing economic activity over several
periods.[14]

An aggregate model may be structurally more unstable than a less
aggregate one, because the parameters obtained through aggregation are
likely to change when changes occur in the aggregated variables.
However, this is not necessarily always true. Indeed, it may happen that
a more aggregate model is more structurally stable than a less aggregate
one inasmuch as certain changes that occur in some parameters of the

---

[11] One problem concerns the criteria for classifying industries in such a way as to obtain
structural parameters that are as stable as possible. A second problem regards certain
specific assumptions that have to be made in order to derive aggregate variables from
individual variables (such as the assumption of constant distribution of income: this is
required in order to be able to associate an aggregate variable labelled global income with
individual incomes). See Theil (1954); Malinvaud (1957); Balderston and Within (1954).

[12] The propensity of individuals to follow fashions or to assume snobbish attitudes
entails interdependence between their utility functions. With regard to interaction between
interdependent choices, see Bjerring (1978).

[13] For example, Wold and Juréen (1952) has shown that such a situation applies to the
aggregate demand functions for single commodities, for which the elasticity theorem does
not hold.

[14] The introduction of lags raises specific difficulties. It is sufficient that one of the
variables explaining individuals' behaviour enters with a lag to make the aggregate
dynamic behaviour quite complex.

latter model counterbalance each other in such a way that no changes are revealed in the parameters of the former.[15]

2.4. *Economic system and social system*

Unlike certain physical systems that can be considered part of an immediately observable external world, the economic system is the product of a process of abstraction—one that starts from pre-analytical knowledge (Schumpeter 1954), or is justified by some criterion established a priori (Robbins 1932). No matter how the economic system is defined, the economy must be considered a subset of the social system. The economic system is usually considered to be open to the social system in a unique direction. The Paretian notion of *tastes* has been suggested in order to take account of all the influences of the socio-cultural system on the economic system. In fact, if it were possible to describe the social system in a matrix form, the matrix would not be decomposable (so that the economic system could be singled out as a subsystem of a larger system, the social system producing individual tastes which are inputs of the economic system). It can be at most nearly decomposable. Then, as I have shown elsewhere (Lombardini 1982: 52–4), while interaction between the two systems may be negligible in the short run, it is not so in the long run. This means that any econometric model that is used for a sufficiently long time needs to be periodically revised in order to take into account the structural changes that cause changes in certain parameters. Certain interactions between the socio-cultural system and the economic system may bring about abrupt changes in some of the parameters of the model.

The distinction between endogenous and exogenous variables is linked to the fact that all economic models are *partial* models in a more general sense than Marschak's (1950: 7–8).[16] Individuals' tastes, for instance, are the result of psychological and socio-cultural processes. Since economists cannot analyse such processes, the parameters reflecting individuals' tastes are structurally unstable.

By changing the sets of endogenous and exogenous variables, we can affect the structural stability of the model. In fact, some of the exogenous variables become endogenous if we consider a larger system,

---

[15] For similar reasons, finer disaggregations may increase the likelihood of systematic errors in computation.

[16] According to Marschak, a model is complete if all the variables can be determined by the relations of the model or by 'subsidiary' relations which are independent of the former relations. I think that a model should be considered partial also if its structural instability is amenable to the fact that certain individuals' behaviour and social mechanisms cannot be explained by economic theories.

and we do so in such a way as to internalize some of the interactions between a smaller system conceived of as a strictly economic system, and the social system.[17]

In fact, by enlarging the model, the system (being a socio-economic system) may turn out to be structurally more stable. However, this is not necessarily always true. The evolution of the socio-cultural system may in fact make the economic system structurally more unstable. This was Schumpeter's (1934) conviction.

We can distinguish three kinds of evolution:

1. evolution that can be internalized, by enlarging the models and/or by having a model characterized by one or more bifurcations;
2. evolution that can be explored, by utilizing the results of sociological and technological research to produce hypotheses about changes that are likely to occur in parameters or relations;
3. evolution that looks possible on the basis of historical analyses.

Evolutionary processes create problems for econometric research. Any econometric model is likely to be structurally unstable if it is used for long-term forecasting. While an economic model may prove to be valid with reference to a certain set of observations, we cannot be sure that it will remain valid when the set of observations is enlarged. This is the main reason why empirical criteria for testing the theory are scarcely applicable in economics. We come back to the reflections already made on the fact that models are all partial models. This feature in some models is explicitly stated by the *ceteris paribus* clause. Ricardo's theory of rent has been refuted, as well as the Schumpeterian theory of development. Yet with reference to historical experience, Ricardo's theory proves to be helpful; with reference to other experiences, Schumpeterian theory seems to be more valid.

3. Equilibrium and Disequilibrium: Theoretical Analysis

3.1. *Equilibrium theory and comparative statics approaches*

Standard theoretical analysis has been carried on the assumption that the economy has a normal (and thereby rational) structure. The essential purpose of economics is to explain such a structure on the basis of individual behaviour. Such behaviour depends both on optimization

---

[17] Such a possibility has been considered by Giannini (1986), who has pointed out that the structure of the model depends on whether the variables are classified as endogenous or exogenous.

processes and on the processes by which expectations are produced. If expectations are rational, and if all markets can clear instantaneously, then equilibrium models can be used to forecast the effects of exogenous changes (such as state intervention).

Comparative statics can be applied to interpret economic processes. We are thus returning to the theoretical approach suggested by Pareto, who was convinced that, at the present stage of development of economic science, the factors that can produce movements of the system (evolution) must be considered exogenous (Lombardini 1989b). It is true that Friedman defines the natural rate of unemployment by referring to some kind of normal process of growth. Yet such a process is simply assumed and is not explained within the theory—contrary to what classical authors and Schumpeter have done.

In the context of equilibrium theory, evolution is amenable to external factors that cause the economy to move from an equilibrium to a new one. The effects of these factors, and thus the evolution of the system, can be analysed essentially by the methods of comparative statics. Economic laws, conceived as meaningful theorems in Samuelson's sense (1947: 3–6), are the result of theoretical simulations that may have an empirical content only if the assumptions of the New Classical macroeconomics are granted.

The validity of such processes of theoretical simulation depends on:

1. the validity of the equilibrium model that has been used;
2. the existence of a unique solution;
3. the stability of equilibrium: in fact, equilibrium must be reached in such a short time as to make it possible to assume that evolution of the system can be described as a passage from one equilibrium position to a successive one associated with new values of external factors.

If we assume that markets clear instantaneously and that sufficient information is available to all agents, whose expectations are rational, then, provided assumptions 1 and 2 are granted, meaningful theorems having an empirical content can be derived by the method of comparative statics.

3.2. *The logical difficulties of a non-unique equilibrium and the processes of adjustment*

Let us assume that all the assumptions set out in Section 2.1 are granted but that of the uniqueness of the solution. That means that, given a specified set of initial conditions, the system can move to either one or another of a set of possible equilibria. Then, even if the hypotheses of the rational expectations economists are granted, there cannot be a *revealing rational expectations equilibrium*. Let us make the extreme assumption that all the individuals know the possible equilibria to which they attach subjective probabilities and that each individual acts on the assumption that the equilibrium position that will eventually be reached is the one having the highest probability. Since the objective individual probability distributions differ, individuals' behaviours are not congruous to any of the possible equilibria.

Let us assume that all the assumptions set out in Section 2.1 are granted except that of markets clearing instantaneously. In such a case, evolution depends not only on the succession of equilibrium positions corresponding to successive sets of values of exogenous variables, but also on the processes by which equilibria are reached (see e.g. Fisher 1983). If we assume that to each set of values of exogenous variables there corresponds one equilibrium position only, and that all individuals know the process by which such an equilibrium position can be reached, then we can visualize dynamic economic laws (internal dynamics). In fact, if the above mentioned assumptions are granted, there is no need to analyse an adjustment process. The New Classical macroeconomics view becomes reasonable: individuals' knowledge is indeed sufficient to make instantaneous clearance of the market possible.

The assumption of instantaneous clearance is incompatible with either (*a*) the assumption of individuals' ignorance of the process by which the equilibrium position is eventually attained, or (*b*) the assumption of the existence of several possible processes by which equilibrium can be reached once the initial conditions are changed.

In the first case, individuals need to learn from the actual adjustment process. In any event, however, the outcome of individuals' actions is not an equilibrium position inasmuch as their expectations are not uniform. For the second case, see e.g. the papers by Woodford (Chapter 8) and Goodwin and Pacini (Chapter 9) in this volume.

When the passage from one equilibrium position to another requires time, an additional problem has to be faced. During the adjustment process changes in the values of exogenous variables can occur. Their effects on the economy cannot be analysed by the method of comparative statics. In fact, they depend both on the particular process of adjustment that has been activated and on the time at which exogenous change occurs. To evaluate such effects, a truly dynamic model is required.

In the models that are required to interpret these complex dynamics, the relations are generally nonlinear. Then irregular, and possibly chaotic, dynamics are produced, dynamics that make prediction unreliable or even impossible (see Goodwin and Pacini, Chapter 9 above).

3.3. *The problem of expectations*

Equilibrium depends not only on initial conditions but also on expectations about the values that endogenous and exogenous variables will take in the future. In the theory of rational expectations, in order for the equilibrium to be restored, agents must know what changes will occur in the exogenous variables and must be able to evaluate the endogenous variables. For such assumptions to be granted, it is necessary—but not sufficient—that, as the rational expectations economists suggest, policy authorities announce credible economic policies in time.

There are systematic reasons for asserting that governments' actions are not oriented to the pursuit of a coherent set of goals on the basis of objective evaluations. But even if we make the heroic assumption that coherent economic policies are announced in time, the future values of many exogenous variables would still remain uncertain. In fact, in a dynamic context there are additional reasons for thinking that individuals' expectations will diverge. People have different opinions not only about the process of adjustment and its speed, but also about the way growth factors operate. All individuals may agree that a certain technical innovation is forthcoming, and yet they may differ on the date and the effects of such a future event.

Divergences in expectations are not only inevitable: they are also necessary for the economy to develop. Uniformity of expectations is incompatible with entrepreneurs being innovators. Moreover, speculation is possible because people have different expectations.

3.4. *The problem of rationality*

When we drop the assumption of instantaneous clearance of markets, the problem of rationality must be reconsidered—even if we adhere to the neoclassical paradigm. As Simon (1976) maintains, in this case the substantive rationality approach is invalidated: we must adopt the alternative conception of procedural rationality. For that, we do not need to go back to the adaptive expectations approach. What we need is to understand those links between the mechanisms that enable us to define the individual decision problem.

(a) *An optimization model*

To be rational, an individual must act so as to reach the goals he is pursuing in the most efficient way. In an uncertainty context there may be some difficulties even in defining the individuals' intermediate goals.

In fact, for a firm, a certain strategy may be preferable to a more profitable one if the former is likely to make structural adjustment to unforeseeable changes easier, or—we can say—if it entails a higher degree of *flexibility*. The goals are not decided once and for all: as we shall see, they will be adjusted on the basis of the experience acquired during the process. Since it is dynamic and interactive, the optimization model is in this case more complex than the usual static maximization models.

(b) A formation-of-expectations model

Individuals have to utilize all available information in order to estimate the variables entering into the optimization model. Such an operation is performed according to the models that individuals have more or less consciously built up in their minds.

(c) A learning mechanism

In the process, individuals acquire experiences and information that enable them to revise:

1. the optimization model (the goals can be revised—the flexibility requirement, for instance, may increase or decrease);
2. the set of facts that are deemed to be relevant and the mechanism by which they are utilized for the formation of expectations and for the acquisition of experience (process of learning);
3. the model for the formation of expectations;
4. the mechanism of learning.

(d) A model of error correction

When expectations are disappointed (for instance if stocks increase faster than was expected), individuals have to make some corrections in their expectations or in the models by which the problem is framed. The model for error correction establishes some links among the other models.

It is usually assumed that the decision process produces continuous relations. Discontinuities are usually associated with economic policy decisions. In fact, however—as Goodwin (1951) has shown—discontinuities may also be a consequence of market decisions. Even at the individual level, there may be reasons for discontinuities. When certain inequalities (such as inequality between the rate of assets rentability and the rate of interest) are reversed, individuals may find it convenient suddenly to change their behaviour (for instance, to stop purchasing assets and to increase their money funds).

Up to now, we have assumed that individuals are autonomous and that they act independently of one another. Furthermore, in this case difficulties arise because individuals are unequal, even with regard to those aspects that are relevant for the process of aggregation. The difficulties in the process of aggregation increase tremendously if interactions between individuals are taken into account. As I have shown elsewhere (Lombardini 1992), problems arise with regard to the choice criteria, the learning mechanism (when interactions are relevant), and the strategy that the various individuals have to adopt concerning the interrelation between their decisions (as in the prisoners' dilemma).

Economists have discussed at length the microeconomic foundations of macroeconomics. Discussion should be enlarged to include the problem of macroeconomic foundations of microeconomics. Institutions cannot be conceived as the result of a game played by all individuals concerned, for we need first to establish the rules of the game; then, however, we enter into an infinite regress (Lombardini 1989a). We thus need to assume a given institutional framework.

This is not the only factor giving rise to the need for a macroeconomic foundation to microeconomics. The rational expectations economists are right when they stress the possible changes in individuals' behaviour produced by changes in economic policy. Such a remark ought to be generalized. The economy is a system whose global behaviour may change because of its connections with the social system. Such changes also affect individuals' economic behaviour.

3.5. *The usefulness of theorizing*

In spite of the limitations associated with the problems mentioned in previous sections, equilibrium analysis is fruitful for the following reasons.

1. It enables us to discover logical connections between economic variables, connections that may help to state the conditions necessary for efficiency. The efficiency criterion is twofold. On the one hand, efficiency entails a principle of conservation. An efficient system is a system that can prevent its structure from changing over time. The Pareto criterion is a specification of such a principle of conservation. It can be defined in the context of the theory of equilibrium. On the other hand, efficiency is associated with evolution. Schumpeter was essentially concerned with the second feature of the efficiency criterion. Yet his definition becomes a much more complex matter and cannot avoid value judgements.

2. Analysis of the logical properties of ideal processes helps us in setting up models for analysing and comparing concrete processes.

3. It helps us to better understand the historical development of economic science and its link with the development of other sciences and of philosophical thought. The roles of analogy (with respect to paradigms and the models of other disciplines) can be better appreciated.

Theorizing and empirical observation are two essential moments of scientific discovery. The link between them is not mechanical. Before comparing theoretical results with actual occurrences as they are observed, we need to analyse all the possible empirical implications of all the models that can be associated with a theory. Divergence between actual occurrences and the empirical implications of theoretical models can offer suggestions for the revision of theories. Therefore the relationship between theorizing and empirical investigation is of a cybernetic type.

Theory produces stimuli for empirical investigation and also offers suggestions for redefining facts. Empirical research, in its turn, may help in producing the theoretical hypotheses that allow the theory to evolve. The solution of practical problems is not the outcome of a mechanical application of the results of empirical research; nor are solutions directly provided by theory. In fact, all choices entail some unmeasurable risk. (They are indeed the results of both intuition and analytical reasoning.) Rationality is essentially an expression of *procedural* rationality, the procedure reflecting, at the level of the individual, the cybernetic approach that should be established between theorizing and empirical observation.

4. Computational Economics

4.1. *An alternative approach: computational economics*

In spite of all the attempts to reduce objective uncertainty, no scientific model can protect our forecasting from the structural instability of the system it describes. This is so for several reasons. Let us merely point out that it is impossible to internalize all interactions between the social and the economic systems.

As we have already noticed, research in economics is limited by both theory and facts.[18] Theories have to be of sufficient simplicity that problems of existence, stability, and comparative statics (and dynamics)

---

[18] Let us remember that the available facts are scarcely correlative with theoretical concepts, just as not all theoretical concepts admit empirical correlation.

can be set up and solved. The facts with which we can confront the results of theoretical analysis are those—and only those—that can be made available through direct observation or by asking agents for proper information.

The simple theories within which we can solve the problems mentioned above are inadequate for interpreting essential features of actual processes, for several reasons (Lombardini 1990).

1. Because of evolution and processes of adjustment, actual processes are disequilibrium processes. By knowing how disequilibria evolve, we can make reasonable guesses as to the (political, social, and economic) reactions possible and necessary to avoid explosion of the system.

2. Interactions between the macroeconomic structure and the behaviour of the various agents (the microeconomic structure) cannot be dealt with by the usual mechanical models.

3. To study evolution of the second kind (see Section 1.4) we need to analyse the implications of possible structural changes that are not inferred directly from the model but are suggested by the analysis of the socio-cultural and political systems.

Models that are conceived in order to satisfy these needs are in general too complex to allow analysis of their logical properties. It is impossible to find sufficient conditions that can assure specific dynamics. Nor can we state, by methods of comparative statics (dynamics), meaningful theorems in Samuelson's sense.

We can often state the necessary conditions for processes in equilibrium (for example, steady growth). There are some advantages in arriving at equilibrium paths of growth by starting from a disequilibrium model. We can visualize more than one path of growth.[19] The disequilibrium model enables us to state a larger set of structural conditions required if the system is to grow along an equilibrium path.

A number of possible disequilibrium paths of evolution can be discovered through simulation. We need only to specify sets of values for the parameters and possible initial conditions. By such simulation processes we can try to determine critical values of certain parameters for a given set of realistic values of others: namely, values that entail qualitative changes in the dynamics of the system.

By sufficiently large explorations, we can infer some relations between sets of the values of parameters (or sets of initial conditions) and specific kinds of movement of the system. Such relations are different both from meaningful theorems (*theoretical laws*)—since, given certain additional conditions, they are not logically implied by the models—

---

[19] In Lombardini *et al.* (1983) various paths of growth are possible, each with a different rate of inflation—a rate that depends on the initial conditions concerning the quantity of money and its rate of increase.

and from *empirical laws*. The simulation processes, indeed, have produced theoretical facts. They are not the result of observation of real events; yet they are more akin to the theoretical data produced by the model than empirical data are akin to concrete facts.

This model-building-for-simulation approach can be labelled, following the term used to designate similar approaches in physics and chemistry, *computational economics*.

Having been produced by nature, empirical facts are supposed to be superior. As we have seen, they are the product of both nature and the scientists who provide the language system (and the associated more or less conscious and more or less latent theoretical context) as well as the procedures that are required to 'perceive' facts. Moreover, the (empirical) facts that are utilized by the economist are, in general, not collected according to his schemes, but are interpreted *on the basis of them*.[20] Theoretical facts are thus superior, being more akin to the theoretical data produced by the model which is supposed to describe reality. By simulation procedures we can obtain a large number of theoretical facts, whereas by observation we can get only a limited set of facts corresponding to the specific structural conditions of the system at the time the observation is made. This is an aspect in which computational sciences are superior to traditional empirical research (or technical experimentation). Empirical laws directly inferred from facts are limited by the set of facts that can be observed during a certain period, given a certain evolution of the system. From the analysis of the theoretical facts, we can infer *hypothetical empirical laws* that are not constrained by the limited capability of nature to produce facts.

4.2. *The purpose of computational economics*

Through simulation processes, computational economics aims at producing theoretical–empirical data that can be utilized to establish hypothetical empirical laws. Given the assumptions, they cannot be as theoretically sound as the meaningful theorems that are derived from an axiomatic theory; yet, for reasons that have been pointed out, hypothetical–empirical laws may be more operational.

These laws are not derived from the observation of facts as the empirical laws claim (but are they?). Yet they may help:

1. to understand those aspects of the working of the system for which no adequate empirical data are available;

---

[20] Sometimes empirical facts are derived from other facts (observations) by means of procedures justified by specific theories. Then they are halfway between the empirical facts and the theoretical facts.

2. by producing suggestions for rebuilding the theoretical model: the cybernetic relations between theorizing and empirical observation can thus be substituted by a cybernetic relation between model-building and an assessment of the theoretical–empirical results of the processes of simulation;
3. to solve problems of economic policy by investigating, in more realistic contexts, the effects of government action;
4. to stimulate the collection of new empirical data.

In computational economics simulation is not confined to comparative statics (or dynamics). It then becomes possible to explore the properties of disequilibrium processes, as well as to determine changes that are capable of bringing the system close to equilibrium (and that can eventually be induced by specific economic policies). Such explorations can offer suggestions:

1. for visualizing possible interactions—ones that are not postulated by the relations of the model—between social and economic systems and between individuals' behaviour and the working of the system;
2. for stating problems of economic policy afresh—in particular, for revising the goals entering into the definition of such problems— also in connection with the above mentioned interactions;
3. for a better understanding of the mechanisms that prevent the economy from moving too far from equilibrium paths of growth;
4. for determining possible scenarios for the future and for stating the conditions that make each of them most likely to occur. Such an approach is more useful than the usual forecasting methods.

In building the models to be used for simulation we can utilize the results of econometric research; in fact, all information that can be obtained on concrete economic processes should be used to define sets of realistic values for the parameters and sets of reasonable initial conditions.[21]

References

ARROW, K. J., and HAHN, F. H. (1971). *General Competitive Analysis*. San Francisco: Holden-Day.
BALDERSTON, J. B., and WITHIN, T. M. (1954). 'Aggregation and the Input–Output Model'. In O. Morgenstern (ed.), *Economic Activity Analysis*. New

[21] An approach similar to the one I am proposing has recently been developed by certain Soviet economists (as Petrakov, and Altaev). Since they are more interested in the possibility of establishing a more fruitful connection between microeconomics and macroeconomics, they have labelled the new approach *synthetic economics* or the *integrated approach*.

York: John Wiley.

BJERRING, A. K. (1978). 'The Tracing Procedure and a Theory of Rational Interaction'. In C. A. Hooker, J. J. Leach, and E. F. McLennen (eds.), *Foundations and Applications of Decision Theory*. Dordrecht: Reidel.

FISHER, F. M. (1983). *Disequilibrium Foundations of Equilibrium Economics*. Cambridge University Press.

FRIEDMAN, M. (1953). 'The Methodology of Positive Economics'. In his *Essays in Positive Economics*. University of Chicago Press.

GIANNINI, C. (1986). 'Sul concetto di variabile esogena e sulla previsione condizionale'. *Politica Economica*, 11: 273–80.

GOODWIN, R. M. (1951). 'The Nonlinear Accelerator and the Persistence of Business Cycles'. *Econometrica*, 19: 1–17.

GRANGER, C. W. J. (1969). 'Investigating Causal Relations by Econometric Models and Cross-Spectral Methods'. *Econometrica*, 37: 424–38.

HAAVELMO, T. (1944). 'The Probability Approach in Econometrics'. *Econometrica*, 12, suppl.: viii–118.

KOOPMANS, T. C. (1957). 'The Construction of Economic Knowledge'. In his *Three Essays on the State of Economic Science*. New York: McGraw-Hill.

LIPPI, M. (1985). 'Sulla dinamica delle relazioni tra variabili aggregate'. *Politica Economica*, 1: 141–66.

LOMBARDINI, S. (1953). 'L'incertezza nella teoria economica'. In *Studi in memoria di Gino Borgatta*, ii. Bologna: Arti Grafiche, pp. 25–57.

——(1954). 'Monopolies and Rigidities in the Economic System'. In E. H. Chamberlin (ed.), *Monopoly, Competition and Their Regulation*. London: Macmillan, pp. 398–420.

——(1982). 'Economics: Past and Future'. In Giorgio P. Szegö (ed.), *New Quantitative Techniques for Economic Analysis*. New York: Academic Press.

——(1989a). 'Market and Institutions'. In Takashi Shiraishi and Shigeto Tsuru (eds.), *Economic Institutions in a Dynamic Society*. London: Macmillan for the International Economic Association.

——(1989b). 'Équilibre et évolution dans la pensée de Vilfredo Pareto'. *Revue Européenne de Sciences Sociales*. 27: 193–209.

——(1990). 'Rationality in Disequilibrium'. In Kumaraswamy Velupillai (ed.), *Nonlinear and Multisectoral Macrodynamics*. London: Macmillan.

——(1992). 'Rationality and Economic Behaviour'. In M. Baranzini and J. Harcourt (eds.), *Essays in Honour of L. Pasinetti*. London: Macmillan.

——DONATI, F., and VILLA, A. (1983). 'Equilibrium, Disequilibrium and Growth'. Centro di Studi sui Sistemi, Politecnico di Torino, Quaderno no. 35.

LUCE, R. D., and RAIFFA, H. (1957). *Games and Decisions*. New York: John Wiley.

MALINVAUD, E. (1957). 'L'Agrégation dans les modèles économiques'. *Cahiers du Séminaire d'Économétrie*, 4: 69–146.

MARSCHAK, J. (1950). 'Statistical Inference in Economics: An Introduction'. In T. C. Koopmans (ed.), *Statistical Inference in Dynamic Economic Models*. New York: John Wiley.

POPPER, K. (1987). 'La Rationalité et le statut du principe de rationalité. In E. Classen (ed.), *Les Fondaments philosophiques des systèmes économiques*. Paris: Payot.

QUINE, W. V. O. (1961). *From a Logical Point of View*. New York: Harper & Row. First published 1953.

ROBBINS, L. C. (1932). *An Essay on the Nature and Significance of Economic Science*. London: Macmillan.

SAMUELSON, P. A. (1947). *Foundations of Economic Analysis*. Cambridge University Press.

SCHUMPETER, J. A. (1934). *The Theory of Economic Development*. Oxford University Press.

——(1954). *History of Economic Analysis*. London: Allen & Unwin.

SIMON, H. A. (1976). 'From Substantive to Procedural Rationality'. In S. Latsis (ed.), *Method and Appraisal in Economics*. Cambridge University Press.

SLUTZKY, E. (1937). 'The Summation of Random Causes as the Source of Cyclic Process'. *Econometrica*, 5: 105–46.

SUPPE, F. (1977). 'The Search for Philosophic Understanding of Scientific Theories'. In F. Suppe (ed.), *The Structure of Scientific Theories*. Urbana, Ill.: University of Illinois Press.

THEIL, H. (1954). *Linear Aggregation of Economic Relations*. Amsterdam: North-Holland.

VERCELLI, A. (1991). *Methodological Foundations of Macroeconomics: Keynes and Lucas*. Cambridge University Press.

WOLD, H., and JURÉEN, L. (1952). *Demand Analysis: A Study in Econometrics*. New York: John Wiley.

PART VI
Epilogue

16

Issues in Contemporary Macroeconomics

DAVID LAIDLER

1. Introduction

The papers in this volume deal with alternative research strategies in macroeconomics and the visions of the discipline that underlie them. Thus, the collection has a strong methodological content. Debates about method *per se* in economics are often sterile, so I approach this topic with some trepidation. Nevertheless, if we treat methodology as a means to an end instead of as an end in itself, perhaps we can get something out of its discussion after all. As readers of Hicks's contribution to this volume will see, ever since the eighteenth century, there has been a tension in economics between the weight to be attributed to deductive argument on the one hand and empirical evidence on the other when judging economic arguments. The contrast between the *Political Arithmetic* of Petty, developed in the late seventeenth century, and the deductivist natural law approach of the Physiocrats is well known, and provides an early example of the tension in question. In our own century, and in macroeconomics, the contrast between the National Bureau methods of Mitchell and the deductive methodological individualism of Hayek and Robbins also comes to mind.[1]

And yet the greatest economists (to my mind at least)—Smith, Mill, Marshall, Keynes, and so on—have always blended deductive reasoning with respect for evidence. One of the most encouraging aspects of the workshop from which this volume developed was the absence of any dogmatic extremism on these matters. None of the participants suggested, as economists sometimes did in earlier times, that the facts can speak for themselves; and if they had, Vercelli's elegant study of the

I am grateful to Bennett McCallum for helpful correspondence about an earlier draft of this chapter.

[1] See e.g. Mitchell (1927), Hayek (1932), and Robbins (1934). I do not mean to suggest here that the deductivists ignore empirical evidence. However, they treat it as an illustration of deductive argument rather than a test of empirical propositions.

links between recent work in the philosophy of knowledge and the notions of statistical causation so often employed by economists would surely have convinced them of the necessity of always interpreting data relative to a clearly stated theoretical framework. This volume's contributors are, after all, members of the same profession, within which discussion is both possible and constructive. Even so, there are strong contrasts in matters of emphasis in the various papers.

Marcet and Sargent, and Silvestre, have a commitment to basing their models on precise assumptions about tastes, technology, endowments, market structure, and the availability of information, and are clearly willing to sacrifice predictive content in order to adhere to these principles (albeit in the expectation that their work will eventually lead to better predictive models than those we now have). The work of Woodford and Phelps falls into this camp too, though their explorations of the consequences of particular anomalies in the nature of available information and the ways in which agents use it, as well as in specific departures from a complete set of markets, have clearly been prompted by a desire to bring micro-based models a little closer to the facts of the world. McCallum and Taylor also make compromises with microeconomic purity in order to come to grips with data. The real business cycle theorists whose work is surveyed by the former are willing to set aside all of those well known problems that were discussed during the so-called 'Cambridge controversy' in order to derive empirical predictions from models centred on an aggregate production function.[2] Taylor has abandoned the idea that wages and prices are set to equate expected supply and demand for the simple reason that, if they are, then it becomes very difficult, perhaps impossible, for any model to generate the persistence in economic fluctuations that is so pervasive a characteristic of the real world. Even so, though both are willing to make such compromises with analytic purity in order to enhance the predictive content of their models, the work that each has presented clearly falls in the tradition of macroeconomics explicitly based on microeconomic premises started by Friedman (1957), Phelps (1967), and Lucas (1972).

At the other end of the spectrum, we have papers from Day and Lin and Goodwin and Pacini which reopen, with new mathematical tools, questions about the dynamics of macroeconomic systems that were central to the business cycle theory of the 1940s and 1950s.[3] Though this

---

[2] But it should be noted explicitly that McCallum at the workshop was expounding theories with which he himself is not altogether in sympathy. Even so, he is not unsympathetic to the insight yielded by the above-mentioned 'Cambridge controversy', to which Harcourt (1969) still provides an excellent guide.

[3] Here I have in mind the multiplier accelerator analysis associated with the work of Samuelson (1939) or Hicks (1950).

work is not of any logical necessity incompatible with microeconomic analysis, as some of Woodford's work and some of Day's work, not presented here, has shown, these authors did not find it necessary to establish explicit links with micro propositions before getting on with their work. They were content to postulate the existence of certain regularities in macroeconomic relationships, embed these in models, and then analyse the consequences of their interaction. Stiglitz too is concerned with the link between micro and macro, but nevertheless seems comfortable with macroeconomics in the mainstream 'Keynesian' tradition. He analyses in detail certain micro phenomena involving asymmetric information, moral hazard, and so on. These he believes to be pervasive enough to justify the apparently *ad hoc* assumptions about wage and price rigidities that underlie that conventional macro approach. He is, then, trying to develop a microeconomic basis for what he regards as stylized facts of macro behaviour, without however finding it necessary to forge the links here in terms of an explicitly formulated Walrasian model. Indeed, the micro phenomena he analyses cannot be encompassed in a representative agent framework of the type now so popular in Walrasian-style macroeconomics, as he explicitly points out.

The issues with which Stiglitz deals are in some ways complementary to the themes of Leijonhufvud's work; for the latter has long insisted that the key insight of Keynes was that macroeconomic theory should concern itself with problems of disseminating information among agents and the co-ordination of their choices, problems which contemporary general equilibrium theory, and that body of macroeconomics based upon it, most often treats as solved 'as if' by an auctioneer.[4] Leijonhufvud remains sceptical about the desirability of sacrificing too much of the empirical content of macroeconomics to microeconomic rigour, at least of the type that we are currently able to handle. Heymann too, dealing as he does with practical policy issues involved in stabilizing hyperinflations, is careful about how hard theory *per se* is pushed as an alternative to, as opposed to a guide to, interpreting empirical evidence. Lombardini shares such worries as these, but whether he will be able to solve the extremely difficult problems he has set himself with the aid of numerical simulation exercises must remain to be seen. Finally, note that Hendry's work does not pretend to throw any light on how economic theories should be built up, or what issues they should address. He is concerned purely with the development of tools for assessing the empirical content of competing theories, regardless of their origin.

---

[4] On these issues, see Leijonhufvud (1968, 1981).

2. Alternative Approaches to Modelling and the Cycle

A wide variety of approaches to macroeconomics is on show in this volume, then, but most of the papers are concerned with why certain macroeconomic variables fluctuate over time, in an apparently systematic fashion, in capitalist economies. These variables include real output, employment, the general price level, investment, and consumption; and their movements together make up that complex phenomenon which we call the business cycle. Even price-level behaviour has been treated mainly in a cyclical context, though hyperinflation does, of course, emerge as a topic in its own right in Heymann's work.[5]

Leijonhufvud's by now well known 'Swedish flag' taxonomy provides a guide to the range of explanations of the cycle that are feasible, and it is helpful to simplify that taxonomy even further and argue that two broad views of the cycle may be identified in the current literature. On the one hand there are models, such as those presented by Day and Lin and by Goodwin and Pacini, which treat the repetitive nature of the cyclical fluctuations as being the result of endogenous properties of an inherently unstable capitalist economy; and on the other there are the real business cycle theorists, whose work was described by McCallum. These regard the capitalist system as inherently stable, but subject to exogenous shocks imposed either by government or by nature. They also regard it as appropriately modelled as if it were continuously in rational expectations equilibrium. In their view, the persistence of the economy's responses within any cycle probably represents an optimal response to such shocks, while Day–Lin and Goodwin–Pacini would presumably regard it as a welfare-reducing phenomenon which policy ought to mitigate.[6]

Somewhere in the middle are those like Taylor, Woodford, Stiglitz, or Phelps, who accept the idea that the impulses driving the cycle are exogenous, but still entertain the possibility that the economy might depart sufficiently far from the Walrasian ideal that the mechanisms propagating the consequences of such shocks can themselves be a source of welfare-reducing trouble. Marcet and Sargent's contribution, emphasizing as it does that, if an economy is to achieve rational expectations equilibrium, agents within it might have to take time to learn about its

---

[5] That is to say, we have not discussed, except in passing, recent developments in the theory of economic growth associated with the work of Romer (1986).

[6] One must be careful with the word 'optimal' in this context. It is easy enough to introduce externalities into a general equilibrium model which generates non-Pareto allocations of resources both in full equilibrium and over the course of the cycle. What I mean here is that the cyclical fluctuations themselves do not introduce any extra loss of welfare into the system but rather represent the outcome of markets working as well as they can.

properties, suggests how this work might be linked to traditional New Classical analysis. Bubbles, sunspots, peso problems, efficiency wages, and such can all lead to non-optimal responses on the part of the economy to exogenous shocks, whether the latter initially affect its supply side by way of productivity changes, or its demand side by way of monetary surprises and the like, and all of these phenomena arise in one way or another as a by-product of information problems.

As will already be apparent, questions about what causes the cycle tend to yield answers with implications about what economists ought to tell governments (among other agents) to do about it. Is government itself the source of the trouble? If not, is it desirable that it act to remove cyclical fluctuations? If it is, how should it act? Should economic policy be a series of rules for the behaviour of the authorities, or should it be discretionary? It is fair to say that the contributions to this volume reveal a rough (but I emphasize 'rough') correspondence between views on such issues and the nature of research strategies. By and large, those who are committed to research strategies that require strong microfoundations, and particularly Walrasian microfoundations, are more likely to regard the cycle as being an optimal endogenous response on the part of the capitalist economy to exogenous shocks, and hence are likely to regard any kind of activist stabilization policy with suspicion.[7] The reasons for this, however, lie more in the specific nature of the models with which they have been working than with any hidden ideological bias in their research agenda.

A proposition that, as a result of discussions at the workshop out of which this volume grew, I have come to think of as 'Woodford's law' may be put as follows: if economic agents want to smooth their consumption over time, and if they find it easy to do so, they will. A corollary immediately follows: economies in which the above-mentioned conditions hold will be unlikely to display large fluctuations in real variables unless they are persistently subjected to exogenous shocks. But Arrow–Debreu economies, and the minor departures from them that have formed the basis for so much New Classical work in monetary economics, all of which are firmly rooted in the Walrasian tradition, fulfil the above conditions well indeed. In such models all markets, including those involving intertemporal trade, clear costlessly, and agents either know, or form uniform and single-valued expectations about, the future values of relevant variables. Hence consumption-smoothing is a straightforward matter. Problems start to arise in such models when obstacles are put in the way of the intertemporal allocation mechanism. If we follow Phelps in making it difficult for agents to form

---

[7] Once more, readers are cautioned to interpret the word 'optimal' with care. See fn. 6 above.

uniquely valued rational expectations because of bubble effects, or Woodford in permitting intrinsically irrelevant information to intrude, or if we follow Woodford and Stiglitz in introducing inefficiencies in capital markets, we quickly find that models based on maximizing premises are well capable of generating fluctuations that amplify, in a welfare-reducing fashion, the effects of exogenous shocks.

There is a striking relationship between these results and the issues on whose prime importance Leijonhufvud has for so long insisted. Sun-spots, moral hazard, and so on are problems having to do with the dissemination of information and the co-ordination of choices. Such problems arise particularly acutely in the context of intertemporal allocation decisions, and when they do they disrupt the smooth function-ing of the capital market. Leijonhufvud has frequently reminded his colleagues that the middle name of the *General Theory* was, after all, *Interest*. This remark is not, of course, intended as a veiled suggestion that we should now forget all about the macroeconomics of the last fifty years and become primitive Keynesians. It is, however, intended to draw attention to the fact that the problems of intertemporal co-ordina-tion of economic activity that were at the centre of the macroeconomics of the 1920s and 1930s, and which vanished with the dominance of *IS–LM* style macro, and seemed for a while to be remaining in limbo during the New Classical revolution, are suddenly returning to centre-stage.[8]

Moreover, we should recall that the *General Theory* had a last name too, namely *Money*. Modern general equilibrium analysis, even that in Silvestre's non-Walrasian style, has great difficulty in finding a role for money except as a store of value, as McCallum in particular has often complained. Agents who are adept at calculating rational expectations of variables hardly miss a unit of account, and if they operate in markets where the auctioneer costlessly mediates all trade, they have no need of a means of exchange either. Even so, I am uncomfortable with any approach that simply adds money to a model where equilibrium prices are set by an auctioneer before the processes of production and trade are permitted to commence. As a formal analytic procedure, the trick works well enough, but it does seem to neglect to a dangerous extent the basic economics of monetary exchange. If one starts with a conven-tional Walrasian economy and removes the auctioneer, one ends up with the kind of chaotic search economy with which analysts such as Brunner and Meltzer (1971), Niehans (1971), or Melitz (1974) began their stories about the usefulness of money. If we then introduce a means of exchange and unit of account into the setup, transaction chains are

---

[8] Interested readers will find this theme developed at considerable length by Howitt (1986).

shortened, search and computation costs are lowered, and the system looks viable. However, we do not get back to the Arrow–Debreu economy or anything much resembling it.[9]

Money as a means of exchange, that is to say, is a substitute institution for those of Walrasian markets, but in a monetary economy there remain substantial information and co-ordination costs that are absent from an Arrow–Debreu setup. That is why money usually emerges only as a store of value in New Classical work, which insists on retaining explicitly general equilibrium premises, and why the alternative above-mentioned solution to this problem of arbitrarily introducing money (perhaps by way of a cash-in-advance constraint) should leave one feeling uncomfortable. Here again, though, the problem arises not from using microfoundations in any generic sense, but only from using a particular class of model. Townsend's 'turnpike model', mentioned during the workshop's discussions of these issues, deals with a spatial, and therefore non-Arrow–Debreu, economy. In it there is a role for a means of exchange (though this role could be played by any durable commodity) and competitive equilibrium when such a means of exchange used is non-optimal. All this suggests that yet another set of problems which macroeconomists of fifty or more years ago thought were important are now beginning to be addressed within the microfoundations research agenda.

3. Microfoundations and Empirical Evidence

To say that a research agenda is beginning to address problems that one thinks important is not to say that it provides the only, or even the best, means of getting to grips with them. Participants in the workshop of which this volume is a partial record spent quite a bit of time discussing how we might choose among competing theories, and here again, methodological issues inevitably intruded. My own sympathies lie closest to the positions taken by Hendry and Taylor, which, though not identical, have one important element in common. Both of them would have us put any theory, regardless of the strength or weakness of its microfoundations, to empirical test in competition with others. Hendry argues this position with particular vigour; but, strongly though I agree with him in principle here, I must express some doubts about whether his chosen method of putting this principle into practice—by applying what he terms the 'encompassing principle', powerful though it is—provides us with all the answers. To begin with, there are technical problems. It is one thing to put alternative formulations of a single

---

[9] I have since developed this line of argument at greater length in Laidler (1988).

linear equation such as a consumption function to torture by microcomputer, and quite another to give the same treatment to a complete model whose estimation involves the imposition of nonlinear constraints on the parameters of the equations that make it up. But of course, a good deal of modern macroeconomics requires that our tests of it be formulated in this latter fashion. Indeed, Taylor's contribution to this conference is a first-rate example of work in this style. No doubt technical progress in computing will solve such problems in due course, but we are not, I suspect, quite there yet.

But there are deeper problems too. Suppose we compare two systems and find that which one wins the contest depends upon how we weight the accuracy of particular equations. And suppose that the better consumption function, say, cannot be embedded in the other model without grossly violating its logic, so that the route of creating an all-encompassing hybrid is ruled out. Such uncomfortable possibilities cannot be neglected by anyone who is willing to concede that the 'best available' equation describing a particular relationship at any time is likely to be just that, and is extremely unlikely to embody any ultimate truth. Or, again, Hendry told the workshop during its discussions that his techniques cannot deal with regime shifts; but how can we define a 'regime' except with respect to a particular model of the economy? Suppose, then, that a model contains an equation which fits well across what its rival identifies as different regimes, while that rival has two separate equations, one for each regime, each of which does better than the equation of model 1 for the subset data to which it is fitted. In due course, a third model that will encompass our two rivals might become available, but what do we do until it turns up? I believe that we will always, as a matter of fact, have to rely on theoretical as well as purely empirical criteria in selecting models, and because reasonable people can disagree about the relative weights to accord these criteria, the tension between deductivism and empiricism that I pointed to earlier will always mark debates in economics.[10]

However, if econometrics does not provide all the answers, it still seems to me to provide a far safer basis for imposing empirical discipline on economic theorizing than the practice of qualitatively comparing a model's predictions to 'stylized facts', whether informally characterized, as in the case of Stiglitz's use of them, or set out in terms of summary statistics, as in the case of the 'tests' of real business cycle models described by McCallum. Stylized facts seem to me to be dangerous tools indeed, if they are used as anything more than preliminary inputs into a

---

[10] This is not to argue that we can never settle debates in economics. It is to say, however, that there is no sure way to come to the 'right' conclusion about any particular dispute. Boland (1989) makes this point very clearly in his discussion of the relevance of the ideas of Karl Popper to economics.

model-building exercise. What is or is not a 'stylized fact' often depends upon who is looking at the evidence. Consider the dominant stylized fact that the classical economists, from Adam Smith to Karl Marx, thought they had to explain, namely the falling real rate of profit. Is it a fact? And if not, was it ever a fact?

And there are other problems. The theorist generally knows the stylized facts before building a model. If the model explains them, this confirms the theorist's logical powers, not the correctness of the model. The latter must be tested against facts that were not considered in constructing it. And if that test is carried out in qualitative terms only, it is more likely to be misleading than if explicit econometric estimation is employed. Let me illustrate. Friedman's permanent income hypothesis did not gain acceptance because it could explain the discrepancy between time-series and cross-section estimates of the marginal propensity to consume: it did so because it could do that and also throw light on to other issues, such as the need to distinguish between durable and non-durable goods when relating the theory of consumption to the facts of consumer expenditure. Moreover, when Friedman (1959) applied the permanent income hypothesis to money, it became clear that the distinction between permanent and measured income could, qualitatively, account for the cyclical fluctuations in velocity that traditional models attributed to interest rate movements. It took explicit econometric estimates to show that both effects were present in the data, however.[11]

But if theoretical as well as empirical criteria are needed to help us select our models, which should they be? Leijonhufvud and Stiglitz in particular remind us of the yawning gap that used to exist in the textbooks between microeconomics and macroeconomics. It was from a desire to close this gap that the currently fashionable penchant for building macroeconomic models with explicit microeconomic foundations stems. No disagreement of general principle about the desirability of closing the macro–micro gap is on display in the contributions to this volume, but there are questions about how far the issue should be pushed in practice. Do we wish to rule out of court theories that can be shown to be inconsistent with micro theory, or are we willing to disqualify from serious consideration those macro models whose micro-foundations have not been established? The first alternative is not quite vacuous, for it does at least rule out models that imply long-run money illusion, but it is certainly weak.[12] The second is extremely strong and would rule out of court almost any macro work written more than fifteen years ago and a good deal that has appeared since. And all this

[11] On this particular issue, see Laidler (1966).
[12] This point was made explicitly by McCallum in discussions at this workshop.

begs a question that surely ought to be asked: Are we so sure of the empirical validity of contemporary microeconomics that we should use it as a touchstone in this way? Why not test micro theory by considering its consistency with macroeconomics?

Though most contributors to this volume would probably assent to the suggestion that we be willing to accept models lacking explicit micro-foundations in cases where they can be shown to perform better empirically than the best available micro-founded alternative, some of them—e.g. Sargent and McCallum—have often, over the years, ex-pressed extreme uneasiness about this. Their preference for explicit micro premises, if not absolute, is certainly very strong. In part this must stem from a distaste for what Sargent has termed 'theories that assume their answers'. But all theories do that, and (to paraphrase a well-known remark usually attributed to Nissan Liviatan) how close assumptions and conclusions have to be to one another before the logical links between them cease to be interesting depends very much upon the IQ of the person making this judgement. Most of us are more easily pleased than Sargent! Something deeper is at stake here, and that something seems to me to be the capacity of a model to deal with that set of problems known as the 'Lucas critique'.[13]

4. The Lucas Critique

The essence of the Lucas critique is this: maximizing agents treat the behaviour of other agents (and particularly the government in standard applications of the idea) as a component of the constraints subject to which they maximize their utility. If that behaviour changes, so will the maximizing strategies of agents. Thus, if economic theory is needed to help in the design of policy, and surely that is an important purpose of macroeconomics, it must be able to take account of the way in which the private sector will alter those strategies when policy rules are altered. Heymann's discussions of the importance of establishing credib-ility for stabilization programmes shows how such thinking has already had an important influence on policy analysis. Moreover, and this is the crucial point, *the more explicit attention to maximizing behaviour does a model pay, the better are its chances of coming to grips with such questions.* Taylor's paper provides a fine example of how an empirically oriented model may be structured to address this issue. How strongly one should insist that a good macro model be one with explicit

---

[13] The *locus classicus* for the 'Lucas critique' is of course Lucas (1976). The well-known Sargent–Wallace (1976) policy ineffectiveness proposition is a special case of it.

maximizing foundations, then, depends on some measure upon how seriously one takes the Lucas critique.

Surprisingly little work has been directly aimed at assessing the empirical importance of the critique. Hendry's methodology, however, makes the Lucas critique a potentially testable hypothesis, and he finds no compelling evidence of the importance of forward-looking expectations in the French consumption function. Moreover, his studies of the UK relationship have yielded a similar result, while he has also found an extremely robust specification of the British demand-for-money function that had held up over a shift from fixed to flexible exchange rates, two oil price shocks, an extensive reform of the domestic monetary system, and the coming to power of a self-styled 'monetarist' government. Some might express scepticism about this evidence on the grounds that the relationship, which is 'well known' to be extremely vulnerable to the critique, is not one of those studied by Hendry, but one describing the inflation–unemployment trade-off, namely the Phillips curve.

One really bad case of policy-makers ignoring the critique and getting into trouble is surely enough to make us take it seriously; and it is widely believed that the disappearance of the Phillips trade-off in the 1960s and 1970s is a clear-cut example of just this phenomenon at work. I would urge a little caution on how we interpret the sad history of the Phillips curve, however. The idea that policy-makers discovered it in the early 1960s, attempted to exploit it, and saw it vanish in a manner that could not be explained until Lucas introduced the rational expectations idea into macroeconomics is, quite simply, a myth, albeit an influential myth.

The facts of the case are rather more prosaic, and lend no support to the view that the Lucas critique was empirically important. To begin with, in its country of origin, the UK, the Phillips curve never influenced policy. In the 1960s and early 1970s the dominant view in policy-making circles interpreted inflation as a cost-push phenomenon that could be mitigated by running the real economy at a higher level of output and a higher rate of growth too. It was this 'labour standard' theory of the inflation rate that came to grief in the early 1970s, not an $IS-LM$ + Phillips curve theory.[14] In the USA matters are less clear-cut, for the Phillips curve as interpreted by Samuelson and Solow (1960) did perhaps have some influence on policy in the early Kennedy–Johnson years. However, the onset and acceleration of inflation in the USA after about 1968 surely had much more to do with the exigencies of simultaneously financing the Vietnam War and the War on Poverty than

---

[14] I have documented the relationship between a prevailing economic orthodoxy and the conduct of policy in Britain during this episode in Laidler (1976).

it did with any nicely calibrated experiment in macroeconomic fine-tuning.

Even more important, though, anyone who entered the 1970s armed with Phelps's (1967) analysis of the need to augment the Phillips curve with (far from rational) endogenously determined inflation expectations found little that was surprising in the data generated by that decade. I would not deny for a moment that Muth's rational expectations idea is more intellectually appealing than error learning as a basis for modelling expectations, but the awkward fact remains that error learning can still cope with a good deal of evidence.[15] And when we look at the economic history of the early 1980s, an old-fashioned backward-looking expectations-augmented Phillips curve, combined with a monetarist model of aggregate demand, provided a better guide to the outcome of policy than did the then available New Classical models. Expectations did not respond rapidly to perceived policy changes (perhaps because of credibility problems which were not then firmly on the New Classical research agenda, or perhaps because the learning processes analysed by Marcet and Sargent were empirically important), and output changes preceded inflation-rate changes in a way that an old-fashioned monetarist model, but not a Lucas–Sargent–Wallace model, predicted.[16] In this case, at least, a model that respected microfoundations to the extent of ruling out money illusion in the long run, but which was not capable of addressing the Lucas critique, did better than one with explicit microfoundations. This is not to say that the Lucas critique is an unimportant idea. It is, however, to say, and quite emphatically, that *better and more explicit microfoundations do not always guarantee more accurate empirical predictions about the outcome of any macropolicy experiment.*

That being said, however, Heymann's discussion of hyperinflation and their aftermath, with its stress on the importance of *ex ante* credibility of stabilization programmes for their success, and its insights about the long-lasting institutional changes that persist in economies even after they have been stabilized, does show that the critique is sometimes crucially relevant. Moreover, its main significance for current macroeco-

---

[15] I do not believe for a moment that the fact that adaptive expectations work owes much to the general public forming their expectations by an error-learning mechanism of this simple variety. It is much more likely that, in introducing distributed lags into economic relationships, this particular formulation enables empirical models to capture in a rough and ready way the inertia that characterizes inflationary processes and which arises from all manner of ill-understood sources, only some of which relate to expectations.

[16] This last observation seems to me to be crucial. If the 'Phillips curve' really is an aggregate supply curve, then quantities should respond to prices and hence should move after them or simultaneously with them. In fact, quantities move first, and this suggests that some kind of sticky price 'Keynesian' mechanism is at work. This observation has from the outset prevented me from moving from a 1960s vintage monetarist position to embrace New Classical macroeconomics.

nomics is identified by Taylor. His paper shows that the idea forces us to think about policy in terms of rules, as at least principles of conduct, rather than in terms of unrelated discretionary acts. In doing so it has given new life, not to mention a much stronger intellectual foundation, to the utilitarian view of economic policy that permeated nineteenth-century classical economics, and which dropped out of fashion in the face of the Meade–Tinbergen approach to the design of policy.

Even so, perhaps we should not quite give up on permitting a discretionary element to persist in the conduct of policy. Classical monetary economists tried to do so in the mid-nineteenth century, but soon learned better. Thus, Sir Robert Peel's 1844 Bank Act was an attempt to put British monetary policy on a completely automatic basis, and it abysmally failed to do so. Its proponents believed that only currency could influence the price level, and sought to make its quantity vary in lock step with the balance of payments by imposing 100 per cent marginal specie reserve requirements on the country's stock of notes in circulation. Even before the measure was enacted, its more perceptive critics were already pointing out that many more instruments than coin and bank notes were functioning as means of exchange and also affected prices. The relative importance of bank deposits continued to grow as the century proceeded, and by the 1870s it was apparent to almost all that having made the behaviour of the note issue automatic was not sufficient to mitigate, let alone eliminate, the cycle or to stave off a financial crisis at its upper turning point. The Bagehot Principle that during a financial crisis the central bank should lend freely to sound borrowers, albeit at high interest rates, was not a policy rule: it was a guideline for the conduct of discretionary policy during emergencies— and these did keep on occurring. The guideline was, however, to be applied against the background of the rules of the gold standard, and discretionary policy was always to be disciplined by those rules.[17]

5. Doubts about 'First Principles'

The problem with the 1844 Act was that the rules it embodied did not quite match up to the structure of the economic system for which it was designed. I think we would run into similar problems today, and indeed at any time, were we to try to design policy rules based on the best available models, even micro-founded models. I say this not just because I believe that the current generation of models is in need of improvement, nor because I doubt that the specific principles upon which they

---

[17] Readers are referred to Fetter (1965) for the classic account of the evolution of British monetary thought in the 19th c.

are built can be guaranteed to provide a sound basis for policy-relevant modelling. The problem is much deeper than this. *I do not believe that any set of modelling principles can ever offer a guarantee that the analysis they yield will be correct and durable.* An economic model has to start somewhere, and has to take technology, tastes, endowments, and the 'rules of the game' as given. To attribute equal amounts of information about these factors to all agents is surely a defensible procedure whose implications for modelling are well worth systematic investigation. Moreover, models built in this way yield an exceptionally rich array of insights, as anyone who reads the above contributions of Silvestre, Woodford, Taylor, and McCallum must agree. And yet, more intellectually appealing than anything we have had before though these foundations might be, one must wonder whether they are quite as robust as they look at first sight.

At the risk of sounding platitudinous, it must be pointed out that technology is not exogenous. Its state at any time is the result of past actions of researchers and firms, and is always evolving. The same may be said of tastes. Any demographer will tell us that the very number of agents in an economy is the outcome of previously made endogenously determined choices, and any psychologist will suggest that the criteria those agents apply in making their own choices are the outcome of complex and ill understood processes of acculturization. Nor are endowments exogenous. Economics is concerned only with endowments of scarce factors, and what is scarce depends upon the above-mentioned endogenous tastes and technology. Nor do the rules of the game remain the same. The nature of property rights, of permissible contracts, and so on is determined by endogenous choices implemented through the workings of political and legal processes. As Heymann's study shows, such institutional factors actually respond to economic experience. As to the state of knowledge, it too varies over time; and in any economy that practises division of labour, knowledge is not equally shared among agents, but is highly concentrated in particular groups. Indeed, much of Stiglitz's analysis hinges on just this fact, which is why his insights cannot be displayed in a representative agent framework.

One must be careful with such arguments. It is easy to fall into a destructive obscurantism which argues that economics, after all, is really a combination of psychology, political science, sociology, history, etc., and has no claim to an independent existence as a discipline in its own right. *Let it be absolutely clear that this is not my position. Economics does have an independent existence, and it is extremely useful.* Nevertheless, what seem to an economist to be first principles from which one can safely reason are, from a broader perspective, anything but that. Immutable premises whose truth can be guaranteed and hence transferred to conclusions do not exist, or if they do we can never know it.

We do have to start somewhere, of course, and it is surely uncontroversial that good economics reasons logically from clearly stated premises to conclusions with empirical content, and perhaps policy relevance too. But good economics, so defined, can still be misleading; well constructed refutable theories do, after all, sometimes get refuted; and even economics that has stood up well to empirical tests in the past might go wrong in the future. In saying this, I do not intend to recommend that economists become nihilists; only that they retain a certain scepticism about the durability of their results, so that when they base policy recommendations upon them, they leave room for those recommendations to be changed in the light of future knowledge.[18]

There is a further, and I hope constructive, implication of my arguments. If those givens of economic theory, technology, tastes, endowments, and institutions change over time, we might learn something about the durability of our models and the way in which they can be applied to policy by studying a little history. And if agents' behaviour depends upon their understanding of the way in which the economy functions, and if it is true, as I believe, that our discipline is in fact the source of that understanding, not just for policy-makers but for society at large, then the study of the history of that discipline might also yield some dividends. This is indeed a plea that we do something to raise the appallingly low standards of historical scholarship among economists to which Leijonhufvud draws our attention, not as a substitute for rigorous economic theory, but as a vital complement to it.

6. Concluding Comments

There is no neat and tidy way to sum up the achievements of the workshop from which this volume stemmed. In modern macroeconomics a wide variety of lines of enquiry are evidently open and flourishing, but their exponents are, as we have seen, capable of engaging one another in constructive dialogue. No one is quite sure where our enquiries are leading, or how the results we have hang together. This is not a sign of a discipline in crisis, however. Disagreement and uncertainty are signs of health. Though very few people knew it at the time, macroeconomics was in a real state of crisis in the 1960s, when, to all but a few dissenters, it seemed to have all the answers.[19] It took the 1970s to

---

[18] Once more, interested readers are invited to consult Boland (1989) on the intellectual foundations of the scepticism I am recommending here.

[19] Among the dissenters, it is worth mentioning explicitly Clower (1965), Tsiang (1966), and Leijonhufvud (1968), not to mention the Cambridge (England) group (see Harcourt 1969), and of course Friedman (e.g. 1968). Needless to say, each of the above dissented for different reasons, and to different aspects of, the then prevailing orthodoxy.

reveal this crisis to economists at large, not to mention the lay public. To be sure, the menu of ideas on offer in this volume seems confusing, but confusion prompts questions, and questions are the starting-point for creative research.

References

BOLAND, L. A. (1989). *The Methodology of Economic Model Building*. London: Routledge.

BRUNNER, K. and MELTZER, A. H. (1971). 'The Uses of Money: Money in the Theory of an Exchange Economy'. *American Economic Review*, 61: 784–804.

CLOWER, R. (1965). 'The Keynesian Counter-Revolution: A Theoretical Appraisal'. In F. H. Hahn and F. R. Brechling (eds.), *The Theory of Interest Rates*. London: Macmillan.

FETTER, F. W. (1965). *The Development of British Monetary Orthodoxy 1797–1875*. Cambridge, Mass.: Harvard University Press.

FRIEDMAN, M. (1957). *A Theory of the Consumption Function*. Princeton University Press for the NBER.

—— (1959). 'The Demand for Money: Some Theoretical and Empirical Results'. *Journal of Political Economy*, 67: 327–51.

—— (1968). 'The Role of Monetary Policy'. *American Economic Review*, 58: 1–17.

HARCOURT, G. (1969). 'Some Cambridge Controversies in the Theory of Capital'. *Journal of Economic Literature*, 7: 369–405.

HAYEK, F. A. VON (1932). *Prices and Production*. London: Routledge & Kegan Paul.

HICKS, J. R. (1950). *A Contribution to the Theory of the Trade Cycle*. Oxford University Press.

HOWITT, P. W. (1986). 'The Keynesian Recovery'. *Canadian Journal of Economics*, 19: 626–41.

LAIDLER, D. (1966). 'The Rate of Interest and the Demand for Money: Some Empirical Evidence'. *Journal of Political Economy*, 74: 545–55.

—— (1976). 'Inflation in Britain: A Monetarist Perspective'. *American Economic Review*, 66: 485–500.

—— (1988). 'Taking Money Seriously'. *Canadian Journal of Economics*, 21: 687–713.

LEIJONHUFVUD, A. (1968). *On Keynesian Economics and the Economics of Keynes*. Oxford University Press.

—— (1981). *Information and Co-ordination*. Oxford University Press.

LUCAS, R. E. JUN. (1972). 'Expectations and the Neutrality of Money'. *Journal of Economic Theory*, 4: 103–24.

—— (1976). 'Econometric Policy Evaluation'. In K. Brunner and A. Meltzer (eds.), *The Phillips Curve and the Labour Market*, Carnegie–Rochester Conference Series, i. Amsterdam: North-Holland.

MELITZ, J. (1974). *Primitive and Modern Money*. Reading, Mass.: Addison-Wesley.

MITCHELL, W. C. (1927). *Business Cycles: The Problem and its Setting*. New York: NBER.

NIEHANS, J. (1971). 'Money and Barter in General Equilibrium with Transactions Costs'. *American Economic Review*, 61: 773–83.

PHELPS, E. S. (1967). 'Phillips Curves, Expectations and Inflation, and Optimal Unemployment Over Time'. *Economica*, 34: 254–81.

ROBBINS, L. C. (1934). *The Great Depression*. London: Macmillan.

ROMER, P. (1986). 'Increasing Returns and Long-run Growth'. *Journal of Political Economy*, 94: 1002–37.

SAMUELSON, P. A. (1939). 'Interactions between the Multiplier Analysis and the Principle of Acceleration'. *Review of Economics and Statistics*, 21: 75–8.

—— and SOLOW, R. M. (1960). 'Analytical Aspects of Anti-inflation Policy'. *American Economic Review*, 50: 177–94.

SARGENT, T. J. and WALLACE, N. (1976). 'Rational Expectations and the Theory of Economic Policy'. *Journal of Monetary Economics*, 2: 169–83.

TSIANG, S. C. (1966). 'Walras' Law, Say's Law, and Liquidity Preference in General Equilibrium Analysis'. *International Economic Review*, 7: 329–45.

Index of Names

Index of Subjects